The Thematic Organization of Our Wonderful World

9	10	11	12	13	14	15	16	17
Your Ears: For Hearing & Balance	Heart, Blood, & Lungs	Digestive System	Your Brain and Nervous System	Wheel of Life	The World and Our Senses	Growth & Glands		
First Aid & Home Care of Sick	Allergy		Mental Health and Illness	About Drugs, Alcohol, & Tobacco	Sleep			Making the Most of Your Appearance
Drives & Needs: Signals for Action	Your Defense Mechanisms		Intelligence	Understanding Your Family				Your Personality
						Planning for College	Schools Here and Abroad	
Careers in Agriculture	Selling & Service Occupations	Law as a Career	Teaching Profession	Careers in Business	Careers in Entertainment	Careers in the Natural and Applied Sciences (Engineering)	Working for the Government	Careers in Fashion
What Is Life?	Engines		Atomic Energy		Science of Sound	Hydraulics: Mechanics of Liquids	Light & Color	Space, Time, and Gravity
Fossils & Prehistoric Animals	Story of Rivers	Earth's Long Past	Mapping the Earth			The Story of Iron	Coal: Basis of Our Industrial Civil.	Story of Weather
A Survey of the Animal Kingdom				World of Fishes Water Animals Without Backbones	Odd & Unusual Animals	Amp...		
Rodents	Unusual Beasts of Burden	Creatures That Never Existed	Cattle, Sheep, and Hogs	Parade of Poultry				
			Exploring for Plants	Know Your Wild Flowers	Plants and How They Adapt to Places	Ho...		
The Solar System	The Sun	Comets and Meteors	Giant Telescopes & Their Discoveries					
		Devel. of Metals	Speed & Motion	Basic Mathematics	Principles of Radio and Television	Applied Mathematics Bridges	Inventing New Plants	Measurement Your Home and Its Furnishings
		Test Tube Revolution: Chemical Industries	Story of Plastics	Story of Glass	Synthetic Materials	What Man Builds With		
Man and His Animals	Geography of the Dining Table				Fun with Food	Food in the Future	How Plants Multiply Art & Science of Agriculture	
Vanishing Animal Life		Ways of Preserving the Past	A Nation Takes Stock of Its Resources	Conserving Human Resources				
	Trade Routes, Ancient Times Until Today	Digging into the Past (archaeology)						Exploration and Discovery
	Trucks & Trucking	Canals & Waterways	Rockets, Jets, & Guided Missiles		Shows That Travel	Story of Tunnels		
Immunity	Hospitals & How They Work	Beginnings of Medicine			Water, Key Resource	Miracle of Modern Surgery	Antibiotics	Keeping Community Healthy Radiation Medicine
Life in African Towns	Business in Action Business Enterprise and Freedom	Life in Ancient Times		Life in Orient Today	Motion Pictures Around the World	Planning Cities To Live In	Co-operatives	
Constitution of United States	Govt. & Business	U. S. Political Parties —Then and Now	Defending the United States	The Executive of the United States	Courts of the United States	Gallery of Presidents	Congress of the United States	
	Banks and Credit				Business of Play (show bus. industry)	What Does Insurance Mean to You?	Marketing Commodities & Corporations	Mail-Order Business
Meat for Your Table	Canada at Work					Our Pushbutton Age (automation)		
				Language at Work	Entertainment as Education			
The United Nations	Nations in Harmony	Olympic Games	World Citizens at Work	Gallery of Peacemakers		International Relations & Diplomacy		
So. Atlantic States South & East Africa	Hawaii & Alaska Pacific Coast States	Northwest Africa Mediterranean World	Lands of Middle East Rocky Mt. States	Nations of the Far East	S. Central States Scandinavia, Iceland, & Greenland	Soviet Union Australia & Neighbors Washington, D.C.	Cen. America & Mexico Caribbean Islands	Temp. So. America Plains States
	Liberty and Justice	Ethics: Study of Right and Wrong	Introduction to Philosophy	Religions of the East	World of Tomorrow			Christian Religion
		Latin Amer. Story	Middle Ages of Europe	Asia and Its Past	On Stage! History of the Theater	Looking Ahead with Cycles & Trends	Man in Revolt The United States: 1870–1900	When Brother Fights Brother: Civil Wars On the Trail of Man
Classical Music & Its Composers Superstition, Folklore & Legend		Gods & Goddesses of Ancient Times Imaginative Literature	Introduction to Poets & Poetry	United States as Others See It	Invitation to the Dance		Renaissance Story of Everyday Things	Names on the Land Holidays
Animal Art & Artists		Ancient Art	Working in the Arts	Musical Instruments		Through the Ages with Architecture	Flowering of European Art (Renaissance Art)	Paintings in America
Fishing & Hunting	Winter Sports	Track & Field	Boxing, Wrestling & Gymnastics	Games of Logic & Luck	Popular Music Circuses & Pageants		Photography	Sports for Everyone

Our Wonderful World

Our Wonderful World

an encyclopedic anthology for the entire family

Volume 9

Grolier
INCORPORATED
New York

ISBN 0-7172-1102-9

Library of Congress Catalog Card Number 75-118652

Contents

volume **9**

In this volume . . .

You can explore the animal kingdom. Here are familiar farm animals and the story of man's search for better ways to raise and use them. Here, too, are the unfamiliar creatures of the prehistoric ages, and the fossils which we study to learn more about the history of life on our planet. Here are some of the many members of the rodent family, as well as some of the rare animals which are fast disappearing from the earth. You will see how animals have inspired artists to recreate them in painting and sculpture, and you will see how hunting and fishing have provided sport and relaxation to people of all ages.

You can also read about strange beliefs of yesterday and today, life in Africa, the solar system, classical music, and the United Nations. And, as you read, you will add many more fascinating facts to your knowledge of our wonderful world.

Here are some of the questions which will be answered in this volume:

How many eggs does an oyster lay? (page 83)
What is the largest rodent in the world? (page 127)
How do the pygmies of the Congo jungle live? (page 273)
How many quills are there on a porcupine? (page 128)
What are the differences between rats and mice? (page 136)
How did the custom of throwing rice at newlyweds begin? (page 288)
What is a male swan called? a female swan? (page 190)
What animal has no mouth, but manages to eat? (page 27)
How does a bird stay on its perch when it's asleep? (page 85)
How many pork chops are there in a pig? (page 420)
Who invented the "hot dog"? (page 420)

It's the red cloth the bullfighter waves that enrages the bull. Fact or fancy? (page 287)

This is a fossil skeleton of Diplodocus, the longest dinosaur in history. Can you guess its length? (page 2)

Denver Mus. Nat. Hist.

The fossil skeleton of Diplodocus, *the longest dinosaur (87 feet) in history. Note the size of it compared to the men. Fossil remains of all types of animals have been uncovered as a result of accidental finds or diligent search.*

Fossils and Prehistoric Animals

The Dinosaur,
A beast of yore,
Doesn't live here
Any more.

Carl S. Junge

Many people think that fossils and dinosaurs mean the same thing. Actually, all dinosaurs are fossils but not all fossils are dinosaurs. What, then, are fossils? They are the bones, tracks, casts or impressions of any animal, or the remains of any plant, that have been preserved through a long period of time. In a general sense, fossils are the remains of, or direct indication of, life during the geologic past. Usually the time is measured in thousands and millions of years. Fossils include far more than dinosaurs: they include the remains of many other animals and plants.

There are many reasons why fossils are important. First of all, they give us a history of life on our planet, Earth; secondly, they point out areas (some of which are now dry as a desert) which were under water—seas, oceans, rivers, lakes—millions of years ago, and they tell us of the great changes in climate throughout the ages (Greenland, for example, once was as warm as Miami, Florida); and finally, they are very important to the petroleum industry in locating oil. Fossils aid in identifying and determining the age of rock strata, one of the most vital steps in oil drilling.

In this section you will read the story of fossils and animals of the past—the types of fossils, where they are found, and how to interpret them. You will also see something of the work of the scientists who have *paleo* ("old") as part of their title—paleontologists (who study fossils), paleobotanists, paleogeologists, and others who investigate the life of the distant past on our planet.

2

How Fossils Are Formed

There are, in general, four main methods by which organisms can be preserved as fossils. In this article you will read about these methods. From **All About Dinosaurs** by Roy Chapman Andrews. Adapted by permission of Random House, Inc. Copyright 1953 by Roy Chapman Andrews.

Fossil comes from the Latin word *fossilis,* which means "dug up"; a fossil, therefore, must have been buried at some time. It is the remains of a plant or an animal that once lived upon the earth.

Fossils are being made today just as they were a million years ago. A bone your dog has buried in the ground may some day become a fossil if it remains there long enough. When an animal dies, there is a great chance that its skeleton will be pulled apart by other animals and destroyed. But that doesn't always happen. Sometimes wind may cover it quickly with sand, or rain may wash mud over it. This heaps up higher and higher. Water, which contains minerals in solution, drips through it. Then a very slow change takes place. Particle by particle the animal matter in the bone is replaced by mineral matter. So it is petrified or "turned to stone."

Quite often an animal may die on the bank of a stream or in the water. The body floats along until it comes to rest on a sand bank or in a backwater. There it sinks to the bottom. The flesh decays, and the bones are gently covered with very fine mud. It fills every groove and pore and preserves the mark of each ridge or furrow. After a long while the sediment is pressed together into rock. The stream dries up or changes its course. The bones are left enclosed in stone, perhaps to be found by some fossil hunter millions of years later.

What Fossil Bones Last Longest?

Some parts of the skeleton are more frequently preserved than others. Because they are hard and solid, skulls and teeth are often found

120,000,000 years ago a dinosaur walked across a mud flat which later hardened into stone, leaving the tracks (below) that a paleontologist is examining. At right is a cast of the remains of an Archaeopteryx, an ancestor of modern birds, which lived during the Jurassic Period, some 135,000,000 years ago. It was warm-blooded and had birdlike feathers.

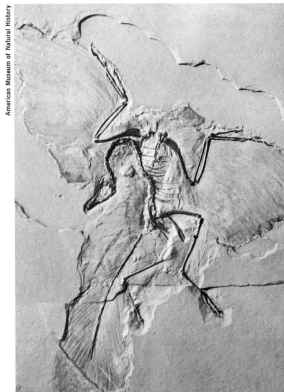

when nothing else is present. Leg and arm bones and ribs are easily broken. Very rarely the flesh, skin, or tendons are entirely or partly preserved.

Quite often fossils are formed as molds, or casts, like dinosaur tracks. In the Gobi Desert, in eastern Asia, I found impressions of plants and insects in what are called "paper-shales." These were made from extremely fine sediment, deposited in horizontal layers, which separate into sheets as thin as paper. In one is the perfect imprint of a mosquito. In another the imprint of a butterfly's wing is so beautifully preserved that you can see the most delicate veins under a magnifying glass.

These paper-shales were formed in sheltered pools of quiet water. Leaves or insects which died upon the surface sank to the bottom and were gently covered with a blanket of extremely fine mud. As the animal matter decayed, their tiny bodies left a perfect impression in the mud. It was exactly like the mold that one makes in plaster.

Mary Anning, who discovered the first marine reptile (in England), was hunting for fossil sea shells at the time of her discovery. These sea shells were actually casts of shells. The shells were pressed down into the mud. After a while all the animal matter was dissolved by the water. But a hole, or mold, was left where the shell had been. Later this mold was filled with sediment which hardened into a cast of the shell. Many of the small animals, like crabs, that lived in the sea or swamps have been preserved in this manner.

Plant Fossils in Arizona

Most of you have seen fossilized wood. In Arizona there is a place called the "Petrified Forest" where hundreds of fallen trees lie on the ground. Some are great trunks thirty or forty feet long. Chips and chunks are scattered about. The vegetable matter in the wood has been replaced by minerals. So completely was it done that, with a microscope, you can see the cellular structure of the wood.

The impressions of leaves, of seeds, and of wood tell an important story. From them it is easy to decide what the vegetation was like when those plants and trees lived. We can even know the climate. If the trees were of desert type, there must have been little rainfall. If they were those of the tropics, like palms, certainly the weather was warm with much rain. So you see how the history of past life on the earth has been written in the rocks. You can read it easily, once you have learned the language.

Fossil bones can only be preserved in sedimentary rocks, like sandstone, limestone, slate, and shale. These rocks are made up of small particles of sediment pressed together. You couldn't find fossil bones in granite or volcanic rocks which have been formed by heat and change (plant fossils, however, are quite often found in volcanic rock). So when we go fossil hunting, we first have to know that we are on sedimentary rocks.

Next, the surface must be cut up into ravines and gullies and canyons. Thus we have a cross section of the land. It is usually desert or dry country with little grass, trees, or other vegetation to protect the soil from the wind and weather, where rain and "flash floods" cut deep gullies in the surface, exposing the bones that lie buried underneath.

 Other Books To Read

Dinosaurs: Their Discovery and Their World, by Edwin Harris Colbert. Published by E. P. Dutton & Company, New York, 1961.
A dinosaur expert from the American Museum of Natural History tells everything about dinosaurs, including theories of how they lived, why they became extinct.

Strange World of the Dinosaurs, by John Ostrom. Published by G. P. Putnam's Sons, New York, 1964.
The world of the giant reptiles was in many ways much different from our own. The author describes this epoch in the earth's history and describes the many types of dinosaurs that lived then.

Earth for Sam, by William Maxwell Reed. Published by Harcourt, Brace & World, Inc., New York, revised edition, 1960.
A lucid and perennially popular history of the earth and its various inhabitants through the ages.

The Tar Pits of California

Near Wilshire Boulevard in Los Angeles, California, lie the Rancho La Brea Tar Pits—a treasure
chest of fossils, which has attracted the attention of fossil hunters the world over. **Brea** is the Spanish
word for "pitch," and that is how Rancho La Brea got its name (when it was part of Mexico).
As early as 1875, Major Hancock, the owner of the property, had known that the pits contained
bones of animals, but he did not know they were fossils. Not until 1905 did paleontologists
recognize the importance of the bones. From "Beasts of the Tar Pits" by W. W. Robinson. Used by
permission of the author.

In southern California, in the heart of present-day Los Angeles, there is a complete record of prehistoric animal life as it existed there fifty thousand years ago, during the Pleistocene Era. It is found in a place called Rancho La Brea.

Here pools of tar, disguised by a thin layer of water, lured huge creatures to their death. These beasts came from long distances to drink. They saw but did not heed the bubbles of gas that rose out of the water and the rainbow-colored streaks that meant oil. Wading or plunging into the cool waters, they were caught in the tar as if in quicksand. The roars and bellowings of these floundering creatures filled the air. Other beasts, attracted by the uproar, came not to aid the victims but to feast upon them. Deadly battles took place, but the attackers sank to their doom as did the victims they had attacked.

Saber-Toothed "Tiger" in California

Among the remains at La Brea, there have been found many fossils of the so-called saber-toothed "tiger," which once roamed not only over North and South America, but over Asia and Europe as well. It was as big as an African lion, but more savage than any lion. Also, it had two great saber-like teeth in its upper jaw, which gave it the name of "saber-toothed." As a matter of fact, it was not a tiger, more nearly it was an enormous wildcat.

The saber-tooth, when hungry, used to slip

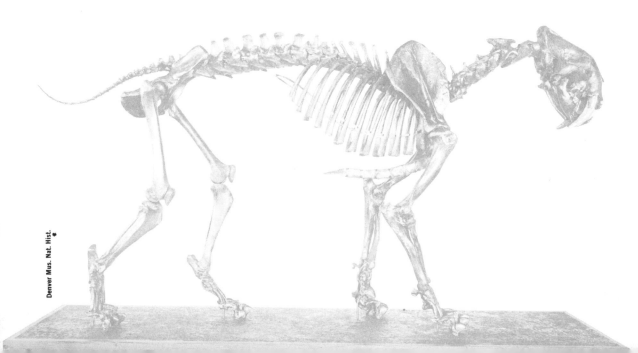

*A "saber-toothed tiger" from Los Angeles! Thirty million years
ago this "tiger" (actually a large cat) roamed over the world, but
the greatest number of its fossil remains have been found in
the Rancho La Brea Tar Pits in Los Angeles.*

down from the mountains to the grassy plains where the water holes were. He had learned that horses, camels, bears, elephants, ground sloths, and all sorts of large creatures came there to drink.

Saber-toothed cats were the enemies of all other great beasts, but they were not so wise as they were strong and cruel. They, like their victims, grew careless of the tar, were trapped, sank down, and died.

Nowadays there are no saber-toothed cats. When the other big animals they lived upon disappeared from the earth, these great cats could not adjust themselves to living on small game, wild vegetables, or other foods. The sabers were then only a handicap. Thus, like their favorite victims, the saber-toothed cats became extinct.

More Strange Beasts from La Brea

One of the strangest beasts of these ancient days was the giant ground sloth, whose fossil remains have also been found in La Brea. It was a huge creature with a heavy body and short, powerful legs. Large claws grew out of its hands and feet. With them it could dig

holes in the ground. The claws were handy in fighting, too, for with them the sloth could rip up a great lion or a saber-toothed cat.

The giant ground sloth fed on wild vegetables and on the leaves and young buds of trees. In fact, it was a vegetarian.

The giant ground sloth was powerful enough to crush slowly any beast it embraced. It had another means of self-protection. In the thick layers of its hide grew many tiny bones, like pebbles. These formed an armor. A distant and smaller cousin of the sloth, the armadillo—living in South America today—also has a protective armor.

The tar pits have yielded many other types of fossil remains. The horse, for example, roamed over the California pits thousands of years ago, but it had disappeared from North America by the time the European explorers arrived. The fossils of mammoths, mastodons, great wolves, vultures, and camels (which resembled llamas) have also been found there.

Today the fossil beds of La Brea have hardened into asphalt. They have been one of the richest sources of fossils that has yet been found.

The ground sloth was one of the largest animals of the Pleistocene period. Its bones show that there were several species, and that it ranged over most of both North and South America. The largest member of the family, Megatherium, was twenty feet long and weighed five tons. Mylodon, shown below as a fossil skeleton and as an artist has reconstructed it, was about 12 feet long and weighed about a ton. Skeletons of Mylodon have been found in the La Brea pits and in other widely separated areas. The skeleton of a ground sloth related to Mylodon has been found in a cave in Patagonia, where Pleistocene men had kept it penned until it was killed for food.

6

Photos, Denver Mus. Nat. Hist.

Brontosaurus

The heavy Brontosaurus must have kept his forty tons of weight in water most of the time, for his legs were certainly too weak to support such a mass. The Brontosaurus soaked his 65-foot-long body in the swamps of Colorado and Wyoming about 150 million years ago, feeding on the plant life his long neck helped him reach. The small, flesh-eating dinosaur on the nearby shore is Ornitholestes, standing barely a yard high, looking for his prey. In the air there flies a curious, bird-like reptile, the Rhamphorhynchus.

Hodgell

Tyrannosaurus

*About 100 million years ago the ruler of the reptile world was undoubtedly
the monster Tyrannosaurus. His six-inch teeth could tear his victim
apart, after which the Tyrannosaurus swallowed the huge chunks whole,
rather than chewing them. The main food of the Tyrannosaurus was
probably other dinosaurs, especially the abundant, plant-eating
ones like the Trachodon in the picture. When the water-dwelling
dinosaurs disappeared, and the climate changed, the Tyrannosaurus
became extinct. The three-horned plant-eater Triceratops munches in
the background, and overhead a Pteranodon, over 20 feet between wing
tips, looks on.*

About Dinosaurs

Nearly two hundred million years ago, dinosaurs roamed across America and other parts of the world. In this well-written selection, one of the world's foremost naturalists tells you about the different kinds of dinosaurs and the story of the discovery of their fossil bones. From **All About Dinosaurs** by Roy Chapman Andrews. Adapted by permission of Random House, Inc. Copyright 1953 by Roy Chapman Andrews.

Dinosaurs were the strangest animals that ever existed on this earth. They were the sort of creatures you might think of as inhabiting another planet or the kind you dream of in a bad nightmare. The word dinosaur means "terrible lizard." It is a good description, for dinosaurs were reptiles—cold-blooded animals related to crocodiles, snakes, and lizards. At one time they ruled the entire world.

Some—like *Brontosaurus*—were of gigantic size, heavier than a dozen elephants. They had long snakelike necks, small heads, and twenty-foot tails. They waded along the margins of lakes and rivers, half sunk in mud and water, feeding on soft plants.

Others—like *Tyrannosaurus*—walked on powerful hind legs, and stood twenty feet tall. Their small arms ended in clutching hands and curved claws longer than those of the biggest bear. Their mouths were more than a yard deep, bristling with great dagger-like teeth. They killed other dinosaurs and tore the flesh off their bodies, gulping it in hundred-pound chunks.

Some were huge, pot-bellied reptiles thirty feet long. They were *Trachodons*, and walked erect, balanced by heavy tails. Their faces were drawn out and flattened into wide, horny beaks like a duck's bill. Two thousand small teeth filled their mouths. They loved to wallow in lake-shore mud, chewing plants and herbs. But they were good swimmers, too.

When a hungry flesh eater leaped out of the forest, they dashed for deep water where he couldn't follow.

Other dinosaurs, like *Triceratops,* were short-legged and square-bodied, as big as an army tank. Long horns projected forward like machine guns from a bony shield over an ugly hooked beak. They lumbered through the jungle, and all other animals fled in terror.

Another fantastic reptile was *Stegosaurus,* a dinosaur which had plates down the middle of its back. On the tip of the ten-foot tail were four huge spikes, about three feet long. At the same time there lived a dinosaur—*Ankylosaurus*—completely armored by a heavy shell. Its thick tail ended in a huge mass of bone. He could swing it like a war club and give a crushing blow.

Some dinosaurs, such as *Ornitholestes,* were slender and swift, skipping over the plains

Trachodon was one of the most unusual dinosaurs because of the duckbill shape of its head. It lived about 70,000,000 years ago, was 30 feet long, 16 feet high. Trachodon had no scales on its body.

9

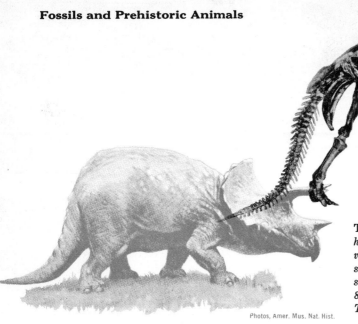

Triceratops gets its name from the three horns on its head. This dinosaur—the last of the horned ones—was a vicious fighter; only Tyrannosaurus *could hope to survive a battle with it. The Triceratops had a heavy, squat body about 30 feet long and a skull that was 8 feet long. On the left is a reconstruction of* Triceratops; *above, a fossil skeleton.*

faster than a race horse. And some were very small, no larger than rabbits. They hid among the rocks or in the thickest forest for protection.

What I tell you about these unbelievable creatures is true. They really did live. We know they did because we find their bones buried in the earth. These bones have been fossilized or turned to stone.

Also we find their footprints in stone. It is just as if you had stepped in soft mud, and the tracks your feet made had become solid rock. In the same way the impressions of plants and trees and insects have been preserved in stone. So we know what the country was like when the dinosaurs lived.

The time was the Age of Reptiles. That was a period in the earth's history which began 200 million years in the past and ended 60 million years ago.

No One Has Ever Seen a Dinosaur

People often ask if there are any dinosaurs living today. The answer is no. They all died out at the end of the Age of Reptiles. Why they disappeared we don't know. We only know they did. When you see pictures in the comic strips of dinosaurs with men, that is all imagination. No human being ever saw a dinosaur alive. They had become extinct 60 million years before man came upon the earth.

The Age of Reptiles lasted 140 million years. During that great length of time dino-

saurs ruled the land. In the air weird goblin-like reptiles, *Pterodactyls,* sailed through the gloomy skies. Some of them had long faces, peaked heads, and twenty-foot wingspreads.

The oceans swarmed with other reptiles. There were great sea serpents with wide flat bodies, long slender necks, and small heads filled with sharp teeth. There were also giant lizards, forty feet long, and others that looked like fish. Truly the land, the sea, and the air were frightening in the Age of Reptiles.

But the earth back in that far dim past was not as it is today. The climate was different. In most places it was tropical or subtropical like southern California or southern Florida. The climate was the same—warm and humid almost everywhere. There were no cold winters. If there had been, the reptiles could not have flourished the way they did. They didn't like cold weather.

When Kansas Was Under Water

In the Age of Reptiles the great mountain systems had not yet been born. The Himalayas, now the highest mountain range in the world, did not exist, and there were no Rocky Mountains. Instead, the low lying country of western America and of central Europe held great inland seas. What are now the states of Kansas, Wyoming, and Montana were covered with water. The land lifted at times and sank and rose again. One hundred and forty million

10

Stegosaurus was one of the most heavily armored of all dinosaurs. It was about 15 feet long and had a very small head and brain. Some of the huge triangular plates on its back were about 3 feet high. On the right is a reconstruction of Stegosaurus; above, a fossil skeleton.

Photos, Amer. Mus. Nat. Hist.

years is a long time, and many changes took place. The continents then were not as they are today, for there were land connections which do not exist at the present time.

That is the reason why dinosaur bones are found over much of the world. They have been discovered in North and South America from Canada to Patagonia, in various parts of Europe, in Africa and Asia, and even in Australia.

The Discovery of Dinosaurs

Scientists had been digging up the fossilized remains of other animals for some years before dinosaurs were discovered. The first ever found, or at least recorded, was unearthed at East Windsor, Connecticut, in 1818. No one knew to what creature the bones belonged.

Years later Professor O. C. Marsh of Yale University gave them the name *Anchisaurus*.

In 1822, the wife of Dr. Gideon Mantell discovered some peculiar teeth in the rocks of Sussex, England. No one at that time, of course, had ever heard of a dinosaur. Dr. Mantell sent the teeth to several other scientists, but they said the teeth belonged to a rhinoceros.

That didn't seem right to Mantell, and he went back to the place where the teeth had been found. There he dug up a number of bones and studied them for a long time.

Finally he decided they represented a new type of large reptile. He described it and named it *Iguanodon* because the teeth looked like those of the living iguana lizard.

But it was Sir Richard Owen who recognized that these extinct reptiles needed a general name. He called them dinosaurs, meaning "terrible lizards."

Strangely enough one of the first discoverers of fossil reptiles was not a scientist, but a young girl named Mary Anning. She lived on the coast of southern England. She used to help her father hunt for fossil sea shells. These they sold to tourists who came to the village in the summer.

In 1811, when Mary was twelve years old, she made a great discovery. It was the petrified skeleton of a reptile that lived in the sea when dinosaurs ruled the land. It was quite unknown. The animal was named *Ichthyosaurus*. (See page 13 for a picture of the fossil.)

Mary's reptile created great excitement among scientists. She searched the rocks near her home and found other petrified marine or sea animals, and when her father died, she went into the business of fossil collecting.

In 1821, Mary Anning unearthed the first skeleton of a sea serpent which was named *Plesiosaurus*. Seven years later she made another important discovery. It was the skeleton of a Pterodactyl, a flying reptile, the first of its kind ever known from England. Mary Anning made quite a little money selling the

11

Pteranodon *was a flying reptile that lived near water. It had no feathers and no teeth. Its wingspread was about 20 feet. Many of its fossil remains have been found in western Kansas. Pteranodon, which means "winged, but without teeth," lived about 90,000,000 years ago.*

Amer. Mus. Nat. Hist.

fossils to museums all over the world and her name became famous in science.

Dinosaurs not only left their bones in the rocks; they also left their footprints. The Connecticut Valley has some of the best preserved dinosaur tracks in the world.

In 1802, a farmer named Pliny Moody ploughed up a block of stone. It showed small imprints like those of a bird's feet. These were called the tracks of Noah's raven. Others were found, but no one paid much attention to them until 1835.

Then Professor Edward Hitchcock of Amherst College studied them and decided they had been made by large extinct birds. Not until later was it understood that they were the tracks of dinosaurs that walked on their hind legs. Professor Hitchcock's mistake was quite natural. Dinosaurs were almost unknown at that time, and the three-toed footprints looked very much like those of birds.

Dinosaur Tracks in Connecticut

The Connecticut dinosaur tracks are very, very old. They were made about 200 million years ago at the beginning of the Age of Reptiles.

The story of these tracks is an important chapter in the history of dinosaurs. That part of the Connecticut River Valley, where the footprints are found, was an ancient river bed. Or it may have been a long shallow arm of the sea; its water level changed greatly. Large stretches would be left dry to bake in the sun for days or weeks. Then suddenly they would be covered with muddy water.

For some reason, dinosaurs liked to come to this river flat. When they walked across it, their feet sank into the soft mud and left

deep imprints. Then the mud dried up and baked in the sun. When the flats were again covered with water, sediment filled the tracks and made casts. After many years the mud became hard rock.

Thousands of tracks have been preserved in this way. The dinosaur footprints show they were of many different kinds and sizes. The largest tracks are fifteen inches long and three feet apart, and were made by very large dinosaurs which walked on their hind feet. Probably the animals had small front limbs like those of a kangaroo. This seems to be true, because there are impressions of dinosaur "hind ends" where they sat down to rest. With these are casts of the smaller forelegs in just the right position where they touched the ground.

It is strange that very few bones of these reptiles have been found. Probably the rocks containing their skeletons lie out to sea. The bodies must have been carried away by tides or currents before they had time to be buried and fossilized on land.

Connecticut is by no means the only place where dinosaur footprints have been found. Texas, Montana, and other states can boast of bigger and better tracks but not so many as in Connecticut. About 1830, in England, dinosaur footprints were discovered in rocks of the same age as those in Connecticut. But no bones of the reptiles that made them have been discovered. For some reason these tracks all go from west to east. Perhaps the dinosaurs were migrating or traveling a regular road to their feeding grounds. Belgium, too, has some very fine tracks of the big Iguanodon, the same type of dinosaur that Dr. Mantell described.

What Do Fossils Tell?

Fossils tell us a story—the history of our planet before man, the kinds of plants and animals that lived here then, and clues about the age of the earth. By permission from **Historical Geology** by Russell C. Hussey. Copyright 1944, 1947. McGraw-Hill Book Company, Inc.

Scientists depend heavily upon a study of the feet and teeth in determining the habits of extinct animals. In many cases, living representatives of the fossils may furnish valuable information. The hoofs of a horse show that the animal would normally live in places where the footing was firm. The long, slender legs, with powerful muscles placed high upon the shoulders and hips, indicate speed; and the long-crowned teeth are perfectly suited for a diet of grasses, such as grow upon the open plains in the West.

The long canines and highly specialized slicing teeth of the cats are useful only in a diet of flesh, while other types of teeth show clearly that the animal to which they belonged was vegetarian.

The majority of reef-building corals are found living today within the tropics and the subtropics, where the water is clear and not colder than 68° F. Most of the fossil corals that grew in great reefs during some of the past geologic periods probably lived under conditions similar to those required by the modern forms; and the presence of such fossils in high latitudes, even within the Arctic Circle, is evidence that those regions enjoyed much milder climates in the past than at present.

Reptiles as a group are sensitive to cold. Those that live in places where the temperature drops close to the freezing point or below it during the winter season must seek shelter in protected places, usually underground. Large forms, such as giant snakes, the great turtles, and crocodiles, cannot find such places of refuge because of their size; consequently, they are forced to live in tropical countries through the entire year. The huge dinosaurs of the Mesozoic Era were doubtless just as sensitive to the cold as any reptiles living today. Therefore, wherever their bones are found we may safely assume that the region had a very mild climate. Some of these dinosaurs were more than 60 feet long and could never have found places of retreat during a cold season.

Fossils and Land Bridges of the Past

The geographical distribution of land animals in the past points to the existence of land connections between the continents in those days, where no such connections exist today. The true camel (*Camelus*) lives at the present time in Asia, but numerous fossil forms found in the western part of North America indicate that the family originated there and migrated to Asia by way of some land bridge—probably the one that formerly connected Alaska and Siberia. The present isthmus that connects North and South America is an excellent example of a land bridge between two continents, but even this land connection has not always been in existence. (See "The Rocks Beneath Our Feet" in Volume 1.)

13

The Ichthyosaurus, *found in Kansas, was a fishlike reptile that swam in warm seas 125,000,000 years ago. Now extinct, its fossil skeleton shows scientists that Kansas was covered by an ocean, millions of years ago. Wherever such reptiles are found, geologists know that a sea must have covered the area at some time in the past.*

Amer. Mus. Nat. Hist.

Fossil Remains of the Plant Kingdom

Many plant fossils can be found near dormant volcanoes as well as in sedimentary rocks. Millions of years ago volcanic ash, which accompanied volcanic eruptions, fell on plants and buried and preserved them as plant fossils. In this article you will read about the main methods of fossilization (both plant and animal). This selection from Gilbert M. Smith and others: **A Textbook of General Botany.** Copyright, 1953, by The Macmillan Company and used with The Macmillan Company's permission.

The term "plant fossils" covers many types of plant remains, such as *impressions, casts, compressions,* and *petrifactions.*

These are big words, but their meaning is simple. An *impression* is a print made by a plant or a part of a plant coming in contact with a soft surface such as that of clay. The material of the plant decays and disappears, but the impression may remain. If the clay later is changed into rock, a record of the appearance of the plant is thus preserved as a fossil.

A *cast* is formed when a plant submerged in water is covered by a crust of mineral matter. This may happen if the surrounding water contains a mineral substance, such as lime. The decay of the plant leaves a mold which may become filled with clay or sand. The hardened clay or sand filling the mold forms a cast that displays the structure of the plant that was in it.

A Familiar Fossil

Did you know that the ordinary coal used for fuel is mostly fossil? Coal occurs when masses of plants or parts of plants pile up and are buried under sand and mud, which later becomes rock. When this happens, the decay of the plants is greatly slowed up. The great pressure of the rocks, and the heat that results from the pressure, produce chemical changes in the plants. Since these changes are due to the compression of the rock, the plants within them are called *compressions,* and millions of years later they may become fossils—which we call coal. (Strictly speaking, coal is a rock which contains a great amount of fossil plants.)

Sometimes it happens that plant fragments become saturated with water containing mineral substances. These mineral substances may completely or partly replace the material of the cells and tissues. Such remains are *petrifications,* which we usually call petrified wood.

The fossil cast of an impression of a fern leaf, about 300,000,000 years old.

The impression of cycad leaves, made about 200,000,000 years ago. These plant fossils are found all over the world—England, Australia, Alaska, and the Antarctic.

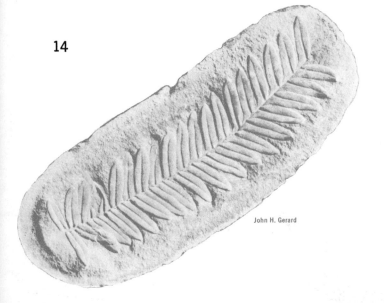

John H. Gerard

When Mammoths Roamed America

What's the difference between a mammoth and a mastodon? In this interesting selection the former curator of fossils at the American Museum of Natural History, tells you about these huge mammals which roamed over America about a million years ago. From "The Mastodon and the Mammoths of New York" by Dr. Edwin H. Colbert, **Audubon Nature Bulletin**, Series No. 9, Bulletin No. 4.

If we were to choose an extinct mammal to represent the past life of New York and the surrounding areas, no better selection could be made than the American mastodon. During the Pleistocene Period, which ended about 10,000 years ago, and which was the age of great glaciers in the northern hemisphere, this animal roamed the length and breadth of the state, wallowing through the marshes of Orange County and crashing through the dense woods of wild Manhattan. Indeed, the remains of the mastodon are among the most common fossils discovered in New York— and along the entire Atlantic seaboard, for that matter. Thus we are justified in believing that these large animals were once unusually abundant in eastern North America, probably wandering over the countryside in large herds, much as the wild elephants of today range across the African grasslands or through the Indian forests.

What Was the Mastodon?

What sort of an animal was this mastodon, whose teeth and bones are so constantly being turned up to remind us of his once common existence? Generally speaking, the mastodon (*Mastodon americanus*) was related to the modern elephant, which belongs to a group of mammals known as the Proboscidea (mammals characterized by a long proboscis or trunk). Like the elephant, the mastodon was of huge size, with a large, barrel-like body, supported by heavy, column-like legs. Like the elephant, the mastodon had a very large, rounded skull, carried on so short a neck that the only method whereby this animal could reach the ground for feeding and drinking was by its trunk. And like the elephant, the mastodon had two greatly enlarged teeth, or tusks, projecting downwardly and forwardly from the skull.

But unlike the elephant, the mastodon was thoroughly adapted to life in a frigid, even an arctic climate. Structurally, the mastodon differed in many respects from the modern elephants. For instance, the mastodon was heavier and stockier than the elephant, but was not so tall at the shoulder; it had a differently shaped skull and its grinding teeth were quite unlike those of the elephants and their near relatives.

At the same time that the mastodon was in North America, there lived several other Pro-

The mammoth had only four teeth, but what teeth! Mammoth teeth have been found which are a foot long and nine inches high. Here you see the fossil skeleton (right) and (below) a reconstruction of a mammoth.

Amer. Mus. Nat. Hist.

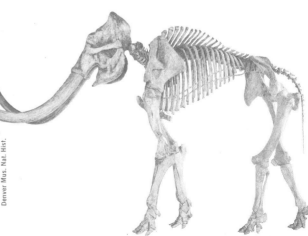

Denver Mus. Nat. Hist.

The mastodon came to America about 25,000,000 years ago, and became extinct about 10,000 years ago. They did not have the same type of teeth as the mammoth.

boscideans which were all very closely related to the modern Asiatic elephant. These were the mammoths, so often confused by nearly everybody with the mastodon. The mammoths were actually taller at the shoulder than the mastodon, and less bulky in their general build. And structurally—in the skeleton, in the skull, and particularly in the teeth—these animals were very similar to the modern Asiatic or Indian elephant.

The mammoths were especially noted for their tremendously long, spirally directed tusks, which projected forwardly from the skull, then followed a downward and outward curve, to sweep upwardly and inwardly.

The Main Kinds of Mammoths

There were, in the main, three kinds of mammoths in North America: *Elephas primigenius,* the woolly mammoth of the far north; *Elephas columbi,* the Columbian mammoth of the north and the temperate regions; and *Elephas imperator,* the gigantic imperial mammoth of the temperate and southern sections. Needless to say, the ranges of these three types of mammoths overlapped a great deal. The woolly mammoth, in addition to its wide distribution through northern and arctic America, extended to the west through Siberia and on into western Europe.

The mastodon and the mammoths, although they lived at the same time, were nevertheless quite distinct, as we have seen. That is, the two types of animals, though both proboscideans, were actually not much more closely related than dogs and cats (both carnivores) or pigs and cattle (both hoofed mammals). If this fact be kept in mind, the confusion that so often arises as to the mastodon and the mammoth may be avoided.

The mastodon is known from many complete fossil skeletons and a great number of skulls, jaws, and teeth. The woolly mammoth is known from equally complete material. And in addition, carcasses of this beast have frequently been found frozen in the ice of the arctic regions, while to complete our picture as to the structure and appearance of the woolly mammoth, the Cro-Magnon cave men of Europe—primitive artists of great ability—made numerous paintings and carvings on the walls of their caves, showing to the last vivid detail what this animal looked like in life. Unfortunately, the earliest men in North America, who were primitive Indians, have left us no clear pictures of the mastodon or of the mammoths with which they were acquainted.

Several fine fossil skeletons of the mastodon have been found in Orange County, New York. That general region is a mastodon graveyard, full of small swamps, in which these animals seemingly were trapped, and preserved until the present day. But remains of the mastodon have been found throughout the state, and even sixty miles or more out to sea—the result, perhaps, of bones and teeth floating out in cakes of ice. A few years ago, a rather complete skeleton of a mastodon was found during the process of making an excavation for an apartment house at the northern end of Manhattan. Unfortunately all of this skeleton was not saved, but part of it was recovered, and the jaws may be seen on exhibit at the American Museum of Natural History.

Similarly, the remains of mammoths have been reported from New York, although these animals are certainly not so common in this region as is the mastodon. But discoveries in the western and the southwestern states indicate that the mammoths were exceedingly abundant throughout North America during the Pleistocene Period, and like the mastodon, were important elements in the "life-picture" of those days.

Where To Find Fossils

You can't collect fossils unless you know where to find them; and finding them requires a knowledge of rock strata. In this article, you will find some valuable tips on where to look for fossils. From "The Amateur Scientist" by Bernard Powell, quoted by Albert Q. Ingals; Scientific American, January, 1954. Used by permission of the author and Scientific American.

Where do you find fossils? Any hunter will admit that luck accounts for part of his success, but a knowledge of the woods and the game helps. The rule holds equally for fossil hunters. Some rocks are full of fossils and others have none. It therefore pays a beginner in paleontology to do some studying before hunting fossils. With a good geology book and a little firsthand observation it is rather easy to identify the major systems of rocks.

With rare exceptions, animal fossil bones are found only in rocks of sedimentary origin. (For more about these rocks, see "The Rocks Beneath Our Feet," in Volume 1.) Sedimentary rocks are formed largely from the deposits of ancient seas. Successive down-warping and uplifting of the earth's crust, along with flooding, drying, and chemical change under great pressure, have built up many layers of sedimentary rock in some locations. The U.S. Midwest is a good example. Other regions appear never to have been flooded. These are covered by rocks of igneous origin which, with rare exceptions, contain no fossil bones. Nor do metamorphic rocks—those of sedimentary origin which have been drastically changed by heat, pressure, and chemical change—for the changes have largely destroyed their fossil record.

A beginner is wise to search first in outcrops of sedimentary rocks. Even where the rock layers are hopelessly entangled and out of order because of folding or erosion, they can be identified and dated by "key" or index fossils. To collect a set of these—made up of at least one specimen from each geological period—is a challenging project.

The key fossils and rock layers with which they are associated, together with the geological time scale and related facts, are listed

in tables of geologic periods which appear in all good geology books. The few minutes required for memorizing it will be repaid many times in hours saved during field trips. Also, a lot of shoe leather can be saved by using the special maps published by state geological surveys. Some of these maps are available through the U.S. Geological Survey, Dept. of the Interior, Washington 25, D.C.

Geology and paleontology have developed a long list of scientific names for their discoveries and findings. These terms, derived from Latin and Greek, frighten some beginners. It is not necessary to learn all the words, but it helps to know a few. They come in handy when the amateur approaches local museums and colleges for advice on likely sites and what to look for in them.

In the northeastern United States good sites include rock quarries, road cuts, building constructions, and similar projects where large-scale excavation is under way. The same is true in the Midwest, where a railroad cut may unearth scores of different fossils within a few hundred feet. Small streams in New York and New England frequently uncover interesting specimens. One of the largest mastodon fossils ever recovered was spotted by a small boy fishing for brook trout.

John H. Gerard

Many different kinds of fossils can be found in limestone bluffs along rivers. The ability to recognize fossil-bearing rock strata is one of the most important steps in locating fossils.

Collecting Fossils

Fossil hunting is a fascinating hobby. It is not an easy one, and requires patience, but it gives great pleasure to those who spend the time in it. Much of the progress in paleontology is due to the findings of amateur fossil hunters. From **A Field Collector's Manual in Natural History** prepared by members of the staff of The Smithsonian Institution. Published by The Smithsonian Institution, 1944.

Fossils are found everywhere in the world. In fact, they are sometimes dug up in backyards.

Many fossils, such as clams, corals, sponges, and brachiopods (marine shell animals that look like clams), may be found embedded in hard rock or loose on the surface of the ground. When they are found in a hard rock, it will be necessary to break the rock to free the fossils. For this a hammer is necessary, preferably one with a square face but, opposite to it, a chisel edge at right angles to the shaft for splitting slaty rocks. In addition one or more cold chisels or sharp points are desirable, as well as a hand lens of six or eight magnifying power.

If there are a lot of fossils which can be easily removed from the rock, a good collection may be made by breaking up the larger rock chunks on the spot. Usually, however, removal of a fossil from its surroundings requires more time and equipment than are available in the field. It is best, therefore, to take chunks of fossil-bearing rock home for more careful breaking. Do not attempt to clean fossils of any kind where they are found.

When broken open, fossil clams, brachiopods, and some other fossils found as impressions often yield an inner kernel or lump representing the ancient mud-filling of the inside of the shell. Inexperienced collectors often preserve only this inner filling, which is nearly worthless without the outer impressions. Both kernel and outer impressions must be saved, the latter to determine shape and ornament, the former because of impressions of internal organs and muscular marks.

In areas where the rocks are broken up, leaving the fossils free, be sure to use the lens to detect microscopic species such as protozoa or young stages of the larger fossils. If microfossils are noted, brush debris from a small area, then collect a small sack of the shale for washing and sorting at home.

18

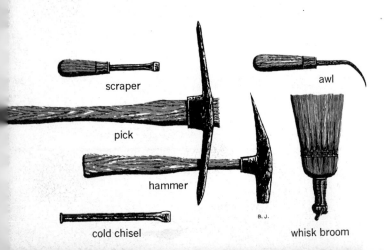

scraper

awl

pick

hammer

cold chisel

whisk broom

B. J.

Some of the important tools for collecting fossils are a hand pick, awl, cold chisel, scraper, hammer, and whisk broom. If fossils are found in hard limestone, a section of the rock containing the fossil should be cut away and carried home, where the rock can be more carefully chipped away. If the fossil bone is in soft rock, expose the top part of the fossil and paint it with thin coats of shellac (to harden it). Then remove the remaining rock underneath.

"Fossiltown, U.S.A."

"Fossiltown, U.S.A." is Ekalaka, Montana—a town where everybody's hobby is collecting fossils (a rare event—the people have already found enough fossil bones to construct a whole dinosaur). Eighty million years ago most of Montana was underneath an ocean; Ekalaka was part of its seashore, where dinosaurs roamed. Today, Ekalaka (population: 900) lies in the middle of a dry prairie. From "Fossiltown, U.S.A." by Gregory Desmond. Reprinted through the courtesy of **Dodge News** magazine, published by Dodge Division of Chrysler Corporation.

MONTANA

Ekalaka ●

The people of Montana laughingly refer to the little wind-blown settlement of Ekalaka in the eastern badlands as "Skeleton Flats." Fanciful as it sounds, the name is well earned. So many fossils have been dug up in the vicinity of Ekalaka, an otherwise ordinary little town, that it has become world famous for its inexhaustible fossil beds. Dinosaur bones have been found nearby, in such quantities that ranchers use the bones for doorstops.

It all began 45 years ago when Walter H. Peck, amateur paleontologist, found the bones of a *Stegosaurus*, a huge vegetarian dinosaur. Soon the entire community became infected with Peck's enthusiasm and everybody started digging for bones.

On weekends, led by the geology teacher from the local high school, young and old would go out in the country looking for new finds. They never returned empty handed. It seems there is no end to fossil riches around Ekalaka.

Dinosaurs in Montana

Among the rarer finds were remains of a *Brontosaurus*, an 80-foot long monster which used to weigh 40 tons. They also found the skeleton of a *Triceratops*. Its head alone weighed 1,000 pounds. A thorough search also yielded fossilized fishes, complete with scales, and remains of a marine reptile of tremendous size —a *Plesiosaurus*. The crown of them all, however, was a *Pachycephalosaurus*, a dinosaur with a peculiar bulbous skull several inches

thick. Local folk simply spoke of it as the "Bonehead."

When descriptions of it were sent back to New York, scientific circles were immediately agog: the Ekalakans had dug up something completely unknown to science at that time.

Many outstanding men of science from all over the country visit Ekalaka at least once during their careers to try their luck at finding something revolutionary.

Ekalaka now has its own fossil museum of which it is extremely proud. It is even toying with the idea of giving its "skeleton flats" national recognition by taking a touring exhibit of rarest fossils on the road, to show all over the nation.

Until then, Ekalaka goes on with its routine of a standard small western outpost, with its cattle roundups, its western talk, and its unhurried western ways. But dinosaurs have left an unmistakable stamp on the inhabitants, for even the plainest cowboy can toss around such big words as *"Tyrannosaurus Rex,"* and before they are interested in dolls, little girls often want to play with toy dinosaurs.

Citizens of Ekalaka discuss a recent fossil discovery in front of one of the town's dinosaurs (the "duckbill" dinosaur, Trachodon; see page 9).

Bringing Fossils Back to "Life"

How do scientists know what a dinosaur looked like? Actually they really don't know—they make very good scientific guesses. In this article, a noted paleontologist tells you how fossils are brought back to "life." From **Life of the Past** by George Gaylord Simpson. Copyright 1953 by Yale University Press.

The rebuilding of a fossil animal requires that all or nearly all the hard parts be found. This is usual for some fossils, such as oysters, or fishes, but quite unusual for others, such as mammals. Even for the latter, however, the fossil hunters have been at it long enough to have gathered together a fair series of skeletons as samples of the more important different sorts. Even these are very rarely complete, but reconstruction of some missing parts is possible without too much guesswork.

Since most vertebrates are nearly symmetrical, a bone missing on one side only can be supplied by a plaster replica modeled after the other side. Two or more partial skeletons of the same species may be at hand. Parts missing on one and present in another can safely be cast or modeled from the latter.

The next step in bringing a fossil back to "life" is to consider what the soft parts were like. In almost all cases these are gone forever. But they were fitted around or within the hard parts. Many of them also were attached to the hard parts, and usually such attachments are visible as sunken or raised areas, ridges or grooves, smooth or rough patches on the hard parts.

Restoring the outside appearance of an extinct animal has little or no scientific value. Such a restoration does not help in finding out what the activities of the living animal were, how fast it could run, what its food was, or such other conclusions as are important for the history of life. However, what most people want to know about extinct animals is what they looked like when they were alive. Paleontologists also would like to know, and they try to oblige.

Animals in which the skeleton is internal present great problems of restoration, and honest restorers admit that they often do considerable guessing. The general shape and outline of the body are fixed by the skeleton and by muscles attached to the skeleton; but surface features, which may give the animal its really characteristic look, are seldom able to be restored with any real chance of accuracy. When possible, the present helps to interpret the past. An extinct animal supposedly looked more or less like its living relatives, if it has any. Extinct members of the horse family are usually restored to look somewhat like the most familiar living horses, domestic horses, and their closest wild relatives. It is, however, possible that many extinct horses were striped like zebras.

No living elephants have much hair, and mammoths, which are extinct elephants, would doubtless be restored as hairless if we did not know that they had thick, woolly coats. We know this only because mammoths are so recently extinct that prehistoric men drew pictures of them and that the hide and hair have actually been found in a few specimens. For older extinct animals we have no such clues.

Length of hair, length and shape of ears, color and color pattern, presence or absence of a camel-like hump, and many other features are shaky conclusions, if not downright guesses in most restorations of fossils, especially those of mammals. At worst, a restoration by a good artist with good help from scientists shows what the animals *may* have looked like, and may be enjoyed without taking it too seriously.

Fossils Through the Ages

If you go hunting for fossils, the chances are that most of the fossils you find will have no backbone. Why? Invertebrate fossils make up about ninety per cent of all fossils found. They are of great importance because 1, they give us a record of early life, and 2, certain types of them aid in "dating" sedimentary rocks. In this article, you will read about some of the fossil discoveries which show us what forms of life were on the earth from 500,000,000 B.C. to 100,000,000 B.C. Compiled from official sources by the editor.

Five hundred million years ago there were no men and no dinosaurs or other reptiles on earth; in fact, there were no vertebrates (animals with backbones) at all. How do scientists know this? In the rock strata of that age paleontologists and other fossil hunters have not found any fossil remains of man, reptile, or fish; but as the layers of rocks decrease in age (over millions of years) the fossil remains of the higher forms of life appear. On the right is a simplified chart which shows when each of the major forms of life appeared in "geologic time."

Sponges are among the oldest fossils known to man, some being hundreds of millions of years old. This group of animals survives to this very day. The fossil sponge (reduced about one-fourth) shown below, left, was found in Texas, but they also have been found in Tennessee, New York, and Missouri, and in Europe.

The fossil coral below, right, (actual size) was found in New York, and is about 340,000,000 years old. Corals such as this one have been found as far north as Greenland, which proves that Greenland at one time had a warm, semitropical climate (in which reef building corals live).

Time Scale	ERAS	Duration of periods	PERIODS	DOMINANT ANIMAL LIFE
0			Recent	Man
20	Cenozoic 60 million years duration	60	Pleistocene Pliocene Miocene Oligocene Eocene Paleocene	Mammals
40				
60				
80				
100	Mesozoic 140 million years duration	60	Cretaceous	Dinosaurs
150		35	Jurassic	
		45	Triassic	
200		25	Permian	Primitive reptiles
		20	Pennsylvanian	
250		30	Mississippian	Amphibians
300	Paleozoic 340 million years duration	65	Devonian	
350		35	Silurian	Fishes
400		75	Ordovician	Invertebrates
450				
500		90	Cambrian	

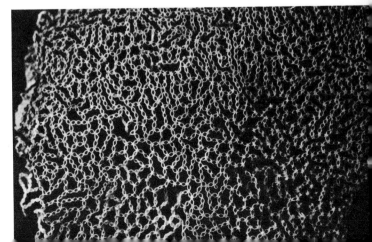

Fossils and Prehistoric Animals

These fossil lamp shells (actual size) are about 400,000,000 years old and were found in Ohio. The lamp shells, known to scientists as brachiopods, are divided into two parts like the clam. They are called lamp shells because, when viewed from above, they look like ancient bronze lamps. They are found in almost every state in the United States.

Trilobites are among the most interesting fossils that you can find. This animal, now extinct, had a large head, long spines, and a jointed body, and belongs to the phylum of arthropods. Like the three fossils just described, the trilobite lived in the sea; its closest living relative today is the horseshoe crab. Here you see the remains of a trilobite (actual size) which lived about 500,000,000 years ago. Trilobites are found in many parts of North America.

This starfish is about 300,000,000 years old. The fossil, which has survived in almost perfect form, was found in West Virginia. A member of the phylum of echinoderms, starfish still survive today.

Fossil insects, such as the one shown here, are frequently found embedded in the volcanic ash beds of the extinct lake at Florissant, Colorado. Many insect fossils have also been found in amber. Millions of years ago the insects were caught in resin which hardened around their bodies in the form of amber. This preserved the insects so well that they can be studied today in almost as much detail as insects we see today.

Ninety million years ago a very large fish ate a smaller fish in the seas over what is now Kansas. The fossil evidence of this meal is shown here; the larger fish, fourteen feet long, is known as *Portheus;* the smaller fish, six feet long, is known as *Gillicus.* Now extinct, both are related to the tarpon (found off the coast of Florida). This remarkable fossil is now on display in the Museum of the Fort Hays Kansas State College.

He ruled Texas 200,000,000 years ago! This finback, known as *Dimetrodon,* was six or seven feet long, and had a "sail" that was two or three feet high. What was the purpose of the sail? This question has baffled paleontologists for a long time, and they still do not know. Some believe that it was used to absorb heat from the sun to warm dimetrodon's blood—but so far this is no more than a guess.

23

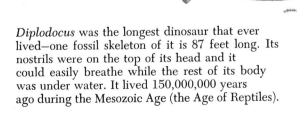

Diplodocus was the longest dinosaur that ever lived—one fossil skeleton of it is 87 feet long. Its nostrils were on the top of its head and it could easily breathe while the rest of its body was under water. It lived 150,000,000 years ago during the Mesozoic Age (the Age of Reptiles).

Bodger Seeds, Ltd.

What Is Life?

L. W. Brownell

Almost everybody at some time has wondered where life started, why some things are alive and others are not, and whether it will ever be possible to make life from nonlife. But the first and biggest question is "What is life?" This question has called forth a stream of speculative answers from all kinds of people in all ages.

This section attempts to answer, "What is life?" from a biologist's point of view. Biology is the science of life, so it is natural for biologists to want to define life. However, they usually put the question in a slightly different way. Garrett Hardin explains why in his article.

Aluminum Co. of Amer.

The cell is the basis of life, and all life activities are carried on by the protoplasm which fills it. Very likely you already know that. But less than three hundred years ago those facts were not known at all. Knowledge of the cell had to wait for lenses strong enough to make cells visible. When Van Leeuwenhoek (see "Bacteria and Disease," in Volume 7) described bacteria as seen through his microscope (1676) he opened a new field of biology. Additional information poured from observers throughout Europe. One of these was Robert Hooke, who described the microscopic compartments in a slice of cork as "cells." After Hooke a long list of workers demonstrated cells in various kinds of living things. But it remained for two German biologists, Schleiden and Schwann, to say that all living things are made of cells, and that the life of the whole organism is the combined life of the individual cells. This is known as the cell theory. It was such an important turning point in biological science that its hundredth birthday (1848–1948) was celebrated around the world.

L. W. Brownell

24

In the pages that follow you will read about cells that live independently (the one-celled animals and plants) and other cells that live as part of a complicated body. You will find an article on viruses—the smallest form of life, so far as we know now. (There is some doubt that some viruses are alive at all.) Finally, you will find the article "Death in Life." Life cannot be separated from death in our experience of the world. The author of this article explains why living things die even though some of their cells could go on forever.

—Anne Norton

Marine Studios, Fla.

Calif. State Fair Ass'n

USDA

Amer. Mus. Nat. Hist.

U.S. Forest Serv.

What Does It Mean To Be Alive?

Scientists run into difficulties when they try to answer such an all-inclusive question as "What is life?" Careful biologists prefer to begin with questions more easily answered. From **Biology, Its Human Implications** by Garrett Hardin. Copyright 1949, 1952 by Garrett Hardin. Used by permission of W. H. Freeman and Company, publishers.

This dog's ears go up when you call him. Living things respond to what is happening around them.

Biology is the science of life. But what is life? There are reasons why it is unwise to do more than begin to attack this question at this point. Experience shows that asking the question, "What is Life?" (with a capital L), all too frequently leads to answers of uncertain sense. Perhaps not all answers to this question need be nonsense, but so many of them are that it is sound strategy to avoid the question at first by asking other questions which are more easily answered. These are: "What are living things? What do we mean when we say living? How can we tell living things from dead?" These questions are less profound than the original question, but they are more easily answerable. A most important part of the strategy of science is asking answerable questions.

It is difficult, perhaps impossible, to state a single rule or test that can be used to tell living from nonliving things. But we can list the chief characteristics exhibited by *organisms,* those things that are commonly recognized as "living."

Movement

Most animals, but few commonly known plants, show marked movements of a sort that we call spontaneous, because we cannot predict them as accurately as we can the movements of a nonliving thing, say a rock. Close microscopic examination of even such apparently nonmoving organisms as plants, however, reveals movements in some parts.

Responsiveness

Speak to a dog, and his ears erect as he turns toward you. Put a plant in a room with only one small window, and the plant, as it grows, bends toward the lighted window. In both of these situations, the first action is called a *stimulus* and the reaction of the organism is called a *response.*

Growth

Every kind of living thing takes from its environment chemical substances, which it changes and combines in such various ways as to cause an increase in its own size. Among such animals as man, growth takes place by *ingestion* (taking in) of food, *digestion* of it (breaking it up chemically into smaller particles), and *assimilation* of the small particles, that is, turning them into larger particles that are now different from the original food particles. The nature of the final product is determined primarily by the organism that takes in the raw material. A dachshund and a St. Bernard puppy may always be fed from the same box of dog biscuits, but they do not, as a result, come to resemble each other. Each grows true to its (not the food's) type.

Reproduction

A most characteristic attribute of living things is their ability to reproduce themselves. But, although it is true that only living things reproduce, an object need not necessarily possess the ability to reproduce to be called liv-

25

Only living things can reproduce.

Crystals grow, but you would never call them alive. The difference is that they add material, unchanged, to the outside, whereas living things change their foods into protoplasm.

Gil Davis

ing. Most ants, for instance, are completely *sterile*, that is, incapable of reproducing themselves; yet, no reasonable man would doubt that they are alive. A given species or kind of plant or animal must always include some reproductive individuals if the species is to continue to exist, but an individual member of the species may be unquestionably alive even though it never reproduces.

Metabolism

Organisms require energy to move and respond. Much evidence indicates that growth and reproduction also require energy. What is the source of this energy?

The immediate source of energy for all these activities is food. Within a living organism the energy from food can be released by a sort of "burning." The energy so released is used for various purposes: movement of the organism or its parts; manufacture of more living material (growth); destruction of harmful bacteria or neutralization of poisons; and so on. Each of these activities is made possible by many biological and chemical reactions. In order to speak of all these reactions, the word *metabolism* has been coined. Metabolism is the name given to the entire complex of chemical reactions taking place inside the living organism.

Wöhler Makes Urea

Friedrich Wöhler (1800–1882) deserves to be more widely known than he is. The material he made by accident in his laboratory changed the scientific thinking of his age. From **Man, the Chemical Machine** by Ernest Borek. Copyright 1952 by Columbia University Press.

Until the middle of the nineteenth century, scientists had explored with zest the nonliving world, but they halted with awe before a living thing. It was believed that the cell membrane shrouded mysterious vital forces that we should never be able to understand. Certainly we could never duplicate a product of such vital forces. An uncrossable chasm separated the realm of the living, organic world and the realm of the nonliving, inorganic world. This was the principle of *vitalism*.

In 1828, a young man of twenty-eight unwittingly bridged that chasm. He made urea in the chemical laboratory, a substance which, until then, had been made only in the body of living animals where it appears as a waste product in the urine. This achievement was the "atom bomb" of the nineteenth century.

Friedrich Wöhler was a student of medicine at Heidelberg in the early 1820's. Under the guidance of his chemistry teacher, Gmelin, Wöhler left medicine and became a chemist. He more than justified his teacher's faith, for, in addition to the great discovery which shook the foundation of vitalism, we owe to Wöhler the isolation of the two elements aluminum and beryllium.

Wöhler had no intention of making urea in a test tube. He wanted to make a new inorganic compound, ammonium cyanate. As the final step, he boiled away the water and some white crystals were left behind. But they were not the new inorganic salt that he had expected; they were the very same urea which animals excrete!

It so happens that in ammonium cyanate there are the same elements in the same number as in urea. The difference is the pattern the atoms form. The pattern of ammonium cyanate was disrupted by the heat of the boiling water and the atoms rearranged themselves to form urea. (The changing of chemical structures by heat is not unusual; indeed it is an everyday household feat—a boiled egg is quite different from an uncooked one.)

Simple? It looks simple now, many years later, when the manufacture of synthetic vitamins is a big industry. But the importance of the finding was not lost to Wöhler or his contemporaries. The homage of history was paid by Sir Frederick Gowland Hopkins, Nobel prize winner in medicine and physiology: "The importance of Wöhler's synthesis can hardly be exaggerated. So long as the belief held ground that substances formed in the plant or animal could never be made in the laboratory, there could be no encouragement for those who instinctively hoped that chemistry might join hands with biology."

The Cell and Its Work

The study of living things begins with the study of the cell, the building block of our bodies and of all other organisms. Rose Wyler and Gerald Ames introduce you to cells by way of that interesting little animal, the amoeba. Reprinted by permission of the publisher, Abelard-Schuman, Inc. From **Life on the Earth** by Rose Wyler and Gerald Ames. Copyright 1953.

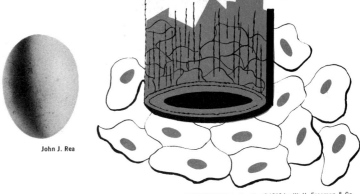

John J. Rea

After BIOLOGY: ITS HUMAN IMPLICATIONS by Hardin, ©1952 by W. H. Freeman & Co.

Cells vary greatly in size. An egg is a single cell. But most cells are so small that they can be seen only under a microscope. Above, right, you can see how skin cells of your cheek compare in size with one of your hairs.

One way to investigate life processes is to put a small organism under the microscope and watch its behavior. Suppose we have taken water from a pond, placing a drop of it on a glass slide under the microscope. The little animal we hope to find is the one-celled creature, amoeba proteus. Actually, this species is not very common, though a favorite for study purposes. We may have to take a domesticated amoeba proteus that has been raised in a flask.

The family name of this creature, amoeba, comes from a Greek word for "changing." Its given name, proteus, is the name of the Greek god Proteus, famous for assuming any shape that he chose. Amoeba proteus has earned both its names. When we catch it in a beam of light, the amoeba looks like a little blob of whitish, transparent jelly. The blob does not keep one shape for long. It is by a constant changing of shape that amoeba proteus manages to function and move about.

The way it appears to us, the amoeba bulges on one side, sending out an extension. This we call a "false foot," a pseudopod. The fluid substance of the amoeba oozes into the false foot until all of it is there and the amoeba now is where the false foot was. It has managed to shift to a new position next to its old one. Then the amoeba starts out on another ooze.

Sometimes amoeba proteus moves in order to get away from a harmful substance in the water, such as an acid. The amoeba takes the avoiding action automatically, through a chemical response to the acid. Other actions, such as movement toward food, also are chemical responses.

Eating Without a Mouth

The little bag of jelly has no mouth, but manages to eat without one. The amoeba simply oozes toward a food particle and flows around it. The particle of food floats about inside the amoeba in a droplet of water, called a food vacuole. For a while, we do not notice anything happening to the food in the vacuole. But as we watch, it gradually melts away and then disappears. The dissolution of the food particle can be explained only in one way. Chemicals from the amoeba's body fluid seeped into the vacuole, acted upon the food and took it apart—digested it. We can see something like this when digestive fluids are drawn from an animal or human stomach and are placed in a flask with a piece of food, which they break up and liquefy before our eyes.

If we watch the amoeba long enough, we may see it reproduce itself. Having eaten well and grown until it is about twice its original volume, the amoeba begins a series of remarkable changes. First, a collection of particles appears in the middle of the body, in a disc formation. This structure, the nucleus, is present at all times, but ordinarily it is hard to see. The particles divide into two equal portions, which move to opposite locations in the body. Then the amoeba pinches

27

The amoeba looks like a little blob of jelly. Some of its parts can be seen in this model.

food vacuole

contractile vacuole

pseudopods

Bausch & Lomb
Optical Co.

centrosome

nucleus {
  nucleolus
  chromatin reticulum
  nuclear membrane
}

cell membrane

cytoplasm

This diagram shows a typical animal cell. The protoplasm is divided into cytoplasm, filling the bulk of the cell and the nucleus. The nucleus governs the activities of the cell; if it is damaged the cell dies. It also carries the hereditary characteristics of the species in the chromosomes, part of a clump of little threads called the chromatin reticulum. When the nucleus divides during cell division, the chromosomes split so that the two daughter cells receive exactly equal shares of the parent's characteristics. This is called mitosis (described in a section on heredity in Volume 13) and occurs in almost all plant and animal life. The tiny centrosome is a sort of secondary nucleus which is also active in cell division. It is found in the cells of most animals but not in cells of higher plants. See page 32 for other differences between animal and plant cells.

together in the middle, dividing itself into halves. Each half possesses its own nucleus. The halves separate, and behold, each half is a new amoeba!

The Cell and How It Lives

Tissues of a large plant or animal body are built of a multitude of tiny units—cells—which are separated from each other by membranes. Each kind of tissue is made of cells of a particular type. Yet all types of cells resemble each other. Every cell has a covering membrane through which water can pass in both directions, carrying materials in solution into the cell and out of it. The cell uses some of these materials to build its own substance.

As the cell grows, a problem arises. How to grow and yet remain small? As the cell grows, its surface area becomes less, in pro-

portion to its volume. Were the cell to grow indefinitely, the covering membrane would become too small to supply it with enough food. A microscopic organism like the amoeba solves the problem by splitting in two. The cell solves the volume-surface problem in the same way. It splits into two new cells of the proper size. This is the mechanism of all organic growth. In plants, animals, and man, tissues grow by the splitting and the multiplication of cells. (A large animal has more cells than a small animal, but not larger cells.) A microscopic organism such as the amoeba or the alga actually is a single cell living by itself.

Protoplasm: The Life Fluid

As we watch the functioning of cells and one-celled organisms, we wonder: what is this

New Cells from a Single Parent

In asexual reproduction, one parent, instead of two, gives rise to new generations. These pictures show three ways in which this is accomplished. *1. Fission.* Nucleus and cytoplasm divide into two equal parts, producing two daughter cells. Sometimes the dividing cell surrounds itself with a tough coat called a spore which enables it to survive drought or cold and germinate when conditions are favorable. (See "Plants That Cannot Make Their Own Food," in Volume 3.) *2. Budding.* A bud begins to form at one end of the parent cell, receiving half of the parent's nucleus and a smaller proportion of cytoplasm. A cell wall forms between bud and parent, and the bud soon grows to adult size. It may separate from the parent or it may remain, to begin a chain of cells. *3. Regeneration.* Many animals can make new body parts to replace those they have lost. In the case of starfish, sponges, and flatworms any part of a cut-up body may regenerate (restore) a new individual. In such cases regeneration is a form of reproduction. Asexual reproduction is common in the plant world but occurs only in simple forms of animals. Most animals reproduce by the mating of two parents.

1 Fission

2 Budding

3 Regeneration

cut here

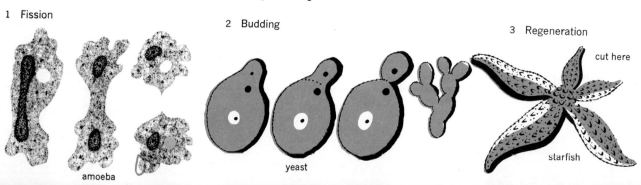

amoeba

yeast

starfish

self-maintaining jelly? How does the bloblet carry on its ceaseless activity, its growth and change and renewal? How does it live?

The life-bearing fluid of the cell is called protoplasm—"first fluid." Though we speak of it as if protoplasm were the same in all plants and animals, actually there are as many protoplasms as there are kinds of cells. Protoplasms have different proportions of their substances and the kinds of proteins they contain are especially varied. Yet we are quite right in speaking of protoplasm in general, for all protoplasm is similar in make-up and behavior.

Ordinary gelatin or glue can help us to understand the functioning of protoplasm. If we dissolve some dry gelatin or glue in warm water, the solution remains an ordinary liquid —a little syrupy, but still free-flowing. But make a simple change in conditions—a change in temperature will do. Cool the solution a little. For a while nothing happens. Then, all at once, the liquid turns into a jelly. Warm the jelly, and it turns into a free-flowing liquid again. The jelly stage of the solution is called a gel, and the liquid stage a sol. The balance between the two conditions may be very delicate. Small changes in pressure or salt content will make the solution go from one condition to the other. A mixture that acts in this way is called a colloid, which simply means "something like glue."

Now we can better appreciate the behavior of the amoeba proteus when some acid touches it. What happens is that a portion of the amoeba's fluid, on the side toward the acid, turns into a gel. The amoeba cannot flow on that side and therefore when it oozes it must ooze from the other side, away from the acid.

The amoeba's whole process of oozing takes place through a shifting of the cell fluid back and forth between the two conditions, sol and gel. The amoeba moves when a part of its outside layer liquefies, allowing the protoplasm to flow out as a false foot. What if the flowing should go on and empty all of the amoeba's protoplasm into the water, leaving an empty bag? This is prevented because the cell fluid, at the surface where it touches the water, turns to the gel state and forms an elastic membrane around the stream of protoplasm.

The amoeba's protoplasm is nicely adjusted to the water of its pond. The water is a dilute solution of a number of salts, including salts of potassium and calcium. These two elements affect protoplasm in opposite ways. Potassium favors the sol state. Using our microscope, we can see how potassium works by adding a little potassium salt to the water. Then we take a glass needle and make a cut in the amoeba's membrane. The fluid streams out in what looks like a pseudopod, but its surface does not gel into a membrane. The fluid just pours out into the water until the amoeba vanishes, entirely dissolved.

If we add a calcium salt instead of potassium and cut the amoeba, the calcium seeps into the protoplasm and stiffens it into a gel. In this rigid, unmoving form the protoplasm cannot function, and the amoeba shrivels up and dies.

It is the colloidal structure of protoplasm that enables all life to adjust so sensitively

What Is Protoplasm Made Of?

This table shows average make-up of several kinds of plant and animal protoplasm. There is considerable variation from one species to another.

required by all organisms	per cent
Oxygen	76
Hydrogen	10
Carbon	10.5
Nitrogen	2.5
	99.00
Sulphur	0.2
Phosphorus	0.3
Potassium	0.3
Iron	0.01
Magnesium	0.02
	0.83
not required by all organisms	
Calcium	0.02
	0.02
not required by plants	
Sodium	0.05
Chlorine	0.1
	0.15
	100.00

In Biology, The Science of Life by MacDougall and Hegner

29

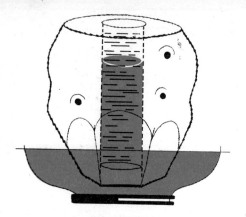

After METHODS AND MATERIALS FOR TEACHING BIOLOGICAL SCIENCE
by Miller & Blaydes, ©1938 by McGraw-Hill Book Co., inc.

How Do Cells Get Their Food?

Water carries food in solution to cells. But how does the water get in? A simple experiment will help you understand. Peel one end of a potato and cut so that it will stand in a bowl of water, as shown here. Then hollow out a deep pit in the top half of the potato and partly fill with corn syrup. After a few hours you will notice that the corn syrup solution has risen and is overflowing. Water has moved from the bowl through the potato cells and into the pit, according to the law of diffusion which states that substances will move from a place of greater concentration to a place of lower concentration. There are more water molecules (greater concentration) in the bowl than in the potato cells, and more water molecules in the potato cells than in the syrup. In the same way blood and lymph—containing more water molecules than protoplasm—enter the cells. Diffusion through living membranes is often called osmosis.

to its environment. In many-celled organisms, the environment of the cells is the fluid that bathes them—a dilute salt solution, like the water in which an alga or an amoeba lives. Calcium and potassium salts are nicely balanced, with potassium inside the cells to keep their protoplasm fluid, and more calcium outside the cells to keep their membranes a gel. With this delicate salt balance inside and outside the cells, the protoplasm can maintain itself as a colloidal system, trembling between the two conditions, sol and gel.

Inorganic substances also form colloids, but the colloid may be destroyed when foreign particles are added. ("Organic" and "inorganic" refer to the presence or absence of carbon in a compound. Presence of carbon is characteristic of living things—hence the name "organic." But many nonliving things contain carbon.) If the foreign particles have

an electric charge opposite to that of the inorganic substance, the two materials will be drawn together (the attraction of opposite electric charges) and will settle in clumps.

In organic colloids, something quite different happens. Particles of opposite charge draw toward each other but do not bunch into a solid. The particles stay a little bit away from each other, so they form only a half-solid, a gel.

Organic colloids behave in this way because their particles are "water loving." Each particle attaches water molecules, which form a loose film around its surface. It is this film that holds particles of opposite charge a little bit away from each other.

How Protoplasm Maintains Life

The colloidal suspension of particles is the key to the working of protoplasm. What the suspension accomplishes is to hold molecules in an arrangement whereby they can touch and work on each other. The particles float in water, which carries to them the molecules of necessary chemicals and carries away by-products.

In protoplasm in the sol state, the molecules move constantly. Big molecules or clumps of molecules are reached from all directions by

30

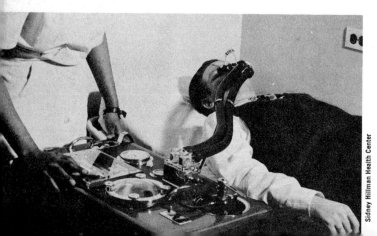

Sidney Hillman Health Center

In protoplasm, molecules are always on the move. Small molecules build up into large molecules of carbohydrate, fat, and protein, and large molecules break down into small ones, releasing energy. These two processes, together, are called metabolism. A person's basal metabolic rate, that is to say, how much energy he uses for simply maintaining his body, apart from exercise or digestion, may be measured by the machine shown here, which records the amount of oxygen taken in during rest.

the smaller molecules streaming about them. We may think of the moving molecules as an assembly line, where smaller molecules join and build up the big carbohydrate, fat, and protein molecules.

The assembly line is reversible. It can go backward and take the big molecules apart again to oxidize their carbon for energy. The whole cycle of building up and breaking down is called metabolism, which means "changing."

In the factory of the cell are special molecules that speed up each process of metabolism, whether it is the building or the dismembering of molecules. These specialists are the enzymes. In construction, the enzymes themselves are protein molecules. They are continually built up in protoplasm.

Since the biggest and most complex molecules in protoplasm are proteins, and since the enzymes which regulate cell chemistry also are proteins, we may wonder: are not proteins the very fabric of protoplasm?

Proteins, it is true, are the most complex structures in protoplasm, but they too can be used for energy, like any other carbon fuel. We know that an animal or a man can live for a long time without food, but the body shrinks. This is because the protoplasm burns up its own proteins, as well as stored fat.

The cells, deprived of new food, still must burn up carbon if they are to supply themselves with energy for living. So the cells consume their protein molecules, releasing energy, and they eliminate waste products.

As the protein content dwindles, the yield of energy diminishes to the point where it can no longer operate the breathing system and other systems of the organism. The oxygen and water supply is cut off; wastes accumulate. Lacking the materials to carry on its activity, and poisoned by an accumulation of wastes, the protoplasm ceases functioning— dies.

An organism lives by dying piecemeal. The protoplasm constantly destroys itself in order to rebuild itself again. It breaks down its molecules and uses some of the energy to forge new molecules.

The energy system of the cell drives on continuously, forward and backward, building and destroying and building again. It is by the eternal cycle of destruction and rebuilding that the colloidal fluid lives, that it gives life to cells and organisms. Truly we can say: Life is the chemistry of protoplasm.

Celebrity of Life Science

Sir Jagadis Chandra Bose   1858–1937

Sir Jagadis Chandra Bose, India's pioneer physicist and plant physiologist, made several important contributions to modern physical science. His researches with electromagnetic waves led to the discovery that plants, animals and metals show similar responses to the stimulus of electromagnetic radiation. For his experiments he designed several highly sensitive measuring devices, such as the cresograph, which records plant growth and demonstrated that plants actually grow in pulses. He further observed that plants are sensitive to environments of air and water, light and temperature. In 1895 he had designed a wireless telegraph system with very sensitive receivers. When these began to show signs of fatigue he studied the responses of many inorganic substances under the stimulus of electromagnetic radiation; his experiments demonstrated that metals can experience fatigue, a then revolutionary concept. Two of his pioneering books are *Response in the Living and Non-Living* (1902) and *Plant Responses* (1906). Born in Bengal, Bose graduated from St. Xavier's College, Calcutta in 1878 and later studied medicine at the University of London. In 1884 he graduated from Christ's College, Cambridge. Upon his return to India he was appointed professor of physics at Presidency College in Calcutta. He retired as professor emeritus in 1915. In 1917 he founded the Bose Research Institute in Calcutta and in that same year was knighted by King George V. At first his data was not accepted; however, as his delicate instruments were perfected, his researches were more appreciated and his ideas attracted commercial interest. He was elected a fellow of the Royal Society in 1920.

The Granger Collection

Plant or animal? That is almost as puzzling a question
as "What is life?" On this page you will see plant cells
both simple and specialized; on the opposite page
are animal cells. So far, so good; biologists could look
at these under the microscope and classify "plant"
or "animal." But when you come to euglena and volvox,
at the bottom of these pages, the arguments begin.

Plant

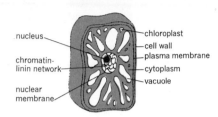

The typical *plant cell* has a thick wall composed of nonliving material (cellulose) secreted by the cytoplasm. Small green bodies (chloroplasts) in the cytoplasm contain chlorophyll, used in food-making and an important part of most plants. (See "We Live on Sunlight," in Volume 4.)

Plant cells, like animal cells, become specialized for definite functions. Plants have a skin, (1) usually consisting of a single layer of epidermal cells which protect other tissues from drying. Guard cells control small openings in the skin (stomata), through which gases pass in and out. The stem of the plant (2) is composed largely of cells adapted for support of the plant. They may be fibers or cells thickened in various ways throughout the wall or at the corners where they touch other cells. At the inside of the stem are cells adapted for transfer of liquid food, sieve cells. These fit end to end like sections of a pipe, the cells separated by sieve plates which allow strands of cytoplasm to pass through. The root of the plant (3) has microscopic hairs composed of very thin-walled cells, specially adapted for absorption of water from the soil.

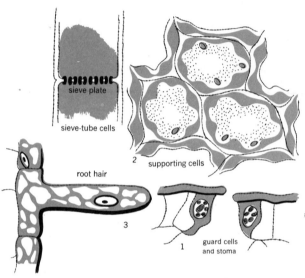

Spirogyra is a threadlike plant that grows on the surface of ponds. The cell walls are marked, and green chloroplasts run spirally through the cell.

Diatoms, although one of the first plants on earth, are still abundant today. They are usually brown, not green, and you can see them in enormous colonies as a yellowish-brown film on the surface of water. Diatoms have many shapes, but all secrete a nonliving shell which lasts long after the cell dies. (Read about diatoms at the bottom of the sea in "The Seas That Lap Our Shores," in Volume 2.) The two halves of the glasslike shell are hinged like a pillbox. Some land deposits of diatom skeletons are as much as 300 feet deep and have been mined for use in polishing powders, tooth pastes, etc.

32

Now we come to the *euglena,* one of the betwixt-and-betweens. The euglena has a mouth and gullet, leading to a "reservoir" stomach. But instead of taking food from the outside into this stomach, the euglena manufactures its own food in its chloroplasts (like a plant) and carries the wastes to the stomach. (The light-sensitive eye spot enables euglena to swim toward the sunshine it needs.) Also like a plant, it spends the winter as a thick-walled resting spore, which germinates in the spring. But euglena's cell structure and its ability to move (by means of the long threadlike flagellum) are characteristic of animals.

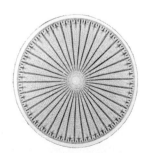

Photos, Bausch & Lomb Optical Co.

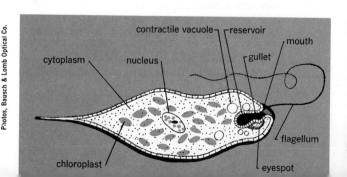

or Animal?

The typical *animal cell* lacks the thick wall of the plant cell. Instead it has only a cell membrane of protoplasm in the gel state. The chloroplasts are lacking; no true animal has chlorophyll. Near the nucleus of the animal cell is a small body called a centrosome, which plays an important part in cell division.

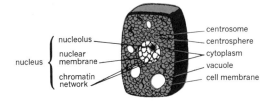

The *paramecium* is a one-celled animal, one of the protozoa. It is often called the "slipper animal." But the single cell has several parts, some of which you can make out in this model. Food vacuoles fill, one at a time, from the mouth and gullet, then move off to carry food around the cell. At each end of the cell are contractile vacuoles which excrete waste products that are brought to them by means of canals. You can see the canals of the contractile vacuole at the toe end of the slipper—the rear end of the animal. The paramecium moves by means of rows upon rows of cilia (projections of the protoplasm). Notice the large nucleus in the center.

Photos on this page, not otherwise credited, by Bausch & Lomb Optical Co.

The *vorticella* looks like a microscopic tulip. The stem coils and uncoils continuously, like a spring. As the cell rises from the coiled position food is swept into its mouth, helped by the action of the cilia.

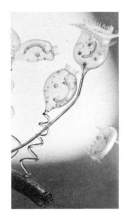

These are a few examples of the many kinds of cells in the human body. *Nerve cells* are the longest cells in the body. Some nerve cell axons (extensions) reach from the lower part of the spinal cord to the toes. *Red blood corpuscles* are coin shaped. The mature red cells in the blood stream have no nuclei and cannot reproduce themselves (discussed in detail in "Death in Life," page 36). *Liver cells* carry on many different functions. They store carbohydrates, manufacture proteins, and collect and excrete bile. The liver cells are arranged in cords in such a way that their walls form tubes to carry blood and bile. *Taste buds* are groups of cells on the tongue, tipped by sensitive hairs and connecting to a nerve at the base. We have about 3,000 taste buds.

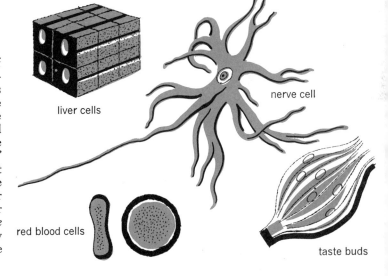

liver cells

nerve cell

red blood cells

taste buds

Volvox is a plant-animal curiosity. The individual cells live together in a ball-shaped colony about the size of a pinhead, hollow on the inside. Each cell has two cilia that roll the ball along in the water. The cells are green; they make their own food by means of chlorophyll. When the colony is mature some of the cells enlarge and divide many times to form daughter colonies. But the volvox reproduces in another way also, a way more characteristic of animals. Some of its cells change into so-called egg cells and swim about in the hollow center of the ball until fertilized by other cells which have become sperm cells.

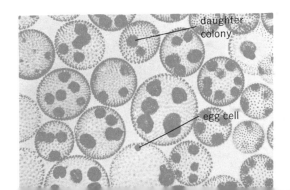

daughter colony

egg cell

Viruses: Living Chemicals

In the preceding article you can read about tiny organisms that seem to walk the line between "plant" and "animal." In this article you will read about much smaller materials, some of which present a more basic question—"dead" or "alive"? These materials are viruses. (Be sure to read also "Bacteria and Disease," in Volume 7.) From **The Science Book of Wonder Drugs**, by Donald G. Cooley. Copyright 1954 by Franklin Watts, Inc.

Polio virus as seen under the electron microscope (magnified 77,000 times). Viruses can live only inside living cells.

Ask an authority what a virus is and you confront him with a most embarrassing question. Is a virus a living organism? Or is it a pure chemical, no more alive than a salt crystal? It seems to fit either description, like a strange something that exists in a shadowy world between life and not-life. A virus behaves like a living chemical.

A virus reproduces itself. Seemingly this power of self-duplication proves that viruses are alive, yet some viruses that have been isolated in pure crystal form contain no water and seem to be as unalive as granite.

Another very strange fact makes viruses different from bacteria that cause diseases. Viruses multiply only *inside* living cells. They cannot live on sugars or meat broth or other foods that bacteria thrive upon. And a virus can use only a particular kind of cell. The cells of human bodies give the polio virus exactly the foods that it needs. The cells of a cat do no such thing. Cats do not have polio, but they have other virus diseases that never bother human beings.

What Are Viruses Made Of?

Viruses are not vegetable matter like bacteria, nor animal matter like protozoa, nor mineral matter. Chemistry cannot tell us what a virus *is*, but it can tell us what a virus is made of. The answer is truly astonishing for it seems to carry us back millions of years to the very beginnings of life on our planet.

Viruses are made of a very special and all-important group of proteins called *nucleoproteins*. These wonderful substances are formed by relatively simple chemicals known as nu-

cleic acids, in combination with proteins. One virus that attacks bacteria has been studied extensively as to its composition. Most of its protein is concentrated in an outside layer which surrounds an interior composed of nucleic acids. The protein "skin" seems to attach the virus to the cell it attacks, while the nucleic acids are concerned with the multiplication or reproduction of the virus.

Nucleoproteins are the chemical material of the chromatin network of the nucleus, of which the cell chromosomes and genes are largely made. (See diagram of the cell, page 28.) The genes control the forces of heredity as they descend from one generation to another. They accomplish this miracle through their remarkable power of self-duplication. We human beings have about 20,000 genes. All of them are contained in most of the billions of cells of our bodies, descendants of the original single cell with which our lives began. (Read more about heredity in Volume 13.)

Both viruses and genes, then, are made from nucleoproteins, the essential chemicals with which living matter duplicates itself. Both viruses and genes have the property of self-duplication. Both may simply be gigantic protein molecules. Just think what this means! As far as their composition is concerned, the genes which gave you the color of your hair and the shape of your nose might be thought of as "good" viruses. And the viruses that cause smallpox or polio might be considered to be "bad," degenerated genes.

Some authorities believe that the very first living structures to appear on earth, ages and ages ago were very similar to present-day viruses. Then, as now, the substances were living chemicals—life in the very smallest of packages. But in those dim days of earth, the primitive living chemicals survived alone and independently. Slowly, as more complicated forms of life arose, certain of those chemicals began to live on other materials. They penetrated cells and stole the food they needed. In time they became utterly dependent upon the host cells. They became, in short, viruses.

Did you ever have a plain, ordinary cold sore? It is caused by a virus that constantly inhabits the bodies of most people from infancy to old age. Most of the time you don't know you have it. Once in a while, when your resistance is low, the virus gets the upper hand.

Many virus-caused illnesses are more annoying than serious, but there are dangerous viruses which cause some of the most devastating diseases that afflict the human race. Infantile paralysis or polio (a shortening of the medical word, poliomyelitis) strikes dread into the hearts of parents. Influenza, encephalitis, mumps, measles, shingles, yellow fever, chickenpox, smallpox, and the common cold are virus diseases of human beings. All living things have their own virus diseases.

Where Do New Diseases Come From?

New diseases appear through the centuries, and old ones disappear or lose their deadly punch. Polio was practically unknown a century ago, although reports of limbs paralyzed after a feverish sickness have been extracted from old records. In the light of today's knowledge, we believe such crippling may have been caused by polio. But widespread polio epidemics which would arrive on schedule every summer were an aspect of twentieth century civilization. (Fortunately, the pattern can now be changed with the help of the Salk vaccine.) Some violent diseases of today may be new forms of old ones. A curious disease called "dancing sickness" once swept some parts of Europe. Was it a virus which caused the uncontrollable, jerky movements of the sufferers? Did it attack the nervous system in much the same way as polio? We cannot know.

What has happened to the influenza virus which caused the deadly, world-wide flu epidemic of 1918? This was one of the most disastrous plagues of history, killing 25,000,000 people in a few months. Today, influenza is not so dangerous a killer. We know that influenza of our time is caused by at least three different strains of flu viruses.

Viruses have the ability to acquire new characteristics (mutation). Therefore we expect that viruses may occasionally change in such a way as to cause a new disease, or to bring back an old one, or to change a mild disease into a violent one.

A Struggle for Existence

A virus gains no advantage by killing its host. That is the equivalent of virus suicide. Quite likely a sort of "you leave me alone and I'll leave you alone" arrangement is struck between our body cells and many harmless viruses we never know about.

Actually, viruses have a pretty fierce struggle for existence. Many viruses do not thrive in human cells. They live on plant cells or those of lower animals or bacteria. And the viruses that do invade our bodies alert a whole series of chemical defenses designed to overwhelm them. The time it takes to organize our defensive chemicals varies with different diseases. Our bodies win the race against time more often than we know. It is quite probable, for instance, that you have already met and overcome virus diseases that you did not even know you had.

35

Other Sections To See

"The Machinery of the Body," Volume 4; "Familiar Diseases," Volume 6; "Bacteria and Disease," Volume 7; "Exercise and Physical Fitness," Volume 8; "First Aid and Home Care of the Sick" and "Immunity," this volume; "What Does Allergy Mean to You," Volume 10; "The Wheel of Life," Volume 13; "Antibiotics," Volume 16; "Keeping the Community Healthy" and "Radiation Medicine," Volume 17.

Death in Life

What is death? Why is it necessary? Does it have any part in the healthy functioning of our bodies? Three kinds of body tissue which thrive by the death of some of their cells are discussed in "Death in Life" by Orville T. Bailey, M.D. **The Scientific Monthly**, February 1944. Used by permission of the author and **The Scientific Monthly**.

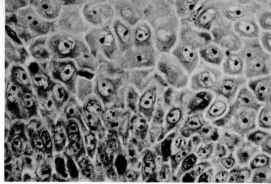

Photos, THE SCIENTIFIC MONTHLY, Feb. 1944

This is how your skin looks in cross section, under the microscope. The various cells are described on this page.

You might think that in growing you simply make more and more cells and that none are destroyed. For the most part, this is true. But there are some sequences in growth that involve the death of all or some of the cells concerned. Without this kind of death, normal growth as we know it would be impossible.

Three groups of tissue illustrate the ways in which death and life, usually regarded as extreme opposites, work together for the good of the whole. In the first group—the skin and nails—substances necessary for the body are produced by the death of cells and changes in the dead material. Hair is another example of this tissue group. In the second group—the blood—cells become so specialized that they no longer divide. After a time they die and are replaced by new cells. In the third group—bone—the death of particular cells causes a defect. Repair of the defect leads to creation of normal tissue.

Skin and Nails

The picture at the top of this page shows a cross section of skin. (See also the cross section in color in "Skin: The Body Covering," Volume 5, page 216.) At the bottom of the picture (the inner portion of the skin) you can see connective tissue cells and blood vessels. This is the part of the skin which supports and nourishes the outer layers. As new cells are formed in the inner portion they push the older cells out toward the surface. Here the old cells are no longer in contact with the cells which furnish nourishment and they

Cross section of a fingernail. At the bottom of the picture are normal skin cells. At the top of the picture are dead cells, full of closely packed fibers, which form the nail.

die. As they die they are transformed into keratin, a firm, horny substance which forms the outer layer of the skin. Keratin is necessary to the body; it keeps the tissue fluids in and foreign materials out.

The change in the cells is first detectable just toward the surface from the growing region. Granules of keratin make their appearance in the cytoplasm; at the same time the nucleus becomes more and more pale. Finally the nucleus is lost altogether and the cell is dead. Meanwhile, the granules of keratin have come to occupy the whole cell. From time to time the keratin layer rubs off somewhat and must be replaced. If much rubs off much is produced to replace it; if little rubs off little is produced. In some parts of the body the keratin layer is thicker than on others, as if to protect against more frequent irritation. The soles and palms are the outstanding examples.

Fingernails and toenails are formed by a particular group of cells of the epidermis (the same tissues which form skin and hair). The nail substance is formed at the base of the nail where there is a plate of cells somewhat thicker than that of the nearby skin. The cells here look like other living cells and divide frequently. As they do so, the older cells are pushed outward and begin to show closely packed fibers. These fibers are made of a chemical substance peculiar to the nails and are the counterpart of keratin in the outer skin layer. The nail substance slides over the lower cells as the nail extends toward the finger tip. The skin cells at the finger tip probably do not contribute to the nail in any way; if you have ever lost a nail you know that replacement comes from the base.

Blood

In certain tissue, particular cells divide over and over again, each generation showing more specialized structure. But with the structural changes the cell gradually loses its capacity for growth. The end of such a series of divisions is a cell well adapted to perform its function but unable to reproduce itself, or even to keep itself alive. It dies and is replaced by other cells which have only partially completed the series of changes. This is death in life—a cycle which must be repeated over and over from the beginning of life to old age.

An example of this type of death in life is the cells of the circulating blood. Different kinds of blood cells undergo slightly different steps, so it will be convenient to discuss the red blood cells only.

There are large cells in the bone marrow which have no specialized features of nucleus or cytoplasm and which multiply rapidly. The daughter cells begin to show differences from the parents, but the variations are not the same. Different kinds of blood cells result from these variations.

One of these groups develops into red blood cells. Here the daughter cells are smaller and more regularly rounded than their parent. These cells divide several times and each time the nucleus becomes more and more compact. At the same time hemoglobin (the blood pigment which carries oxygen to the tissues) appears in the cytoplasm as a yellowish material (which looks red when we see it in large amounts). After many divisions the cell apparently loses its capacity to divide. Then a curious thing happens which has not been observed in the maturation (growing to maturity) of any other cell in the body. The nucleus is expelled through the outer membrane of the cell. The cell, minus its nucleus, is now in its adult form and is ready to enter the blood stream.

In this series we do not know where life ends and death begins. This is one of the places where the ordinary definitions of life

A drop of blood showing one immature red cell. A normal mature red blood cell has no nucleus. When the body is making many new red cells, as when recovering from anemia, some immature red cells enter the blood stream. They are recognized by their large nuclei and different staining properties.

and death are insufficient. It is in investigating just such situations as this—where accepted definitions must be strained if they are to fit at all—that new discoveries are to be expected.

The mature red blood cells begin to disintegrate. Some are taken up by certain cells of the spleen; others are removed from the blood stream by other cells. At this time the red blood cells must be dead, for no cell engulfs another cell of the same organism unless the cell engulfed is dead.

In spite of all the various stages which must be passed before the adult red blood cell appears in the blood stream, the number of red blood cells remains almost the same as long as a person is in normal health. Even where there is a tremendous loss of red blood cells in a short time, as in hemorrhage (heavy flow of blood) the number returns to normal very quickly. How can this be done? The answer is that not all of the daughter cells from the unspecialized cells of the marrow proceed in their development. Some remain in a resting state at various stages of the cycle of development. When a sudden need arises, they become mature cells without the delay that would be necessary if they had to go through the entire cycle.

Bone

A third way in which death enters into growth is in creating a defect, the repair of which leads to normal tissue. The formation of the long bones (ribs, arms, and legs) is the best example of this phenomenon.

These bones grow in length only at the points where bone and cartilage meet (see "The Story of the Skeleton" in Vol. 6). Cartilage

37

changes into bone in a series of steps which must be carried out in a definite order if normal bone is to be formed.

First the cartilage cells divide in such a way as to produce straight columns of close-packed cells like rows of soldiers. At this point a form of cellular death intervenes. The nucleus of each cell shrinks, the cytoplasm breaks up and the cell is dead. This does not mean that growth of the bone has ceased or is abnormal. On the contrary, it is an essential step in the creation of normal bone. Meanwhile, other cartilage cells are formed and the process is repeated, over and over. It is as though the soldiers at the end of the column were constantly being shot and replacements were taking their place at the rear. The loss of the soldiers at the front would leave a vacant place unless the column moved forward or unless the enemy moved in to fill the space.

In the case of bone, the enemy (that is to say, another kind of tissue) moves in to fill the space. Small blood vessels, accompanied by a kind of connective tissue, come in to repair the defect. Thanks to this process, the new tissues are brought into contact with the cartilage. Meanwhile the cartilage has been receiving deposits of calcium, and the bone grows.

The relationships of these processes are not understood; they can only be guessed at. But it is known that if one fails, the pattern of

bone cannot be attained. When vitamin D is deficient, as in rickets, the cartilage cells do not die. Consequently, there is no defect, no repair, and no new bone. When vitamin D is restored to the diet repair begins almost immediately, and the first evidence of it is the death of cartilage cells at the margin nearest the bone!

What Is Death?

What is death, anyhow? We shall not know the answer until we know how the inactive products of the test tube differ from the living cell. Why is death a biological necessity? With this question there can be some start toward an answer.

It is possible to say something about the permanence of living cells by the study of growth of cells in the laboratory. The cell is the unit of life as it is the unit of growth. It has within itself the capacity to perform all the functions which we think of as belonging to living things. Can cells under favorable conditions continue to grow indefinitely, or does the pattern of the cell finally break up? Classical researches on this problem were done by Alexis Carrel. He began work on the problem as soon as a method was available for cultivating and maintaining cells outside the body. (This is known as tissue culture and is done by means of special nourishing fluids and careful protection from bacteria, etc.)

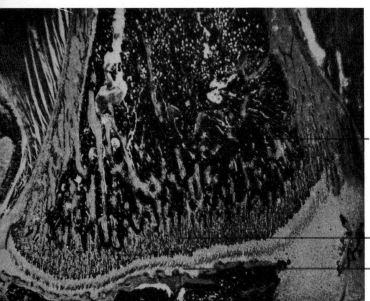

Normal growth of bone is a dramatic contest between different kinds of tissue. Cartilage cells are pushed out from the growing area, where they are formed, and die; small blood vessels, accompanied by connective tissue, take their place.

Small blood vessels and connective tissue

Dying cartilage cells

Normal cartilage cells

On January 17, 1912, he removed a piece of heart from a chick embryo. At first the fragment of heart tissue continued to beat in the tissue culture, indicating that some of the heart muscle fibers were growing. Microscopic examination showed that there were many connective tissue cells among the muscle fibers. Gradually the connective tissue cells overgrew the more slowly growing muscle cells as weeds overgrow a garden. After a time a pure culture of connective tissue cells was obtained. For many years subcultures were taken from these connective tissue cells. There was no change in the power of growth of the cells; for 34 years they continued to reproduce themselves. When the experiments came to an end, in 1946, the cells were still growing. There is no more convincing proof that connective tissue cells can reproduce themselves indefinitely as long as the environment is favorable. Once life is established it continues until conditions required to maintain the organism are no longer met.

In nature there is even more striking evidence of the immortality of protoplasm. First, all forms of life are continuous. Parents die and offspring grow, but this is not discontinuity because the young arise from living cells of their parents. On the cellular level, the chain of life is not interrupted. All life comes from life which existed before.

A second instance of immortality of the isolated cell is the growth of bacteria, which are single-celled organisms. They grow in the laboratory on artificial foods, multiplying at different rates. Like Dr. Carrel's tissue cells, bacteria, if kept in a favorable medium, would overrun the world. Life ceases only when the environment no longer supplies the substances the organism needs, or no longer removes the wastes produced in its growth.

Thus, there is a place in the scale of living things at which there is no death. How is it that death creeps in? When organisms become more complex they are composed of many cells, some cells nearer, some farther from the source of materials required. As specialization continues the requirements become more exacting; the capacity to adjust to extreme

The French scientist, Alexis Carrel (1873–1944), became known for his important investigations into the life of cells. He won the Nobel prize in 1912 for his success in transplanting organs and in suturing blood vessels together. He kept a section of chicken heart tissue alive for years in a special apparatus. His book Man the Unknown *contained many controversial ideas about man and life, and proposed researches and theories far beyond those which other scientists would accept.*

Malvina Hoffman

conditions becomes less. Here, then, is a system which carries within itself the seeds of its own destruction. Only those portions go on which have become specialized for the purpose of reproduction.

Death is the inevitable result of a high degree of specialization. Man pays the price of death in order to know and control his environment. Without death during life, many of his tissues could not be created. Without those characteristics for which he pays with death, man would still be as the bacteria.

Other Books To Read

Chemical Origin of Life, by Alexander I. Oparin. Published by Charles C. Thomas, Publisher, Springfield, Illinois, 1964.
Life: Its Nature, Origin and Development, by Alexander I. Oparin. Published by Academic Press, Inc., New York, 1962.
These two books, both translated by Ann Synge, present the research and ideas of one of the most prominent scientists in this field.

What is Life?, by Edwin Schrödinger. Published by Cambridge University Press, New York, 1963.
While most of his work lies in the field of physics, this scientist's views on the nature of life are stimulating and thought-provoking.

Adventures with a Microscope, by Richard Headstrom. Published by J. B. Lippincott Co., Philadelphia, 1941.
This book has become a classic in its field, and presents numerous explanations of what things look like through a microscope and how to use one.

Search for Life on Other Worlds, by David C. Holmes. Published by Sterling Publishing Co., New York, 1966.
Life Beyond Our Planet, by Daniel Q. Posin. Published by McGraw-Hill Book Co., New York, 1962.
Two books which deal with the fascinating question of whether life exists elsewhere in the solar system or in the galaxy, and if so, what it might be like and how it might compare with that on earth.

Your Ears: For Hearing and for Balance

In Washington, D.C., people were spending a winter afternoon watching a movie. Outside it was snowing hard. Suddenly there was a cry, "Get out! Get out!" and a man scrambled to his feet and made for the door. Others followed him, just in time; a few minutes later the roof, overstrained by the weight of the snow, collapsed onto the seats below.

Several people were killed in this terrible accident. Those who escaped owed their safety to one man's good hearing plus ability to analyze a sound. The man who gave the warning was a miner. His ear had caught faint sounds from the roof, and his brain had interpreted them as being the same kind of sounds that mean "cave-in" in the mine.*

If you think you can't use your ears as well as the miner did, you will probably find it is a matter of training. Your ear is an almost unbelievably sensitive instrument. You can hear sounds ranging from 0 to 120 on the decibel scale (shown on the opposite page). Ten points on the scale represent a tenfold difference in loudness of sound. That means that your ears can stand sounds a million million times as loud as the tiniest sound you can hear.

The other great service that your ears perform for you is that of detecting motion and helping you keep your balance. The pretzel-like structure that is responsible for this "equilibrium sense" is described in detail in "Steady Now!" page 45. Fortunately for us, disturbances of equilibrium sense are very rare indeed. We can and do get used to hearing less well as we get older. Getting used to falls and dizziness would be much harder.

How your ears hear, some tips on training them to hear better, and how you keep your balance are discussed in this section. Of course, there is a great deal more that can be said about sound, presented in Volume 14.

—Anne Norton

*This story appears in *Science for Better Living* by Brandwein, Hollingworth, Beck, and Burgess. Harcourt Brace, 1952.

Ears, ears, ears! They look quite different outwardly, but the part inside the head is almost identical among higher animals. Many animals can move their ears to help catch sound. Perhaps we could do this once; some people can still manage a wiggle!

What Do We Hear?

How Much Do Different Animals Hear?

(Frequency in cycles per second)

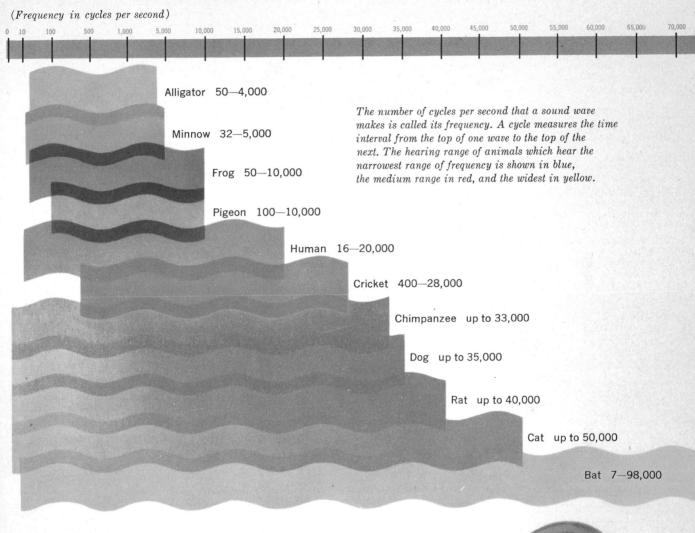

0 10 100 500 1,000 5,000 10,000 15,000 20,000 25,000 30,000 35,000 40,000 45,000 50,000 55,000 60,000 65,000 70,000

Alligator 50—4,000

Minnow 32—5,000

Frog 50—10,000

Pigeon 100—10,000

Human 16—20,000

Cricket 400—28,000

Chimpanzee up to 33,000

Dog up to 35,000

Rat up to 40,000

Cat up to 50,000

Bat 7—98,000

The number of cycles per second that a sound wave makes is called its frequency. A cycle measures the time interval from the top of one wave to the top of the next. The hearing range of animals which hear the narrowest range of frequency is shown in blue, the medium range in red, and the widest in yellow.

Where Do We Hear Sounds?

The drawing on the right uses color to indicate where sound waves of certain frequencies are changed into nerve impulses in the human cochlea (see the next page for more about the cochlea). The low tones are shown in blue, the medium in red, and the high tones in yellow.

How Loud Do Things Get?

The relative loudness of sounds is measured in decibels. A low number on the decibel scale means that the sound is relatively soft; a high number means that the sound is relatively loud. Below are the decibel ratings of some familiar noise-makers.

threshold of hearing (at a 1,000 cycle tone)

rustle of leaves

whisper

quiet garden

average dwelling

quiet office

average office

quiet automobile

vacuum cleaner

ordinary conversation

busy street

average motor truck

heavy street traffic

pneumatic drill

elevated train

riveting machine

boiler shop

airplane engine

thunder

0   10   20   30   40   50   60   70   80   90   100   110   120

The Human Ear

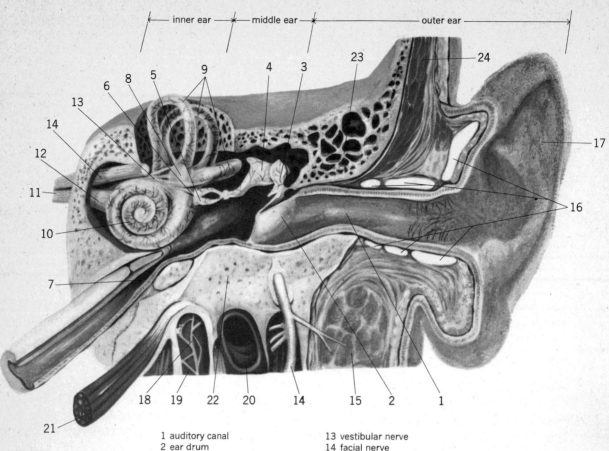

inner ear ✻ middle ear ✻ outer ear

1 auditory canal	13 vestibular nerve
2 ear drum	14 facial nerve
3 hammer	15 salivary gland
4 anvil	16 cartilage of ear
5 stirrup	17 helix
6 oval window	18 sympathetic nerve plexus
7 Eustachian tube	19 internal carotid artery
8 vestibule	20 internal jugular vein
9 semicircular canals	21 soft palate muscle
10 cochlea	22 mastoid process
11 auditory nerve	23 petrous-type bone
12 cochlear nerve	24 temporal muscle

The Cochlea

Similar in appearance to a spiral staircase, the cochlea (left) contains thousands of cells that look and work something like piano keys. These make up the organ of Corti (below) and are what help you hear. A sound wave movement in the cochlear fluid vibrates the hairs of the hair cells, which activate the auditory nerve, and a message is sent to the brain.

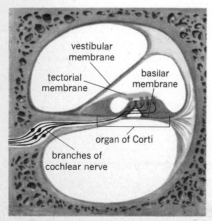

vestibular membrane
tectorial membrane
basilar membrane
organ of Corti
branches of cochlear nerve

Magnified Cross Section of Cochlea

Magnified Cross Section of Organ of Corti

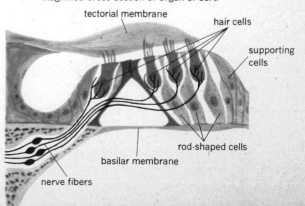

tectorial membrane
hair cells
supporting cells
rod-shaped cells
basilar membrane
nerve fibers

How Do We Hear?

Ears are like icebergs—more out of sight than on the surface. The ear drum and the little bones of the middle ear are just barely out of sight. But the cochlea, the real organ of hearing, is hidden away inside the head, in a twisted tunnel hollowed out of the temporal bone. Professor Guilford, of the University of Southern California, traces the path of sound waves from the external ear to the cochlea, and on to the brain. From **General Psychology**, J. P. Guilford, second edition, copyright 1952, D. Van Nostrand Company, Inc.

The colored picture on the opposite page shows the arrangement of the outer, middle, and inner ear. Sound waves enter the auditory canal and set into vibration the eardrum stretched across the canal at the entrance of the middle ear. The middle ear carries the vibrations on to the inner ear by means of the hammer, anvil, and stirrup bones. The base of the stirrup bone is attached to the oval window, the entrance to the inner ear, where the vibrations must be transferred to the liquid that fills the inner ear. The middle ear opens to the throat by means of the Eustachian tube. By means of this tube, air pressure inside the middle ear can be made equal to air pressure outside the drum.

The inner ear has three main parts: the vestibule, the semicircular canals, and the cochlea. All are carved-out areas in the bones of the skull and are filled with liquid. The vestibule, with the utricle and saccule, and the canals with their ampullas serve as organs of balance. The liquid of the vestibule also transmits sound vibrations onward to the cochlea. The cochlea contains the receptor cells for hearing. It is really a tube that is wound up snail-like. On the opposite page you see a cross section of the cochlea. You will notice that across the middle runs a shelf or partition. If you imagine the cochlea tube unwound, as in the picture at right, below, the position of the shelf is made clear. It extends almost to the upper end of the tube.

The organ of Corti is the real organ of hearing. It lies on the basilar membrane, which in turn is part of the shelf running the length of the cochlea. The basilar membrane is composed of a very large number of fibers, varying (1) in length, (2) in the amount of tension under which they are suspended, and (3) in the amount of loading attached to them. The basilar membrane with its fibers suggests a stringed instrument. This has been the key to the understanding of how the ear works.

How Do Sound Impulses Reach the Brain?

It is believed that each part of the basilar membrane responds most completely to some one frequency. (Frequency refers to pitch—the highness or lowness of the sound.) We cannot say that each fiber in it vibrates alone, for the fibers are bound together and it is known that a single frequency may agitate many fibers. However, for each frequency there is a point on the membrane which responds more than the points around it. Once the basilar membrane is in vibration, certain hair cells in the organ of Corti that rest upon it are also agitated. In touch with these cells are the receptor cells, the sensitive nerve endings that connect with nerve fibers to form the auditory nerve. This nerve is like a cable composed of millions of strands; the entire bundle is no thicker than the lead of a pencil. The auditory nerve carries the impulses to a special part of the brain, the cerebrum, which interprets the sound.

43

The inner ear, shown in its actual form (left)
and with the spiral cochlea straightened and laid open (right).

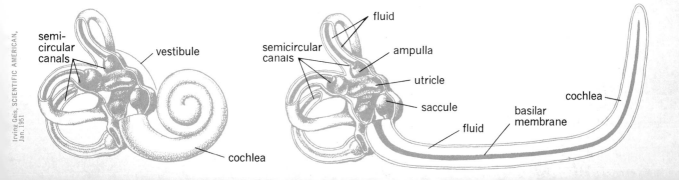

semi-circular canals   vestibule   cochlea

fluid   semicircular canals   ampulla   utricle   saccule   fluid   basilar membrane   cochlea

What Can You Hear?

How Far Can You Hear?

The next time you and your friends get together, try this. Blindfold the person to be tested and hold a ticking watch next to the left ear, while he covers the right ear with his hand. Now slowly walk away from him with the watch and ask him to tell you when he no longer hears it. Then move the watch back until he *just* hears it. Measure the distance from watch to ear with a yardstick. Repeat with the right ear. To make a good test, you ought to run it at least three times and average your measurements. If you think your subject is faking, you can walk farther off with the watch when he thinks you are coming back!

You will probably find that no two people have the same measurements. Don't forget that many different degrees of good or not-so-good hearing are still "normal."

What Sound Is It?

This one is fun from two points of view: how keenly you can hear, how well you can identify a sound. Pass out paper and pencils, set a five minute limit, and ask your friends to write down all the noises they can hear—in the house, outdoors, or wherever you are playing. Score a point for each sound heard and a point for each sound correctly identified. For instance, "soft, whispery sound" scores 1, but "whispery sound, maybe the phonograph turntable running" gets 2.

steady now!

People are likely to think of hearing as the most important business of the ears. However, ears have another function: maintaining balance. People can and do get along without their hearing, but they are almost helpless without a sense of equilibrium. This article describes the neat little structures that keep us steady. Reprinted by permission of the publisher, Abelard-Schuman, Inc., from **The World Through Your Senses** by Sarah R. Riedman, copyright, 1954.

If you were perched at the top of a skyscraper, you would sway with it from side to side. Does this seem strange? It may seem so, but engineers tell us that if it weren't constructed to have this sway the building might topple with the force of the wind. The Empire State building, although firmly rooted in the ground, still sways a few inches at the top. If you held a yardstick upright on a flat table and tilted it from side to side ever so slightly, you would see that, like the skyscraper, it sways at the top and barely moves at the bottom. Your head too moves more than the rest of your body whenever there is the slightest danger of losing your balance. The apparatus controlling your equilibrium, located as it is in your head, is in the best possible position to "sense" motion.

Canals and Sacs for Balance

Attached to the cochlea in each ear, but unrelated to our hearing, are three little canals. Shaped like tiny horseshoes, they are called the semicircular canals. They are arranged in three directions or planes, as shown in the diagram above. This arrangement is important, because if you turn your head from right to left, downward and to the right, upward and to the left, or if you just rotate your head, the sense organ in one or more pairs of the canals will be stimulated.

The semicircular canals, like the cochlea, are bony tunnels filled with fluid. Suspended in each is a membranous canal also filled with fluid. One end of each canal has a swelling. Inside this swelling, or ampulla, is a little protruding hill of cells. The cells are topped with stiff hairs, and they receive nerve end-

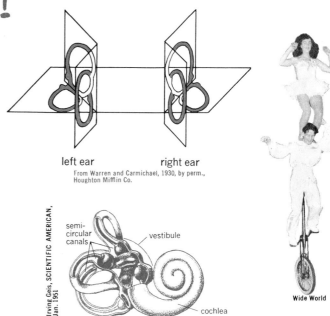

left ear   right ear

From Warren and Carmichael, 1930, by perm.,
Houghton Mifflin Co.

Irving Geis, SCIENTIFIC AMERICAN, Jan. 1951

semicircular canals

vestibule

cochlea

Wide World

Could you ride a monocycle? Not without the help of your semicircular canals, which are described in this article. The small diagram shows how the arrangement of the canals helps us sense head movement in any direction.

ings from a branch of the auditory nerve. Whenever the head moves, these hairs are free to swing in the fluid that surrounds them.

How To Keep from Falling

The hair cells in the semicircular canals are stimulated by a *change* in the speed of motion of the body. The earth is constantly turning, and we with it, but because its motion is at the same *rate* all the time we don't feel it. However, if you turn someone in a swivel chair, the rate of motion changes, sometimes slower, sometimes faster; such changes in the rate of motion are felt, because the hair cells are stimulated. How?

When the head is rotated, the fluid in the semicircular canals presses on the hair cells, which then discharge a nerve impulse from the nerve endings. In one ear the pressure is heightened; in the other it is reduced. Together the two nerves start a reflex movement of the muscles which prevents you from falling.

The fluid in the semicircular canals does

45

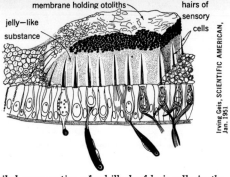

Irving Geis, SCIENTIFIC AMERICAN, Jan. 1951

Detailed cross section of a hillock of hair cells in the utricle. The pressure of otoliths upon the hairs gives the sense of up or down. Similar cells appear in the saccule.

not move as fast as the head itself. After rotation has stopped, the lag in the movement of fluid makes you feel as if you were still turning. Then the fluid catches up and gives a sensation of turning in the opposite direction.

Which Way Is Up?

The sensory organs in the semicircular canals are stimulated when you are spinning, whirling, or swinging. But other structures in the inner ear tell you which way is up and which way is down. For instance, if you do a handstand or handstand, you know the position of the body because these little structures are stimulated by the pull of gravity.

Two little membranous bags, the utricle and saccule, connect with the membranous semicircular canals. They contain fluid and a hillock of hair cells just like the ones in the ampulla. The only difference between this structure and the one in the semicircular canals is that the hairs are weighted with the tiniest stones made of lime. These are called the otoliths, meaning ear stones. How do the otoliths work in response to changes in the pull of gravity? One scientist studied similar ear structures in a crayfish. The equilibrium organ of the crayfish is a little sac of cells with hairs on which the otoliths rest. The sac opens to the surface of the animal

A

at rest

B

beginning of movement

C

continued movement

D

movement stopped

E

at rest

These diagrams show how body movement affects the hair cells in the semicircular canals. When movement begins (B) fluid and hairs are backed up, away from the direction of motion. If movement is continued at an even rate (C) the fluid will soon "catch up" and hairs will come upright. After movement has stopped (D) the fluid wells up in the opposite direction, carrying the hairs with it. This gives rise to aftersensations of opposite movement.

After Boring, Langfeld and Weld, 1935, by permission of John Wiley & Sons, Inc.

and so it was possible to do this clever experiment.

When the animal is upright, the otoliths rest upon the hair cells and stimulate them by their weight. Now the scientist played a trick upon the crayfish. He removed the otoliths and put iron filings into the sac instead. When he brought a magnet close to the sac, the iron filings moved in the direction of the magnet, pressing down on different cells. If the magnet was held to the left of the animal, even though the animal was in an upright position, it behaved as if it were pulled to the left. The animal attempted to "right" itself, when it was already upright, thereby actually upsetting itself.

We have evidence that the utricle and saccule in human beings are also stimulated by changes in the gravitational pull. Even with eyes closed you know whether you are up or down in a roller coaster, because the hair cells are stimulated by the pull of gravity on the otoliths.

The utricle and saccule give us clues about the position of our body; the semicircular canals adjust the body to movements that are likely to upset our balance. Disturbances in the inner ear structures, caused by movements of the head, produce reflex movements of the neck muscles which set the head "right" again.

Do You Get Seasick?

When you walk, run, swim, skate, glide, or ride a bicycle you are moving in a horizontal direction, which you are used to. But if you are on a Ferris wheel you are going up and down. The same is true in an airplane during "bumpy" weather, on a ship in a rough sea, or even in a fast-moving elevator during sudden starts and stops. The semicircular canals are excessively stimulated by these unnatural motions, which also stimulate certain other nerve centers in the brain. The result is nausea and seasickness. Lying down often helps, because when the body is in the horizontal position these very same up-and-down movements are more like the ones the body undergoes during horizontal (walking) motions.

How to Tell
Where a Sound
Is Coming From

While the ears are not as adept as the eyes at locating objects, they can do a pretty good job and you can help them. This article, written for soldiers, explains how sound waves of different lengths reach the ears. Be sure to read also the section on sound in Volume 14.

From **Psychology for the Fighting Man**, prepared by National Research Council with the collaboration of Science Service. Copyright 1943 by National Research Council and Combat Forces Press (formerly Infantry Journal Press). Revised by editor, 1963.

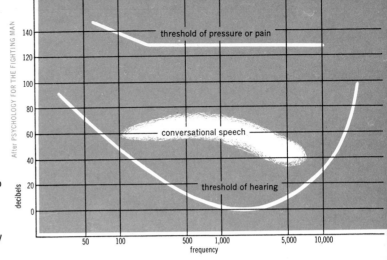

This graph shows the area of audible sounds, ranging from the lower threshold of sounds that can just be heard, to the upper threshold at which sounds cause pain. The white shape shows the area of ordinary speech.

All sounds start with the vibration of something. The vibrating object presses the neighboring molecules of air, and these in turn, press against their neighboring molecules, thus starting a pressure wave, or compression. Sounds differ from one another. It is sometimes important to distinguish different sounds.

What Kind of Sound Is It?

One way sounds are distinguished is by their highness or lowness—their *pitch*. Pitch depends on the frequency of the vibrations that make up the sound.

Loudness helps in judging the distance of familiar sounds. Loudness is governed by the amount of energy behind the sound. For instance, the engines of a plane have more energy than that of an automobile.

More important than pitch or loudness is what is known as the quality of a sound. It is the *quality* rather than the pitch that permits you to know one man's voice from another's. The quality of a sound depends on the mixture of tones that make it up.

What Sounds Can We Hear?

There are many sounds that human ears cannot pick up. The best ears cannot generally hear sounds with frequencies below fifteen waves a second. And at the other end of the scale people can seldom hear tones much above 20,000 waves per second. Notes too low to be heard are sometimes felt as vibrations on the body and may be annoying or even terrifying. Notes too high to be audible—sometimes called the "death ray"—are damaging to small organisms such as germs. Experiments are in progress to test the effect of "supersonics" on the nervous system of higher animals.

Physicists and engineers measure the energy of sound in decibels. (The decibel scale is explained and illustrated in color on page 41.) The graph on this page shows the frequencies and decibels at which audible sounds occur. The lower curve represents the threshold of hearing—the faintest sound that can be heard at each frequency. The upper curve shows the threshold at which uncomfortable pressure or pain is felt. At 120 decibels, a sound is pretty close to the ceiling of hearing. You can have more energy and more pain, but not much louder sounds.

It is astonishing how sensitive your ears are to sounds in the frequency range of 1,000–4,000. At a frequency of 3,600 your eardrum has to move only one one-billionth of an inch to make a sound just audible.

Locating Objects by Sound

The ear is not as good as the eye for locating the position of objects. A ventriloquist talks without moving his lips while the dummy on his lap makes the mouth movements. The dummy seems to be talking, because the eyes of

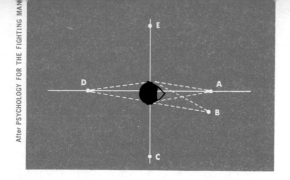

We place most easily the sounds that come from the side (E and C) because they arrive at one ear before the other. A sound at an intermediate point (B) is placed the same way, but less easily. Sounds from A and D are hard to place because they arrive at both ears at once.

the audience locate the speaking mouth exactly, whereas the ears cannot give such accurate information.

Nevertheless the ears can do a good job in telling whether a sound is from the right or the left or from some intermediate position, although they make mistakes about the difference between front and back, or up and down, and in estimating distances.

The capacity to locate sound depends on the fact that people have two ears, one on each side of the head. The sound gets to the far ear after it arrives at the near ear, and it is louder at the ear it reaches directly than at the ear that is screened by the head.

Look at the picture at the top of this page. A sound at E is loud in the left ear, faint in the right; and it gets to the left ear first. The opposite is true for a sound starting at C.

If the sound comes from A, it gets to both ears at the same time and with the same intensity, a relationship which leads the hearer to localize the sound halfway between left and right. The same relation holds for a sound from D, and the result is that sounds in front (A) and in back (D) are apt to be confused. The sound from in back may be a little fainter than the one from in front because the outer ears screen the sound from the rear. That clue works, however, only if you know how loud the sound ought to be.

A sound from B is a little earlier and a little louder at the right ear. The two ears, working together, localize it correctly.

The low frequencies (as in thunder) are localized mostly by the difference in time of arrival at the two ears. Since these sound waves are long, there is considerable difference in arrival time at the two ears. But, being long, the sound waves slip easily around the head so that there is little difference in loudness at the two ears.

On the other hand, the high frequencies (as in a whistle) are localized almost entirely by loudness difference. The waves are very short and do not leave much chance for differences in time to operate, but, being short, they cannot easily get around the head. Thus the ear that is wholly or partly screened by the head hears only a faint sound.

Both principles operate together for most sounds, because most sounds have both low and high frequencies.

The Seeing Ear

Adapted with permission from **Science News Letter** © 1962 by Science Service.

As long ago as 1793 it was discovered that bats determine distance by listening to echoes of their rapidly repeated cries. In the same way, the bottle-nose dolphin or porpoise uses a train of underwater sonic pulses to navigate the ocean.

Now, experiments conducted by Dr. W. N. Kellogg, professor of experimental psychology at Florida State University, Tallahassee, show that blind people, too, can detect obstacles by bouncing echoes off them.

To perform this human sonar, blind people and blindfolded "controls" talked, sang, whistled, hissed, snapped fingers, clicked tongues, or made other noises to judge both the kind and distance of objects from which the echoes were bounced.

Metal, wood, denim, cloth, and velvet "sounded different." Denim cloth and velvet could be differentiated by the blind 86.5% of the time.

Sound Detectives

Animals can use hearing far more expertly than human beings. Ira M. Freeman explains how in this excerpt from **All About Sound and Ultrasonics**, copyright, 1961, by the author. Reprinted by permission of Random House, Inc. **All About** books are published in England by W. H. Allen & Company.

Most people think of such words as *voice* and *speech* in connection with human beings only, but many animals can "sing" and "talk," too. This does not refer to parrots and myna birds that can be trained to give a fair imitation of human speech. Many animals have a kind of speech of their own, and they use it for more purposes than people do. It is now known that animals use sounds not only for communicating with each other, but for finding food and for navigation.

Some of the biggest animal "blabbermouths" are fish and other creatures that live in the oceans. When scientists put a microphone down into the sea, they may hear a tremendous racket—a mixture of grunts, whistles, barks, groans and other noises. Although many of these noises can be traced to certain undersea animals, scientists still do not know where some of the sounds come from.

One of the simplest underwater sounds is made by the toadfish. The "visible speech" record of this sound shows how simple it is compared with the human voice. Another fish, the goby, has had its voice recorded. A scientist studying these sounds made tape recordings of them and then played the sound back, under water. Male gobies flocked toward the place where the sound came from, and a great free-for-all fight took place. Other fish, too, produce sounds that their own kind will recognize. Sea croakers make a noise like the "rat-tat-tat" of a machine gun.

During the Second World War, American coasts were protected by explosive mines that would be set off by propeller noises from enemy submarines. The coast defense stations found that often these mines exploded when no submarines were around. It was discovered that the sounds that set off these explosions were the "conversations" of toadfish or of snapping shrimps. The U. S. Navy is now doing research to develop controls against such underwater interference.

Sea creatures are not the only animals that can talk to each other. A farmer found that the squealing of a trapped "king" rat would warn other rats to stay away from his barn. A tape recording of the cries worked just as well, and even kept mice and squirrels away.

This diagram shows how a bat locates its prey by sending out sounds and listening for echoes. The squeaks have such high sound frequencies (50,000 vibrations a second) that you cannot hear them. Each bat knows its own sounds, ignores those of other bats.

Irving Geis

How Bats Use Sonar

Most animals seem to depend on sight or smell to find their food, but some use sound as a kind of sonar for this purpose. Over 200 years ago, an Italian scientist wanted to find out how bats track down the insects that they feed on. Having released some blind bats in a room, he noticed that they avoided things that were in their way, just as if they could actually see them.

Then the experimenter allowed the blind bats to fly outdoors. When they returned home, he found that there were freshly caught insects in their stomachs. The bats were certainly using something other than their eyes to find their way around, but the scientists of that time had no idea what this might be.

Only a few years ago, American scientists were able to solve the puzzle. First, they checked the fact that bats can fly around just as well when blindfolded as when they are able to see. Next, they covered the ears of some bats. The animals did not seem willing to fly; and when they did, they kept bumping into things.

The experimenters had the idea that the bats themselves made sounds that were reflected back to them from nearby objects, just as in sonar. So the next thing they did was to cover the nose and mouth of a bat, leaving its ears free. Again, the result was that it kept bumping into things. This was pretty good proof that bats make voice sounds that they use as sonar.

When ways were found to record the sound, it proved to be a series of sharp, ultrasonic "squeaks." The actual sound frequencies go up as high as 50,000. Bats also make sounds of around 5,000 vibrations a second, and these are the squeaks that your ear is able to hear.

But they are not used for navigation or for locating insects in flight, because the ultrasonic waves are better for this purpose.

Further experiments showed that bat sonar is so sensitive and accurate that a bat easily finds his way in the dark through a maze of fine wires stretched across a room. And each bat seems to be able to recognize his own sounds and ignore all those made by other bats.

Porpoise Sonar

The porpoise is another animal that uses sonar for finding food. The underwater sound waves made by this animal can even tell him the difference between two kinds of fishes. In fact, porpoise sonar is better than any system that man has been able to build, and U.S. Navy scientists are studying it in order to find ways of improving their own. Besides being able to use sonar, porpoises can be trained to give an imitation of some human speech sounds.

Bird Language

Of all animal sounds, the songs of birds are probably the most beautiful. Scientists believe that birds use their musical songs for communication, and also "just for fun." Besides his true song, a bird has a special call note that he uses to warn others when an enemy, such as a hawk or owl, is near. The young of some birds have a kind of "baby talk" made up of a great variety of sounds. As they grow older, they drop the sounds that they do not hear older birds use—just as human babies do. What is left is the grown-up song pattern.

There is certainly much more to be found out about the wonderful sounds that animals make. With modern electronic ways of recording and studying these sounds, progress should be very rapid in the next few years.

50

American Museum of Natural History

Famous Flo and her offspring, Flicker, of the Lerner Marine Laboratory in the Bahamas, like all porpoises and dolphins, locate food by undersea sonar.

Deafness

Once there was a man who was just a little hard of hearing. So he bought a plastic button at the ten cent store and wore it in his ear. Worked fine, he reported. Everybody was careful to turn toward him and speak clearly, and that was all he needed!

It's too bad that people who need real hearing aids do not adopt this casual manner. Too often they refuse to admit that they need an aid. Sometimes the trouble is just that they do not understand their deafness or realize how much can be done for them. Reprinted with permission from Edwin Garrigues Boring, Herbert Sidney Langfeld and Harry Porter Weld: Foundations of Psychology, 1948, John Wiley & Sons, Inc.

Normal hearing, like normal intelligence, is something which exists only in the averages of the statistician. All ears differ more or less from the average ear. The ability to hear usually starts out quite near "normal" in small children and declines through the natural processes of aging or, sometimes, through accident or disease.

A relatively small number of children are born deaf, perhaps one in six thousand. They are also mutes, that is, without speech, because without hearing they do not have the natural means of learning to speak words. A somewhat larger group of people lose their hearing entirely, often as a result of infection or disease, less often through degeneration of the inner ear because of a little-understood hereditary defect.

With no hearing the totally deaf person has to rely on his eyes or his sense of touch. The easiest form of communication to learn is a sign language which is an elaborate system of manual gestures and finger spelling invented for the deaf. Better schools for the deaf, however, insist on speech and lip reading, more difficult skills to acquire, but skills that permit a far more normal adjustment of the deaf to ordinary life. (You can read about deaf children in school in "Exceptional People and Their Problems," in Volume 7.) The speech of persons who are totally deaf is generally intelligible, but it has a characteristic single-tone quality and other peculiarities that are due to the fact that the speaker cannot hear his own voice.

A far larger group than the totally deaf may be described as hard-of-hearing. Persons in this group have a measure of hearing, but their sensitivity is below normal. These are the people who may benefit from medical care or from the use of well-designed hearing aids. One in four over age 65 falls in this group.

What the Audiogram Shows

Loss of sensitivity for the hard-of-hearing is commonly shown by a chart called an *audiogram*. Some sample audiograms are shown at the top of the next page. In this chart "normal"

Transistor hearing aids are smaller than those which use vacuum tubes. They also cost less to operate. Read about transistors in "Transistors: Mighty Midgets," in Volume 4.

Sonotone Corp.

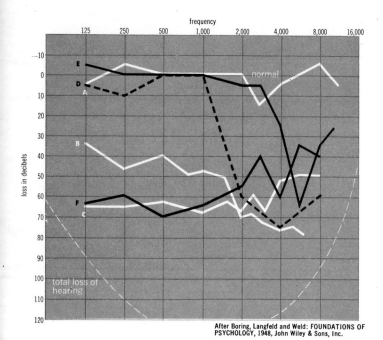

frequency

After Boring, Langfeld and Weld: FOUNDATIONS OF PSYCHOLOGY, 1948, John Wiley & Sons, Inc.

Two Kinds of Deafness

The cause of the deafness may be located in either the middle ear or the inner ear. If, for instance, scar tissue has grown over the ear-drum, as a result of long-continued infection of the middle ear, or if the joints between the little bones of the middle ear become fixed through otosclerosis, the resulting deafness we call conduction deafness. Sound is blocked before it reaches the inner ear, and the audiogram shows a large loss at all frequencies. On the other hand, if some acute infection, such as comes with scarlet fever or meningitis, happens to strike at the inner ear, the hair cells and the connecting nerve fibers may be destroyed over some part of the basilar membrane. The result is a "perceptive," or better, a "nerve" deafness. Particular frequencies are no longer heard. The resulting audiogram may show a sharp dip, most often at high frequencies but sometimes at the lower end or in the middle.

When a person has pure conduction deafness, sound can still be transmitted to the intact cochlea by means of *bone conduction*. The sound waves pass readily through the bones of the head and by compressing the walls of the labyrinth set the fluids of the cochlea in motion. Anyone can hear bone-conducted sound by touching a vibrating tuning fork to his teeth.

Tremendous improvements in the design of hearing aids have been made recently. Unfortunately these devices are still not so common as glasses, and too many people struggle along with an unnecessary handicap. The choice of a suitable hearing aid depends largely on the degree of hearing loss. Moderate losses are helped by almost any good aid. Purely conductive deafness can be overcome by the use of a bone conduction receiver which rests on the mastoid bone just back of the ear. Other forms of deafness merely require great enough amplification. To be sure, there must be wide-range, high-fidelity amplification, which is not always easy to attain.

hearing is represented by the zero line near the top of the audiogram. A person who can just hear the tone heard by the average listener is represented by points along the normal line. The curve *A* shows a typical audiogram with the ups and downs of a normal ear. Losses of sensitivity are then shown below this line in terms of the number of decibels by which a tone must be increased above the normal level in order to be heard.

Abnormal audiograms are grouped into three or four loosely defined classes. Curve *C* illustrates, for instance, a "flat" loss in which all frequencies are equally difficult to hear. Another common picture is shown in *B* where the loss gradually gets worse as frequencies from low to high are tested.

A sudden drop in the audiogram, as shown in curve *D*, is common among soldiers whose ears have been injured by very close explosions. Some ears develop such losses without injury, as illustrated in curve *E*. The loss often starts near 4,000 cycles (or vibrations—a measure of frequency) per second. On the diagram the line makes a wide, deep notch. The rarest type of audiogram is the one shown as *F;* it is down most at low frequencies, gradually rising toward the high end. It is more usual for people to miss high frequency sounds.

MacKinlay Kantor tells how . . .

Joth Countryman Retires

MacKinlay Kantor is an Iowan who knows his old soldiers. The Civil War is his particular interest; and **Joth** was the first of many stories to make use of this background.

Not all deaf people have the good sense to meet their handicap as Joth Countryman did. But if you think you know **what** he did—well, you may be mistaken. Condensed from "Joth Countryman Retires" from **Author's Choice** by MacKinlay Kantor. Copyright, 1944, by MacKinlay Kantor. Reprinted with permission of Coward-McCann, Inc.

. . . two, or even three times to come to dinner.

Joth Countryman was getting deaf. In fact, he was already deaf. No one, he was sure, except himself knew it. His wife had to call him two or even three times to come to dinner, and when he asked for plug tobacco at the grocery and the clerk inquired, "Thin, medium, or thick?" old Joth would mumble a reply about somebody being sick.

It would not have set the town of Rock River agog, this newly discovered infirmity of Joth's, had it not been for Rock River's most highly prized musical organization—the fife and drum corps. When the straggling lines of white-haired men who made up the National Encampment of the G.A.R. (Grand Army of the Republic, men who served on the Union side in the Civil War) marched through the streets of Des Moines in 1922, the Rock River drum corps led. It was a proud day for all concerned, and no veteran enjoyed it more than Joth Countryman, who played a fife with the same inspiring reverence that he had at a little Tennessee town, sixty years before.

But now old Countryman was an object of general concern. At a Washington's Birthday program in Council Bluffs, Joth's fate was sealed. Had not Ethan Lee, the fife major, given out the name of the next tune—"Village Quickstep"—in perfectly audible tones? And had not Comrade Countryman played "1776," unaware that the sudden rests of the gay "Quickstep" (B flat) did not harmonize with

the shrill grace notes of "1776," played in the key of F?

On Hoseah Haverhill, Joth's brother fifer, fell the distasteful task of informing old Countryman that he was to retire—with all honor, of course, but that he was positively to retire from the drum corps. His blue eyes would twinkle no more as he tapped the ground with his toe while "Turkey in the Straw" clattered on the rims of the battered drums.

"Aw, why pick on me?" growled Hoseah. "I'd make a mess of it sure—Joth would tell me t' go t' blazes. He don't know he's deef!"

Ethan Lee's snowy-eyebrowed scowl became almost threatening. "Hose, I done lots of things fer you. Joth wouldn't take it from me, being as I'm leader. But you're different. You've known him fer years—you was in the war with him. Now, a little hint on the side—"

Thus the matter stood in March. By April, Ethan Lee began to watch Joth's face for the signs of surprise and indignation which would inevitably follow the "hint" from Hose.

Came the middle of the month. It was Joth's birthday and his daughter invited the eleven able-bodied members of Winfield Scott Post, Number 157, to an A-1 dinner at which her father was the guest of honor. As yet he appeared to be unconscious of the shadow that had fallen on him, and no one was willing for him to come to the realization that night

53

if it could be helped. One and all shouted; the conversation at the table resembled a continuous thunderstorm.

Hoseah Haverhill tried to elude Ethan Lee at the conclusion of festivities, but was not successful.

"I can't do it yet, Ethan," mourned the ambassador, "I simply ain't got the nerve. Maybe Monetery Cooter—"

"I wish to land there was some other way out of it," muttered Lee. "But thunderation, he wouldn't want to spoil our music on Decoration Day! It seems awful, but I reckon we're all getting old, and we'll all have to quit sooner or later. Joth's time has come now."

And so the matter rode—and Memorial Day burst upon Rock River with a wealth of floating flags, and white-clad children and Legion boys in uniforms too tight for them. Shortly after the noon hour, the Corps gathered in front of G.A.R. headquarters and began a preliminary concert for the benefit of the crowd. The eleven veterans who could march were all active; eight were members of the fife and drum corps, while the remaining three had formed a pathetic escort for the colors, borne aloft by the gnarled hands of Otto Yaus. A line of automobiles carried the rest of the old soldiers. This was their day of days.

In the middle of "The Belle of the Mohawk Vale," Joth Countryman pushed his way through the circle of listeners, with his face beaming and his old metal fife clutched in his hand.

"A little bit late," he chuckled when the music had ceased, as he carefully wiped his fife in preparation for service, "but Addy would rub my coat with gasoline; said it was awful dirty."

Ethan Lee felt a great, choking wave around

his heart. But right was right—the honor of the Corps was at stake. He motioned to Hoseah Haverhill, and the latter reluctantly detached himself from the players and walked toward Joth. All eyes were on the scene; everyone knew with regret what the outcome must be.

"Come upstairs to the hall a minute, Joth," shouted the white-faced Hoseah, "I got something I want t' tell you." He wiped his brow freely as they climbed the stairway and entered the G.A.R. room, where cavalry sabres and pictures of Lincoln covered the walls. "Joth did you ever think that you might—sometimes—perhaps, quit playing in the fife and drum corps?"

Joth was suddenly very pale. "Hose, what do you mean?"

Haverhill felt stricken and weak. He could not rob his old comrade of the great joy to which he clung. The Corps must find another way. . . . The walls of the room seemed to fade away, and great clouds of sour smoke filled the air. There was a roaring and thrum and whirling about Hoseah—a flashing mist that the distant musicians could not pierce. The face before him . . . not old Joth Countryman, deaf and dispirited, but a boy! A boy with burning eyes and light bronze hair. And how the ancient wound in his own shoulder seemed to throb in response . . . Shiloh! He heard again the rattle of the old Greyhounds' muskets in the fierce horror of the battle. His shoulder hurt a great deal, and only the wild shriek of his bronze-haired comrade seemed to pull him back to life.

"Git—Git! Ye—ye devils! He's my pardner—ye can't have him!"

Hoseah had gripped the boy with his hands in a last, despairing hold on life—he was shaking him, dragging him. And the sixty years passed in a muttered rumble. Joth was questioning, "What was that, Hose? What was you saying?" Down the dusty stairway, into the crowd, the waiting crowd. "Why are we back down here, Hose? And you didn't tell me what you wanted. . . ."

The parade had formed and the mayor was lifting his hand as a signal for the Corps to strike up.

"Joth can play!" Hoseah kept muttering, as he shoved his comrade into place. "Joth can play. . . . I don't give a damn if he does make some wrong notes! What's the tune?" he hissed into Ethan Lee's astonished face. "Tell me what you're gonna play!"

"Jefferson n' Liberty," Lee answered, and once again the words seemed to come down sixty years.

Hoseah gripped Joth's elbow. "The tune is Jefferson n' Liberty!" he shrieked, in a tone that many townspeople afterward swore was heard over by the electric light plant. Countryman nodded and glanced toward the leader's baton. It dropped with a jerk, and the bearded lips of Joth Countryman carressed the mouth-piece of his instrument as the notes shrilled on high. There was not a variation, not a false chord. The other members of the Corps played on in grim anticipation of the break. But none came. The marshal lifted his hand for another song.

"Hell on the Wabash!" yelled Hoseah in Joth's ear.

Again the old man nodded, and again his eyes sought the baton of the leader as it jerked down to begin the song.

How that flag carried by Otto Yaus streamed in the wind! Like a banner of spirited music, almost—and here was Joth Countryman, marching in perfect step, playing with never a false note. It was almost unbelievable.

They reached the cemetery; the flags above the rounded graves rippled in the soft breeze. The drummers were slipping handkerchiefs under the snares to muffle their drums; the parade had come to a halt. Joth Countryman did not need to be told the name of the tune he should play. He knew well enough. Beneath that velvety sod, other old men would be listening, listening . . .

It was after the ceremony when Joth turned to Hoseah Haverhill. Ethan Lee hovered near and was summoned by an imperious wave of Countryman's hand. "Come over here," called the old man, "you other fellers, too." His sweep included the querulous members of the disbanding drum corps.

"Boys," said Joth, "I got something to tell you. I'm getting a little hard of hearing, and I wanted to admit it before you all. Hain't noticed it, have you? Probably not—But what I was going to say was—you might git a piece of paper and put on it the names of the songs we play. Then when you was going to play, Hose could take the paper and point me out the name, and I'd know what it was. All the way up here today he bellered in my ear like an Angus bull, and I'm afraid that I'm deafer in consequence. I don't need to hear the rest of you playing; I can watch Ethan's baton."

Hoseah Haverhill drew a long breath. "Joth," he replied, "I'm the biggest fool in Rock River, or Hamilton County, or pretty near all Ioway. Ethan gets second place. Can you hear me, Joth? Well, no matter; I'll write it down . . . or beller, like an Angus bull!"

"Boys, I got something to tell you."

Ear Troubles

Probably you have had an earache some time in your life. Would you like to know more about what caused it? This article discusses some of the more common ear troubles, and what can be done for them. From **The Book of Health**, compiled and edited by Randolph Lee Clark, Jr., M.D., and Russell W. Cumley, Ph.D. Copyright 1953 by Elsevier Press, Inc.

The wrong way to blow your nose—and it may lead to an earache. Blow both nostrils at once, not one at a time.

Earache may arise from many causes and may occur in numerous forms. The most usual pain in the ear, aside from that caused by mechanical injuries, arises from some type of bacterial infection. Although painful, most forms of earache are not dangerous, but because some types can become fatal, it is wise to consult a physician whenever symptoms arise.

In many cases, earache is caused by a foreign body that has become trapped in the ear. If the foreign body plugs the auditory canal, there may be a temporary deafness which is relieved on removal of the object. Such foreign bodies should be removed by a physician. Sometimes earache may be caused by hardened wax in the ear. This, too, should be treated by a physician.

Sometimes, following a cold or other respiratory infection, shooting pains are felt in the ear. The eardrum, which divides the outer ear from the middle ear, may become inflamed. The physician probably will use a medicated solution to clear the inflamation. Normal hearing may continue throughout the course of the disease.

Infections of the Middle Ear

The middle ear is located between two avenues of possible infection. Bacteria may enter through a broken eardrum, but the Eustachian tube is the more common route, since it opens into the cavity behind the nose. Respiratory infections often invade the middle ear through this route. Blowing the nose incorrectly is sometimes responsible for middle ear infections. Both nostrils should be blown at the same time, for blowing only one side at a time may force infecting material into the Eustachian tube.

At the onset of a middle ear infection, the Eustachian tube closes. It is then that the first symptoms arise. Sharp, stabbing pains shoot through the ear, and a heavy feeling is noticed on that side of the head. Yawning or blowing the nose relieves the pain for a short time. This kind of middle ear infection may last a few days or a few weeks.

Sulfonamide drugs and antibiotics are used with much success in the treatment of middle ear infection; still it may be necessary for the doctor to make a cut in the eardrum and drain the fluid which may have accumulated. After the inflammation subsides, it is sometimes necessary to remove or add air to the middle ear chamber in order to attain the correct pressure there.

Other forms of middle ear infection are not so severe, but may last longer. The Eustachian tube, through which the infection is carried, is usually swollen, although pain may be slight, and waves of deafness are felt at some times and not at others. A ringing sound (tinnitus) may be heard, and a fullness felt in the affected ear. Attacks may sometimes be prevented by removal of infected tonsils.

Hearing may be damaged in later life if a person has repeated attacks of middle ear infection.

Chronic Infections

A chronic (long continued) middle ear infection may develop as a result of repeated ear infections or from respiratory diseases. It may

56

also be caused by diseases such as tuberculosis and measles. Other causes are obstructions in the nose, improper blowing of the nose, washing out the nose, or diseased tonsils or adenoids.

One of the main symptoms of chronic middle ear infection is a ringing sensation in the ear. It comes at intervals at first, then gradually the ringing becomes constant. The sounds vary both in pitch and intensity. Nausea may accompany the ringing. Hearing is usually affected, but total deafness seldom occurs. The only hope of complete recovery lies in early treatment. Draining of the middle ear can be accomplished successfully and safely by surgery, by which a small cut is made in the eardrum.

Statistics show that ten per cent of severe deafness in adults arises from middle ear infection in childhood. Boys and girls should practice good health habits which will increase their resistance to respiratory diseases.

Mastoid Trouble

Infection of the mastoid process (a part of the temporal bone right behind the ear) has become much less frequent in the past few years, as a result of the use of antibiotics such as penicillin, streptomycin, and aureomycin. Mastoiditis, as this infection is called, involves the middle ear, for the infection must invade this part of the ear in order to reach the mastoid process.

The inflammation in mastoiditis involves the lining of the mastoid cells. Drainage, which eventually turns into pus, is a characteristic of the disease. The causes of mastoiditis include respiratory infection, abnormal formation of the ear, improper channels for ear drainage, and lowered resistance to infection. Mastoiditis may occur as a secondary infection following various diseases.

The chief symptom of mastoiditis is pain, intense pain lasting six or more days if untreated. Fever may or may not be present. Hearing may be lessened to some degree.

During the past decade, the use of antibiotic drugs in the treatment of patients with middle ear infections has practically eliminated mastoiditis. If the disease does occur,

the physician may perform an operation in which the infected mastoid cells are removed.

Motion Sickness

Seasickness, airsickness, and elevator sickness are forms of motion sickness caused by irregular and unusual motion which upsets equilibrium. The usual symptoms are dizziness, nausea, vomiting, and thirst.

The semicircular canals of the inner ear are responsible for adjusting the body to changes in motion and adapting the body to them. The rate of these changes normally allows sufficient time for the canals to maintain bodily equilibrium. When motion is rapid or irregular, the canals are not able to function properly, and motion sickness results.

During World War II, in an effort to prevent seasickness, many experimental tests were performed on troops going overseas in which a large number of drugs were investigated. Dramamine was found to be the most effective. More than half of the men who received this drug did not become seasick or were relieved even after seasickness had begun. (Other drugs have been found to work pretty well if the person is not already seasick.) In practically all the cases, the ordinary severity of the illness was lessened.

Other Books To Read

How We Hear: The Story of Hearing, by Judith Fryer. Published by Medical Books for Children Publishing Company, Minneapolis, 1961.
An elementary but complete description of the complicated mechanisms that regulate hearing.

Wonders of Sound, by Rocco V. Feravolo. Published by Dodd, Mead & Company, New York, 1962.
What sound is and does, ranging from simple vibrations to ultrasonics. The author suggests easy experiments to demonstrate the principles of sound.

Science and Music: From Tom-Tom to Hi-Fi, by Melvin Berger and Frank Clark. Published by McGraw-Hill Publishing Company, New York, 1961.
The role of science in music explained for high-school students and music lovers. The authors clarify the phenomena of sound, including pitch, resonance, and sound waves, and their book would be helpful to anyone who operates a hi-fi or stereo record player.

A Survey of the Animal Kingdom

Did you know that:

A porpoise is not a fish?
A turtle is a reptile?
A snake never chews its food?
An earthworm eats dirt?
A cheetah, the fastest of all land animals, can run 70 miles per hour?
A hummingbird burns up food so fast that it eats almost constantly while awake?

In this survey of the animal kingdom, you will find these and many other facts discussed. Here you will find how the animal kingdom is divided into groups, what animals belong in each group, how animals reproduce, and something about unusual animals.

No discussion of the animal kingdom would be complete without an answer to the question: What is an animal? To this day, zoologists (scientists who study animals in general) can give no all inclusive answer, for there are some forms of life (such as the euglena, see page 32) which have properties of both animals and plants. In general, however, we can say that most animals would be included in the following definition: An animal is a living organism which can move about, which can take in and digest food, and which lacks chlorophyll and cannot perform photosynthesis. For more about animals, consult the entry on "Animals" in the Index.

—Herbert Kondo

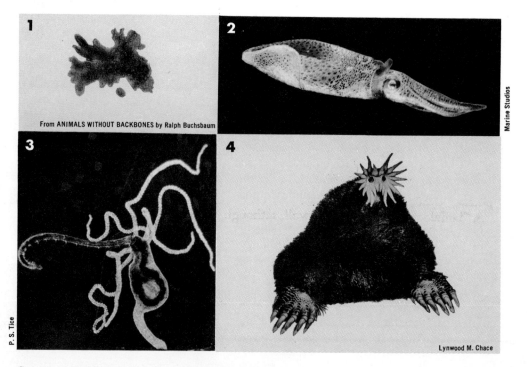

From ANIMALS WITHOUT BACKBONES by Ralph Buchsbaum

Marine Studios

P. S. Tice

Lynwood M. Chace

Can you identify these members of the animal kingdom?
They are 1, an amoeba; 2, a squid; 3, a hydra (shown here
eating a worm); and 4, a star-nosed mole. All are
discussed in this section.

The favorite food of giraffes is the leaf of the acacia tree. These leaves grow among three- to four-inch thorns, and are neatly plucked by the giraffe with its tongue and upper lip. Mature Tanganyika giraffes, like these, stand about 18 feet high, and will weigh up to 1¾ tons.

The Flamingo and the Giraffe: How They Eat

For part of the year, Lake Nakuru, in Kenya, Africa (where this picture was taken), is home for countless flamingos. The flamingo plunges its beak into the water, and then, lifting its head, lets the water run out. Inside the long, deep beak remain the thousands of tiny plants and animals which are the flamingo's food.

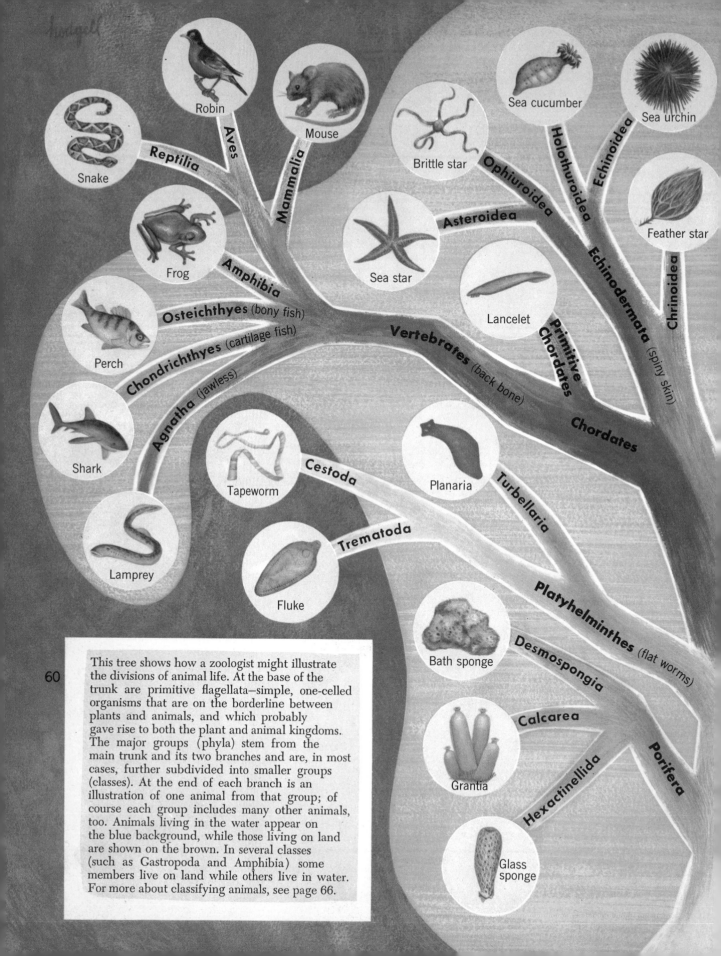

Robin

Mouse

Snake

Reptilia

Aves

Mammalia

Sea cucumber

Sea urchin

Brittle star

Holothuroidea

Echinoidea

Ophiuroidea

Frog

Amphibia

Asteroidea

Feather star

Osteichthyes (bony fish)

Perch

Sea star

Chinoidea

Lancelet

Echinodermata (spiny skin)

Chondrichthyes (cartilage fish)

Vertebrates (back bone)

Primitive Chordates

Agnatha (jawless)

Shark

Cestoda

Tapeworm

Planaria

Turbellaria

Chordates

Lamprey

Trematoda

Fluke

Platyhelminthes (flat worms)

Bath sponge

Desmospongia

Calcarea

Grantia

Porifera

Hexactinellida

Glass sponge

60

This tree shows how a zoologist might illustrate the divisions of animal life. At the base of the trunk are primitive flagellata—simple, one-celled organisms that are on the borderline between plants and animals, and which probably gave rise to both the plant and animal kingdoms. The major groups (phyla) stem from the main trunk and its two branches and are, in most cases, further subdivided into smaller groups (classes). At the end of each branch is an illustration of one animal from that group; of course each group includes many other animals, too. Animals living in the water appear on the blue background, while those living on land are shown on the brown. In several classes (such as Gastropoda and Amphibia) some members live on land while others live in water. For more about classifying animals, see page 66.

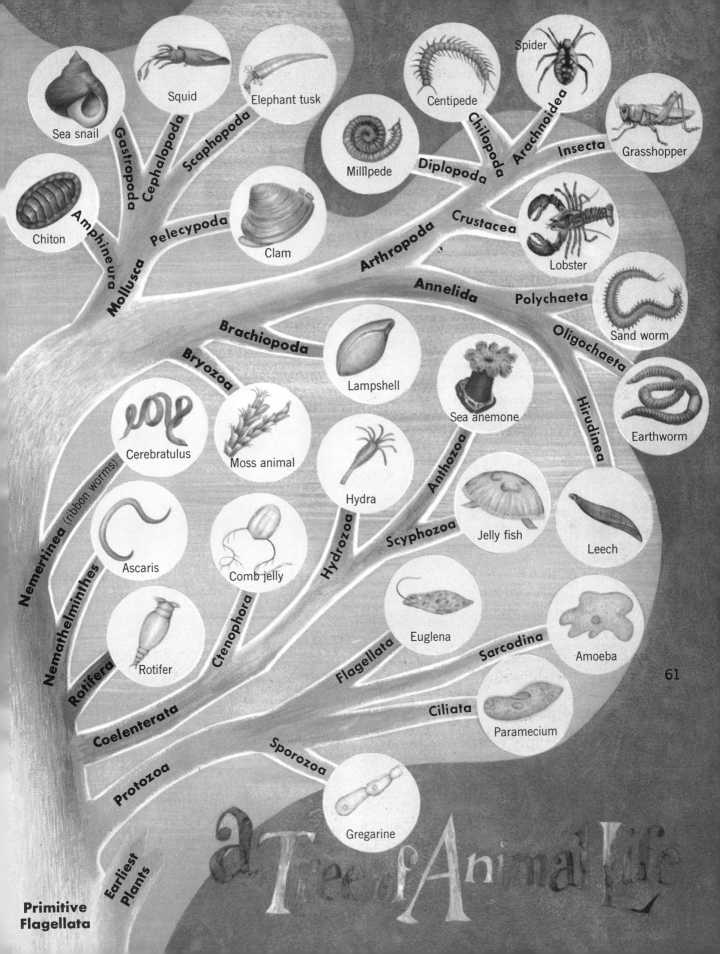

Sea snail

Squid

Elephant tusk

Centipede

Spider

Chiton

Grasshopper

Clam

Lobster

Lampshell

Sea anemone

Sand worm

Cerebratulus

Moss animal

Hydra

Earthworm

Ascaris

Comb jelly

Jelly fish

Leech

Rotifer

Euglena

Amoeba

Paramecium

Gregarine

Gastropoda

Cephalopoda

Scaphopoda

Chilopoda

Arachnoidea

Insecta

Amphineura

Pelecypoda

Diplopoda

Mollusca

Arthropoda

Crustacea

Annelida

Polychaeta

Brachiopoda

Oligochaeta

Bryozoa

Hirudinea

Anthozoa

Nemertinea (ribbon worms)

Scyphozoa

Hydrozoa

Nemathelminthes

Rotifera

Ctenophora

Flagellata

Sarcodina

Coelenterata

Ciliata

Protozoa

Sporozoa

Earliest
Plants

A Tree of Animal Life

61

Primitive
Flagellata

Animals in the Sea

The handsome starfish (left), four or five inches across, is seen from above. Oyster fishermen do not like the starfish, which feeds largely on shellfish, and can therefore do great damage to oyster beds.

Above, *this little* Porpita linneana *is a deep-sea jelly fish only half an inch across. They are sometimes seen in such quantities that the ocean is flecked with their bright blue color for miles. This specimen was picked up in a hand net in the Gulf of Mexico.*

Below, *this cancroid crab (one of whose ten legs is missing) was fished up from a depth of 1,200 feet in the Gulf of Mexico. Its hindmost legs are oval shaped at the end, which helps greatly when the crab swims about. Crabs, like other members of the phylum Arthropoda, have no closed blood vessels; the space between their body organs and outer shell is filled with blood.*

Dibranchus atlanticus *is the full name of this deep-sea fish (below) with foot-like fins. Dibranchus probably uses these specialized fins to shuffle along the sea bottom.*

Photos by Harvey Bullis, U. S. Fish and Wildlife Serv.

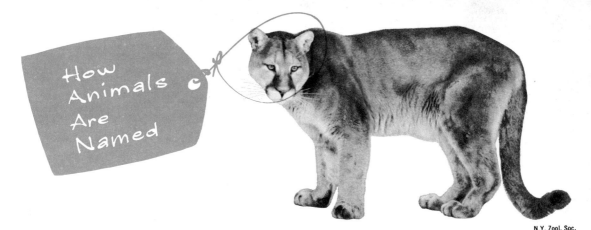

How Animals Are Named

Why do zoologists use such complicated scientific names for animals? And how do they get these names? This article gives you some answers. From **Zoology** by Robert F. Lane. Published by the Boy Scouts of America. Copyright 1941.

Is it a mountain lion? A cougar? A puma? A panther? Actually this animal is all of them, depending on where it is found. To avoid such confusion in names, we have Latin scientific names for animals—names which are used by zoologists throughout the world.

Most people give animals familiar or common names, like pack rat, boomer, fisher, buffalo runner, barking rabbit, mud puppy, earthworm, black bear, etc. Some of these you know. Most of them receive their names because of a peculiarity of color, habit, size, shape or locality.

But here's the catch. You might not be able to go far from your own home and still find people who know these animals by the same names you call them. Of course you would know the animals if you saw them. But imagine that you are from Oregon, going down to Texas to visit another friend. You both go for a hike, and later spot an animal.

"There's a mountain lion," you say.

" 'Tis not! It's a panther," argues the Texan; and he thinks he ought to know.

Well there you are! Both of you are right. To the people of the Northwest this animal is known as a "mountain lion"; to Texans it goes by the name of "panther." Mexicans call it a "puma." Others call it a "cougar."

A "buffalo runner" is a prairie wolf, although some people misname it a coyote. If everyone said "prairie wolf" in the first place, there'd be no confusion. The common name of "buffalo runner" comes from its habit of running with a herd of buffalo until a calf or an old animal falls behind. Then the prairie wolf makes an easy kill.

Sort of confusing, isn't it? Especially when both names are used for the same animal. No group of people can get together and talk unless they all use the same language. For example, the common names of animals just mentioned identify the animals for a certain section but not for the whole country. A "boomer" down South is a red squirrel but a special kind of red squirrel. Calling him a boomer, or even a red squirrel, makes it hard for a scientist to say positively which he is, because "boomer" is a purely local name, and while he *is* a red squirrel he is a special kind of red squirrel.

But if we classify him according to some sort of system there will be no mistaking who he is, even to a scientist of another country.

That doesn't mean he has to have a long, complicated name for ordinary conversation, but his correct common name describes him exactly. The squirrel mentioned is the *Tamiasciurus hudsonicus loquax,* the southern Hudsonian red squirrel. Correctly naming an animal makes it possible for you to make yourself understood.

How Are Animals Classified?

Classification became necessary when man in his early days found he had to group things together because there were so many of them coming within his range of knowledge that he couldn't remember them all.

Aristotle, the Greek philosopher, was one

63

Carolus Linnaeus (1707–1778), Swedish botanist, developed the "binomial system" of naming plants and animals. Before him, another Swedish botanist, Caspar Bauhin (1560–1634) had introduced a similar system for plants only. Linnaeus had a passion for classifying things—he once classified all scientists in a military order, with himself as general.

of the earliest scientists to make an attempt to classify animals into groups. His followers later divided all animals into two groups, those which had red blood and those which did not. Many other ideas on classification have since been proposed, but only one has been retained. This is the Linnaean system, devised by Carolus Linnaeus, a Swedish naturalist who lived in the eighteenth century.

His system, which is still in use, is very convenient and eliminates much confusion. His method is called the binomial system (binomial means two names). In this system every animal can be identified by giving it two names. However, in this system there are never two John Joneses.

But animals are not given just any name that happens to suit somebody's taste; their scientific names are based on their differences. In fact, the entire animal kingdom is divided into many groups and subgroups on this basis. Here's how the system works:

All animals belong to one great *kingdom*— the animal kingdom. This is the broadest classification of animals.

However, from this point onward animals begin to differ. Therefore we divide the animal kingdom into large groups, called *phyla* (the singular is *phylum*).

Some scientists claim that there are thirteen phyla, other scientists say that there are fewer than thirteen, and still others say that there are more than thirteen. This is a dispute which need not bother you at present.

Animals within a phylum differ from one another, so those with the same characteristics are put into a *class*. As you've probably guessed by now, this process goes on, certain differences placing animals in still other groups. Classes are divided into *orders* which in turn are separated into *families*. Then come the *genera* (*genus*, the singular form is probably more familiar to you) and finally the *species*.

You will find, if you read any books on zoology or biology, that many scientists divide each main group into subgroups because they see additional differences between animals. So while two animals may belong to the same phylum, these differences place them in a subphylum. In some instances differences and similarities are so striking that some of the subgroups may be skipped in designating an animal. In others, however, slight but important differences make subgrouping advisable in order to name the animal accurately.

The genus and species are usually enough to identify an animal but when there are several similar types, a subgenus and subspecies are often necessary.

Let's Take an Example

To illustrate this method of classification, let us consider the red squirrel (scientific name: *Tamiasciurus hudsonicus loquax*). We shall start with the animal kingdom and indicate the phylum and other subgroups to which this squirrel belongs, ending with the genus and species.

Southern Hudsonian Red Squirrel

(Tamiasciurus hudsonicus loquax)

Kingdom—Animalia

This includes *all* animals from one-celled protozoa to many-celled man.

Phylum—Chordata

Chordates, at some time during their life history have a notochord or rod lying above the digestive organs. They have a hollow nerve cord. This narrows the field, eliminating all animals from sponges to insects. But our animal can still be a fish, amphibian, reptile, bird; or mammal.

Subphylum—Vertebrata

These are vertebrates that also have a brain case, true skin, bone, red blood, hair or feathers, and body cavity separated into two parts. This eliminates some wormlike animals and the sea squirts.

Class—Mammalia

This confines us to one general type of animal, namely, those that are covered with hair, and whose females supply milk to raise their young.

Subclass—Eutheria

The duckbill waddles out here as does the opossum. All other mammals are in. We ought to be getting near a more definite name.

Order—Rodentia

Now we've got something! This puts our animal in one type—the gnawers. All carnivores (flesh-eaters), and man are out now.

Family—Sciuridae

The family will allow only squirrels, woodchucks, and a few others. Mice, rats, and beaver are eliminated.

Genus—*Tamiasciurus*

Here's his street address. He's a *red* squirrel and has edged almost all other animals out. This will be part of his scientific name.

Species—*hudsonicus*

Ah! the Hudsonian red squirrel. But wait—this fellow comes from the north (Hudson Bay region) and the one we're tracing lives farther south. So a subspecies is added to tell us this.

Subspecies—*loquax*

We've got him! Name and address. He's the only one! His name is *Tamiasciurus hudsonicus loquax,* or in English—the southern Hudsonian red squirrel.

It is the name of the genus and species which gives the animal its scientific name; the

Amer. Mus. Nat. Hist.

The Hudsonian red squirrel (Tamiasciurus hudsonicus loquax)*, described in this article, is shown here. Its back is red, its breast is white.*

genus is the first name and the species is the second name. In case these two aren't enough to identify the animal, the name of the subspecies is added.

Other Sections To See

"How Animals Survive," Volume 1; "Human and Animal Tools" and "Birds of Sea and Shore," Volume 2; "The Story of Horses," Volume 3; "Whales," Volume 4; "Land Birds of North America," Volume 5; "The World of Reptiles" and "Dogs," Volume 6; "Insects" and "Cage Birds," Volume 7; "Big Game Animals" and "The Cat Family," Volume 8; "Rodents: Animals that Gnaw," this volume; "Unusual Beasts of Burden," Volume 10; "Cattle, Sheep and Hogs," Volume 12; "The World of Fishes," "Water Animals Without Backbones" and "Parade of Poultry," Volume 13; "Odd and Unusual Animals," Volume 14; "Amphibians," Volume 15; "Animal Behavior" and "Pests of the Animal Kingdom," Volume 16; "Presenting the Primates," Volume 17.

Other Books To Read

Colby's Nature Adventures, by Carroll Burleigh Colby. Published by Dial Press, Inc., New York, 1961. An alphabetically arranged collection of brief articles about animals, ranging from aardvarks to zebras.

The Language of Animals, by Millicent E. Selsam. Published by William Morrow and Company, Inc., New York, 1962. Animals do talk to one another, and this author reports on how various animals manage to communicate with their fellows.

Wild Animals of North America, edited by National Geographic Book Service. Published by National Geographic Society, Washington, D. C., 1960. Articles by various writers cover the many categories of North American wild life.

What Are the Main Groups of Animals?

The animal kingdom is divided into major groups called **phyla**, in order that the animals may be better described and studied. In this selection, the ten important phyla and their main classes are described. The phyla are given in a definite order: from the simplest one-celled animals to the most complicated. Adapted from **Exploring Biology**, third edition, by Ella Thea Smith, copyright, 1938, 1942, 1943, 1949, by Harcourt, Brace and Company, Inc.

Phylum Protozoa: The One-Celled Animals

The first large group in the animal kingdom consists of all the one-celled animals, which together make up the phylum Protozoa (protozoa means "first animals"). The most familiar group of protozoa are the amoebas, which live in backyard ponds and other places where there is water containing green plants.

The whole amoeba is a single cell, most of which is cytoplasm (for more about cytoplasm, see "What Is Life?" on page 24). Floating in the cytoplasm are a small nucleus, bits of food enclosed in a *food vacuole* (or "bubble"), and one or more clear "bubbles" called *contracting vacuoles*. The food vacuoles digest food and the contracting vacuoles give off liquid wastes.

Other One-Celled Animals

There are many other kinds of protozoa, some of which are more complicated than the amoeba. Two of these are the paramecium and the vorticella. The hairlike projections on them are called cilia (singular, cilium). The paramecium uses its cilia both in moving around and in taking in food. The vorticella uses them in food-getting and occasionally in moving around when it breaks loose from its base and swims away. Each animal has a definite opening or mouth through which the food enters. Each animal has one or more small contracting vacuoles. The vacuole fills with liquid waste material, which is discharged from the cell when the vacuole contracts. The vorticella has a curved nucleus. The paramecium has two nuclei, a large one and a small one. Both animals are composed of just one cell, as the amoeba is.

Protozoa in General

Fifteen thousand species of protozoa have been described and named, and new ones are being discovered each year. They abound in water and in moist places everywhere. The red snow that is sometimes observed in Arctic regions or on high mountains owes it color to the presence of many one-celled animals that are red in color and can live and thrive in snow. They are called "bloodberries." The orange glow of the surface of the sea at night in some locations is due to the protozoan called the "nightlight," which gives off light.

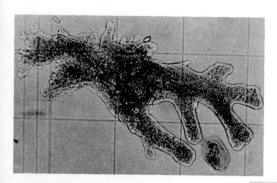

How does an amoeba eat? Merely by surrounding the food it encounters with its body. The amoeba then absorbs the food. Here you see an amoeba eating another protozoan, shown in green color.

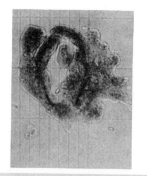
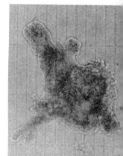

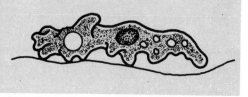

How does an amoeba walk? The amoeba has no definite legs, but it can make some temporary ones by merely pushing its body out. This forms pseudopods (false legs), which the amoeba uses to walk on.

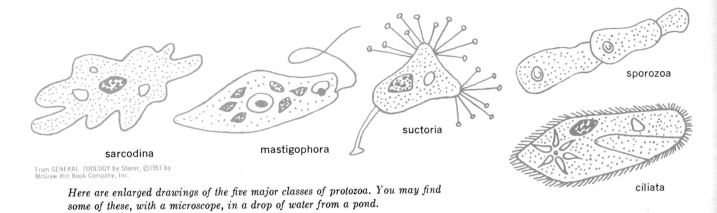

sporozoa

suctoria

sarcodina

mastigophora

ciliata

*Here are enlarged drawings of the five major classes of protozoa. You may find
some of these, with a microscope, in a drop of water from a pond.*

Phylum Porifera: Sponges

You are familiar with one kind of sponge, at least. You have probably used one often to wash a car, but the thing you used was not a whole sponge. You used only its skeleton—its bones, as it were. The living cells that once covered and lined every hole in that sponge were dead and gone when you used it. When the sponge was alive, it was slimy, and except for color, resembled a piece of raw liver. A sponge differs from an amoeba or any other protozoan in that it consists of many cells that live together in one body. These cells are very loosely connected, but they do depend upon one another to some extent. When you examine a sponge for some special feature by which to identify all sponges, you can hardly select any feature except the holes. There are holes all over the surface of a sponge, even when it is alive.

For a long time sponges were considered plants because they are often green when alive. When it was discovered that the greenness is due to microscopic green algae (simple green plants) in the bodies of sponges, and that the cells are bounded by typical animal cell membranes, sponges were classified as animals.

How Sponges Make Water Currents

You may be able to collect living fresh-water sponges for yourself in nearby lakes. Look for specimens on the underside of floating objects or on the submerged parts of water plants or on other underwater objects in shallow fresh water. One type, called spongilla, is likely to be green in color because of the algae imbedded in its body. Here is an experiment you can do with a spongilla, should you find one.

Place a living spongilla in a dark-colored pan and add enough clear water to cover it. Powder a piece of chalk until you have a fine white dust. Drop some of this white powder close beside the sponge and watch carefully. You should be able to see currents of water entering the tiny holes or *pores* on the sides of the animal. Soon you should be able to see the specks of chalk dust being thrown out of

*What's inside a sponge? On the far left A is an external view of the Grantia sponge, which is
usually about three-fourths of an inch long. At B is a lengthwise section of the same sponge, and
C is an enlarged section of part of the wall, showing pores and canals. A collar cell from the lining
of the canal is shown at D.*

A

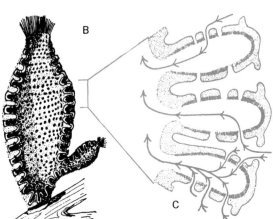

B

C

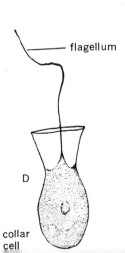

flagellum

D

collar
cell

The horny (bath) sponge repre-
sents one of the three kinds
of sponges.

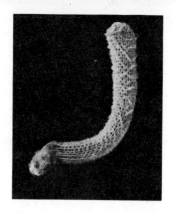

The glass sponge represents another class of sponges. Above are two genera:
Euplectella (Venus's-flower-basket) (left) and Staurocalyptus (right). Adult
sponges spend their life attached to rocks or other hard objects.

the larger openings in the surface of the sponge. How are these currents of water kept flowing through the sponge's body?

The currents of water are set up and kept flowing by certain cells that line the canals and the cavities all through the body of the sponge. Each one of these cells has a collar around the top and a flagellum (a hairlike whip projecting from a cell) projecting from the middle of the collar. The waving of the flagella makes the water currents. These currents bring oxygen and bits of food to the internal cells of the sponge. One scientist found that some 45 gallons of water will pass through the body of a marine sponge of average size in a day.

Other Kinds of Sponges

Only a few species of sponges live in fresh water. The rest of the 3,000 known species live in shallow seas. They are collected in abundance in the water off the Florida coast and

Spongilla, which you see below, is a member of the
only fresh-water sponge family known. Spongilla
grows in streams, lakes, and ponds.

around the Bahamas and in the Mediterranean Sea.

Sponges vary a great deal among themselves. Some of them make glassy skeletons. Others, like the common bath sponge, make a horny skeleton. Still others, such as the Grantia, make lime skeletons. Venus's-flower-basket is one of the most beautiful. In spite of their differences, all sponges have pores and belong to the phylum of pore-bearing animals.

Phylum Coelenterata: Jellyfish and Their Relatives

68

Most of the animals of this phylum live only in the sea. If you have done much ocean bathing, you may have been stung by a jellyfish, or you may have seen one floating nearby. In the water a living jellyfish looks something like an inverted glass cup or dish with a fringe hanging from the rim. A few kinds of jellyfish live in fresh water, but most are marine.

What Is a Hydra?

It is not necessary, however, to go to the seashore to find animals of this phylum to study.

There is one genus that lives in almost any fresh-water pond. It is called the *Hydra*. If you will collect some pond weeds in a glass dish, or a jar of pond water, you may be able to find living hydras to study. Living hydras and prepared microscopic slides can be purchased from any biological supply house.

You will have to look closely to see the hydras, for when at rest they are only about as big around as a coarse white thread and about one-tenth of an inch long. Look for something that resembles a short, white thread with the ends frayed out. The frayed appearance is due to the half-dozen arms that surround the mouth of the animal. Each arm is called a tentacle.

The body of a hydra is shaped much like the finger of a glove. The hollow space inside is a kind of "stomach" (called a coelenteron), since food is digested in it. The body wall that surrounds the "stomach" consists of only two layers of cells. The inner layer is called the endoderm, which means "inside skin." The outer layer is called the ectoderm, which means "outside skin." In the endoderm, there are gland cells that have digestive juices, and there are flagellated cells that keep the liquid in the "stomach" in constant motion, much as the collar cells of sponges maintain the water currents. In the ectoderm, especially that covering the tentacles, there are many stinging cells. Each stinging cell contains a sharp-pointed coiled hair and a little poison fluid. When the tentacles grab a water flea, the hairs are released and sting; they inject poison into the water flea, thus numbing it. The stinging cells of the hydra are unable to prick human skin.

What Is a Jellyfish?

Like the hydra, the jellyfish has a hollow body with ectoderm and endoderm, and tentacles that have stinging cells. The tentacles form a fringe around the rim of the cup. The stinging cells are capable of stinging the human skin, as many an ocean bather has discovered, to his discomfort.

There are many different kinds of jellyfish. Some of them are as large as washtubs, but even these have only two layers of cells. Most of the mass of the body is water. Many jellyfish give off a sort of golden light, much like that of the firefly. They swim slowly close to the surface of the sea, by a kind of pulsation of the whole body.

Corals and Other Forms

You may have seen a string of beads made of bits of coral, and you have undoubtedly read about the coral reefs of the South Seas. You are probably wondering how animals that grow into coral reefs or produce the materials used in making coral beads can be classed in the same phylum with hydras and jellyfish.

What you call *coral* is only a limy secretion of the coral colony. The living corals take a compound of lime out of sea water, and use this lime compound in manufacturing the secretion. The living tissue is supported by the

There are three main classes in the phylum Coelenterata, one of which is the class Hydrozoa, represented by the hydra. Here is a lengthwise and cross section of a hydra, showing the central body cavity, which is typical of members of this phylum.

Here is an unusual picture, showing a hydra eating a worm. Part of the worm is in the stomach and can be seen through the thin body walls. The bumps on the tentacles of the hydra are the stingers.

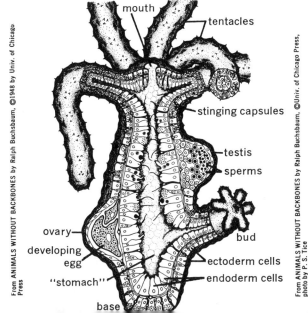

From ANIMALS WITHOUT BACKBONES by Ralph Buchsbaum, ©1948 by Univ. of Chicago Press

mouth

tentacles

stinging capsules

testis

sperms

ovary

bud

developing egg

ectoderm cells

"stomach"

endoderm cells

base

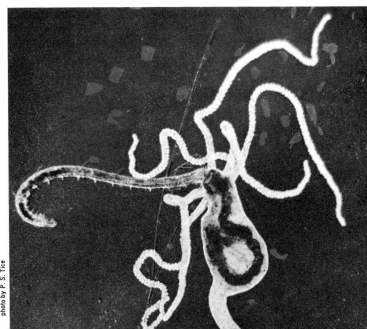

From ANIMALS WITHOUT BACKBONES by Ralph Buchsbaum, ©Univ. of Chicago Press, photo by P. S. Tice

On the left, you see a Portuguese man-of-war, which is carried along the water by the wind blowing on its "sails." This jellyfish belongs to the class Hydrozoa, but most jellyfish belong to the class Scyphozoa. Above are the sea anemone (center) and coral (right), both of which represent the class Anthozoa.

hard secretion. In each cup in the coral skeleton, there once lived a little animal, with tentacles and stinging cells and a hollow body very similar to those of the hydra and the jellyfish.

There are still other animals in this phylum. Sea anemones, sea fans, sea pens, and other strange forms, such as the Portuguese man-of-war, belong here.

The Phylum as a Whole

Altogether, the animals of the third phylum are an interesting, colorful lot. In their bodies some cells are specialized in one function, others in another. There are primitive nerves and muscle fibers and gland cells. There are flagellated cells in the lining of the "stomach" and stinging cells all over the surface, particularly on the tentacles.

This phylum has been named the Coelenterata which is a descriptive name meaning "hollow intestine." The name refers to the fact that the cavity in the body is the digestive tract. All forms have tentacles and stinging cells. Some 5,000 species of coelenterates are known.

Life with the Worms

You may think that a worm is a worm, regardless, and that all of them are alike. This is not so, for they differ a great deal—so much, in fact, that they have been sorted into three different phyla. These are the *flatworms* (phylum Platyhelminthes), the unsegmented *roundworms* (phylum Nemathelminthes), and the *segmented worms* (phylum Annelida), which are discussed later in this article.

It is quite true that worms are alike in some ways. They are long, and they have a head end that goes first and a right and a left side to the body. But the flatworms are flat like a ribbon, as in the tapeworm and planarias. Both the roundworms and the segmented worms are round, but the body of a segmented worm is made up of a series of rings, called segments, whereas roundworms are unsegmented.

A Study of a Fresh-Water Flatworm

Try to collect living planarias from a pond. If you have a goldfish pond with water hyacinths in it, you ought to be able to find living planarias. Partially fill a large white dish or enamel basin with pond water. Carefully lift a water hyacinth out of the fishpond and place it in the dish. After it has stood half an hour or more, the planarias, if present, will be seen against the white of the dish. They are little, flat, brownish worms usually less than half an inch long. You may now replace the hyacinth in the pond, and bring the dish of planarias into your room. Keep a lid over the dish to protect the worms from the light. Two or three times a week place a few very small pieces of raw meat in the dish and watch the worms feed. When the worms move away from the meat, remove it from the dish and change the water carefully.

What Is a Tapeworm Like?

Tapeworms live inside the body of some other animal and get their living from that animal. Animals (or plants) that live directly on or in another living thing, and at its expense, are called parasites, and the organism whose body they inhabit is called the host. A tapeworm in the human intestine is a parasite, and the human being is then called the host. All tapeworms are parasites and most other flatworms (such as the fluke) are, too.

The tapeworm that most often infests the human intestine consists of a head and many sections. New sections are constantly being formed just back of the head, thus making the worm longer and longer. Often specimens from five to ten feet in length are found, and lengths of 25 feet are recorded. The tapeworm looks something like a white, jointed ribbon. Sections of the worm that contain eggs pass out of the host's body.

What Are the Roundworms?

Among the roundworms, there are some that are parasites and others that are not. In the dregs from a vinegar jug you are nearly sure to find the small roundworms known as vinegar eels. Often similar small roundworms will be found in the jars of pond water collected for the study of protozoa. Hookworms are also examples of parasitic roundworms.

Another parasitic roundworm of considerable fame is the trichina. Trichina lives one part of its life in one animal and another part in another animal. It alternates between two hosts. Adult trichinas may live by the millions in the intestines of some animal such as a pig. Occasional female trichinas bore into the wall of the pig's intestine and there produce young. The young spread through the body and lodge in muscles and form cysts, which lie there, quite inactive, until the host dies or the meat is eaten.

If the muscle of a pig containing trichina cysts (usually called "measly" pork) is thoroughly cooked, the young trichinas will be killed, but if a person eats measly pork which is not thoroughly cooked, the young trichinas will emerge from the cysts in the human intestine. Females in turn bore into the walls, and young individuals eventually reach the person's muscles, where they produce inflammation. The resulting disease, called trichinosis, may be severe and even fatal.

Hookworms Cause Disease

These small worms live in the human intestine. They bite into its lining and suck the

The planaria is of interest because it is the lowest animal having something like a brain. Here you see a planaria and a close-up of its head.

The hookworm is a parasite belonging to the phylum Nemathelminthes. (Nema is the Greek word for "thread.") Hookworms live for five or six years.

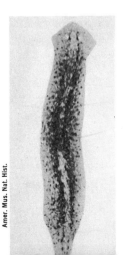

P. S. Tice

Amer. Mus. Nat. Hist.

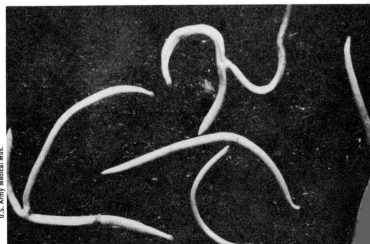

U.S. Army Medical Mus.

blood of the human host. The worst of it is that the sores caused by the bite of the hookworm do not heal as soon as the worm lets go its hold, but keep on oozing blood. As a result, persons infected with hookworms are pale and listless.

The hookworm is a roundworm, less than half an inch long, that spends its early youth as a free-living organism in moist soil. Men and women and children who go barefooted to work in the fields in the warm southern parts of the United States, and in Mexico and South

America, are likely to develop "ground itch" or "dew sores" on their feet. A dew sore marks the spot where a young hookworm is entering the body. The worm gets into the blood vessels, is carried to the lungs, climbs the windpipe with the help of the hairlike cilia on the lining of the windpipe, and gets itself swallowed. Once in the intestine, the hookworm lives at the expense of its host. Hookworms can be killed and eliminated from the human intestine with the proper medicines given under a doctor's direction.

Phylum Echinodermata: The Spiny-Skinned Animals

Animals Built Like a Star or a Wheel

There are a number of animals that are built like a star or a wheel. They have no head or tail, no right or left side. Most of them have a rough outer covering with projections (spines) all over themselves. We call animals of this phylum the *spiny-skinned animals*. They include the starfish, sea urchins, sea cucumbers, sea lilies, brittle stars or feather stars, sand dollars, and others—all of which live in the ocean.

The best-known animal in this phylum is the starfish. It has many odd features, but probably the most interesting feature to a biologist is its method of moving around. On the lower side of the starfish you can see the rows of

tube feet down each arm. These tube feet are like small rubber tubes, and are closed at the outer end and connected at the inner end to water vessels inside the starfish. These water vessels are always kept full of sea water. The feet are called tube feet because they are little tubes used as feet. When the starfish moves about, it forces some of the water out into the tube feet, causing them to lengthen out. On the end of each foot is a little sucker with which the starfish sticks to objects.

Among oyster fishermen, starfish are notorious as enemies of the oysters. How can a starfish attack an oyster? It simply folds its arms around the shell of the oyster, takes hold of the two half shells, and pulls by means of

The starfish gets its name from its starlike appearance, but it is not a fish. Its body consists of five "arms" (or multiples of five, such as ten or fifteen) which meet at a central disk. The starfish has no head, but has a mouth opening directly into the stomach, which is located in the disk; it lives mostly on clams and oysters.

72

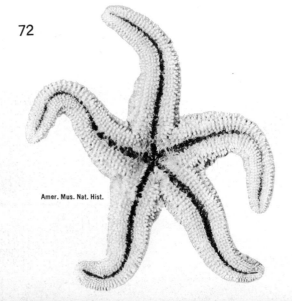

Amer. Mus. Nat. Hist.

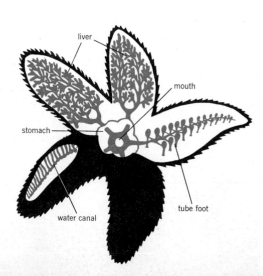

liver

mouth

stomach

water canal

tube foot

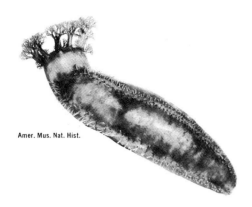

Other echinoderms are shown here: on the left is a sea cucumber which belongs to the class Holothurioidea. The treelike growths at the left end are tentacles, which surround its mouth. In the center is the sea urchin, which belongs to the class Echinoidea. On the right is the sand dollar, which belongs to the same class as the sea urchin. It eats sand and absorbs the organic matter contained in the sand.

the suckers that are on its tube feet. At first the much stronger muscles of the oyster hold tight and nothing happens, but the tube feet keep pulling. After twenty minutes or so the oyster muscles get tired, in much the same way that the muscles in your hand would tire if you clenched your fist for twenty minutes. Then the shell opens. Even now the starfish cannot swallow the soft body of the oyster, for the oyster is too big to go into its mouth. So the starfish just turns its stomach inside out through its mouth, which is in the center of the lower side. Thus it covers the oyster's soft body with the stomach lining and digests and

absorbs it. Then it returns its stomach to its normal place inside the body.

The spiny-skinned animals are different from all other animals. They are well-organized cell communities, with muscles and nerves and stomachs and livers and many other special tissues and organs. In these features they resemble the vertebrates and other more complex animals. But they differ from vertebrates in that most of them have spiny skins and water-vessel systems of locomotion, and are built around a central point as a wheel is. Approximately 5,000 species of this phylum have been identified and named.

Phylum Mollusca: Soft-Bodied Animals

At some time or another you must have seen a collection of sea shells. Perhaps you have collected them yourself. Animals that live in shells belong to the phylum Mollusca. The shell is the feature by which most people know the mollusks, although some outgrow their shells.

These animals are called soft-bodied animals. Just think of a raw oyster out of its shell and you will see how well the description fits.

The squid belongs to the phylum Mollusca, class Cephalopoda. It moves backward as well as forward, and when in danger, darts backward by shooting a jet of water forward.

73

(The name given to this phylum of animals, mollusks, comes from the Latin word *mollis*, meaning "soft.") Some 80,000 species of this phylum have now been named.

Most mollusks live in the water. The fresh-water mussel (often called a clam) is very common. Many kinds of snails live in fresh and in salt water, and some of the most beautiful sea shells are those of snails. Air-breathing snails and slugs creep about over the land.

The octopuses, the squids, and the land slugs are mollusks which have no shells when fully grown. In their very early youth they start to form shells. Then the shell stops growing but the body grows on and on. The giant octopus is one mollusk that may be a source of danger to men who dive for pearly oysters or go down in diving helmets to collect specimens from the ocean floor. Land slugs are mollusks which may often be found on cabbage plants.

Phylum Annelida: The Earthworms

In the phylum Annelida are included all the segmented worms, of which the most familiar example is the common earthworm. (See also "Our Friend the Earthworm," Volume 3, page 38.) Right in your own yard there are probably hundreds of them in the soil.

No doubt you have heard that "the early bird always catches the worm." And maybe you've heard some one answer back: "it's the early worm that gets caught by the bird." This last item is not true, however, for the earthworm is a nocturnal (night) animal, so that if he stays out too late—into the early hours of the morning—he is apt to get caught. The earthworm lives in moist soil and does not usually leave its hole. It breathes through its skin and eats dirt for its food. The dirt passes through the digestive tract of the worm, and the food in the dirt (seeds, eggs or larvas, decaying plants) is digested. The remaining dirt is then expelled.

The earthworm has a very tiny brain. The structure of its body is more complicated than any of the animals mentioned in any of the phyla before this. Many segmented worms live in the ocean.

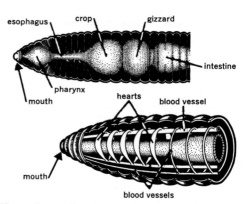

The earthworm has five pairs of hearts as you see in this drawing, which shows the digestive system (top) and blood vessels (bottom).

Phylum Arthropoda: Animals with Jointed Legs

The animals of this phylum are often called the animals with jointed legs because they have three or more pairs of legs with several joints in each. Insects, spiders, lobsters, and centipedes are examples. The name of the phylum is Arthropoda. Some 700,000 species are known and more are being discovered and named every year. Of these, more than 650,000 are insects.

All arthropods are alike in the following ways:

1. They have three or more pairs of jointed legs.

2. They are divided up into segments.

3. They have an external skeleton, called an exoskeleton.

The major classes of this phylum are:

1. The Insecta

2. The Crustacea, which includes crabs, crayfish, lobsters, shrimps, water fleas, barnacles

3. The Arachnida, which includes spiders, scorpions, and ticks

4. The Centipedes and Millipedes

The "Thousand Leggers"

This is the class of the centipedes and the millipedes. You must have turned over a stone or

A

B

C

D

Here are representatives of the four largest classes in the phylum Arthropoda: A, the centipede (class Chilopoda) which has from 24 to 340 legs; B, the insect (class Insecta); C, the lobster (class Crustacea); and D, the spider (class Arachnoidea). Insecta is the largest single class in the animal kingdom.

a log sometime and observed what looked like a worm with a "thousand legs" go scampering away. If you had captured the runaway, you would have found that it wore a light exoskeleton and had, not a thousand legs, but from 24 to 340 legs. Centipedes have one pair of legs on each segment of their bodies; millipedes have two pairs on each segment. Millipedes are called the myriapods or many-footed animals.

The Crayfish Class

This class includes the crayfish, lobsters, crabs, and shrimps. These animals have a horny exoskeleton which forms a hard crust over the body. Most of these animals, like the lobster, have no neck but have the head and the thorax fused firmly together. The name of the class is Crustacea, a name which refers to the hard crust over the body. There are a great many kinds of crustacea, most of which live in the water. The water fleas upon which the hydra feeds are very small crustacea often found in pond water. The fresh-water crayfish is often

wrongly called a crab. It is famous for its ability to swim rapidly backward.

The Spider Class

This is the class of spiders, daddy longlegs, mites and ticks, and scorpions. All of these have eight legs, in contrast to the six that insects have. You need never again mistake spiders for insects. Just count the legs. Like the crustacea, spiders have no neck. There are many kinds of spiders, some of which are the common garden spider (which has a black and yellow abdomen), the tarantula, the black widow, and the trap-door spider.

The Insect Class

Insects are alike in many ways. The most obvious similarities are these:

1. All insects have three pairs of jointed legs.

2. All insects have three body regions: a *head* in front, a *thorax* to which the legs and wings are attached, and an *abdomen*.

3. All insects have a tough (not brittle) exoskeleton.

75

Phylum Chordata: Mostly Backboned Animals

There is a little animal that does not fit into any of the phyla discussed so far. Because it does not have a backbone, it cannot be called a backboned animal. This animal is the lancelet, so called because it is shaped somewhat like a surgeon's lance. In many ways the lance-

let is like a little fish, but it has no backbone. Where the backbone ought to be there is a long rubbery rod of cartilage which is called the notochord. Above the notochord lies the hollow nerve cord. Since none of the animals so far studied has a notochord or a hollow

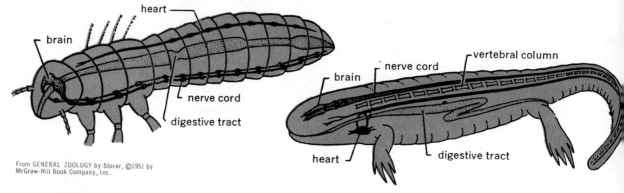

Here we see the main difference between the invertebrate and vertebrate divisions of the animal kingdom. On the left you see the interior of an insect; on the right, the interior of a salamander.

nerve cord, the lancelet cannot be placed in any of the first nine phyla. What, then, is the lancelet?

The lancelet is classified in the phylum Chordata because of the notochord. Chordates are the only animals that have a notochord and a hollow nerve cord running along the back. They constitute a large phylum which includes some 40,000 known species. Most of the animals that are classified in this phylum have a notochord only while they are in the very early stages of growth. As the young develop, the cartilage in the notochord, and certain other tissues, gradually grow around the nerve

What is it? A star-nosed mole, which belongs to the same phylum and class that you do: phylum Chordata, class Mammalia. The mole lives in dark tunnels, and detects objects by feelers at the end of its nose. Here you can see the feelers and two nostrils plainly.

76

Lynwood M. Chace

cord and finally encase it. Then the animal has a backbone. Animals that have backbones are called *vertebrates*.

The Class of Vertebrates

Most of the animals with which you are familiar are vertebrates. Dogs, cats, horses, birds, turtles, frogs, and fish are all vertebrates. Perhaps you know from experience what a cat's backbone feels like. If you have ever been served the neck of a roasted turkey the day after Thanksgiving, you know what the bones in the backbone of the neck look like. Each bone is called a vertebra (plural, vertebrae). You may have seen the vertebrae of the backbone of a fish, like trout or bass, when you have pulled the meat away from the bones; and often one finds several vertebrae in a serving of salmon. A snake has a great many vertebrae—over 300 in some species. All animals that have vertebrae belong to the subphylum Vertebrata of the phylum Chordata.

Vertebrates are alike in many other ways. *1.* Nearly all of them have two pairs of limbs, usually legs. In fish, however, the limbs are fins; in birds and bats, one is a pair of legs and the other a pair of wings; in seals and whales they are flippers; and in snakes there are no limbs at all. Some snakes, like the python, still have "hips" that indicate where the legs used to be. In spite of these and a few other exceptions, vertebrates generally have two pairs of limbs. *2.* They have a brain encased in a skull. *3.* They have their bones on the inside instead of outside their bodies. (For more about vertebrates, see pages 77 and 78.)

Animals with Backbones

Animals with backbones are those belonging to the phylum Chordata, and the subphylum Vertebrata (the vertebrates). They are the most highly developed and complicated members of the animal kingdom. In this article, you will read about five of the most important classes in this phylum. Some of the animals are referred to as cold-blooded, and others as warm-blooded. Cold-blooded animals are those whose body temperatures change with the temperature of the environment; warm-blooded animals are those whose body temperatures remain more or less the same regardless of the temperature of the environment.

N.Y. Zool. Soc.

Fishes are the lowest class of animals with backbones. (Most scientists believe they were the first animals to have a backbone.) They belong to the class Pisces (from piscium, *Latin for fish). All of them live in water and nearly all take oxygen out of the water by means of gills. This class does not include whales or porpoises, for these are mammals. Many zoologists now classify fishes into two classes, instead of one: the class Chondrichthyes, which are the "cartilaginous" fishes, and the class Osteichthyes, the "bony" fishes. In the former class, the skeleton is not made of true bone, but of cartilage; the shark, for example, has no true bones and belongs in this class. In the latter class, the skeleton is made of true bone. Fishes usually have scales that cover their body, and are cold-blooded.*

Lynwood M. Chace

Amphibians are animals that live part of their life in the water and part of it on land. The scientific name for this class is Amphibia, and it includes frogs, toads, and salamanders. In early life the amphibians breathe by gills, but in adult life they become air-breathers. They are cold-blooded and live in fresh water or damp places. None of them live in or near salt water. Amphibians prefer moist temperate climates; if the weather becomes very cold in winter, frogs and aquatic salamanders will hibernate by swimming deep into lakes and streams that do not freeze. Most amphibians have neither scales nor claws.

Reptiles belong to the class Reptilia, which includes snakes, lizards, alligators, crocodiles, and turtles. They are cold-blooded, are covered with scales, and breathe by lungs. Some reptiles grow to great lengths—an anaconda 38 feet long has been measured in South America for example, and is the largest reptile known today. Snakes do not have legs, while lizards usually have them. Snakes swallow their food whole; they do not bother to chew or tear it up. Lizards have movable eyelids and external ears; snakes do not.

L. W. Brownell

What is a bird? It is a vertebrate with feathers, and belongs to the class Aves. (Aves is the Latin word for bird.) Birds are warm-blooded, have two legs and—with a few exceptions, such as the ostrich—they can fly. The ostrich of Africa, the largest known bird, is 7 feet tall and weighs up to 300 pounds. The hummingbird of Cuba, the smallest known bird, is 2¼ inches long and weighs 1/10 of an ounce. The giant condors of the Americas have the longest wing spread: ten feet.

N.Y. Zool. Soc.

Mammals

The highest class in the animal kingdom is Mammalia. The name mammal refers to the mammary (milk) glands in the females. Mammals all have hair and the females supply milk to suckle their young; all are warm-blooded. On this page you will find a brief discussion of four important orders of the class Mammalia.

U.S. Fish & Wildlife Serv., by E. P. Haddon

Squirrels, rats, and mice are among the animals which belong to the order Rodentia, the rodents or gnawing animals. They have a pair of sharp, chisel-like teeth, in the front of their mouths, for gnawing. They breed frequently and are very numerous. Most of the rodents eat vegetables and grain, but they also eat meats and fruits. This order also includes guinea pigs, woodchucks, beavers, porcupines, and muskrats.

TVA

The hoofed mammals (ungulates) include many of our domestic animals. The ungulates have grinding teeth, and they all eat plants only. One part of this group has an even number of toes (cloven or divided hoof): sheep pigs, deer, cattle, goats, giraffes and buffaloes. The other part of this group has an odd number of toes: horses, zebras, rhinoceroses, and tapirs. Nearly all of the latter group are good runners.

N.Y. Zool. Soc.

Lions, tigers, cats, dogs, weasels, seals, and walruses belong to the flesh-eaters or order Carnivora. All of these animals have long, strong canine teeth and live mainly on meat. Some of the carnivores—such as the seals, sea lions, and walruses—live in the sea and on land; the rest live wholly on land. Most of the land members of this order are fast runners, have sharp claws, and are cunning hunters. All bears belong to this order.

78

N.Y. Zool. Soc.

The primates make up the highest order in the animal kingdom. It includes the lemur, tarsier, monkey, ape, and man. The lemurs make up one of the three divisions of the primates; the tarsiers make up another, and the anthropoids—monkeys, apes, and man—make up the third. Nearly all of the primates have an "opposable thumb," that is, a thumb which can be placed opposite to the other fingers. The primates are the most intelligent members of the animal kingdom.

Record-Breakers Among Animals

Here's a short quiz you can take to find out if you're familiar with some record-breakers among animals which are some of the fastest, the biggest, and the smallest. Take a sheet of paper and write down your selection; then check it with the answers at the bottom of the page.
From "Record-Breakers Among Animals" by Osmond P. Breland.
Natural History Magazine, September, 1953. Reprinted by permission of the author.

1. What is the largest animal that ever lived?
    A. *mammoth*   C. *whale*
    B. *dinosaur*   D. *mastodon*
2. What animal lives the longest?
    A. *tortoise*   C. *elephant*
    B. *whale*   D. *carp*
3. What animal can run the fastest?
    A. *antelope*   C. *deer*
    B. *cheetah*   D. *greyhound*
4. What is the fastest flying bird?
    A. *duck hawk*   C. *Indian swift*
    B. *carrier pigeon* D. *bald eagle*
5. What is the largest fish?
    A. *ocean sunfish* C. *manta ray*
    B. *tuna*   D. *whale shark*
6. What is the longest snake?
    A. *boa constrictor* C. *python*
    B. *king cobra*   D. *anaconda*
7. What is the smallest creature in the animal kingdom?
    A. *protozoan*   C. *coral*
    B. *rotifer*   D. *worm*
8. The smallest backboned animal is a kind of
    A. *reptile*   C. *mammal*
    B. *fish*   D. *amphibian*
9. What is the mammal that is smallest at birth?
    A. *mouse*   C. *opossum*
    B. *shrew*   D. *pika*
10. The smallest living mammal is a kind of
    A. *chipmunk*   C. *mouse*
    B. *ground squirrel* D. *shrew*
11. What is the largest amphibian?
    A. *African bullfrog* C. *hellbender*
    B. *siren*   D. *Japanese salamander*
12. What animal has the sharpest eyes?
    A. *goldfish*   C. *insect*
    B. *rhinoceros*   D. *bird*
13. What animal had the longest horns?
    A. *buffalo*   C. *deer*
    B. *mountain sheep* D. *mountain goat*
14. The part of the mammalian body that has grown to be the longest:
    A. *antler*   C. *claw*
    B. *horn*   D. *tooth*

---

1. C. *whale.* Specimens over 100 feet long have been captured. The dinosaurs were neither so long nor so heavy as a blue whale.

2. A. *tortoise.* One giant tortoise is thought to have lived 152 years. Some may have lived as long as 200 years.

3. B. *cheetah.* Cheetahs can often catch the fastest antelopes in a *short* race. They have been timed at 70 miles per hour.

4. C. *Indian swift.* These birds have been timed at speeds of from 170 to 200 miles per hour.

5. D. *whale shark.* One 45 feet long has been measured. May possibly grow to more than 60 feet.

6. D. *anaconda.* An anaconda 38 feet long has been reported. The regal python may be as long as the anaconda, but the longest python observed was 33 feet.

7. A. *protozoan.* All have only one cell in their bodies. Most cannot be seen without a microscope.

8. B. *fish.* The dwarf pygmy goby of the Philippines has a body length of only two-fifths of an inch when fully grown.

9. C. *opossum.* When first born, young opossums are smaller than a honey bee, and weigh only ¹⁄₁₅ of an ounce.

10. D. *shrew.* Some have a body length of 1¾ inches and weigh less than half an ounce.

11. D. *Japanese salamander.* Some specimens are over five feet in length and weigh almost 100 pounds.

12. D. *bird.* Particularly the birds of prey have unusually sharp eyes and can spot their victims at unbelievably great distances.

13. A. *buffalo.* Indian buffaloes have been known with horns over 6 feet long.

14. D. *tooth.* Elephant tusks, which are really teeth, of more than 11 feet are on record.

Some Wild Animals

and Where They Live

The picture map at right shows the general locality of some of the wild animals in nature. On this page and the next you will find a key to the animals which are numbered. The general area where the animals usually live is indicated in the parentheses. All the animals shown here belong to the phylum Chordata.

1. Ostrich (All drier and sandier parts of Africa)
2. Bactrian camel (Steppes of central Asia)
3. Northern fur seal (Migrates from northern Pacific, near Pribilof Islands, to California coast in winter)
4. Grizzly bear (Rocky Mountains and arctic region of North America)
5. Moose (Northern forests of North America, Asia, and Europe)
6. Walrus (Coasts and ice floes of Arctic Ocean)
7. Sea otter (Sea coast from central California to Kurile Islands)
8. California condor (Remote areas of Coast Range of central California)
9. Beaver (Europe, central Asia, and North America)
10. Skunk (In the Americas, from Canada to Patagonia)

11. Rattlesnake (Almost every portion of the temperate and tropical Americas)
12. Alligator (In southeastern United States, particularly Florida and Georgia, and Yangtse River of China)
13. Brown pelican (Florida, the Gulf states, California, and South America)
14. Humming bird (North and South America, from Alaska to Cape Horn)
15. Sloth (Brazil to Nicaragua)
16. Jaguar (Arizona to Argentina)
17. Great anteater (Forests of South and Central America)
18. Anaconda (Guianas, Brazil, and Peru)
19. Armadillo (Texas and southern Mississippi River Valley to Patagonia)
20. Sperm whale (Warmer oceans)
21. Marine turtle (Warmer oceans)
22. Humpback whale (In all seas)

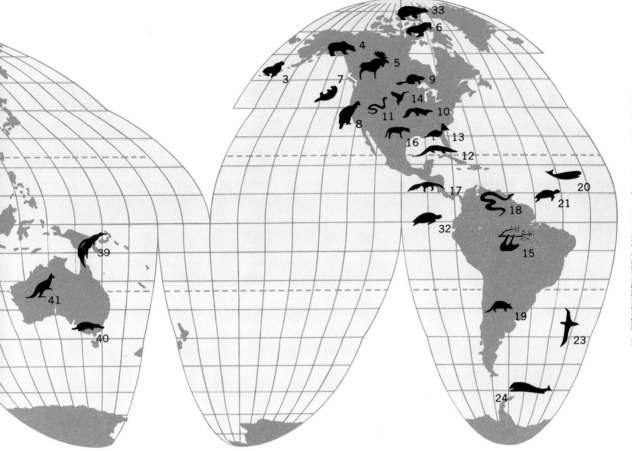

After THE WONDERFUL WORLD, ©1954, by James Fisher, by perm., Garden City Books

23. Wandering albatross (Southern oceans, chiefly between 60 and 30 degrees south)

24. Blue whale (Arctic and Antarctic oceans in summer; warmer waters in winter)

25. Chameleon (North Africa, Israel, the Arab countries, islands of eastern Mediterranean, India, southern Spain, and Madagascar)

26. Lion (Africa south of the Sahara, apart from the Congo)

27. Zebra (Open plains of eastern and southern Africa)

28. Hippopotamus (Big rivers of Africa)

29. Giraffe (All of Africa, south of the Sahara)

30. African elephant (In the forests of Africa, south of the Sahara)

31. Gorilla (Forests of equatorial Africa, from Cameroons to the lakes of east Africa)

32. Giant tortoise (Galapagos Islands, and off coast of South America)

33. Polar bear (Arctic region of Europe, Asia, and America)

34. Wolf (Northern Hemisphere from arctic regions to Mediterranean; Arabia, India, and Mexico)

35. White stork (Europe, North Africa, and Asia)

36. Hyena (Plains of Africa, Palestine, Arabia, and India)

37. Cobra (Africa, India, China, Malay Archipelago, and Philippines)

38. Tiger (Asia, from Mongolia and Korea to Caucasus to Java and southern India)

39. Bird-of-paradise (New Guinea)

40. Platypus (Eastern Australia and Tasmania)

41. Kangaroo (New Guinea, Tasmania, and Australia)

42. Indian elephant (India, Ceylon, Burma, Thailand, the Malay Peninsula, and Sumatra)

81

How Animals Reproduce

One of the most interesting things in nature is the manner in which different animals reproduce their own species. A few of the many methods of reproduction in the animal kingdom are described in this selection from J. Darrell Barnard, Lon Edwards: **Basic Science.** Copyright 1951 by The Macmillan Company and used with The Macmillan Company's permission.

In some animals the process of reproduction is quite simple. Certain of the protozoa reproduce just as bacteria do—by simple cell division. Some groups of animals can reproduce parts of their bodies after those parts have been removed. Flatworms can be cut into dozens of pieces and each new piece will develop into an entire flatworm. If a sponge is cut into small pieces, each piece of the animal may develop into another sponge. Lobsters which have lost a foot or claw may produce another to replace it. This process of growing missing body parts is called regeneration.

Most of the animals that we are familiar with, however, reproduce by the union of a male sex cell, called the sperm, and a female sex cell, called the egg. Such a process is known as *sexual reproduction.* (For more about this, see "Wheel of Life," in Volume 13.)

How does an amoeba reproduce? Merely by splitting itself into two parts. The nucleus splits first, and each nucleus moves to opposite ends of the amoeba. The amoeba then splits in half with a small amount of protoplasm with each nucleus.

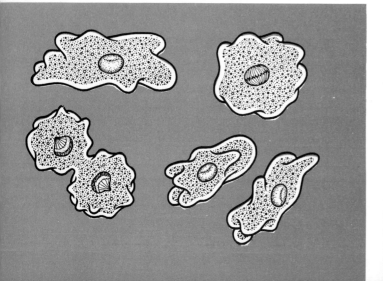

How Mammals Reproduce

Two sexes, male and female, are necessary for reproduction in mammals. The female produces egg cells, and the male produces sperm cells. The egg is fertilized within the female's body by the sperm. After an egg is fertilized, it begins developing into a young animal, which during its early development is called an embryo. The females of some mammals, such as cats, dogs, and hogs, produce several egg cells at one time, each of which may develop into an embryo after it is fertilized. Mares and cows usually produce only one egg cell at a time.

The developing embryo obtains food and oxygen from its mother's blood stream. The length of time it takes the embryo to develop into a young animal that is ready to be born varies among mammals.

After birth, hogs and sheep complete their growth when they are about one year old. Cows and horses do not complete their growth until they are about two years old.

How Birds Reproduce

Birds reproduce by laying eggs in which the embryo develops. The egg cell, produced by

Hydras may reproduce by growing a bud which later separates and forms a new hydra. This type of reproduction is asexual; *another type is* sexual, *in which the male produces sperms only and the female, eggs only. In some species of hydra, however, sperms and eggs grow in the same individual. When both are discharged into the water, the sperms fertilize the eggs and later a hydra is formed. Below you can see rows of testes on the hydra, as well as two long seeds—one on each side.*

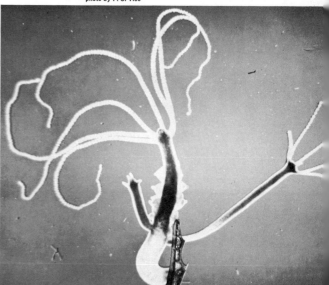

Length of Pregnancy of Certain Mammals

	donkey 12 months			**hog** 4 months
	horse 11 months			**dog** 2 months
	cow 9½ months			**cat** 2 months
	man 9 months			**rabbit** 1 month
	sheep 5 months			**opossum** ½ month

The planaria is a good example of the ability to regenerate. If it is cut into many pieces, each piece can form a new planaria; this ability to regenerate decreases from the front to the back end.

the ovary of the female bird, is fertilized in her body. The yolk and white of the bird's egg along with the fertilized egg cell are covered by a shell within the female's body before the egg is laid. After the egg is laid, it must be kept warm or *incubated* until the fertilized egg cell develops into a young bird ready to be hatched. By the time the egg is hatched, all of the yolk and white of the egg have been used by the young bird as food.

How Do Oysters Reproduce?

Oysters are invertebrate animals that reproduce sexually. The female of one kind of oyster lays her 50 to 60 million eggs in sea water.

The male also releases the sperm cells into sea water. The fertilization of the eggs is uncertain under such conditions.

The oyster eggs hatch in from eight to twelve hours, and the newborn oysters begin to form shells in about two days. When the oyster is about two weeks old, it attaches itself to some object at the bottom of the ocean water where, if undisturbed, it will develop into a full-grown oyster.

How Does a Fish Reproduce?

Fish reproduce sexually in much the same manner as oysters. The female fish spawns her eggs in the water. The male fish releases sperm, called *milt*, into the water nearby. Under these conditions only a few of the many thousands of eggs laid by the female may be fertilized. Many of those which are fertilized may later be eaten by fish and other animals. The number of fish, therefore, produced under natural conditions is small compared to the large number of eggs laid by the female.

The earthworm's sex organs, located near the front of the body, contain both the male and female organs. In warm, moist weather, two earthworms meet and clasp each other A, while discharging sperms into the sperm sacs of the other. They separate and later a slime tube and cocoon form over the sex organs, B. The eggs enter the cocoon which slides toward the front end of the earthworm, C. As the slime tube and cocoon slip forward, the sperms stick to the cocoon. Soon the whole cocoon, containing both sperms and eggs, slips off over the head of the earthworm. The sperms fertilize the eggs in the cocoon, D, and the eggs later hatch young earthworms.

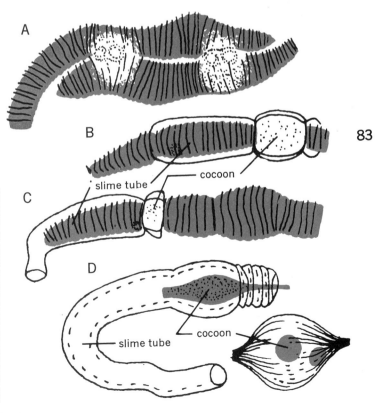

A

B

slime tube — cocoon

C

D

slime tube — cocoon

83

The life cycle of a frog, from tadpole to full-grown frog. The cycle, from birth to maturity, takes from two months to two or three years, depending on the species of frog.

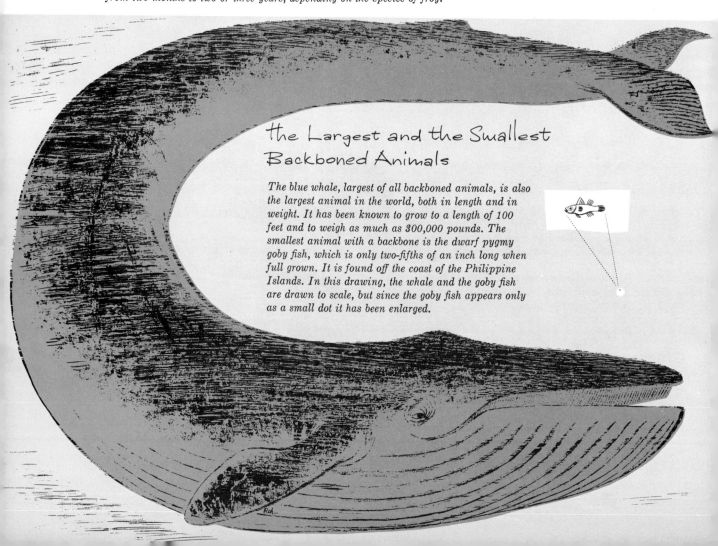

the Largest and the Smallest Backboned Animals

The blue whale, largest of all backboned animals, is also the largest animal in the world, both in length and in weight. It has been known to grow to a length of 100 feet and to weigh as much as 300,000 pounds. The smallest animal with a backbone is the dwarf pygmy goby fish, which is only two-fifths of an inch long when full grown. It is found off the coast of the Philippine Islands. In this drawing, the whale and the goby fish are drawn to scale, but since the goby fish appears only as a small dot it has been enlarged.

Who's Who in the Family?

There's a difference between a gander and a goose and a stallion and a mare.
In this table you can see at a glance the family relations between these animals.

When we talk about these kinds of animals:	The male is called	The female is called	The young are called	With these animals:	The male is called	The female is called	The young are called
Deer	Buck or stag	Doe	Fawns	Lions	Lion	Lioness	Lion cubs
Horses	Stallion	Mare	Colts	Foxes	Fox	Vixen	Fox cubs
Donkeys	Jack	Jenny	Colts	Dogs	Dog	Bitch	Puppies
Goats	Billy	Nanny	Kids	Cats	Tom cat	Cat	Kittens
Sheep	Ram	Ewe	Lambs	Rabbits	Buck	Doe	Rabbits
Swine (Pigs and Hogs)	Boar	Sow	Pigs or Shoats	Poultry			
Cattle	Bull	Cow	Calves	Chickens	Rooster	Hen	Chicks
Bison	Bull	Cow	Calves	Ducks	Drake	Duck	Ducklings
Elephants	Bull	Cow	Calves	Geese	Gander	Goose	Goslings
Whales	Bull	Cow	Calves	Turkeys	Gobbler or Tom Turkey	Hen Turkey	Poults

Did you know?

Here are some interesting facts about animals that you may not have known before. Adapted from "Beastly Devices" by Paul Steiner, **The New York Times Magazine**, October 18, 1953. Copyright 1953 by The New York Times Company.

A bird has an automatic lock mechanism in its foot which keeps it on its perch when it is asleep.

About 40,000 muscles are in an *elephant's trunk*. (Man has only 500 in his whole body.)

Bees smell with the last eight joints of their legs.

The *horseshoe crab* is not a crab at all; its nearest living relatives are the spiders.

In Sumatra *macaque monkeys* are trained to assist in harvesting of coconuts.

A whale's nostrils do not match; the right one is always larger than the left.

A wren builds several dummy nests so his mate can choose the one she likes best.

The nest of *a bald eagle* may eventually weigh as much as a ton because the eagle adds to it each year.

Wild pigs not only swim but duck their heads under to catch fish.

Hummingbirds burn up food so fast that they must eat almost constantly while awake.

Butterflies have a better taste for sweets than humans; they can detect one part of sugar in 300,000 parts water, the average human one part sugar in only 200 parts water.

A moose's neck is so short and his legs so long that he must kneel when grazing off the ground.

The female ostrich and the male divide egg-sitting duties; she sits by day, he by night.

An elephant cannot get all four feet off the ground at the same time and so is unable to jump.

The jumping jerboa, a rodent, has stiff hairs on its feet to act as "skid chains" on the sandy desert.

85

First Aid and Home Care of the Sick

First aid is defined by the American Red Cross as "the immediate care given to an injured or sick person until the services of a physician can be obtained." It is important for you to know how to give first aid correctly because you will be able then to help others when they need it. If you have ever seen an accident take place, you know that people will crowd around the victim quickly but most of them do not know the correct first-aid techniques to help the patient. The first aider knows what to do to relieve the patient's pain until a doctor comes. The trained first aider knows how to help save life, decrease the possibility of crippling, and lessen suffering as a result of the accident. The first aider helps himself, too, because his knowledge of accidents and illness helps him to prevent them from happening.

In this section you will learn some of the most important principles of first-aid treatment as well as getting some ideas on how to make confinement to the home a pleasant experience for the sick person. You will probably find this section easier to understand if you have already read "The Machinery of the Body," in Volume 4. Other sections that will interest you are "Familiar Diseases" and "Accident Prevention," in Volume 6.

—Carol Zeman Rothkopf

Why You Should Know About First Aid

In one recent year more than 9,000,000 people were involved in accidents in the United States. This fact alone explains the importance of knowing some first aid, for the chances are great that sooner or later you will be at the scene of an accident and your aid may help to ease the pain of the victim. From **The Book of Health**, compiled and edited by Randolf Lee Clark, Jr., M.D. and Russell W. Cumley, Ph.D. Copyright 1953 by Elsevier Press, Inc.

Often, ill or injured persons are in a place where considerable time may elapse before medical aid can be secured. Therefore, it is essential that every individual have a thorough knowledge of the basic rules of first aid before an emergency occurs. The purposes of first-aid knowledge are threefold. *First,* it enables the individual to determine the nature and extent of an injury. This does not mean that he will be able to make a full, accurate diagnosis that a physician can make; but it should enable him to make some intelligent decision as to the type of injury or illness occurring during an emergency. *Second,* first-aid training helps the person to know the proper thing to do at the proper time, and also what not to do. *Third,* first-aid training is one of the best means of preventing accidents.

General Directions in Case of Emergency

Considerations to be taken into account in the event of injury or illness may be listed as follows:

Keep the patient lying down: this prevents fainting and may help prevent development of shock (see page 90). If the patient is vomiting, turn his head so that he will not become choked.

Keep the patient warm: this is also important in preventing shock. In cold weather, it is important that the patient is covered under as well as over the body.

Look for stoppage of breathing and hemorrhage: if the patient has stopped breathing, from any cause, artificial respiration (see page 104) is the immediate treatment. In examining the injured person to look for signs of bleeding, remove only enough clothing to determine the possible extent of the injury. It is preferable to cut clothing away, since removing clothes in the usual manner may cause further pain and aggravate the injury.

Never try to get an unconscious person to drink any liquid: water or liquid stimulants should be withheld, since fluids may enter the windpipe and cause strangling. If a person has no visible injury and is unconscious, search of his pockets or wallet may be necessary, since many patients with chronic disorders carry papers on their persons with

If you must move a patient (and it is usually best not to) here are three methods of transportation you might use: (left) stretcher, (center) pick-a-back, and (right) the fireman's carry. These methods of transportation are described in detail in this article.

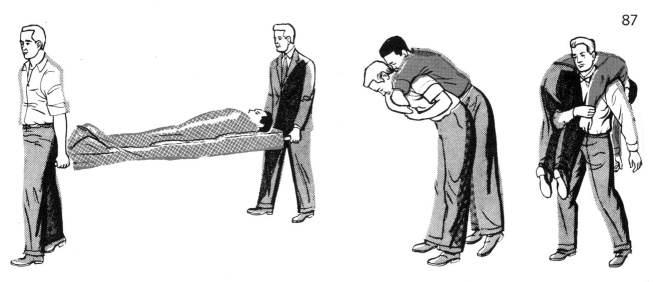

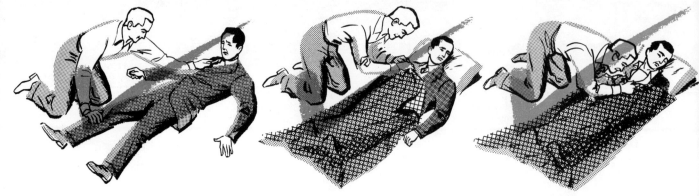

keep the patient lying down   keep the patient warm   look for stoppage of breathing and hemorrhage (severe bleeding)

information regarding a likely seizure or collapse.

Do not move the patient unless it is absolutely necessary: this is especially important in the event of injury; if it is necessary that the patient be moved, be certain that the method of moving him will not cause further injury.

Summoning medical aid: send someone to call a physician or ambulance as soon as possible and be prepared to give complete information concerning the emergency. The exact location of the patient; the extent of injury or nature of illness; what medical supplies are available at the site; and what first-aid measures have been taken should be told to the doctor. This will enable him to bring necessary medicines and equipment and to give possible directions to be carried out before he arrives at the scene.

In critical situations, whether a physician is needed or not, it may be necessary to contact other community services. The first page of every telephone directory lists the numbers of local fire and police departments, as well as state and federal law-enforcement agencies. There is usually listed also a means for obtaining help from city, county, Red Cross, and other first-aid corps which carry such equipment as oxygen supplies, resuscitators, etc.

Gaining the patient's confidence: before medical help arrives, the person giving first aid should try to keep a composed and efficient attitude. Gaining the patient's confidence helps his co-operation and aids his recovery by lessening the degree of shock. It is important to ease his fears and also, in severe cases, it is important not to let him know the seriousness of his condition. In addition, by soothing and calming the patient, the person giving first aid may also overcome his own natural excitement or worry over the situation.

Transportation Problems

In most situations requiring first aid, there is little problem involved in moving the patient to a place where he may receive medical treatment. Often the patient is able to walk, or he can be transported by ambulance. In serious accidents, it is always best *not to move the patient* until the ambulance arrives. Improper methods of moving an injured person may increase the severity of the injury and can even cause death. In many cases of automobile accidents, the patient is literally tossed into the first available automobile and driven at breakneck speed to the nearest hospital. This is a serious mistake and can result in death. Especially in cases of head injury or back injury extreme care must be used in moving the patient in a lying-down position. In instances of injury to the back of the head, the patient should be moved gently to one side.

Occasionally accident or illness may occur far from the source of medical treatment, for example on hunting or fishing trips. In such instances the kind of transportation should be determined by the injury. In general, a stretcher is the desired method of carrying seriously ill or injured patients.

For moving a patient long distances on foot,

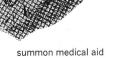

summon medical aid

never try to get an unconscious
person to drink any liquid

do not move the patient unless
absolutely necessary

it may be necessary to improvise some kind of stretcher. A blanket wrapped and tied around two poles makes a suitable litter. Articles of clothing, such as shirts, skirts, or trousers, may also be used if a blanket is not available. When no poles are available, a stretcher may be made by placing the patient in the center of a blanket and rolling the edges toward him. This requires at least two bearers on each side. Whatever type of stretcher is made, it should be tested to see if it is strong enough to bear the patient's weight. Extreme care should be exercised in loading, carrying, and unloading a stretcher. A convenient method of carrying an ill person without a stretcher is to seat the patient in a chair. This is particularly useful in carrying a patient to another floor level, where a stretcher cannot be used because of narrow, winding stairways or small elevators.

In some cases a patient may be able to support part of his own weight if one of his arms is placed around the neck of another person, who then offers further support by placing his hand under the patient's other arm. In the *pick-a-back* carry, the patient is transported on the carrier's back with his legs held through the carrier's arms, and his arms slung crosswise around the carrier's neck and held by the latter's hands.

In the *fireman's carry* the patient is carried with his torso across the carrier's shoulders. The patient's body is held in place by the carrier encircling one of the patient's legs and grasping the patient's arm which is thrown over his shoulder. By alternating one or sev-

eral of these methods with frequent periods of rest, it is possible to cover a considerable distance even when the victim is a fairly heavy person.

First-aid Kits

A good first-aid kit should be kept at home and in the automobile. The automobile kit need not be elaborate, but should be ample to allow treatment of several injuries. Around the house, first-aid equipment is usually scattered and not readily available. A definite amount of first-aid material should be kept in a metal box of convenient size, preferably in or near the medicine cabinet. Such an arrangement will keep bandages clean and safe to use.

A good first-aid kit should contain most of the following articles:

1-inch compresses on adhesive
gauze squares—about 4″ x 4″ in individual
    sterile packages
sterile triangular bandages
burn ointment—nonoily, such as anesthetic
    jelly
mild solution of iodine or mercurial anti-
    septic
aromatic spirits of ammonia
a tourniquet
scissors
splinter forceps
2-inch roller bandages
roll of adhesive tape
roll of absorbent cotton
70% alcohol
clinical thermometer

89

SHOCK

Shock is one of the more serious conditions in which first aid can be of use. Read this article so that you can learn the symptoms of shock and what can be done to help an injured person in this condition. From the American Red Cross **First Aid Textbook for Juniors** by Carl J. Potthoff, M.D., M.P.H. Copyright 1949 by The American National Red Cross.

When a person is badly injured, he may develop a serious condition called shock. In shock cases, the blood flow in the body is disturbed, even in parts distant from the injury. The brain does not get enough blood. Thinking is difficult, digestion of food is slowed, and all body processes are at a low level. The injured person feels exceedingly weak. Unless he receives proper care, he may die of shock, or his recovery may be greatly delayed.

Causes of Shock

Any serious injury may cause shock. Bad burns, loss of much blood, broken bones, and large cuts are often followed by shock. Shock may also occur because of serious illness. Emotional disturbance sometimes leads to a temporary state of shock. During the last war millions of Americans gave some of their blood through the Red Cross for use by doctors in treating shock resulting from war wounds.

Signs of Shock

The skin of a person in shock feels cool and is whiter than usual. Sometimes perspiration appears, especially on the forehead or chin, or above the mouth. Sometimes the victim feels like vomiting or actually does vomit.

First Aid for Shock

Whenever you give first aid to a seriously injured person, always try to prevent shock. Act immediately. Do not wait for shock to appear.

Make the victim lie down at once, so that his head is level with or lower than the rest of his body. However, if his breathing in this position is difficult because of chest injuries, raise the head and shoulders by placing pillows under them.

Cover him properly. Carefully place a blanket under him. If the weather is not hot, place a coat or blanket over him. If the weather is very cold use several blankets, but don't make him sweat; too much covering is undesirable.

Ordinarily you should not use hot water bottles or electric heating pads on accident victims. However, you may use them if the weather is very cold and there aren't enough blankets. The best places to use them are under the armpits or about the chest. Take care not to burn the skin.

Give warm water to drink if an hour or more will pass before the doctor sees the victim. But if the doctor will see him soon, give nothing to drink. In any case, don't give water if the person is unconscious or has an injury in the stomach region. Stimulants such as ammonia have no value in shock.

Don't disturb the injured person unnecessarily. Try to avoid measures that would cause more pain. Unnecessary handling and careless transportation make shock worse. It is best not to question the victim much or to discuss his injuries. Don't feed him. He should lie as quiet as possible.

These first-aid measures—having the victim lie flat and providing the proper amount of covering—are very important. They help prevent shock; therefore, apply them at once. They also help if shock does develop.

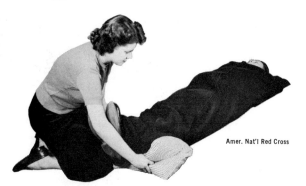

Amer. Nat'l Red Cross

This first aider has taken the proper steps in caring for a person in shock. How would this picture be changed if the victim was suffering from shock due to a chest injury?

90

Unconsciousness

Is there any first-aid treatment for unconsciousness? What may cause this condition? You will find the answers to these questions in this selection. From the American Red Cross First Aid Textbook for Juniors by Carl J. Potthoff, M.D., M.P.H. Copyright 1949 by The American National Red Cross.

Accidents or illnesses sometimes result in unconsciousness. An injury to the brain because of a blow on the head is called a *concussion.* If severe, it may cause unconsciousness. Most people who become unconscious following an automobile accident or following a fall in which the head is struck are suffering from concussion. Sometimes interference with the blood supply to the brain occurs in older people, and they have a stroke, becoming unconscious. People may become unconscious because of severe bleeding, drinking alcohol, taking poisons, or because of heart disease, and many other illnesses or injuries.

In case of unconsciousness, first find whether the victim is breathing. If not, you should give artificial respiration, provided the victim's condition was caused by drowning or some other type of accident for which artificial respiration is recommended. Cases of stroke and of concussion are, in general, not helped by artificial respiration, even though the person has stopped breathing.

If, as is usually the case, the victim does not need artificial respiration, you should provide covering over and under him. Be careful, because a broken bone may be present. If the victim's face is red or purplish, raise the head and shoulders slightly by pillows or other supports. If the face is pale, the victim should lie flat. Do not try to arouse an unconscious person by shouting at him, shaking him, or throwing water upon him. Let him lie undisturbed while you summon help.

Simple Fainting

People who are in crowded rooms, who are hungry, tired, fearful, or see blood may faint even though they are in good health. The immediate cause is an insufficient supply of blood to the brain. As soon as they lie flat, they recover consciousness, because then the brain gets enough blood.

If you feel faint, bend forward at the waist, bringing the head down between the knees, or better yet, lie down.

Keep the victim lying flat. If he gets up soon, he may faint again. Loosen his collar. After he recovers consciousness, a drink of tea or coffee may bring further relief. If he does not recover very soon, the case is not one of simple fainting, and a doctor should be consulted.

Epileptic Convulsions

Many people suffer from an illness called epilepsy. In this illness they may have an epileptic convulsion; that is, they become unconscious, fall, and thrash around on the ground. Usually the attack ends quickly, but the patient may seem sleepy and confused for a time. Doctors can help these patients very much.

If a person has an epileptic attack, he may bite his tongue or injure himself by striking against something. Do not try to hold him, but see that he does not strike anything. If possible, place a folded cloth or a strong stick between the teeth so that he does not bite his tongue. But be very careful in doing this, lest he become injured.

After the attack, do not question the victim unless absolutely necessary. He should lie down undisturbed and sleep.

A good remedy when you feel faint is to bend over from the waist and bring your head down between your knees, then raise your head very slowly. If possible, you should lie down.

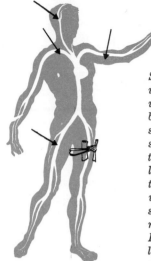

Severe bleeding from an artery, which can be recognized by the way the blood spurts can usually be controlled by applying pressure at one of the pressure points shown on the left. Notice the tourniquet applied to the left leg. Remember, however, that a tourniquet should not be used unless there is no other way to stop bleeding or unless you cannot locate the pressure point. If a tourniquet must be used, loosen it gently for a few seconds every ten minutes.

A spiral reverse bandage for a limb injury. Anchor the bandage with a few turns at the base of the limb, then spiral the bandage upward. If a gap appears, hold the lower edge of the last turn of gauze and make a neat half-twist or lap which changes the direction of the gauze and continue.

92

Wounds

In this article you will read about the first-aid steps that may be taken to stop bleeding and that help eliminate the possibility of infection in various kinds of wounds caused by cuts, rubbing, puncturing, or the bites of animals and insects. (You will also want to read "Wounds and How They Heal" in Volume 5.) From **The Book of Health**, compiled and edited by Randolf Lee Clark, Jr., M.D. and Russell W. Cumley, Ph.D. Copyright 1953 by Elsevier Press, Inc.

A wound is an injury in which the outer or inner surface of the body is cut or penetrated. The danger of infection is present in every wound, but fortunately the danger of hemorrhage (serious bleeding) is present only in very severe wounds or when a sizable blood vessel has been cut. Whenever the skin of the body is broken, germs may enter the break. These germs grow not only in the wound, but also in the tissues surrounding it. Usually, these bacteria are of the *staphylococcus* or *streptococcus* groups of organisms, although many other types may be involved. Heat, pain, swelling, redness, and the formation of pus result. This is infection. The infection may enter the blood stream and cause *septicemia,* or *blood poisoning.* Many serious infections and cases of blood poisoning begin in very small wounds. Therefore, it is important to have each wound, no matter how insignificant it appears, properly treated *at once*. First-aid treatment of wounds varies, depending upon whether the wound is bleeding seriously.

Wounds Which Bleed Severely

Hemorrhage can usually be controlled by direct pressure applied to the wound by a thick sterile gauze. Application of pressure at the pressure points (see illustration above) is an efficient method of controlling arterial bleeding in the arm or leg. Bleeding from a severed

Direct pressure into an open wound is the safest and most common way to stop severe bleeding.

artery can be recognized by the blood flow, which occurs in spurts that correspond to each heartbeat. If bleeding of an arm or leg cannot be stopped readily, a tourniquet or constriction may be used.

To apply a tourniquet, soft flat material at least two inches wide should be used. A tourniquet can be improvised from bandages, a necktie, stocking, or strip of cloth. The tourniquet is placed between the body and the bleeding point. Wrap the cloth around the limb twice, tie a half knot, and place a short strong stick or similar lever in the knot. Tie a square knot over it and twist the stick enough to tighten the tourniquet sufficiently to control the bleeding. The tourniquet should be loosened gently for a few seconds at ten minute intervals. The best places for applying a tourniquet are around the upper arm, about four inches below the armpit, and around the thigh about the same distance from the groin. The use of a tourniquet may be dangerous unless applied correctly. It cuts off the blood from the injured area, and if circulation is cut off for too long a time, the tissues are destroyed, and *gangrene* may develop. Gangrene is a serious complication, which may require amputation of the part or, if unchecked, may lead to death.

Bleeding from a vein is a slower and steadier hemorrhage than that from an artery and is much easier to control. Usually, venous bleeding can be controlled by placing a compress over the wound and bandaging it. A bleeding arm or leg should be elevated to help slow the blood flow.

In cases of bleeding, *do* apply pressure to the proper point. If the pressure points are not known, apply a tourniquet or tight band to the upper arm or upper leg, as the case may be, between the cut and the body. Elevate the limb.

Do place thick, sterile gauze pads or a clean towel over the bleeding point and apply pressure.

Do not leave a tourniquet or band in place longer than ten minutes at a time. After fifteen minutes, the tourniquet should be loosened and then replaced if necessary.

Abrasions and Cuts

Abrasions are wounds made by rubbing or scraping the skin or mucous membrane. The most common are "scuff burns," "floor burns," and "mat burns." These are not really burns, but actual wounds that become infected easily. If the abrasion is extensive, simply cover the area with sterile gauze and let the physician do the rest. If the injured area is small, cleanse with warm water and soap or a mild antiseptic and apply a light bandage.

Cuts are inflicted by sharp-edged objects such as knives or broken glass. These wounds usually bleed freely as the small blood vessels have been completely severed. Frequently, only a small amount of tissue around the cut is damaged, and cuts are not so likely to become infected as other wounds. Cuts should be treated in the same way as abrasions. If the cut has been made by a very dirty, rusty, or penetrating object, the physician may administer tetanus antitoxin.

Lacerations

Injuries that are inflicted by blunt instruments, machinery, or falls against angular surfaces *tear* or *lacerate* the flesh. As a rule, bleeding is not so severe as in cuts. The danger of infection, however, is greater, because dirt and debris are often ground into the tissues and damage to the surrounding tissue is more extensive. If the laceration is extensive or very dirty, the wound should be covered by sterile gauze and the cleansing left to the physician. If the wound is small, cleansing with soap and water, application of mild antiseptic solution, and bandaging should be done.

In case of cuts, *do* wash well with soap and water and apply a sterile bandage or a clean, freshly ironed piece of cloth if the wound is small.

Do cover with sterile gauze; press gauze firmly over wound to control bleeding, if wound is large, and hold in place until the doctor arrives.

Do not use strong antiseptics. Fresh tincture of iodine (half strength) or 70% alcohol may be used if desired. Soap and water is an excellent antiseptic.

93

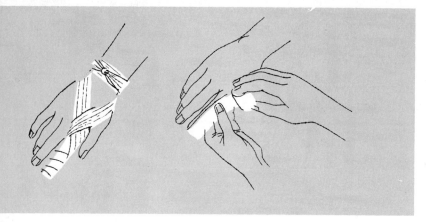

A spiral bandage for a finger (or toe) injury. Using one-inch gauze cover the finger as shown, then neatly spiral the gauze. The bandage may be held with a figure-eight anchor around the wrist.

If wound is large, cover with sterile gauze, then control bleeding, and call the doctor.

Puncture Wounds

Puncture wounds are caused by any penetrating object such as nails, pieces of wire, bullets, etc. Puncture wounds usually do not bleed freely. The edges of the wound tend to turn inward, making the wound difficult to clean. This tendency of puncture wounds to close makes the danger of infection much greater than in cuts and other wounds, since air cannot reach the injured tissue. This lack of air in a puncture wound enhances the growth of those germs causing *tetanus* or *lockjaw*. First-aid treatment of a puncture wound consists of inducing bleeding by the application of light pressure around the edges of the wound and then applying a mild antiseptic solution. In addition to treating the wound, the physician may give tetanus antitoxin to prevent lockjaw.

Powder burns and gunshot wounds are treated as other puncture wounds. Treatment to prevent shock and prompt proper transportation to a physician or hospital are the proper measures in such instances.

In case of puncture wounds, *do* try to encourage bleeding by gently pressing again and again just above wound and, in the case of a finger or toe, by gently squeezing it.

Do ask the doctor in every case if he thinks tetanus antitoxin advisable.

Do not ever try to close a puncture wound with bandage, adhesive, or anything else. A sterile gauze pad may be placed loosely over the wound until the doctor comes.

Do not forget to tell the doctor if the patient has had any kind of serum before.

Dog and Cat Bites

First-aid treatment of animal bites which are usually puncture wounds but may be a laceration, consists of washing the saliva from the wound and applying a sterile gauze dressing over the area. The physician will give the wound any further treatment.

In case of dog bite, *do* hold the wound under running water and wash it thoroughly. Dry it with clean gauze and cover it with gauze dressing. Since the doctor will probably want to cauterize the wound, do not use antiseptics before he arrives.

Insect and Spider Bites

Many insect bites cause irritation, swelling, and inflammation. These stings may be painful and poisonous. Infection may occur from scratching. Remove the "sting" if it is still present and apply a paste made of baking soda and water. Insect bites about the face may require medical treatment.

Spiders in general have been considered poisonous for many years, but apparently the "black widow" or "shoe button" spider is the only one capable of causing death in North America. A characteristic crimson "hourglass" marking is found on the abdomen of the female spider. Few first-aid measures seem effective, besides those of keeping the patient quiet and warm until the physician arrives. Severe abdominal pain may develop. Death seldom occurs except in very young or very old and infirm persons.

Injuries from Heat and Cold

Exposure to extreme heat or cold may cause serious injuries. Here you may learn some of the first-aid remedies for such things as heat exhaustion, sun stroke, and frostbite. From the American Red Cross **First Aid Textbook**, revised edition. Copyright 1933, 1937, 1945, by The American National Red Cross. Revised by editor, 1959.

Injuries caused by heat contact are burns. A burn caused by a hot liquid or a hot, moist vapor is called a scald.

Most burns are caused either by dry or moist heat, or frequently by electricity. There are two kinds of electric burns: *(1)* when the current passes through the body, burning or destroying tissue as it goes, making a deep burn which may be smaller on the surface than below and slow to heal; *(2)* when the cause is an electrical flash, but these are not deep and are usually first or second degree.

Such chemicals as strong acids and alkalies destroy body tissues, and, although the injury is produced by direct action of the chemical rather than by any heat produced, the injury is always called a chemical burn.

Degree

Burns are classified according to degree, that is, the depth to which the body tissues are injured. Remember the classification, because the terms are useful in describing the seriousness of an injury.

First degree—skin reddened.
Second degree—skin blistered.
Third degree—deeper destruction of tissue, as charring or cooking.

First Aid for Burns

Shock and infection are the chief dangers from burns. Death in the first day or two after a burn is usually the result of shock. Death later is chiefly the result of infection.

Remember: The first aider's duties are to relieve pain, prevent infection, and treat shock.

The danger from a small, deep burn—the size of your palm, for example—is not nearly so great as from an extensive burn of much less degree, like one that covers the chest and abdomen.

Burns of limited extent. The exclusion of air from a burn by the application of a thick dressing relieves pain and, if the dressing is sterile, prevents further contamination. Use several layers of dry dressings. They should be dry, because wet dressings stick more. *Use no ointment* before a doctor has seen the patient.

Extensive burns. These are much more serious. Shock is always present. Keep the patient lying down, with his head down, and avoid exposure or cold. If the patient got his burn in a fire or automobile accident, don't attempt to treat it locally on the street or in a public building. Leave his clothing on, cover him with blankets, and get him to a hospital by ambulance or car as quickly as you can. Again, keep the patient lying down.

It is usually best to remove all loose clothing from the burned area, but not if it sticks to the burned area. Cut around it and leave the adhering clothing for the doctor to remove. Do not try to undress the patient in the usual manner.

When the burn is extensive, involving the trunk or a large part of an arm or leg, wrap a clean sheet or large towel around the part. Do not wet the sheet or towel nor apply any ointment. In cool weather keep the pa-

Accidents never take a vacation. When you go on a trip or a picnic where someone could possibly be burned, take along a clean white cloth which can be tied loosely over a burned area.

Amer. Nat'l Red Cross

tient covered and warm until the doctor arrives. This leaves the doctor an opportunity to treat the wound as he chooses, and the wound will be as little contaminated as is possible.

Don't use absorbent cotton directly on a burn. It will stick, and it will further injure the tissues when it is removed. If wax or metal-like substance has caused the burn, don't attempt to remove any portion that sticks. Large blisters should be opened only by a doctor.

It is important to give shock the usual care. If you have to care for an extensively burned patient for some time before a doctor comes, water should be given to the patient—best as small drinks at frequent intervals. If the burn is extensive or deep, a physician's services are always needed.

Chemical Burns

Burns caused by an acid, alkali, or any other chemical should be washed immediately and continuously with large quantities of water, until the chemical is thoroughly washed away. Many chemical plants have large showers well distributed over their buildings so that only a few seconds is spent in getting a burned person under a shower. Large scissors or shears should be provided at such places for the rapid removal of clothing soaked with the chemical causing the burn.

Apply a dry dressing after the chemical is thoroughly washed off and get to a doctor.

These burns, like all burns, should not be exposed to direct sunlight until healed.

Chemical Burn of the Eye

Any chemical in the eye, including lime, cement, and "battery fluid," should be washed out immediately with large quantities of water. A drinking fountain set so that it throws a stream from four to six inches high is an excellent device for this purpose. Another way is to make the patient lie down; then gently pour cupful after cupful into the inner corner of the eye, letting it run to the other side. Continue this process until the chemical is removed. Then put several drops of clean olive oil, mineral, or castor oil into the eye. Cover

with a sterile compress and get a doctor at once. Milk is valuable as an eyewash, especially in burns caused by lime and other alkalies.

Ill Effects of Excessive Heat

Exposure to excessive heat usually results in one of three definite conditions: sunstroke, heatstroke, heat exhaustion, or heat cramps. People likely to be affected seriously by too much heat include those suffering from any general disease, alcohol addicts, the very young, the very old, or the very fat.

Sunstroke and Heatstroke

These conditions have the same symptoms, although the cause may be slightly different. It is sunstroke if the cause is direct exposure to the sun's rays, heatstroke if the cause is excessive indoor heat.

If you notice the beginning of any symptoms, find a cool place to rest immediately. If you have ever had sunstroke you are particularly vulnerable and should exercise proper caution.

This chart will help to distinguish between sunstroke and heat exhaustion:

Sunstroke and Heatstroke

cause:	Exposure to heat, particularly the sun's rays.
symptoms:	Headache, red face, skin hot and dry, no sweating, pulse strong and rapid, very high temperature, usually unconscious.
treatment:	Call a doctor, cool body with a sponge bath or lukewarm applications, patient lies with head elevated, no stimulants.

Heat Exhaustion

cause:	Exposure to heat, either sun's rays or indoors.
symptoms:	Pale face, skin moist and cool, sweating profuse, pulse weak, temperature low, often faint but seldom remains unconscious for more than a few minutes.
treatment:	Keep head level or low. Give salt solution, a half teaspoonful in a half glass of water. Coffee or tea may help. In severe cases, call doctor.

96

Heat Cramps

The cramps occur usually in the abdominal muscles or in the limbs. They are extremely painful and may or may not be accompanied by the symptoms of heat exhaustion.

First aid is the same as for heat exhaustion. Give the patient salt water, a teaspoonful to a pint, in small drinks at frequent intervals. Firm hand pressure applied to the muscles of the limbs will often relieve the cramps.

(You will want to read "Sunburn and What To Do for It" in Volume 5, page 217.)

Frostbite

Frostbite is the injury produced by the freezing of a part of the body. Usually the area is small in which the tissue is actually frozen, but it can be of considerable size. Places most frequently frosted are the nose, cheeks, ears, toes, and fingers.

The cause is exposure to cold, particularly with insufficient clothing. A person with poor circulation or one who is exhausted is always less resistant to cold.

Frostbite is more likely to occur when a high wind is blowing, which takes heat from the body rapidly. There is usually considerable pain if the hands or feet are frosted, but often frosted cheeks, ears, or nose are not painful and the victim is not aware of his condition until someone tells him. The frosted area becomes a peculiar grayish white because of the ice actually frozen in the tissues.

First Aid for Frostbite

The experience of many Arctic explorers has demonstrated clearly that rubbing after freezing has taken place is *not* the proper treatment. Rubbing with snow is particularly bad. The frozen tissues are bruised, and gangrene is apt to result.

Until the victim can be brought indoors, the frozen part should be covered with woolen cloth. Bring him indoors as soon as possible, give him a warm drink and begin to rewarm the frozen part if it is still cold and numb by immersing it in water at body temperature (90°F. to 100°F.) *but not hot* water. If this is not possible, gently wrap the part in warm blankets. Handle the frozen part with the greatest care. Do not apply hot water bottles or heat lamps, nor place it near a hot stove, because excessive heat may increase the damage. Once the part is rewarmed, encourage the patient to move injured fingers or toes. Do not disturb blisters.

First Aid for Prolonged Exposure to Cold

When a person is exposed to severe cold, he becomes numb, movement is difficult, and irresistible drowsiness overtakes him. He staggers as he walks, his eyesight fails, he falls and becomes unconscious.

Bring the victim into a warm room quickly. If breathing has stopped, begin artificial respiration. Rewarm him by wrapping him in warm blankets or by placing him in a tub of warm (78°F. to 82°F.) *but not hot* water. When he reacts, dry his body thoroughly if water was used to rewarm him and put the patient in a warm bed. Give him a hot drink— tea, coffee, or cocoa.

In cases where the patient is only chilled and parts of the body are not frozen, and he is not unconscious, put him in a warm bed and give him hot, stimulating drinks.

When the frostbite patient is recovering, place him in a warm bed and give him a hot drink.

97

Common Injuries

You probably know what to do in case of a nosebleed, choking, or a speck in the eye but it might be a good idea to make sure your information is accurate.
From **Safety in the World of Today**, by Herbert J. Stack, Don Cash Seaton, and Florence Slown Hyde. Copyright 1941 by Beckeley-Cardy Company. Used by permission of the publishers.

Nosebleed: In cases of nosebleed have the patient sit up with head thrown slightly back, breathing through the mouth. Apply wet, cold compresses to the forehead, the back of the neck, and the bridge of the nose. If bleeding continues for more than a few minutes send for a doctor. This is especially important in the case of older people or young children.

Objects in ear or nose: Do not attempt to remove foreign objects from ears unless they come out easily. In most cases the object should be removed by a doctor. Never use a hairpin or a similar article to pick wax out of the ear. Remember, your ear is a delicate mechanism which can easily be injured. Hearing is too valuable to run any risks of impairing or losing it.

If an object in the nose cannot be removed by gentle blowing, it is best to consult a doctor as soon as possible. A few drops of mineral oil will relieve the irritation and help to prevent swelling. If done carefully, one nostril may be held shut while blowing the other nostril.

Choking: If an object has become lodged in the throat or windpipe, it can in many cases be dislodged by lowering the person's head and slapping him sharply on the back. A child may be lifted up by his feet. An object can sometimes be removed by reaching into the throat with the finger, but care must be taken that the object is not pushed farther down. If the object cannot be removed and breathing stops, artificial respiration should be applied without delay (see page 104). As a rule an object that is lodged in the air or food passages can best be removed by a doctor with special equipment for this purpose.

Something in the eye: Nearly everyone gets "something" in his eye now and then. When this happens do not rub the eye. First try closing both eyes so that tears may accumulate and wash out the object. If this does not help, pull the upper lid out and down and blow the nose hard at the same time. If still unsuccessful, have someone look at the lower lid, turning it down gently. Wash out the eye with a solution of boric acid, made by using a rounded teaspoonful of boric-acid crystals to one pint of water that has been boiled. Use a medicine dropper or an eyecup. If these measures do not give results and a doctor is not within reach, try rolling the upper lid back on a pencil. If the object can be seen, remove it with a small swab dipped in boric-acid solution. Be sure to scrub your hands thoroughly before attempting to remove an object from the eye. Boric acid or a couple of drops of sterile castor oil will soothe the eye after an object has been removed.

If an acid or other chemical, including lime, iodine, or battery fluid, has entered the eye, wash out immediately with large quantities of cool water. A good way to do this is to have the patient lie down and then gently pour water from a cup or glass into the inner corner of the eye, letting it run out on the other side. Hold the eye open while doing this and use several cups or glasses of water. When you are sure that the chemical has been washed out, put several drops of sterile olive oil or castor oil into the eye. Milk is a good eyewash for alkalis. In all cases of eye injuries it is wise to see a doctor. No one can afford to run any risks with eyesight.

Black Star, by Marvin Koner

Be sure to wash your hands thoroughly before attempting to remove an object from the eye.

Injuries to Bones, Joints, and Muscles

What is the difference between a simple and compound fracture of the bone? What kind of first aid can be given to ease the pain of people who have broken a leg, sprained an ankle, or dislocated a joint? (See "The Story of the Skeleton" in Volume 6.) This selection from Sidney J. Williams, W. W. Charters: Safety. Copyright 1940 by The Macmillan Company, and used with The Macmillan Company's permission.

Avoid making broken bones more serious by rash handling. First aid should be applied to make the injured person more comfortable until the doctor arrives. It is very important not to rush first aid for fractures in such a way that damage and shock are increased. You should not attempt to turn doctor and set a fracture yourself, for you may only increase the injury. Be extremely cautious about moving anyone with a broken bone until he is prepared to be moved. Too frequently an injured person is picked up, set up in a car, and rushed to a hospital with no adequate protection for his possible fractures. If possible let him rest until a doctor or an ambulance can arrive.

There are two kinds of fractures: simple and compound. In a simple fracture the bone is broken, but there is no connecting wound from the break in the bone to the skin. In a compound fracture the bone is broken and in addition there is a wound from the break to the surface of the skin. The wound may be made either by the sharp end of the bone being pushed out through the flesh or by some object, such as a bullet, passing in from the outside.

What To Do for Simple Fractures

A simple fracture has various symptoms. Often the person feels his bone snap, and the break is tender and painful. The broken part swells up. It usually looks deformed and different from the corresponding member which is uninjured. The first aider has three jobs to perform before the arrival of the doctor: *(1)* He should try to prevent further damage, for a simple fracture which is treated improperly may turn into a compound fracture; *(2)* he should make the person comfortable; and *(3)* he should take care of shock.

If the doctor can come right away, and if the person is not bleeding, it is not necessary to remove his clothing. If the clothing ought to be removed, cut or tear it off very gently. Cut off a shoe instead of trying to unlace it. Do not move a person with a broken arm or leg unless it is absolutely necessary. Cover him with blankets, put a pillow under his head, and leave him alone until the doctor arrives.

However, if the injured person must be moved, a "fixed traction" splint should be applied to his injured limb. Fixed traction is pulling against a fixed point at the base of the limb, where it joins the body, by means of an apparatus like a splint. It takes two people to put the splint on. Have the splint ready; then, taking hold of the wrist or ankle, pull it to straighten the limb and put the hand or foot in its normal position. Keep on pulling

99

Temporary splints for fractures can be made with materials you have around the house. A leg splint (right) made of a long wooden board, cushioned with rolled cloth, and held in place with strips of cloth knotted outside the wood. Below, a splint for the lower arm can be made of rolled newspaper and held in place with strips of cloth.

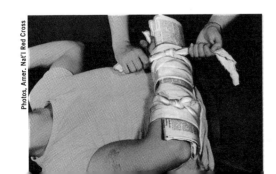

Photos, Amer. Nat'l Red Cross

until the splint has been applied. This traction prevents the muscles, nerves, and blood vessels from being damaged any more, and thus reduces the person's pain and shock. Never move a person without putting on a splint, and do not try to set the bone.

If it is impossible to use fixed traction, there are other splints which may be applied. The splint should be made of some rigid material like a board and padded with something soft. It should extend beyond the joints above and below the broken bone, and be tied against the broken bone with bandages which are not so tight that they stop the circulation.

What To Do for Compound Fractures

A compound fracture has all the symptoms of a simple fracture, as well as a wound through which the bone may or may not protrude. If there is bleeding from an artery (which comes in spurts), stop it by pressing between the wound and the heart and then applying a tourniquet. Do not press directly on the fracture. Since there is the same danger of infection from a compound fracture as there is from any other wound, treat it with tincture of iodine and bandage it with sterile gauze. Straighten the limb by traction and apply a traction splint. Do not worry if the end of the bone disappears; just tell the doctor that it has protruded.

First Aid for Other Fractures

So far we have been talking about fractures to the extremities: the arms, legs, hands, and feet. Other breaks need first aid just as much.

A fractured skull may be accompanied by a bump or cut on the head, unconsciousness, difference in the size of the pupils of the eyes, and bleeding from the ears and nose. The color of the face and the pulse beat depend upon the seriousness of the fracture. The person should be kept lying down: his head level with the rest of his body if his face is pale, higher if it is red or normal. Handle him very carefully and keep him lying down if he has to be moved. Put ice bags or cold compresses on his head. Keep him warm, but do not give him stimulants. If blood is coming from a wound

on his head, apply enough pressure to stop or lessen it, but not enough to drive pieces of bone into the brain.

Fractures of the nose cause pain, swelling, and often deformity. Do not try to put on a splint. Bandage the wound (if there is any) very gently.

A fracture of the lower jaw is indicated by irregularity of the teeth, difficulty in jaw movement, pain, swelling, and bleeding. Raise the lower teeth to their normal position against the upper teeth, and keep the jaw there with a bandage from the chin to the top of the head. Take off the bandage if the person begins to vomit; put it on again when he stops.

A person with a fractured collarbone usually cannot raise his arm above the shoulder. You can feel the broken ends when you pass your fingers over his collarbone. Put the arm on the injured side in a sling and bandage it tightly against his body. If possible, leave at least the ends of his fingers uncovered so you can see more readily if the circulation is cut off.

Fractured ribs cause pain when the person coughs or takes a deep breath. He usually holds his hand over the broken rib to keep it from moving. If a lung has been punctured, he may cough up blood. If he is expelling blood keep him warm, quiet, and lying down with his chest high enough to let him breathe easily. Do not move him unless it is absolutely necessary. If he is not bleeding, however, tie two or three broad bandages tightly around his chest and back to limit chest motion. Put a pad under the knots to prevent bruising. A pillow slip or towel drawn tightly around him over the broken rib will serve the same purpose of limiting the painful motion of the chest.

If a person cannot move his legs, his back is broken; if he cannot move his fingers, his neck is usually broken. If he is unconscious and it is impossible to know where he is paralyzed, treat him as though he has a broken neck. A person with any of these fractures should not be moved until the doctor arrives, except to be rolled easily over on his back. If he has to be moved, he should be tied onto

If you sprain your ankle and must walk some distance for aid, this is what you should do; first bathe your ankle in cold water and then apply a sprained ankle bandage with a scarf or any cloth you have available. The bandage should always be used with the shoe on.

a very rigid stretcher with coats or sweaters packed around his head and shoulders. Six or eight men are needed to lift him onto the stretcher; his body must be kept in a straight line and not allowed to bend.

Fractures of the pelvis are very painful. These should be treated in the same way as a spinal fracture, that is, the person should not be moved unless it is necessary, and then only on a stiff stretcher. His knees and ankles should be tied together, and his knees should be either raised or straightened, depending upon which position is the more comfortable.

What To Do for Dislocations

Dislocations occur when the ligaments which hold the bones together in a joint are torn and the bones pulled apart. Ligaments are heavy, strong bands of white tissue. They extend from one bone to another around a joint. The joints are enclosed in flexible sacs, and are lubricated by a fluid secretion. A dislocation is very painful. Torn ligaments may take a long time to heal. Usually the joint is deformed and swollen and cannot be moved. Cold compresses help to reduce the pain and keep down the swelling.

A dislocated hip is very serious. If you have to move a person with such an injury, put pads under his weak knee. A dislocated shoulder should be supported by a loose sling. Shoulder and hip dislocations must always be treated by a doctor.

Dislocations of the lower jaw or of fingers and toes can sometimes be taken care of by a first aider. To put a lower jaw back into place, have the person sit in a chair. Standing in front of him, place your thumbs, which should be covered with a protective bandage, on his lower back teeth. Keep your fingers under his chin; pull up with them and press down with your thumbs. Get your thumbs out of the way before the jaw snaps back. Put a bandage under the person's chin and up around the top of his head. To set or "reduce" a dislocated finger, pull it out in a straight line with the hand until it slips into place. If a dislocated joint is open or bleeding, do not try to reduce it. Put on a bandage and send the person to a doctor.

What To Do for Sprains

Sprains are dislocations which go back into place by themselves. If ligaments are torn, sprains are very painful; all are accompanied by some pain, especially when the injured joint is moved. They swell up quickly, and get black and blue. The first thing to do for a person with a sprained wrist or ankle is to raise the sprained joint: an ankle by putting it on pillows, a wrist by placing it in a loose sling. Next, keep the joint cold with running water, cold compresses, or ice bags. Finally, do not let the person use the injured part until a doctor has seen it.

Other Books To Read

What to Do Until the Doctor Comes, by William Bolton, M.D. Published by Reilly & Lee Company, Chicago, revised edition, 1960.
A useful reference book on what to do and how to do it in case of accident, injuries, or illness.

Home Nursing Text Book by The American National Red Cross. Published by Doubleday & Company, Inc., Garden City, N. Y., 6th ed., 1950.
An excellent book on all phases of home nursing.

You can obtain more information by writing either of the addresses below and requesting pamphlets about first-aid treatment.
The American National Red Cross
17 Street, N.W.
Washington 13, D.C.
Metropolitan Life Insurance Company
1 Madison Avenue
New York City, New York

101

Poisons and Poisoning

Many of the poisons which may cause physical damage if taken internally or inhaled in large amounts are found around the home. "Warning—Poison!" on the label of a bottle is not always enough to prevent a dangerous accident, and you will want to know exactly what to do to help in case of such an emergency.
From **The Book of Health**, compiled and edited by Randolf Lee Clark, Jr., M.D. and Russell W. Cumley, Ph.D. Copyright 1953 by Elsevier Press, Inc.

A poison is any substance which produces a harmful or deadly effect on living tissue. The effect of most poisons depends on the amount consumed and the age and physical condition of the victim. Substances which prevent the action of the poisons are *antidotes.*

Poisons may be classified in a number of different ways, but perhaps the most useful classification is on the basis of their physiological action. Under this simplified classification poisons fall into four classes: *corrosives, irritants, neurotoxins,* and *hemotoxins.*

The corrosives include the strong acids and alkalis, the chief action of which is the local destruction of tissues. The irritants are those which cause too much blood to gather in the organ with which they come in contact. The largest group, the neurotoxins, affect the nerves or some of the basic processes within the cell. Neurotoxins include the narcotics, barbiturates, alcohols, and anesthetics. Among the hemotoxins are carbon monoxide and hydrogen cyanide. These substances combine with the blood and prevent oxygen from forming hemoglobin. Thus death may occur from "internal suffocation," since the blood is deprived of oxygen that nourishes the tissues and brain.

Emergency Treatment of Poisoning

Do dilute the poison by inducing the patient to drink a large amount of water.

Do bring about vomiting by giving large amounts of soapy water, warm salt, soda, or mustard water (which are known as emetics).

Do gag the patient by tickling the back of the throat with the finger. Then give more emetic fluid and do the same thing again.

Do keep up the vomiting until the fluid that is vomited is clear as when swallowed.

Do give artificial respiration if breathing ceases.

Do consult chart in this article and administer specific treatment if the substance swallowed is known.

Do use the universal antidote given below if poison is not known.

Do not lose your head.

Do not waste precious time trying to look up an antidote when you don't know what has been swallowed. If you can bring about vomiting, it will greatly reduce the danger. The physician will give the proper antidote.

Universal Antidote

Two parts of burned, powdered toast.
One part of milk of magnesia.
One part of strong tea.

The substances included above are found in most households. The burned powdered toast is the source of *carbon,* the milk of magnesia a source of *magnesium oxide,* and the strong tea a source of *tannic acid.* The carbon absorbs poisons; the magnesium oxide has a soothing effect on the mucous membranes of the stomach and a laxative action that tends to neutralize acid poisons, and the tannic acid tends to neutralize caustic alkaline substances.

Food Poisoning

Food poisoning occurs particularly during the summer months. It is caused by poison-producing bacteria in food. Certain poisonous plants may cause irritation. The symptoms are an uncomfortable sensation in the upper abdomen, pain, cramps, nausea and vomiting, and, occasionally, prostration. First-aid treatment is the same as for chemical poisons.

Call local health department; save container (can, wrapper, etc.); save samples of vomitus and stool.

(You will want to read about how to treat snake bite wounds in "First Aid for Snake Bite" in Volume 6.)

Some Common Poisons

	Chemical Poison	Chief Signs and Symptoms	Emergency Treatment
Acetone	Nail polish remover Paint and varnish remover	Nausea, vomiting, decreased pulse, difficulty in breathing, irritation to kidneys, stupor.	After patient has vomited, give stimulant such as strong coffee or tea.*
Acids	Acetic Hydrochloric (muriatic) Nitric Phosphoric Sulphuric	Corrosion of membranes of the mouth and throat and esophagus. Vomiting, intense pain, collapse. Feeble heartbeat, rapid pulse.	Give liberal doses of milk of magnesia, milk, soapy water, or egg whites.*
Alkalis	Sodium hydroxide (lye) (caustic soda) Potassium hydroxide (caustic potash) "Saniflush," etc.	Corrosion of mucous membranes of the digestive tract. Vomiting. Intense pain. Feeble heartbeat. Rapid pulse. Blood often present in vomit and in stools.	Give strong solution of vinegar or citrus juice followed by olive oil, melted butter, or other non-toxic oil. Emetic not indicated.*
Alcohol, methyl	Wood alcohol Paint or shellac thinner	Depression, lack of muscle co-ordination, headache, disturbed vision, nausea, blindness, delirium, collapse; often fatal.	After patient has vomited, give large dose of baking soda followed by a dose of epsom salts. Have the patient inhale spirits of ammonia if available.*
Amyl acetate	Banana oil Pear oil Lacquer thinner	Irritation of eyes, coughing, abdominal pain, vomiting, difficulty in breathing.	Give strong stimulants, such as coffee or tea.*
Arsenic	Fly paper Fowler's solution Paris green Lead arsenate Ant or rat poison	Metallic taste, burning pain in esophagus or stomach, vomiting and diarrhea, thirst, choking sensation, garlic odor on breath, cold skin, rapid weak pulse, collapse, convulsions, coma.	Give strong stimulants, followed by castor oil or epsom salts.*
Barbiturates	Barbital, Phenobarbital Seconal, Nembutal Amytal, Pentothal "Yellow birds, Blue birds"	Small doses produce sleep. Large doses produce headache, mental confusion, coma, blue lips and fingernails, dilated pupils, slow or irregular breathing.	Administer strong stimulants. If breathing remains normal, patient will probably sleep off the effects of the drug.*
Benzene, benzol	Toluene Xylol Floor wax or polish Some shoe polish	Nausea, vomiting, headache, irregular pulse, dizziness, excitement, depression, coma. Heart failure. Damage to blood-forming organs.	Give large amounts of mineral oil, and have the patient inhale spirits of ammonia.*
Benzine	Gasoline Kerosene Petroleum ether Cleaner's naphtha	Inhalation produces flushed face, coma, dilated pupils and respiratory failure. Swallowing produces burning of mouth, nausea, vomiting, drunkenness, thirst, slow pulse, difficult breathing, convulsions, and coma.	If swallowed, induce vomiting and give the patient strong coffee or tea. If the substance is inhaled, treat patient in same manner except for the emetic, which is omitted.*
Canabis	Marihuana Hashish	Exhilaration, hallucinations, delirium, mania, muscle weakness, slow respiration, dilated pupils, convulsions, coma.	Administer strong coffee, protect from shock, and restrain the patient.*
Carbon monoxide	Coal gas Automobile exhaust	Dizziness, weakness, headache, stupor, throbbing pulse, increased blood pressure, skin dusky, lips pink, paralysis, coma.	Remove patient to fresh air and begin artificial respiration. Protect from shock.*
Carbon tetrachloride	Non-inflammable cleaning fluid Fire extinguisher fluid	Headache, drowsiness, confusion, coma. Abdominal pain, dilated pupils. Kidney and liver damage follows acute symptoms.	Give strong coffee or tea in addition to the treatment listed below for induction of vomiting and prevention of shock.*
Chlorine	Sodium hypochlorite Bleaching solution of "Clorox" type	Inhalation produces irritation of lungs and eyes, spasm-like cough, choking, vomiting, collapse. Swallowing produces irritation of the gastrointestinal tract and extreme pain.	If inhaled, remove patient to fresh air, give artificial respiration, and have the patient inhale spirits of ammonia. If swallowed, treat as listed below for production of vomiting and prevention of shock.*
Copper salts	Copper sulphate Blue stone Blue vitriol Zinc salts	Nausea, vomiting, purging, severe abdominal pains, cold clammy skin, delirium, coma, convulsions.	The patient should vomit repeatedly. Then, give egg white or magnesia followed by strong coffee or tea.*
Cyanides	Hydrocyanic acid Cyanogen Some insect poisons Gopher poison	Large doses produce instant death. Small doses cause vomiting, diarrhea, difficult breathing, glassy eyes, pale face, blood-stained foam on mouth, stupor, coma.	After patient has vomited, give dose of hydrogen peroxide.*
Fluorides	Cockroach or insect poison	Nausea, vomiting, abdominal cramps, weakness, fall in blood pressure, deep, rapid respiration, convulsions, coma.	Give calcium tablets, lime water, chalk, or milk.*
Formaldehyde	Home disinfectant Preserving fluid for natural history specimens	Swallowing produces irritation of mouth and intestines. Irritation of lungs. Severe abdominal pain, nausea, vomiting, rapid pulse, blood in urine, intense irritation of eyes and lungs upon breathing fumes.	Before having patient vomit, give him diluted ammonia water, egg whites, or milk. After he has vomited, give large doses of baking soda in water.*
Iodine	Tincture of iodine Iodex salve Lugol's solution	Brown color on lips and mouth. Burning pain in stomach, vomiting. Bloody purging, heart depression, cold skin, convulsions, collapse.	Give large quantities of starch (bread, flour, corn starch, etc.) followed by strong coffee or tea.*
Lead	Red lead White lead Paints	Pain in stomach, thirst, blood in stools and vomit, weakness, paralysis, convulsions, collapse.	After patient has vomited, give him calcium tablets, powdered chalk, or milk, followed by epsom salts.*
Mercury	Bichloride of mercury	Severe pain in mouth, throat, stomach, increase in saliva, blood and mucus in vomit. Watery, bloody diarrhea, followed in 1 or 2 days by inflammation of colon, blood in urine, coma, collapse.	Give egg white immediately.*
Opium	Codeine Heroin Laudanum Morphine	Mental exhilaration followed by drowsiness. Pupils of eyes pin point. Slow shallow breathing, slow onset of unconsciousness, muscles relaxed, skin pale, cold sweat, blue lips, irregular breathing.	After patient has vomited, give him a dose of charcoal and aluminum hydroxide. Follow this with strong coffee or tea, and keep the patient awake and warm until a physician arrives.*
Phenols	Carbolic acid Creosote Lysol	Burning pain from mouth to stomach, white patches in mouth, depression, weakness, nausea. Blood in urine, fall in body temperature. Pale, clammy face.	Give patient large quantities of any non-toxic oil (olive oil, mineral oil, cooking oil, etc.). Also give lime water and egg whites. Emetic not indicated.*
Phosphorus	Matches Rat poison (read label)	Gastrointestinal pain, garlic odor, vomiting of blood, bloody diarrhea. If patient survives, symptoms will go away in 2 to 3 days. Later symptoms: skin eruption, enlarged liver, jaundice, pulse weak, heart weak, convulsions.	Give large amount of mineral oil, followed by epsom salts.*

*In every type of poisoning, immediate medical aid is essential. Further, vomiting should be induced if the poison is swallowed (except in those cases noted where it is not indicated) by causing the patient to gag or by administration of warm soapy water or a tartar emetic (a liquid which induces vomiting). Every patient must be kept warm until the physician arrives, and other standard means to combat shock should be instituted. Should the patient cease breathing before medical aid is available, artificial respiration should be given.

Artificial Respiration

The correct administration of artificial respiration has saved lives. This article describes how artificial respiration is given and when to use it. From Until the Doctor Comes . . . Or First Aid in a Nutshell, by Louis H. Merker, M.D., published by Sheridan House. Copyright 1953 by Louis H. Merker. Revised by editor, 1961.

Most people think that artificial respiration applies to drowning cases, only. Many doctors have never used it for a drowning case, but have given artificial respiration many times for other conditions. For example, electric shock cases need it.

When Someone Stops Breathing

First of all, have someone call a doctor or an ambulance. As soon as you reach your victim: act fast, act sensibly, don't delay.

Drop him on his belly, on the floor, wherever you are. Get to work immediately. Don't start dragging him into some room on a bed. You'll have less space to work in. Your assistant can cover him with a blanket, loosen his clothes, and remove his false teeth, or chewing gum.

Artificial Respiration Technique

The American Medical Association, the Army, Navy and Air Force, the Red Cross, the Boy Scouts, and the Girl Scouts, have all agreed to abandon the Schaefer Method, known as the "prone pressure method." Instead, they teach two new methods, said to be twice as effective as the Schaefer Method. They are: (1) the Holger Neilsen Method: "back pressure—arm lift", (2) the Silvester Method: "chest pressure—arm lift."

Back-pressure—Arm-lift Method

104

a. *Position of the victim.* Place the victim in the face-down (prone) position. Bend his elbows and place his hands one upon the other. Turn his face to one side, placing his cheek upon his hands.

b. *Position of the operator.* Kneel on either the right or left knee at the head of the victim and facing him. Place the knee at the side of the victim's head close to the forearm. Place the opposite foot near the elbow. If it is more comfortable, kneel on both knees, one to either side of the victim's head. Place your hands upon the flat of his back in such a way that the heels of your hands lie just below the lower tip of the shoulder blades. With the tip of the thumbs just touching, spread the fingers downward and outward.

c. *Compression phase.* Rock forward until the arms are approximately vertical, and allow the weight of the upper part of your body to exert slow, steady, even pressure downward upon the hands. This forces air out of the lungs. Keep your elbows straight and exert pressure almost directly downward on the back.

d. *Expansion phase.* Release the pressure, avoiding a final thrust, and commence to rock slowly backward. Place your hands upon the victim's arms just above his elbows, and draw his arms upward and toward you.

Apply just enough lift to feel resistance and tension at the victim's shoulders. Do not bend your elbows, and as you rock backward, the victim's arms will be drawn toward you. The arm lift expands the chest by pulling on the chest muscles, arching the back, and re-

These pictures show the steps in the "back-pressure —arm-lift" method of artificial respiration described in this article. Study the pictures carefully and, if possible, practice this method with a friend.

Drawings courtesy Amer. Nat'l Red Cross

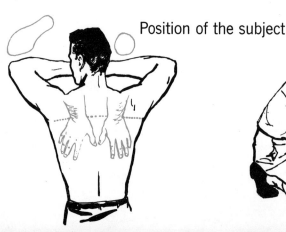

Position of the subject

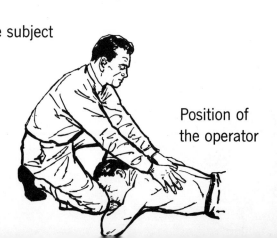

Position of the operator

lieving the weight on the chest. Then drop the arms gently to the ground or floor. This completes the full cycle. You are now ready to repeat the cycle.

e. Cycle timing and rhythm. This cycle should be repeated about ten to twelve times per minute at a steady uniform rate to the rhythm of *press, release, lift, release.* Longer counts of about equal length should be given to the "press" and "lift" steps of the compression and expansion phases. The release periods should be of minimum duration.

f. Changing position or operator.

(1) Remember that either or both of your knees may be used, or you may shift knees during the procedure with no break in the steady rhythm. Observe how you rock forward with the back pressure and backward with the arm lift. This rocking motion helps to sustain the rhythm and adds to the ease of operation.

(2) If you get tired and another person is available, you can "take turns." Be sure, however, that you do not break the rhythm in changing. To change operators, move off to one side while your replacement comes in from the other side. The replacement begins the press-release after one of the lift-release phases, while you move away.

The Silvester Method is practically the same as the Neilsen Method. The only difference is that the patient is on his back. It's important to know this method for one reason. Suppose your victim has a severe abdominal wound; he cannot be put with the abdomen on the floor (or face down). He is on his back, and must remain that way. Then the Neilsen Method cannot be practiced. The victim's arms are folded on his chest, and you, the rescuer, kneel at his head. The arms, grasped above the wrists, are drawn upward, above the head, until they touch the ground. This makes the victim exhale. This is repeated until the vic-

tim is revived and is breathing normally again.

Caution—When the victim is on his back, he may swallow his tongue. This means that his tongue may fall back in his mouth, and block air traffic. So, to play safe, make sure his tongue is pulled out, and protruding slightly from his mouth.

Now, how long are you going to continue artificial respiration? The rule says at least four hours. There are many reports on record where success finally came after eight hours of artificial respiration.

Mouth-to-Mouth Method

However, the method of artificial respiration which is gaining favor over all others is mouth-to-mouth breathing. It is easy to perform, provides oxygen quickly, and can be used even when there is a chest injury. The method is as follows:

a. Place the victim on his back, remove any foreign matter from his mouth, and tilt his head backward as far as possible so the front of the neck is stretched.

b. Lift his jaw upward so that the lower teeth are higher than the upper teeth and hold the jaw in this position.

c. Approach the victim from the side, take a deep breath, place your mouth over his mouth and your cheek against his nose to make airtight contact, and blow. With small babies, place your mouth over both nose and mouth. Blow *forcefully* into an adult, *gently* into a child.

d. When his chest moves, take your mouth away and let him exhale, then blow in the next deep breath. Repeat every three to five seconds in an adult, and every two to three seconds in a child. Rhythm is less important than the amount of air blown into the lungs.

105

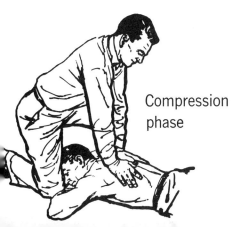

Compression phase

Position for expansion phase

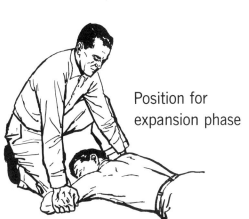

Expansion phase

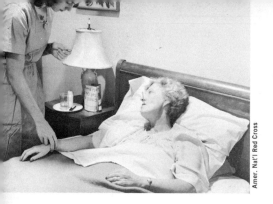

Home Care of the Sick

Sooner or later everyone spends a few days or perhaps a few weeks in bed because he is ill. Do you remember how uncomfortable the bed began to feel after a while, how dull the food seemed to taste, and how bored you were with everything? If you do you will want to help yourself and others to be happier the next time they are confined in bed for more than a day. (See also "Familiar Diseases," in Volume 6.) From **Enjoying Health** by Evelyn G. Jones. Copyright 1952 by J. B. Lippincott Company.

Everyone should have some nursing skill because the comfort and recovery of a sick person often are dependent more upon a nurse than upon a physician. The latter examines, diagnoses, and prescribes. Carrying out directions, administering medicines, and noticing changes in the condition of the patient are responsibilities of those who care for him. The physician can see the sick person only briefly and must rely on reports from the nurse for conditions the remainder of the time. Intelligent teamwork is an important factor.

A Record for the Doctor

A patient's chart is a carefully kept record of his condition and progress through the day. Hospitals and registered nurses make a graphic chart of symptoms and treatment so that a physician can tell at a glance how his patient is getting along. If the one who is taking care of a sick person in the home will keep a record of the most significant symptoms, it will be of great value.

Some symptoms that can be observed are the color of skin (whether the face is pale or flushed), the expression of the eyes, restlessness or unusual quiet, and the degree of appetite. The patient himself can tell about his feelings of pain, nausea, or dizziness.

Temperature is one of the symptoms that a home nurse should record. Slight variations have so much significance to the doctor that the nurse should not trust them to memory.

Every home should have a clinical thermometer. This is a sensitive instrument that registers body heat usually between 94° and 110° F. The scale is divided to read at intervals of two tenths of a degree. An arrow on the side of the scale and red figures above the normal point, 98.6° F., call attention to fever temperatures. Readings should be made morning and late afternoon and oftener if the doctor so requests.

To use a clinical thermometer, hold it firmly at the end away from the bulb. Snap the wrist quickly, several times, until the mercury has dropped below 96° F. Rinse the thermometer in cold water and place the bulb under the patient's tongue. Have him close the lips and hold the thermometer at least two minutes. Then remove the thermometer and wipe with a piece of cotton or tissue, rubbing from the upper end down to the bulb. Hold it on a level with your eye, with the triangular edge toward you. This gives an opaque background against which the point at the end of the column of mercury may be read. Record the reading and the time of day.

A thermometer should be washed carefully by rubbing with a bit of cotton or tissue, soap, and cold water. It should be kept in its case for protection.

Pulse (rate, strength, and regularity of heartbeat) may be recorded while the thermometer is in the patient's mouth. The pulsation of blood may be felt in any artery that is close to the surface of the body. The wrist, temple, and base of the throat are convenient places. Probably pulse is counted in the artery leading to the patient's thumb more frequently than in any other place.

To take the pulse, the tips of two fingers (not the thumb) of one hand should be placed

A thermometer

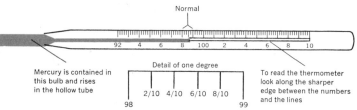

After HOME NURSING TEXTBOOK, ©1951 by Amer. Nat'l Red Cross

on the underneath side of the patient's wrist. After the pulse is located beats should be counted for half a minute. Multiply the result by two to get the rate for a whole minute, then repeat for another half minute. The average of the two counts should be recorded.

While counting the pulsations notice whether they come at regular intervals and if they are strong or weak (hard to detect). Pulse rate varies in different individuals, at different ages, and under varying conditions. The pulse rate is 140 at birth and drops as the person becomes older. The range for adults is from 66 to 88. Young people usually have a pulse rate of 80 to 85.

Other items may be noted as the physician requests. These include the food eaten, the amount of liquid taken, bowel movements, urination, and treatments.

Follow the Directions!

Directions for administering medicines should be followed exactly. The rule that one should read the label three times, every time a dose is given, is particularly important if a patient has several medicines. Measurements should be exact and medicine should be given at the time indicated. Pills and capsules should be taken from the box with a spoon and offered to the patient. A glass of water should be at hand when the medicine is given.

Heat or cold may be ordered as a form of treatment for a part of the body. Neither should be used without a doctor's order as the effect may be harmful. Dry heat is applied with hot-water bags or electric pad. A bag should be filled only about one third, and air pressed out before the stopper is tightened. This makes the bag more flexible and soft. If the patient is very ill, or sleeping, the nurse must watch to see that skin is not becoming red from too much heat. Moist heat is applied by compresses. A clean washcloth makes a good, small compress; a turkish towel is good for a larger one. The compress is wrung out of hot water, kept in as many folds as possible to retain heat, and placed lightly where needed. Cover it with a dry towel. Compresses are changed after two or three minutes and treat-

A simple cardboard carton can be used three different ways to make a patient more comfortable—as a backrest, footrest, or tray.

ment is usually continued about twenty minutes.

Cold may be applied by filling an ice bag with chopped ice. A compress may be chilled by laying it on a piece of ice or by wringing it out after immersing in ice water.

Pillows for Comfort

One of the advantages of hospital care over that given at home is the equipment for comfort and convenience of both patient and nurse. Many substitutes in home care may be devised by a thoughtful nurse.

Several pillows may be used to make a patient comfortable. One placed under the knees is very restful. When a patient is lying on one side, a pillow at his back and one between the knees adds to comfort. Small pillows, that may be tucked in to support parts of the body, often relieve strain or fatigue. An alert nurse will place pillows to make a patient comfortable without waiting to be asked. Often the patient is vaguely unhappy but does not know just exactly what is wrong with him.

A pillow or a box may be placed under the covers at the foot of the bed. This gives a support against which the feet may be pressed.

Two pillows may be arranged in an inverted V, with a third pillow across the center, to make a back rest when the patient wishes to sit up. This same arrangement is good in a chair when the patient can get out of bed.

107

After drawing, Amer. Nat'l Red Cross

Bacterial toxins are the strongest poisons we know; yet for many of them the body can build an army of antibodies that makes such poisons harmless! It takes only .00000005 grams of purified tetanus toxin to kill a mouse, as compared to .00016 grams (3,200 times as much) strychnine.

Immunity

section 6

As recently as the opening years of the 1700's most people accepted diseases such as smallpox as unavoidable. Whether or not one became a victim was largely a matter of chance. London, with a total population of about 600,000 people, had over 2,000 deaths a year from smallpox. But eventually some people began to wonder if such a terrible toll was necessary. They had ideas for prevention and were willing to work to give their ideas a try. For instance, the idea of inoculation against smallpox was born. It took work to get it started; on the prolonged pleading of Lady Mary Montagu, seven criminals in Newgate prison were given their liberty in return for allowing themselves to be inoculated. By so doing, they helped show anxious Londoners that inoculation itself was not dangerous. That was 1721. By the end of the century an even better immunization was known—vaccination— though it was not generally accepted for many years. Not until the 1880's, when vaccination was required by law in England, could it be said that smallpox was practically under control there. Then England's death rate due to smallpox fell from about 4,000 per million to less than twenty. In the United States today, almost 2,000,000 people are vaccinated for smallpox every year. Contrast the twenty or so annual cases of smallpox in our enormous population, with the thousands in eighteenth-century England!

You probably know that by now diphtheria, tetanus (lockjaw), typhoid fever, whooping cough, and—most recently—poliomyelitis have entered the ranks of controllable diseases. This section will help you understand how people can become immune to these diseases. You will also read about times when "immunity" takes an unwanted turn: when a blood transfusion does not work, or when the once mysterious Rh factor causes complications. These kinds of reactions are discussed in more detail in "What Does Allergy Mean to You?" in Volume 10. You will also find more about immunity in "Bacteria and Disease," Volume 7; and "Pioneers of Medicine," Volume 8.

There are still a great many diseases for which no immunity is yet known. Men and women all over the world are working to conquer them, too. Your part is small but important. Cooperate with the various immunization programs. Keep up your vaccinations whether or not your state requires them. Many a young doctor has never seen a case of smallpox. We have made diphtheria just as rare, and now polio is being added to the list. It depends on you. —Anne Norton

Vaccination:

A Country Doctor's Discovery

Often people observe that something cures or prevents a disease before they have any idea why it should be so. That was the case with vaccination. Edward Jenner saw that it worked, but because he could not explain it, he had a hard time getting his fellow doctors to accept the practice. This is Jenner's story, as told by a well known English writer. From **The Romance of Medical Science** by Patrick Pringle. Used by permission of Roy Publishers, New York.

Jenner's first vaccination. The "boy named Phipps," a hero in his own right, is being inoculated with pus from a milkmaid's cowpox pustule.

An outbreak of smallpox today would be so rare that it would rate front-page news; yet in the eighteenth century, some 40,000 people in England died of it every year—and that figure is nothing compared with the numbers that lost their sight or were disfigured for life.

There was no known cure for it. There was only one consolation, and that was a small one: if a person survived one attack he was not likely to catch it again.

No one knew why it was so, but that did not stop the very earliest doctors in history from trying to turn the knowledge to good account. In its mild form smallpox was anything but pleasant, but at least the sufferer knew that he was unlikely ever to experience anything worse. Thus began man's first attempts at protective inoculation, that is to say, deliberately infecting himself with a mild form of the disease in order to escape a more severe attack. The principle of immunity was put into practice long before it was first preached.

This sort of inoculation was practiced among the early Hindus, Chinese, North Africans, and various other people. However, it seems to have been almost unknown in Europe until early in the eighteenth century, when it was introduced to England by Lady Mary Wortley Montagu. This lady accompanied her husband on his assignment as England's ambassador to Turkey, and it was from Constantinople that she wrote the letter that was to gain her a place in the history of medicine.

The smallpox (she wrote), so fatal and so general among us, is here entirely harmless by the invention of ingrafting, which is the term they give it. . . . They make parties for this purpose, and when they are met (commonly fifteen or sixteen together) an old woman comes with a nut-shell full of the matter of the best sort of smallpox, and asks what vein you are pleased to have open. She immediately rips open that you offer to her with a large needle (which gives no more pain than a common scratch) and puts into the vein as much venom as can lie upon the head of a needle, and after binds up the little wound with a hollow bit of shell, and in this manner opens four or five veins.

The resultant fever, said Lady Mary, was invariably mild, and she found no record of any fatal consequences.

Lady Mary was a person of some consequence in England, and her report attracted great attention. Eventually the College of Physicians gave inoculation their blessing, but French doctors condemned the practice. The French had good reason for this. Although the inoculation saved a good many individual lives, it caused a greater number of deaths among the community as a whole. There was no effective quarantine system, so inoculation started off fresh epidemics. As the disease had a habit of getting stronger as it was passed on, the death rate went up instead of down. In 1802 a Dr. Lettson reported to Parliament that since the introduction of the practice in England the smallpox death toll had risen from 72 to 89 per thousand.

109

But by 1802 vaccination had been discovered.

The Country Doctor

Edward Jenner was born in 1749, in the village of Berkeley, Gloucestershire. Born and bred in the country, he was a countryman all his life. Natural history especially interested him, and he soon began to acquire a large collection of fossils and birds' eggs.

After a preliminary education, Edward was sent to learn medicine under a Dr. Ludlow at Sodbury, near Bristol. From there he journeyed to London, and at the age of twenty-one he began to study under the great surgeon, John Hunter.

After qualifying as a doctor Jenner returned to his native Berkeley to set up in practice. He was a good doctor, popular in every class of society. He had several offers of town and overseas appointments, which would have paid more than his country practice ever could. He was not tempted. However, although he had little worldly ambition, he had an active and inquiring mind. He occupied himself with some private researches in medicine and pharmacy. At the same time quietly and methodically, he was studying a disease common among cows.

Cowpox and Smallpox

Jenner's interest in this subject was first aroused when he was still a student, even before he went to London. While in Dr. Ludlow's house in Sodbury he heard a chance remark that was to haunt him for over twenty years. The conversation was about smallpox—a topic as common as the weather in those days; and a milkmaid who happened to be present remarked carelessly: "I cannot take that disease, for I have had the cowpox."

The young student made no comment, but the remark set him thinking deeply. Inquiry revealed that it was based on a popular belief in the neighbourhood that smallpox never attacked a person who previously had had cowpox. Now, as a general practitioner, Jenner mentioned this to other doctors, but they showed little interest in the legend. Country

people were full of superstitions and absurd beliefs.

Jenner was not so sure, and he began to study cows. Cowpox normally shows itself in the form of spots or pustules on the udders of the animals. It is contracted by human beings during milking. The disease is trivial in humans; apart from a few spots or sores on the hands, the sufferer hardly notices it.

If, thought Jenner, this infection could really prevent smallpox, why could it not be substituted for the dangerous inoculation that was then in use?

As a doctor he was regularly called on to administer the ordinary smallpox inoculations, and his observant mind noticed something that made him certain that the peasants were right. The inoculations sometimes failed to "take," and no symptoms of smallpox developed at all. When this happened Jenner asked the person concerned if he or she had ever had cowpox. The answer was nearly always in the affirmative.

Now Jenner began to expound his suggestion of cowpox inoculation to his colleagues. They were not impressed. When Jenner mentioned the subject at the local medical society he was actually threatened with expulsion if he did not keep his ridiculous views to himself!

Thinking perhaps that London doctors might be more ready to give a new idea a hearing, Jenner paid a visit to the capital. His reception was not encouraging. He was held in high esteem as a naturalist, but this idea of cowpox inoculation did not increase his reputation as a doctor.

The London doctors cannot altogether be blamed. This country doctor had not brought any practical proof in support of his theory—indeed, on his own admission he had never put it into practice at all.

On May 14, 1796, Jenner put his theory to the test.

The Crucial Test

For simplicity and clearness Jenner's own account of the experiment cannot be bettered. It was written in a letter to a friend:

A boy named Phipps was inoculated in the arm

from a pustule on the hand of a young woman who was infected by her Master's cows. Having never seen the disease but in its casual way before, that is, when communicated from the cow to the hand of the milker, I was astonished at the close resemblance of the pustules in some of their stages, to the variolous (smallpox) pustules. But now listen to the most delightful part of my story. The boy has since been inoculated for the smallpox which, as I ventured to predict, produced no effect. I shall now pursue my experiments with redoubled ardour.

Jenner made two further successful experiments, and in the spring of the following year he submitted his results in the form of a paper to the Royal Society. The paper was not published. The Royal Society explained to him that it was in his own interests that it should not appear. He had made a good impression with his other papers, notably one on the life history of the cuckoo, and it would be foolish of him to risk his reputation on this cowpox idea.

But there was no stopping the country doctor now. In 1798 he published his results at his own expense.

The paper was not well received. It looked as if the Royal Society had been right about Jenner's reputation. Then one London doctor was moved to try the experiment himself— and Jenner had one follower. Others came soon after, and the profession began to take sides. Vaccination (from the Latin word *vacca*, meaning "a cow") had arrived. Jenner was becoming famous. His friends urged him to make his fortune in London. But Jenner, the country doctor, refused.

Whether he wanted to go or not, however, London needed him. London doctors did not have Jenner's extensive knowledge of cowpox. Mistakes were being made over the collection of the vaccine, and failures were reported. It took Jenner three months to get the Londoners working on the right lines.

In 1800 Jenner published his latest figures. Under his supervision 6,000 people had been vaccinated, and were later inoculated with smallpox. Not one had contracted smallpox. Jenner also made the important observation that vaccination could save people from smallpox even if given after exposure to infection.

Now the name of Jenner became a household word. The societies that had made fun of his theories now begged him for lectures. He was summoned to audiences with the King and Queen and appointed physician extraordinary to His Majesty. But he did not stay in London. Berkeley was his home, and to Berkeley he returned.

To the last Jenner remained the simple, retiring country gentleman he had always been. He ended his days in his beloved Berkeley, as the ordinary country doctor again, vaccinating the poor in his garden, and spending his leisure hours in the study of birds and animals. He died in 1823, seventy-one years old, and was buried quietly in the village churchyard.

The Microbe

Like any other science, bacteriology has provided plenty of fun for scoffers. Hilaire Belloc wrote this poem a hundred years after Jenner's discovery of vaccination. "The Microbe" by Hilaire Belloc, **Cautionary Verses.** Reprinted by permission of the publishers, Gerald Duckworth & Co., Ltd., England, and Alfred A. Knopf, Inc.

The Microbe is so very small
You cannot make him out at all,
But many sanguine people hope
To see him through a microscope.
His jointed tongue that lies beneath
A hundred curious rows of teeth;
His seven tufted tails with lots
Of lovely pink and purple spots,
On each of which a pattern stands,
Composed of forty separate bands;
His eyebrows of a tender green;
All these have never yet been seen—
But Scientists, who ought to know,
Assure us that they must be so. . . .
Oh! let us never, never doubt
What nobody is sure about!

Different Kinds of Immunity

Jenner saw that people could be made immune to smallpox by a small dose of the germ (in a changed and weakened form) that causes it. But how did it work? Were there other ways to become immune? What accounted for the rare person who didn't catch smallpox, even when unvaccinated and living near those who had it? These questions are not easy to answer even today. Here is a discussion of some of the basic facts of immunity and the various kinds of protection your body can give you. Compiled from official sources by the editor.

"This hurts me more than it does you." But at least it keeps a fellow's dog safe from rabies.

The body's resistance to disease is commonly known as immunity. Perhaps immunity could better be called an inner resistance, because there are also outer defenses against disease, which are not properly called "immunity." Unbroken skin, for instance, is a pretty effective barrier to germs; the mucous membrane of your mouth, nose, and eyes is another; the coughing or sneezing that expels irritating substances is a third.

If we successfully combat such a disease as diphtheria it is because of one or both of two inner defenses: (1) certain white corpuscles called phagocytes which destroy invading germs (the phagocytes are a kind of white blood cell and are discussed in "The Heart, Blood, and Lungs" in Volume 10), (2) antibodies which accumulate in the blood and kill bacteria or counteract the harmful effects of their toxins (bacterial poisons). Generally, antibodies work with the white corpuscles in destroying germs.

Antibodies are substances which are produced by the body cells and are contained in the liquid part (the serum) of the blood. Antibodies have never been seen with the microscope. That they exist, however, is known by the definite results that they produce.

Natural and Acquired Immunities

There are two important types of immunity to disease: natural immunity and acquired immunity. If a person *inherits* a permanent resistance to a disease, he is said to possess a natural immunity to the disease. This means

that his body possesses certain protective substances, such as antibodies, that fight and destroy the germs of the disease, thus preventing the disease itself.

Acquired immunity may be either active or passive in form. The active form is a result of the formation of antibodies which are produced to resist the germs or the toxins of a disease. In this case the body cells actually fight the disease. The passive form is the result of injecting antitoxin or immune serums into a person's body to keep him from taking a certain disease.

How active acquired immunity is produced: Frequently a person acquires immunity to a disease by suffering an attack of the disease itself. While he is ill with some such disease as smallpox, diphtheria, or typhoid fever, enough antibodies are produced in his body not only to bring about recovery but also to protect him against further attacks of the disease for many years and often throughout life.

Active acquired immunity may also be brought about by vaccination, or inoculation with a vaccine. A vaccine consists of a virus or of a solution that contains either dead or weakened disease-producing bacteria. The purpose of inoculation is to bring about immunity to a disease by stimulating the body cells to produce antibodies. The bacteria in the vaccine are weakened just enough so that they will cause the body to produce antibodies but will not cause the disease itself.

In the case of smallpox a weakened living

Your Guide to Vaccinations

Disease	Immunizing Material	Type of Immunity*	How Long Does It Last?	For Whom	When
Smallpox	Cowpox virus	Active	5 to 10 years	All normal persons	1st—3 to 9 months of age 2d—entrance to school Later: every 5 or 6 years and during epidemics
Diphtheria	1. Toxoid	Active	5 to 10 years	All normal children and exposed adults	1st—3 to 6 months of age 2d—entrance to school and at 5-year intervals to age 15 For susceptible adults such as nurses and physicians
	2. Antitoxin	Passive	2 to 3 months	Infants and young children	If not immunized and closely exposed to disease
Typhoid and paratyphoid fever	Dead germs	Active	2 to 3 months	Anyone especially exposed	When exposed to disease or to unsafe drinking water.
Whooping cough (pertussis)	Dead germs	Active	Several years	Infants, children	4 months of age
Tetanus	1. Toxoid	Active	Probably 5 to 10 years	Children Adults	In infancy When likely to be exposed
	2. Antitoxin	Passive	Few weeks	Children Adults	After injuries likely to be contaminated, if toxoid has not been administered
Rabies	Weakened virus	Active	Undetermined	Anyone	When exposed to saliva of animal suspected of being rabid.
Combined Immunization**	Diphtheria and tetanus toxoid and whooping cough vaccine	Active	5 to 10 years	Infants	3 months of age Repeat at school age without whooping cough vaccine
Poliomyelitis	Dead or attenuated virus	Active	Undetermined	Anyone under 40	Infancy or later
Measles	Immune blood serum, gamma globulin, or placental extract†	Passive	Few weeks	Infants	When exposed to disease.

After TEXTBOOK OF HEALTHFUL LIVING by Harold S. Diehl, © 1960 by McGraw-Hill Book Co., Inc.

*Defined in this article
**Combined Immunization may also contain poliomyelitis vaccine

†By mid-1962 a measles vaccine of weakened live viruses together with gamma globulin was given its first community-wide testing.

virus is used for inoculation. In typhoid fever dead typhoid bacilli in a salt solution are used.

Active immunity may also be assured by the injection into the blood stream of toxins—poisons from which the bacteria have been removed by a filtering process. In immunization against diphtheria a changed and weakened toxin, called a toxoid, is used.

How passive acquired immunity is produced: Passive immunity differs from the active type in that the antibodies have been produced in another person or animal and are merely transferred. Pooled blood serum from many adults (gamma globulin) contains antibodies for a variety of diseases and is helpful, although not as effective as antitoxin or immune serum. Passive immunity usually does not last long.

What Are Antibodies and Antigens?

Antibodies cannot be seen under the microscope nor located by chemical tests. However, it is known that they are carried in the cell-free part of the blood called the serum. When experiments are made with the serum, the presence of antibodies becomes apparent.

What sort of substance causes formation of antibodies, that is to say, what sort of substance acts as "antigen"? After many experiments with laboratory animals which were inoculated with all kinds of materials, bacteriologists can say that the substances which start the body cells producing antibodies are foreign proteins. By a foreign protein is meant one which does not occur naturally in the body. For instance, if you inject rabbit red blood cells (a protein) into a rabbit, no antibodies are produced. But if you inject red blood cells of any other animal into a rabbit, the rabbit's blood will make antibodies which will attack the red cells of that particular species. This fact is the basis of blood identification tests.

Immunity of the Future

Constant experimentation is being carried on in medical and bacteriological laboratories in all the civilized countries of the world. Each year brings to light some new method or weapon of defense with which to conquer our foes, the microbes. If you are interested in taking part in the great fight to produce immunity to disease, you will have plenty of opportunity to find out something new. There are many unknown phases of the problem yet to be solved. It is a fascinating field and attracts some of the greatest scientists in the world.

How Immune Reactions May Help the Law

Suppose a man has been accused of hitting a pedestrian and failing to stop. He says he didn't do it—that the blood on his tires came from hitting a dog. The technician, shown below, makes a salt solution of some of the blood in question and runs tests on it. He says the man is lying. How does he know?

To answer this question, we must go back a little and see what kind of testing materials the technician has at his disposal. He works in a laboratory where 25 to 50 rabbits are kept in separate cages. Each cage is numbered and the technician has already spent about three weeks immunizing each rabbit to a different kind of animal blood. Rabbit *1* has been getting injections of dog red blood cells; rabbit *2* of horse red blood cells, and so on. In each rabbit's body, antibodies have been produced in response to the particular kind of foreign blood received. Now the technician takes

some blood from each rabbit, allows it to clot, and pours off the remaining clear fluid (the serum) into numbered test tubes. These serums are his testing materials.

Now he is ready for the test. Taking salt solution of the unknown blood from the tire, he adds a tiny amount to each of test tubes 1, 2, 3, and 4 (below). The reaction he is looking for is a deposit of material on the bottom of the tube. This deposit will occur *only* when dog red cells meet the serum with anti-dog antibodies or when horse red cells meet the serum containing anti-horse antibodies—in other words, the reaction, like all immune reactions, is *specific*. You can see for yourself what happened, as you look at the four tubes. Tubes 1, 2, and 4 contain no deposit; therefore the unknown blood was not dog, horse, or deer blood. Tube 3 contains a deposit; so the unknown blood is human.

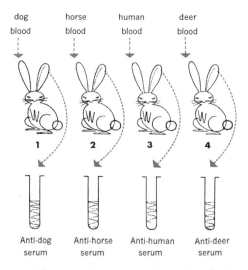

Your Blood Groups

Compiled from official sources by the editor.

On the opposite page you can read how antibodies to the red blood cells of other animals are manufactured in a rabbit's blood. Do you know that your own blood contains antibodies that would react against the red blood cells of many other people? You did not receive injections of other bloods to produce these antibodies; you were born with them. You belong to one of four blood types: A, B, AB, or O, and if you ever need a blood transfusion from someone else, a sample of your blood will be typed by a technician to make sure the blood you get will be right for you. Otherwise there would be an antigen-antibody reaction.

To go back a little now, the types O, A, B, and AB, get their names from factors A and B which are antigens and are contained in the red blood cells. People who have antigen A belong to type A; those who have antigen B belong to type B; those who have both antigens belong to AB, and those who have neither belong to O. There are also corresponding antibodies carried in the serum (the clear part of the blood that has no cells). The chart below shows you how the antigens and antibodies are distributed. Of course nobody has antibodies which would react against his own red cells, because the red cells would then be useless.

Let's take a specific example from the chart below. Suppose you have a friend, Al, who was thrown from his bicycle and is in shock. He needs some blood. You would like to help. Al is type B, and if you are type B, that is fine, obviously. But by looking at this chart you also see that type O blood could be used. How come? The answer is that type O blood has no antigens; therefore there is nothing to react with the antibodies in Al's serum. If you are type O you could equally well give blood to an A, B, or AB person. You are called a "universal donor." Suppose, however, that you are an A type. Then you cannot help Al at all; in fact your blood might kill him. Your anti-B antibodies will cause his B red cells to clump.

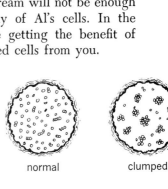

What's the Catch?

There is a catch to this "universal donor" business. Perhaps you have already seen it. You may say, "My blood is O and therefore has no antigens to react with Al's antibodies. But what about my *antibodies?* Won't they destroy Al's red blood cells?" You are right; they will, to some extent, and that is why *transfusion of exact type blood is always best.* The reason that your O blood can be used in an emergency is that incoming blood is so rapidly diluted by the greater volume of Al's blood that the proportion of your antibodies in the whole blood stream will not be enough to destroy very many of Al's cells. In the meantime he will be getting the benefit of many new, healthy red cells from you.

Blood typing depends upon the recognition of the clumping reaction discussed in this article. This reaction is easy to see with the naked eye, but it may also be observed by microscope (as at right). To do the typing, the technician needs only a single slide, holding a drop each of anti-A and anti-B testing serums. He adds a tiny amount of your blood to each of the testing serums, and watches for a reaction. Follow the testing procedure for yourself, with the help of the four slides pictured below, and the chart adapted from Medical Milestones *by Henry J. L. Marriott. The colored circles represent clumping reaction.*

normal   clumped

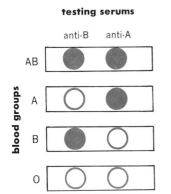

testing serums

anti-B   anti-A

blood groups

if cells contain	group is called	serum will contain	patient can be transfused with	patient cannot be transfused with
A and B antigens	AB	no antibodies	AB, A, B, O	—
A antigen	A	anti-B antibodies	A, O	B, AB
B antigen	B	anti-A antibodies	B, O	A, AB
neither A nor B antigens	O	both anti-A and anti-B antibodies	O	A, B, AB

The Vanishing Lady

Here is a great storyteller at his best. If you've never read "The Vanishing Lady," you're in for a treat. Condensation from **The Portable Woollcott**. Copyright, 1946, by The Viking Press, Inc. Reprinted by permission of The Viking Press, Inc., New York.

Then there was the story—told me some years ago as a true copy of a leaf from the secret archives of the Paris police—of the woman who disappeared during the World Exposition.

As I first heard the story, it began with the arrival from Marseilles of an Englishwoman and her seventeen-year-old daughter. The mother was the frail, pretty widow of an English officer who had been stationed in India, and the two had just come from Bombay, bound for home. The mother decided at the last minute to shift her passage to a Marseilles steamer in order to take care of business in Paris.

Paris was so tumultuously crowded for the Exposition that they counted themselves fortunate when they learned that their telegram from Marseilles had miraculously caught a room at the Crillon—a double room with a fine, spacious sitting-room looking out on the Place de la Concorde.

The mother had seemed unendurably exhausted from the long train ride, and was now of such a color that the girl's first idea was to call the house physician, hoping fervently that he spoke English, for neither she nor her mother spoke any French at all.

The doctor, when he came—a dusty, smelly little man with a wrinkled face lost in a thicket of whiskers, and a reassuring Legion of Honor ribbon in the buttonhole of his lapel—did speak a little English. After a long, grave look and a few questions put to the tired woman on the bed in the shaded room, he called the girl into the sitting-room and told her frankly that her mother's condition was serious; that it was out of the question for them to think of going on to England next day; that on the morrow she might better be moved to a hospital, etc., etc.

All these things he would attend to. In the meantime he wanted the girl to go at once to his home and fetch him a medicine that his wife would give her. Unfortunately, he lived on the other side of Paris and had no telephone. After a talk with the hotel manager, the doctor put her into a carriage, armed with a note to his wife.

It was then that the girl's agony began. The ramshackle victoria crawled through the festive streets, more often than not in the wrong direction. The doctor's house seemed to stand at the other end of the world when the carriage came at last to a halt in front of it. The girl grew old in the time which passed before any answer came to her ring at the bell. The doctor's wife, when finally she appeared, read his note again and again, then stationed the girl in an airless waiting room and left her there so long that she was weeping for desperation before the medicine was found, wrapped, and turned over to her.

A hundred times during that wait she rose and started for the door. A thousand times in the wretched weeks that followed she loathed herself for not having obeyed that impulse. But always there was the feeling that having come so far and having waited so long, she must not leave without the medicine.

The snail's pace trip back was another nightmare, and it ended only when she leaped to the street and appealed for help to a passing young man whose alien tweeds and boots told her he was a compatriot of hers.

He was still standing guard beside her five minutes later when, at long last, she arrived at the desk of the Crillon and called for her key, only to have the very clerk who had handed her a pen to register with that morning look at her without recognition and blandly ask, "Whom does Mademoiselle wish to see?" At that a cold fear clutched her heart, a sudden surrender to a panic that was born when, after the doctor had casually told her he had no telephone, she heard the fretful ringing of its bell on the other side of his walnut door.

The clerk was gazing at her as though she were some slightly demented creature demanding admission to someone else's apartment.

The doctor was a dusty little man with a wrinkled face lost in a thicket of whiskers.

But, no, Mam'zelle must be mistaken. Was it not at some other hotel she was descended? Two more clerks came fluttering into the conference. They all eyed her without a flicker of recognition. Did Mam'zelle say her room was No. 342? Ah, but 342 was occupied by M. Quelquechose. Yes, a French client of long standing. He had been occupying it these past two weeks and more. Ah, no, it would be impossible to disturb him.

She demanded the registration slips only to find in that day's docket no sign of the one she herself had filled out that morning.

From then on she came only upon closed doors. The same house physician who had hustled her off on her tragic wild-goose chase across Paris protested now that he had dispatched her on no such errand, that he had never been summoned to attend her mother, that he had never seen her before in all his life. The same hotel manager who had so sympathetically helped her set forth on her fruitless mission, denied her now as flatly. Mam'zelle must be tired, she should let them provide another chamber where she might repose herself until she could recollect at what hotel she really belonged.

There was in his polite voice the unspoken reservation that the whole mystery might be a thing of her own disordered invention. Then, and in the destroying days that followed, she was only too keenly aware that these evasive people—hotel personnel, embassy attachés, reporters, officials—were each and every one behaving as if she had lost her wits. Indeed there were times when she felt that all Paris was rolling its eyes behind her back and significantly tapping its forehead.

Her only aid was the Englishman who, because a lovely lady in distress had come up to him in the street and implored his help, elected thereafter to believe her against all the evidence which so impressed the rest of Paris. He proved a pillar of stubborn strength.

There slowly formed in his mind a suspicion that for some unimaginable reason all these people—the hotel attendants and even the police—were part of a plot to conceal the means whereby the missing woman's disap-

A cold fear clutched her heart . . .

pearance had been effected. This suspicion deepened when, after a day's delay, he succeeded in forcing an inspection of Room 342 and found that there was no detail of its furnishing which had not been altered from the one etched into the girl's memory.

It remained for him to prove that plot and to guess at its motive—a motive strong enough to enlist all Paris in the wiping out of a woman of no importance, moreover a woman who, as far as her daughter knew, had not an enemy in the world. It was the purchased confession of one of the paper hangers, who had worked all night in the hurried transformation of Room 342, that started the unraveling of the mystery.

By the time the story reached me, it had lost all its content of grief and become as unemotional as an anagram. Indeed, a few years ago it was a kind of circulating parlor game and one was challenged to guess what had happened to the vanished lady. Perhaps you yourself have already guessed that the doctor had recognized the woman's ailment as a case of the black plague smuggled in from India; that his first step had been to find time to spirit her out of the threatened hotel. When she died that afternoon, the doctor's trick widened into a conspiracy on the part of the police to suppress an obituary notice which, had it ever leaked out, would have emptied Paris overnight. The city that had gambled heavily on the great Exposition would have been ruined.

117

The Rh Factor:

End of a Mystery

Until the early 1940's doctors were occasionally puzzled by a newborn baby with a mysterious case of jaundice, a disease characterized by many damaged red blood cells. The baby's mother was healthy, the baby himself was otherwise perfectly normal; what could have happened? Here J. D. Ratcliff tells the story of a troublesome and sometimes serious immune reaction which many people do not yet understand. From "The Rh Factor in Blood," by J. D. Ratcliff. **Woman's Home Companion**, September, 1945. Copyright, 1945, by Crowell-Collier Publishing Company.

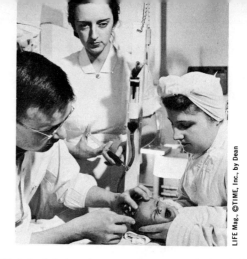

This baby is being given an exchange transfusion. While safe Rh negative blood is flowing in through a scalp vein, the baby's own damaged blood is being allowed to run off through an opened artery. A complete exchange cannot be made, but it can be carried far enough so that the baby's condition is strikingly improved.

The story of Rh goes back to the work of the late Dr. Karl Landsteiner, a giant of medical research. One of his triumphs was the discovery of the major blood groupings—types A, B, AB, and O—which made safe transfusions possible. With a sharp-eyed young assistant, Dr. Alexander Wiener, Dr. Landsteiner was working in his Rockefeller Institute laboratory in 1936, studying the blood of a rabbit that had just been transfused with a small amount of rhesus monkey blood. They noted an entirely new chemical stuff hidden in the red cells, and named it Rh after the rhesus monkey. Landsteiner then returned to his main job. Rh was a sidetrack.

But to Dr. Wiener the sidetrack was fascinating. Would human blood have this Rh stuff? He found it in the blood of 85 out of every 100 white Americans! An even larger percentage of Negroes had it, and 99 per cent of all Chinese.

Those Mysterious Reactions!

The discovery caused a small amount of interest among research men. But nothing very practical promised to come from it. Wiener, however, kept thinking about the transfusion accidents that sometimes happened. A patient's blood would be typed and matched with the blood of a donor. But instead of getting better, the patient would have a fearful reaction. There would be chills, fever, anemia. And sometimes the patient would go into shock and die. Could these symptoms be the result of mixing blood containing Rh factors with blood which did not possess them?

Wiener's theorizing, tested by experimentation, proved correct. Mix Rh positive (containing the Rh factor) with Rh negative blood (containing no Rh factors) and under certain conditions open warfare developed. There was fearful destruction of red cells, in some cases 80 per cent or more. The result was a general poisoning and death.

Meanwhile, another research man—Dr. Philip Levine—was on the track of a disease which had baffled medical men for years: erythroblastosis (meaning "destruction of red cells"). It struck at unborn or at newborn babies. In its most severe form it would kill the baby in the first months of pregnancy. Or a baby would be born apparently healthy, then in a short time become jaundiced and die. Since the jaundice was a mark of red blood destruction, physicians had one weapon against this sickness—transfusion. In rare instances it worked wonders. But oftener it brought violent reaction and death.

Some thought this ugly disease was a malignant process. Others thought it was an inherited sickness of the blood. Levine made a new guess. Wasn't it reasonable to suppose that Rh negative mothers might have babies with Rh positive blood inherited from fathers? Then, *under certain conditions,* wouldn't the mother's blood actually declare war on the blood of her own baby?

Levine checked the blood of mothers who had borne dead babies. He checked the blood of the fathers. Over and over again the story was repeated: mothers Rh negative, fathers Rh positive. And the story was tragic. One woman had two miscarriages, then a normal child, then a stillbirth. She was transfused with her husband's blood and died.

What Is the Certain Condition?

The picture added up grimly but convincingly. Rh had explained transfusion accidents and it now seemed to explain a killing disease. But there was a flaw in the picture. *What was the certain condition that brought it about?* By the law of averages nine per cent of all white American marriages are between Rh negative women and Rh positive men. Yet erythroblastosis occurs only once in every 40 of these pregnancies where it might occur, or about once in every 400 births.

Levine remembered a discovery he had made in 1939. An unborn infant has a heart action and circulatory system of its own. But Levine had found that a woman may have a tendency to develop a defective placenta which permits an exchange of red blood cells or other cells between herself and her unborn child. What if such a woman was Rh negative and her child Rh positive? That was the clue.

The red blood cells that went from an Rh positive infant to an Rh negative mother created something in the mother's blood that turned on and destroyed the baby's red blood cells. Or, more commonly, it turned on the blood of the next child the mother carried.

The sequence is very much like the way our common vaccines act. They jolt the blood into building protective factors called antibodies. Getting minute doses of the Rh chemical from the red cells of her baby's blood, the mother builds antibodies which attack red cells containing Rh in the unborn infant's blood. When her first baby is born, Levine reasons, the blood of an Rh negative mother probably would not contain enough antibodies to do material damage. In the course of later pregnancies, however, more antibodies would be created, until there might be enough to cause trouble.

One explanation for the rarity of erythroblastosis therefore, is that most women today do not have many pregnancies. Another explanation is that there is only one mating of Rh factors that *can* make trouble. There is trouble *only* if the mother is negative, the father positive.

One point of caution should be injected here. If the Rh negative woman received a whole blood transfusion as a child, the chances are five to one that she received Rh positive blood. So her blood even before pregnancy contains antibodies ready to declare war on any Rh positive infant she might conceive. Rh-typing is now standard procedure before transfusions. Serum is always safe because it contains no red cells, hence no Rh factors.

Doctors now know what precautions to take. An Rh negative woman married to an Rh positive man can usually expect two babies without difficulty. (And remember, always, that the child may be Rh negative, in which case there is no difficulty.) If a third child is desired, her physician can watch her blood for a telltale rise in the antibodies which spell Rh trouble. If they stay within safe limits he can permit a normal delivery; otherwise he may deliver the baby early. He will have a stock of Rh negative blood on hand for immediate transfusion.

119

The most common course of Rh difficulty is shown here.

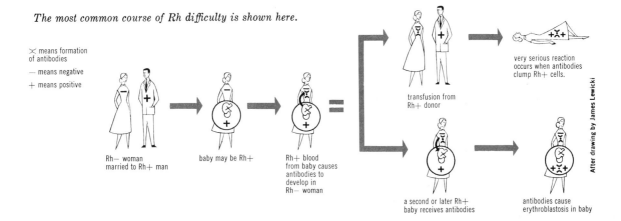

✕ means formation of antibodies
— means negative
+ means positive

Rh— woman married to Rh+ man

baby may be Rh+

Rh+ blood from baby causes antibodies to develop in Rh— woman

transfusion from Rh+ donor

very serious reaction occurs when antibodies clump Rh+ cells.

a second or later Rh+ baby receives antibodies

antibodies cause erythroblastosis in baby

After drawing by James Lewicki

The Diphtheria Story

Von Behring

The story of the conquest of diphtheria begins in 1884 when Friedrich Löffler started to investigate a microbe that his colleague, Edwin Klebs, had found in the throat of a diphtheria victim. It was a rod-shaped bacterium, belonging to a general group called bacilli. To prove that a particular microbe is actually the cause of a disease, it must be shown microscopically on slides of material taken from the person with the disease. Then it must be grown artificially in a "culture" outside the body. The final step is to produce the same disease in a laboratory animal, using the artificially grown microbe. This cycle of proof took Löffler two years, but at the end of that time he could definitely announce: "The Klebs bacillus is the only and the specific cause of diphtheria." That was step one in the story.

Step two came when Emile Roux in 1889 made a brilliant suggestion as to how the diphtheria bacillus killed and then set about—with Alexandre Yersin— to prove it. The most puzzling of questions in connection with Löffler's research had been: How can diphtheria bacilli cause paralysis of the heart muscles when they never move from the tough gray diphtheria membrane which they form in the throat? Roux suggested that the bacilli must produce a poison— a toxin—and that the poison, traveling in the blood stream must cause the disease symptoms. He and Yersin proved this theory by growing diphtheria bacilli in broth, then filtering out all bacilli and injecting the broth into healthy guinea pigs. When the guinea pigs sickened and died, never having come into contact with actual bacteria, the two men knew that they had the answer. This article picks up the story at this point. From Milestones of Medicine by Ruth Fox. Reprinted by permission of Random House, Inc. Copyright, 1950, by Ruth Fox.

Guinea pigs are excellent research animals because they are very susceptible to bacterial poisons. One milligram (1/1000 gram or 1/28000 of an ounce) of pure botulinus toxin will kill 1,000 tons of guinea pigs.

120

Emil von Behring was busy shooting a dying guinea pig full of iodine trichloride. For weeks he had been hard at work filling guinea pigs first with diphtheria toxin, then with whatever chemical was currently engaging his attention. He hoped to find one that would kill the diphtheria bacilli without killing the patient. Thus far, there was little choice between the disease and the remedy.

Iodine trichloride was different. It narrowly missed killing the guinea pig, but it most decidedly killed whatever diphtheria germs were in him.

Behring was too realistic to believe even for a moment that he had found a practical cure for diphtheria. "Can one save a child from death by scalding his veins with a poison which is as dangerous in its way as the toxin of diphtheria?" he asked himself. The iodine trichloride experiment would have been unimportant save for one thing: Emil von Behring now had a laboratory animal which had recovered from diphtheria.

The Guinea Pig That Lived

"Do you suppose that this poor creature is now immune to diphtheria?" he asked, thinking out loud. He filled a syringe with a fresh culture of diphtheria bacilli and pumped the uncomplaining guinea pig full of it.

Nothing happened.

He tried injecting the animal with pure toxin. Still nothing happened. He repeated the experiment he had originated on the other animals. Those which were not killed, either by the disease or by the iodine trichloride, were safe from a second attack of diphtheria.

"What protects them the second time that wasn't around to protect them the first time?" Behring asked himself. The science of immunology dates from that moment of curiosity.

"Whatever it is," he reasoned, "is certainly located in the blood stream, where the toxin itself circulates. Would it work *outside* the body that originally produced it?"

From his convalescent guinea pigs he drew some blood and separated the clear serum from the cells. To the serum he added an equal amount of deadly pure toxin, calculated to kill any nonimmune guinea pig in forty-eight hours. He injected the mixture into the veins of a fresh laboratory animal. The guinea pig was bothered by it no more than by the prick of a needle.

"Now Let's Try a New One!"

Behring, suddenly in possession of an animal that had no right to be alive, according to the science of the day, pondered his next move with care. In Koch's laboratory no discovery was credited even with grudging attention until it had been subjected to a systematic debunking by the entire staff. (You can read about Robert Koch in "Bacteria and Disease" in Volume 7, page 175. Behring was one of Koch's pupils.)

"Draw five cubic centimeters of blood from a guinea pig," he told his assistant, "and separate the serum from the cells."

"From one of these?" the assistant asked him, nodding at the cage where the immune animals were kept.

"No, no. From a new one! From one that hasn't even been inside the laboratory."

To the blood serum of this animal Behring added some diphtheria toxin. He injected the mixture into several nonimmune guinea pigs. Two days later, as he stood with his colleagues observing the dead bodies of these animals, he said to Robert Koch, "Blood serum from an immune animal neutralizes the toxin of diphtheria, but blood serum from a nonimmune animal does not."

Another Kind of Proof

"Now," said Koch, "you must prove it forward as well as backward. See what happens when you provide the prevention first and then the poison."

Behring did. He gave serum from an immune animal first, then toxin to a fresh guinea pig. He found that he could not determine which shot affected the animal less. The unimpressionable laboratory rejoiced.

Few scientific communications have been of so much significance to so many people as the paper published in the *German Medical Journal* on December 4, 1890: "On the Production of Diphtheria Immunity and Tetanus Immunity in Animals." The paper, written by Behring in collaboration with the Japanese bacteriologist Kitasato, a great name in tetanus research, stated for the first time the underlying principle of immunity. "The immunity of animals," they wrote, ". . . consists in the power of the cell-free blood [the serum] to render [harmless] the toxic substances which the . . . bacillus produces." In a footnote, the two men suggested the name "antitoxin."

The diphtheria story did not begin with Behring, nor does it end with him. Usually it takes many minds and many interweaving lines of research to conquer a disease, and diphtheria was no exception. While Behring turned to the problem of a cure with antitoxin, Dr. William Park of the New York City Health Commission and his assistant, Dr. Anna Williams, worked on prevention. They found a diphtheria bacillus that produced strong toxin which in turn called forth a particularly effective antitoxin. A mixture of toxin and antitoxin caused immunity if three shots were given. With general use of the inoculation, the death rate dropped from 270 per 100,000 in 1900 to 14 per 100,000 in 1930.

Other Sections To See

"Familiar Diseases," Volume 6; "Bacteria and Disease," Volume 7; "Pioneers of Medicine," Volume 8; "Antibiotics," Volume 16.

Other Books To Read

The New You and Heredity, by Amram Scheinfeld. Published by J. B. Lippincott Co., Philadelphia, 1950. Here you can read more about the various blood groups and blood typing.

Edward Jenner and Smallpox Vaccination, by Irmengarde Eberle. Published by Franklin Watts, Inc., New York, 1962.
A biography of the great Englishman who was the first European to make practical use of an immunizing vaccine.

Great Moments in Medicine, by Lawrence J. Ludovici. Published by Roy Publishers, New York, 1961.
The great moments include Roentgen's discovery of X-rays and Banting's isolation of insulin.

The Search for a Polio Vaccine

A book started Albert Sabin on the career that led to the discovery of the first successful oral vaccine. This account of his research is condensed from **Today's Health**, published by the American Medical Association. It is from **The Scientific Life** by Theodore Berland. Copyright © 1962 by Theodore Berland and published by Coward-McCann.

Theodore Berland

Dr. Albert Sabin arrives at his Cincinnati office promptly at eight each morning. In the laboratory, he works slowly, carefully, deliberately. He finds that writing up experiment results is often the most important part of his work.

In 1926, a young dental student at New York University read a book that changed his life. It was *The Microbe Hunters* by Paul de Kruif, which tells the exciting story of men who spent their lives tracking down germs, and trying to prevent or cure infectious diseases.

Ever since he read that book, Albert Sabin has been a microbe hunter. He has lived his life as a further, unwritten chapter, hunting germs around the world. His vaccines—the culminations of his hunts—prevented thousands of soldiers and sailors stationed on Pacific islands from getting sleeping sickness; by swallowing spoonfuls of cherry-flavored syrup, children the world over can be free of that dread disease, paralytic poliomyelitis.

Sabin was born in Bialystok, Russia. His parents, an older brother, and two younger sisters were among the last Jewish families to flee Eastern Europe's violent persecutions. When his family arrived in Paterson, New Jersey, in 1921, he was 15. After graduating from high school in 1923, he took a year of predental courses and entered the New York University School of Dentistry. Then he read *that* book and caught the thrill of the microbiologist's life. He switched to medical school and found a job to help pay his way.

A professor of bacteriology let him use a corner of his laboratory to do research. Through his microscope young Sabin studied bacteria gathered from everywhere: from the air in the laboratory, from his home, and from the subway. By working in the lab in the morning and early afternoon, going to class in later afternoon, and holding down a job and studying at night, he earned his M.D.

First Discoveries

In 1935, Sabin joined the staff of the Rockefeller Institute. Here he was successful in growing *for the first time* test tube tissues in which polioviruses could live.

At this time it was thought by other researchers that polioviruses invaded the body through the nose. Sabin disproved it by showing that if the inside of a monkey's nose was first coated with certain chemicals before poliovirus was swabbed on, the nose route wasn't followed. But if the monkeys were with others sick with polio, they still contracted the disease.

In 1939 Sabin took a job with the Children's Hospital Research Foundation in Cincinnati, where he still does his research. The question in his mind was still: How did polioviruses get into people and where did they live? To find out, he conducted research of heroic proportions. He was able to prove that polioviruses not only grew inside and alongside nerves but also proliferated in the small intestines. Thus was born the concept of enteroviruses and the idea for an oral vaccine.

At work for the Army during the war, he developed a vaccine against two forms of encephalitis. He then went on active duty as a major with the assignment of combating epidemics of exotic diseases among our troops fighting in strange hot lands. His missions included fighting sandfly fever in Italy, dengue fever in New Guinea, sleeping sickness in Okinawa, and polio in China.

After the war, he started his laboratory workers back on the poliovirus track. Some of the questions to be answered now were: Why did so many people contract polio and not become paralyzed? Why did so many people who had apparently never been sick with polio have germ-neutralizing antibodies against polioviruses in their blood?

To help solve some of these problems, Sabin and his staff gathered and studied data from polio epidemics all over the world. One of his important findings was that the virus was spread by contaminated food and drink.

In 1948 the National Foundation for Infantile Paralysis appointed Sabin to a committee to type and list all of the known kinds of polioviruses. Three years, 30,000 monkeys, and $1,370,000 later, the committee decided that there were three types, each of which produced its own distinct antibody.

Polio Is a Parasite

Sabin was convinced that the poliovirus was "a parasite that maintains itself in nature only in human beings. Rob it of its soil of multiplication and you eradicate it."

To do so would mean making the human intestines a hostile home for polioviruses. Now, it had been suspected that avirulent, or non-disease producing, polioviruses existed naturally. This was one answer to why people had antibodies yet had never had polio. Sabin focused all his efforts on finding natural weakly virulent polioviruses and making them avirulent. This was an arduous job.

At the end of 1953 he had several safe viruses of each type. But when he fed them to monkeys, he suffered a heavy disappointment. They wouldn't grow in the intestines. He moved his feedings up a notch on the evolution ladder and tried chimpanzees. Big doses of live viruses were needed, but it worked. The next step was to test the mutants on a group of human volunteers. Sabin turned to the Federal Reformatory at Chillicothe, Ohio.

In May, 1955, Sabin reported on tests with prison volunteers that "there was no evidence even of minor illness," and that only two drops of his vaccine produced intestinal immunity. By 1957 Sabin was ready for large-scale tests of the world's first successful oral vaccine.

By 1959, four and a half million persons had swallowed Sabin vaccine—in small tests in Sweden, Louisiana, and New York, and in field trials in England and Singapore. By the end of 1960, over 77 million youngsters in Russia, Latvia, Estonia, Czechoslovakia, Poland, Hungary, and East Germany had swallowed the mutants and were protected.

The Salk Vaccine

In the United States, however, Sabin vaccine was not approved for public use. Instead a killed-virus vaccine developed by a man whose life somewhat parallels Sabin's—Jonas Salk of Pittsburgh—was in use. In 1951 Salk perfected the procedures of making his killed-virus vaccine. In the two years following he tested it on small groups of children with encouraging results. In April, 1954, a mass trial to Salk-inoculate almost two million grade school children began. A year later the Salk vaccine was announced a success.

It was not until August, 1960, that the Public Health Service, after the most careful scrutiny, approved the Sabin live vaccine. In June, 1961, an American Medical Association report cited the added benefits of oral vaccine—longer protection, gastrointestinal immunity, and the obliteration of carriers. It stated that oral vaccine "may safely be given to all persons six weeks of age or over regardless of whether or not they have received Salk vaccine." The report recommended that until the oral vaccine was generally available . . . "physicians should encourage, support, and extend the use of Salk vaccine on the widest possible scale." Licenses for the oral vaccine were issued in 1961.

Dr. Sabin's work, however, is by no means ended. He has completed his poliomyelitis research only to begin a new adventure that is equally challenging—investigating the mysteries of human cancer.

123

Most famous rodent in the world is Mickey Mouse, created by Walt Disney in 1927. The adventurous little rodent is shown here as he appeared in the motion picture, Fun and Fancy Free. *The mouse is the smallest of all the rodents.*

Rodents:

Animals That Gnaw

section **7**

The largest group of animals among the mammals are the rodents. Rodents include many familiar animals, which few persons suspect are rodents. The beaver and the porcupine, for example, are rodents; so are the chipmunk, the woodchuck (ground hog), the chinchilla, the tree squirrel, the prairie dog, and the pocket gopher.

What about the rabbit? Zoologists usually do not consider the rabbit as a rodent, for the outstanding characteristic of the rodent is that it has two long, chisel-like front teeth in its upper jaw, and two in its lower jaw. The rabbit has four such teeth in its upper jaw.

Rodents play a very important part in man's life. Some of them are valuable for their fur, and the beaver aids in the conservation of natural resources. Others—like the house rat and house mouse—are detested because of the great destruction that they leave behind them.

Rodents are usually very small animals. Most of them eat vegetable matter, especially seeds and nuts. Some of them, like porcupines, dormice, and squirrels, live in trees; others, like the beaver and the capybara, spend most of their lives in or near water; and some, such as the rats and mice, woodchucks, gophers, prairie dogs, and chipmunks, burrow underground to make their homes.

124

In this section you will read about squirrels, porcupines, hamsters, rats and mice, and some unusual rodents around the world. Three rodents—the beaver, the chinchilla, and the lemming—are described in other volumes. For more about the beaver and the chinchilla, see "Fur Animals and Furs" in Volume 3; and for more about the lemming, see "The Lemmings of Norway and Sweden" in Volume 1.

—Herbert Kondo

What Is a Rodent?

The word "rodent" comes from the Latin rodere, which means "to gnaw." Starting from this fact, the following selection tells you about rodents, their habits and characteristics. From **The Animal Kingdom**, Volume I, edited by Frederick Drimmer. Copyright 1954 by The Greystone Press.

A rodent is an animal that gnaws. To most people the name suggests only rats and mice. But it describes, just as accurately, many other creatures—squirrels, beavers, woodchucks and marmots, prairie dogs, chipmunks, gophers, muskrats, hamsters, lemmings, and porcupines.

There are more kinds of rodents—about 6,400 in all—than there are members in any other order of mammals; in actual numbers they may exceed the combined total of all other mammals alive on the earth today!

The Work of the Rodents

The rodents represent a mighty force in the world, and their strength lies in numbers. You may be surprised to learn that the combined efforts of these industrious creatures play an important part in making and keeping the earth livable for us.

How do they help us? Rodents aid greatly in natural conservation of our water supply. Digging and burrowing, they sometimes change barren wastes into fertile soil.

On the other hand, rodents have directly and indirectly taken the lives of more people than all the wars this world has ever known. Many rodents carry lice and fleas that spread various diseases such as typhus, infectious jaundice, and bubonic plague.

The Rodents Have Traveled Far

The rodents have entered most fields of animal activity and have covered the face of the earth from the border of the Arctic ice fields to the last tip of dry land north of the Antarctic Continent. Somehow, house rats and mice, as well as other rodents, bridged the gap between Australia and mainland Asia which most other land mammals failed to do.

Rodents have entered the water, climbed into treetops, burrowed underground; some, while not actually able to fly, have learned to glide. Most of the smaller rodents are of the scurrying type, but there are fast runners, hoppers, and highjumpers in their ranks, as well as some that are slow-moving.

Rodents build the finest nests of any mammal, breed the fastest, and probably live the shortest lives. They are harvesters and hoarders. Vegetable matter is their food, but they are not all vegetarians; they supplement their diet with insects and other forms of animal life. One interesting mouse is credited with devoting much of its efforts to hunting scorpions.

All Kinds of Rodents

One thing you will notice among the rodents is the great differences in their appearance and habits. The texture of the rodent hair varies from the soft, downy fur of the chinchilla to the barbed quills of the porcupine—yet both are rodents. The body structure of these animals varies amazingly, too.

Some of the groups of rodents are distantly related, and other than the fact that they are

The rodent's incisor teeth are shown here. If these teeth were not worn down by constant gnawing and sharpening, they would increase in length about five inches a year.

Federal Works Agency

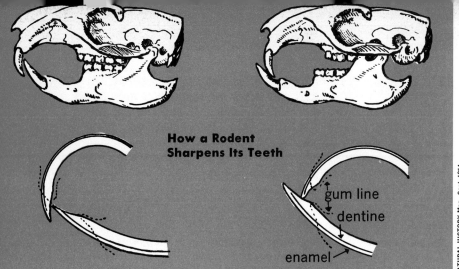

**How a Rodent
Sharpens Its Teeth**

gum line

dentine

enamel

NATURAL HISTORY Mag., Sept. 1954

How does a rodent sharpen its teeth? Usually by gnawing as it eats. Sometimes, however, a rodent will swing its lower jaw far forward to sharpen its cutting teeth, as shown in the two upper drawings. The teeth have a hard enamel on their outer surface, soft dentine on the inner surface. By scraping the teeth together, the outer enamel wears away the softer dentine on the inside.

classified as rodents, seem to have little in common with the rest of their order (Rodentia). Others, although they may seem very different, are actually closely related. Anyone can see that the tree squirrel and the beaver are very different animals both in appearance and habits—yet the beaver is a close kin of the squirrel.

Teeth Like Chisels

The chief feature by which we can tell the rodents from all other mammals is the pair of large, chisel-like incisor teeth they have at the front of both their upper and lower jaws. They use these front teeth constantly in gnawing. Subject to severe wear, the incisors would soon be mere useless stumps if they did not continue to grow throughout life. A precious possession, they often mean the difference between living and dying to the rodent. If it damages an incisor, the rodent cannot feed properly until the incisor grows to proper length.

The rest of the rodent's teeth are placed well back in its mouth, and a wide space separates them from the incisors. The hares and rabbits are often mistaken for rodents because they have a similar dental arrangement, but they possess another pair of teeth behind the upper incisors.

Rodents of Today and Yesterday

All in all, we find that these animals fall into three main groups or suborders. The first contains the squirrels and their relatives

(Sciuromorpha), the most primitive of the rodents.

The second group is much larger—it would take a six-hundred-page book just to list the members of the 186 groups here. They include the typical rats, mice, voles, lemmings, and like creatures (Myomorpha).

The last group is the most specialized—in it we place the porcupines, guinea pigs, and their kin (Hystricomorpha). To this third division also belong such curiosities as the mole rats and gundis.

Rodents are a very ancient order—their history dates back to the beginning of the Age of Mammals. Well-formed rodents existed on the earth sixty million years ago, and at that early date they had already learned to climb, as the squirrels and so many others still do today.

Other Books To Read

Paws, Hoofs, and Flippers, by Olive L. Earle. Published by William Morrow & Co., Inc., New York, 1954.
This book contains a good chapter on rodents. It describes the beaver, porcupine, capybara, and kangaroo rat.

Golden Hamsters, by Herbert S. Zim. Published by William Morrow & Co., Inc., New York, 1951. An easy-to-read book on the care and habits of hamsters.

126

The Family Tree of Rodents

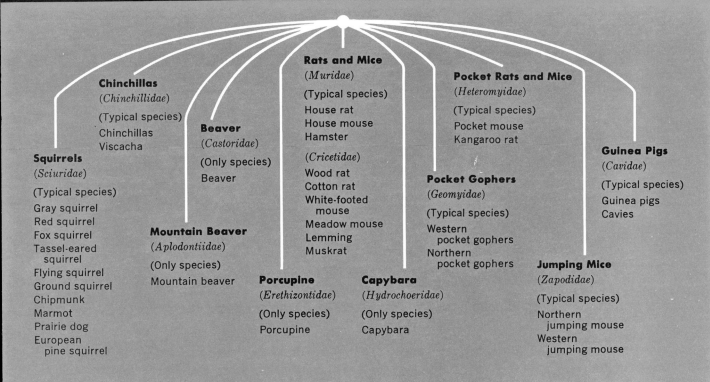

Squirrels
(*Sciuridae*)

(Typical species)
Gray squirrel
Red squirrel
Fox squirrel
Tassel-eared
 squirrel
Flying squirrel
Ground squirrel
Chipmunk
Marmot
Prairie dog
European
 pine squirrel

Chinchillas
(*Chinchillidae*)

(Typical species)
Chinchillas
Viscacha

Beaver
(*Castoridae*)

(Only species)
Beaver

Mountain Beaver
(*Aplodontiidae*)

(Only species)
Mountain beaver

Rats and Mice
(*Muridae*)

(Typical species)
House rat
House mouse
Hamster

(*Cricetidae*)
Wood rat
Cotton rat
White-footed
 mouse
Meadow mouse
Lemming
Muskrat

Porcupine
(*Erethizontidae*)

(Only species)
Porcupine

Capybara
(*Hydrochoeridae*)

(Only species)
Capybara

Pocket Rats and Mice
(*Heteromyidae*)

(Typical species)
Pocket mouse
Kangaroo rat

Pocket Gophers
(*Geomyidae*)

(Typical species)
Western
 pocket gophers
Northern
 pocket gophers

Jumping Mice
(*Zapodidae*)

(Typical species)
Northern
 jumping mouse
Western
 jumping mouse

Guinea Pigs
(*Cavidae*)

(Typical species)
Guinea pigs
Cavies

From *Animals of the World*, edited by J. W. McSpadden. Copyright 1917 by
Doubleday & Company, Inc.; used by permission of Garden City Books Division.

A Pair of Unusual Rodents

Here are two of the most unusual rodents in the world—the capybara and the pocket mouse—which represent the large and the small among the rodents of North and South America. You can find them in the chart above. Compiled from official sources by the editor.

The capybara (*Hydrochoerus*) is the largest rodent in the world. A native of South America, it stands about 21 inches tall at the shoulder, is four feet long, and may weigh as much as 100 pounds. It lives near the banks of rivers and eats grass and water plants. The capybara has no tail, is partly web-footed, and is an excellent swimmer. In captivity, it eats bananas, carrots and peanuts.

The tiny pocket mice (*Perognathus*) are found only in the western part of North America. They never weigh more than an ounce. One type— the Pacific pocket mouse—weighs one-third of an ounce and is the smallest rodent in North America. The pocket mouse is a vegetarian.

Chicago Nat. Hist. Mus.

George McClellan Bradt

The Porcupine:
A Barbed Rodent

The North American porcupine is a tree climber. It can swim and climb easily but shuffles along very slowly when walking. It carries from 20,000 to 30,000 quills on its body.

Anyone who has traveled in the woods of the northern United States is familiar with the porcupine or quill pig. In appearance he is not attractive. His shape is similar to that of a beaver covered with long stiff quills. His tail, too, is broad and flat, but not so wide as that of a beaver.

Although found in deciduous and in mixed forests (a deciduous tree is one that sheds its leaves in the fall), the porcupine prefers the evergreen woods. The hemlock is his favorite food tree, and, in winter, he lives almost entirely upon the bark of this and other trees. In summer, however, he will eat almost any vegetable matter, and will go to considerable trouble to get lily pads.

In one respect, however, the porcupine is not a strict vegetarian. He will brave all dangers to get salt or anything that has the suggestion of a salty flavor. Repeatedly during the night he will return to a camp from which he has been driven, in order to gnaw flooring, door jambs, ax handles, or any article which has been handled by human beings. (These articles will have a salt flavor if perspiration is on them.)

Except during the coldest weather, the porcupine does not hibernate. He may stay in his "den" until the worst is over, but a slight increase in temperature will bring him out, and his wanderings may be traced by his tracks in the snow and by chips and pieces of bark under the trees where he has fed. Nor does he confine himself to the night hours for roaming, but may sometimes be seen during the day. Once he has gotten into a favorite tree, he is not likely to leave it until he has explored its food possibilities.

What Are the Quills Like?

When attacked the porcupine does not roll itself into a ball, as has often been stated. It does, however, arch its back, erect its quills, and put its head under a log or root, if one happens to be handy; otherwise it puts its nose between its forepaws. Then if approached closely or poked with a stick, it waves its tail defiantly. Woe betide the animal which is rash enough to get in the way of that tail. Wherever it strikes flesh the quills penetrate, stick, and cause great pain. More pain will come later when an attempt is made to pull the quills out. The point is very sharp, and below it are hundreds of little barbs pointing backward. This means that they must often be cut out of the flesh or the points broken off in it. In the latter case these points often "work through" the injured part. The quills separate easily from the skin of their owner, but he *cannot throw them* at an enemy.

A close-up of a porcupine's quill.

The Squirrel Family

Did you know that the woodchuck, the prairie dog, and the chipmunk are squirrels? They are actually ground squirrels, which together with the tree squirrels make up the squirrel family. This interesting selection describes some important members of this family of rodents. From **The Animal Kingdom**, Volume I, edited by Frederick Drimmer. Copyright 1954 by The Greystone Press.

The fox squirrel (Sciurus niger) *lives in the eastern half of the United States and is the largest tree squirrel in that area. Its fur may be gray, red, brown, or black in color.*

The squirrel family (Sciuridae) is a very great one. It includes all tree squirrels and flying squirrels, and many animals that people do not commonly think of as squirrels at all—the squirrels that live on the ground, such as the woodchuck, marmot, chipmunk, and the prairie dog.

The tree and flying squirrels are mostly small, slender-bodied creatures, a foot in length or shorter, with bushy tails often as long as the body. Their relatives, the ground-dwelling squirrels, are bigger as a rule, but have smaller tails.

The squirrels are equally at home in the Old World and the New. We meet them in Europe, Asia, Africa, North America, and South America, but not in Australia or Madagascar.

The Tree Squirrel

Every man, woman, and child is familiar with the tree squirrel, its long, bushy tail, and its habit of hoarding nuts. Its nervous movements, its rapid flight, its sudden appearances and disappearances are famous.

All true tree squirrels have a showy tail, and in some it is magnificent. But the tail is not just for decoration alone; it is a vital necessity, and its purpose is to maintain and correct the balance of the animal in its daring leaps from branch to branch.

The accuracy with which a squirrel can leap from one swaying bough to another and rarely fail in its estimate of the distance to be covered is amazing. In a leap, the squirrel first fixes the direction, judges the space, and hurls itself in the air with feet extended forward, body flattened, and tail held straight out be-

hind as a rudder to keep the course. At the end of the jump, the animal lands with its head up, ready to scamper away.

Not all squirrels climb trees in exactly the same manner, but, in general, squirrels go up at a gallop, the fore and hind feet being used in pairs, one after the other. Coming down, the squirrel travels head first and is more careful as it moves, setting its feet down one at a time.

The tree squirrels are active by day. They are hoarders of nuts, seeds, fruits, and other types of vegetable food. Often they have a number of storage places, making them in holes in trees or underground, or next to logs or rocks. To save storage space, they usually shell the nuts and take the seeds and the corn from the husks. Edible mushrooms and toadstools are first sun-dried and cured in the fork of a tree before storage.

Tree squirrels are spread over the world in a rather surprising pattern. They are perhaps best represented in Central America and Mexico; the rest of North America is a good second. South America has a fair share of tree squirrels, but Russia, Siberia, and most of Europe have but a single species, the so-called European pine squirrel.

Ground-dwelling Squirrels

Did you know that the woodchuck, the chipmunk, and the prairie dog are really squirrels?

129

Actually they are ground-dwelling members of the squirrel family.

The large, heavy-bodied animals known as marmots—the American species are called woodchucks or ground hogs—are ground-dwelling squirrels. Too big and clumsy to climb trees easily, they live in burrows in the ground or have their dens among rocks. You will see them up and doing mostly in broad daylight during the summer months. Loving a life of comfort and ease, they sleep all night, and all winter, too.

When summer has gone, the marmot retreats to its deep winter den. It will not see the light of day again until the spring sunshine warms the earth. It packs a rather small amount of green fodder into the underground chambers. Then it plugs all entrances to the burrow securely, with a foot or more of earth mixed with straw. Usually two to four marmots hibernate together, but as many as fourteen have been found in one winter den.

"Ground-Hog Day"

There is a tradition that on the second day of February the ground hog comes out of its den for the first time in the year. If the sun is shin-ing and the animal sees its own shadow, it will retreat underground for another six weeks of slumber. Accordingly, the forecast is for continued cold and a late spring. If the day is cloudy and the ground hog fails to see its shadow, it is a sign that the cold weather is over and there will be an early spring. (For additional reading on the ground-hog superstition, see "Superstitions Old and New" on page 286.)

Despite its love of warmth and its dread of cold, the marmot does not live in tropical countries, and none has crossed the equator. In fact, it favors the temperate regions of the Northern Hemisphere. Most of the United States and Canada is marmot or woodchuck country. In the Old World these rodents are found in the Alps of Europe and eastward in the mountains to China and northeastern Siberia.

The woodchuck, or ground hog, *Marmota monax*, is the smallest of the American marmots, weighing about eight or nine pounds. In the fall, however, when it is fat, it may weigh up to fourteen.

Mating begins in March, when the woodchuck comes out of hibernation. Three to five one-ounce baby chucks are born a month later. At first they are quite naked and sightless, and it is a month before they open their eyes.

The woodchuck's life is one we might well envy. While the day is still young—but not too early in the morning—the chuck is out feasting on the fresh, tender leaves of grass, clover, and other sweet, green vegetation. When the sun rises high overhead, the chuck, its belly now full, stretches out lazily on the shady side of some cool rock or under a leafy tree. As the shadows begin to lengthen in the afternoon, the animal feasts once more. At sundown it retires to the seclusion of its warm nest for a night's sound slumber.

In the United States, we find the woodchuck from the Atlantic Coast west to the Great Plains, with the exception of the Gulf States. In Canada, its range stretches almost all the way across the continent, and extends north to Alaska.

The woodchuck, or ground hog, is about twenty inches long when full grown, and has brownish-gray fur. Like the squirrel, it stores food in its den in the fall. Why it does this is a mystery, since the woodchuck hibernates.

Lynwood M. Chace

Prairie Dogs and Their Dog Towns

The prairie dog, *Cynomys* ("dog mouse"), of the midwestern United States, is not a dog but a ground squirrel. A fat little bobtailed rodent, it was as much a part of the Old West as the Indian and the buffalo. Like the others, it has all but vanished. It did not fall before the guns of the frontiersmen; the cattlemen killed it off with strychnine poison, for it fed on the forage they needed for their herds.

In early pioneer days, the prairie dogs were famous for their "towns." These were actual underground cities, with miles and miles of well-worn tunnels and dens extending in every direction beneath plateaus and upland prairies. The horde of individuals in a big town was almost incalculable; a large one may have had millions. A few towns still persist in out-of-the-way places, but their numbers are small.

The fat prairie dogs are hunted by badgers, coyotes, foxes, ferrets, and wild cats. Eagles and hawks swoop down to grab them from the air.

Rattlesnakes and small burrowing owls sometimes take up residence with the prairie dogs in their towns, but it must not be supposed they are really their friends. Each of these predators will eat the others' offspring, and a baby prairie dog is a juicy morsel for them.

At the first sign of a stranger, a prairie dog utters a shrill whistle of warning. All its fellows stop whatever they are doing and look about to see what the trouble is. If there seems to be any danger, they plunge to the safety of their underground home. Each individual has its own particular den and makes a scramble for it.

Like the marmot, the prairie dog feeds on green vegetation. If this gets scarce, it digs down to the roots and eats them. When there is a plague of locusts or grasshoppers, the prairie dog will join forces with insect-eaters to eliminate them.

The prairie dog is not strictly a hibernating animal. At high altitudes and on the colder parts of its range, it will sleep through the winter, but in southern localities it is active the year round.

The young—usually four to six in a litter—come early in May, in an underground nest. Four to six weeks later they are getting their first glimpse of the upper world and seeing how plants taste in comparison to mother's milk.

The entrance to the prairie dog's burrow goes almost vertically down, three to fourteen feet, before it levels off. It builds mounds of earth high around the entrances to prevent flooding, a very serious menace to animals that live underground. Sometimes, before leaving its burrow, the prairie dog sits in the "listening post" to listen for possible enemies on the surface.

Prairie dogs live in the western plains of the United States, in southern Canada, and northern Mexico. They are about fourteen inches long (full grown) and live to be about seven or eight years old.

131

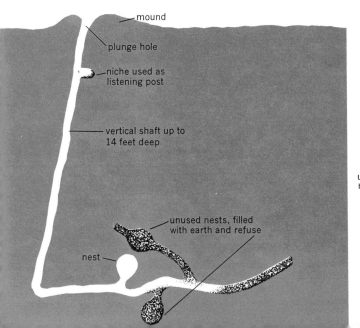

mound

plunge hole

niche used as listening post

vertical shaft up to 14 feet deep

unused nests, filled with earth and refuse

nest

U.S. Fish & Wildlife Serv., by D. A. Spencer

Chipmunks

The curious, pert little chipmunks, with their bright colors and friendly disposition, add a warm, cheerful note to the countryside. They are creatures of sunlit woods and pastures. The shrill, lively call of one will bring responses from another and another until the woods ring with their chatter.

Chipmunks do not live in the trees; they favor stone walls, rocks, and fallen timber, especially naked branches bleached by the hot summer sun. Like most other ground squirrels, we find them only in the Northern Hemisphere; Asia and North America are the home of the chipmunk tribe.

The American chipmunks are separated into two distinct groups that have divided the continent between them.

The eastern chipmunk, or *Tamias,* is a small ground-dwelling squirrel, nine or ten inches long; almost half of this is bushy tail. We can readily recognize this fellow by the five heavy black lines running down the back.

The chief foods sought by the chipmunk are seeds, grains, nuts, and berries. All summer long, and especially in the fall, these busy little squirrels are out gathering food and transporting it to their storehouses underground. A chipmunk can carry as many as seventeen hazelnuts at a time in its cheek pouches.

The chipmunk's storerooms often contain half a bushel of nuts, dried fruits, and seeds. This extensive storing of food clearly shows us that the chipmunks do not pass through a long period of complete hibernation during the winter; real hibernators fatten up in advance and live off the fat on their bodies, while they are asleep. Spring is the mating season.

By March most of the females have mated, and five weeks later about three to five babies are born. After about eight days the stripes are visible under the babies' skin. They can recognize sounds when three weeks old and open their eyes at the end of the first month. At the ripe old age of three months, the young are well developed and able to look after themselves.

If you look at an eastern chipmunk closely, you will see that the central stripe on its back is bordered on each side by a brownish line, while the two outermost stripes are separated by white. The head, with two white stripes on each cheek, is rather pointed for a squirrel. The ears are low and rounded, and the tail bushy and flattened. The warm rusty-red shades on the hips add to the colorful appearance of this little sun worshiper.

The eastern chipmunk is spread over the greater part of eastern Canada and the eastern United States except Florida. It is found west to the Great Plains, but here the range stops abruptly.

The western chipmunk, *Eutamias,* is more slender than the eastern chipmunk, and has a longer tail. The general impression is that it has many more stripes, but its normal pattern consists of five blackish and four whitish stripes, all approximately equal in width, and all but the outer pair extending from the shoulders to the rump; the middle line reaches the head. This creature occupies all of North America, west of the plains regions. Its range extends from the Yukon south into central Mexico and overlaps the range of the eastern chipmunk in Ontario, Michigan, Minnesota, and Wisconsin.

132

The eastern chipmunk is a timid ground squirrel, which is easy to tame. Its worst enemies are weasels, snakes, foxes, and hawks.

N.Y. Zool. Soc.

The Muskrat:

The Beaver's Little Brother

The muskrat (**Ondatra**) is one of the most valuable of all fur-bearing animals in North America. A member of the mouse and rat family (**Cricetidae**), it is called the beaver's little brother because it does everything a beaver does except build dams. Beavers, however, belong to a different family, the **Castoridae**. (For more about the beaver, see "Beaver on the Move" in Volume 2, page 378.) From **Lives of Game Animals**, by Ernest Thompson Seton, published by Charles T. Branford Company. Copyright, 1909, 1928, by Ernest Thompson Seton. Used by permission of Julia M. Seton.

The muskrat gets its name from the musky odor that it gives off. It is about twenty inches long, weighs around two or three pounds, and has partly webbed hind feet which aid it while swimming.

There is an old Indian legend which tells that the muskrat once gave great service to the Indian sun god, Nanabojou, during a flood. So the sun god said: "You may have any part of the country to live in that you please." The muskrat took the deep blue lakes.

But next day, he came back, and said: "I made a mistake; I want the grassy banks where there is something green to eat." These were given him.

The next day, he was back to say that he was again mistaken, as the banks offered no chance to swim, and he wanted the deep water again.

Nanabojou replied: "One day you want land; the next day, water. You don't know your own mind, so I will decide. Henceforth, you shall live in the between-land of the marsh—where there is long green grass to eat, and water deep enough to swim in." And so it has been ever since.

Wherever, on this vast continent, there is slow water with rushes or weeds, we find the muskrat. And far from these, he is never found, except when seeking a new home.

What Do Muskrats Eat?

By all the rules of dentistry, the muskrat should be strictly a vegetarian. As far as is convenient and agreeable, the beaver's little brother lives up to this understanding, and the food of the species is chiefly vegetable matter. The bleached ends of long reeds, lilies, stalks, and roots of irises are his basic food; but nearly every green thing in the marsh is a bag of vitamins for him.

There is a backwoods saying: "A pile of empty clamshells by a hole means a fur cap inside"; and there is much evidence that clams are a favorite food of the muskrat. He is clever in his ways of getting at the clam. He can, indeed, cut the hinge and force it open; but, when not pressed for time, he lets the clam die on the dry bank, then it opens itself.

Where Do Muskrats Live?

When a new nest is to be made, muskrats select a place in the weeds or rushes, where there is about two feet of water; and begin to drag to one spot the vegetation and mud from ten feet around. In this way, a little island of rubbish is gradually piled up, and the water around is deepened and cleared of rushes, etc. As the island rises above the water level, less mud and more reeds are used—this is probably accidental, as the reeds are easier to carry than mud. Now the island is made a little wider, and becomes like a low haycock (pile of hay) on a small base of mud and trash. As soon as it is a few inches above water, the builder begins to dig a tunnel into the side of the island and under the water level. The tunnel goes through the rushes, then up to the surface of the mud island and into the thin haycock.

This now answers for a house, although the roof is so open that the muskrat can see out. But the process of building goes on; each day, a few more bundles of reeds are dragged onto the pile. The muskrat's house, after a slow growth during perhaps four months, is now ready for winter.

133

How To Raise Pet Hamsters

The hamster is a member of the rat family. A native of Syria, it was first brought in large quantities to the United States in 1938. Today, it is so popular as a pet and so valuable in the laboratory that it is being bred in all parts of North America. In this selection you will read about hamsters as pets. From **Home-Made Zoo** by Sylvia S. Greenberg and Edith L. Raskin. Copyright, 1952, by Sylvia S. Greenberg and Edith L. Raskin. Courtesy of David McKay Co., Inc.

The hamster is a little rodent with large cheek pouches and a short tail. It has been compared to a toy bear, a chipmunk, and a field mouse, because of its small, stout body, soft fur, and alert black eyes. However, when the hamster fills its cheek pouches to overflowing, so that the face puffs out, it resembles no other animal. It is this characteristic that earned the hamster its name. The German word, *hamstern,* means "to hoard."

A Hamster in the Home

A full-grown hamster fits comfortably into the palm of your hand. It is easy to handle as it responds readily to affection. Not only are the natural pranks of a hamster appealing, but also it quickly learns new tricks.

Raising hamsters requires little work, little room, and little money. A hamster is a clean animal with no body odor, no lice, and no fleas. They are perfectly safe to keep in the house. A hamster can be boarded in a small cage, taking up very little space. They are economical to feed since they eat sparingly of inexpensive foods.

A hamster should be three weeks to two months old when you buy it. At three weeks it is independent of its mother. At two months it is an adult and at the best age to start breeding. Two years is ordinarily a ripe old age for a hamster, but with proper care it may live to be three or four years old. It is best to buy them young, as it is easier to train them, and of course you can enjoy their company for a longer period of time.

Hamsters live comfortably at normal room temperatures, 68° to 70° F. Keep them in a warm part of the room away from drafts. When the temperature drops to 45° F., they may either hibernate or become extremely drowsy, dull, and slow moving. Hamster cages may be kept on porches or out of doors in the summer.

What Do Hamsters Eat?

The best diet for keeping hamsters active, alert, and in good health is a combination of a leafy green vegetable or fruit and a prepared pellet food, daily. The following menu is suggested:

1. Vegetable or fruit—cabbage, lettuce, celery tops, beet tops, grapes, apples, or apple peelings.
2. Pellets—puppy biscuits, laboratory chow, or poultry feed (½ ounce each day).

All the necessary vitamins and minerals are conveniently supplied in these pellets, which may be obtained at the grocery store or the local pet shop. A one-pound package will provide a month's daily servings for one hamster.

Hamsters eat sparingly but like to have a hidden hoard. Therefore give them as much of the fresh vegetable or fruit as they will take at one feeding. Remove the perishable food when it spoils.

Occasionally hamsters enjoy a change from the daily diet. Table scraps of cooked or uncooked foods are a treat. Any one of the following items may be added at any time:

1. Grains, cereals, bread—corn, oats, wheat germ, rice, whole wheat, corn flakes, oatmeal, dry bread.
2. Succulent vegetables—white or sweet potatoes, carrots or carrot peelings.
3. Beans and nuts—chick peas, limas, string beans, peanuts, hickory nuts.

Hamsters get most of their water from the green vegetables they eat, but fresh water should be kept before them at all times.

134

Hamsters Are Fun

Hamsters like to play and are always ready to put on a show for you. They are so good-natured that even though you awaken them from a nap in the middle of the day, they are willing playmates.

When you first get your hamster, he will be excitable and a little frightened of his new environment. He will draw away from your touch and make squealing noises. Try to make friends with him. A few days of feeding and allowing him to arrange his sleeping chamber and food pile to his own taste will relax and reassure him. Your hamster will be friendly and contented if he is cared for properly.

In a hamster playground, the little fellow will get plenty of exercise, have a good time, and entertain you with his amusing tricks. A hamster can move backward as well as forward like an ice skater. One "toy" that will appeal to him is a treadwheel.

Hamsters will run round and round on a treadwheel, for hours at a time. A plastic treadwheel, nine inches in diameter, is available at hamsteries. If the cage is high enough, it can remain as part of the equipment. There are many other toys you can get for your hamster. For example, hamsters like to climb toy ladders and slide down toy chutes. Hamsters, indeed, are very enjoyable pets.

Hamsters are about five inches long when fully grown and weigh around four ounces. They reach maturity when they are about two months old. Hamsters have four toes on each front foot, five toes on each hind foot; when eating, they sit up on their hind legs and hold the food with their front feet.

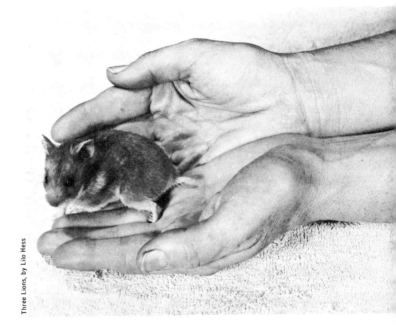

Three Lions, by Lilo Hess

You can make a good hamster cage with two pie pans and some quarter-inch or half-inch wire mesh. Cut the wire mesh into the shape of a rectangle, then roll it into a cylinder large enough to fit the pie pans. Place the pie pans on top and bottom. Wire cages are better than wood cages since hamsters can gnaw through wood easily.

135

What is the difference between a rat and a mouse? There are two main classes of rats and mice: (1) Old World, and (2) New World. The most familiar are the Old World rats and mice, which include the domestic rat and the house mouse. Among these the main differences are that the rats are larger than the mice, usually two or three times as large, and the rats have tails that are longer and more scaly than those of mice. Although domestic rats and mice belong to the same family of animals (Muridae), they belong to different genera. Domestic rats belong to the genus *Rattus*, whereas house mice belong to the genus *Mus*.

After drawing by Robert W. Hines, U.S. Fish & Wildlife Serv.

Rats and

Of all the animals that roam the earth, none do more damage or spread more diseases than domestic rats and mice. Wherever man goes or lives, the rats follow, devouring food and property. Rats and mice are nocturnal animals that eat practically any kind of food: grain, fruit, milk products, meat, vegetable, or fish. They contaminate more food than they eat. Although rats and mice do great damage, certain types of them have been used by scientists in the laboratory for experiments in fighting disease. Thus these rodents are also of great benefit to man. In this article you will read about the different kinds of rats and mice, the harm they do, how they are controlled, and their use in the laboratory. Compiled from official sources by the editor.

The gray rat (*Rattus rattus alexandrinus*) is a very good climber. It can scamper up trees and telephone poles, and walk telephone wires with ease. It uses its tail for balancing. Both the black rat and the gray rat spread bubonic plague and typhus fever.

U.S. Fish & Wildlife Serv., by E. R. Kalmbach

The Norway rat (*Rattus norvegicus*), also known as the brown rat, is one of the most vicious of all rats. It can swim and climb, and often burrows into the ground. The Norway rat is usually grayish-brown in color, with a gray or light brown belly, and is about twelve to nineteen inches long. It is found in practically all parts of the world, but only in areas where human beings live. In many areas of the world, such as the United States, it has virtually driven out the black rat. It spreads bubonic plague and typhus fever.

The black rat (*Rattus rattus rattus*) is more slender in size than the Norway rat. It is black in color, has large ears and a long tail. The black rat prefers tropical weather, and usually shuns cold climates. It is about thirteen to seventeen inches long, and is a good climber. The best way to tell the black rat from the brown rat is by the tail lengths. The brown rat's tail is shorter than its head or body, while the black rat's is longer.

U.S. Fish & Wildlife Serv., by H. J. Spencer

U.S. Fish & Wildlife Serv., by J. Silver

After drawing by Robert W. Hines, U.S. Fish & Wildlife Serv.

Mice

The white-footed or deer mouse (*Peromyscus*) is one of the most beautiful of all mice. It is easily recognized by the white under parts of its body and white feet. The upper part of its body is brown or gray, or a mixture of these colors. The white-footed mouse eats seeds, nuts, and insects, and lives in woods and meadows. Like many other mice, it is very clean. (Some mice spend a large portion of their lives cleaning themselves. They do this by licking the fur with their tongues, like a cat.)

John H. Gerard

The common house mouse (*Mus musculus*) has followed man wherever he has made his home. It will eat almost any type of food, but prefers food in groceries and pantries, as well as grain. Its worst enemy is the cat. The house mouse is about four inches long (with a three inch tail).

The most common of the field mice is the meadow mouse (*Microtus pennsylvanicus*). It lives on grain, corn, roots, and grasses. The meadow mouse is about five or six inches long, has small ears and a very short (two inches) tail, is gray or reddish-brown above and whitish-gray below. These mice do considerable damage to farmers' crops each year.

137

Fish & Wildlife Serv., by E. R. Kalmbach

Chicago Nat. Hist. Mus.

Graphic House, Inc., by Jack Gorman

Do Cats Kill Rats?

Worst enemy of mice and rats (except for man) is the cat. Cats will readily pounce on a house mouse, as shown here, and kill it. Some cats, however, will not attack a domestic rat. Certain dogs also make good rat catchers—especially when they are trained.

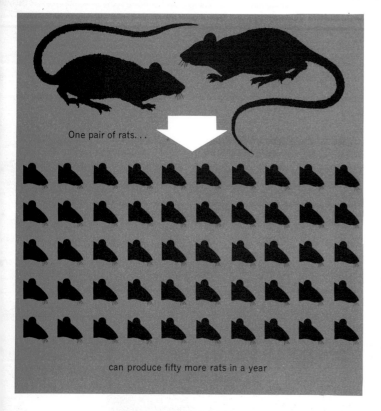

One pair of rats...

can produce fifty more rats in a year

Why Are Rats So Abundant?

One important reason is that they reproduce very fast; one male and one female rat alone can produce fifty young rats in a year! And there are billions of rats in the world. Another reason is that rats can eat almost any kind of food. Rats start to breed when they are less than four months old, and have seven to nine babies in a litter.

Rats Cause Disease

Rats, if infected with typhus fever or plague bacilli, spread these to man by means of fleas, ticks, and lice which they carry on their bodies. Rats live in filth; they thrive near uncovered garbage cans, and dump-heaps in backyards and alleys. (For more about rats and plagues, see "The World and the Black Rat" in Volume 6.)

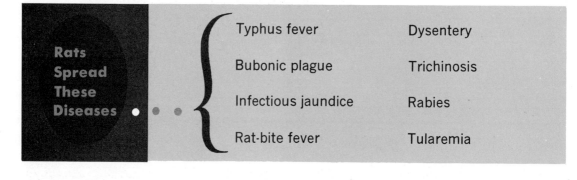

Rats Spread These Diseases

Typhus fever	Dysentery
Bubonic plague	Trichinosis
Infectious jaundice	Rabies
Rat-bite fever	Tularemia

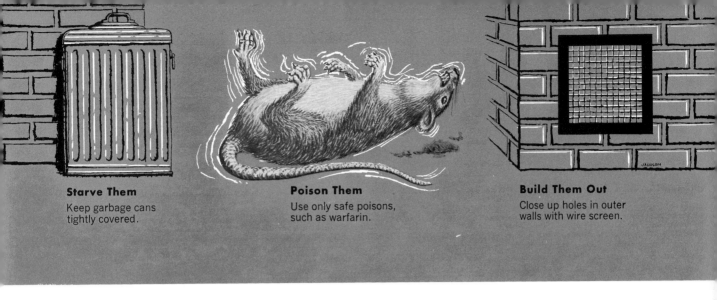

Starve Them
Keep garbage cans tightly covered.

Poison Them
Use only safe poisons, such as warfarin.

Build Them Out
Close up holes in outer walls with wire screen.

How To Control Rats

Rats destroy property by gnawing wood and other building material, and by starting fires (rats gnaw electric wires, causing short circuits). Rats may be controlled by traps, poison (warfarin, carbon monoxide), sanitary garbage and refuse cans, cleanliness, and proper building methods (no double walls, use of wire netting and concrete). Cleanliness and sanitation is the best control method, as it is easier to prevent rats from breeding than it is to kill them later.

Rats and Mice Can Be Useful

Rats and mice are widely used in scientific laboratories to study the effect of diseases on them and cures for diseases. They thus have a beneficial use to man. Not all rats and mice are good for laboratory use; certain types, such as the albino rat and white mouse, are preferred. The mouse is used in medical research, particularly in cancer research, and the rat is used to study the effect of drugs. The rat is a rather intelligent animal, and is widely used by animal psychologists to test learning ability. Other rodents used in laboratories are the guinea pig and the hamster.

139

The South Atlantic States

Base map copyright by Jeppesen & Co., Denver, Colorado, U.S.A. All rights reserved.

Virginia, North Carolina, South Carolina, Georgia, and Florida are the South Atlantic States. They have a combined coast line of about two thousand miles and are located south of the Mason-Dixon line (the Maryland-Pennsylvania border.)

Four of these South Atlantic States were among the original thirteen which formed the United States; Florida was not admitted to the Union until 1845. This section of the country contains some outstanding landmarks of American history (see "Landmarks of America" in Volume 4, page 296). St. Augustine, Florida, the oldest city in the United States, was founded in 1565. Roanoke Island, North Carolina, was the site of the first English settlement (1585) in what was to become the United States. Jamestown, Virginia, was the site of the first permanent English settlement (1607) in the United States. And, of course, these five states bear the scars of the War Between the States (1861–1865), also called the Civil War, about which you can read more in Volume 17, page 221. If you visited these five states today you would find that they have much to offer in addition to such historical landmarks as these. They are important centers for the raising of cotton and the processing of cotton and other textiles. Florida and Georgia are renowned for their fruits—citrus fruits from Florida and peaches from Georgia. Industry is growing in the South and it is becoming one of the many important industrial regions in the United States.

The South Atlantic States have many scenic attractions to offer: beautiful beaches from the southernmost tip of Florida to the northernmost corner of Virginia, mountain ranges such as the Great Smokies and Blue Ridge, natural wonders such as the Dismal Swamp, the Everglades, and Okefenokee Swamp. All these can be found in the South Atlantic States.

Here then are the South Atlantic States where you will find an exciting mixture of yesterday and today, of historic shrines and bustling industries, high mountains and long stretches of beach—a land of fascinating contrasts.

—Carol Zeman Rothkopf

The South Atlantic States

VIRGINIA

Arlington
Alexandria
Mt. Vernon

Potomac River
Shenandoah R.
Rappahannock R.
Chesapeake Bay

Rockfish Gap
Charlottesville
York River
Richmond
Yorktown
DELMARVA PENINSULA
Lynchburg
James River
Williamsburg
Appomattox
Fort Monroe
Roanoke
Norfolk
Virginia Beach
Dismal Swamp
Kitty Hawk

CLINCH MT.
WALKER MT.
APPALACHIAN
MOUNTAINS
MOUNT ROGERS
STONE MTS.
Blowing Rock
BLUE RIDGE MOUNTAINS
PLATEAU

Roanoke River
Albemarle Sound
ROANOKE ISLAND

GREAT SMOKY MT. NAT. PARK
GREAT SMOKY MOUNTAINS
MT. MITCHELL
Asheville
Tryon

Greensboro
Durham
Winston-Salem
Chapel Hill
Raleigh
NORTH CAROLINA
Pinehurst
Southern Pines
Lake Mattamuskeet
Pamlico Sound
CAPE HATTERAS

SASSAFRAS MT.
PIEDMONT
LOOKOUT MT.
BRASSTOWN BALD

Rock Hill
Charlotte
Spartanburg
Cape Fear River
CAPE LOOKOUT

Anderson
SOUTH
Lake Murray
Columbia
Pee Dee River
Wilmington
CAPE FEAR

Rome
Stone Mountain
Athens
CAROLINA
Lake Moultrie
Winyah Bay

Atlanta
Augusta
Savannah River
Charleston

GEORGIA
Warm Springs
Macon

Columbus
Pinehurst

Albany
Altamaha River
Jesup
Brunswick
Waycross
SEA ISLANDS

Thomasville
Okefenokee Swamp
Marys R.

FLORIDA
Escambia R.
Apalachicola R.
Chattahoochee River
Suwannee R.
St. Johns R.
Tallahassee
Jacksonville
St. Marks
St. Augustine
Apalachee Bay
Escambia Bay
Pensacola

Silver Springs
Ocala
Lake George
Daytona Beach

Orlando

Tarpon Springs
Winter Haven
Lake Kissimmee
Tampa
St. Petersburg
Tampa Bay

Sarasota

Lake Okeechobee
Caloosahatchee R.
Palm Beach
West Palm Beach

The Everglades
Fort Lauderdale
Miami Beach
Ten Thousand Islands
Miami
Coral Gables
Biscayne Bay
Ponce de Leon Bay
KEY LARGO

Florida Bay
Key West
Florida Keys

Gulf of Mexico

ATLANTIC OCEAN

N
S

statute miles

0 25 50 75 100 200 300 400 500 600 700 800

What Do You Know About the South Atlantic States?

Before you start reading about the South Atlantic States why not test your knowledge of this part of the United States? Twenty or above is an excellent score and would entitle you to be an honorary Southern Colonel. Anything below that means you've got a lot to learn about one of the oldest and most interesting parts of the United States. Answers to the quiz appear on page 159.

A. Virginia has been called the "Mother of Presidents." Can you name the eight presidents of the United States who were born in Virginia? (Total: 8 points—1 point for each part)

B. Three other South Atlantic States have been the birthplace of presidents. Can you name the presidents and the states in which they were born? (Total: 3 points—1 point for each part)

C. What are the capital cities of the South Atlantic States of Virginia, North Carolina, South Carolina, Georgia, and Florida? (Total: 5 points, 1 point for each part)

D. Many familiar songs have been written which use the name of a South Atlantic State or a site in the state in the title. See if you can match the proper name with the blank in the song title.
1. "Carry Me Back to Old . . ."   a. Carolina
2. "Marching Through . . ."   b. Georgia
3. ". . . Moon"   c. Carolina
4. "Way Down Upon the . . . River"   d. Virginny
5. "Moon Over . . ."   e. Miami
6. "Nothing Could be Finer Than   f. Suwannee
   To Be in . . . in the Morning"
(Total: 6 points—1 point for each part)

E. Four of the South Atlantic States were named for rulers of a famous nation. Can you name the ruler and the country for which these states were named? (Total: 4 points—1 point for each part)

F. In the pictures below are some very well-known landmarks of the South Atlantic States. Can you name them and describe why they are well-known? (Total: 4 points—1 point for each part)

1

2

WILBUR WRIGHT ORVILLE WRIGHT

3

4

N.C. Dept. Conserv. & Development

Although the South Atlantic states produce many crops, a large part of the earnings of many people in these states comes from the growth and sale of tobacco. In this South Carolina tobacco shed, the leaves of the plant are cured by air and sun.

The Color Camera Visits the South

Industry, moving from the crowded, expensive locations in the northern states to the roomy southland, has built huge factories throughout the former cotton and tobacco kingdoms. First opened in 1939, this plastics factory (right) in Florida has expanded to keep pace with greater demands for its products.

The Blue Ridge Mountains extend across the state of Virginia from the northeast to the southwest. From Deep Gap, where this photograph was taken, we can see the pine and hemlock covered mountains which form a part of the Appalachian range.

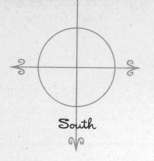

South

A large farm in the Smokies near Asheville, North Carolina. North Carolina is one of the leading states in the value of its crop production. Most of this value is accounted for by large crops of tobacco, corn, cotton, and peanuts.

Standard Oil (N.J.)

Sunny Florida is justly famous as a playground for those who prefer summer the year around. This mansion, one of the more elaborate resort homes, is located at Fort Lauderdale, on Florida's southeastern coast. Other well-known Florida vacation spots include Miami, Palm Beach, St. Petersburg, and the Florida Keys.

Virginia:

The Old Dominion State

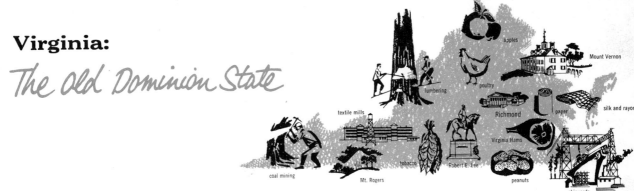

apples

Mount Vernon

lumbering

poultry

textile mills

Richmond

paper

silk and rayon

Robert E. Lee

Virginia Hams

coal mining

tobacco

Mt. Rogers

peanuts

shipyards

Virginia has many nicknames: "Old Dominion State," "Mother of Presidents," and "Mother of States." The name "Old Dominion" comes from the fact that this phrase was often used in early writings about Virginia. Virginia has been the birthplace of eight Presidents of the United States which explains the second nickname. The third—"Mother of States"—comes from the fact that many other states were formed from land held by Virginia. From **Northeastern Tour Book**, copyright 1954 by the American Automobile Association. Revised by editor.

Situated in the Atlantic coastal plain and the Appalachian Highlands, Virginia may be divided into five regions. The Coastal Plain, historic "Tidewater Virginia" which occupies about one-fourth of the area of the state, includes the three peninsulas formed by the Potomac, Rappahannock, York, and James rivers, and part of the Delmarva Peninsula, across Chesapeake Bay, known as the Eastern Shore.

The central part of Virginia is a region of rolling hills accounting for nearly one-half of the land area of the state. The Blue Ridge, which extends from the junction of the Shenandoah and Potomac rivers southwestward to the North Carolina line, contains Virginia's highest peaks—Mount Rogers, 5,719 feet, and White Top, 5,520 feet. The famous Skyline Drive follows the crest of the Blue Ridge through Shenandoah National Park, and connects at Rockfish Gap with the Blue Ridge Parkway which continues along the mountain tops through Virginia and North Carolina to the Great Smoky Mountains National Park.

Extending southwestward from the junction of the Shenandoah and Potomac rivers for about 360 miles to the Tennessee line is the Appalachian Ridge and Valley province. The eastern part is a series of valleys, called the "Valley of Virginia," of which Shenandoah Valley at the north is best known. The western part is composed of a series of high, narrow ridges, known as The Valley Ridges, some of the most prominent being North, Shenandoah, Walker, and Clinch Mountains. Only the extreme southwestern part of the state lies in the Appalachian plateaus, a broad uplifted area, underlaid by coal-bearing strata and deeply cut by streams into a pattern of winding ravines, gorges, and narrow ridges.

The Land and Its Products

Even though the state possesses various industries, Virginia is still largely agricultural. More than half of the land is devoted to farming and a relatively large portion of the population is engaged in agriculture. The state's principal crops are corn, hay, apples, wheat, white potatoes, and peanuts. Tobacco, the "pleasant, sweet, and strong" leaf which was introduced into Europe by seventeenth-century Virginians, is still grown in great quantity. Because of the mild climate, livestock can graze in the open most of the year in Virginia. The livestock industry is especially important to farmers in the hilly and mountainous areas.

From the standpoint of the total value of products, the most important industries are tobacco processing, and the manufacture of chemical and allied products, textiles, transportation equipment, food, lumber, and wood

145

products. Other industries include paper and allied products, apparel, metal products, leather, electrical equipment, rubber products and stone, clay, and glass.

About 150 different minerals are found in Virginia, the most important of which is coal. The bituminous fields in southwestern Virginia produce much of the state's supply, and semi-anthracite coal is found in the valley. Limestone and its products, derived chiefly from the huge deposits underlying the valley, rank second in commercial importance. Other commercial resources include aplite, barite, cement materials, clays, feldspar, glass sand, granite, greenstone, gypsum, black marble, mica, pyrite, salt, sand and gravel, slate, soapstone, talc, and titanium minerals. Lead, manganese, and zinc are the chief metallic resources mined.

Valuable forest land is another of Virginia's natural resources. The state's two national forests, George Washington and Jefferson, cover about 1,500,000 acres.

Eastern Virginia is noted for its seafood industry with oysters, crabs, and finfish the principal products.

Virginia's Vacationland

Virginia, which was the site of the first permanent English settlement in North America, is today an ideal vacationland because it contains both seashore and mountain resorts, forest retreats and many natural wonders within its varied landscape. The state of Virginia offers numerous recreational opportunities.

Among the scores of well-preserved or restored historic attractions are such shrines as Mount Vernon, Washington's home; Monticello, Jefferson's home near Charlottesville; Arlington National Cemetery; a number of national military parks; and Williamsburg, the Colonial capital of Virginia.

Splendid fishing, especially for trout and bass, is to be had in the mountain streams, fresh-water lakes and ponds. The eastern rivers, salt-water bays, and the ocean are famous fishing grounds offering sport for edible game fish—black drum, bluefish, bonito, channel bass, croaker, gray and spotted sea trout, striped bass, and summer flounder. The finest stretch of beach found east of Norfolk, extends from Willoughby through Ocean View and Ocean Park on the Chesapeake Bay to Cape Henry and Virginia Beach on the Atlantic.

Chesapeake Bay, the tidewater rivers, the tidal flats on the Eastern Shore, and the famous Back Bay offer as good waterfowl and rail shooting as can be found anywhere on the Atlantic Coast. Duck, geese, and brant are plentiful in winter when they are driven south by cold. Quail may also be found in the Tidewater and Piedmont sections. Deer roam the swampy areas bordering some of the eastern rivers, as well as the great Dismal Swamp—also well known for its wild turkey and bear hunting. Ruffed grouse and pheasant are the principal fowl in the mountains; deer, raccoon, opossum, skunk, otter, and mink are among the game animals.

146

Cornfields near Newmarket. About one-half the population of Virginia is engaged in agriculture.

During the War Between the States this building, in Richmond, was the home of Jefferson Davis, President of the Confederate States. Today it is the Confederate Museum.

Rotunda of the University of Virginia (in Charlottesville). The university was founded by Thomas Jefferson in 1819.

Standard Oil (N.J.)

Two photos, Eunice Sawders from Cushing

North Carolina: *The Tar Heel State*

There are many interesting explanations for the origin of North Carolina's nickname. One is that General Robert E. Lee used the expression "tar heel" to describe the sticking qualities of the North Carolina troops in the War Between the States (1861–1865). Another explanation is that in the days before the war one of the chief exports of the state was tar, and since the preparation of tar is so messy the workers came barefoot and were nicknamed for the way their feet looked after a day at work. From **What to See in the Southeastern States**, copyright 1954 by the American Automobile Association. Revised by editor.

Three distinct regions are found within the borders of this South Atlantic state: the Appalachian Highlands, the Piedmont Plateau (the area between mountains and coast), and the broad Coastal Plain.

The mountain region consists of about 6,000 square miles in the western part of the state. Five peaks rise above 6,600 feet in altitude and 223 are 5,000 feet or over. Mount Mitchell, the highest point in eastern United States, attains an elevation of 6,684 feet. The Great Smoky Mountains, so called from the haze that usually hangs over them, are the master chain of the Appalachian Range. East of the Great Smokies are the rolling, forest-covered mountains of the Blue Ridge cut by many rivers and valleys. Numerous lakes have been created by damming mountain brooks and streams.

East of the mountains lies the Piedmont Plateau region, covering almost one-half of the state, sloping gradually from an elevation of about 1,000 feet at the edge of the Blue Ridge to approximately 500 feet at the fall line. In the southeastern part of the plateau is the sandhills region, a narrow strip of sandy soil, dry climate, and the beautiful long-leaf pine.

Along the coast and for miles inland is the level Coastal Plain, with an average elevation of less than 500 feet at its western edge, and sloping down to the shallow coast lagoons, of which Pamlico and Albemarle Sounds are the largest. Lake Mattamuskeet, the largest of the many lakes in this region, covers an area of about 100 square miles. The 320-mile coast line is marked offshore by a chain of long, narrow islands.

The Land and Its Products

Although rapidly expanding as an industrial state, North Carolina's basic importance is still in agriculture, and it leads the nation in tobacco production, growing about seventy per cent of all the bright-leaf (known also as "Virginia") cigarette tobacco produced in the country. Cotton ranks second, with peanuts third, and corn fourth. Hay, Irish and sweet potatoes, small grains, soy beans, and truck crops are grown extensively. Swine, mules, poultry, and dairy products are important.

Over eighteen million acres of the state's land area are classed as forest land. Of this area about a million acres are in federal ownership, in the Croatan, Nantahala, and Pisgah National Forests. Western North Carolina's hardwood forests and eastern North Carolina's pine and gum timberlands are among the richest supplies of timber in the eastern half of the United States.

North Carolina's commercial mineral wealth is centered in the nonmetallic minerals such

147

as mica, feldspar, and asbestos. The state ranks high in the production of kaolin clay (used in manufacturing china), granite, and sand and gravel. Talc and pyrophyllite, used in making talcum powder and pottery, are found in large quantities. Gold has been mined since 1799 and until the California discoveries, North Carolina was a leading producer of this mineral.

The rapid growth of industry in recent years has placed North Carolina among the leading manufacturing states of the South. The major industries—textiles, tobacco products, and the manufacture of wooden furniture—depend on the resources of the state for raw materials. Mountainous western North Carolina leads in the manufacture of forest products. Much of the textile production is centered in the heavily populated Piedmont while the Coastal Plain, chiefly a tobacco-growing area, supports several large food processing plants.

North Carolina is an important sea food producer. The enormous fresh- and salt-water sounds and lakes furnish some of the finest fishing grounds in the United States. One of the most profitable fish caught in this area is the menhaden, whose oil is used in the production of paint, fertilizer, insect killers, and waterproofing liquids.

Holidays in North Carolina

North Carolina, well known for its variety of holiday spots, has three major resort areas— the mountains of the west, the sandhills, and the coast. The many mountain resorts have settings of great loveliness. In the sandhills, where the climate is dry and bracing and the winters exceptionally mild, are the famous resorts of Pinehurst and Southern Pines. Tryon and Blowing Rock are also popular resorts. Along the coast with its 320 miles of surf-washed shore are several beach resorts.

Some of the best sport fishing in North America may be found in the waters of this state. Surf and deep-sea fishing are excellent from early spring through fall, particularly at the famous fishing grounds of Oregon Inlet, Ocracoke and Capes Hatteras, Lookout and Fear. Bluefish, flounder, weakfish, sea trout, Spanish mackerel, and channel and striped bass are among the varieties taken from the sounds. Deep-sea fishing yields amberjack, dolphin, sailfish, barracuda, and bonito. Large-mouth bass and bream may be caught in the streams of the Piedmont Plateau and Coastal Plain, and trout and small-mouth bass are taken from the swift mountain streams.

Quail, ducks, geese, grouse, doves, foxes, deer, bear, raccoons, rabbits, and squirrels are among the prey for hunters. While game conditions vary widely from county to county, big game is confined generally to the far east or far west. Small game is found in most sections, the cottontail and squirrel being taken throughout the state.

Roanoke Island, site of the first English settlements in America. In the theater a play is presented each summer which tells the story of "The Lost Colony." Fort Raleigh which guarded the colony is on the left.

The Blue Ridge Parkway and the Great Smoky Mountains National Park meet in western North Carolina near Mile-High Overlook, offering a famous view of the Smokies.

The capitol of North Carolina at Raleigh was completed in 1840. The building was captured and occupied by General Sherman's Union Army during the War Between the States.

N.C. Dept. Conserv. & Development, photos by Gus Martin and Sebastian Sommer

South Carolina:

The Palmetto State

South Carolina, one of the original thirteen states, was the first state to secede from the Union (December 20, 1860) more than three months before the outbreak of the War Between the States. A state of many "firsts"—the first free library in America (1698), the first cotton mill in America (1789), and the first city college in the United States (1770)—it gains its nickname from the palmetto tree which grows on its islands and along the seacoast. From **What To See in the Southeastern States,** 1954–55 edition. Copyright 1954 by American Automobile Association. Revised by editor.

South Carolina, flanked by the cool Atlantic beaches, extends to the Blue Ridge Mountains to provide a variety of recreational facilities. Several state parks and recreational areas in national forests offer a wide choice of recreational and sight-seeing centers from the seacoast to the mountains.

World-famous gardens and expansive plantations link modern South Carolina directly with the historical days of the buccaneers and baronies. Azaleas, camellias, and other flowers bloom today where rice and indigo grew during the seventeenth century. Gay beach resorts offer swimming, fishing, golf, and sailing—plus the opportunity to see historic or other interesting sights. Numerous lakes, the largest formed by power dams, provide swimming, fishing, and other recreation.

South Carolina offers excellent hunting and fishing. Hunting seasons are long, opening in September for deer, and on Thanksgiving for almost all other game, and closing the first of March with some exceptions. White-tail deer are plentiful along the coast, and a few bears are left in the swamps. Opossum, fox, raccoon, rabbit, and squirrel are found in all parts of the state. Game birds include quail, duck, and goose.

Principal fresh-water fish in streams and lakes are large-mouth bass, striped bass, bream, crappie, and white perch. Salt-water fishing off the coast is excellent.

In general, South Carolina is divided into the nearly level Coastal Plain, or "low country," and the Piedmont Plateau, or "upcountry." The fall line dividing the low country from the upcountry runs diagonally across the state about 125 miles inland. Approximately following the fall line is a sandhill belt, an area ten to thirty miles wide, which was once the shore line.

At the shore line the Coastal Plain is low and level, gradually rising to an average elevation of 150 to 250 feet in the west. The highest altitude reached in the sandhill belt is 500 feet at its western edge. Many fine beaches line the shore where it stretches straight and almost unbroken from the northern boundary of the state to Winyah Bay. From this point south, the coast line is very irregular, indented by numerous inlets and estuaries and bordered by sea islands. The harbor at Charleston is one of the best on the Atlantic Coast.

The upcountry is generally rolling in character, the average elevation rising gradually from 500 feet in the east to about 1,200 feet in the northwest. In the northwestern corner is the eastward-facing escarpment rising abruptly 2,000 feet or more to the peaks of the Blue Ridge Mountains.

Industry and Agriculture in South Carolina

Agriculture is an important occupation in South Carolina, although its products bring

149

in only about one-fifth the income produced by industry. About fifty-seven per cent of the state's land area is farmland.

Indigo and rice, the main staple crops of the early settlers, soon gave way to cotton, chief money crop of the state since the early nineteenth century. Tobacco ranks next in importance today. Peaches, melons, and berries are the leading fruits.

Many large areas have been turned into pasture land and fine beef and dairy cattle are raised. Hogs have been raised since the earliest settlement and are still important.

Approximately 11,587,000 acres, or three-fifths of the entire land area of South Carolina, is wooded, including woodlots on farms. The two national forests, the Francis Marion and the Sumter, comprise over 585,000 acres. Saleable softwoods, including pine and cypress, cover 3,288,000 acres, and hardwoods cover 1,813,000 acres. Of this timber, the southern yellow pine comprises ninety per cent of the softwoods; while red gum, oak, yellow poplar, soft maple, tupelo, and black gum are the predominant hardwoods. Forest products include poles, piling, lumber, logs, veneer, furniture stock, crossties, pulp, fuel, turpentine, rosin, and tar.

Minerals are the least important of the state's natural resources, but a few valuable kinds are found in abundance. South Carolina contains some of the world's largest deposits of kaolin. Other large industries are paper and tire manufacturing. Almost inexhaustible supplies of fine granite and large deposits of phosphate are found. Extensive areas are underlaid with limestone and marble.

Of the more than 2,100 industries operating in South Carolina, textile manufacturing is by far the largest single industry. The state now has some of the largest textile plants in the world, produces more finished cotton goods than any other southern state, and has the South's greatest finishing plant. The processing of raw wool, as well as the manufacture of wool, rayon, nylon, and other synthetic fibers is increasing.

Other important industries include lumbering and woodworking, cottonseed oil mills, the manufacture of food products, iron and steel plants, chemical plants, pulp and paper mills, printing and publishing houses.

South Carolina ranks second in the packing and shipping of oysters, producing approximately twenty per cent of the country's total. Shrimp are also shipped. Other products of the fisheries are mullet, clams, crabs, menhaden, and shad.

Turpentine sap dripping into a cup. Turpentine is one of the important products of South Carolina's more than 11,000,000 acres of forest.

Cotton is South Carolina's leading crop. At the time of the harvest in South Carolina, upland cotton is brought to the gin in mule carts and trucks.

Cypress Gardens near Charleston. South Carolina was the birthplace of the gardenia, named for the man who first developed it, Dr. Alexander Garden.

Cushing photos by Edward Van Atena and James Sawders

Georgia:

The Peach State

Georgia, the largest state east of the Mississippi, derives its nickname from the fact that it is one of the leading producers of peaches in the United States.
From **What To See in the Southeastern States**, 1954–55 edition. Copyright 1954 by American Automobile Association. Revised by editor.

Georgia, with rock and mountains to the north, a heart of ribbed clay hills against dark pine forests, and sand and marshlands to the south, is an Atlantic Coast state, although it has a coast line of only about one hundred miles.

Here the Appalachian Mountain system extends into the northeastern part of the state, with peaks from 2,000 to nearly 5,000 feet above sea level, separated by wide fertile valleys and ridges. Brasstown Bald (4,784 feet) is the highest peak within the state. On the west and south the high mountain region ends in a sudden drop of 500 to 2,000 feet.

In the northwest corner of the state Lookout and Sand Mountains, long plateaus several miles wide, rise about 1,000 feet above their valleys and about 2,000 feet above sea level.

The Piedmont region (the land between mountains and coast) of central Georgia is characterized by broad, rounded ridges and fairly narrow valleys. Some of the mountains of this part of the state stand out in bold relief, particularly Stone Mountain (1,686 feet). The fall line, forming the boundary between the Piedmont region and the Coastal Plain, is so named because most of the rivers crossing it have falls or rapids at this point.

The Coastal Plain, which takes in the southern three-fifths of the state, is generally level, having a maximum elevation of about 700 feet at the fall line, and decreasing gradually to sea level at the coast. In the low, flat sections are a number of swamps and ponds. West of a broad sand ridge, which parallels the coast from Jesup south to the great bend of the St. Mary's River, lies the Okefenokee Swamp, parts of which are very little known.

The coast of Georgia is bordered by the famed Sea Islands—low, sandy, and marshy islands, separated from the mainland by a series of lagoons, sounds, and narrow channels which are navigable by small craft the entire length of the coast.

What Georgia Produces

About 25,000,000 acres in Georgia are classified as farmlands, of which nearly 8,000,000 acres are actually crop producing. Cotton and cottonseed oil are the leading cash products.

Following in order of their cash importance are corn, tobacco, peanuts, hay, oats, peaches, and truck crops. Georgia is surpassed only by California and South Carolina in the production of peaches, and many leading varieties of the fruit were originally developed in this state. Georgia ranks first in the production of papershell pecans, peanuts, and is second in the production of sugar cane. The state also ranks high in watermelon and sweet potato yield.

Georgia has more meat packing plants than any other southeastern state. Dairying and poultry raising are also growing in importance. Georgia ranks first in the production of commercial broilers. Ranking third in the United States in the manufacturing of cotton, Georgia has about three hundred textile mills.

Chemical industries produce fertilizers, pine

oils, refined sugar, and similar goods. Georgia leads the nation in the production of naval stores (rosin and turpentine), supplying more than one-half of the country's output. Steel and its products, machinery, leather, furniture, candy, transportation equipment, and wearing apparel are also made.

As a result of the large deposits of clay and limestone in the state, other large industries have developed. Clay products include face brick, sewer pipe, roofing tile, and building tile. Georgia limestone, the basis of an immense cement and lime industry, is used as a base in road building and as crushed stone in concrete structures.

Georgia's timbered acres cover almost two-thirds of the state, giving Georgia the largest forest acreage of any state east of the Mississippi River. The pine and hardwood forests supply raw materials for Georgia's wood product industries.

The lower Coastal Plain is the most important commercial forest area, where there are great naval stores and pulpwood industries. Other important forest products in the state are saw logs, crossties, poles, piling, veneer, cooperage, plywood, and furniture. Among the leading commercial trees are yellow pine, used for naval stores; slash pine, important in pulp and paper production; and white oak, which is used for interior furnishings.

The state's mineral products include thirty-five types of minerals and clays which are produced in commercial quantities.

Georgia is the largest producer of kaolin for use as china clay, accounting for about 75 per cent of the domestic production of such kaolin. Georgia marble, known for its high quality, is widely used as an ornamental building stone. One of the largest deposits of marble in the world is found in Pickens County.

Georgia—a Vacationland

Georgia has both winter and summer resorts. The coast and the southern part of the state, being low and warm, have an ideal winter climate. Augusta, Savannah, Brunswick, the Sea Islands, Albany, Thomasville, and other centers are winter resorts. The mountains of north Georgia offer a delightful summer vacation area.

Georgia has a wide variety of game and fish. Quail is the most highly prized of native game birds, although doves are in abundance all over the state. Wild turkeys are found in the mountains and the coastal section, and ruffed grouse in some sections of the mountains. Other game birds are duck, goose, and woodcock. Virginia deer inhabit the mountains and coastal area, and bear may be found along the river banks near the coast. Squirrel, opossum, raccoon, rabbit, and fox are plentiful.

There is excellent trout fishing in the streams of twelve mountain counties, while muskellunge may be caught in the mountain lakes. The winding rivers of south Georgia offer all native species of bass and bream. Along the Sea Islands, off the coast, there is excellent surf fishing, and three miles out are the deep-sea fishing grounds.

The Entrance Gate to the University of Georgia at Athens. This was the first state university to be chartered by a legislature (1785).

A lady farmer at work among the mountains of Georgia.

Georgia ranks high among the cotton textile manufacturing states and has about 175 spinning, weaving, and finishing plants.

Ga. Dept. of Comm.

Carolyn Carter

Georgia Power Co.

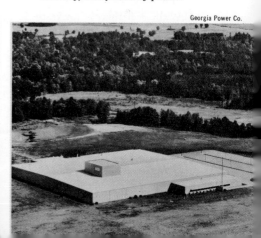

Florida: *The Sunshine State*

Florida is the southernmost state in the mainland United States and one of the leading vacation areas of the nation. Its nickname comes from its excellent year-round climate which averages about 69°F. From What to See in the Southeastern States, copyright 1954 by the American Automobile Association. Revised by editor.

Florida is a year-round resort state. Its ideal winter climate ranges from warm-temperate to semitropical, and except for brief cold spells, it is warm enough for surf bathing and all outdoor sports.

Both fresh- and salt-water fishing are excellent. Probably nowhere else in the country is there such variety, for six hundred kinds of fish are taken from the state's salt waters, lakes, and streams. Deep-sea fishing in the Atlantic or the Gulf is about the best in the sport, both for the size of the fish and the skill required in landing such varieties as sailfish, tarpon, marlin, amberjack, tuna, kingfish, barracuda, and dolphin.

Florida's fresh-water lakes provide some of the best black bass fishing in the world. Lakes and streams also are well stocked with varieties such as bream, speckled perch, and crappie.

Good hunting for rabbit, opossum, fox, and raccoon, as well as for quail and dove, is common in all parts of the state. Duck, goose, jacksnipe, and marsh hen are found along the streams and lakes and on the coast. In the more remote districts are deer, black bear, wildcat, panther, and wild turkey.

The Pistol-shaped State

Florida is sometimes called the Peninsula State because it is a pistol-shaped state extending southward with the Atlantic Ocean on one side and the Gulf of Mexico on the other. Because of the broken character of its coast line, with deep bays, inlets, and lagoons, and the thousands of islands off shore, it has the longest tidal coast line of any state, 8,426 miles (detailed). All of the state is included in the rather flat Coastal Plain, and elevations vary from sea level to 325 feet.

The east coast is characterized by a series of long, narrow beaches, broken at intervals by inlets from the ocean and enclosing on the mainland side a continuous waterway. Along the seaward side is an almost uninterrupted string of beaches, with some of the most famous winter resorts in the world. A few miles south of Miami, the Florida Keys, a group of coral limestone islands, curve around the tip of the peninsula to the city of Key West.

Florida's west coast, deeply indented by bays from the Suwannee River south to the mouth of the Caloosahatchee, becomes low and swampy where it borders the Everglades. South of Naples along the coast are the Ten Thousand Islands set in a maze of tidal channels which sometimes flood the smaller, low-lying islands.

Florida has more lakes than any other state, a total estimated at 30,000; most of them are scattered down the middle of the peninsula in what is known as the central lake region or the highlands. The lakes range in size from tiny ponds to the great expanse of Lake Okeechobee, one of the largest lakes entirely within the limits of any one state, covering about 730 square miles of water surface. In the limestone regions of central Florida are most of the

153

A view of the ocean near Palm Beach. It is scenes like this that make Florida so popular with vacationers.

large springs for which the state is famous, among them Silver Springs, near Ocala, and Rainbow Springs, near Dunnellon.

From Lake Okeechobee south are the Everglades, the most truly tropical portion of the mainland of the United States. The highest land is only a few feet above sea level, and most of it is covered by shallow water, cypress swamps, and saw-grass morasses. A labyrinth of waterways honeycombs the swamps and hummocks. Much of the Everglades is included in Everglades National Park, but a large area has been drained and opened to agriculture.

The Gulf Coast of northwest Florida is marked by sheltered bays, many islands, and long sandy points of land. Occasionally high bluffs break the generally low level of the coast, particularly at Escambia Bay, northeast of Pensacola.

Animal Life

More than 435 kinds of birds have been found in the state, including migratory species that spend part of the year here. Some of the more unusual varieties are the great white heron, the sandhill crane, white ibis, blue heron, and egret. Gulls, pelicans, and ospreys are seen along the coast.

Largest of Florida's reptiles is the alligator, found in almost all parts of the state in fairly large numbers. These huge creatures have much the appearance of prehistoric monsters. The full grown alligator is eight to twelve feet long and may weigh over eight hundred pounds. Crocodiles, once plentiful in the state, only occasionally are seen in the coastal

area between Biscayne Bay and Cape Sable.

Fruits and Forests

Florida's range of climate and soils enables a greater variety of crops to be produced than in any other state. Altogether two hundred kinds of crops, fruits, and nuts are grown in this state, which ranks second in the value of crops per acre. In order of acreage, the principal crops are corn, citrus fruits, vegetables, hay and forage, peanuts, cotton, sugar cane, and tobacco.

Field and forage crops are grown principally in the northern and northwestern parts of Florida. The Suwannee River Valley and Gadsden County are the leading tobacco raising areas. Central Florida produces the greatest amount of citrus fruits and watermelons, and Seminole and Sarasota counties most of the celery. The flat prairie lands north of Lake Okeechobee are the principal beef and cattle raising areas, but this industry is also growing along the west coast. The introduction of Brahma cattle has been so successful that Florida now ranks thirteenth among the beef producing states, with more than 1,265,000 head of beef cattle. The rich muck lands of the Everglades yield tremendous quantities of winter vegetables and sugar cane.

Florida ranks first in the production of grapefruit, tangerines, and oranges. Subtropical fruits raised on a commercial scale are pineapples, mangoes, avocados, papayas, guavas, bananas, and sapodillas. Strawberries are grown extensively in several central and northern counties.

Winter truck crops are of great commercial value in Florida. The state ranks high in the production of snap beans, eggplant, peppers, tomatoes, cucumbers, celery, potatoes, and lettuce.

Florida's climate and vegetation show a mingling of the characteristics of the temperate and tropical zones. Pines, cypress, oaks, palms, and mangroves are all native, but pines

*Oranges, a citrus fruit
for which Florida is famous.*

are by far the most common trees and grow throughout the state. Botanical novelties are the rare Torreya tree and Florida yew, which grow only along the Apalachicola River. Dense forests of mangroves grow out of the shallow water in southern Florida, particularly in the Ten Thousand Islands. The largest area of cypress is in the big Cypress Swamp.

Most of the 21,451,000 acres of commercial forest land have been cut over but the forests are still a great natural asset. More than a million acres of forest and potential forest land are protected by its three national forests. In addition, over 200,000 acres are in four state forests.

Various kinds of pine and cypress represent 75 per cent of commercial forest acreage; hardwoods about 25 per cent. The state produces more cypress lumber than any other state and about 23 per cent of the national total.

Florida ranks second in the production of naval stores (turpentine and rosin). Revenues from lumber, naval stores, poles, piling, crossties, fuelwood, pulpwood, and other forest products amount to more than $310,000,000 annually.

An important nonmetallic mineral producing state, Florida is a leading producer of phosphate rock and fuller's earth. About 80 per cent of the country's supply of phosphate comes from the state.

Several kinds of clays of commercial importance are found, including fuller's earth, used by the oil industry in its filtering processes, and kaolin. Other minerals found in commercial abundance include titanium oxide, diatomite, peat, sand, and gravel.

Florida's Fish

Florida waters yield more than sixty varieties of food fish for commercial purposes, besides nonedible fish from which oil and fertilizer are manufactured. Of the food fishes, mullet is the most important and comprises about 40 per cent of the total fish volume. Other top-ranking marketable food fish are mackerel, groupers, red snappers, sea trout, catfish, king whiting, bottom fish, kingfish, and bluefish.

Two species of nonedible fish, menhaden and sharks, are very important. Three menhaden plants operate in the state, extracting the oil and producing meal for fertilizers and poultry feed. Sharks are becoming increasingly important for their valuable oil.

Of sea foods other than fish, shrimp is the most important, with Florida producing nearly half of the country's supply. Approximately 75 per cent of the catch is frozen, 15 per cent canned, and the rest sold as fresh shrimp. Oysters are more widely distributed than any other sea food, but the beds have been seriously depleted in some sections. Crabs, crawfish, clams, scallops, and sea turtles also are found.

For over 50 years Florida waters have been producing nearly all of the sponges harvested in the United States. The coastal area from St. Marks to Key West represents the great producing area. Markets are at Tarpon Springs and Key West.

Other Industries

Although not essentially a manufacturing state, Florida is one of the largest producers of cigars. Ybor City, at Tampa, is the center of the industry. Jacksonville is also a cigar manufacturing city.

Nine large pulp mills manufacture paper and containers and one manufactures raw rayon. There are three large sugar mills in the Everglades region. Other important products of the region are cans, canned and packed foods, furniture, boats, wearing apparel, livestock feeds, vegetable oils, and cement.

Cape Kennedy, from which missiles and space vehicles are launched, has stimulated many space age industries.

155

The cattle industry is growing in Florida; the state ranks thirteenth in cattle production. Zebu cattle, which have grayish coats and drooping ears, were introduced to the cattle ranches of south central Florida because of their ability to withstand heat and insects.

The Okefenokee Swamp

The South Atlantic States have three large swamps: the Dismal Swamp in Virginia and North Carolina, the Everglades in Florida, and the Okefenokee in Georgia and Florida. The Okefenokee has been known as a region of unusual beauty since the late eighteenth century, but it was not designated as a wildlife refuge until 1937. Here is the story of this strange area which is home for hundreds of different kinds of animals and birds, but which has never been completely conquered by man. It is also the home of the imaginary animals that people Walt Kelly's popular comic strip, Pogo. From Georgia: A Guide to Its Towns and Countryside, compiled by WPA of the State of Georgia. Copyright, 1940, by the University of Georgia Press. Revised by editor.

The Okefenokee Swamp, 660 square miles of fresh water and timber, extends from a point a few miles south of Waycross, Georgia to an indefinite end several miles south of the Florida state line. It is approximately forty miles long and averages twenty miles wide. It was once the hunting ground of the lower Creek and Seminole Indians and its name is a corruption of the Indian word Owaquaphenoga which means "trembling earth." Geologists believe that the Okefenokee was once a salt-water sound that was shut off from the ocean by a barrier reef now called Trail Ridge and that in its earlier stages it probably resembled the much younger Dismal Swamp in North Carolina and Virginia and the Everglades in Florida.

The swamp is an unconquered wilderness despite repeated efforts to use its resources. In 1889 the Suwannee Canal Company bought the area from the state for about $62,000, intending to drain the swamp into St. Marys River, cut the rich timber and turn the great "prairies" (submerged trembling earth covered by a heavy growth of grass) into farmlands. After more than a million dollars had been spent digging miles of canals with steam shovels and dredges, the corporation failed and abandoned the project. The next effort was made in 1908 by the Hebard Lumber Company, which forced into the swamp a railroad built on pilings, with branch lines leading to the principal islands and "bays." For several years the work continued but eventually was stopped because the expense of cutting and shipping the timber became too great. In 1937 President Roosevelt designated the area as a wildlife refuge, which now contains more than 330,000 acres.

"Prairies" and "Houses"

In the vast swamp, large bodies of water stretch through labyrinths of moss-covered cypress trees. The great expanse of swamp is broken by several lakes and islands, by many acres of "prairies," and by "houses" (clumps of bushes and trees and thick undergrowth growing on more solid areas).

The prairies are threaded by a maze of water runways which lead from lily-covered cypress bogs to alligator holes. The houses are formed and the bogs extended by a phenomenon known locally as a "blow-up." This occurs when gases formed beneath the water by decaying vegetable matter force masses of vegetation, some a hundred feet square, from the bottom of the water. Helped by the rise and fall of the water level, the surface of the mass, resembling muck, rises several inches above the water and becomes covered with grass, briars, small bushes, and water weeds. When it has accumulated this covering, the entire mass floats until caught in a clump of trees; sometimes it is forced beneath the surface by the pressure of growing cypress roots. During its floating period this earth-raft collects seeds from cypress and other trees and in time develops into a house; many never become stable but sway and tremble under the slightest weight.

Islands in Swampland

Floyd's Island is one of the more than twenty-five flat, white-sand islands in the swamp. They differ little from the surrounding mainland. All are covered with a thick growth of saw palmettos, huckleberries, blueberries, gallberries, sedges, and various small herbs. Long-leaf and slash pines grow in the central part

156

A close-up and a long view of the lovely water lilies which grow in parts of the Okefenokee Swamp.

It is possible for visitors to see parts of Okefenokee Swamp Park by walking around or from boats operated by park guides.

of the islands but in the richer soil along the margins are live oak, magnolia bay, and sweet-gum trees. So dense are the bogs of muck and moss around some of the islands that it is possible to walk on them. Here growing to the unusual height of three feet are great numbers of the spotted greenish pitcher plants that ensnare small flies in their tubelike leaves by means of a sweetish liquid, imprison them with a projecting flap, and slowly digest them.

On some of the islands the Seminole, driven to the swamp by invading colonists, have left mounds. A few hardy settlers later ventured here and made a meager living by marketing lumber and pine resin and by raising cattle. Cowhouse Island, named for Billy Bowlegs, a Seminole chief, is one of the largest islands—four miles long and one mile wide. For two generations it was the home of the Lees, who for many years were the only white people living in the interior of the swamp; fifteen children were born in their isolated home, which was never visited by a doctor. When timber crews first came into the swamp in the latter part of the nineteenth century, the Lees moved outside but were so home-sick that they returned within a year. A lumber camp with a store, school, and a motion picture house thrived for a short time on this island, but it is now deserted.

"The Booming of the Swamp"

The Okefenokee is drained by two small rivers. The St. Marys drains the southeastern part of the swamp during periods of high water and winds to the Atlantic Ocean, and the Suwannee drifts southwestward to empty into the Gulf of Mexico. As the Suwannee River courses through the swamp, first through high banks and then in open channels, patches of dense shade and brilliant sunshine dapple dark, cypress-stained water. Through the entire area the eerie stillness is broken only by the splashing of water fowl, singing of birds, bellowing of alligators, hooting and screeching of owls, and the faint rumbling of mingled sounds known as the "booming of the swamp." Alligators, some of them eight to ten feet long, are found in the canal, the lakes, the river, and in the deeper pools of the prairies. Their deep throated bellowing is a familiar sound throughout swampland. Generally harmless unless prodded into attack, they are unmolested because they are useful in keeping the mud from accumulating in the lake bottoms and in building wallows inhabited by fish.

The Daughters of the Sun

There is a legend that some Indian hunters, lost in the swamp, found an enchanted island. Suddenly a group of beautiful women appeared and placed before them delicious fruits, marsh eggs, and corn pone, warning them that their husbands would kill intruders, and pointed out a path by which the lost Indians could return safely home. No sooner did the hunters set foot on the path than the women vanished, and in spite of many efforts the Indians were never able to rediscover the island or find these "Daughters of the Sun."

157

Florida's Great Coral Reef

Along the curve of Florida's island Keys lies a reef of living coral—the only one of its kind in the continental United States. An area of this reef about 24 miles long and four miles wide has been made into an undersea park—The John Pennekamp State Park. Benedict Thielen describes the beauty of the reef in this excerpt from "The Florida Keys." Reprinted by special permission from **Holiday,** copyright 1962, by The Curtis Publishing Co.

For more than 100 miles the Florida Keys stretch southwestward in a sweeping curve between the shallow waters of Florida Bay and the Gulf of Mexico to the west and the 500-fathom depths of the Straits of Florida to the east.

Once the Upper Keys from Key Largo to Bahia Honda were a living coral reef, and if you pick up a stone, it is often imprinted with the fossil outlines of coral or seaweed or sea fan. This reef has been long dead but today, following the eastern shore, forming Hawk Channel, a younger reef, alive and still building, stretches along the curve of the Keys. Its presence shows that the Keys, though they lie just outside the tropics, are tropical. It is only now and then, and for short periods, that the water temperature falls below 70 degrees.

Along this series of coral reefs, the ocean bottom is strewn with the wrecks of ships, of West Indiamen and privateers, of Spanish galleons that sailed north from Havana with the gold of Mexico and the silver of Peru in their holds. Looe Key, Fowey Rocks, Carysfort Reef are all named for sunken British frigates or ships-of-the-line.

The reefs lie just below the surface and in smooth weather are unmarked by breakers. On their seaward side the water shoals abruptly. You can take soundings from the color of the water as it changes from deep blue to pale green or from the bright reflected light above the white sand.

Though you are looking at the Atlantic and the Gulf, the waters are Caribbean. No waters north of the Keys have colors like these. On still days their greens and blues are glassy clear. When the wind blows they turn cloudy as jade, opaque and dully polished as the skins of limes. The Gulf Stream's blue is so

158

Underwater garden: A tree of green elkhorn coral dominates a landscape of reddish brain coral, purple fan coral, and gorgonians (giant sea whips).

Photos, Jerry Greenberg

deep that the people of the Keys call it The Purple Water.

Drifting on the surface with mask and snorkel above the reef off Marathon, the water is green-gold. You can see the enameled cowries crawling or the big rosy-lipped conchs heaving themselves forward with jerks. You survey a watery kingdom in which 30 different kinds of coral grow.

Where the tides flow strongly north and south, they have cut deep canyons, whose walls of living stone glow with the salmon-pink flower shapes of the anemones, the brick red and sulphur yellow of sponges and corals. The purple sea fans sway in rhythm with the sea; and there are the reef fish—demoiselles and sergeant majors and rainbow parrot fish and fish striped with colors that shine like luminous paint. Barracudas, too, live among the reefs, and no matter how many times one swims among them, one never quite gets used to their fixed cold stares. The expression on the face of a moray is not especially engaging either. But the small jets of adrenalin they produce in the system have an exhilarating effect and probably account for the speed with which time passes when you hang suspended over these magic depths.

Silver spadefish, striped with black, escort an aqualunged photographer along the reef, 20 feet below the surface of the sea.

Answers to quiz on page 142.

A. 1. George Washington
2. Thomas Jefferson
3. James Madison
4. James Monroe
5. William Henry Harrison
6. John Tyler
7. Zachary Taylor
8. Woodrow Wilson

B. 1. Andrew Jackson—South Carolina
2. James Knox Polk—North Carolina
3. Andrew Johnson—North Carolina

C. Virginia—Richmond
North Carolina—Raleigh
South Carolina—Columbia
Georgia—Atlanta
Florida—Tallahassee

D. 1. d
2. b
3. a or c
4. f
5. e
6. a or c

E. Virginia   Queen Elizabeth I   England
(the virgin queen)

Georgia   King George II   England

North Carolina   King Charles I   England
(from Latin *Carolus*, meaning Charles)

South Carolina   King Charles I   England

F. 1. The Governor's Mansion, Williamsburg, the Colonial capital of Virginia
2. Wright Brothers National memorial at Kitty Hawk, North Carolina. The site of the first sustained powered flight by men. (See "Man Learns To Fly" in Volume 5, page 156.)
3. Monticello, the home of the third President of the United States, Thomas Jefferson.
4. The Okefenokee Swamp is famous not only as the home of Walt Kelly's Pogo and his friends, but also is one of the largest and most famous swamps in the U.S.A.

159

Celebrities of the States

Willa Cather

Though born in Winchester, Virginia, Willa Cather (1876–1947) became a chronicler of the Midwest. Brought to Nebraska as a child and brought up with foreign children on the prairie, she saw how the immigrants' courage and moral strength helped them to tame the stubborn land. Whether as newspaperwoman, magazine editor, schoolteacher, traveler in France, or as author, she kept her quick sympathy with the needs, frustrations, and hopes of the person in foreign places and among strange people, from the Bohemian girl in Nebraska or the American soldier in France, to the priest among the Indians. Some of her best-known books are *O Pioneers! My Antonia, Shadows on the Rock,* and *Death Comes for the Archbishop*—the latter based on the life of Archbishop Lamy of New Mexico.

O. Henry

O. Henry, who was born William Sydney Porter (1862–1910) in Greensboro, North Carolina, was a rancher, editor, and banker. Charged with embezzling funds, he escaped to Central America; but when he heard that his wife was dying, he returned and was imprisoned. A master of the surprise ending, no one was more surprised than he when prison changed him overnight from an ordinary newspaperman into a full-fledged and successful author—one of the most popular short story writers the world has known. Jack London described O. Henry's style as "to the point, with snap, go and life, crisp and crackling and interesting." His best-known collections of stories are *Cabbages and Kings, The Four Million,* and *Roads of Destiny*. His best known short story is *The Gift of the Magi*.

Sidney Lanier

Sidney Lanier (1842–1881) was born in Macon, Georgia. During the Civil War he spent four years in the Confederate Army. A lover of the flute, he carried that instrument concealed in his sleeve—in battle and even when captured trying to run a blockade and sent to a Northern prison camp. After the war he was released —with tuberculosis. The life that was left to him he described as "merely not dying." Knowing that time was running out, he left his job in his father's law firm and turned to poetry, earning his living by joining the Peabody Symphony Orchestra of Baltimore. Those who heard him play said he was one of the world's greatest flutists. These two passions—music and words—he tried somehow to merge in the thought that "Music is love in search of a word."

▶ Other Sections To See

Famous Cities in the South Atlantic States

Asheville, North Carolina (population in 1960: 60,192), is the resort center of the state (right). The city is named in honor of Samuel Ashe, Governor of North Carolina, 1795–1798.

N.C. Dept. Conserv. & Development, by Morton

Charleston, South Carolina (population in 1960: 65,925), is an important seaport and was at one time the capital of the state. Interesting sights in this old city are the College of Charleston, the first city college in the United States; the Citadel, a military college, and many other historic buildings such as the Dock Street Theater (left) built in 1736 and the first building in America devoted wholly to the drama.

Two photos, Southern Rwy. System

Atlanta, Georgia (population in 1960: 487,455), the capital of Georgia, is a bustling, modern city (left). Atlanta was burned by General Sherman on his march to the sea (1864) during the War Between the States and as a result the city has few historic buildings. Atlanta is today an important railroad, financial, and communications center.

161

Richard B. Hoit from Cushing

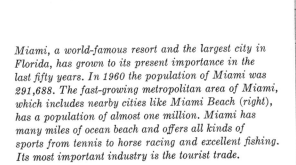

Miami, a world-famous resort and the largest city in Florida, has grown to its present importance in the last fifty years. In 1960 the population of Miami was 291,688. The fast-growing metropolitan area of Miami, which includes nearby cities like Miami Beach (right), has a population of almost one million. Miami has many miles of ocean beach and offers all kinds of sports from tennis to horse racing and excellent fishing. Its most important industry is the tourist trade.

From Sand Dunes to Spaceport

The biggest birds in the world fly at Cape Kennedy, Florida—because "bird" is the missileman's slang for the rockets which thunder upward from the launching pads into space. Tove Neville describes what a trip around America's first spaceport is like in this excerpt from "Cradle of the Space Age," **Science News Letter,** February 24, 1962. Reprinted by permission of Science Service, © 1962. Revised by editor, 1968.

A Saturn rocket, gleaming in the early morning light and waiting to carry three astronauts to the moon, is a far cry from the first missile fired from Cape Kennedy. The first firing from the now world-famous Cape was a German V-2 with a WAC-Corporal second stage on top. The rocket was shot up on July 24, 1950, under the most primitive conditions. It was fueled directly from tank trucks, and an old army tank was used as the blockhouse controlling the flight. Since that day hundreds of Polaris, Thor, Titan, Atlas, and other rockets have been launched from the Cape, bearing space vehicles on missions as distant as the sun and the other planets.

The barren sand dunes on a point of land near the center of Florida's east coast were chosen in 1947 as a test site for long-range guided missiles. The location was then called Cape Canaveral. In 1963, shortly after President John F. Kennedy was assassinated, it was renamed in his honor.

Today, the U.S. Air Force Missile Test Center is spread over more than 100,000 acres at and near the Cape. It is the control point of the Atlantic Missile Range (AMR) which extends southeast from Cape Kennedy 9,000 miles, going beyond the Cape of Good Hope at the southern tip of Africa and into the Indian Ocean.

The Atlantic Missile Range is managed by the Air Force, which launches both military and nonmilitary space vehicles for missions

All photos, NASA

The first men to circle the moon were the three United States astronauts (left to right below) James A. Lovell Jr., William A. Anders, and Frank Borman, in a world-thrilling flight of the Apollo 8 during Christmas week, 1968. At left, their Saturn V space vehicle is readied for launching; at right, above, Commander Borman at the controls during the flight, and at right below, the earth from 120,000 miles away.

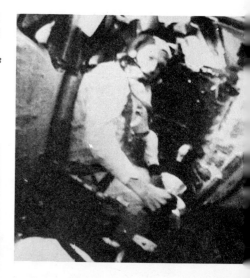

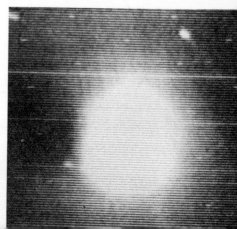

The vehicle assembly building at Cape Kennedy can be seen from a distance of many miles.

of the National Aeronautics and Space Administration. Several dozen launch complexes have been built, each with its launching pad and supporting facilities. Some pads are used constantly; others are now inactive because the missiles for which they were laid out have passed the testing stage and are now operational. Especially big facilities have been built for Project Apollo, the manned mission for landing on the moon.

Launching a rocket is a complicated business. It requires huge gantry towers to erect the missile when it is brought onto the launch pad after at least one month's extensive checkout of all parts and systems. The gantry envelops the erected rocket and is used as a work platform and for further checking. Under the test stand area of a launch pad are supply systems for the rocket, telemetry and electrical systems, and monitoring equipment for testing the rocket's "innards."

Close to the test stand are storage tanks for the lox (liquid oxygen), or other oxidizer, and fuel for the rocket.

Cape Kennedy is a magic name that stands for the last frontier. It catches the imagination of the thousands of people who watch from the white sand beach and other vantage points well away from the pad when a launching is scheduled, and of the millions around the world who watch the giant rockets soar spaceward on their television screens.

Other Books To Read

Gentlemen of Virginia, by Marshall W. Fishwick. Published by Dodd, Mead & Company, New York, 1961.
Four hundred years of Virginia history retold in biographical sketches of 12 prominent Virginians including George Washington, George Mason, Robert E. Lee, and George Marshall.

South Carolina: Annals of Pride and Protest, by William F. Guess. Published by Harper & Brothers, New York, 1960.
A readable, witty history of South Carolina from the colony's beginnings until the present.

A Guide to Everglades National Park and the Nearby Florida Keys, by Herbert S. Zim. Published by Golden Press, Inc., New York, 1960.
This brightly colored pocket-size volume is full of fascinating facts about the history, geology, plant and animal life, and points of interest in Florida and the Southeast.

The following guides to the South Atlantic states were compiled and written by the Federal Writers' Project of the WPA. They are the best sources of historical and factual information about the states.
Virginia: A Guide to the Old Dominion
The North Carolina Guide
South Carolina: A Guide to the Palmetto State
Georgia: A Guide to Its Towns and Countryside
Florida: A Guide to the Southernmost State

163

The signing of the Constitution, 1787. George Washington, who presided over the Philadelphia Convention, watches one of the delegates putting his name to the final draft of the Constitution.

SIGNING OF THE CONSTITUTION by Hintermeister, from the Libr. of Congress collection, ©The Found. of Amer. Gov't

The Constitution of the United States

The American Constitution is one of the most surprising pieces of writing in existence. It is the oldest written constitution in the world. The Swiss, Canadian, and Australian federal constitutions are modeled on it. It is the basic law behind all others in the United States. It is revered by Americans and admired by foreigners.

Many changes, called "amendments," have been made in the original Constitution of 1787. Sometimes these amendments replace parts of the old Constitution, and sometimes they are merely additions to it. But some basic practices of American government are not mentioned in the Constitution. There is nothing there, for example, about party nominating conventions, which play such an important role in presidential elections. There is very little about how much control the United States government shall have over industry, trade, or the relations between businessmen and their employees. Yet these are basic questions in the world of today.

It was not possible for the Fathers of the Constitution to foretell the future with its special problems and needs. Since they had to leave so much unsaid—and since some parts of the Constitution are framed in very general terms—somebody has to judge, in any special case, exactly what the Constitution means. This job, called "interpreting the Constitution," is done by the Supreme Court of the United States.

The Court has sometimes given an interpretation of some part of the Constitution which is the exact opposite of its previous interpretation of the same part. Times change; so does the Supreme Court. The Constitution is more than it appears to be, for its meaning changes with the times, although its words remain the same. If it didn't change in this way, it might have been scrapped long ago.

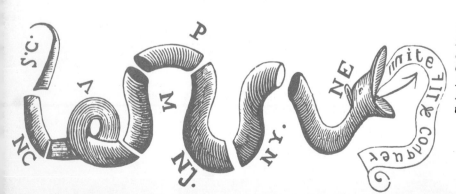

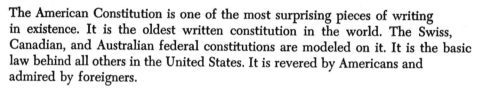

This snake, broken in pieces, was Benjamin Franklin's idea for a symbol of the disunited American Colonies of Great Britain as they were in 1754. In that year, Franklin's "Albany Plan" for a union of the Colonies was turned down.

The Making of the American Constitution

The story of how the American Constitution came to be made is one of the truly great chapters in modern history. After the British Royal Air Force had saved England from Nazi invasion in 1940, Prime Minister Churchill spoke the famous words: "Never in the field of human conflict was so much owed by so many to so few." The same might be said of the Fathers of the American Constitution. The thirteen original states were in conflict one with another. A mere handful of men carried through the great act of statesmanship which made the United States a really united nation, under a truly national government. From Gavian and Hamm: The American Story, 1951. Reprinted by special permission of D. C. Heath and Company, Boston.

The new republic of 1776 was like a weak and sickly infant. Few outsiders thought it would live. The years from the end of the war to the adoption of the Constitution in 1788 were the most critical of our nation's history. They are known as the "Critical Period," for no one could say that the United States would remain united.

The First United States Constitution

The thirteen states were bound together in a "league of friendship," or confederation. The Articles of Confederation, which were drawn up in 1777 but not ratified (approved) by all the states until 1781, provided for a weak central government. It was headed by a one-house congress in which each state had an equal voice. Congress had few powers. It could not levy taxes, enlist troops, punish lawbreakers, or compel the states to follow its orders. It could not regulate commerce between the states. This first constitution of the United States made the states strong and the union weak—a situation which did not help the ideal of unity held by many colonists.

Congress had the greatest difficulty in getting funds to support the government and the armed forces. From 1781 to 1783, for example, Congress asked the states for $10,000,000, but they furnished only $1,500,000. Government officials and members of the armed forces seldom received their pay.

Congressional leaders were not blind to the weaknesses of this "league of friendship." Congress appealed to the states in vain for power to levy a small duty on imports. Congress also begged for power to regulate commerce; this, too, was refused. A change in the Articles re-

The Albany Plan for Colonial Union

As early as 1754, Benjamin Franklin became concerned with the problem of the separated colonies under British rule. He therefore drew up a proposal, which was presented to a group of delegates meeting at Albany, New York, which suggested a form of federation. The delegates accepted it, but the colonies felt that it involved the surrender of too much power, and therefore it was not submitted to the Crown. The plan itself, brief excerpts from which follow, may be said to foreshadow both the Articles of Confederation and the Constitution of the United States.

It is proposed that humble application be made for an act of Parliament of Great Britain, by virtue of which one general government may be formed in America, including all the . . . colonies, within and under which government each colony may retain its present constitution, except in the particulars wherein a change may be directed by the said act . . .

That the said general government be administered by a President-General, to be appointed and supported by the crown; and a Grand Council, to be chosen by the representatives of the people of the several Colonies met in their respective assemblies.

That these representatives shall choose members for the Grand Council in the following proportion . . . (Editor's note: Eleven colonies were to have a total of 48 members) who shall meet . . . at the city of Philadelphia, being called by the President-General . . . after his appointment.

quired the consent of all the states. To every suggestion that the Articles be amended, one state at least said "no."

Why were the states so unwilling to strengthen the national government? There were several reasons. First, there was the strong loyalty felt by the people of a state to their state government. The state governments had been in operation since the first settlement of the country. The people regarded their state assemblies as their own mouthpieces, for in endless squabbles with royal governors the legislatures had stood for liberty. Second, there was the fear that the central government might interfere with the people's liberties. The war had been fought to end interference by Parliament; interference by Congress was equally unwelcome. Third, there was scarcely any feeling of national unity now that the war had been won. Communication and commerce between the states were slight. A sense of national unity was needed before the people would wish to strengthen the central government.

1781–1788: The Confederation Was Weak

The new republic had hardly a friend in the world. Every European king hoped it would collapse. Even our ally, France, hoped we would remain so weak that we would do as she said.

The weakness of the Confederation was also shown by quarrels between the states. Connecticut and Pennsylvania nearly went to war over a boundary dispute. An argument over the frontier between Vermont and New York resulted in the calling out of troops. Several states made commercial war upon one another. Connecticut laid duties on imports from Massachusetts. Pennsylvania laid duties on goods from Delaware and New Jersey. New York taxed all imports from other states and charged a fee for every out-of-state boat which landed on her shores. Such signs of ill will between the states led to a fear that the Confederation would soon fall apart.

Of all the troubles suffered during the years of the Confederation, the one which bothered the most people was the scarcity of money. The paper money issued during the war had become entirely worthless and had ceased to circulate. Most of the small supply of "hard" money—gold and silver—was being sent abroad to pay for imported goods. Money became very scarce and very dear, that is, only a little money could be obtained by selling a large quantity of goods. Prices and wages dropped, and there were three years of hard times.

The poorer people demanded that the state governments print paper money to revive trade and make easier the payment of their debts. They also asked for laws delaying the collection of debts through the courts. In seven states paper money was issued. Since no one really knew what it was worth, creditors did not wish to accept it. Some of the states passed laws requiring creditors to take paper money in full payment for debts. Men of wealth complained that these laws were unjust. They wanted to strengthen the central government so that it could protect them from such laws.

1786–1787: Shays's Rebellion

In Massachusetts the legislature refused to issue paper money and to delay the collection of debts through the courts. Farms were being foreclosed (sold to pay off debts of their owners) daily. When the farm brought less than the mortgage, and the farmer could not pay the balance, he might be sent to jail. In 1786 the farmers in the western part of Massachusetts rebelled. They released debtors from prison and broke up sessions of the courts where cases against debtors were being tried. Early in 1787, under the leadership of a Revolutionary captain, Daniel Shays, they tried to break into an arsenal at Springfield in order to get muskets and cannon. The governor sent troops and the uprising was put down. Thoughtful men feared that the trouble might spread and that the states might not be able to keep order. They thought the only remedy was to strengthen the central government.

Governing the Public Lands

Difficulties with foreign nations, quarrels between the states, and disorders within the

In the 1780's, the United States got a huge area of western land from the separate states. The central government now became the keeper of the "public domain," the property of the people of the United States as a whole. Here you see the public domain as it was by 1800, and the areas given up by the various states which had claimed land in the West.

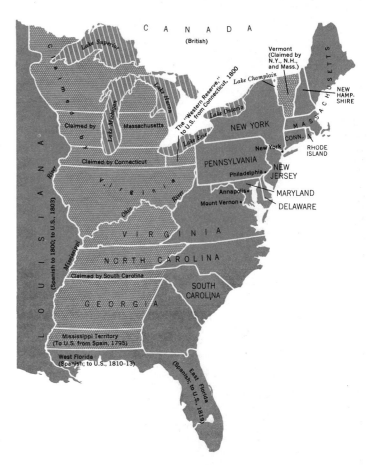

states showed the need for a stronger national government. But the event which did most to develop national unity, and so prepared the way for a stronger national government, was the creation of a domain, or territory, belonging to all the states in common.

Seven states claimed land west of the Appalachians and six did not. The states having no claim to western land argued that all such claims should be ceded (given) to the nation, which could then sell the land to pay national debts and support the national government. In 1780 New York agreed to cede its claims. Congress then recommended that all the states having western claims follow this example. Virginia, Connecticut, and Massachusetts gave up their claims, and in 1786 the vast Northwest Territory became a national domain. Common ownership of this rich territory drew the states together with a new feeling of national pride.

The Mount Vernon and Annapolis Conferences

George Washington was one of a small group of Americans who constantly considered the good of the whole union. After returning from the wars to his home, Mount Vernon, in 1783, Washington gave most of his time to plans for improving transportation between Virginia and Maryland and the West. At Washington's suggestion Maryland and Virginia appointed commissioners to work out an agreement concerning navigation on the Potomac—a matter over which there had long been difficulty. The commissioners met at Mount Vernon. They drew up an agreement which was later approved by the two state legislatures. The Mount Vernon Conference ended its work by proposing a convention on navigation and

trade to which all the states would be invited to send delegates.

A few months later the Virginia assembly invited all the states to take part in a convention at Annapolis to consider trade and navigation. General Washington, James Madison, James Monroe, and Alexander Hamilton were among those who hoped great things might come from this convention.

At the appointed time, September 11, 1786, delegates assembled from five states—Virginia, Pennsylvania, Delaware, New York, and New Jersey. With only five states represented, the convention could not accomplish the purpose for which it was called. Yet it did something which proved of far greater importance. At the suggestion of Alexander Hamilton the delegates recommended a second convention to meet in Philadelphia the following year for the

167

purpose of considering much-needed changes in the Articles of Confederation.

The Virginia legislature chose George Washington as a delegate to the proposed convention at Philadelphia. The news was greeted with joy throughout the land. New Jersey, Pennsylvania, North Carolina, and Delaware appointed delegates. Congress decided to fall into line by sending out a formal call for a convention. All the remaining states except Rhode Island then made plans to take part.

1787: The Philadelphia Convention Meets

The convention called to revise the Articles of Confederation met at Philadelphia in May, 1787. The states sent their most distinguished citizens.

The majority of the fifty-five delegates were lawyers, most of them with considerable experience in public life. There were also wealthy landowners, planters, moneylenders, and merchants, and a sprinkling of college professors, physicians, and retired ministers. The delegates represented the conservative, propertied class. Small farmers, wage earners, and frontier settlers were not represented.

The convention chose George Washington as its presiding officer. Although he could take no part in the debate, his opinions carried great weight. James Madison of Virginia, a scholar

Poorly printed paper bills like these were issued by the states in the late 1770's to make up for the shortage of cash in circulation. But the merchants did not trust them, because too many were issued, and they swiftly lost value. This period of "inflation," or "cheap money," made many men turn to the idea of a stronger central government—one which would be able to control the currency of the Colonies as a whole.

in the field of government, took a leading part in the convention's work. He made careful notes of the proceedings day by day, and these were published after all the delegates had died, as Madison's *Journal of the Constitutional Convention.* Madison's *Journal* is our chief source of information concerning the debates and discussions in the Constitutional Convention. Another well-known delegate was the aged Benjamin Franklin, whose wit and homely common sense kept the members in good humor during the most trying hours. Gouverneur Morris of Pennsylvania, brilliant in writing and debate, was responsible for the final wording and arrangement of the Constitution.

Although the convention had been called for the sole purpose of recommending changes in the Articles of Confederation, most of the delegates believed that a new plan of government must be developed. The convention therefore simply threw aside the Articles and decided to write a wholly new constitution.

Ironing Out Differences of Opinion

One of the major disagreements in the convention resulted because the states were unequal in area, wealth, and population. The small states were fearful that the large ones would control the new national government.

A second question dividing the delegates was whether the national government or the states should be supreme. The experiences of the Confederation had shown the necessity for a stronger central government, but many people still believed that each state should be sovereign, that is, supreme. The small states were more anxious to keep their complete independence than the larger ones, since they feared that they would never have enough influence in the new government to prevent the passage of bills which they thought might injure them.

A third difference among the delegates was in their attitude toward democracy. Should the new constitution enable the masses of people to control the government, or should it give control to wealthy landholders and other men in important positions? Most of the delegates were afraid of democracy, believing that the masses of people were inclined to be rash and lawless.

The differences in the convention appeared in two general proposals of union. These are now called the Virginia and New Jersey plans or the "large-states plan" and the "small-states plan." James Madison prepared the Virginia plan, which called for a strong central government in which the states should have representatives in proportion to their population or their wealth. Delegates from the small states said that they would never accept this proposal. William Paterson of New Jersey proposed another plan, reserving more power to the states and giving them equal representation in Congress.

The two plans were debated for days. The most difficult question to settle was how the states were to be represented in the new government. At times there seemed no hope of reaching an agreement. Finally the convention adopted what has come to be known as the "Great Compromise." It was agreed to have two houses in Congress—the House of Representatives, in which the states are represented according to their populations and the Senate, in which the states are represented equally. It was then decided to form a federal government —one in which the powers of government are clearly divided between states and central government.

How Power Was Divided

The powers of the federal government were carefully listed. Among these powers are the right to lay taxes, to borrow money, to coin money, to fix weights and measures, to regulate foreign and interstate commerce, to raise and support an army, and to declare war. Congress was also given the power to "make all laws which shall be necessary and proper for carrying into execution the foregoing powers."

To prevent confusion, certain powers were denied the states. The states are not to coin money, to issue bills of credit (that is, paper money), to lay duties on imports, to enter into treaties, or to violate contracts (for example, by preventing the collection of debts). Many

of the difficulties that had arisen during the Confederation were due to these very actions by the states.

The convention intended that all powers not granted to the federal government and not prohibited to the states should be considered as reserved to the states. Despite this concern of the convention about division of power, many cases have arisen where it was not clear whether the power to do a certain thing belongs to the federal or to the state governments. Such cases often come before the Supreme Court for decision.

The convention decided that the federal government should have three branches—the *legislative*, to make the laws; the *executive*, to see that the laws are carried out; and the *judicial*, to administer justice and safeguard the rights of individuals. The three branches were to be separate; each was to be a check on the others.

Because of the controls that each branch has upon the others, our federal government is often said to be a system of "checks and balances." By creating checks and balances the framers of the Constitution hoped to prevent the government from taking hasty and unwise actions that might be demanded by the masses of people.

The delegates realized that the Constitution was not perfect and that changes might become necessary. The delegates intended to make the amending process difficult, and they succeeded. A small number of states can block a change desired by the rest. Of the hundreds of amendments which have been proposed, twenty-three have been adopted.

In September, 1787, after nearly four months of wearisome work, the Philadelphia convention held its last meeting. Only three of the delegates present refused to sign.

Getting the Constitution Adopted

According to the Articles of Confederation any change in the government had to be ratified by the legislatures of all thirteen states. The delegates at Philadelphia thought it unlikely that all the state legislatures would accept their work, so they proposed that each state hold a convention to consider the Con-

169

stitution. When such conventions in nine states had given their approval, the Constitution would go into effect for those states, no matter what the other four decided.

As soon as the Constitution was published, people divided themselves into two groups—the Federalists, who wished to ratify the Constitution, and the Antifederalists, who opposed ratification. The Federalists were chiefly from the commercial, moneylending, and planting classes, which had tried so long to strengthen the central government. The Antifederalists were chiefly from the debtor and small farmer classes. Both parties had strong, able leaders.

The country was flooded with pamphlets and newspaper articles. Some of the ablest articles in defense of the Constitution were written by Alexander Hamilton, James Madison, and John Jay. They were printed in New York newspapers and were later gathered together in a single, famous volume called *The Federalist*.

The three states in which the contest was closest were Massachusetts, Virginia, and New York. The Federalists won in Massachusetts by a narrow margin after they promised to recommend adding a bill of rights to the Constitution. Massachusetts was the sixth state to ratify. Every state but one which ratified after Massachusetts recommended similar amendments.

In Virginia the influence of George Washington and James Madison brought victory after a hard struggle. By 1788 then every state but New York, North Carolina, and Rhode Island had ratified. The Constitution was now certain to go into effect. Yet without central and powerful New York the Union might be hopelessly handicapped. When the New York Convention met in June, two-thirds of its members were Antifederalists. After a month of fiery argument Alexander Hamilton converted the best speaker on the Antifederalist side. Then other Antifederalists changed sides. New York ratified by the close vote of 30 to 27. North Carolina did not ratify until November, 1789, and Rhode Island held out until May, 1790. Government under the new Constitution was launched in the spring of 1789.

The Fathers of the Constitution

Here is a list of the men who went to the Philadelphia Convention of 1787 to help make some changes in the Articles of Confederation. About 75 men were appointed delegates by the states, but only 55 ever showed up. Of these, the 39 marked with stars stayed to sign the entirely new Constitution which the convention drafted. The names of the 55 who attended are arranged according to the states from which they came. Rhode Island did not send any delegates.

Connecticut:	Delaware:	Georgia:	Maryland:
William Samuel Johnson* Roger Sherman* Oliver Ellsworth	George Read* Gunning Bedford, Jr.* John Dickinson* Richard Bassett* Jacob Broom*	William Few* Abraham Baldwin* William Pierce William Houston	Dr. James McHenry* Daniel Jenifer* Daniel Carroll* John Francis Mercer Luther Martin

Massachusetts:	New Hampshire:	New Jersey:	New York:
Elbridge Gerry Nathaniel Gorham* Rufus King* Caleb Strong	John Langdon* Nicholas Gilman*	David Brearly* William C. Houston William Paterson* William Livingston* Captain Jonathan Dayton*	Robert Yates John Lansing Alexander Hamilton*

North Carolina:	Pennsylvania:	South Carolina:	Virginia:
Alexander Martin William R. Davie Richard D. Spaight* Dr. Hugh Williamson* William Blount*	General Thomas Mifflin* Robert Morris* George Clymer* Jared Ingersoll* Thomas Fitzsimmons* James Wilson* Gouverneur Morris* Benjamin Franklin*	John Rutledge* Charles Pinckney* Charles Cotesworth Pinckney* Pierce Butler*	George Washington* Dr. James McClurg Edmund Randolph James Blair* James Madison* George Wythe George Mason

Alexander Hamilton and the Constitution

Alexander Hamilton was born on the island of Nevis in the West Indies in 1757, and studied at King's College in New York. After the American Revolution began he served on George Washington's staff, and was later a member of the Continental Congress. He was secretary of the treasury, 1789-1795, and was killed in a duel with Aaron Burr in 1804. His part in the Constitutional Convention of 1787 is described here.

On the afternoon of June 18, 1787, a group of the most influential men in the new United States sat in the Pennsylvania State House and listened to a speech by Alexander Hamilton.

Hamilton was the minority member of a three-man delegation from New York. The other members, and many of the other delegates to the Constitutional Convention, did not share his views; but he was listened to for almost five hours on that June afternoon, while he spoke brilliantly and strongly on how he thought the new nation should establish its system of government.

There was no discussion when he had completed his speech. "Committee rose and the house adjourned," noted James Madison, who had taken notes during the session; and another delegate said, "The Gentleman from New York is praised by everyone, but supported by no one."

Shortly after this presentation of his ideas Hamilton left Philadelphia; there was, he felt, nothing he could do as one lone man against many to influence the course of events. But his ideas had been heard and would bear more fruit than he knew.

Hamilton had favored two houses for the national legislature, and suggested that the Supreme Executive be chosen "by Electors chosen for that purpose by the people in the Election Districts." When this aspect of the selection of a president arose (during debate in July), there was some hesitation; but the final wording of the part of the constitution concerning election of the president was almost exactly what Hamilton had proposed.

Another of Hamilton's proposals was that the president should have with the advice and approbation of the Senate "the power of making all treaties." This point does not appear in notes on convention proceedings during the summer; but a committee report made in September used the phrase "by and with the advice and consent of the Senate," and it was so written into the constitution.

That the president should have the power of pardoning all offences except treason was another of Hamilton's proposals which was written into the constitution almost as he stated it. And still another was that, in the event of the death, resignation or removal of the chief executive the "President of the Senate" would exercise his duties until a successor was selected.

The committee report of late July on this part of the constitution made just such a proposal, stating that "the President of the Senate [that is, the vice-president] shall exercise those powers and duties until another President of the United States shall be chosen, or until the disability of the President be removed."

A final point of Hamilton's suggestions was one which would prohibit individual states from possessing their own land or naval forces, and this was incorporated into the constitution much as he proposed it.

Thus, when Hamilton returned to Philadelphia in September 1787, he was to find that although he had not been present in person, his ideas had made a contribution to the development of several phases of the new constitution.

While it is usually considered that Alexander Hamilton played no part in the making of this vital document of our nation's history, it would appear that he had shaped the thinking of the delegates more than he had realized at the time of the speech which presented his plan. And he was soon to begin to explain and defend the constitution of the United States in the *Federalist Papers,* which did much to make its adoption a reality.

What Does the Constitution Say?

The United States Constitution was drawn up by lawyers, who tried to put it in language which the eighteenth-century legal mind could clearly understand. For the average man of today, the Constitution is rather hard to read and follow. Below you will find an outline of the Constitution and its amendments in simpler language than the originals. Compiled by the editor.

Article I Is About Congress

Article I is the longest of the seven articles of the Constitution. It constitutes the Congress. In other words, it says how Congress shall be elected, who may sit in Congress, and what powers Congress shall have. (For more about Congress, see "The Congress of the United States" in Volume 16, page 342.) At the end of Article I there are a few general clauses. The first was intended to gain the support of the South for the Constitution. It forbids Congress to stop the import of persons whom the states see fit to admit (meaning slaves) before the year 1808. The next two provisions were intended to secure the liberties of the individual. The fourth requires any direct tax laid by Congress to be levied in proportion to the population of the states as given by the census. Then come some more rules for handling money and taxes. Another clause forbids the United States to grant any titles of nobility. The last section of Article I lists certain powers which the states must not exercise.

Article II Is About the President

The second article is the second longest. It constitutes the executive, that is, the Presidency. Article II lays down how long a presidential term shall be (but not how many terms one man may hold the office of President; the 22nd amendment does that), how the President and Vice-President shall be elected (changed slightly in 1804 by the twelfth amendment), the presidential succession in the event of death in office, the form of the inaugural oath, and the powers and chief duties of the President. (For more about the Presidency, see "The Executive of the United States" in Volume 13, page 261.)

Article III Is About the Federal Courts

Article III requires Congress to set up a judiciary, or system of courts of justice, and lays down certain rules for running them. The article says there shall be a Supreme Court and such lesser courts as Congress shall establish. The jurisdiction of the United States courts is outlined—that is, what kinds of cases they can try. Article III requires that all crimes

The original draft of the United States Constitution may now be seen in a special, airtight case (doors open in front), which stands over the originals of the Declaration of Independence and the Bill of Rights in the National Archives Building, Washington, D.C.

Nat'l Archives

be tried by jury, defines treason against the United States, and protects the rights of the heirs of traitors.

Article IV Is About the States

Article IV lays down certain rules affecting relations between the states, and between the states and the United States. All the acts, records, and judgments of any state are to be recognized in all the other states. A citizen of any state is entitled to the privileges of citizenship in all the states. States must deliver up criminals, who have fled from another state, for trial in the state where their crimes were committed. Fugitive servants or slaves ("persons held to service") who run away to a state where the laws don't allow enforced service are not to be freed, but to be handed over on demand to the person who has a claim on their service. New states can be admitted to the Union, but these are not to be carved out of existing states, nor to be formed by joining together existing states or parts of states, unless Congress and the state legislatures concerned agree on the move. Congress is to have control over the territory and property of the United States. The United States shall make sure that every state has a republican form of government and shall protect every state against invasion. If the legislature or governor of a state asks for help in putting down a rebellion or other civil disorder, Con-gress shall go to the aid of that state in quelling the disturbance.

Article V Is About Amendments

Article V gives the procedure for amending the Constitution. An amendment can be put forward in two ways: (1) when two-thirds of each house of Congress proposes one or (2) when one is proposed by a convention called by Congress on the application of two-thirds of the state legislatures. An amendment will become valid and a part of the Constitution when ratified by (1) three-fourths of the state legislatures or (2) popular conventions held in three-fourths of the states. Congress is to propose which method of ratification shall be followed. But no amendment restricting the slave trade, says Article V, is to be made before 1808. This provision is out of date and so no longer valid. No amendment is to be made which takes away a state's equal representation in the Senate.

Article VI Is About Several Matters

Article VI deals with the debts, laws, and oaths of office of the United States. The United States under the new Constitution is to take over and pay all debts of the central government under the old Constitution. The Constitution, laws, and treaties of the United States are to be the supreme law of the land. State judges are to be bound by this rule, what-

Separation of Powers

The power of the federal government in the United States is divided in three parts, as shown below. This "separation of powers," as it is called, is required by the Constitution, and is meant to prevent too much power being concentrated in any one man or group of men.

". . . all legislative power granted herein shall be vested in a Congress . . ."

"The judicial power shall be vested in a Supreme Court and in such inferior courts as Congress may from time to time ordain and establish."

"The executive power shall be vested in a President . . ."

173

The amendments of the "Reconstruction period" after the Civil War (the 13th, 14th, and 15th) gave freedom to the slave, made him a citizen of the United States and of his home state, and gave the United States power to protect his rights of citizenship, including the right to vote. Here you see Uncle Sam pulling off "Mr. State Legislature," when he tries to interfere with the freedman's rights.

ever their state constitutions or laws say. All congressmen, United States officials, state legislators, and state officials are to take an oath to support the Constitution of the United States. But nobody shall ever be made to take any kind of religious test as a requirement for service with the United States government.

Article VII Is About Getting the Constitution Accepted

Article VII lays down the way in which the new Constitution is to be ratified. Fearing that all thirteen states might never reach agreement to adopt the Constitution, the Fathers in Philadelphia made the rule that conventions in only nine states need ratify the Constitution. When they had done so, the Constitution would be in operation as far as those nine states were concerned. Thus four states might be left out in the cold. (As it turned out, North Carolina and Rhode Island, the twelfth and thirteenth states, did not ratify the Constitution until after it had gone into operation in 1789.)

The original Constitution ends with the date (September 17, 1787) and 39 signatures, which represent all twelve of the states that sent delegates to Philadelphia. (Rhode Island was the only state that sent no delegates.)

The Amendments Begin

The first ten amendments (the Bill of Rights) of 1791 were concerned with safeguarding the liberty of the individual. The tenth says that all powers not given to the United States by the Constitution are reserved to the various states or to the people. This is the famous "reserved powers" rule, which stresses the fact that all power comes ultimately from the people.

The eleventh amendment (1795) says that the federal courts have no jurisdiction (right to try) over cases arising out of a suit brought against one of the states by the citizen of another state or of a foreign country. The twelfth amendment (1804) changed the system for electing the President and Vice-President.

The Reconstruction Amendments

The thirteenth amendment (1865) abolished slavery in the United States. The fourteenth amendment (1868) declared all persons born in the United States to be citizens of the United States and of the state where they lived. No state was to pass laws taking away the privileges of United States citizens. These provisions were intended to safeguard the rights of the freed slaves. The states were prohibited from taking away anybody's life, freedom, or property without "due process of law," that is, a properly conducted trial by qualified judges. If the states denied the vote to any of their citizens (the freedmen, for instance), they were to have the number of their congressmen reduced in proportion. Those persons found guilty of rebellion were not to be allowed to hold any office in the United States government. The debts of the Confederacy (the states in the South which were in rebellion from 1861 to 1865) were to be held illegal and void. The fifteenth amendment (1870) forbade the United States or the state governments to deny the vote to anybody on account of his race or former condition of

In 1920, the 19th amendment forbade the states to prevent women from voting, and gave Uncle Sam the power to enforce this rule.

By the 18th amendment of 1919, Uncle Sam prohibited the use of alcoholic beverages, but did away with prohibition by the 21st amendment of 1933. States still have the right to prohibit such beverages.

slavery. In other words, the Southern States must allow the freedmen to vote. As you can see, Amendments XIII, XIV, and XV were intended to settle matters arising out of the Civil War.

The Eight Amendments Since 1913

The sixteenth amendment (1913) gave the United States the power to collect a tax on incomes without the restrictions mentioned in Article I of the Constitution. The seventeenth amendment (1913) introduced election of United States senators by the people, instead of by the state legislatures. The eighteenth amendment (1919) introduced the prohibition of alcoholic beverages. The nineteenth amendment (1920) gave women the vote.

The twentieth amendment (1933) put the inauguration date for presidential terms back from March 4 to January 20. This did away with the "lame duck" session of Congress, between January and March. (Under the old system, when the newly chosen President took office many weeks after the new Congress, the lawmakers couldn't get much done until things settled down after March 4, the date when the new President was always inaugurated.) The twenty-first amendment (1933) repealed the eighteenth, so as to make it once more legal to make and sell alcoholic beverages. The twenty-second amendment (1951) gave legal force to the old custom, started by Washington, by which no man held the office of President for more than two terms. This amendment allows a man to succeed a President who dies in office more than half way through his term, and then to run for election

twice; however, if a man serves as President for more than half a term, he can be elected only once. The twenty-third amendment (1961) gave residents of Washington, D.C., the right to vote in presidential elections.

The twenty-fourth amendment (1964) abolished the payment of poll tax as a requirement for voting in Federal elections. The twenty-fifth amendment (1967) stipulated the line of succession if the President dies, resigns, or becomes disabled.

Other Sections To See

"Documents of American Democracy," Volume 3; "Free Elections: Keystone of Democracy," Volume 7; "Business in Action," "Business Enterprise and Freedom," and "Government and Business," Volume 10; "The Executive of the United States," Volume 13; "The Courts of the United States," Volume 14; "The Congress of the United States," Volume 16.

Other Books To Read

Your Rugged Constitution, by Bruce Allyn Findlay and Esther Blair Findlay. Published by Stanford University Press, Stanford, California; available in several editions.
A clause-by-clause explanation of the United States Constitution and its amendments.
The Supreme Court, by Gerald W. Johnson. Published by William Morrow and Company, Inc., New York, 1962.
A description of the history and duties of the branch of government that has the deciding voice in interpreting the Constitution and applying its clauses to our daily lives.

175

Dodo bird, symbol of vanished animals.

Smithsonian Inst.

Vanishing Animal Life —

Why do certain kinds of animal life disappear from the earth when they were once abundant and played a useful or interesting part in our world?

In the geologic past, tremendous changes in the earth's surface, the waters, the soil, and the climate must have blotted out many animal species by destroying their natural food and cover. Other species died out because the course of their evolution had brought them to a stage where they could not successfully compete for existence with other animals. But always, as the millions of years rolled by, there was room enough for the new animals which appeared as other species died out.

Since man began to populate the earth it has become more and more difficult for many forms of animal life to survive. Reshaping the earth's surface for his own use, man has robbed animals of living space and food. We drain marshes, cut down forests, clear underbrush from our fields, often pollute waters with our industries, plow up prairies, and cover once wild areas with our networks of cities, towns, villages, farms, and roads. With man whittling away their old territories, many animal populations have shrunk to the point where an epidemic of sickness or a catastrophe of weather can wipe out the remaining few at one blow.

People have also destroyed wildlife for food, clothing, and sport. We need animal food and products to live, but we have killed more than we needed and have not cared for the wildlife that was left. Passenger pigeons once existed by the billions in the eastern two-thirds of the United States, but they were shot and sold by the barrel until they became extinct. Trappers, unmindful of their own future livelihoods, have almost killed off many small fur-bearing animals. Unsportsman-like hunters, who could not resist bringing down something big, have almost robbed us of such species as the whooping crane, the grizzly bear, the elk, and the caribou.

In this section you will find a surprising survey of the damage that has been done to North American and also some world species. There are articles on species we have lost, such as the dodo bird pictured here. (See page 187 for more about the dodo.) You will find articles on wildlife saved just in time, on other wildlife that is still threatened, and information on how conservation methods are helping to save animal life. This volume also contains many other interesting sections on animals.

—Margaret Tomec Zamiska

Photos, Allen D. Cruickshank from Nat'l Audubon Soc.

In a few places on the coasts of Texas and Louisiana, and in southern Florida, the roseate spoonbill makes its home. The adult spoonbill, over thirty inches long, is fairly quiet, except for an occasional croaking sound. Spoonbills were once hunted for their plumes, which were used on women's hats, and the bird was near extinction. Today, the spoonbill is protected in guarded sanctuaries.

Animals That Man Protects

The beautiful wild turkey, once found throughout North America from New England to the Mexican plateau, now is seen only in a few areas along the eastern seaboard, and in the Aransas National Wildlife Refuge in Texas. It can be distinguished from the domestic turkey by the chestnut-colored tips of its tail feathers. The tips of the domestic turkey's tail are white or brownish-yellow.

U. S. Forest Service photo by Leland J. Prater

No history of western America would be complete without the story of the bison, or buffalo. At one time over 50 million bison roamed the open spaces between the Appalachians and the Rockies. With advancing settlement their numbers inevitably decreased, and in the late 19th century they were slaughtered in vast quantities. Under government protection, the few hundred bison left in 1900 have multiplied until there are now over 10,000 in the United States and about 15,000 in Canada.

Allen D. Cruickshank from Nat'l Audubon Soc.

The pure white plumage of the great white heron makes it an easy target for hunters. Because its feathers have been prized for women's hats, and because of droughts and storms, the number of herons in America dwindled to a few living in southern Florida. Now, under legal protection, the great white heron population is increasing.

Chicago Nat. Hist. Mus.

Fisher

Wildlife in Peril

Almost everyone can think of some form of wildlife that is vanishing from the American scene. But perhaps few people realize the great numbers of North American species that are almost past hope of survival unless man helps. Here is a detailed report on the situation. From **Conserving Endangered Wildlife Species** by Hartley H. T. Jackson, using material from the Smithsonian Report for 1945. Revised by editor, 1963.

North America has a long list of endangered wildlife races—perhaps fifty in number. All of them, except for one or two marine forms, occur in the United States.

Several of the grizzly bears have vanished, and, except for Canada and Alaska, it seems that Yellowstone National Park and Glacier National Park offer about the only real hope for their preservation. Black bears as a group are reasonably safe, yet the Florida black bear is extremely rare and is decreasing in numbers. That frosty-gray bear of the black bear group, the glacier bear of Alaska, is so scarce as to face extinction, but its remote and almost inaccessible habitat may save it.

Fur Fatalities

The fisher, the marten, and the wolverine have all been trapped so extensively for fur that except for a few fishers in New England and New York they are almost gone from the United States and have been reduced to the danger point everywhere in North America. The black-footed ferret, with a geographic range almost like the prairie dog's, was never a common mammal, but has become rarer and rarer, until now it is seldom reported. The southern sea otter was a few years ago believed to be extinct, when unexpectedly a small herd was discovered south of Carmel, Monterey County, on the coast of California. This herd now numbers about a thousand or more. It is protected and guarded carefully, and with proper management the race may be saved from extinction.

The little kit fox of the western plains was not only easily trapped for its fur but also frequently was caught in traps set for coyotes and other animals. No restrictions seem to have been placed on killing it, and what was once a common mammal is now rare, and in many regions gone.

The timber wolf of the northeastern states could hardly be expected to withstand settlements and civilization and has almost given up the fight. In fact, all the large wolves of the United States are endangered. The eastern puma, or cougar, has been almost exterminated. Among the other cougars, the Florida subspecies is the most endangered, there being almost none left.

Several of our seals are so reduced in numbers as to cause serious concern for them. The Guadalupe fur seal of the west coast of Mexico has reached too low a population for its safety, a few hundred at the last count, and both the West Indian monk seal and the Pacific monk seal have become rare and reduced to local habitats. The oddity of seals, the elephant seal of the Pacific Coast, has shown some recovery, but is still in an endangered condition. On the North Atlantic Coast, the beautiful hooded seal has been hunted for oil and fur until it, too, is in danger. The Pacific walrus, while in some danger, is not reduced to the vanishing stage, as appears to be the case with the Atlantic walrus.

Game Animals

We correctly think of the white-tailed deer

179

as our most abundant big-game animal, yet they became scarce in many parts of the country because of slaughter. Since laws were passed protecting them, they have increased until they now number about 5,000,000. The key deer, inhabiting a few of the lower Florida Keys, was very rare, local in distribution, and probably did not number more than 100 individuals a few years ago. It was reduced by the hurricane of 1937, and was overhunted and subjected to poaching (illegal hunting) until only a few remained. Now, it is increasing, however.

When the mad rush for gold was on in California during the middle of the nineteenth century, the great valley of California, the combined valleys of the San Joaquin and the Sacramento rivers, abounded in a small elk with simple antlers, the California valley or tule elk. It soon became scarce. A remnant was protected on the Miller and Lux Ranch, Buttonwillow, Kern County, California. In an effort to save these animals, which may have reached a low of 350 or 400 animals in 1921, some were transplanted to Yosemite and Sequoia National Parks. In 1933 all of these, and several from the Buttonwillow herd, were transferred to a reservation with good elk-pasture features in Owens Valley. Today there probably exist only very limited numbers of these elk, confined mainly in huge refuges in several California counties.

Last of the Caribou and Bighorns

The last woodland caribou seen in Maine were near Mount Katahdin in 1908. They had disappeared from New Hampshire and Vermont about the middle of the nineteenth century. Fifteen occurred in northern Minnesota in 1938, only two of which were native, the others being from stock brought in from Saskatchewan. This herd is now believed to be extinct in the United States. In Canada, also, the woodland caribou is vanishing. The eastern moose, while not in so much immediate danger as the woodland caribou, is nevertheless rapidly approaching a dangerous situation.

All our bighorn sheep should give us cause for worry. Two forms are in especial danger.

The Sierra bighorn has been reduced to a very low level, and the Texas bighorn, at one time thought to be totally destroyed, is reduced to a remnant scattered in six or eight mountain ranges. Its fight for survival, in competition with domestic sheep and goats and in the face of illegal hunting, is almost hopeless. The desert bighorn apparently has been saved by the establishment of national refuges for its preservation in Arizona, Nevada, and New Mexico. Hunting laws and ranges are also helping to save the Rocky Mountain bighorn.

Saving the Musk Ox

Unique among all mammals, the odd-looking musk ox, which resembles a miniature shaggy-haired buffalo and combines certain features of cattle and sheep, is dwindling except for a few places in Canada. Although formerly occurring in the barren grounds from northern Alaska to eastern Greenland, it is at present found native only on the east coast of Greenland and in Arctic barrens directly north and northwest of Hudson Bay as far as about latitude 83°. Even within these ranges musk oxen inhabit only certain areas, and there are immense expanses where none occur. A herd of 31 Greenland animals introduced in 1936 on the Nunivak Island National Wildlife Refuge, Alaska, is prospering. The Canadian government has also set aside a refuge, and the herds there are also increasing.

The Disappearing Mermaid

Stories and legends about mermaids originated in superstitions about those peculiar aquatic mammals, the dugongs and the manatees. In their present distribution, dugongs inhabit only parts of the Eastern Hemisphere, whereas the three species of manatees occur only in the Atlantic coastal waters of America from Florida to Brazil. The manatees are harmless mammals that feed on aquatic vegetation. They were once killed for meat and oil. The most northerly form, the Florida manatee, is now protected by law. Manatees migrate south because they dislike cold water. Sudden drops in temperature to freezing, or two or three nights of freezing weather, often kill manatees. Even some of our smaller game mammals need especial protection if we expect them to continue as a part of our wildlife. The northeastern fox squirrel and the mangrove fox squirrel are both at the vanishing point.

Vanishing Wings

There are many North American birds that are in a more or less uncertain situation as to their future existence. Some of these, such as Leach's petrel, reddish egret, Franklin's grouse, southern white-tailed ptarmigan, sage hen, golden plover, and upland plover, it would appear are holding their own. Possibly they are even on the uptrend, though once greatly reduced in numbers and hard pressed. Others are in the more threatened class. The great white heron population of extreme southern Florida appears to have become stabilized in relation to the habitat available on the Great White Heron and Key West national wildlife refuges, where most of the nesting occurs. The roseate spoonbill, beautifully colored and grotesque of bill as the name implies, is possibly in more danger as a nester in the United States than the great white heron, though actually at present more birds exist. It is found in the same general region of Florida as the great white heron, but has another chance for survival in a larger colony in Texas and a few small ones in Louisiana. There are also a considerable number of the birds in Mexico. The Florida nesting birds are decreasing in numbers. The Texas nesters have increased, but are in constant danger of destruction through oil development. (You may be interested in these: "Birds of the Sea and Shore and Other Water Birds," in Volume 2, and "Land Birds of North America," in Volume 5.)

Preying on Birds of Prey

Many of our birds of prey, even though actually beneficial species, have been shot on sight as harmful, or considered legitimate targets on which to test marksmanship. Practically all species of this group have been reduced in numbers. Probably the most seriously endangered is the California condor, masterful airman of graceful flight and grandeur, and man's benefactor as a destroyer of carrion. The California condor formerly ranged west of the Sierra Nevadas from Washington to Lower California, and in the days of the forty-niners was not rare. It is now reduced to alarmingly few survivors, most of which make their home in a 35,000-acre sanctuary within the Los Padros National Forest. Two other birds of graceful flight and beauty and both of harmless habits, the white-tailed kite of the southwestern United States and the Everglade kite of Florida, are extremely reduced in numbers. The whitetail is probably in less danger than the Everglade, since its present distribution is more extensive and it is known to nest in several scattered colonies. The Everglade kite, however, is known to nest in the United States only in the vicinity of Lake Okeechobee, Florida, where there are only a few pairs of birds.

Threatened Wildfowl

Three of our ground-dwelling fowl are approaching the vanishing point. None of the existing races of prairie chickens is in any too satisfactory a position. One of them, Attwater's prairie chicken, is reduced to approximately a few thousand birds inhabiting scarcely more than five per cent of the former range of the race on the Gulf Coast area of Texas. The population of these prairie chickens has been reduced not only by hunting but also by general agricultural and grazing practices. The masked bobwhite, formerly occurring in fair numbers within the United States near the Mexican border, has almost disappeared except for a few local colonies. The eastern wild turkey, a few years ago had all but disappeared as a pure-strain wild turkey. It is now re-established in parts of its former range —the region of the lower Santee River in South Carolina, in Francis Marion National Forest. Under the direction of the United States Fish and Wildlife Service, fifteen birds from this region were placed on Bull's Island, South Carolina, a national wildlife refuge, in 1939–40. The annual increase from this refuge is being used to establish other flocks of pure-strain wild birds.

181

Man-sized Target

The whooping crane, a white bird nearly man high, formerly occurred during migration from the Atlantic Coast south to Georgia and west to the foot of the Rocky Mountains, was known to nest from Iowa and Nebraska north and northwest to Hudson Bay and Mackenzie, and wintered in huge flocks in the Gulf States. Being big and conspicuous, and an inhabitant of the open places, it afforded "something to shoot at" for the unprincipled gunner who was out only to kill. Its population is still only a few dozen birds, although strenuous efforts have been made to protect them.

The Florida sandhill crane, a grayish bird confined to a few nesting areas in Florida and one in Georgia, is dwindling in numbers.

Some shore birds are becoming scarce, even though protected through the Migratory Bird Treaty Act. The last specimen record of an Eskimo curlew for the United States was in Nebraska in April, 1915, though a bird was collected in Argentina in January, 1925. One was reported as a sight record from Hastings, Nebraska, April 8, 1926. There are no reliable records since then, and the species is probably gone. Of other shore birds, the Hudsonian godwit seemed to be near the vanishing point. It nests on the barren grounds from Alaska to Hudson Bay, and migrates to South America where it winters. It became greatly reduced during the game-marketing days of the eighties and nineties, but is now making a comeback.

Largest and most magnificent woodpecker in the United States, the ivory-billed woodpecker is now reduced to a few individuals, and may even be extinct. If any are left, they are in a heavily forested tract in Louisiana. Dense forests of large trees are essential for the existence of the ivorybill. Unless its Louisiana home can be saved from the lumberman's ax, the ivorybill is surely doomed.

Three of our small perching birds have approached the danger line. One of these, the dusky kinglet, a midget bird of Guadalupe Island, Lower California, may now have followed other vanished birds on that island. Bachman's warbler of the southeastern United States, always in recent times a rare bird,

barely maintains its population, and in general its status causes concern. The Ipswich sparrow, a species related to the savanna sparrow, has a breeding range restricted to small Sable Island, Nova Scotia, and in winter is found from there south along the sand dunes of the Atlantic Coast to Georgia. On Sable Island it nests only near the beach. Waves from severe storms may at any time destroy its nesting habitat.

Tears for the Crocodile

The American crocodile has decreased in numbers. The crocodile never occurred within the United States boundaries proper except in extreme southern Florida. It differs from the alligator in its longer and slenderer body, its much more pointed snout, and longer teeth. Both the crocodile and the alligator have been hunted for their hides for use in leather manufacture. Many of them have also been wantonly killed out of sheer prejudice and hatred for an ungainly reptilian with an unfriendly appearance. The catching of the young of both species and their sale as pets to be transplanted to an unsuitable northern climate has killed hundreds of them. The crocodile is almost a relic of the past.

Of our highly edible fishes, two species of sturgeons, the common and the lake, have been so reduced in numbers, largely by commercial fisheries, that they have not only become of little commercial importance but are in actual danger of extinction. And on our eastern coast, the thousands of Atlantic salmon that formerly, early in summer, ascended many of the New England streams to spawn, now migrate only by hundreds to one or two rivers, more notably the Penobscot.

Other Sections To See

"How Animals Survive," Volume 1; "Big Game Animals," Volume 8; A Survey of the Animal Kingdom," Volume 9; "Odd and Unusual Animals," Volume 14; "Animal Behavior," Volume 16; "Presenting the Primates," Volume 17.

Where Are Our Vanishing Animals?

*These maps show how the ranges of many species of wildlife have shrunk in the United States.
On each map, the species shown inhabited approximately the shaded and solid black
areas at one time. Now, the species inhabits approximately the area shown in solid black.
Three maps show the former range of species that have disappeared completely, the
passenger pigeon, the woodland caribou, and the heath hen. The eastern turkey, almost extinct, is
occasionally seen. Big-game mammals and other wildlife threatened with extinction in Alaska
now have the protection of 11½ million acres of National Wildlife Ranges.*

pronghorn   heath hen

grizzly bear   Florida black bear

bison

black-footed ferret

kit fox

fisher

mountain lion (including Florida cougar)

marten

bighorn sheep   woodland caribou

timber wolf

wolverine

California condor

Florida sandhill crane

whooping crane

Attwater's prairie chicken

roseate spoonbill

passenger pigeon

eastern turkey

183

U.S. Fish & Wildlife Serv., by Susott

Passenger Pigeon

Though the American passenger pigeon is believed by some naturalists to have lived in greater numbers than any other vertebrate land animal on record, it was wiped out by 1914. The 17-inch long bird lived in great colonies in eastern and middle North America. Used for food, it was over-hunted during its breeding season.

California Condor

Original habitat: Pacific Coast; height: 4 ft.; wingspread 9-10 ft.; color: dark gray-black; lives on carrion (decaying flesh or refuse); uses rock nests. Now found in only one California valley. This bird lives in a zoo.

184

Prairie Chicken

Habitat: North America; height: 18 in.; color: rust, gray; lives and nests on ground; hunted for its fine meat. (See Volume 1 for more information about the prairie chicken.)

Texas Game & Fish Comm'n

Amer. Mus. Nat. Hist.

American Crocodile

Habitat: tropic, southern Florida; length: about 12 ft.; color: green-brown; lives in water and swamps; sluggish. Hunted for leather, and because people often dislike reptiles.

N.Y. Zool. Soc.

Lake Sturgeon

Habitat: Northern Hemisphere; length: 5-6 ft.; weight: 30-40 lbs.; rough hide, long snout; lives in deep fresh water; rapidly decreasing.

Amer. Mus. Nat. Hist.

Atlantic Salmon

Habitat: North Atlantic and its margins; length: 4 ft.; thick shape; spawns in rivers; lives on other fish; a popular game fish; few left.

Whooping Crane

Original habitat: North America; height: 4-4½ ft.; wingspread: 7½ ft.; color: white with some black; migratory; eats fish; noted for booming cry and leaping courtship dance. This female was photographed at the Aransas National Wildlife Refuge in Texas.

U.S. Fish & Wildlife Serv., by Howard

Elephant Seal

Habitat: sea margins of the Southern Hemisphere; once abundant on islands off Lower California; length: up to 20 ft. for old males; hunted for oil. This is a zoo specimen.

Black Star, by Seidenstucke

Woodland Caribou

Habitat: Canada; formerly northern United States, also; length: 7 ft.; color: brown-white; antlered forest animal; eats lichen. This Minnesota animal was one of the last in existence in the United States. Now believed extinct.

Minn. Dept. of Conserv., by Wettschreck

Pronghorn Antelope

Habitat: Great Plains; height: 4 ft.; color: sandy white; swiftest of American grazing animals, they are found only in North America. They are now sheltered in government refuges, and hunting is controlled.

The Great Auk:

Dead as a Dodo

The dodo bird's quick and complete disappearance from the earth, once it was discovered by the white man, has made its very name mean "extinct." It was a huge, grotesque member of the pigeon tribe, said to have been discovered first by the explorer, Vasco da Gama, in 1497 on the Indian Ocean island of Mauritius. Potbellied and awkward, it had lost the power of flight, laid its single egg on the ground, and was unsuspicious to the point of stupidity. The great auk, a bird far more useful to man than the dodo, was erased almost as quickly, as you will find in this article. From *Our Amazing Birds* by Robert S. Lemmon. Copyright 1951, 1952 by the Literary Guild of America, Inc.

Mounted specimens of the great auk and its egg.

What the larger penguin species are to the antarctic, the great auk, standing nearly three feet tall, once was to the North Atlantic from the Arctic Circle southward as far as Massachusetts and Ireland. Both birds resembled each other in some respects, black above and white below, incapable of flight because of their extremely small wings, but superb divers and underwater swimmers. The penguins survive, but the great auk is believed to have become extinct about 1844, the victim of relentless persecution by fishermen who raided its breeding islands for eggs and meat, by feather hunters seeking a substitute for eider down, and by unrestricted shooting. Today there are no more than 80 mounted specimens anywhere in the world, and about the same number of their five-inch, buffy, mottled eggs.

Not too much is known about the habits of this strange big diver, for detailed records in the days of its abundance were few and often unreliable. It was, of course, a colony nester, laid but a single egg, and, when on shore, walked or sat erect in much the same way a penguin does. It must have been a skilled underwater swimmer, probably able to catch any fish it went after, as well as to escape most of the sharks and other big ocean enemies that tried to gobble it. In this subsurface life it used feet as well as wings for propulsion, unlike the penguins, which swim underwater only with their wings and use their feet for steering.

The great auk was not as many people believe, a truly arctic bird. On the contrary, two of its most populous breeding areas were near Labrador and Newfoundland, and apparently considerable numbers of the birds used to spend the summer in the region of Cape Cod. It is believed, too, that a definite southward movement took place in the fall and winter, carrying a few of the birds even as far as Florida. It is not known whether this was a true migration such as motivates so many of our flying birds, or merely a following of some favorite food fish which sought warmer waters during the cold weather. In either case, it was an amazingly long distance to swim, for the auk could not fly at all.

The world has seen many instances of man's reckless destruction of other forms of life which surrounded him, but somehow the case of the great auk is particularly discreditable. That millions of such harmless, half-helpless birds should have been exterminated is a far from pretty picture for us to acknowledge.

187

Saving the Trumpeter Swan

Trumpeter swans in flight over Red Rock Lakes, waterfowl refuge, Montana. There are now about 650 trumpeters in the United States.

U.S. Fish & Wildlife Serv., by Banko

Here is the story of how an unusual assortment of people—a president, hunters, and radio announcers—helped conservation officials rescue the beautiful trumpeter swan. The selection from Daniel B. Beard, chairman of a committee of the United States Department of the Interior, National Park Service: **Fading Trails.** Copyright 1942 by The Macmillan Company and used with The Macmillan Company's permission.

Trumpeter swans are the largest of North American waterfowl. Their weights run from 20 pounds to as high as 36 pounds. They are usually over 55 inches long, with a wing of more than 23 inches. The trumpet call of the adult can be heard for over two miles.

Unfortunately for these great North American swans, the pioneers and trappers who lived in the United States and Canada lacked the reverence and superstition which their Old World ancestors held for them. Swan's-down was discovered to be excellent material for stuffing pillows, lining muffs, edging babies' hats, and for making powder puffs. Swans' feathers set off the fragile daintiness of the nineteenth century belles, in the form of useless trimmings on dresses and hats. Consequently, traffic in swanskins (trumpeters' and whistler swans') from interior North America started early.

It has been estimated that between 1853 and 1877 the Hudson's Bay Company sold a total of 17,671 swanskins. The number sold annually ranged from 1,312 in 1854 to 122 in 1877.

It is impossible to determine just how many of the skins taken in that particular span of years were trumpeters'. However, it is certain that many were killed because the range of trumpeter swans corresponded with the areas occupied by man, or where heavy trapping and hunting were taking place.

Trumpeter swans were found in British Columbia and northwestern Canada, east through the prairie country, and south into the United States to include mountainous sections of Idaho; and east through most of North Dakota, South Dakota, and parts of Minnesota and Iowa. The southern boundary of their breeding area has been mapped through the northern half of Nebraska and about the northern two-thirds of Wyoming. In general, this was the original distribution of trumpeter swans, although casual records of them were made elsewhere. This is also an area now taken over by farms, ranches, and other forms of human enterprise. In the mountains, trappers plied their trade and the plains became easily accessible. The trumpeter was probably never as common as its relative the whistling swan, so that when humans began to use the breeding grounds year-round, in addition to shooting the swans, the trumpeter population dropped rapidly.

How Many Are Left?

Serious doubts began to arise as to whether trumpeter swans could survive, if, indeed, they were not already gone.

In 1931, an early fall came to Yellowstone National Park. "Squaw winter" weather brought snow flurries to the valleys, to be followed by beautiful Indian-summer days. National Park

Service biologists had made a determined effort in the preceding summer to take a census of the last remaining trumpeters in the United States. Search as they might, they had found only about fifty birds. Of this number a mere five pairs had been known to nest. During the summer the young swans, called cygnets, had grown to maturity. A crop of eighteen was counted. In the frosty air of that Indian summer only thirteen young remained. It was a dark day for our largest waterfowl. How many of the surviving cygnets withstood the ensuing winter we do not know, but it is certain that some were lost.

Action!

George Wright, in charge of the wildlife work of the National Park Service, began to write letters and to see people about saving the trumpeters. The press gave willing assistance. Wright, at his own expense, traveled or sent his assistants scurrying here and there, giving talks before sportsmen's clubs and building up interest in the cause. It set off the spark, and from all corners of the country conservationists became concerned about the future of this bird. The Montana Fish and Game Commission offered a reward of fifty dollars for the apprehension of anyone caught disturbing or killing trumpeter swans.

At least seventeen trumpeters were killed by gunshot in 1933. Sportsmen, probably mistaking the great birds for other game, had killed them and, upon discovering their error, beat a hasty retreat, leaving the dead swans where they fell. George Wright secured framed pictures of trumpeters and sent them to hunting clubs with a plea not to shoot the rare birds.

It was found that the greatest concentration of trumpeters was not in Yellowstone National Park, where they received protection, but a few miles west at the Red Rock Lakes. These lakes did not freeze over completely in winter because they contained springs. The sedges, bulrushes, and other vegetation near the lake shores helped screen the swans' nests, which are built on open ground. However, the practice of cutting the bordering vegetation for

N.Y. Zool. Soc.

The unique call of the trumpeter swan is due to its long windpipe (sometimes five feet) that is looped like a French horn under a hump in its breastbone.

hay and permitting horses to cross frozen parts of the lakes to graze on the small islands somewhat spoiled the area for the trumpeters. The Red Rock Lakes were famous for their waterfowl: Canada geese, mallards, baldpates, pintails, teal, and others. Some local hunters soon recognized trumpeter swans and avoided killing them, but the waterfowl hunter who came from other parts of the state was not always as careful. Because of the efforts of George Wright and J. N. "Ding" Darling, at that time Chief of the Bureau of Biological Survey (replaced by Fish and Wildlife Service), President Roosevelt, in 1935, created by executive order the Red Rock Lakes Migratory Waterfowl Refuge.

Government biologists began to concentrate on better trumpeter swan counts. They chose August as the best month because no whistling swans were present and the cygnets were large enough to be conspicuous. A total of 211 of the huge birds were counted in August, 1941.

Naturalists in Yellowstone and biologists at Red Rock Lakes were requested to study the life history of trumpeter swans in order to ascertain their requirements and determine

189

how the species might be encouraged to increase.

Watching for Enemies

Yellowstone naturalists watched the nesting swans from a distance with binoculars. Elk, moose, and beavers that appeared along the shore line or fed in the shallow lake did not especially excite the swans. Even when an old bear prowled nearby, the trumpeters just watched it and went on feeding. One day a coyote came along searching for mice in the meadow that bordered the pond where a pair was nesting. The coyote glanced at the swans and both birds raised their long necks to watch the prowler. But the coyote went on stalking mice and the swans paid no more attention to it.

The Biological Survey found it necessary to exclude human beings from the Red Rock Lakes area between the first of May and the first of August. The problem was not so simple in Yellowstone. At one place in the park, where the birds were nesting near a highway, Memorial Day visitors who stopped to see the swans kept them away from their nests so long that the eggs cooled and the clutch was lost. The National Park Service has excluded people from certain swan nesting grounds, but visitor disturbance at other nesting sites remains a serious problem.

Not infrequently, a dead adult is found. Sometimes the cause of death cannot be determined although the birds are usually in an extremely thin condition, indicating hunger or disease. In several cases, however, the gizzard contained lead shot that the bird had picked up while feeding in an area around a duck blind. The importance of lead poisoning as a factor in the decline of the species is still unknown. Lead poisoning has been shown to cause sterility as well as death among waterfowl.

The trumpeter population in Canada has a better chance of survival than that in the United States, owing to the inaccessibility of their range as well as to protection afforded by the Mounties.

The localized migration of surviving trumpeters has been an important factor in permitting concentrated effort upon their protection. The national park, federal waterfowl refuge, and national forests where the birds still exist are regularly patrolled.

The one most vulnerable point is the vital winter area that is largely outside of both Red Rock Lakes and Yellowstone Park. To protect swans, the Federal Government closed the season on snow geese in part of this area in 1941. The reason was that hunters who killed swans often made the excuse that they thought the birds were snow geese. The National Park Service and Fish and Wildlife Service sponsored a poster admonishing hunters in the area to shoot no all-white birds. In 1940, the Emergency Conservation Committee made funds available for a series of lectures on the trumpeter swan throughout the vital winter area. The story of the swans was also broadcast over radio stations in an effort to save the trumpeters.

A recent census conducted by the Fish and Wildlife Service reported that the population of the trumpeter swan is showing an encouraging annual increase, and has reached a total of about 650 birds. All but a few were found in government refuges such as Red Rock Lakes and Yellowstone National Park.

190

The pen (female) sitting on the nest, while the cob (male) searches for food. Trumpeters nest at lake borders or on islands as soon as winter ice recedes. Old nests are usually repaired for a new season, when four to eight buff-white eggs are laid.

N.Y. Zool. Soc.

Living Room for Wildlife

One successful way of saving our vanishing animals is to set aside areas where man and his way of life cannot interfere with them. This is the story of Mattamuskeet, one of the United States' many national wildlife refuges. Text and illustrations from **Mattamuskeet, A National Wildlife Refuge,** by Rachel L. Carson, Conservation in Action Number Four. Published by the United States Department of the Interior, Fish and Wildlife Service.

The Mattamuskeet Wildlife Refuge includes about 50,000 acres of land and water in this Carolina coastal country, in the county of Hyde. The dominant geographic feature of the refuge is Lake Mattamuskeet—a shallow, sluggish body of water more than fifteen miles long, five or six miles across, and some 30,000 acres in extent. Being little more than three feet deep anywhere, the lake is stirred deeply by the winds and its waters are usually muddy. Silt-filled waters support little plant life, and so the best feeding grounds for the waterfowl are not in the open lake but in its surrounding marshes. Cypress trees form most of the northern border of the lake, but its eastern and southern shores pass into low swamplands.

This land was acquired for a waterfowl sanctuary by the United States government in 1934.

The Visiting Waterfowl

Whistling swans are the most spectacular birds to be seen at Mattamuskeet. With their wing spread of six to seven feet, they are the largest of all North American waterfowl except the related trumpeter swan.

The whistling swans arrive at Mattamuskeet sometime in November, remain several months, and usually in February begin their northern migration. When they leave Mattamuskeet, they have a trip of 2,500 to 3,500 miles before them, for most of them breed north of the Arctic Circle.

For the Canada geese of the Atlantic Coast, Mattamuskeet is one of the chief wintering places, with a population of about 40 to 60 thousand of these handsome birds from November to the middle of March.

Magnificent though the swans are, the person who visits Mattamuskeet in midwinter is likely to come away with impressions of geese uppermost in his mind. Throughout much of the day, their wings pattern the sky above you. Underlying all the other sounds of the refuge is their wild music, rising at times to a great, tumultuous crescendo, and dying away again to a throbbing undercurrent.

A large majority—probably three-fourths—of the Mattamuskeet geese breed along the eastern shores of Hudson Bay, smaller numbers in the Maritime Provinces.

The ducks that winter at Mattamuskeet are largely the marsh or dabbling ducks—the shallow-water feeders. Pintails are the commonest of these, and it is a beautiful sight to see 10,000 or more of these graceful ducks wheeling above the marshes. Small flocks of wigeons appear in spring along the lake road. Black ducks, green-winged teal, mallards, and blue-winged teal spend the winter here in

191

varying numbers, from a few hundred to a few thousand.

Most of the ducks found in winter, from Delaware Bay south, nest in the prairie provinces of Canada or in the flat country of the Dakotas and Minnesota. All of this country is subject to periodic droughts; then many ponds and marshes dry up, few ducks nest successfully, and few ducklings survive to join the fall flights south.

The bird life of Mattamuskeet includes about 200 different species, with water birds and water-loving land birds predominating.

Why Have Refuges?

What does the Mattamuskeet refuge do for the waterfowl that could not be done in the same area of wild country without management? This is a fair question, and its answer gives one of the chief reasons for establishing wildlife refuges throughout the country.

The answer is this: by cultivating or managing the marshlands by scientifically tested principles, the land within the refuge is made many times as productive of natural foods as outside areas not under management.

Underlying and determining the character of the management activities are the great recurrent rhythms of nature. Moving over the marshlands as over a stage, the passing seasons bring the sweep of two great series of events, one in the animal world, the other in the world of plants. The two cycles are directly related. In the spring the marshes that have been brown and desolate come alive with fresh green shoots of plants like the sedges, bulrushes, and salt grass. Spring yields to summer, the hot sun is over the land, the plants grow, flower, mature their seeds. By the time autumn begins to paint the leaves of the gums and the swamp maples, the marshes are loaded with food—the roots, seeds, and shoots of the plants that waterfowl eat.

Now the fall migrations of the birds—the sweep of the animal-cycle—fill the marshlands with ducks, swans, and geese from the north. Here in the marshes they find the food they must have if they are to survive the winter.

By late winter or early spring the food

supplies are exhausted. But once more the urge to migrate is stirring among the waterfowl, and soon the marshes are left empty. In the stillness and heat of summer the recuperative powers of nature set to work to build up a new food supply.

To get the largest possible production of waterfowl foods out of the marshes at Mattamuskeet, the manager operates the refuge with certain aims in mind. Among the most important, he must keep down the brush that is forever moving into the marshes. Geese, swans, and ducks feed in marshes but not in thickets, so every foot invaded by the fast-growing brush is a corresponding loss of waterfowl pasture. Today at Mattamuskeet you can see hundreds of acres of productive marsh which have been won back from the thickets by burning, disking, and cutting.

Control of the water level is another method used by the refuge manager to increase the production of food plants. In the spring he lowers the water by manipulating the gates in the canals that lead from the lake to Pamlico Sound, about eight miles distant. This lays bare extensive areas where three-edge, four-square, and other food plants can grow. In the fall the gates are closed, and the marsh areas flooded to serve the food plants in the way the birds prefer—under a few inches of water.

By late January or early February, most of the natural marsh food has been eaten. The thousands of birds that remain must have food to fuel their bodies on the long spring migration. This is a season of busy activity on the refuge. Crews of men move out into the marshes, starting fires in the marsh grass. Keeping the fires carefully under control, many hundreds of acres are burned. Less than a week later, new green shoots are coming up all over the marsh. Within ten days the geese have moved in to harvest this new food supply.

By thus co-ordinating the management of the refuge with the natural cycles of plant and animal life, the Fish and Wildlife Service has developed Mattamuskeet to the point where it now supports much larger flocks of waterfowl than came to this region in former years.

Vanishing Wildlife Around the World

Within the past 2000 years about 200 species of animals and birds have become extinct.
Many more than that are in danger of extinction today. Here, his Royal Highness, Prince Philip,
Duke of Edinburgh and head of the World Wildlife Fund in Great Britain, explains some of the reason
why. These paragraphs are from a speech launching a Fund drive in the United States. The World
Wildlife Fund has been formed in order to try to conserve the world's rapidly diminishing
wildlife of all kinds.

193

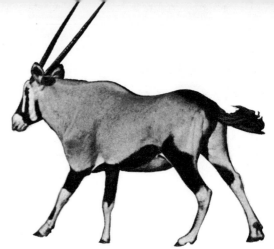

Ewing Galloway

Once prevalent throughout the Middle East, the white oryx, a large species of antelope with ringed, tapering horns, exists in small numbers only in Saudi Arabia. An Arab superstition that the killer of an oryx inherits its courage partially accounts for its near-extinction.

Today, 250 species of animals and birds are in danger of extermination by the sheer callousness of mankind. There are five reasons why wild animals are in danger all over the world.

First, physical conditions are changing; human population is increasing, forcing the animals out. Industry and science are polluting the air, the soil, and the water, unintentionally maybe, but nonetheless effectively, killing off vast numbers of animals and fish.

Second, the means of controlling those creatures which are considered to be pests and nuisances are very much more powerful than ever before in history. They are, in fact,

National Audubon Society

Zoological Society of N. Y.

no longer means of control; they are methods of extermination. Even then things might not be so bad if they only affected the so-called pests; the trouble is that they set up a chain reaction in nature which takes in many innocent creatures and in some cases man himself.

Third, there are the killers for profit, the poachers. In Africa they are rapidly getting rid of the rhino. In Africa and elsewhere, these thoughtless exploiters are slaughtering vast numbers of elephants merely because they can get 50 cents a pound for their ivory.

Fourth, the status killers. Who hasn't heard the man boasting about his latest hunting or fishing success—not because he gets any pleasure out of it, but merely because he thinks it is the thing to do. At least the sportsman is concerned that the source of his sport is not destroyed; the status killer couldn't care less.

Finally, and probably most important, are the inadequate game and conservation laws and the means of enforcing them.

What is needed, above all, are people all over the world who understand the problem and really care about it: people with courage to see that the letter and the spirit of the conservation and game laws are obeyed and, where necessary, improved.

Not just a few people, here and there, but literally hundreds of thousands of ordinary people, as well as naturalists and sportsmen, game wardens and zoologists, so that we shall be able to say with satisfaction that, at least in this one endeavor, mankind was able to correct its mistakes in time by a conscious and deliberate effort of will and generosity.

All over the tropical world, the rhinoceros has been ruthlessly hunted for alleged magical powers of its horn. The World Wildlife Fund is attempting to save the last white rhinos (left, above) in Uganda. Giant tortoises of the Galápagos Islands (left) are also protected.

The Passing of the Buffalo

Hamlin Garland (1860-1940) was a midwestern poet, novelist and farmer who used conservation themes in much of his literary work. When he wrote this lament at the turn of the century, the buffalo was almost extinct; conservation has helped increase its numbers. Used by permission of Mrs. Constance Garland Doyle.

Going, the wild things of our land.
Passing, the antelope and the buffalo.
They have gone with the sunny sweep
Of the untracked plain!
They have passed away with the untrammeled
Current of our streams!

With the falling trees they fell,
With the autumn grasses they rotted,
And their bones
Lie white on the flame-charred sod,
Mixed with the antlers of the elk.

For centuries they lay down and rose
In peace and calm content.
They were fed by the rich grass
And watered by sunny streams.
The plover called to them
Out of the shimmering air,
The hawk swooped above them,
The blackbirds sat on their backs
In the still afternoons;
In the cool mud they wallowed,
Rolling in noisy sport.

They lived through centuries of struggle—
In swarming millions—till the white man came.
The snows of winter were terrible!
The dry wind was hard to bear,
But the breath of man, the smoke
Of his gun were more fatal.

They fell by the thousands.
They melted away like smoke!
Mile by mile they retreated westward;
Year by year they moved north and south
In dust-brown clouds;
Each year they descended upon the plains
In endless floods;
Each winter they retreated to the hills
Of the south.
Their going was like the ocean current,
But each spring they stopped a little short—
They were like an ebbing tide!
They came at last to meager little bands
That never left the hills—
Crawling in somber files from canyon to canyon—
Now, they are gone!

Conservationist Contradictions

Sometimes the actions of people contradict their words, often purposely but on other occasions simply because they have not thought through all of the aspects of their position and taken a truly consistent stand. Reprinted by permission from **Time, the Weekly Newsmagazine.** Copyright Time Inc., 1969.

The four-day conference was billed as a "creative dialogue between sportsmen and scientists who share a deep and growing concern for vanishing wildlife species." Into Monte Carlo winged 300 of the world's leading sportsmen, wildlife scientists, game biologists, conservationists and professional hunters to demonstrate their concern by feasting at a sumptuous banquet on wild boar, pheasant, partridge and turkey. And on to the dialogue. One speaker, lamenting the wanton slaying of alligators, apologized profusely for the belt he was wearing. Alligator, of course. Equally well made was a point about the dangers that the fur trade poses to the world's great cats; on view among the ladies were eight leopard coats, two ocelot coats, a cheetah suit and a tiger jacket with matching handbag. Their hostess, Princess Grace of Monaco, even showed up splendidly attired in a coat made of wild mink, with matching turban.

 Other Books To Read

Last of the Thundering Herd, by Bigelow Neal. Published by Dodd, Mead & Company, New York, 1960. For younger readers, an account of the vanishing herds of bison in North America.

Serengeti Shall Not Die, by Bernhard and Michael Grzimek. Published by E. P. Dutton & Company, New York, 1961. This account of the work of the author and his son to save Serengeti National Park, Tanzania, is a plea to forbid human beings to enter the last great strongholds of animal life, in order to save the world's few remaining wild animals from extinction.

No Room in the Ark, by Alan Moorehead. Published by Harper & Brothers, New York, 1959. Another plea to grant more living space to the dwindling numbers of wild animals in Africa. This fascinating account of a trip south of the Sahara is illustrated with magnificent photographs.

Drives and Needs: The Signals for Action

Tom, Dick, and Harry are running down a road. Tom is running home because he is very hungry and wants to eat. Dick is running just as fast as he can to get away from a skunk. Harry is running because he wants to get to football practice on time. Although you will probably never see these three boys running down the road at the same time for such different reasons it does tell you something about what psychologists (scientists who specialize in the study of behavior) call "motivation." Motivation may be defined simply as the study of what makes people do the things they do, when they do.

A psychologist might tell you that Tom is motivated to run because he feels a *need* for food; this need, if it is great enough, stimulates a *drive* to seek food. The drive, which may be defined as a state of bodily tension, would not be relaxed in Tom's case until he had eaten something and satisfied his need for food. Drives for food, sleep, excretion, liquids, and air are often classified as *biological drives* because they are concerned with internal bodily needs. Dick is running because of a need to get away from the possible shower from the skunk; this creates a drive to escape. It may be said that Dick has an aversion for (will try and avoid because he dislikes) skunks. Many of our needs and drives arise from our likes and dislikes which psychologists sometimes classify as *appetites* and *aversions*. Harry who is running for football practice may be motivated by a need for success, that is, he wants to be best at something and that creates the drive to practice his favorite sport. Many of our needs and drives are classified as *social motives*, one of them is like Harry's need for success. Other familiar socially motivated drives are the desire for approval and the desire to be like others.

Much of man's behavior, as well as that of Tom, Dick, and Harry's, can be explained in terms of drives and needs, which, as you see, are signals for action. You will find interesting descriptions of how many of these important needs and drives affect our daily life in this section.

Needs, Drives, and Incentives

You have probably heard the words "need," "drive," and "incentive" many times before this, but they have a special meaning in the study of psychology (why man behaves as he does). You will find the articles in this section more interesting if you know exactly what psychologists mean when they use these words. Adapted from **Introduction to Psychology** by Ernest R. Hilgard. Copyright 1953 by Harcourt, Brace and Company, Inc.

Each of us tries to understand the motives of those about him. The student running for the class presidency tries to understand and appeal to the motives that control the behavior of his classmates. The real-estate salesman tries hard to understand the motives that lead people to buy houses. A wife may never succeed in understanding her husband's passion for hitting a small ball around a four-mile golf course. Men do countless things for which the motives are complex and not always clear: they build bridges, compose music, climb mountains, fight one another, compete, and co-operate. One of the central problems of psychology is to discover why men do what they do.

The most dramatic human motives are revealed in daring and heroic action—when determined men explore new lands, when one man sacrifices his life to save another, when a man withstands the pains of torture rather than renounce an ideal. We might begin by trying to give a psychological account of noble human motives, but we would soon find our tools inadequate to the task. So we start much more modestly and simply by trying to find ways of studying commonplace motives such as those of hunger and thirst. If we come to understand these simpler motives we may hope eventually to understand the bolder, more complex motives that characterize man at his best.

The tendencies to eat when hungry and drink when thirsty are shared in common by man and the lower animals. Motives like these for which the bodily needs are obvious are called *biological* or *physiological* motives. Much of the behavior of the newborn baby

can be explained on a physiological basis. He is primarily occupied with satisfaction of the needs for food, water, sleep, and excretion of wastes.

But before long new needs are acquired. The infant cries when hungry. The crying, he finds, brings the mother and food. Her presence leads to the satisfaction of physiological needs. After many such experiences the infant may cry when he is not hungry or otherwise physically uncomfortable. He cries, we say, because he has been left alone. The presence of his mother has come to be an end in itself. The desire for the mother's presence is a motive without basis in an obvious bodily need. It represents a learned or acquired need. Parental attention or approval comes to be needed in and of itself. Motives such as the need for approval of other people are called *personal-social* motives to distinguish them from physiological or biological motives. The distinctively human motives, such as those which control behavior guided by ideals, are personal-social.

Needs and Drives

We use a great many words to describe motivation: needs, urges, impulses, desires, goals. They all refer in some way to the forces that energize behavior and give it direction. The

197

In the early days of life the baby is concerned mainly with his bodily needs for food, water, sleep, and excretion.

Gerber's Baby Foods

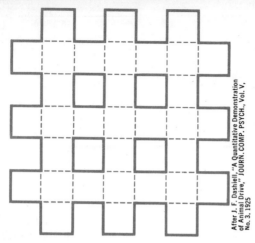

first step in studying motivation is to see what we mean by needs and drives.

If a rat that has been deprived of food for several hours is placed in a checkerboard maze, such as the one illustrated in the drawing above, it will be active. We may keep track of its movements and find how many squares it covers. A well-fed rat placed in the same maze may move about a little, but it will cover much less ground than the hungry rat. We may say that a food-deprived rat is an *active* rat. Now if the same rat is placed in a maze consisting of several alleys, one of which leads to food, it will run about until it happens to reach the food. Then it will eat. We may say now that a food-deprived rat is also a *hungry* rat. After eating it is no longer restless. If returned to its cage, it is likely to curl up and go to sleep. When it is again hungry, its activity cycle will begin again.

How shall we talk scientifically about the behavior of the rat just described? We may refer to the food-deprived state as a state of *need*. The organism needs food, and when the rat has not eaten for a while there are chemical changes in its blood which are indicators of its need. The need for food is bodily, not psychological, but a bodily need has psychological results. The psychological consequence of a need we call a *drive*. Thus the food-need in the rat leads to the hunger drive.

Drive does not necessarily become more intense as need gets stronger. A starved organism may be so weakened by its great need that drive is weakened. Men who have fasted for a long time report that their hunger pangs come and go, though, of course, their need continues.

The checkerboard maze has been used in experiments; the results of which showed that a hungry rat is likely to be more active and restless than a well-fed rat. Differences in behavior are recorded by counting the number of squares each rat enters.

Typical physiological needs are those for food, air, water, and moderate temperature. These lead in turn to corresponding drives.

Incentives

Something that can satisfy a drive is called an *incentive*. When we bait a trap, we place an incentive there. Such words as "lure," "reward," "goal-object," refer to incentives. Food as an incentive satisfies the hunger drive, water as an incentive satisfies the thirst drive. In general, an appropriate incentive is one that can reduce the strength of a drive. A state of aroused drive is an active, restless state; after the incentive has been responded to, usually the state is less tense and more relaxed.

Needs and drives are inside the individual; incentives are outside. Incentives, because they lie in the environment, can be controlled by parents or teachers or animal trainers.

Motivated behavior consists of a pattern of activity in which drives and incentives become related. There are two parts to motivated behavior: the activity that leads the person with a drive into the presence of the incentive and the activity that takes place in the presence of the incentive. We distinguish, for example, between food-seeking behavior and eating behavior. Food-seeking brings an individual and food together; eating relieves the individual's hunger. That portion of the behavior prior to the incentive is the *preparatory* behavior or the *goal-directed* behavior; the behavior in the presence of the incentive is known as the *goal-activity*. The incentive makes possible the goal-activity.

We have now completed our introduction to the need-drive-incentive formula that is to guide us as we study the physiological background of motivation. Need gives rise to drive. Drive is a state of tension leading to restless activity and preparatory behavior. The incentive is something in the external environment that satisfies the need and thus reduces the drive through goal-activity.

The Biological Drives

When you are hungry, you go to the refrigerator and get some bread and butter to relieve your hunger. When you are tired you go to bed, and when you are thirsty you take a drink. All this may seem quite obvious to you, but have you ever stopped to think what happens in your body to make you realize and do something about the fact that you need food, drink, or sleep? In this article you will read about these and other biological drives and how they affect your behavior.
From **Psychology and Life,** fourth edition, by Floyd L. Ruch. Copyright, 1953, by Scott, Foresman and Company, and used with their permission.

Biological drives start with the bodily needs of the individual. These drives may be considered as stimuli associated with bodily needs. They center the behavior of the individual on the satisfaction of those needs. For example, the hunger drive motivates the individual to seek and eat food. Prolonged failure to satisfy a drive finally results in disease or death.

Drives are observed from birth. A biological drive is inborn, although the actions the individual uses to satisfy a drive are generally learned.

The drives which have been recognized and studied include our needs for food, water, oxygen, rest, sleep, warmth when cold, cooling when hot, and relief of bowel and bladder tensions.

The Hunger Drive

Of all the drives, hunger has received the most study. Yet the answers to the problem of what makes people feel hungry is still somewhat of a mystery.

From our own examination of the gnawing sensations which we call "hunger pangs," we assume that hunger consists of a mass of sensations coming from the region of the stomach. But just what changes in the condition of the stomach are associated with the sensation of hunger which we feel and report? And is the stomach the only source of the sensations of hunger?

Understanding of the mechanism of hunger has been advanced through the combined efforts of psychologists and physiologists, who have performed various types of observations on the behavior of the empty stomach. They have definitely shown that when the stomach is empty, contractions set in and the person feels "hungry."

But this does not tell the whole story of the nature of the hunger drive. Recent research suggests that hunger pangs have several causes. Stomach contractions are only one source of hunger pangs, and not even a necessary one.

It may be that the hunger drive can operate

The hunger drive has been studied by having a subject swallow a thin, rubber stomach balloon attached to a long, rubber tube. The balloon is inflated until it touches the wall of the subject's stomach and so will reflect any changes in the shape of the stomach during hunger contractions. The long, rubber tube is connected to a recording device (left) which shows any changes in the stomach. The subject hits a key when he feels hungry, and it has been shown that there is a close correspondence between the hunger pangs the subject reports he feels and the period when stomach contractions are at their height.

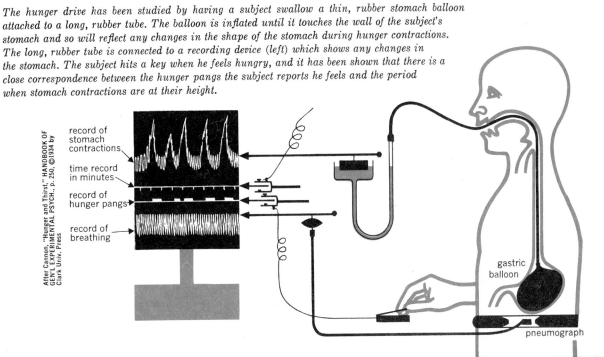

After Cannon, "Hunger and Thirst," HANDBOOK OF GEN'L EXPERIMENTAL PSYCH., p. 250, ©1934 by Clark Univ. Press

record of stomach contractions

time record in minutes

record of hunger pangs

record of breathing

gastric balloon

pneumograph

Scientists believe that the hunger drive may be caused by some change in the chemistry of the body. In order to show this, a well-fed dog was given blood from a starving dog. The result was that the well-fed dog started eating again, although he was known to be "full."

without stomach contractions, that is, they may be important to the individual merely as a useful sign or signal of hunger.

Some findings suggest that the origin of the hunger drive is chemical in nature. Studies have shown, for instance, that blood transfused from the body of a starving dog to that of a recently fed one can cause stomach contractions under certain conditions. But these experiments will have to be carried much farther before we can definitely say that hunger has a chemical basis. The hunger drive, for all the study devoted to it, is still far from being completely understood. We are still only in the beginning stages of understanding many basic phenomena in psychology—the hunger drive is but one example.

Effects of the Hunger Drive

We are much more aware of hunger sensations when we are eating very little than if we eat nothing at all for a day or more. After several days of eating nothing hunger pangs disappear almost entirely, but in cases of prolonged semi-starvation where a small but inadequate amount of food is available, hunger grows until it almost entirely dominates the individual's thoughts and actions.

Actual famine is a personal and social catastrophe which is capable of producing striking changes in the behavior of its victims. History is rich in accounts of famines, such as the following excerpt from a thirteenth-century chronicle describing a famine in Russia:

"A brother rose against his brother, a father had no pity for his son, mothers had no mercy for their daughters; one denied his neighbor a crumb of bread. There was no charity left among us, only sadness, gloom, and mourning dwelt constantly within and without our habitations. It was a bitter sight, indeed, to watch the crying children begging in vain for bread, and falling dead like flies."

In modern times, famine has plagued war-torn Europe and Asia. During World War II (1939–45) in countries occupied by the Germans such as Belgium and the Netherlands, the average daily civilian food ration, in calories, was cut to about half the normal daily requirement, and among prisoners of war the daily food intake was even lower. Near the end of the war in 1945, for instance, prisoners at the notorious German concentration camp in Dachau were receiving the following weekly menu:

Soup, noon	1750 calories
Soup, evening	300 calories
Bread	1680 calories
Total per week	3730 calories
Per day (average)	533 calories

In other words, the calorie content of a week's diet at Dachau was nearly equal to that required by a normal, active human being *in a single day.*

The effects of such a diet upon war prisoners were drastic. Their hunger which could not be satisfied directed all their thoughts toward food. The drastic psychological effects of extreme and unsatisfied hunger have been well summarized by a captured medical officer imprisoned by the Germans who has remarked, "None of the other hardships suffered by fighting men observed by me brought about such a rapid or complete degeneration of character as chronic starvation."

The Thirst Drive

Although man can live for many weeks without food, he can survive only a few days without water. Men who have been completely deprived of both food and water for long periods of time report that the sensations of thirst soon became maddening, while pangs of hunger actually tend to disappear after a few days.

The sensation of thirst is a device which serves to control the intake of water into the body in such a manner as to maintain the water content of the body at a constant level. Exactly what all the factors in thirst are—just how the lowered water level of the body sets up the thirst drive—is still only partially understood by scientists. It is known, of course, that thirst operates as a drive. When the supply of water in the body becomes low, the individual sets forth in search of water. A lack of water occurring as a result of such processes as perspiration and urination results in increased activity by the individual, which is kept up until water is found and taken into the body, thereby bringing the water level of the body to normal.

Our present knowledge of the mechanisms that regulate drinking behavior is far from complete. Dryness of the mouth and throat tissues is one of the most obvious signs of thirst. As the water supply in the body becomes low, the tissues of the mouth and throat become drier and drier, stimulating the tiny nerve endings embedded in them and producing awareness of thirst. Yet, although dryness of the throat may lead an animal to seek water and drink, it seems to have nothing to do with *how much* the organism drinks. Dryness of the throat and mouth seems to be important in starting drinking behavior but the amount of water which an individual will consume seems to be regulated by the amount of water which is needed to maintain a steady water

USAF School of Aviation Med., Randolph Field, Tex.

Vision is one of the first bodily functions to be affected by oxygen starvation (or air hunger) at higher altitude. This chart shows that the symptoms of oxygen hunger appear very soon after one leaves the ground and at 15,000 feet the oxygen loss becomes dangerous.

level in the body, particularly the water supply of the body cells themselves.

Air Hunger

One of the most basic requirements of the human body is air, a need which must be continually and constantly satisfied. Yet the need for air is relatively unimportant as a motive in everyday life, simply because air is usually easy to get, and actual air hunger is therefore rarely experienced. But when our need for air is not met, as in suffocation, air hunger is the most intense of all human drives and is capable of producing violent activity on the part of the individual struggling for oxygen.

The importance of a continual oxygen supply to the body cannot be overemphasized. Although the nervous system, at rest, consumes

201

oxygen in very small amounts, this consumption goes on constantly, and a severe lack of oxygen for periods as brief as a minute can result in actual damage to the nervous system.

When oxygen starvation occurs in an atmosphere without excessive carbon dioxide—as at mountaintops or in high-altitude flying—a peculiar sort of drunkenness, or confusion, comes on. The person loses control and may shout, fight, or burst into tears. Memory does not work well, the senses function poorly, and paralysis is common, especially of the legs. Yet the person feels confident of his abilities and fails to realize how serious his condition is.

Fatigue and the Sleep Drive

We all know how desperate the need for rest can become; yet the physiology of fatigue is so complicated that very little is known about it. As a result of long periods of exercise, the chemistry of the blood is changed in several ways, including an increase of the concentration of lactic acid in the muscles. Presumably this condition stimulates the nervous system directly or activates certain receptors. The picture is enormously complicated by the fact that much of our fatigue seems to result not from physical exertion but from frustration, worry, or boredom. Some people, for example,

are continually exhausted, no matter how little activity and how much rest they have.

Tired people go to great lengths to obtain rest. Where fatigue is due to physical exercise, rest brings a readjustment of the body and an end to the stimuli which are causing the awareness of fatigue and the efforts to rest. Where fatigue is emotionally based, relief will probably not be gained by rest.

Sleep, like rest, is an important need of the body, but it, too, is still not very well understood. It is not even known, for instance, what or how many kinds of sensory receptors (if any) are active when we feel sleepy.

Certain drugs, such as chloroform and ether, produce a relaxed condition resembling sleep, which suggests that its basis may be chemical. It may be that in sleepiness our nerve and brain centers are directly stimulated by chemical conditions within the body. The muscles are also affected, for one of the outstanding conditions bringing about sleep is a general relaxation of the body.

But whatever the chemical factors in sleep, it is definitely known that sleepiness can be caused by injuries to certain parts of the brain, particularly some of the lower brain centers, which may be the nerve centers controlling the sleep drive. Besides a variety of physiological theories of sleep, there is also

Early in your life you become adjusted to a 24-hour day. To find out if this is due to inborn factors, two scientists spent more than a month in Mammoth Cave, Kentucky where the light, temperature, and sound remain fairly steady. The graphs (right) show that one of the scientists, K, continued to have seven peaks of temperature corresponding to a seven-day week (based on the 24-hour day). Subject R became used to a new schedule of six days, each of 28 hours.

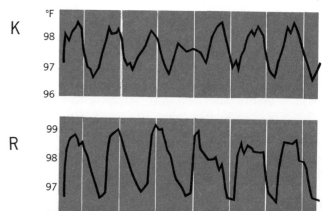

| K | °F 98 97 96 | | | | | | |
| R | 99 98 97 96 | Sun. | Mon. | Tue. | Wed. | Thur. | Fri. | Sat. |

a theory which explains this need as a conditioned (learned) response.

Warmth and Cold As Drives

Everyone everywhere is affected by the weather. Clothes, houses, sports, agriculture —and sometimes, it is said, even temperament —are affected by how hot or cold the climate is. No one can dispute the importance of warmth and cold as drives. Just what is their physical origin?

First of all, there are some receptors in the skin which are sensitive to contact with warm objects and others which are sensitive to cold. In addition, there is a structure in the brain, the hypothalamus, which, among its many functions, responds directly to the temperature of the blood flowing through it. This center is vital in the adjustment of the body to warmth and cold.

The temperature of the human body is regulated by a complex mechanism that balances heat loss against heat production. Thus two temperatures are always involved: the amount of heat in the surrounding environment and the heat produced by the body itself. Our bodies obviously can lose less heat to their surroundings on hot, humid days than they can on cold days.

When the body is cold—that is, when external temperature falls below about 57° F. —bodily activity is stimulated. Increased muscular activity takes place; the blood pressure rises. Blood is driven from the surface of the body to the deeper tissues, where it will not be exposed to cold air. The reaction to heat is pretty much the opposite. When external temperature is raised, bodily activity slows down. The arteries at the surfaces of the body dilate, thus exposing a greater volume of blood to the air for cooling. The circulation rate is increased.

All these automatic bodily changes act in various ways to keep the temperature of the body tissues fairly constant at about 98°–99° F., no matter what the temperature of the environment. But besides these continuous, automatic adjustments to warmth and cold, there are many things we deliberately do to keep our bodies at a comfortable temperature. Electric fans, air conditioning, ice water, lightweight suits—oil burners, hot drinks, and fur coats—all are familiar results of man's drives to adjust to warmth and cold.

Pain As a Drive

To serve most effectively as a drive, pain must be prolonged and not too strong. If you touch a hot iron accidentally, you draw back your hand. This is a simple already-organized response: the *withdrawal reflex*. The localized pain which lasts only a short time is not, properly speaking, a drive any more than all stimuli are drives. But suppose that even after you have withdrawn your hand the burn continues to smart and you go to the doctor to get it dressed. Here pain is serving as a drive.

Pain has an important biological significance in that most harmful situations produce pain as well as injury. The desire to avoid pain and protect others from pain has been one of the important motivating forces in the history of mankind.

Bowel and Bladder Tensions

When the bladder or the lower colon become distended, receptor cells in their walls are stimulated and produce drives. These drives ordinarily have little importance because there are seldom obstacles to their relief. They have, however, all the characteristics of the other physiological drives: (1) they may be defined as the conditions surrounding some bodily need; (2) they grow out of the physiological state of the tissues; (3) they stimulate sensory receptors and thus set up activity in the nervous system and brain; (4) they produce by this stimulation a restless activity which continues until the tissue needs have been met.

Other Sections To See

"Three Stages in Growing Up," Volume 5; "Adolescence," Volume 6; "How We Learn," Volume 8; "Your Defense Mechanisms," Volume 10; "Intelligence," Volume 12; "Your Personality," Volume 17.

203

Appetites
and
Aversions

The noise of many horns loudly honking all at once is so annoying to some people that they will try to get away from the noise as fast as they can. The same people who run away from the sound of honking horns may sit happily listening to the sounds of a symphony an hour later. We may say that some people have an aversion (dislike) for some sounds and display an appetite (liking) for other sounds. In this article you will read more about the way in which appetites and aversions regulate our behavior. From **Psychology and Life**, fourth edition, by Floyd L. Ruch. Copyright, 1953, by Scott, Foresman and Company, and used with their permission.

Like the biological drives, the appetites and aversions are internal conditions that bring about and direct activity immediately concerned with the biological comfort of the individual. Unlike the drives, however, the objects and actions which the appetites and aversions lead the individual to seek or avoid are not vitally related to the life, growth, and continued activity of the individual. Many of our biological likes and dislikes are products of growth; that is, they are present at birth or appear later in life in the absence of opportunity to learn. Many others, however, appear to be determined primarily by learning rather than by growth. For example, Philippine tribesmen would relish a meal of dog flesh which would disgust most Americans. A major practical difficulty is finding out how far likes and dislikes are determined by heredity and growth and how far by learning. But we all know that people seek what they feel to be pleasant and avoid what they feel would be unpleasant.

Although the appetites and aversions direct human behavior in exactly the same way as do the basic biological drives, psychologists are not entirely agreed upon the items to be included in a list of likes and dislikes, nor upon what to name them. Probably the most satisfactory terms are *appetite*, if some object is willingly met or actively sought, and *aversion* if it is avoided.

The Appetites

Many stimuli produce pleasant conscious experiences and are therefore actively sought by the individual. Among them are musical notes as opposed to noise; certain colors and color combinations, tastes, flavors, and odors; and sexual stimulation.

The Sexual Appetite

The sexual appetite is second only to the hunger drive in its importance for social living. While our society does not place many restrictions upon our eating habits, sexual expression is governed by both law and social conventions. This conflict between the sexual appetite and the cultural restrictions on its outlets makes sex one of the most powerful forces in human behavior. Although sexual activity is necessary to the survival of the race, it is not actually essential to keeping an individual alive. Most modern physicians and psychologists, however, believe that sexual satisfaction leads to the best physical and mental health. (See also the section on heredity in Volume 13.)

Other Appetites in Man

The other human appetites have not been so well surveyed and cataloged as have the biological drives (see page 199). This is because they are less essential to life and provide fewer problems in normal human adjustment. Also, they are so easily influenced by learning that it is not entirely clear exactly how they begin. In fact, some psychologists feel that the category of appetites is not necessary, classifying some of them instead under drives and some under social motives.

Appetites for specific foods and flavors exist

even in the absence of general hunger drive, as is shown by the way people reach for a sweet at the end of a heavy meal and make liberal use of various seasonings and condiments. Various observations show that people also respond differently to different kinds of things they hear. The young human infant cries when he hears high notes and smiles and coos when he hears low ones. Since learning cannot be called upon to explain the preference in babies who have had no opportunity to learn, we must conclude that this reaction is inborn. Another inborn preference is for musical tones as against noises. Specific musical appetites, however, seem to be determined largely by experience. The Chinese, for example, have been brought up to like musical combinations that the trained European ear finds unpleasant, and people who have heard nothing but dance music all their lives often find classical music boring.

Psychological experiments show that appetites for specific colors also appear in the absence of opportunity to learn and continue to develop all during life through the interaction of growth and learning. It has been found that babies show greater interest in colored papers which are held before their eyes than they do in gray ones. Among preschool children, red appears to be the favorite color; from grade school on, blue replaces red. Also, as the child matures, the preference for yellow appears to decline. In the human adult, there is no good method of separating the influences of inherited tastes, but it would be difficult to explain the preferences of young babies on any other than an inborn basis, for the simple reason that infants have not yet had an opportunity to learn to prefer one color to another. In summary, the appetites have very much the same function in directing human behavior as do the basic biological drives. The individual will continually seek to keep the pleasure gained from an appetite and will actively seek it when it is not present.

The Aversions

An aversion is a negative appetite: appetites direct an individual to seek pleasant forms of stimulation, aversions lead an individual to avoid unpleasant stimuli. The aversion is much less important than the appetite, because it is usually quite simple to avoid an unpleasant situation merely by moving away from it. There are many simple actions which will remove the individual from the presence of the stimulus which arouses aversion. In the case of an appetite, however, behavior must be much more precise and more definitely organized to achieve its goal. A young boy must run an errand in order to earn money which will buy candy that will taste good when placed in his mouth—a complicated chain of reactions. The same boy might, of course, try equally hard to avoid having an unpleasant tasting substance thrust into his mouth. The point is that the first situation is frequently met in life, and the second is seldom met and if met, is usually overcome. But even though the aversions are not among the strongest of our motives, nor among those most important to daily life, they can be—as we all know from our daily experience—a source of great annoyance. Putrid smells, loud or screeching traffic noises, and bitter medicine have aroused aversion in most of us.

205

Our "five senses"—sight, touch, smell, hearing, and taste—are often offended by things for which we have an aversion.

Shrill railroad whistle

Loud colored suit

The aroma of a skunk

CASTOR OIL

Dentist's drill

castor oil

H. Armstrong Roberts

Our Desire for Approval:

A Social Need

The desire for approval, for success, and to be like others are called "social motives" by psychologists. In this interesting article you will read about the first of these needs or social motives, the desire for approval, and how it affects man's behavior. This and the following two articles from **Understanding Ourselves** by Helen Shacter, Ph.D. Copyright, 1940, 1945, 1952, by McKnight & McKnight Publishing Company.

One of the social needs is the need for approval. (And remember, the order in which our social needs are discussed in this section does not imply that one of these needs is more important than another.)

Think how much better you felt when your father was pleased with the way you managed to carry through a difficult errand for him, as compared with that time when you felt that he was definitely vexed with you.

Do you remember how satisfying it was when the dramatics coach pointed out an instance of especially good acting on your part, since in the last play you could not seem to measure up to the requirements of your role?

And that day when you came home with a new hat which you had selected all alone: it was certainly far more pleasant to hear your mother praise your good taste than it had been to hear her question in no uncertain terms the judgment you used in the last purchase you made "on your own"!

Social Approval Influences All Activity

It is not only the approval of adults in which you find pleasure. You are normally just as eager for the approval of your classmates, whether they are discussing a play in football, the results of a mathematics quiz, the way your new suit fits, or the attractiveness of your new hair style. Their attention is pleasant; their sympathetic agreement is enjoyable. Sometimes their reaction seems even more important than the reaction of the grownups.

We rarely stop to think about this desire for approval; we do not put into specific words any vague thought we may have concerning it. But recall several recent incidents in which approval or disapproval figures. You will agree that you felt pleased when you knew that what you had done was praised. Compare this experience with the time when your actions were not received with favor and you were aware of criticism.

In larger issues, too, much more significant than playing football, buying a new hat, or taking part in a school play, the approval of others is a powerful influence upon your actions. Your friendliness to that new student in class, your helpfulness to the cripple you passed yesterday, your co-operation in group undertakings, are reactions sensed by you as particularly agreeable when they are recognized by others. Not that it is essential that someone notice that we are doing the decent, the courteous, or the friendly thing in order that we may experience satisfaction from so doing. But somehow, if we are honest with ourselves, we will admit that approval of a good deed does make us feel pleased.

Some people are so eager for the good will and approbation of others that they will not do or say anything which they feel might be contrary to what their companions accept. Such individuals are so dependent upon the approval of others that they hesitate to think or act in ways which are unusual to them. Even though they may be convinced in their own hearts and minds that their somewhat different point of view is a correct and justifiable one, they hesitate to express a "different" opinion for fear of disapproval. This is so extreme a manifestation of the common characteristic of a desire for approval that it is to be regretted.

One girl in high school was acutely uncomfortable if she wore anything but the prevailing anklets, saddle shoes, sweater, and skirt. To appear in a dress other than what seemed to be almost a uniform among the other girls made her quite miserable and dreadfully self-conscious. She was apparently unable to feel sufficiently sure of herself to risk even *looking* any different from her classmates. It bolstered up her feeble self-assurance to know that in appearance, at least, she matched the others.

More serious was the case of the first year student who was uncomfortably certain that his friends were going contrary to both school regulations and good sense by their secret indulgence in smoking. Yet he felt insecure in his inner conviction of behaving foolishly. He was not sure enough of himself to go contrary to the group opinion. He continued to

Another reaction to feeling unapproved is to try to attract attention to ourselves.

join the other fellows in their escapades because he feared to arouse their laughter or their disdain. He feared, too, that he might lose their fellowship, and he depended upon association with his "gang" to maintain his feeling of self-importance.

Certainly such an attitude is undesirable. Whether it is in regard to our clothes, what we read, or what we think about current events, we should not be too ready to conform, too willing to refrain from independence of thought and action. Such spineless behavior is a mark of weakness and of immaturity.

When Social Approval Is Lacking

It is equally inadvisable to be at the opposite extreme, to go completely contrary to the

One reaction to the feeling that we do not receive enough approval is to comfort ourselves by eating a lot of food.

207

*Meeting people halfway and
sharing their interests are
important steps in gaining the
interest and approval of others.*

opinion of others, to be oblivious to what
others are thinking. That is the way of the
person with peculiarities which are outstandingly opposed to the judgment and conduct of
the group. And of the person who, merely to
be known as "different," ignores the suggestion
of others and insists on his own way of carrying out a plan or of reacting to a situation.

Here the "being different," "being individualistic," is not the result of a firm inner conviction that one's point of view is sound and
has been carefully thought through. As a
matter of fact, the person who insists upon
following discordant ideas very often is voic-
ing his differences because he is uncertain of
his importance in a group and is eager to
attract attention.

Oddly enough, much as people covet the
good will and approval of others, they frequently find it more desirable to forfeit approval in order to win recognition, than to
remain ignored entirely. Nothing seems harder
to bear than to be overlooked. Hence when
one is being disregarded there is occasionally
a tendency toward extreme dissension, because
that is certain to attract at least *some* attention
even though the attention be not wholly
approving.

To Be Ignored Hurts Most

Does that point seem difficult to understand?
Do you think that to behave thus would be
most peculiar and unusual? We see it even in
little children. The youngster who whines,
clowns, or nags will often become cheery and

docile if his mother devotes more time and
interest to him. It is when she ignores him
that the whining, cutting-up, and nagging
serve a purpose. Then attention is directed
toward him for *mis*behavior.

The same motive is back of the discourtesy
or impudence that is sometimes seen in the
high-school student. It is also the answer to
the behavior of the girl who talks too much
and laughs too loudly at a party and is generally too boisterous. So often behavior of
this kind has as its object the attracting of
attention. To be recognized in some way seems
to be even more significant in such instances
than to be recognized with approval and
admiration.

We must enlarge upon our interpretation,
then, of the desire to be approved by others.
We must have it include the desire to be
noticed by others. This applies to all of us.
It accounts for much of our own behavior
which sometimes we find difficult to explain.
It is the explanation of much of the behavior
of our friends and acquaintances which has
seemed so pointless and incomprehensible.

Most people, of course, go to neither of
these extremes which we have discussed. Most
of us are interested in having others think
well of us; therefore we regulate our behavior,
at least in part, by the attitudes of others.
We are wary of behaving in ways that will
expose us to criticism or to disfavor, even
while we earnestly strive to maintain our own
self-respect and display the courage of our
own convictions.

208

Our Desire for Success:

Another Social Need

Everyone of us, quite naturally, wants to be best at something, whether it be as a Boy Scout, or as a writer, or any one of a thousand other areas of human activity. This article describes how this desire to succeed affects our behavior.

Boy Scouts of America

Which do you like to play best, tennis or baseball? Which would you rather do, mathematical problems or an English theme? How do you prefer to go to the movies, to go swimming, or out for a hike—alone or with companions?

If you prefer tennis to baseball, it is fairly certain that you play a better game of tennis than you do of baseball. If you do "math" in preference to composition, it is probable that you are better at figuring than you are at putting thoughts down in writing. If you would rather do things alone than with others, it is pretty good evidence that you get along with yourself better than you do with other people.

We are inclined to *like* to do best that which we *do* best. This is only another way of saying that we like the experience of success.

That is why a very small baby shakes a rattle and enjoys it, but shows no interest in a complicated picture puzzle. He can play successfully (hence happily) with his rattle, but he has no understanding of a puzzle, and so he is not made happy by it.

That may be why you like to make a batch of fudge, but are not at all inclined to bake a layer cake. You perhaps have experienced making good fudge, and thereby enjoyed satisfaction in your success. But that cake you tried once fell and was tough; therefore it did not give you a feeling of success or of having mastered the cakemaking problem.

This same feeling of success in certain undertakings explains why some students volunteer to do the various jobs connected with school plays. Some offer to do the publicity and posters, others to take care of the lights, fixtures, costumes, etc. Each one volunteers for the thing in which he feels most competent.

Success: An Unconscious Need

The poster volunteer has the pleasant reaction of being successful in his art work. The one who likes to act usually acts well; the girl who prefers to make the costumes is successful at designing and sewing. The artist with brushes or crayons is not inclined to do the sewing; the expert designer of costumes is not inclined to try out for a part to act; the good actress has no desire to have charge of the lighting, and so on. We are all inclined to do that which we feel fairly sure we can do well. We desire to try that which will give us some measure of success and which will help us feel we have accomplished something with merit.

Two boys went on a weekend visit to the summer home of a classmate. They had all been together in their city environment many times, but had never been together in the country. They arrived, exchanged greetings, and unpacked. Then the host suggested that they go fishing, but one of the guests said he would rather play tennis. The other indicated that as far as he was concerned he would prefer to try the golf course. Now, of course, all of these boys, as is true of most fellows, enjoyed many different activities. But the host had only recently learned the trick of casting; one of his friends was an excellent tennis player, while the other was particularly skillful at golf. Their first suggestions for activity concerned the particular things at which each was most adept, at which each would achieve the greatest success. They were not thinking of "showing off" their accomplishments; they were merely reacting to an underlying general motivation. We all have the desire to be successful. We enjoy doing what we do well.

Two girls were discussing plans for an

209

evening party for a few school friends at the home of one of the girls. One girl suggested that they turn on the radio, roll up the rugs, and dance. The other, a rather large, awkward girl who was not very light on her feet, was insistent that they get together some games which would be played around a table. How easy to understand the reasons back of each suggestion!

We Enjoy Most What We Do Best

It is not strange that we *like* to do best that which we *do* best. We are fulfilling our unconscious desire to satisfy one of our needs, that of being successful in what we undertake.

Do you ever have science assignments which make it necessary to look up material in the library? You select a reference which sounds helpful in the card catalogue, but it turns out to be full of long words and complicated explanations which you do not understand. What do you do when that happens? Generally, you give up that special book. Your struggle with material which is too technical is a decidedly unpleasant experience. Your efforts to understand are in vain, and you are only too well aware of a lack of success. You find another book which uses less difficult terms and which really tells you what you want to know. You are happier with this book because you are successful with it.

Have you ever been asked if you could fix a lock which does not work? You may have considerable skill at that kind of undertaking. You may have been able to turn keys easily in a lock which seemed very stubborn. You may

These three winners in the Olympic games excel in sports. It is a natural need in everyone of us to wish to excel in our chosen field.

enjoy working with tools and being precise and careful in your movements so that your job is expertly done. But here is something different—here is a lock which is not at all like any you have seen before. You examine it carefully, and you try and try to get it to work. Finally, you become impatient, or annoyed, or out of sorts. You are not enjoying this experience of being unsuccessful.

Did you ever see a small boy playing with his big brother's electric trains? When a complicated procedure interferes with the youngster's efforts at making the trains switch properly, what does he do? Generally, he gives up after a period of time. He may just walk off in disgust, or he may hurl the train from him in his keen disappointment. But he is very happy with his wind-up trains, because he can manipulate them successfully.

Success Brings Self-Satisfaction

When you attempt to complete an assignment in translating a passage in French, you are dissatisfied and perhaps greatly disturbed if you cannot put the subject matter into clear, understandable English. If you are able to work out the meaning of the French translation correctly, you experience a feeling of satisfaction. Therefore, you experience pleasure at your success in this undertaking.

Perhaps you have wondered at the persistence of laboratory workers in their research projects, or at artists in their particular fields of activity. Perhaps you have been amazed at the years of study and experimentation that have been consumed in perfecting great scientific discoveries, in the completion of great symphonies and works of art, or the construction of a bridge or skyscraper. The satisfaction of work successfully accomplished, whether in actual construction or in abstract thought, is a powerful motivating factor back of the endeavor each represents.

It really does not matter whether we are concerned with placing a drop kick, playing a violin concerto, designing a bookplate, or trimming a hat, the significant factor is the job of successful achievement. It represents one of the social needs felt by all of us.

Our Desire To Be Like Others:

A Third Social Need

Everyone who has read Daniel Defoe's book about Robinson Crusoe marvels at the fact that Crusoe could stand to live alone without any human companionship for so many years. On the other hand we find it easy to understand such animal behavior as that of the giraffes who herd together. Most human beings desire to be like their fellow humans—it is one of the important social needs. This article will tell you more about our desire to be like others.

Why do you suppose that most of the girls wear their hair in a particular fashion each season? One year they wear little curls all over their heads, another season they slick back their locks, and another year they wear long, wavy bobs.

Why is it that the boys seem to buy the same kind of clothes to wear to school? One year, you may remember, Mackinaws were the thing; another year, it was leather windbreakers. One year coats and trousers have to match or the boys are mildly uncomfortable; another season, unless the material of each is different in weave and color they feel "out of style."

Why is it that when fashion decrees long skirts, practically all girls and women wear long skirts, but when short skirts are "the thing," up they go on all femininity? Last year's dresses and coats are made longer or shorter, in order to conform with this year's styles, and they seem strange when they are worn at last year's popular length!

We can find many other examples of the common tendency to conform, to do what others are doing: current dance steps, widespread use of slang, collections, and hobbies. All of these furnish further evidence of the constant demand for individual adjustment. How absurd we would feel on a dance floor today if we knew only the minuet, or the polka, or the gavotte. How ridiculous our friends would think us if we spoke in the slang and colloquialisms of our grandmother's day. Today, we do the foxtrot, the rhumba, or that new step you learned only last week.

Most of Us Want To Be Like Our Group

All of these everyday bits of human behavior illustrate the ever-present human tendency to be like one's fellows. And this urge to conformity goes even deeper than when shown in clothing, dance steps, or collecting fads. It appears, also, in more meaningful social behavior that involves us every day of our lives. Think how abused you felt when your parents refused you permission to join that excursion. That was because it made you seem different from the others who were going. Remember how annoyed your whole class was when your faculty advisors would not sanction a dance in a downtown hotel. The seniors had enjoyed one off-campus, and you younger students wanted to be like them.

This urge to be like others is not present in the same degree in all individuals, any more than are other characteristics. So we always find some people—usually only a few —who glory in being as different as possible from all others. We also find a few folks who are frankly miserable unless they can do just what others are doing, and who follow sheep-like the formula of the majority. Extremes are rarely to be desired. Not that we would seek to make all boys and girls alike! But to be radically different from all others seldom makes for happy adjustment in living.

Is It Sometimes Wise To Be Different?

You may ask, what of the expressions which seem so complimentary to a person: "He had the courage to be different," and "He had the courage of his convictions"? Is it always right to conform? Is it not sometimes wise to be different? Of course the answer to the last question is yes. The problem lies in knowing when to insist upon being individualistic in your reaction. Of course, progress in any field lies in the courage to experiment, in the imagination which suggests experimentation. The first man who conceived the idea of a train, of a steamboat, of an automobile, of an airplane—was he not laughed at in scorn by his contemporaries? Had each one not had the "courage of his convictions," our means of transportation would be very different today and would lack the speed and safety which we accept so casually.

It is not easy to ignore the basic tendencies of human nature. It takes courage to be different. And, obviously, we must be very sure of the wisdom of insisting upon certain differences.

Had Louis Pasteur not had the courage to go contrary to the opinion of his day, science would have been impeded in its advance and mankind would have continued to suffer ills which had been misunderstood until Pasteur's research. Had Marie Curie not had the tenacity to carry on in the face of contrary convictions, the same results would have followed. These scientists were not merely objecting; rather, they were attempting to establish truths which they were convinced were indisputable. Their conviction was based upon the evidence of scientific laboratory investigations.

In such individuals it is highly laudatory to be different, and to be different in the extreme. Of course, most of us are not Pasteurs or Curies. Most of us follow the underlying human tendency to conform. We lack the reasons for nonconformity which these and similar outstanding individuals have had. That

does not mean that we are all just alike. There are always differences, but not always are these *marked* differences.

It Is Not Always Easy To Be Different

There are many occasions when we are disinclined to follow a certain activity because others we know are not active in that particular direction. We do many things which we hate to admit, because we know others do them differently.

Do you recall the time your parents would not permit you to join a group of your acquaintances in an evening jaunt? The next day you said, casually, that you had not felt like going, or that some guests dropped in and you had to stay at home. Either of those statements might of course have been quite true. You were more comfortable offering such reasons than you would have been in saying that you were "different" from the others in that your parents had not agreed with the group plan.

Whether or not it is wise or desirable to "conform," to follow group inclinations, depends upon so many circumstances that each instance must be considered apart in order to be judged.

We should recognize the tendency to be like others as an urge that motivates much of our behavior and the behavior of our friends. It may explain your resentment at a parental or school regulation which seems to make you or your group "different." It underlies your reluctance to look, to plan, or to think in ways which vary from those of your friends and acquaintances.

However, the desirability of following blindly the driving force of *any* of our social needs is not our immediate problem. *What interests us here is the existence of these needs and the explanation they provide for human behavior.* They are the reason, in some measure, for the conduct of your school group and of any other group. They are the answer when we look for an explanation for the reactions of children and of adults. For we are all human personalities and hence are all motivated by similar forces.

212

How Simple Drives Are Measured

Compiled from official sources by the editor.

The Columbia Obstruction Box

An ancient fable tells us that a young man once swam the Hellespont, the broad channel which separates Europe from Asia, to join his ladylove. This story is told to illustrate how strong the young man's love was. Today, psychologists use an electric Hellespont to study the strength of drives in animals. A rat is put in a device such as the one shown at right. From its place in the entrance chamber (A), the goal box (C) is visible. In it the scientists have placed some food. The rat has not eaten in 24 hours. Before the animal can get to the food it must cross the metal grid (B) separating the entrance chamber from the goal box. But the metal bars of the grid are charged with an electric current. When the rat steps on the metal it gets a shock. The electrical Hellespont is known as the Columbia Obstruction Box. In building it the scientists reasoned that by counting the number of times the animal crossed the electric grid they would get a measure of how strong the animal's drive was. The number of times the animal crosses the electrical barrier in twenty minutes (the rat is returned to the entrance chamber as soon as it reaches the goal box) steadily increases with the time it has gone without food. A male rat will cross on the average about eighteen times in a twenty-minute period when it has gone without food for about two days. That is about one crossing every minute. As the period of starvation increases beyond two days the number of crossings slowly begins to decrease. This is probably because the strength of the animal slowly begins to fail. It is interesting to note, however, that human beings who have gone without food for a long time also report that after the first day or so hunger pangs are not so bothersome. (See "The Biological Drives," page 199.)

The Columbia Obstruction Box and similar devices have also been used to measure thirst, the sexual drive, and even the strength of a mother rat's drive to join her young.

The reason psychologists are interested in obtaining an accurate measure of drive is that drive is closely related to the way animals learn and behave. For example rats who have practiced in a maze perform more efficiently and quickly as the number of hours the animals have gone without food increases. Further, hungry animals are less likely to give up a response which is no longer rewarded by food than are animals who have recently been fed. Because drives have such an important effect upon behavior, rats cross electrical Hellesponts in many laboratories today.

Other Books To Read

The Hidden You: Psychology in Your Life, by Arthur Alexander. Published by Prentice-Hall, Inc., Englewood Cliffs, New Jersey, 1962.
For younger readers, an introduction to elementary psychology that offers explanations for certain kinds of behavior and various behavior patterns. The author stresses that the individual personality can surprise even its owner, and that no ironclad rules about human behavior can be laid down.

The Science of Ourselves: Adventures in Experimental Psychology, by William N. McBain and R. C. Johnson. Published by Harper & Row, New York, 1962.
Ten psychologists explore the mysteries of the human personality. The methods employed by experimental psychology are described and some theories that have grown out of it are explained. The authors suggest a few experiments that readers can carry out.

Psychology, by Ross Stagner and T. F. Karwoski. Published by McGraw-Hill Book Company, Inc., New York, third revised edition, 1961.
Chapter 2 is good advanced reading for anyone who is interested in learning more about the biological drives.

The United Nations Headquarters, as seen from across New York City's East River. The monumental Secretariat Building looms over the smaller Library (just left of center) and the Conference and General Assembly buildings, which extend to the right. The Headquarters occupies 18 acres along the river's edge and contains gardens and fountains. In the background are the skyscrapers of midtown Manhattan.

The United Nations

Every year hundreds of thousands of people from all over the world visit the strikingly modern United Nations Headquarters on the banks of the East River in New York City. But the beautiful glass and steel buildings are only a symbol. The United Nations is a world organization whose power lies only in the willingness of its members to meet together, discuss, and then suggest a plan of action on the particular problem before them. As a forum (and perhaps a safety valve) for the statesmen of the world, it has played and continues to play an important role in many of the crucial issues of our time—Indonesia, Korea, Suez, the Congo, disarmament, to name just a few. Under the circumstances it is not at all surprising that the United Nations should have its detractors as well as its admirers. Some criticize it for doing too little, some for doing too much. One thing is certain, however; since its foundation in 1945 the United Nations has more than doubled its membership. To many of the new members acceptance means introduction to a complex new world in which they will learn much.

There have been other attempts in history to form organizations of nations and states for the sake of peace. There have been many leagues and alliances, but these were usually meant only to give the allies more power against their enemies. After Napoleon's defeat in 1815, Europe's statesmen tried a plan called the Concert of Europe, under which countries held conferences (called congresses) to settle their differences without going to war. After World War I, the League of Nations was set up as a means of preserving peace. These peace organizations were too weak for the big problems they were expected to solve. The United Nations has done better than any previous body in its peace-keeping efforts. But it has many other important tasks apart from preserving the peace, and they are discussed in some of the pages that follow.

The Road to
San Francisco:

How the UN Was Born

In April, 1945, fifty nations which were fighting together in World War II against the Axis dictatorships sent representatives to San Francisco to work out a plan for world peace. After two months' hard work they agreed to a constitution for a new world organization. They signed the United Nations Charter. Poland, which did not attend the conference, became the fifty-first nation to sign. From **One World in the Making: The United Nations,** by William G. Carr, copyright 1946, 1947. By permission of the publishers, **Ginn and Company. Revised by editor.**

For many hundreds of years people have been trying to find a way to prevent wars. After World War I ended, in 1918, the winning nations held a meeting in Paris to plan a League of Nations. Woodrow Wilson, the President of the United States at that time, was the leader in working out the plans for the League. He wanted the United States to join the League of Nations, but the Senate decided that the United States ought not to join. Most of the other nations of the world did join the League of Nations. Much good work was done by the League, but it was not strong enough to prevent World War II.

When a terrible war is being fought, people think most eagerly about how to secure and keep peace among the nations. As soon as World War II started, the leaders of the nations began to plan together for the peace that would follow. Many important meetings were held while the war was still being fought.

Drawing Up the Atlantic Charter

In August, 1941, Winston Churchill, the British Prime Minister and Franklin D. Roosevelt, President of the United States, met on a battleship in the North Atlantic. They wrote a statement called the Atlantic Charter. They said:

that they did not want their countries to take land away from any other nation;

that they did not want any nation to take new lands against the wishes of the people living there;

that all people should have the right to decide how they should be governed;

that nations should work together to make better living conditions for all their people;

that they wanted to establish a peace under which "all men in all lands may live out their lives in freedom from fear and want";

that everyone should have a right to travel in safety across the seas;

that nations which threaten the peace should not be allowed to have weapons;

and that all nations should as soon as possible reduce their armies and navies.

They looked forward to "a permanent system of general security," that is, to some definite plan to keep the peace.

When the Atlantic Charter was written, the United States was not actually at war. In a little over three months, however, on December 7, 1941, the Japanese attacked Pearl Harbor and certain American islands. Then the United States entered the war against Germany, Italy, and Japan.

On New Year's Day, 1942, at the White House in Washington, the representatives of twenty-six nations signed a paper called "Declaration by United Nations." Other nations signed it later. These nations all agreed that they approved what was in the Atlantic Charter, that they would all fight the Axis to a finish, and that no one of them would make peace with their enemies until victory was won. This was the first time that the term *United Nations* was used. There was no real organization of these nations then. They were indeed *united,* but only for the purpose of winning the war.

Planning for Peace

In October, 1943, Cordell Hull, Secretary of State of the United States, flew to Moscow for

215

a meeting with representatives of China, Great Britain, and the Soviet Union. These men held twelve meetings about how to win the war and the peace. Among other things they decided:

that they would establish, as soon as they could, "a general international organization," which all peace-loving countries could join on an equal basis, "for the maintenance of international peace and security."

In November, 1943, at Tehran in Iran (Persia), President Roosevelt, Prime Minister Churchill, and Marshal Stalin met for the first time. They agreed that they must make a peace that would "banish the scourge and terror of war" and create a "world family" of democratic nations.

In order to work out these plans for peace more completely, the representatives of the Big Four nations (China, Great Britain, the Soviet Union, the United States) met again, in Washington, D.C., in August and September, 1944. Because the place where they met was a beautiful home and garden called Dumbarton Oaks, the plans they prepared were called the Dumbarton Oaks Proposals.

The men who met at Dumbarton Oaks were not able to agree on one very important point—namely, how the voting should be done in the Security Council through which the big nations were to preserve peace. President Roose-

In February, 1945, Winston Churchill, Franklin D. Roosevelt, and Joseph Stalin met at Yalta, on the Black Sea, U.S.S.R., and agreed to call a conference at San Francisco in April, 1945, for the purpose of organizing the United Nations.

velt, Prime Minister Churchill, and Marshal Stalin, therefore, met again the following February at Yalta, a seaside resort in the Crimea. There they did clear up the question of voting in the Security Council, and decided to invite all the United Nations to consider the Dumbarton Oaks Proposals at San Francisco, beginning April 25, 1945.

The Atlantic Charter, the United Nations Declaration, the Moscow Declaration, the meeting at Tehran, the Dumbarton Oaks Proposals, the Yalta Conference—these were the principal milestones along the road to San Francisco.

Food and Shelter for Millions

While these events were happening, the United Nations held several special meetings to consider special problems relating to winning the war and keeping the peace.

In June, 1943, the United Nations had a meeting in Hot Springs, Virginia, to consider how enough food could be produced and sold so that everyone could have enough to eat. In August, 1944, the United Nations formed a Food and Agriculture Organization to help them work together to grow and buy enough food for all.

In October, 1943, the United Nations held a special meeting in Atlantic City, New Jersey, to plan how best to get food, clothing, shelter, medicines, and other needed help to the people in the countries which the enemy had invaded. They decided to form a United Nations Relief and Rehabilitation Administration to give that kind of help as soon as the enemy was driven out. This agency, usually called UNRRA for short, later gave aid to the victims of war in many different parts of the world. It arranged for over three billion dollars' worth of relief supplies for use in seventeen different countries. It managed camps where people who had been driven from home by the war could live. The great work of the United Nations Relief and Rehabilitation Administration was ended in 1947.

In July, 1944, at Bretton Woods, New Hampshire, the United Nations arranged to have an International Bank and an International Mon-

The flags of the countries that met to form the United Nations ring the stage of the San Francisco Opera House as the delegates sign the UN Charter on June 24, 1945. Here, Joseph Paul-Boncour signs for France while other delegates wait to sign the vital document.

etary Fund. The International Bank lends money to increase the production of goods and to encourage trade among the nations. The International Monetary Fund is used to help to keep the value of money steady in all parts of the world.

In November, 1945, the United Nations met in London to plan an international organization for education, science, and culture. This organization is called the United Nations Educational, Scientific, and Cultural Organization (UNESCO). It has its main office in Paris. UNESCO helps the peoples of all the nations to know one another better, to have better schools, and to exchange their best work in science, music, art, literature, and education for the good of all.

Fifty Nations Meet at San Francisco

After all the years of preparation, the San Francisco Conference met on the afternoon of April 25, 1945. Fifty nations were represented there by about sixteen hundred delegates and their assistants. The conference met in San Francisco's War Memorial Opera House.

The work of the conference was complicated. Over sixty different committees worked on special parts of the United Nations plan. These committees met a total of 335 times. In the busiest part of the conference ten of these committee meetings were held every day.

Difficulties were increased by the different languages. There were five official languages of the conference: English, French, Spanish, Russian, and Chinese. The important speeches were translated several times, and all important papers used by the conference had to be translated into five languages. This work was done by 120 interpreters and translators.

Every nation was invited to suggest changes in the Dumbarton Oaks Proposals. There were over four hundred pages of these suggestions. Printed in the five languages of the conference, they made a very heavy book. Every one of these suggestions had to be considered carefully. Most of them had to be discussed at length.

Each of the clauses of the Charter was written several times before it was agreed upon. Finally, on June 26, 1945, the final draft of the Charter was signed by delegates of the assembled nations. Later that year, on October 24, the Charter came into force. This day is now known as United Nations Day.

The United Nations moved several times before it secured the majestic headquarters on the East River in New York which it occupies today. Its membership has more than doubled since 1945, and it has had to cope with many problems which did not exist then. But it has done much to prevent wars, to help nations, and to unite the world's people.

217

Workshops of Peace

United Nations Headquarters in New York City was planned by an international team of architects. The 39-story Secretariat Building dominates the General Assembly Building (background) and the Library Building.

The Economic and Social Council chamber was designed by Sven Markelius, of Sweden. With the chambers of the Security Council and the Trusteeship Council, it occupies the Conference Building, a long, low structure which is obscured by the Secretariat Building in the photograph at the left.

The newest structure, the Dag Hammarskjöld Library, is shown at left and also in the view of UN Headquarters (above left). Like the Secretariat Building, its front and back are of glass and metal and its sides are of marble. Housing up to 400,000 volumes, it is a world reference center.

Architectural harmony at UN Headquarters is apparent even in this view of the rear, northern plaza. You are facing the corridor that connects the General Assembly Building (right) with the Conference Building (left).

218

The Meditation Room in the General Assembly Building is a room of peace for those of many faiths in the service of peace. A large fresco by Swedish artist Bo Beskow is placed slightly in advance of the front wall. Like most other areas, this room is open to the public.

How Does the UN Operate?

The United Nations is a complex organization, because keeping the peace of the world is a complex task. The commissions, committees and agencies of the UN perform a great variety of useful and humanitarian work. Here is a survey of the divisions of the UN, with notes on the responsibility of each division. Based on "Key to the United Nations," published by **Senior Scholastic**, by permission of the editors. Copyright 1954 by Scholastic Corporation. Revised by editor.

The purpose of the United Nations, according to its Charter, is to maintain peace, prevent war, encourage respect for human rights, and promote the social and economic welfare of all mankind.

Member Nations in the Assembly

The General Assembly is the parent body that holds together the UN structure. It is not a legislative body in the sense of the United States Congress or the British Parliament. The Assembly is the place for airing and discussing all the world's problems. Since the UN is not a world government, but merely a loose federation of independent nations, the Assembly cannot pass laws binding on all nations or their citizens. It can only suggest action either by the Security Council or by individual member nations.

Every member nation is represented in the General Assembly. Each nation large or small, has one vote, but may send five delegates to the sessions of the Assembly. The Assembly must meet at least once a year. It may hold special sessions whenever an urgent need arises.

Decisions on major issues in the Assembly are made by a two-thirds majority; on smaller issues, by a simple majority. The Assembly elects its own president annually.

After the North Korean Communists attacked the Republic of Korea in the summer of 1950, the General Assembly took an important step. It adopted a plan proposed by U. S. Secretary of State Acheson called the "Uniting for Peace" Resolution. This resolution, passed by the General Assembly in November, 1950, empowers the Assembly to deal with any breach of peace by an aggressor nation if the Security Council should fail to take action because of a veto by any of the Big Five countries which sit permanently in the Council.

Flags of the member states flying in front of the United Nations Headquarters in New York City. Each new member means an additional flag.

A. Devaney, Inc.

How the United Nations Is Organized:

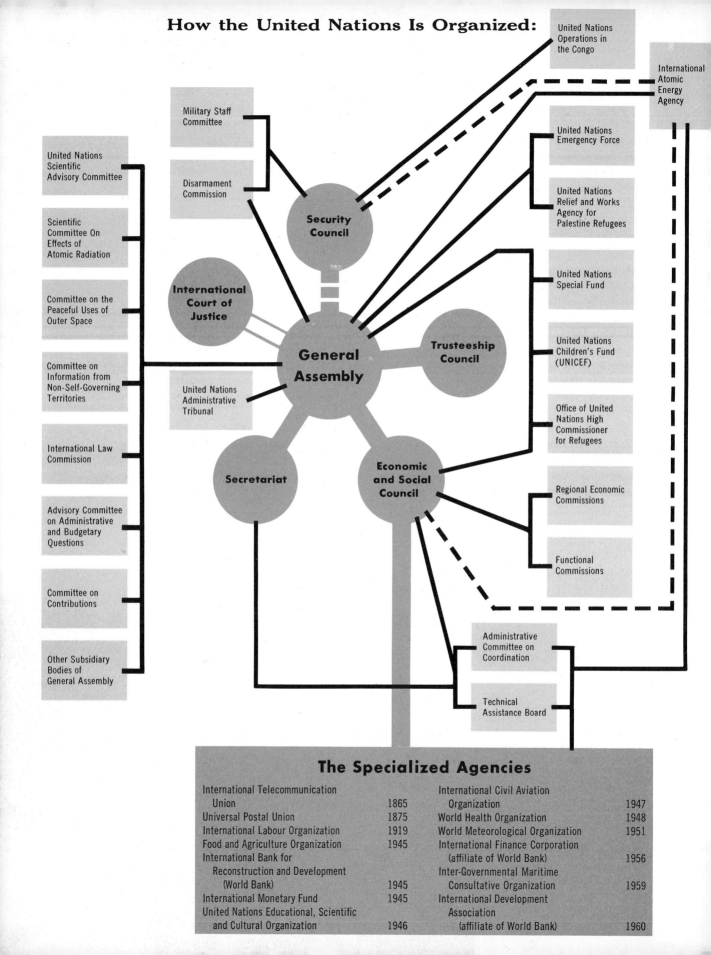

United Nations Operations in the Congo

International Atomic Energy Agency

Military Staff Committee

Disarmament Commission

Security Council

United Nations Scientific Advisory Committee

Scientific Committee On Effects of Atomic Radiation

Committee on the Peaceful Uses of Outer Space

Committee on Information from Non-Self-Governing Territories

International Law Commission

Advisory Committee on Administrative and Budgetary Questions

Committee on Contributions

Other Subsidiary Bodies of General Assembly

International Court of Justice

United Nations Administrative Tribunal

General Assembly

Secretariat

Trusteeship Council

Economic and Social Council

United Nations Emergency Force

United Nations Relief and Works Agency for Palestine Refugees

United Nations Special Fund

United Nations Children's Fund (UNICEF)

Office of United Nations High Commissioner for Refugees

Regional Economic Commissions

Functional Commissions

Administrative Committee on Coordination

Technical Assistance Board

The Specialized Agencies

International Telecommunication Union	1865	International Civil Aviation Organization	1947
Universal Postal Union	1875	World Health Organization	1948
International Labour Organization	1919	World Meteorological Organization	1951
Food and Agriculture Organization	1945	International Finance Corporation (affiliate of World Bank)	1956
International Bank for Reconstruction and Development (World Bank)	1945	Inter-Governmental Maritime Consultative Organization	1959
International Monetary Fund	1945	International Development Association (affiliate of World Bank)	1960
United Nations Educational, Scientific and Cultural Organization	1946		

Countries in the Security Council

In theory the Security Council is the most powerful organ of the United Nations. Under the charter the Council is empowered (1) to settle disputes among nations peacefully, if possible by persuasion; (2) to use all powers at its command, including force, to punish aggressors and prevent the spread of war. It can call on any member nation to contribute armed forces for this purpose.

The Security Council is in session the year around. The Council consists of fifteen members. Of these, five are permanent members—Britain, Nationalist China, France, Russia, and the United States. The other ten are non permanent members, elected for two-year terms by the General Assembly. Each of the fifteen members presides over the Council for one month at a time.

The permanent seat assigned to China has been held since the beginning by the Nationalist government, regardless of its defeat by the Chinese Communists on the mainland. This situation has led to continuous protest by the Soviet block of countries that Communist China should have the Chinese seat.

The voting procedure in the Security Council has been the subject of great argument. The rules provide that small decisions may be made by a majority of nine members—any nine, whether they are members of the Big Five or not. On important matters, however, the majority of nine must include the votes of all five permanent members. Any one of the Big Five can veto (vote down) a proposal. This veto power has been the Council's chief source of weakness.

The Economic and Social Council

This body was set up to "build a better life" —to promote the welfare and improve the living conditions of the peoples of all countries.

Accordingly, ECOSOC (as it is called) studies economics, social, and cultural, health, and related matters, and makes suggestions to the General Assembly or to the individual members of the United Nations. However, it has no power to enforce its plans. The Council supervises, but does not control, the work of the specialized agencies which are independent bodies.

ECOSOC is composed of twenty-seven members elected by the General Assembly for three-year terms. Voting in ECOSOC is by simple majority, each member nation having one vote. It meets at least twice a year.

The Trusteeship Council

The Trusteeship Council is progressively working itself out of a job. Its purpose is to protect the interests of the inhabitants of de-

A typical meeting of the Security Council. Each member sits at a place marked with the name of his country. The striking mural on the left of the chamber is by the Norwegian artist, Per Krohg.

Wide World

In the North Lounge of the Conference Building members of various delegations often meet and converse informally.

pendent territories placed under its supervision and to lead them to self-government or independence. Of the eleven territories once under trusteeship, only three remain.

The UN Trusteeship System applies to: (1) territories taken from enemy nations in World War I (the so-called "League of Nations mandates"); (2) territories taken from enemy nations in World War II; and (3) other territories voluntarily placed under the Trusteeship System.

The Trusteeship Council is composed of *a,* countries which administer trust territories; *b,* the five permanent members of the Security Council; and *c,* a variable number of other countries elected by the General Assembly.

When Pope Paul VI arrived at United Nations Headquarters in New York on October 4, 1965, he became the first supreme pontiff of the Roman Catholic Church to set foot in the New World. Here he addresses the UN General Assembly; Secretary-General U Thant is seen at left.

Voting in the Trusteeship Council is by simple majority.

The World Court Judges Nations

The International Court of Justice, popularly called the World Court, is designed to settle legal disputes which may arise among nations. Only nations, *not individuals*, may bring cases before the Court.

The Secretariat

This is the executive and office staff of the United Nations. It is composed of a Secretary-General (who is appointed by the General Assembly upon the recommendation of the Security Council) and an international force of civil servants.

The Secretary-General is the chief administrative officer of the United Nations. He is assisted by several under-secretaries. The Secretariat is divided into offices and departments corresponding in general to the principal UN organs. The 4,400 men and women who work for the Secretariat are international civil servants; about 3,000 are at New York headquarters. The UN Charter requires that "in the performance of their duties, the Secretary-General and the staff shall not seek or receive instructions from any other authority" outside the organization.

The Specialized Agencies

There are a number of independent international agencies that are associated with the United Nations. These are known as the Specialized Agencies. Some of them were founded long before the United Nations came into existence. These specialized agencies work closely with the UN and with each other.

Other Sections To See

"World Action for Man's Health," Volume 6; "Warfare and Weapons," Volume 8; "Nations in Harmony," Volume 10; "The Olympic Games," Volume 11; "World Citizens at Work," Volume 12; "A Gallery of Peacemakers," Volume 13; "International Relations and Diplomacy," Volume 15.

The planting of mimosa trees in the barren sands of Gaza by the UN Relief and Works Agency for Palestine Refugees has reclaimed land for cultivation.

This earth mover is operating on the railway embankments of the Gongola River, Nigeria. World Bank loans are helping the country expand its railway facilities.

Words Into Deeds: The Work of the UN Agencies

Some of the most important accomplishments of the United Nations are often unknown to the general public. One does not hear too much about the dedicated men and women patiently working on a great variety of projects. Here is part of this exciting story. From **The Story of the United Nations**, by Katharine Savage. Copyright © 1962 by Katharine Savage. Reprinted by permission of Henry J. Walck, Inc., and The Bodley Head Ltd.

At first there may not seem to be much connection between building dams, curing people of leprosy, and keeping the world at peace. But history has shown that peace and prosperity go hand in hand. The United Nations hopes through its many agencies to banish ignorance and poverty and promote better living so that people all over the world will be contented enough that they will not want to go to war.

When a government sends in a request for United Nations aid the agency concerned, working with the Economic and Social Council and the General Assembly, dispatches experts to examine the situation on the spot. They may find a desperate shortage of doctors and teachers or an urgent need for up-to-date equipment and technical advice. Despite the spread of education and the advances of science, there are still many regions in the world today where sickness and hunger are commonplace and very few people can read or write. It requires skill and perseverance to introduce learning to a community where no one has ever seen a book or imagined that a vehicle could run on wheels.

Adventures in Technical Assistance

This work is mainly paid for with money which has been pledged for the Expanded Program of Technical Assistance or the Special Fund. But each project is a combined effort, and the country receiving the aid has to guarantee part of the cost.

The Technical Assistance Board (TAB) is one of the most adventurous of the UN agencies. It answers calls from remote areas, far from the beaten track, and sends out small but enterprising teams with expert knowledge. Life is hard in many of these isolated communities, and the TAB teams try to give the people technical assistance. Sometimes they can discover minerals and start a new industry; or drain swamps; or increase the water supply by uncovering hidden streams. Often up-to-date tools make the whole difference to potters or weavers or farmers. A new fertilizer can turn poor crops into plentiful ones, and a couple of bulldozers in expert hands can save months of back-breaking toil.

What Does UNESCO Do?

The United Nations Educational, Scientific and Cultural Organization (UNESCO) has responded to appeals from many nations. The name speaks for itself. UNESCO links the work of other agencies, for its staff teaches everything from simple cleanliness to higher education. It is sensible for a child to learn first how to wash its hands and then how to

223

The provision of safe drinking water is an important step in the elimination of disease among refugees. The World Health Organization assists in this task.

Moroccan students at the Center for Training of Telecommunication Technicians. The Special Fund is helping the Government finance this training.

read, and clean drinking water is even more important than arithmetic. UNESCO works with governments which are striving to fit people for life in the modern world. It encourages learning for men and women of all ages, as well as many trades, and special instruction for people who are handicapped. Through UNESCO the blind and the crippled in many lands have won new hope. UNESCO tries to safeguard treasures as well as people. One year it worked with Interpol (International Police) studying robberies of famous pictures from art galleries all over the world, and devising new ways both to catch the thieves and to prevent future robberies.

Labor Around the World

The International Labor Organization (ILO) does the same kind of educational work. By organizing international conferences it brings together workers and managers from many different countries. Governments and businesses can send miners and millers, tanners and steel workers, clockmakers and electricians who work thousands of miles apart to ILO meetings where they compare their troubles and techniques. ILO instructors suggest ways to improve working conditions, bring in new

equipment, and show people how to use it. Spinners learn to work new looms, and carpenters to improve their skill; miners learn to respect safety measures and avoid accidents. The ILO also works with schools and colleges helping to train young people for the kind of jobs that they will be good at and opening up new careers for them. As countries develop, horizons are widened, and boys whose fathers were warriors or coolies become engineers and doctors. Girls qualify as nurses, cooks, and secretaries in countries where their mothers could only beg for a living or slave in the fields.

Taking Care of the Refugees

The United Nations has always had to deal with millions of refugees. Each war is more devastating and moves more swiftly than the one before. The number of refugees increases, and they are driven farther from their homes. After the Second World War the problem seemed almost insoluble. A multitude of people, homeless through no fault of their own, were living in dismal camps, and without the help of the United Nations Office of the High Commissioner for Refugees (UNHCR) they probably would have remained in them for

Most of the agencies affiliated with the United Nations have a symbol to identify them. Here (top to bottom) are the symbols of: United Nations Children's Fund (UNICEF); United Nations High Commissioner for Refugees (UNHCR); International Atomic Energy Agency (IAEA); International Labour Organisation (ILO); Food and Agriculture Organization of the UN (FAO); World Health Organization (WHO); Universal Postal Union (UPU); Intergovernmental Maritime Consultative Organization (IMCO).

Preparing yoghurt for delivery in Salonika, Greece. FAO and UNICEF helped to establish this milk pasteurization plant.

These children in a village school in Afghanistan are learning to read. This is part of the Government's rural development program, which is helped by UN agencies.

the rest of their lives. It has taken many years of dedicated work to find new homes and new jobs for these displaced people. May, 1959, to May, 1960, was a special World Refugee Year, and more than $84,000,000 was raised. This was enough to pay for clearing the European camps, and today all the refugees from the Second World War have been moved to better surroundings.

Refugee camps in the Middle East have been crammed to overflowing since the Arab-Jewish war which followed the partition of Palestine and the foundation of the state of Israel in 1948. More than half a million Arabs fled from Israel, leaving their homes and all their possessions behind, into the neighboring states of Transjordan, Syria, Lebanon, and the narrow Gaza strip, which runs between southern Israel and the Mediterranean. There they set up encampments of ragged tents on wasteland that no one else wanted. In May, 1950, the United Nations Relief and Works Agency for Palestine Refugees (UNRWA) was formed.

UNRWA has two main tasks: the day-to-day struggle to provide food, shelter and medical care to keep the refugees alive; and the long-term effort to settle them in jobs where they can support themselves and their families. The better educated among them have mostly decamped and found work in the many Middle Eastern countries. They still call themselves Palestinians and plan to return to the land which they consider is their birthright; but in the meantime they are usefully employed. The rest are a long-term liability. With money from the governments in whose countries the camps are situated and generous donations from benefactors all over the world, UNRWA teams have put up houses in place of tents, and built hospitals, schools, and workshops. They have brought in water and planted gardens in desert land where nothing has ever grown before. Many of the young people are learning trades. Most of the older ones, however, stubbornly refuse to be helped.

How the World Bank Spends Its Money

Perhaps the most tangible results of United Nations planning are achieved through the International Bank for Reconstruction and Development (the World Bank). Many of them stand in steel and concrete, bricks, stone and mortar. They can be seen and their usefulness assessed. United Nations money is behind all kinds of big building projects. The money is deposited with the bank by members of the

Other agencies (top to bottom) are: United Nations Educational, Scientific and Cultural Organization (UNESCO); International Bank for Reconstruction and Development (World Bank); International Development Association (IDA); International Finance Corporation (IFC); International Monetary Fund (IMF); International Civil Aviation Organization (ICAO); World Meteorological Organization (WMO); International Telecommunication Union (ITU). Some agencies do not have symbols.

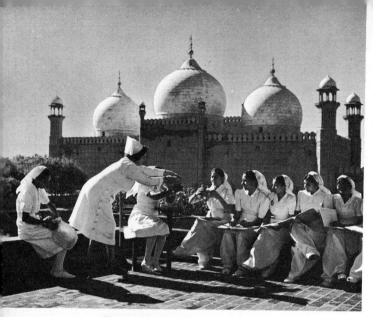

Pakistani girls in a midwifery class are instructed by a WHO expert. This is part of the Government's effort to improve maternal and child health services.

Afghan students prepare to release a weather balloon. The meteorological equipment has been made available through the World Meteorological Organization.

United Nations, and the directors of the bank must make very careful investigations before they promise to support a new venture. They have to be sure that they are making a good investment both for the nations that lend and the nations that borrow. When a government applies for a loan it must promise to provide a share of the manpower, money and materials. Railways driven through hitherto impassable country, new enterprises and factories in countless cities, fine harbors and vast irrigation schemes, hydroelectric plants and oil wells, mines in Mexico, highways in Iran, the Kariba Dam in Africa, the Lunersee Dam in Austria, bridges, viaducts, and tunnels show how World Bank money has been spent.

A Variety of Activities

The United Nations takes part in many different activities. It employs experts to study world aviation, atomic energy, and shipping in all its forms, from primitive sailing junks to modern luxury liners. Helped by United Nations funds, scientists are experimenting with new drugs and trying out industrial designs. In meteorological offices they are poring over charts of tides and winds and collecting data on the eruptions within the earth, the disturbances of the oceans, and the currents in the air. They hope to make travel safer and, by giving

warning of earthquakes, tidal waves, and hurricanes, to save millions of lives.

There is a United Nations commission that defends the rights of women and encourages their education in countries where they have been treated as inferior beings. It also helps women to claim equal pay for equal work in countries where they hold important and responsible jobs. Another commission concentrates on crime and juvenile delinquency, striving to find the causes and cures.

Helping to Improve the World's Health

The United Nations Children's Fund (UNICEF) tries to bring health and happiness to children all over the world. It was started after the Second World War and has been growing ever since. UNICEF depends entirely on voluntary contributions, and it receives generous gifts from governments, businesses, and private individuals to carry on its work. Artists give their services free, and everyone who buys a UNICEF Christmas card helps a child somewhere.

In 1953 the United Nations made a public declaration that every member nation supported. It is a document which concerns grownups and children everywhere, those who are fortunate and those who are in desperate need. It sets out the rights of children all over

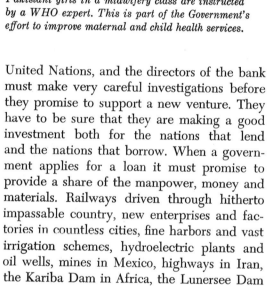

the world and claims that, without exception, they should have a heritage of freedom and grow up without fear. They should have names and a nationality of which they can be proud, enough to eat, good homes, schools to attend, games to play, doctors to give them medical care, and parents or guardians to look after them.

UNICEF tries to help the millions of children who have none of these advantages and whose governments apply for aid.

The World Health Organization (WHO) shares this task with UNICEF and the International Red Cross. WHO has its headquarters in Geneva, and governments send in appeals for help in training medical students and nurses, for doctors to work in their hospitals, scientists to set up laboratories, and medical teams to fight epidemics and famine. These teams establish medical centers in remote areas, often traveling thousands of miles along jungle tracks, across arid deserts, over mountain ranges, or through steaming, swampy country to carry out their work. (For more on UNICEF and WHO see "World Action for Man's Health," Volume 6.)

The Road to International Understanding

Men and women of many nations work for the United Nations, visit each other's territories, and pool their knowledge. In mine disasters in India, Italian engineers have helped to repair the damage; farmers from Japan have consulted with those in Latin America and Swiss shepherds have inspected ailing flocks in Nepal. More than half the population of the world lives mainly on rice, and there is universal exchange of opinion on how to grow the best grains in the most economical way. The Food and Agricultural Organization (FAO) helps to teach farmers new methods of cultivation and to wage scientific war on pests that destroy all kinds of crops.

Many people who are struggling for a bare existence in underdeveloped countries have never heard of the United Nations and have no picture of international understanding. But though they may not be able to grasp the full meaning of the Charter these people can see

Indonesian girls at the Bandung Regional Housing Center, which is partly financed by the Special Fund.

in their homes the practical value of UNESCO, UNICEF, and WHO. They can appreciate the electric power that comes to them through the World Bank or the Special Fund. It is their first glimpse of world planning, and they usually approve of it.

Other Books To Read

The United Nations and What It Does, by Paula Schlining. Published by Lothrop, Lee and Shephard Co., Inc., New York, 1962.
An informative description of the world organization and its activities told by means of text and colorful illustrations.

The Pool of Knowledge, by Katherine B. Shippen. Published by Harper & Row, New York, revised edition, 1965.
How the members of the United Nations share their resources and skills in such fields as health, education, and agriculture; their aims and how they do their work.

Yearbook of the United Nations. Published every year by the Department of Public Information, United Nations, New York.
This is the place to look up the latest work of the United Nations. It is also something of an encyclopedia of the organization from its beginnings in 1945.

227

UN Personalities—Past and Present

UN

Sir Gladwyn Jebb   1900–

Herbert Matthews of *The New York Times* wrote of Jebb: "It is generally agreed
the UN discovered a remarkable civil servant in this British . . . official." Born to a family
of English landed gentry, Jebb went to Eton School and Oxford University.
After serving in the British Foreign Office (State Department) as a diplomat for twenty
years, Jebb went to San Francisco in 1945 to help organize the United Nations.
He became secretary of the top organizing committee and had a hand in all the big
decisions that went into the building of the United Nations. Although often mentioned
as a possible choice for Secretary-General of the UN, Jebb was too busy helping
with the Italian peace treaty and building a democratic alliance in Western Europe
to take up more UN work until 1950. From then until 1954 he sat in the UN
Security Council as permanent representative of the United Kingdom. In 1954, the UN
lost him again when he was appointed British ambassador to France.

Gov't of India Info. Serv.

Mrs. Vijaya Lakshmi Pandit   1900–

This remarkable Indian (whose name is pronounced "Pundit") was the first woman to
hold a top position in the United Nations. She was elected President of the General
Assembly in 1953, for a one-year term. She is the sister of the late Prime Minister
Jawaharlal Nehru of India. Born in a palatial home in Allahabad, in northern India,
she was the daughter of a rich lawyer. When Gandhi rose to fame in India as the
leader of a peaceful independence movement against Great Britain, the entire Nehru
family joined him. In 1949 Mrs. Pandit became ambassador to the United States.
In 1952 she was elected to the Indian Parliament, but soon went to the UN as chief
delegate from India to the General Assembly. After her election as the Assembly's
president in 1953, she said hopefully of the UN: "The very fact that people have
been talking to each other here for eight years is a sign of progress."

UN

Ralph J(ohnson) Bunche   1904–

An outstanding scholar in the field of race relations, a U.N. diplomat, and a Nobel laureate,
Dr. Ralph Bunche was born in Detroit on Aug. 7, 1904. He was educated at Columbia and
Harvard Universities and then taught for several years. In 1941 he entered the State
Department as senior social sciences analyst for the Office for Coordination of Information
(later the OSS). During his years at the State Department he rose to the post of associate
chief of the Division of Dependent Area Affairs; he was the first Negro to hold such high
office in the State Department. Bunche also served as adviser or delegate to many
conferences, including the U.N. General Assembly in London, The Dumbarton Oaks
conference and the International Labor conferences. In 1946 he served as director of the
Trusteeship Division of the U.N. Secretariat. The next year he was appointed to the
Special Committee on Palestine and was acting mediator of the committee after the
death of Count Bernadotte in 1948. He was instrumental in enforcing the truce in Palestine,
and for his work in making peace between the Arabs and Israelis he received the 1950
Nobel Peace prize. Dr. Bunche was appointed U.N. undersecretary in 1954. He was a
special U.N. representative to the Congo in 1960 and headed the U.N. mission to Yemen in
1963. Since 1961 he has served as one of U Thant's inner Cabinet of eight undersecretaries.

Adlai E. Stevenson   1900–1965

Adlai Stevenson was chief U.S. delegate to the UN from 1961 until his death in London in
1965. (He was replaced by Arthur Goldberg, former Supreme Court Justice and Secretary
of Labor.) Mr. Stevenson, after a distinguished career as a government official in World
War II, was appointed press spokesman for the U.S. delegation to the United Nations
Conference on International Organization in San Francisco in 1945. There he was
instrumental in much of the work of forming the UN. He served a term as governor
of Illinois and was twice a candidate for President of the United States, in 1952 and 1956.

Anna Eleanor Roosevelt

1884–1962

Mrs. Franklin D. Roosevelt, first lady of the United States from 1933 until 1945, was perhaps best known for her good will trips around the world and her ardent support of the United Nations. Eleanor Roosevelt fought poverty and inequality among people, both at home and abroad, since before her marriage in 1904. Mother of five children, she was active in women's groups supporting the welfare of youth, promoting rights of minority groups, and fighting unemployment and bad housing. She also wrote a newspaper column for many years. From 1945 to 1953 and again in 1961, Mrs. Roosevelt served as a delegate to the United Nations. As chairman of the UN Human Rights Commission, 1946–1951, she helped to draft the Universal Declaration of Human Rights.

Wide World

Trygve Halvdan Lie

1896–1968

A respected statesman in Norway and the first secretary-general of the United Nations, Lie was born in Oslo on July 16, 1896. He worked at the national headquarters of the Norwegian Labor Party as a young boy and held a party post at the age of 16. From 1922 to 1935 he served as legal adviser to Norway's trade unions, and during this period he notably made peaceful settlement of most of Norway's labor disputes. Lie was minister of justice from 1935 to 1939, after which he served as cabinet minister both in Norway and in exile (1940–45). He headed the Norwegian delegation to the 1946 meeting of the U.N. in London and was elected secretary-general there. As the first secretary-general, his task was to establish the powers of this post. During the Soviet-Iranian dispute he established the right of the secretary-general to make statements to the Security Council about any question under consideration by it. He established the right of the secretary-general to express opinions on the admission of new nations, and, as in the case of the Greek border dispute, to reopen certain questions whenever he deemed it necessary. Lie resigned in 1953 and in 1954 published *In the Cause of Peace*.

Dag Hjalmar Agne Hammarskjöld

1905–1961

A Swedish aristocrat and son of a prime minister of Sweden, Dag Hammarskjöld was born in Jonkoping, Sweden on July 29, 1905. He was trained in financial and economic affairs and held several governmental posts in these areas, including that of undersecretary of the Department of Finance (1936–1945) and economic counsellor to the Swedish Government (1937–1948). He entered his country's diplomatic service in 1946; in 1952 he joined the Swedish delegation to the U.N. and headed this delegation in 1953, and later that year he was unanimously elected secretary-general to succeed Trygve Lie. During his term he created the role of secretary-general as an "international civil servant" and personal mediator-at-large. He practiced preventative and private diplomacy in averting many world crises. During his eight and one half years as Secretary-General, he travelled on 76 missions for the U.N. In 1957 he was unanimously reelected to his post. Hammarskjöld was killed in a plane crash in Africa on Sept. 18, 1961, while on a U.N. mission to the Congo. His spiritual diary *Markings* was published in 1964.

UN

U Thant

1909–

Elected in November, 1961, as acting secretary-general for the unexpired term of Dag Hammarskjöld, U Thant was elected secretary-general in November 1962. At the expiration of this term in 1966, he did not wish to stand for reelection; however, he was persuaded to change his mind and was reelected to a second full term. U Thant was born at Pantanaw, Burma on Jan. 22, 1909. His early career was that of journalist and teacher; he also held educational posts in the Government. In 1947, after Burma voted for independence, Thant entered the interim government as press director. He was a member of the Burmese delegation to the U.N. in 1952 and at home rose to the post of adviser to the prime minister. In 1957 he returned to the U.N. as permanent representative of Burma. Thant's election as secretary-general represented a compromise between U.S. and Soviet blocs. In his role as secretary-general, U Thant has considered himself "impartial, but necessarily neutral." As a result, he has not hesitated to criticize the actions of member nations when he thinks it necessary. His main concerns at the U.N. have been world disarmament; financial solvency for the U.N.; restoring peace and unity to the Congo; and attempting to mediate the Vietnam war.

Leo Rosenthal-PIX

229

The United Nations Guide Service

Very few visitors come to New York without having a tour of the United Nations on their program; and ever since the UN buildings on the East River were opened in the early 1950's, a group of young women—the UN tour guides—have done much to explain the workings of the international organization to the thousands of tourists who every day pass through the bronze doors of the General Assembly building.

The tour guides come from many nations; a typical profile of one would show that she graduated from college, speaks at least two languages (one of which is English) and will remain in the guide service for about two years. Before coming to the UN she has become well acquainted with international affairs.

Applicants must submit forms and recommendations which are carefully studied. If they are selected they undergo a training period of several weeks, during which they learn all about the UN machinery, the personalities, and the issues, so that they can answer almost any question put to them by a visitor.

There is no memorized speech which the guides give; instead, they try to respond to the interest of the group in explaining about the work of the world body. They do not give personal opinions, neither do they try to act like preachers or teachers. They can handle criticism of the UN in a diplomatic manner, and can cope with almost any emergency that might arise during a tour.

A tour starts with a guide taking a group of from 15 to 25 people to a model of the UN enclave and pointing out the three buildings that make it up. They then pause at the Peace Bell, donated by Japan; pass briefly through the Secretariat Building to the low structure which houses three major meeting chambers—Security Council, Trusteeship Council, and Economic and Social Council. On the way the group pauses to examine many art objects which have been donated to the UN by its member countries. Then, after visiting the great General Assembly hall, the group descends to the public area on the lower floor and disbands there near the post office, book store, gift shop and souvenir shop. The UN library is not included in the tour.

Regular guides wear blue uniforms with a loop of dark blue cord on the left shoulder, their names embroidered above the jacket pocket. Apprentice guides may wear dark street suits while their uniforms are being readied, but guides from India, Japan, or other countries with a distinctive national dress may wear this.

For the many people who visit the United Nations, the guide is often the only contact with a member of the organization. What she puts into her presentation is often the primary source of information and impression that the visitors take away with them; and as such, the guides perform a vital service in the work of the United Nations.

At the start of a tour a UN guide, wearing the costume of her native country, points out the buildings of the UN complex on a model.

A guide in regular uniform leads a group of visitors along a corridor. All signs in the UN buildings are in both French and English.

A Record of Accomplishment

The peacemaking mission of the United Nations is its primary function. In the years that have passed since the end of World War II there have been a number of occasions when it seemed that war might begin anew. In several instances the United Nations was able to dampen the fires. This article by the late Adlai Stevenson tells us about some of these important accomplishments of the UN. Reprinted by permission from **THINK** Magazine, copyright 1962 by Adlai E. Stevenson.

The Netherlands foreign minister shakes hands with the Indonesian ambassador at UN headquarters in New York after signing the agreement on West New Guinea (West Irian).

A UNESCO expert teaches a group of young Congolese journalists in Kinshasa. This is a joint project of the Republic of the Congo Government and UNESCO.

Today, a rifle shot on a critical frontier could conceivably trigger a thermonuclear war; a new discovery or a crop failure or a tariff can bring prosperity or disaster to the most widely separated areas. But emerging from the welter of political, national, and racial rivalries there are deeper forces. These make for co-operation in the interest of survival and of a better world. And that is why, fundamentally, the United Nations has absorbed the shocks of the postwar era and has increased the scope of its operations from year to year. Peacekeeping is its primary business. And in spite of the use, and abuse, of the Soviet veto in the Security Council, the United Nations has built up an impressive record of accomplishment.

Helping to Settle the Postwar Disputes

The ink was hardly dry on the Charter when the Security Council was plunged into a historic debate that ended with the withdrawal of Soviet troops from northern Iran. In quick succession, United Nations observers, negotiators and truce supervisors helped to counteract outside Communist support of insurrection in Greece; brought into being the new nation of Indonesia, among the world's largest, without large-scale hostilities; stabilized the dispute between India and Pakistan over Kashmir; and began to patrol the chronically disturbed armistice lines around Israel.

Korea, the Middle East, and Africa

In Korea the United Nations exposed and branded flagrant Communist military aggression, and provided a framework within which 15 nations could help the United States and the Republic of Korea to thwart the attack.

In the Middle East a United Nations emer-

gency force has helped maintain the peace and has calmed impending crises. The United Nations has also been involved in the handling of crises in Lebanon, Jordan and Kuwait. The abrupt departure of the Belgians from the Congo subjected the United Nations to a stringent test. And this is far from a complete catalogue of the trouble spots with which the United Nations has been concerned.

Sometimes Only Words Are Possible

In fairness it must be admitted that the United Nations has sometimes had to limit itself to words rather than deeds in coping with aggressive acts. For years on end, the United Nations can keep the spotlight of free world condemnation turned upon the brutal repression of the Hungarian uprising, and on the conquest of Tibet, but it cannot rectify the evil acts committed. Nor, let us add, is any organization or any state able and willing to do so. Even though the United Nations has not fully secured the peace, it has done much to prevent conflict.

Laying the Economic and Social Base

Peace and tranquillity are not dependent on political and military dispositions alone. They rest equally on sound economic and social foundations. Ignorant, teeming populations living at the subsistence level are not the stuff of which a stable international society can be compounded. This is the basis for the extensive United Nations effort in the economic and social field. Quietly, steadily, the United

Nations and its family of specialized agencies have embarked on a whole series of services to less developed countries.

United Nations agencies are prominently engaged in combating disease, helping to preserve monetary stability, wiping out illiteracy, training skilled personnel, protecting children, facilitating transportation and communications, encouraging better social services, and fostering human rights.

It is an impressive roster of activities. And, as it happens, it is carried on predominantly with the personnel and resources of the free world countries. Currency and personnel restrictions in the Soviet bloc countries have sharply limited Communist participation.

Assisting the Birth of New Nations

What we are witnessing in the underdeveloped areas is an exceedingly rapid transition into the modern world. The United Nations did not create the deep-seated driving forces that underlie this movement. It may be able to influence and channel and stimulate them to some degree, but they would inevitably have made themselves felt in any case.

This is the vantage point from which we must view the passing of the colonial system in Asia and Africa since 1945. In that period, a billion people have been swept into independence, in over forty new states, and the process is continuing apace. Few would have predicted the speed of this development; fewer still that it could be accomplished with so little violence.

For this the United Nations must be given a share of the credit. The Charter established and sanctioned the objective; United Nations membership set the seal on national independence; participation in the United Nations gives voice to each new nation's personality; and aid mechanisms help to meet essential needs.

232

A jeep of the UN Military Observer Group in India and Pakistan on a road in Kashmir.

Participants in the United Nations Training Program for Foreign Service Officers are seen here arriving at UN headquarters, New York, after studying at Geneva.

Careers with the United Nations

For those who wish to work toward the goal of the brotherhood of man, the United Nations offers many opportunities—but they are opportunities which require training in specialized fields, and for which the applicant must compete with others from all over the world. The information in this article was provided by the Office of Personnel of the United Nations.

The United Nations has a steady need for competent staff in various fields. While it is impossible to list in detail the different types of positions for which the Organization recruits, the major categories of staff are described below.

The majority of professional posts in the Secretariat are closely related to the nature of the work required by Resolutions of the General Assembly and its principal organs. As a result the need is largely for specialized professional candidates, with the concentration in economics and related fields.

In filling vacancies, special attention is paid to the development and maintenance of a proportionate balance among the different member states, several of which, particularly countries that have joined the Organization recently, still have few or no nationals on the staff. In addition to professional personnel, there is a continuous need for stenographic help and linguistic staff, such as translators and interpreters, who are not subject to geographical distribution considerations.

The notes given below are aimed only at highlighting the situation with regard to each of the principal categories of staff employed by the United Nations. If, on the basis of this information, a potential candidate wishes to put forward his name, he should send a brief description of his background to: Office of Personnel, United Nations, N.Y.

Professional posts: The professional vacancies that occur call for persons of real professional talent in fields related to the work of the United Nations. Normally, the United Nations consults professional bodies and universities or makes press announcements in the countries from which applications are desired. A junior professional candidate must have an advanced university degree from a North American university, a *Licence avec mention* from a French university, an honours degree from a British university, or the equivalent in other countries. For higher level professional posts candidates are expected to have attained, in addition to their educational background, a recognized standing in their fields.

Technical Assistance experts: The United Nations Programs of Technical Cooperation are administered by the United Nations, including

233

the United Nations Conference on Trade and Development and the United Nations Industrial Development Center, and nine of the specialized agencies under the supervision of a coordinating authority, the United Nations Development Program. Requests from countries for technical assistance are distributed to the participating organizations on the basis of fields of specialization. The United Nations deals with areas of economic development, welfare, public administration, trade and development (UNCTAD), industrial development (UNIDO) and other technical assistance not specifically the concern of the specialized agencies. The requests are normally for senior expert advisers. Experts are normally required to have reached the highest professional standing after long experience in their fields. Candidates who are relatively junior, or who do not have sufficient experience in their fields, are seldom nominated.

Administrative posts: Administrative vacancies are few and far between and, in any case, are normally filled by the reassignment of existing staff.

Public Information posts: Applications for appointments in the Office of Public Information are particularly numerous and, consequently, competition is keen. Professional posts in this office call for substantial experience in

The Personnel Records Unit, Communications, Archives and Records Service of the UN Office of General Services, maintains the personnel records of all UN staff members.

United Nations

the information media of press, publication, radio, films and visual information. Even the junior posts require professional experience, not merely a degree in journalism. Preference is given to candidates able to work in more than one of the United Nations official languages. At the higher senior level, all-around information experience is taken into account together with specialization in one information medium.

Posts in the Office of Legal Affairs: The Office of Legal Affairs has a relatively small staff with a small turnover. Only candidates with specialization in public international law are considered, and preference is given to those with a working knowledge of English, French or Spanish. No vacancies are expected for persons whose main experience has been in civil, commercial, administrative or penal law.

Translators: Recruitment is by annual competitive examination. A candidate is required to translate into his mother tongue, which must be one of the five official languages of the United Nations (English, French, Spanish, Russian and Chinese). Translation into the English is from French and either Russian or Spanish; into French or Chinese, from English; into Spanish or Russian, from English and one other official language. A university degree and relevant experience are required. The maximum age for appointment is fifty.

Interpreters: Interpreters are recruited by individual examination. A university degree and a thorough knowledge of at least three of the official United Nations languages are required. Candidates may either be trained interpreters, capable of passing the qualifying examination immediately, or they may be persons of suitable linguistic and general cultural background who can be trained up to the required standard in a few weeks or months.

Social Welfare personnel: Few openings occur in social welfare work at Headquarters.

Posts in United Nations offices outside the Headquarters area: Aside from administrative personnel, who are usually provided through the reassignment of existing staff from Headquarters or from one of the other offices, the United Nations offices outside the Headquarters area require primarily specialists experienced in economics, statistics, sociology and various phases of industry. The clerical and secretarial staff of each field office is recruited locally, that is, from among residents of the area in which the particular office is located.

United Nations Field Service: This is a corps of men responsible for servicing the various United Nations field missions. Its personnel is subject to rotation from mission to mission in any part of the world. The Field Service comprises five main occupational groups: security officers, vehicle mechanics, radio technicians, radio operators and male secretaries. The age limits are from twenty-three to forty years. Newly appointed staff are not permitted to be accompanied to their duty station by their families.

Military personnel: Observers and other military personnel who are attached to United Nations missions are not recruited by the Organization. Instead, they are made available to the United Nations by member governments who have been asked to assist in this connection.

Many inquiries are received from officers of the armed forces of various countries who have completed or are about to complete distinguished careers with wide experience in many parts of the world and progressively increasing responsibility. It is very seldom that appropriate assignments can be found for these officers.

Clerical and secretarial posts: Most vacancies are for secretaries and typists, preferably bilingual (English plus French or Spanish). Vacancies for clerks occur very infrequently. Graduation from high (secondary) school or the equivalent is required. Candidates for service at Headquarters are chosen from among successful competitors in examinations which take place every Tuesday and Thursday in New York. If candidates living outside this area wish to take the examinations, they must pay their own travel expenses. The minimum requirements for secretarial posts are a typing speed of 50 to 60 words per minute and a stenographic speed of approximately 100 words per minute. A list of eligible applicants is maintained and candidates are considered as vacancies arise. Success in the examinations does not guarantee appointment; it only ensures consideration for such openings as may arise.

Guides: Guides are recruited on a local basis, usually once a year, and begin their training early in March. Only female candidates, twenty to thirty years of age, with college education or equivalent, are considered. They must be fluent in English, with a good speaking voice. Knowledge of other languages is desirable. No application forms are mailed to guide applicants; they are handed to them prior to the interview which is absolutely necessary and is given only at Headquarters.

Summer employment: The United Nations seldom recruits staff for the summer months. Occasionally, however, a few guides are added to the Visitors' Service. Competition for these posts is extremely keen.

Interne program: A summer interne program at United Nations Headquarters is conducted for college students and recent graduates specializing in international relations, political science, law, economics, sociology and related subjects. Each year, about fifty candidates are selected to participate in the program held in New York and about eighty for the program in Geneva.

For the New York program, each candidate should make written application to his own college or university, or to his country's Permanent Mission to the United Nations. For the Geneva program, application forms should be obtained from the candidate's own university or from the nearest United Nation's Information Centre. The United Nations does not pay any stipend whatsoever to the internes, but the program itself is free. The expenses of travel and living accomodation are the responsibility of the students and/or their sponsoring institutions or governments.

Specialized agencies: The specialized agencies of the United Nations conduct their own recruitment programs. Candidates should write directly to the appropriate agency. It should be noted that their clerical and secretarial personnel is also recruited locally from among residents of the area in which the particular agency is located.

235

Geographers in Afric maps,
With savage pictures fill their gaps;
And o'er unhabitable downs
Place elephants for want of towns.
—Jonathan Swift

section **13**

South and East Africa

The teasing verse above, by a great English writer of the eighteenth century, shows how little his world knew about parts of Africa—the southern and eastern parts you will read about in this section. Northern Africa has been known to Europe for more than two thousand years. Another part of Africa became familiar between the tenth and fifteenth centuries when the Arabs, Persians, and Chinese visited the east coast of Africa to trade for gold and ivory—and for tragic cargoes of slaves. Then the Portuguese and the Dutch began to settle the fringes of the lower half of Africa. But it was not until the middle of the last century that Europeans began in earnest to explore and colonize here.

Africa is a continent alive with the thrust of once primitive peoples toward a place in the technological world of the twentieth century. The native Africans began in the 1950's to demand a voice in governing their own affairs. One by one they shed their status as colonies or territories of European powers and achieved the status of independent, self-governing states. This transition was not an easy one. Often they had the will to be free but did not have the skills necessary for the administration of freedom. The turmoil in the Republic of the Congo when it became independent in June, 1960, is an example of such a problem.

The European minority, which had held Africa for almost a century, did not easily give up its hold on some of the African possessions. As you will see when you read the article on the Union of South Africa, friction between native African majorities and white minorities may continue to plague Africa for some years to come.

236

Changing East Africa

East Africa is not just the land of fabled Mount Kilimanjaro and Lake Victoria. It is a land of change, where people who once depended upon farming for their livelihood are learning to develop industries, to build schools and colleges, modern towns and cities. Here Leonard S. Kenworthy describes modern East Africa. Condensed from "Changing East Africa," **Current History** Magazine. Copyright 1962, by Current History, Inc. Revised by editor, 1965.

Political leaders waving to a crowd in Tanzania. The figure on the right is Julius Nyerere, the country's first president. Politicking in East Africa appears to be much the same as politicking elsewhere.

What we call East Africa is actually a vast and varied territory. In area it comprises approximately 680,000 square miles, north and south of the Equator, a region equal to a quarter of the continental United States. It includes Kenya, Uganda, and the United Republic of Tanzania, Tanzania being a union of the countries of Tanganyika and Zanzibar. (The two countries joined together in 1964 after a revolt against the formerly Arab-dominated government of Zanzibar.)

Within that territory are tremendous variations in land and climate. Along the Indian Ocean is a coastal plain, 10 to 40 miles wide, where the climate is hot and humid. Then the land rises until it reaches the East African Plateau, which occupies a large part of East Africa and is anywhere from 2,000 to 5,000 feet high. Next comes the Lake Victoria area, with the lake itself as large as Scotland or The Netherlands, making it the second largest fresh-water body in the world. Finally, in the extreme west are the mountains bordering on Rwanda, Burundi, and the Congo. In most of this vast expanse the weather is very comfortable, with warm days and cool or cold nights.

Since East Africa must depend almost solely upon agriculture, the amount of rainfall is highly important. About 60 per cent of Kenya has less than 20 inches of rain per year, and there are long periods of drought and then torrential floods. The Tanzanian area is somewhat saucer-shaped, with good rainfall at the rim and less than 20 inches in the center. Uganda gets more rain, which is one reason for the wealth of that area compared to the other two major regions.

The People

About 97 per cent of the people are Africans, and most of them are Bantu in background. But there the similarities end and the differences begin. There are scores of tribes in East Africa. The Tanzanian area alone may have at least 120. Some of them are very small, a few are very large, like the Kikuyu in Kenya, with a million and a half persons; the Luo in Kenya, with around a million; and the Sukuma in Tanzania, which has over a million. Among the most modern or westernized tribes are the Kikuyu and Luo in Kenya, the Chaggas in

A typical family in Uganda.

Here in Tanzania, the strong white fibers of the sisal plant are dried in the sun and then baled for shipment.

These two Kikuyu girls picking the blossoms of the pyrethrum plant are members of the largest tribe in Kenya.

Tanzania, and the Buganda in Uganda.

In contrast, there are several pre-literate tribes, leading a nomadic life. These less-developed groups fear the domination of the more modern tribes, especially in lands like Kenya and Uganda.

Religiously there are vast differences. Most of the Africans are animist, but large numbers of them are Christians. Then there are Moslems and Hindus to complicate the picture.

However, the real complication in East Africa, as far as people are concerned, is the plural or multi-racial nature of these nations. The situation is most acute in Kenya, where the large-scale shopkeepers are mostly Asian and the farmers are mostly European. Conditions are less tense in the Tanzanian area, where there have been far fewer Europeans and where they have not owned the major part of the best land. (In Uganda they do not own land.)

A Land of Poverty

In the economy of East Africa, one fact stands out above all others: the widespread poverty of this entire area. Its land is poor, its mineral resources limited, its industrialization meager, its health conditions deplorable, and its educational standards low. Measured by the standards of West Africa, for example, this region is far down the economic scale.

The average middle-class African hopes to purchase a bicycle if all goes well, and there are thousands of bicycles in and around the larger towns and cities. Automobiles are owned almost exclusively by Europeans. People live in mud or dried brick houses, eat inadequate meals, and fall prey to the many diseases, old and new, which are prevalent in East Africa.

Crucial as economic questions are, they have been shunted largely into the background. At the moment politics is more important. That is inevitable, at least until all the areas attain their independence.

Mineral Resources

The nations of East Africa have very restricted mineral resources. Tanzania is the most fortunate for it has some diamonds, a little gold, salt, silver, and mica. Kenya's mineral resources are drastically limited. It has some copper and a little diatomite and graphite. But soda is its one big product. Lake Magadi furnishes the largest source of soda in the world, with the soda crystallizing faster than it is mined. Uganda has some tin, beryl, galena, and apatite, but copper is its chief mineral. The Kilembe Mines were opened in 1956, and already the export of copper has jumped to third place, after coffee and cotton.

The search for more minerals continues, but it does not look as if East Africa can count on mineral wealth for much improvement economically.

An Agricultural Land

This is an agricultural part of the globe, and any advances economically are likely to be

238

The Owen Falls Dam at Jinja, Uganda, serves as an important source of power for Kenya as well as Uganda.

dependent upon improvements in agriculture and upon secondary industries based on farm products.

In Kenya about 80 per cent of the cash income of the country until recently has been produced by the European farmers on their large plots of ground, using fairly modern methods and machinery. This has come from coffee, tea, and sisal for the most part, with increasing income in recent years from pyrethrum, used in the manufacture of insecticides. Cotton, tobacco, and rice are also grown.

The Africans have lived largely on tiny plots of ground, ranging from one to three or four acres, on which they have grown just enough to subsist. Poor farming methods, poor seeds, the lack of rotation of crops, and the lack of fertilizers have reduced their production.

But all that is changing fairly rapidly in Kenya today. The land consolidation and village program which was forced on the Kikuyu at the time of the Mau Mau rebellion has now gained ground elsewhere by free choice and is making larger plots of ground possible. Newer methods of farming are gradually being introduced, and some farmers are beginning to make a few hundred dollars a year on small farms of 10 to 15 acres. New crops are being introduced, and the old restrictions against Africans raising the highly lucrative crop of pyrethrum have been relaxed.

But the pressures on the land in Kenya are still terrific. Much of the good land is owned by Europeans; in a section like the Nyanza Province in the west, there are as many as 3,000 persons to the square mile in some places. Just what the final adjustment will be on the ownership of the White Highlands in

independent Kenya is still not clear, but there is no doubt that the Africans will gain some fertile farmland in that section.

The Dominance of Sisal

In Tanzania, 80 per cent of the export earnings are from agriculture, and 45 per cent of the total output of the country is from agricultural products. Sisal is the largest export crop. This new nation produces two-thirds of the world's sisal, with the plantations owned largely by Europeans. On the other hand most of the coffee is owned by Africans and marketed by co-operatives.

Much of the coffee is grown on the slopes of Kilimanjaro by the Chagga tribe, which is a comparatively well-to-do group. In Moshi they built a $600,000 College of Commerce (actually a technical high school) a few years ago with profits from their coffee co-operatives and later a $250,000 elementary school in the same way. Cotton is also grown, as well as tea, tobacco, and pyrethrum. One of the great strengths of Tanganyika—now united with Zanzibar—had been its co-operative movement, among the most powerful in the world.

A Few Export Crops Are Not Enough

239

In Uganda, cotton and coffee are the main crops for export, with tea a poor third. In fact, Uganda is the largest coffee producer in the Commonwealth. But the growing realization that two export crops are a rather shaky basis for a country's economy have caused planners to turn more and more to industrialization.

Prior to its union with Tanganyika, Zanzibar existed largely on her clove market and on clove-stem oil. This was aided a little

A palace on Zanzibar—now part of Tanzania—reflects some of the enchantment of this clove-scented island off the East African coast.

Agricultural machinery is unloaded at the port of Dar-es-Salaam, capital of Tanzania. The name of this city means "haven of peace."

by a small fishing industry. Now, through union with Tanganyika, Zanzibar is achieving greater economic stability.

But even vast improvements in agriculture will not provide the firm economies these nations need. So, in recent times, there has been a trend toward more and more industrialization in East Africa. This has been particularly noticeable in Kenya and in Uganda.

The Owen Falls Dam

Industrialization has been made possible largely by the erection of the mammoth Owen Falls hydroelectric plant near the source of the Nile in Uganda, which supplies power to the new industries of that nation and much of the power for Kenya. Uganda's new industries include copper mining and smelting, asbestos, hollow-ware, and the production of phosphates.

Kenya is turning more and more to secondary industries, such as processing farm products and tea, canning fruits and vegetables, and freezing fish. There are also factories which produce automobiles, tires, beer, cigarettes, chemicals, bricks, cement, pottery, and glass. In Mombasa oil refineries supply the factories of Kenya and the ships which come to the port there.

In all of this development of industry Kenya is highly dependent upon neighboring nations,

for she obtains most of her power from the Owen Falls plant and from a smaller plant at the Pandani Falls in Tanzania.

Tanzania has not made this much progress as yet in industrialization, but a ride from the airport to the center of Dar-es-Salaam reveals some of the most modern factories in the world, with striking modern architecture as well as modern machinery. They turn out a wide variety of products, among them shoes, metal containers, leather goods, textiles, canned goods, and cement.

Unifying Factors

Despite the many differences several factors foster unity among these separate parts of East Africa.

One of the most important of these is the common language of Swahili, spoken by most Africans in this entire area. English is another common language for the educated people of East Africa.

A second factor has just been mentioned—the dependence of Kenya on Uganda and to a lesser degree on Tanzania for power. Similarly there is an interdependence on common ports, with Kenya and the north Tanganyikan region using Mombasa for their shipping, and all three using the ports on Lake Victoria for transportation.

In the past the only college in this area has been Makerere College in Uganda, to which students from all three areas have gone. Now the three regions have combined to form the University of East Africa, with separate campuses in Dar-es-Salaam, Nairobi, and Kampala.

Their common experience with the rule of the British has given these nations much in common, too. But above all is their common experience since 1948 in what is now called the East Africa Common Services Authority. They have had common postal services and telecommunications, customs and excise taxes, income taxes, railways and harbors, statistics and research, publications, and health services.

Of all the areas of Africa today, East Africa has the most promise of evolving some kind of federation, economic if not political.

Mozambique and the Malagasy Republic

Mozambique was once a stepping stone on the trade route between Europe and the Orient. If you
don't count Australia, the Malagasy Republic is the fourth largest island in the world. Most people
are more familiar with the island's former name, Madagascar, used until October, 1958. Reprinted
by permission of the publisher, J. B. Lippincott Company, from *Picture Map Geography of Africa*,
by Vernon Quinn. Copyright, 1952, by J. B. Lippincott Co. Revised by editor, 1963.

Mozambique

Vasco da Gama, the Portuguese navigator, sailed around the southern tip of Africa on his way to India in 1497. On up Africa's east coast he came to a small island which the friendly inhabitants called Mozambique.

A few years later there was a Portuguese trading post there, and then colonists began to arrive. Other navigators stopped at other villages along the mainland coast. All of them reported that the Negroes were wearing ornaments made of gold! The Portuguese at home were greatly excited. Cargo ships with trade goods set out for the rich land, and soon there were many trading posts along the coast.

Portugal then claimed country far enough inland to extend beyond the gold mines—wherever they might be. By that time the mainland, as well as the island where the Portuguese first stopped, was called Mozambique.

Today it is a Portuguese overseas province greater in size than Texas. The stormy waves of Mozambique Channel roar in upon fifteen hundred miles of coastline. Beyond the coast there are forested mountains and wide plateaus. Two great rivers, the Zambezi and the Limpopo, coming from far inland, cut across Mozambique to reach the sea.

There are many fine harbors, many seaports. The busiest seaport and the largest city is Lourenço Marques, the capital of Mozambique, so named because the first trading post there was opened by a Portuguese named Lourenço Marques.

Those early Portuguese, all along the coast, tried their best to find the mysterious "Land of Gold," with its rich mines. But the Makalanga and other tribes were keeping its location secret. They cheerfully agreed to guide groups of white men there, far inland—and then led them in the opposite direction!

Three centuries passed before the ancient golden land was discovered, near the Rhodesia border. Today gold is being mined there and in other parts of Mozambique. In those same mountains there are mines yielding copper, tin, silver, asbestos, and coal.

But crops are more important in Mozam-

Tananarive, a jumble of stone mansions and straw-thatched wooden houses, is the capital of the Malagasy Republic. This view shows the Ikopa River to the south of the mountain city.

French Embassy Press & Info. Div.

bique than minerals. Maize and oil-bearing seeds—sesame, groundnuts, castor beans—rank first. Sugar cane and coconut plantations spread over the lowlands near the sea. Cotton is one of the big crops.

The hard-working people grow coffee for export, and collect wild honeycombs. They eat the honey and sell the beeswax to exporters. They collect wild rubber latex—thick milky juice—from vines in the forests and harden it into crude rubber. They gather gum from acacia trees and bark from mangroves, which are plentiful in seaside swamps. Its chief use is for tanning leather.

Those swamps that edge the sea are fine feeding grounds for many kinds of birds. Long-legged flamingos flash their bright color among long-legged cranes and herons wading beside them into the water. The pelicans nearby are too busy catching fish to notice them. But often a hippopotamus, splashing too close to their feeding place, will frighten all the big birds away. Elephants and rhinoceroses, buffaloes and zebras, antelopes, leopards, and lions are plentiful in this Portuguese province.

Mozambique's several million Africans are industrious Bantu Negroes. The ancestors of nearly all the tribes south of the Zambezi River were Zulus, a tribal division of the Bantus. The Zulus were among the last of the Bantu to arrive, centuries ago, from central Africa. They had to fight for choice locations that Bantu tribes ahead of them had chosen. And in time they became noted as the greatest of all African warriors, the most daring, the most courageous, and the most dreaded.

Today Zulu children attend government or mission schools, but in the evening, they listen, fascinated, to their elders telling of the days when all of that land was a mighty Zulu kingdom.

Malagasy Republic

Across Mozambique Channel—240 miles wide at the narrowest place—lies one of the world's largest islands. As Madagascar it was a French protectorate from 1896 until 1958, when it became the Malagasy Republic, an autonomous member of the French Community. In 1960 it became an independent republic within the Community.

Most of the island is mountainous or high plateau, but bordering the shore is rich lowland. Here many crops are grown. Rice, sugar cane, vanilla, tobacco, cacao, coffee, cloves, and other crops cover more than three million acres. Cattle graze over large areas of grassland, and there are great forests, rich in timber-woods, gums, resins, and wild honeycombs.

Tananarive, the capital of the country, sits high in the mountains. A railroad winds down to connect it with a seaport on the Indian Ocean, and there are many airports scattered along the coast, with one high in the mountains at Tananarive.

Other Books To Read

Tradition and Change in African Tribal Life, by Colin Turnbull. Published by World Publishing Co., Cleveland, Ohio, 1966.
How the winds of change are sweeping over Africa and reaching into the villages, bringing the people into closer contact with modern life.

The Peoples of Africa, by Colin Trumbull. Published by World Publishing Co., Cleveland, Ohio, 1962.
A scholarly but very readable survey of Africa's chief tribal cultures; the hunters, the grazers and the cultivators.

Young People of East and South Africa, by Charles R.

Joy. Published by Duell, Sloan and Pearce, Inc., New York, 1962.
African teen-agers report on their families, schools, amusements, and ambitions.

Africa, by David Hapgood. Published by Ginn & Co., Boston, Massachusetts, 1965.
An excellent survey book of the continent, its people and problems.

Other Sections To See

"Countries of the Nile," Volume 5; "The United Nations," this volume; "Nations in Harmony," Volume 10; "Northwest Africa" and "The Mediterranean World," Volume 11; "World Citizens at Work," Volume 12.

Natal National Park is often called one of South Africa's national playgrounds. South African citizens and thousands of tourists enjoy its magnificent scenery. The mountain formation in the background is known as the "amphitheater." The park offers facilities for riding and camping, as well as the excellent lodgings which are seen in the foreground.

South African Scenes

243

Deep in the vast equatorial forest of the Congo are small villages like Bilota, built near jungle rivers and lived in mainly by hunters.

Victoria Falls are shown here as they
appear when the Zambezi River is at its
lowest (before the rainy season). Visible in
the right foreground is a bridge between
Zambia and Rhodesia.

About 200 miles south of the Equator the
twin peaks of Kilimanjaro—Mawenzi
and Kibo—rise suddenly from the wide,
hot plains. In the picture above is Mawenzi,
the second highest peak. In the
foreground is the flat prairie separating
Mawenzi from Kibo.

244

This view of Cape Town, South Africa's
oldest city (founded in 1652), was taken
from the top of Table Mountain. Cape
Town is a world-famous harbor and
international trading center.

Rhodesia, Zambia and Malawi

These three Central African territories mirror a number of the problems that are present in the emerging African countries—the attempt of the white settlers to maintain their privileged position, the struggle of the Negro population to assert itself, the necessity of achieving a balanced economy in spite of racial emotions. All these are familiar issues in the Africa of the second half of the twentieth century. Here is a picture of this area in crisis. From **The Story of Africa South of the Sahara,** by Katharine Savage. Copyright © 1961 by Katharine Savage. Reprinted by permission of Henry Z. Walck, Inc. and The Bodley Head Ltd. Revised by editor, 1964.

Rhodesia, Zambia and Malawi are troubled areas in southeast Africa today. After their foundation, in the scramble of the 1880's, the three territories were administered by Britain under separate constitutions; but in 1953 they were joined together in the Federation of Rhodesia and Nyasaland. Each territory had its own parliament but was linked to a central government in Salisbury, the capital of Southern Rhodesia.

The Fight Against Federation

Africans in Northern Rhodesia and Nyasaland violently opposed the idea of federation. They used to enjoy greater freedom and hoped for a larger share in the government than their African neighbors in Southern Rhodesia. Now they were afraid that the white rulers in Salisbury would not only refuse to extend political power to Africans in Northern Rhodesia and Nyasaland, but would deprive them of their existing rights.

The leaders of the Conservative Party in Britain drew up the plans and carried them through. They were aware of native opposition, but decided that Africans are easily swayed by persuasive politicians of their own race who do not necessarily know what is good for them. The British aim was to form a state in central Africa prosperous enough to be self-supporting and strong enough to withstand a possible attempt by Afrikaners to extend the frontiers of South Africa.

Each of the three territories has something the others lack, and it was clear to the men who favored federation that if the rich tobacco lands of Southern Rhodesia were combined with the mineral wealth of the Northern Rhodesian copper belt, and if the hard-working, but impoverished, Nyasalanders helped to man both industries, everyone concerned would be better off. They hoped that the rebellious Africans would realize this and would soon be converted to federation.

These hopes were not fulfilled. The federation ended in January, 1964. That year, Nyasaland became independent as Malawi, Northern Rhodesia as Zambia. Southern Rhodesia became Rhodesia.

One completed project was the Kariba Dam, built at enormous cost, across a wide gorge of the Zambezi River. The waters from

245

View of the Kariba Dam in Rhodesia. This great hydroelectric project was planned to spur the industrialization of Rhodesia and Zambia. Its cost has been estimated at over $300,000,000.

Left, Dr. Hastings Banda, the political leader of Malawi, waves his hat in greeting to the people of Mzuzu during a tour of the northern area. Below, African workers in the tobacco fields of Rhodesia. This particular farm covers about 6,000 acres and is managed by an Englishman.

this great dam operate the most powerful hydroelectric plant in Africa for the immense benefit of all three territories. The money was contributed by the British Government, the Northern Rhodesian copper industry, and the World Bank.

The Land of Cecil Rhodes

The pioneers who opened up the Dark Continent in the nineteenth century handed a grave responsibility to their countrymen. The tribes who had been conquered by the gospel or gun were dependent on the wisdom and efficiency of the white men who came to rule over them.

Rhodesia is the land opened up by Cecil Rhodes. He began British occupation by buying "the right to dig" and completed it by crushing the Matabele and Mashona in battle. After this defeat there were no native chiefs strong enough to stand up for their tribal rights, so the white settlers took over the country and ran it their own way, giving the Africans no voice in the government. Little has arisen to destroy this mastery, so white supremacy still exists in Rhodesia.

The color bar is almost as harsh as in the Republic of South Africa. The tobacco plantations are all owned by white farmers and worked by black labor. Many of the natives live in overcrowded reserves and few manage to get enough education to take skilled jobs. In the towns there are pass laws, and prohibited areas where no black man may live. Africans are not forbidden to vote, but before

they can register they must attain a certain level of education and possess a certain amount of money.

There are, however, signs of a new and more enlightened approach to race relations. A brave and important venture is the fine university college near Salisbury which admits both black and white students. Well-planned houses are creeping in among the ramshackle hovels. Hospitals and Christian churches are spreading through the land. But there is, as yet, little opportunity for Africans to take part in government.

The Copper Belt of Zambia

The foundation of Zambia was far more gradual and also more peaceful. Toward the end of the nineteenth century prospectors who were disappointed by the failure to uncover rich reefs of gold in Southern Rhodesia made their way northward. They concluded treaties with the ruling chiefs and settled down to develop the country. At the beginning of this century they struck a promising belt of copper, but it was not until 1928 that big mining companies were formed to exploit this new wealth. By this time a constitution had been worked out in which the British administered the territory, working through the authority of the local chiefs. This arrangement continued peacefully until independence.

The Hard-Working Malawi

Malawi, the third and poorest member of the group, is a long, ragged territory, curling

Left, surface view of a part of the Nchanga Copper Mine in Chingola, Zambia, one of the world's leading exporters of copper. Above, a typical African copper miner.

along the shores of Lake Malawi. Mountainous and wooded, the land has not yielded gold, diamonds, copper or abundant crops. The farms are owned by Africans and worked in small plots. The people cannot live off their land, and they travel to distant cities and mines to find work. It is two thousand miles as the crow flies from central Malawi to Capetown in the Republic of South Africa, but many of them make the journey on foot. They are strong, industrious workers and greatly in demand.

Rwanda and Burundi

By the editor.

On July 1, 1962, the Republic of Rwanda and the Kingdom of Burundi joined the list of newly independent African nations. Both countries had been administered by Belgium for nearly 40 years as the single territory of Ruanda-Urundi, first as a League of Nations mandate and later as a United Nations trust territory.

This region of high plateaus and spectacular lakes, situated between the republics of the Congo and Tanzania, is smaller in area than the state of West Virginia, yet it has the highest density of population on the African mainland. The soil is harsh and the scanty exports, mainly coffee, are not enough to provide essential revenue.

The two leading tribes are the lean, aristocratic cattle-owning Watusi, who sometimes reach a height of seven feet, and the hard-working Bahutu cultivators of the soil. There are a small number of pygmy hunters, the Batwa. Centuries ago the Watusi drove their long-horned cattle south to this area and made virtual slaves of the Bahutu. There were two kingdoms ruled by a *mwami,* or king. In 1959 the Bahutu of Rwanda, who outnumbered the Watusi six to one, rebelled against their overlords. Many of the Watusi, including their *mwami,* fled north to Uganda driving their cattle with them. In a 1961 referendum the people of Rwanda voted in favor of a republic. Kigali is the capital.

The people of Burundi voted to keep their *mwami.* Usumbura, overlooking Lake Tanganyika, is the capital. It has some small industry and the country's best high school, the Collège du Saint-Esprit.

247

Congolese villagers wade into the waters of the river to sell their bananas, pineapples, and other fruits to the passengers of a Congo river boat.

The Republic of the Congo (Kinshasa)

For a period of nearly three years, 1960-63, the Congo held a place on the front pages of the world's newspapers. The abrupt grant of independence without adequate preparation was soon followed by the mutiny of the Congolese army, the headlong flight of Belgian personnel who were so essential to the running of the country, tribal warfare and starvation, secession movements in various provinces—the most prolonged being that of Moise Tshombe in Katanga—and the murder of the first premier—Patrice Lumumba. The strain on the United Nations to whom Lumumba and President Joseph Kasavubu had originally appealed for help caused near bankruptcy. Why did all of this take place? Most important, what is the Congo like? What is its history? Here are some answers to these questions. Condensed from **Congo: Background of Conflict**, by Alan P. Merriam. Copyright © 1961 Northwestern University Press. Revised by editor, 1967.

Few who have visited the Republic of the Congo come away with an adequate picture of its immense variety. The Congo covers an area of more than 900,000 square miles, one-fourth the size of the United States, or equal to almost all of Western Europe. Its climate ranges from the hot and sultry Congo basin, saturated with tropical rains, to the high mountain ranges of Kivu in the east, where vegetables of the temperate climate are grown and sweaters must be worn.

The people number somewhere around 15,000,000, from the pygmies of the Ituri Forest and other regions through the many Bantu tribal groups who are primarily agriculturists and whose ways of life present a variety of cultural patterns.

Its history counts scandals and triumphs, the high adventure of exploration, determined campaigns against slavery and, finally, independence.

The Mighty Congo River

The principal river is, of course, the Congo which rises in Katanga on the Congo-Zambesi divide. From its point of origin, the river runs north and then turns to the west, where there are several navigable stretches up to several hundred miles in length. At Kisangani it runs over a series of seven cataracts known as Stanley Falls and enters the central Congo basin. Until it reaches Kisangani the river is known as the Lualaba. Then it takes the name of Congo and begins a long navigable section of over a thousand miles. Here its two biggest tributaries are the Ubangi and the Kasai. The navigable stretch of the river continues to Stanley Pool at Kinshasa, where it is broken by a series of 32 cataracts which drop a total of 870 feet out of the basin to the sea. The cataracts—broken by one navigable stretch of 80 miles—continue to Matadi, which is the terminus for seagoing craft. At its mouth, the river is about six miles wide.

The Portuguese explorer, Diego Cão, discovered the mouth of the Congo River in 1482. He returned in 1485 and made contact with the people along the river and also with the ruler of the Kingdom of the Kongo, which covered a considerable territory on the south bank of the river.

Until the arrival of Henry Morton Stanley in the nineteenth century, explorers had not penetrated into the interior of the Congo basin, except to touch some small portions of its eastern region. Stanley set up and fought through expedition after expedition.

The Congo Free State

King Leopold II of Belgium became interested in the Congo through Stanley's work. The two met and formed the "Survey Committee for the Upper Congo." Stanley then returned to Africa and established stations all along the Lower Congo region. He went on to Stanley Pool where Léopoldville, which he founded, is now situated, and inland to Lake Leopold II.

The committee was now replaced by the International Congo Association, which adopted a flag of blue with a single gold star. Stanley then returned to the Congo and with several chiefs entered into a series of treaties for recognition of the association. At the Berlin Conference, 1884–1885, the major powers recognized the association as a sovereign state.

For 23 years Leopold II ruled the Congo as his personal possession. This was the era of the Congo Free State, which was considered by outsiders the worst possible example of brutality. Partly because of this, the Congo was transferred to Belgium as a colony in 1908. Its huge area was divided into six provinces: Katanga in the southeast, Kivu in the central east, Eastern in the northeast, Kasai in the south central, Equator in the north and west central, and Léopoldville in the west and southwest. The Congo remained a colony until June 30, 1960, when it became independent.

Sources of the Congo's Wealth

The principal reason for the Congo's prosperity is the mineral wealth which normally accounts for two-thirds of the value of its exports. The Congo is one of the world's largest producers of copper, which is found primarily in Katanga, where the Union Minière controls most of the production. Gold is found in Katanga and other areas, diamonds in Kasai—in gem stones the Congo is the world's second largest producer, and in industrial stones, its largest producer. Tin, manganese, zinc, tungsten, tantalum, coal, and iron are of varying importance. Katanga's pitchblende originally constituted almost a monopoly until the discovery of other sources in Canada, and the Congo at one time provided over half of the free world's supply of uranium. In recent years it has been producing an estimated 55–75 per cent of the world's supply of cobalt.

Mineral products are not, of course, the Congo's only wealth. A great variety of timber is cut, and there is copal, palm oil, coffee (especially in the Kivi area), cacao in restricted areas, rubber in Eastern and Equator provinces, quinine, pyrethrum, tea, sisal, sugar, perfumes, tobacco, cotton, stock raising, citrus fruits, and a variety of smaller crops.

Growing Their Own Food

The pygmies (see page 273) represent only a small proportion of the people of the Congo. The Bantu are much more numerous, and make up the great bulk of the population. Almost all the Bantu grow their own food. The practice is to cultivate a plot of ground over a period of several years until the soil is exhausted and then to move to another. The chief crops are manioc, rice, sorghum, millet, peanuts, beans, yams, maize, sweet potatoes, sugarcane, and bananas. The Bantu also

Congolese students at the National Institute of Buildings and Public Works listen attentively as a UNESCO expert demonstrates Hooke's Law, as applied to torsion. The institute is operated jointly by UNESCO and the Public Works Division of the United Nations Operations in the Congo.

249

United Nations

A Congolese worker at the copper smelting plant of the famous Union Minière du Haut Katanga in Lubumbashi, capital of Katanga province. Copper is one of the sources of the Congo's wealth.

gather, hunt, and fish. In addition, they keep small domesticated animals but these are usually considered capital goods rather than an immediate source of meat or milk. By Western standards most people are undernourished.

Arts and Crafts

The Congo is one of the great art areas of Africa. The plastic arts are represented by all sorts of objects: masks, statuettes, carved posts, batons, and other symbols of office. Painting on canvas after the European traditions of fine arts has produced some splendid results.

The Congolese are known throughout the world for their craft productions, including those in woods, such as masks, statuettes, and products of daily use. They are also proficient in pottery, ironwork, basketry, and weaving.

The Languages of Trade

Almost every tribal group has at least its own dialect. To make things easier four trade languages are widely spoken as second languages. They include Swahili in the east, Kongo in the west, Luba in the south, and Lingala in the north. French, of course, is the language of the educated.

The Congo Before Independence

Belgian policy was like that of a stern parent. Neither the African nor the Belgian residents of the colony had a voice in the government, which was directly responsible to the Belgian Parliament in Brussels. The chief emphasis was placed on economic development. The Belgians recognized the necessity of providing workers for the new economy and launched a strong policy of technical training. As a result many Congolese held highly technical jobs. But there was not an equal amount of liberal education. In looking back on the Congo before the movements toward independence began, one sees a "model" colony in which the Africans were regarded as children virtually incapable of guiding their own destinies, and in which the Belgians made provision after provision for the welfare of their charges.

Mass Education

The Belgians kept building more and more primary schools in which a larger and larger percentage of Congolese could be trained. The idea was to bring the entire population through grade and high school before any substantial elite could be created by a university education. The result was that while millions of Congolese attended primary school, very few had gone through high school before independence, and almost none were college graduates. In the 1950's two universities were established at Léopoldville (Kinshasa) and Elisabethville (Lubumbashi).

Why Belgium Failed

The Belgian system accomplished much in the way of health and material benefits. Its basic weakness was that it failed to prepare the Congolese for independence. It failed to instruct them in the Western systems of government which, it was assumed, they would undertake once independence came.

The shaping of a nation is difficult under any circumstances, but in the Congo the problem has been especially complicated.

Countries Around the Kalahari Desert

The Kalahari Desert dominates much of southern Africa, just as the Sahara does northern Africa. Here are three countries of this region, Botswana, Angola, and South West Africa. Reprinted by permission of the publisher, J. B. Lippincott Company, from **Picture Map Geography of Africa** by Vernon Quinn. Copyright 1952 by J. B. Lippincott. Revised by editor, 1967.

Botswana

Botswana, the former British protectorate of Bechuanaland, became independent on September 30, 1966. It is a vast tableland and entirely landlocked. The most fertile part of the country comprises the central watershed and the lands between it and the Limpopo River. The rest of the country is very dry. The vast Kalahari Desert spreads over nearly one half of it. There is just sufficient rainfall for the growing of food crops.

The entire surface of the Kalahari Desert is red sand. It is not really a desert, for the roots of grass tufts, wild flowers, shrubs, even occasional forest trees, reach down to the damp sand below the surface and turn the desert into a vast plain, scattered with grass-covered sand dunes. The Kalahari Desert plain is the delight of wild animals—lions, leopards, elephants, buffaloes, hyenas, jackals. And the animals are the delight of Botswana hunters; they supply the villages with food and skins to sell to traders. Their wealth is in the million cattle, sheep, and goats they herd on rich grasslands in the desert.

Near their villages of beehive-shaped huts, sometimes enclosed with a reed circular fence, they grow enough maize and kaffir (a variety of sorghum) to keep their children well fed. The Botswana tribes in the east, where the land is richer, plant kaffir and maize in large fields, and keep fewer cattle than their western kin.

In 1965 Gaberones was made the capital of Botswana. This small city of some 6,000 inhabitants is located in the southeastern section of the country. The former capital of Bechuanaland (Botswana) was Mafeking, over the boundary in South Africa.

Angola

Angola, discovered and claimed by the Portuguese in 1482, is three times the size of California. It lies between the Republic of the Congo and South West Africa, with a thousand miles of coast on the Atlantic Ocean. Scattered along the coast are thriving Portuguese towns. The largest are Benguela and Luanda; Luanda is the capital of Angola.

An overseas province of Portugal like Mozambique, Angola is a troubled land. A growing independence movement among the Africans has been the cause of much bloodshed.

Reaching inland from the coast for many miles the land is low and sandy, almost desert in many places. Then in broad terraces with rich soil it rises to a high plateau of rolling grassland edged with hills and mountains. There are tropical forests in the north. Many wild animals roam through them and over the grasslands.

In the desert-like south there are a few tribes of nomadic Bushmen. Elsewhere the people are stalwart, hard-working Bantu Negroes. They grow nearly all of the maize that is exported; from forest trees and vines they collect whatever wild rubber is exported abroad; and they search for wild honeycombs to get wax for export. Thousands work on white men's plantations, or go out with the fishing fleets, or help in the dried fish sheds and the sugar factories.

Sugar cane, coffee, and maize are the leading crops. But there are also many plantations of coconut palms and oil palms, of cotton, tobacco, and groundnuts. Many cattle, fattened on the rich grass of the highlands, are shipped off to foreign markets.

Diamonds are mined; four per cent of the

251

world output. A railroad connects the diamond fields with the Atlantic Coast; there are many airfields and good motor roads where Europeans have settled.

A small part of Angola is quite separate from the rest of the country. It edges the Atlantic Ocean some distance north of the Congo River. The Portuguese call it *Cabinda*, but the natives cling to the ancient name for their land, Ngoya, and call themselves *Ba-Ngoya*, "Ngoya People."

South West Africa

Mountains, plateaus, plains, and vast expanses of desert give variety to this large country. It extends from the Orange River to Angola, and from a long coastline on the Atlantic Ocean to Bechuanaland and South Africa. It is more than five times the size of New England.

It was a German colony until World War I, when South African troops captured it. In 1920 it was assigned to South Africa as a League of Nations mandate. The South African government has refused to transform it into a United Nations trusteeship.

A high plateau, scattered with mountains that rise still higher, separates the eastern desert from the much larger Namib Desert. Even the southern part of the plateau is almost desert. But Hottentots who live there find enough vegetation for their herds of sheep and goats. And those skilled hunters of wild game, the Bushmen, seldom go hungry.

In the north, conditions are very different. There is abundant rain and the soil is richer. Crops, chiefly maize, cover large areas. There are almost tropical forests. And there are very big depressions called salt pans, which hold shallow water during the rainy season but are usually dry in winter.

Windhoek (Dutch for "windy corner"), on the high inland plateau, is the capital of South West Africa. A wandering railroad connects it with three seaports. The largest one is Walvis Bay, where whaleboats still go far out in the Atlantic and return with one or more of the big creatures.

A refrigeration plant at Walvis Bay handles tens of thousands of cattle and sheep from the herds of Africans and white men who have settled in the country.

The ships loaded with meat sometimes carry a more exciting cargo—diamonds! Diamonds and silver are South West Africa's most valuable mineral exports. Tin ore comes next.

The southern third of the country, known as Great Namaland, is the home of Nama-Hottentots. In the semidesert southern part of their land, only their sheep and goats can thrive, but they graze cattle farther north.

Bushmen wander here and there over the Hottentot country. If there is game to be had, and bulbs for vegetable food, it matters nothing to them whether the land is desert or thorn-covered hills.

In the northern part of the country in rich Ovamboland, where crops grow readily, there are high grassy plains, where the Bantu-Negro Ovambo graze large herds of cattle. They are the most advanced, and the most industrious, of South West Africa's people. Besides the all-important maize, which is their chief crop and their main food, they have large fields of potatoes, beans, and pumpkins.

Sandwiched between Ovamboland in the north and Great Namaland in the south is Damaraland. The people of Damaraland call themselves *Ova-Herero*, the "Merry People." Fields of maize checker their land, but they are chiefly stock raisers.

Kalahari Desert scenes like this cover half a million miles of southern Africa. Its bush and grass make it one of the finest territories in Africa for wild game.

British Info. Serv.

Conflict in the Republic of South Africa

The Republic of South Africa (made up of the provinces of Cape of Good Hope, Transvaal, Orange Free State, and Natal) is wealthy and important, but it has a tremendous problem. Like the rest of Africa it was built by people from many races, but here the races do not live together in harmony. From The Limits of the Earth, by Fairfield Osborn, by permission of Little, Brown and Co. Copyright 1953 by Fairfield Osborn. Revised by editor, 1963.

The Republic of South Africa is the only independent state in Africa that is controlled by the descendants of settlers from European nations. About one-fourth of the population consists of white people of European origin. Two-thirds of these are Afrikanders, or Boers, originally Dutch, with over 300 years of history in South Africa behind them. They have their own language, Afrikaans. The remaining third have English forebears, some of whom came over 150 years ago.

Native-born Africans form the largest part of the population. About one million of them have intermarried with other races. The rest of the nonwhite population consists of Asiatics, mostly descendants of imported Indian laborers.

The inhabitants of the Republic of South Africa live not so much *with* as *among* each other. There is suspicion between white and nonwhite, between Afrikanders and English-speaking whites, between the Afrikanders who control agriculture and the British who control industry, and between all of these and the Asiatics.

South Africa is not the land of wide-open spaces, as is sometimes thought. It has large modern cities, with skyscrapers, luxury shops, and slums. Its Africans are poorly fed farm and industrial workers. Except in the splendid national park system, its once rich heritage of wild animal life has virtually disappeared.

Rapidly becoming industrialized and filled with cities, the Republic is the richest gold and the second richest diamond country in the world. Besides gold exports, it accounts for nearly 20 per cent of the total African merchandise foreign trade, and for about 25 per cent of the trade within Africa. It has the only significant iron and steel industry on the continent.

Serious Conflicts Arise

But there are serious economic, political, and cultural problems in the country. The gap between the people and their natural resources is an important part of these problems. Each year there are two hundred thousand more people in the country, and as each year passes it becomes more and more doubtful whether the productivity of the land is even holding its own.

By nature the land of South Africa is relatively low in fertility. Much of the country is semiarid and the few rivers are mostly seasonal and spaced far apart. Agricultural conditions, at best, were not originally favorable, and the effects of long years of improper farming make reclamation doubly difficult. Many areas, more suitable for grazing than for crops, have been so seriously overstocked with animal herds that there has been wholesale loss of the natural growth. Heavy seasonal rainfalls have caused so much soil erosion that

253

The skyscrapers of Johannesburg rising over a dump from the mines of the Witwatersrand gold fields.

Paul's Photos

the very character of the country's water supplies is being changed.

Some explanation of the present gap between the population and its resources can be given by examining the past. The development of South Africa has been held back by inherited racial conflicts. It is a story of climate, soil, gold, and slavery. Especially it is the story of the Boer, for in his development can be found many of the seeds of the country's present problem.

The first Dutch settlers at the Cape (1652) expanded rapidly and were given land by the Dutch East India Company for farming along the Liesbeek River. The founder of the Cape settlement, Commander Van Riebeek, wanted a small, tightly knit, self-supporting community with as few contacts as possible with the original populations. But the Boers, as the descendants of the original settlers were called, gradually began to move farther and farther into the interior of the Cape colony.

On the Move

Various reasons are given to explain this pioneering among people who were not naturally adventurers.

Many Boers grew restless under the regulations of the Dutch East India Company and moved on. With new lands available it was easier, too, to exhaust one farming or grazing area and then start another elsewhere than to use this land carefully. More suited for grazing than farming, the land did not permit close settlement. Few villages developed, and large families in their large acreages were widely separated from each other. In an area of mild climate, rich game, and fresh lands beyond, hard work was not necessary. It was easy to forget the old Dutch habits of thrift and intensive cultivation. As the Boer saw his needs, they were land and cattle, and both were available.

The Boers moved into lands which already supported several populations. Among these were the Bushmen, who ranged as nomads throughout the area. Very primitive, they lived on game, wild fruits, and herbs. More powerful were the Hottentots, found along the western and southern coasts of the country. They did not cultivate crops, but lived on wild game and domestic cattle and sheep. The Bushmen could not long survive. The Hottentots—and later the Bantu—became Africa's richest natural resource, a cheap labor force. This resource, together with slaves, profoundly affected the Boer outlook and way of life.

South African production and lack of in-

South Africa State Info. Off.

Thousands of men leave homes and families in southern and eastern Africa for the Republic's mining towns. Crowded living conditions add to South Africa's racial tensions.

Sheep raising is an important agricultural industry in Cape province. It provides South Africa with one of its most valuable exports—wool.

South Africa Consul.

tensive agriculture did not require slavery. Through shipping, the Cape had contact with the two great slave-trading coasts of the world, however, and as the Boers became acquainted with slavery, they came to accept it.

In a poor and unprosperous land, the surplus of Africans and slaves, uneducated in European ways, became a means for gaining privilege and importance. It soon became common practice that the Africans should do the hard labor. Little was done to improve their lot, and their work, as a rule, was wasteful and inefficient. The population grew larger but not richer. As time went on the Boers came to think of manual labor as degrading, and getting land became the goal for the young Afrikander. In this attitude we find another reason for Boer trekking.

On his farms, the Boer lived separated from his white neighbors. He had the courage and hardiness of a pioneer. He enjoyed the wide spaces, the slow movement of his life, and the lack of bothersome change. An old-fashioned family man, he was stern, aloof, and religious. Cut off from the Cape, he did not hear of new theories and ideas. The Bible was his only literature, and he saw himself in the biblical story of the chosen people in the wilderness. The Boer felt that he was an individual and he wanted freedom, but freedom for himself alone—freedom from society, from efficient government, from culture, science, and thought.

As the Boers trekked northward, they were met by the Bantu tribes moving south. Like the Boer, the Bantu way of life demanded wide expanses of grazing land. With both groups, animals and soil worked against each other—overstocked animals injuring the land, the ill-cared-for land unable to feed animals properly.

The big conflict between the Boers and the Bantu came toward the end of the eighteenth century. Both groups wanted water, land and grass, and the clash caused war among the tribes themselves and between the tribes and the Boer. Insufficient space caused diseases among the herds and starvation among the Bantus. Both groups had become so involved that whatever happened to one affected the other. Black and white were closely linked.

When, in 1795, an English force took the Cape colony, it found a still primitive country with only one town worthy of the name and five or six little villages. Most of the population was scattered over an immense area.

The British brought with them something of the progressive outside world—humanitarianism, missionary work, and the ideas of law and order. The slave trade was stopped in 1807 and slavery in 1834. British missionaries began to educate the Africans. Law was extended to protect the non-Christian. The new ways of the nineteenth century suddenly broke in.

The British policies were greeted by the Boer with feelings of injustice and outrage. Education brought questions to the minds of Africans. Previously they had accepted without thought the rule of the white men who had taken the place of tribal leaders. Abolition of slavery upset the labor market. Resentment was felt especially on the farms and frontiers.

Many Boers, resenting the foreigner, resenting restrictions, resenting advice, again moved on to new lands—a move called the Great Trek. On the trek Africans were pushed ever into narrower, poorer areas of land both by the Boer who was fleeing and by the British military, who thought that the only way to preserve order was by force of arms. As for the Bantu, they lost not only much of their land, but their entire way of life.

Industrial Problems

So even before the discovery of gold and diamonds, the present pattern of life of the Africans—forced to leave overcrowded, unproductive areas for rural labor—had been established. When diamonds were found in Hope Town in 1867 and gold in 1884–1885 in the Transvaal, Africans were recruited into city labor as well.

Mining demanded skill, precision, science and business organization—requirements strange and out of place to the conservative, still eighteenth-century Boer. His simple society was challenged by a new industrial and

255

commercial way of life, and by the arrival of aggressive Europeans, mostly English, who wanted to make money from the mines. Many Boers reacted as they had when the British first came; they sold their diamond- and gold-laden lands and fled. Today the mines are owned largely by British shareholders who do not live in Africa—another cause for resentment.

So important is gold to the economy of the country that the government makes up part of its trade deficit by exporting bullion. In addition to the Transvaal, the Orange Free State is also an important gold mining area. A number of the mines also produce uranium.

Land Division

Today in the Republic, about one-third of the Africans live in the reserves which have been set aside for them, one-third work in industry and mining, and one-third on European farms.

Despite the poverty of the reserves, life there is usually better for the African than on the outside. He suffers from overcrowding, poverty, eroded farm lands, malnutrition, and, sadly, some of the diseases introduced by the white man. But some sort of tribal life still exists and he has a family life. Usually uneducated, he continues his old, wasteful agricultural methods. His wife does most of the work except for plowing. At present he owns about 40 per cent of the country's cattle, a useless show of wealth since he is discouraged by his social custom from using them for food. Overstocking spoils large areas and the Bantu is even reluctant to use manure as a fertilizer.

The number of cattle in reserve areas is large, the last official reports showing a total of some 3,700,000 animals.

A labor-tenant system for European farms arises out of reserve policies. When there is a drought or when the reserve farmer is unable to provide the barest minimum, he often leaves to hire himself out to a Boer farmer. Formerly he was paid in use of land for personal farming and grazing and could have his family with him. This system has partly disappeared, and he is now often paid in wages. Legislation passed in 1932 provided that every farm servant must give not less than 180 days' work to his master each year. To insure his staying, he must work on days of his employer's choice. Because of this law, service can be spread over a term of an entire year.

If the African, forced to leave his reserve, does not wish to work on a farm, he may go to the mines or to the city, where he is likely to be better paid—another cause for friction between British industry and Boer farming. At the mines the workers live in compounds, separated from their families. Industry or domestic work lures the tribesman to the cities, where he lives in "locations," often badly overcrowded slums. When large numbers of able-bodied men are kept away from the reserves, there is even less care of the soil.

Since the late 1940's the government has passed a number of legislative measures to enforce the much-criticized policy of "apartheid," or separation of the races. In 1961 South Africa became a republic and withdrew from the Commonwealth of Nations.

Whether, in the three-century history of men and events, a more just and humane solution for the African peoples could have been evolved is not within our present consideration. The fact remains that the Negroes in the Republic of South Africa are considered chiefly as a natural resource to be used for the benefit of a white minority.

South Africa is an example, even though a somewhat extreme one, of a country where, in the face of existing social and political conditions, science and technology have done little for the native-born population.

South Africa Gov't Info. Off.

A Boer farm homestead near Capetown, built in the Netherlands style of their original homeland.

Leaders of East and South Africa

Jomo Kenyatta   1893?–

". . . the African . . . has a worthier essential way of life than the European."

Jomo Kenyatta's belief in the superiority of the African way of life cost him seven
years in prison and two years' confinement. Still, he has managed to take his place as
an influential African leader. Kenyatta was born in a Kikuyu tribal area near Nairobi.
In 1922, he became active in the Kikuyu Central Association as its general secretary.
Later he studied both at the University of Moscow and the University of London. In
1939 the Association was declared illegal. In order to promote negro advancement,
Kenyatta became president of the Kenya African Union in 1947. The Mau Mau uprisings
followed shortly afterward, and Kenyatta was tried and sentenced for his alleged
associations with them. He was released in 1961 and in 1963 became prime minister of
an independent Kenya.

Albert John Luthuli   1899?–1967

"South Africa is large enough to accommodate all people if they have large enough hearts."

Albert Luthuli was probably the most influential black African of his time.
For over ten years he was confined to his house near Groutville by order of the South
African Government, for fear that his appearance anywhere might incite riot and
rebellion. This was a strange consequence for a man who advocated "change without
bloodshed" and who was the winner of the 1960 Nobel Peace Prize. Born into the African
aristocracy, Luthuli served as chieftain of a Zulu tribe for 17 years, beginning in 1937.
The help that he gave to African freedom organizations during this time provoked
disfavor in the South African Government. He was deposed as chieftain and forbidden
to visit major towns and cities.

Julius Kambarage Nyerere   1923?–

"I am a troublemaker, because I believe in human rights strongly enough to be one."

As president of the United Republic of Tanzania, Julius Nyerere is one of the most
respected of African leaders. He was born in Butiama on the eastern shore of Lake
Victoria, the son of a Zanaki chief. He attended Makerere College and the University
of London. Nyerere's work with the Tanganyika African National Union and his
nonviolent policies gained him a temporary seat on the Tanganyika legislative council
in 1954. In 1962 Nyerere was elected President of Tanganyika, and in 1964 he became
the President of Tanzania. Nyerere's programs have been aimed at developing the
resources of his country in the directions of agriculture, mining and light industry
in accordance with his motto "Uhuru na kazi" (Independence and work).

Kenneth Kaunda   1924–

*"Zambia . . . where people of all tribes, races, beliefs and opinion, political and
otherwise, will be able to live happily and in harmony."*

"The Black Lion of Africa," Kenneth Kaunda, was born near Chisali. His Presbyterian
education was carried out with the goal of teaching in mind. Later, he joined the
struggle for Negro independence and, as a result, was jailed several times by the
British. He was secretary-general of Northern Rhodesia in 1953 and leader and
president of the United Independent Party in 1960. In 1964, he became
prime minister of Northern Rhodesia, and when the country gained independence
and was named Zambia he became president. Kaunda is a moderate who favors a
policy of nonalignment, or "positive neutrality," but opposes the "black racism" being
practiced by other new African states.

statute miles

100

500

1000

1500

2000

2500

3000

3500

4000

ATLANTIC OCEAN

INDIAN OCEAN

REPUBLIC

OF

THE

CONGO

Congo River

Lake Leopold II

Kisangani

UGANDA

Lake Rudolf

Lake Albert

MT. ELGON

KENYA

Kampala

Entebbe

MT. KENYA

Lake Edward

Lake Kivu

Lake Victoria

Nakuru

Nairobi

RWANDA

Kigali

MT. GELAI

Usumbura

BURUNDI

Arusha

MT. MERU

MT. KILIMANJARO

Malindi

Shinyanga

Mombasa

Tanga

Kabalo

Albertville

Lake Tanganyika

UNITED

REPUBLIC

OF TANZANIA

Zanzibar

PEMBA

Dar es Salaam

MAFIA ISLAND

Lukuga River

CABINDA

Kinshasa

Matadi

Boma

Luanda

ANGOLA

(PORTUGUESE WEST AFRICA)

Benguela

Nova Lisboa

KATANGA

Lubumbashi

Lake Mweru

Luapula River

Lake Bangweulu

Chambezi River

Lake Rukwa

Tukuyu

Luangwa River

Zambezi River

MALAWI

Lake Malawi

Mozambique

Nkana

Luanshya

ZAMBIA

Lusaka

Shire River

Zomba

MLANJE MTS.

MOZAMBIQUE (PORTUGUESE EAST AFRICA)

BAROTSELAND

Bindura

Salisbury

Victoria Falls

Zambezi River

RHODESIA

OVAMBOLAND

SOUTH WEST

OKOVANGGO SWAMP

Bulawayo

MATABELELAND

DAMARALAND

Windhoek

Francistown

MALAGASY REPUBLIC

Tananarive

WALVIS BAY

NAMIB DESERT

AFRICA

BOTSWANA

Gaberones

Limpopo River

SOUTH

AFRICA

TRANSVAAL

Mbabane

SWAZILAND

Lourenço Marques

KALAHARI DESERT

NAMALAND

Mafeking

Pretoria

Johannesburg

ZULULAND

ORANGE

Bloemfontein

FREE

STATE

REPUBLIC OF

Orange River

BUSHMAN LAND

LESOTHO

Maseru

Pietermaritzburg

Durban

NATAL

CAPE OF GOOD HOPE

Capetown

Port Elizabeth

CAPE OF GOOD HOPE

N

S

A Map of South and East Africa

	KENYA	TANZANIA	REPUBLIC OF THE CONGO (KINSHASA)	RWANDA	BURUNDI
GOVERNMENT	Republic	Republic, united with Zanzibar in 1964 to form United Republic of Tanzania	Republic	Republic	Constitutional monarchy
LOCAL NAME					
CAPITAL	Nairobi	Dar es Salaam	Kinshasa	Kigali	Usumbura
POPULATION¹	9,470,000	10,738,000	15,912,000	3,140,000	2,650,000
AREA	224,960 sq. mi.	362,688 sq. mi.	905,380 sq. mi.	10,474 sq. mi.	10,842 sq. mi.
HIGHEST ELEVATION	Mt. Kenya 17,040 ft.	Mt. Kilimanjaro 19,565 ft.	Mt. Ruwenzori 16,795 ft.	4,500— 10,000 ft.	4,500— 10,000 ft.
AVERAGE TEMPERATURES² COLDEST MONTH WARMEST MONTH	Kabete (near Nairobi) 60° F. (July) 67° F. (Mar.)	75° F. (July) 82° F. (Feb.)	73° F. (July) 80° F. (Mar.-Apr.)		72° F. (July) 78° F. (Mar.)
RAIL MILEAGE	1,625 miles	1,601 miles	3,200 miles	none	none
MAJOR RELIGIONS	Animistic, Moslem, Christian	Animistic, Moslem, Christian	Animistic, Christian	Animistic	Animistic
PREDOMINANT LANGUAGES	Bantu, Hamitic, Swahili	Bantu, Hamitic, English, Hindi, Swahili, Arabic	Bantu, Luba, Kongo, Lingala, Swahili, French	Bantu, Swahili, French	Bantu, Swahili, French
LARGEST CITIES	Nairobi, Mombasa, Nakuru	Dar es Salaam, Tanga	Kinshasa, Lubumbashi, Matadi, Kisangani	Kigali	Usumbura
UNIVERSITIES	1	1	2	1	1
NATURAL RESOURCES AND INDUSTRIES	Gold, asbestos, diatomite, graphite, salt, soda, silver, processed foods, dairy products, lumber, leather, beer, soap, limestone, cement manufacturing.	Diamonds, gold, tin, mica, ivory, lead, processed agricultural products, meat packing.	Industrial diamonds, cobalt, manganese, copper, cassiterite (tin), gold, silver, cadmium, iron ore, uranium, processed foods, refined ores, sugar, textiles, soap, quinine, lime, leather goods, chemicals, hides, insecticides.	Agricultural processing, tin, wolfram, gold	Agricultural processing, tin, wolfram, gold, pharmaceuticals
AGRICULTURAL PRODUCTS ¹Based on UN estimates, 1966 ²At capitals, unless otherwise stated	Cotton, maize, wheat, sisal, coconuts, sugar, tea, coffee, barley, oats, livestock, pyrethrum.	Sisal, cotton, coffee, tobacco, peanuts, hides and skins, beeswax, bananas, rice, millet.	Cotton, palm oil, coffee, rubber, fibers, peanuts, cocoa, cinchona, palm kernels.	Coffee, manioc, bananas, sweet potatoes, beans, maize, sorghum, peanuts, cotton, tobacco, kapok	Coffee, manioc, bananas, sweet potatoes, beans, maize, sorghum, peanuts, cotton, tobacco, kapok

259

Editor's note: See Volume 5, page 328, for facts about Uganda.

Facts About South and East Africa	ZAMBIA	RHODESIA	MALAWI	MOZAMBIQUE	MALAGASY REPUBLIC
GOVERNMENT	Republic	Independent state	Independent state	Portuguese overseas province	Republic, independent member of French Community
LOCAL NAME				Moçambique	Grande-Île or Grande-Terre
CAPITAL	Lusaka	Salisbury	Zomba	Lourenço Marques	Tananarive
POPULATION¹	3,744,000	4,306,000	4,056,000	7,147,000	6,428,000
AREA	292,323 sq. mi.	150,333 sq. mi.	47,949 sq. mi.	297,731 sq. mi.	227,602 sq. mi.
HIGHEST ELEVATION	Muchinga Mts. over 6,000 ft.	Mt. Inyangani 8,517 ft.	Mt. Mlanje 9,843 ft.	Namuli Mts. 7,936 ft.	Tsaratanana Massif 9,450 ft.
AVERAGE TEMPERATURE² COLDEST MONTH WARMEST MONTH	(Livingstone) 64° F. (July) 80° F. (Oct.)	57° F. (July) 71° F. (Oct.)	62° F. (July) 75° F. (Nov.)	65° F. (July) 78° F. (Feb.)	70° F. (July) 85° F. (Dec.-Mar.)
RAIL MILEAGE	655 miles	3,000 miles	300 miles	1,834 miles	534 miles
MAJOR RELIGIONS	Animistic, Christian	Animistic, Christian, Hindu	Animistic, Christian, Moslem	Animistic, Christian, Moslem	Animistic, Christian, Moslem
PREDOMINANT LANGUAGES	Bantu (Upper Zambesi), English	Bantu (East Bantu), English	Bantu (Nyanja), English	Bantu, Portuguese	Malay-Polynesian
LARGEST CITIES	Nkana, Livingstone, Lusaka	Salisbury, Que Que, Bindura, Umtali	Limbe, Blantyre, Zomba	Beira, Mozambique, Lourenço Marques	Tananarive, Majunga, Tamatave
UNIVERSITIES	1	1	1	0	1
NATURAL RESOURCES AND INDUSTRIES	Copper, cobalt alloy, zinc, vanadium, lead, gold, silver, lumber products, soap, chemicals, brick, leather, flour.	Gold, asbestos, coal, chrome ore, mica, tungsten ores, brewery products, sugar, wood products, metalwork, fertilizer, clothing, leather goods.	Corundum, coal, bauxite, gold, cigarettes and tobacco, tea, soap, sisal rope, furniture, bamboo and reed products, butter.	Gold, coal, beryl, tin, silver, graphite, bauxite, mica, sugar, flour, tobacco, textiles, rubber, wood products, cement, bricks, lime, hides and skins.	Graphite, mica, quartz, gold, corundum, beryllium, semi-precious stones, processed agricultural products, fiber bags and mats, soaps, oils, coal.
AGRICULTURAL PRODUCTS ¹Based on UN estimates, 1966 ²At capitals, unless otherwise stated	Maize, wheat, tobacco, coffee, millet, animal products.	Tobacco, peanuts, wheat, citrus fruits, maize, vegetables, livestock, fish, cotton, potatoes.	Tobacco, tea, cotton, sisal, rubber, coffee, beeswax, chilies, maize, potatoes, fish, peanuts.	Maize, oil-bearing seeds, tea, sisal, copra, sugar cane, fruits, cotton, peanuts, beans, cottonseed, rice, millet, bananas.	Rice, manoic, sweet potatoes, coffee, maize, beans, vanilla beans, spices, fibers, animal products, sugar cane, cloves, tobacco, sisal.

ZANZIBAR	ANGOLA	BOTSWANA	SOUTH WEST AFRICA	REPUBLIC OF SOUTH AFRICA	LESOTHO	SWAZILAND
United with Tanganyika in 1964 to form United Republic of Tanzania	Portuguese overseas province	Republic	Former German territory mandated to South Africa	Republic	Republic	Constitutional monarchy
			Suidwes-Afrika	Republiek van Suid-Afrika		
Zanzibar	Luanda	Gaberones	Windhoek	Pretoria	Maseru	Mbabane
350,000	5,288,000	565,000	587,000	18,182,000	763,000	302,000
1,020 sq. mi.	481,350 sq. mi.	275,000 sq. mi.	317,725 sq. mi.	472,494 sq. mi.	11,716 sq. mi.	6,705 sq. mi.
Masingini Ridge 390 ft.	about 6,000 ft.	over 3,000 ft.	Brandberg Mtn. 8,550 ft.	Champagne Castle 11,075 ft. (Natal)	Thabantshonyana 11,425 ft.	over 5,000 ft.
76°F. (June-Sept.) 84°F. (Dec.-Mar.)	68° F. (Aug.) 80° F. (Feb.-Mar.)	47° F. (July) 88° F. (Jan.)	55° F. (July) 75° F. (Jan.)	51° F. (July) 72° F. (Jan.)	(Mafeteng) 45° F. (July) 69° F. (Jan.)	53° F. (July) 68° F. (Jan.)
none	1,665 miles	394 miles	1,493 miles	14,068 miles	16 miles	none (some railway motor buses)
Moslem	Animistic, Christian	Animistic, Christian	Animistic, Christian	Animistic, Christian	Animistic, Christian	Animistic, Christian
Swahili, Arabic, English	Bantu (Umbundi) Portuguese	Bantu (Batswana) Bushman	Bantu, Bushman, Afrikaans, English	Afrikaans, English, Bantu, Bushman	Bantu (Kaffir), Sesuto	Bantu, Swazi, English
Zanzibar, Wete	Luanda, Nova Lisboa, Lobito	Kanye, Serowe	Windhoek, Lüderitz, Swakopmund	Johannesburg, Capetown, Durban, Pretoria	Maseru	Mbabane
0	0	0	0	9	0	0
Clove oil, pottery, soap, jewelry, mats, vegetable oil, hides and skins, rope, baskets	Diamonds, manganese, copper, mica, gold, salt, fish products, sugar, alcohol, paper products, soap, shoes, rubber, wax, agricultural processing	Beef, small timber, gold, silver, asbestos, dairy products, hides and skins	Diamonds, vanadium, tin, lithium ores, lead-copper-zinc concentrates, hides and skins, dairy products, fishing, gold, cadmium, graphite, salt, silver.	Gold, diamonds, coal, copper, manganese ore, chrome ore, tin, asbestos, platinum, processed foods, beverages, chemicals, iron and steel, textiles, leather goods, iron ore, silver, tungsten, metal products, wool.	Wool, mohair, hides and skins.	Timber, wood pulp, iron ore, asbestos, wool, barytes, silver, gold, hides and skins.
Cloves, coconuts, copra, fruits, tobacco.	Maize, coffee, sisal, cotton, sugar cane, cocoa, palm oil, wheat, palm kernels, cottonseed, peanuts, livestock.	Livestock, maize, sorghum, beans, pumpkins, melons.	Maize, potatoes, beans, pumpkins, cattle, horses, donkeys, mules, sheep.	Maize, wheat, oats, barley, rye, potatoes, sugar cane, tobacco, fruits, peanuts, cotton, sunflower seeds, animal products.	Maize, wheat, peas, livestock, wool, sorghum, beans, barley, oats, Kaffir corn.	Maize, sorghum, wheat, rye, oats, barley, fruit, cotton, tobacco, livestock.

261

Life in African Villages and Towns

What would your life be like if you woke up one morning in Africa? That would depend on *where* you woke up, because Africans, like most other people, fit their work and customs to their geographic surroundings—desert, mountain, plain, or shore. In this section you can take a trip down one side of this great continent and up the other, sampling African life in villages and towns as you go.

The tour starts in the Sahara Desert of northern Africa, where you may attend a great wedding festival, an event people everywhere seem to celebrate. Next, you will find yourself in eastern Africa with the Masai, who live in the highlands of Kenya and Tanganyika. They are as interested in cattle as the cattle ranchers of the American West. Then, you are invited to a party for young people in southern Africa, where the Kafirs, Zulus, and Basutos live.

An exciting article on the pygmies will take you to the Congo jungles of central Africa where daily life is probably almost completely different from yours, except for the personalities of the people you will meet. You will complete your tour of African villages with a visit to Dahomey on the west African coast. Dahomeans fish and farm for a living, much as many people who live in warm, shoreline areas.

For contrast to the village life of Africa, pay a call, in pictures, on some of the African cities south of the Sahara.

By the time you have finished your trek through this section you will probably have found that *how* Africans do things is different from your way, but *what* they do is not as different as you might have thought.

This exquisite head, about 500 years old, was sculptured in Ife, part of the ancient kingdom of Yoruba, Nigeria, where some of Africa's finest sculpture was produced. The head is made of terra cotta, a fine, baked, brownish-orange earthenware.

Jos Mus., Jos, Northern Nigeria, B.W.A.

262

Wooden headdress illustrating modern African artistry represents an antelope. It is worn during dances of the sowing and harvest feasts in Mali. The dancer mounts the carving on a basket-work cap in order to wear it comfortably.

Courtesy Louis Carre Collection, Paris, photo
Mus. Modern Art, N. Y.

A Berber camel caravan (called "ships of the desert") riding out of the Atlas Mountains with a cargo of wool for market.

French Embassy Press & Info. Div.

The Berbers of the Sahara

The hardy, courageous Berbers, who wring a living out of the great Sahara Desert, are among the most colorful and romantic people of the world. They trade their wool in the big cities of North Africa but actually they are country people who wander through the heart of the Sahara, and all along the north African coast, from Egypt to the Atlantic. As you will find in this article, their lives are as varied as the Sahara itself which combines burning sandy wastes, snow-covered mountains, wheat fields and orchards, and palm-dotted oases. Reprinted from **Across the Great Deserts** by P. T. Etherton, copyright 1948. Published by the McGraw-Hill Book Company, Inc., N. Y. C., and Lutterworth Press, London.

The people who live in the Sahara are not all Arabs, as is popularly supposed, but are mostly Berbers, who lived in North Africa long before the coming of the Arabs. The old name for them was Moors, and though they are still often called by this name, that title is really confined to persons of Arab blood who live in the cities of North Africa.

Where the Berbers themselves came from no one knows, for they were living in North Africa when history began. Neither Romans nor Arabs were ever able to conquer them completely, but both employed them in their armies, for, as we shall see, the Berber is a fine fighting man. Berber warriors crossed over the Alps in Hannibal's march against Rome (218–202 B.C.), and the armies with which the Arabs conquered Spain were largely composed of Berbers (A.D. 711). The name of Hannibal is still to be found among them.

The Berbers are of the white race, but exposure to the burning sun makes them look dark-skinned. Blue eyes and fair hair are not uncommon among them. In fact, one theory of their origin is that they are the descendants of the Vandals, the Germanic race who founded a kingdom in North Africa in the fifth century and who vanished mysteriously from the pages of history a century or so later

The Berber is an independent sort of man and has always been "agin the government," whatever that government may be. He fights for the sheer love of it, and many Berbers took part in World War I and World War II. Although brave and cruel, he is a sportsman and bears no resentment towards those who have defeated him in war.

Berbers differ from Arabs in many respects: in their methods of fighting, in the treatment of their womenfolk, and principally in their attitude towards modern civilization. Like the European or American, the Berber has a mechanical turn of mind and is extremely interested in aircraft, engines, and machinery.

Castles in Africa

Although many of the Berber tribes live in tents, Arab-fashion, they are really house dwellers, living in villages of stone or mud, or in big, many-turreted houses, which are actually castles.

These castles of the northern Sahara are unique; there is nothing to compare with them. With their thick walls and tapering towers, they are one of the striking forms of present-day African architecture. They are

263

really fortified communal storehouses. The members of one Berber tribe, who are nomads for one half of the year and farmers for the other, cannot carry about with them everything they possess, especially reserves of food. So each family group has its own particular fortress, which it leaves in charge of trusted guards during its wanderings.

Outside the *ksar*, or fortified tribal house, is the *nuadder*, or threshing floor. The grain is flung down upon this wide mud platform and then trampled upon by horses and mules driven round and round. Straw and chaff are thrown into the air, to be blown away by the wind, so that finally only the seed remains.

In these mud strongholds the old patriarchal mode of life (where the father is absolute head of the household) prevails; when invited inside you sit cross-legged on a reed mat beside a glistening samovar (a teakettle with a burner built in under the bottom) and drink the three cups of mint tea required by Berber etiquette. There is often considerable difference in the social and political organization of the tribes; many are ruled by *Kaids*, or lords, who exercise complete authority; others are organized as republics.

Warfare of the Past

Water played an important part in Berber warfare. Villages lying a mile or two from a river depended upon canals for their water supply, and the diverting of this canal to another community naturally led to war. When a *ksar* was besieged the attackers first tried to cut off the water supply, thus forcing the besieged to come out into the open. Or, a canal

would be dug along the walls of the stronghold and in a few hours the earthen building would start to crumble into ruins, *tabia* being unable to withstand the effects of moisture.

To prevent an enemy's seizing the canals, watch-towers were built on mounds along the banks. These square-loopholed forts were garrisoned by small bands of men equipped with water and provisions to withstand a siege.

The Berber tribes warred constantly among themselves. Blood feuds were frequent. If a man were killed his kinsmen were compelled to kill the slayer. In turn *his* relatives must avenge his death. This went on until nearly all the male members of a family had been exterminated. (After the French began to rule the Sahara in 1830, this type of war and feuding gradually disappeared.)

Goats and Date Palms

The nomad Berbers dwell in tents woven from the hair of goats and camels, and carry their homes with them when leading their flocks and herds to other pastures. They have their summer and winter pastures, and spend their time traveling back and forth between them.

The oases scattered about the desert at irregular intervals vary in size, some being only large enough to shelter a family and its animals, others supporting changing populations of up to fifty thousand people. Some contain a dozen or so villages and cover hundreds of square miles. Often these people added to their scanty livelihood by making raids on each other's cattle or on passing caravans. In the days when large caravans crossed the desert with loads of salt, gold dust, slaves, and

264

The walled Berber city of Marrakech in Morocco. Marrakech is a big town, but its baked mud buildings are like those of any small oasis village.

Paul's Photos

ivory, this was a very profitable business, but the advance of European civilization has put an end to raiding and slave trading.

The date palm is the mainstay of life, and one can sometimes see hundreds or thousands of trees growing in an oasis. The date is an important article of trade, and it is an interesting sight at harvest time to see boys run nimbly up the tree trunks to cut off the clusters of red-gold fruit.

Berber Banquet

The Berbers are an hospitable people, and if you are invited to dine in one of their camps or houses it is an entertaining affair.

Imagine a banquet in one of the big tents of a Berber chieftain in central Morocco. There are brightly-colored carpets on the floors and embroidered cushions for the guests to recline on. A slave brings soap, water, and towel for you to wash your right hand. "Blessed is the food eaten with the hand," says the Koran (the "bible" of the Islamic faith, to which they belong), and so no knives or forks are used, only the right hand. To use the left when eating is a breach of etiquette.

The chieftain's sons wait upon the guest. The courses are many and varied; as well as the main dish there will be side dishes consisting of strips of mutton served on wooden skewers, hard-boiled eggs, honey, nuts, almonds, and cakes of various kinds.

Later on a dish of *cous-cous*, a favorite Arab delicacy made of broken grains of wheat mixed with meat and vegetables, will be brought in. To eat *cous-cous* is a difficult art for a foreigner. The idea is to scoop up a little of the mixture in the fingers of the right hand, and twist it neatly into a ball; but as it is hot and slippery, unless you have got the knack of doing it properly, you are more likely to drop it into your lap.

Every now and again the host, to mark his appreciation of his guest, will plunge a hand into the pot and pick out some delicacy which the guest must eat, whatever it may be, for a refusal would give great offense.

To the beat of their tambourine drums and the tinkle of their jewelry, these Berber girls of Azrou, in central Morocco, sing and dance at a festival.

With the Berbers, eating is regarded as a serious business, and nothing must be allowed to interfere with it. At long last everybody seems to be full, and slaves then bring water and towels again for you to wash your hands.

Finally, mint tea is served; this is ordinary tea with mint leaves chopped up in it. It is sweet and hot, and not until you have drunk the three cups required by etiquette will you be allowed to depart.

A Royal Wedding

The Berber loves a festival, and particularly a wedding. The recent wedding of a sultan's son was marked with Arabian Nights' splendor. It was a flashback to the old Berber days of golden glory, a revival of their once splendid past. For this the sultan had set aside a large sum and had adjusted his budget in accordance with the amounts certain districts could supply. Successful candidates for government posts were those who got the utmost out of the area committed to their charge.

The sultan's daughter-in-law was one of four lawful wives, as allowed by the Koran; she was the daughter of the governor of Marrakech. For two or three days Marrakech was illuminated with candles, lamps, and lanterns, and on the wedding eve, the bride left her home for that of her future husband. She was enclosed in a box like a dovecote, placed on a mule covered with rich decorations. The procession was headed by the chief priests of the mosque, with the friends and families of both parties.

An immense orchestra was distributed along the route. The town was on holiday and thou-

265

French Embassy Press & Info. Div.

sands of guests carried lamps of silver, brass, copper, and colored paper, while luminous fountains in every square shot forth vari-colored water.

As the bride left her father's home, all the lights in the house were extinguished, as a sign that the light of love and beauty had left forever.

Arriving at the home of her future husband, she was taken to her rooms, where the final touches were put to her complexion, her feet were recovered with henna (a red dye), and a dish of the national *cous-cous* was placed before her by the mother-in-law. Apparently etiquette demanded that she eat only a morsel, but must put a little on her nose and wish herself luck. The bridegroom then took over the lady, still veiled, and served up more of the *cous-cous*, which she ate. Following this came the unveiling, when the husband would get a view of her for the first time in his life.

Two days later the dovecote was placed on the roof, as a signal that she was "at home" to her women friends. A reception followed, and high jinks went on for some days; everyone gave dinners to everyone else, and every variety of Berber dish was served; alms were distributed to the beggars; the poor were entertained, and tea, flavored with mint and verbena, was dispensed. The presents at this marriage included everything from bracelets, anklets, and gold ornaments, precious stones, brocades, and rolls of silk, down to the humble bag of almond nuts from the Berber shepherd.

In the Town

After midday prayers the bazaars and streets are crowded. Shopping is easy, for the jewelers and silversmiths are in one street, the potters in another, and cloth, brocades, shoes, saddlery, swords, hardware and leather, each in its own domain. The shops are like kennels, open to front and sides, and the shopkeeper sits among his wares with an air of complete indifference. In fact, he hardly bothers to notice the customer.

Women in their long gowns and hoods, with two round holes for the eyes, pass to and fro.

Streets are irregular and frequently not more than four or five feet wide, running in and out and leading in every direction. Houses lean drunkenly, shutting out the sun. After sunset it is pitch dark, the night air emphasizing the smell from the open drains.

Here and there are the fortunetellers and sorcerers. They gather the crowd and for a halfpenny or so deal out lifelong prosperity to their clients. Here also is the professional letter writer, an institution in all Berber towns and villages. He sits crosslegged with pen and paper spread out upon his knees; clients gather round and narrate the text of documents, petitions, and letters, and the scribe commits it all to paper. Education being poor, the letter writer comes into his own on market days when the terms of a bargain have to be recorded and deeds of sale drawn up.

There are schools in most towns, though the mosque is usually the seat of learning. With the exception of reading and writing and the religious teaching of the Koran, practically nothing is learned, for the instructors themselves are in need of education and it is really a case of the blind leading the blind. The pupils sit on the ground, or, at the more pretentious schools, on wooden forms, with desks made from logs. They sing whatever is set for study, for the Berbers have the fixed idea that the mind absorbs knowledge through the ears rather than the eyes.

These Berber boys of Morocco's High Atlas Mountains will soon be hard-riding tribesmen, but meanwhile they don't seem to mind a little baby-sitting.

The Greed of the Old Man and His Wife:

A Masai Folk Tale

This favorite folk story of the Masai concerns cattle, because to these cattle herders of Tanganyika and Kenya, food from cattle is highly regarded. Since the Masai must help each other in order to survive, they believe that terrible punishment will come to those who do not share prized things such as the meat of oxen. "The Greed of the Old Man and His Wife" was originally published in *The Masai* by A. C. Hollis, 1905. Used by permission of the Clarendon Press, Oxford.

There was once upon a time an old man who lived in a village. He had a wife and a small child, and possessed a very fine ox.

One day he said to himself, "How shall I slaughter my ox?" And he said aloud to his wife, "My child! I will call the men and tell them that I am going to move. We can then slaughter our ox all by ourselves."

His wife agreed and, in the evening, the old man blew his horn as a signal to his friends that he had something to tell them. His neighbors came together, and he told them that he wished to move, as the air did not agree with him. The others consented, and in the morning he saddled his donkeys, separated his cattle from the rest, and started off, accompanied by his wife, who was carrying the child.

When they had gone some distance, they halted and erected their cattle pen after which they rested.

At dawn on the second day the old man called his wife and asked her why they had not yet slaughtered their ox. The woman replied, "My husband! How shall we manage to slaughter the ox? There are two things to be considered—the first is that we have no herdsman and the second that I am carrying the baby."

The old man then said, "Oh, I know what we will do. I will stab the ox in the neck, then I will leave you to skin it, and I will carry the child to the grazing ground. But when you have skinned the animal, roast some meat so that it will be ready on my return."

The old man then killed the ox, then put the child on his back, and drove the cattle to the grazing ground.

In the afternoon, as the child was asleep, the old man put it down in the grass, and went to drive back the cattle, for they had wandered far. But when he returned to the spot where he had left the child, he was unable to find it, so he decided to set fire to the grass. "When the fire reaches the child, it will cry," he thought, "and I will run to the place and pick it up before it is burned."

He made a fire, and it traveled to where the child was. He ran to the spot, but when he reached it, he found that the child was dead.

The old man had left his wife in the morning skinning the ox. And while she was skinning it the knife slipped, and she stabbed herself in the eye. She went and lay down, and the birds came and finished the meat.

After the child was burned, the old man drove the cattle to the pen, and when they were opposite to the gate, he heard his wife weeping, and saying, "Oh, my eye!" He therefore asked her who had told her the news.

"What news?" she inquired.

"The child has been burned," he replied.

The woman exclaimed, "Oh, my child!"

The old man then asked where his meat was, and his wife informed him that the birds had eaten it, whereupon he cried out, "Oh, my meat!"

They both wept, the old man crying, "Oh, my meat!" and the woman, "Oh, my child! Oh, my eye!"

Look well at these people. It was for their greed that they were punished. They lost their child and their ox, the woman lost her eye, and they had to return in shame to their home.

267

 Other Sections To See

"Countries of the Nile," Volume 5; "The Family: Cornerstone of Everyday Living," Volume 6; "South and East Africa," this volume; "Northwest Africa" and "The Mediterranean World," Volume 11; "Cattle, Sheep, Goats, and Hogs," Volume 12.

A Party in the South African Veld

On the rolling veld or grasslands of southern Africa live tribes like the Kafirs, Zulus, and Basutos, who are farmers and cattle herders with similar customs. The party described here could have taken place among any of these tribes. From **Savage Childhood** by Dudley Kidd. Used by permission of the publishers, A. & C. Black, Ltd., London.

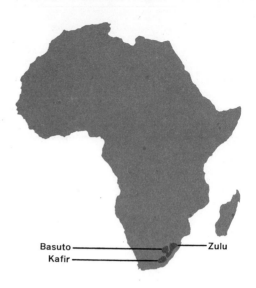

Basuto
Kafir
Zulu

When a party is to be held, the parents have to consider very carefully which *kraals* (villages) should be invited. There are frequent feuds between certain families, and if the boys and girls from these rival kraals were to meet, quarreling would be sure to follow; there would be bruised limbs, and probably broken heads, before the party broke up. It is therefore necessary to consider what kraals are on good terms with one another.

The Kafirs (this name is often applied to all Africans not of the Islamic religion) have no written language, and therefore invitations have to be sent out by word of mouth. As a rule the boys invite the boys, and the girls invite the girls.

It is always understood that the invitation is addressed to all the boys and girls of the kraal, for no one expects a separate invitation; only the infants are kept at home and not allowed to go out to the party.

The invited guests tell by the time allowed for preparation how great a party to expect, and how to dress up. When the party is to be a great affair, the invitation is sent out two weeks in advance; if only a few days' notice be given, every one knows that the party will be a small one. At these great parties fully a hundred children may be present, and every one does his very best to look as smart as possible so as to attract attention.

Getting Ready for the Party

For several days before a party, the children are very busy in the kraal; the girls bring out small grinding stones very similar to those used by grown-up women for grinding corn; soft white stone is then broken into little pieces which are ground into a fine powder between the grinding stones. This white powder is mixed with water, or fat, and smeared on the body. The children frequently paint their bodies in very fantastic ways. In Lesotho the girls are fond of red paint. In this tribe the boys do not often paint themselves for parties; but in Zululand the boys frequently smear their head, trunk, and legs with white paint, the girls only painting a white circle or band round their waists, sometimes adding a few touches of white on the cheeks.

The bigger children make extremely pretty beadwork, choosing attractive combinations of color. Bangles are made with grass, or with brass wire, and are worn round the ankle, calf, knee, waist, neck, elbow, and wrist. Blankets are well rubbed with red clay, and often have their edges prettily ornamented with beadwork. The skins of wild animals are worked up with grease until they are very soft and supple, and the tails of wild cats are made into ornaments for the loins. The children frequently tattoo themselves specially for these parties, using a pointed stick, which makes whitish marks in the skin; these marks only last for a few days.

The anxious mothers are also busy for days in advance of the party, telling the boys to be sure not to quarrel with other boys, lest it should be said they come from a quarrelsome kraal, and so the whole family should be disgraced publicly. They specially impress on the children not to eat too much; they tell them that if they show any signs of greediness the people will all say, "See, those children come from a kraal where there is famine." After that cutting sarcasm no one in the kraal could look the world in the face for many a day. But in spite of these days of coaching by anxious mothers, the children always eat too much, and the boys always quarrel and fight. As the children go off to the party the parents finally impress on the boys that they must not annoy the girls, nor forget to be very polite to the owners of the kraal who are giving the party.

As the twilight dies and a rich afterglow of the deepest purple or violet suffuses the sky, there can be seen a string of young people all silhouetted against a few low-lying clouds of orange color—and hurrying over the veld in single file along the narrow Kafir footpath. At length this thin, wavy line of excited, talkative, chattering children arrives at the kraal.

At the Party

On arriving at the kraal the guests have to salute the headman of the place. If there should happen to be a chief present, the children walk up to him in single file, and as each child passes the chief, he or she has to stand still, shuffle the feet, point to the sky with the right hand, and say, "Bayete." If the greatest man present is only an ordinary headman, the children shuffle their feet, and say, "Numzaan," rarely pointing with the hand to the sky. In some tribes it is not correct etiquette for guests to speak first on arriving at a kraal; it is expected that they should sit down in silence until the headman first addresses them.

When the guests have saluted the great person, they next go and shake hands with his "great" wife (the first wife), and after that they shake hands with the other women present and with the various guests. When this process is over, the guests are told which huts are set apart for the evening, and, if the weather is cold, the children are ushered into one of the other huts, where the girls of the kraal usually hang up their blankets on a leather thong stretched between two poles. The guests pile their blankets on these leather ropes; they will not need their blankets again till the morning, for there are fires kept burning in every hut all night.

Since the party is to last till dawn, any children who may get tired are free to go to one of the huts and enjoy a sleep whenever they like; when rested they can return to the party. If the party does not last the whole night, the children all sleep at the kraal of the person inviting them. Beds are quite unknown, for the people sleep in their blankets on grass mats, using blocks of wood for pillows. It is a simple matter to find floor space for a hundred visitors.

The children creep into the huts through a low doorway on their hands and knees, and find themselves in a large round hut with a fire burning in the center of the floor. The smoke wanders round the blackened rafters

Zulu kraals, *or villages, are spread over the veld. The Dutch who settled in southern Africa called cattle pens* kraals. *(Western Americans use the Spanish word* corral.) *Since the village houses are built around the cattle enclosure, the whole village is called a kraal.*

South African Gov't Info. Off.

and fills the hut, escaping through the dense thatch, which may be several feet thick. The walls of the hut are made of woven branches plastered with mud, and the floor consists of dried mud. Everything is of the color of the earth, and at the back of the hut are to be seen some earthenware pots and calabashes (gourds). A tiny calf or a few goats may be tied up to one of the poles which support the roof, and a number of hens and dogs are sure to be found prowling round the hut, hunting for any small pieces of food they may chance to find.

The first great interest of the evening centers in the food. The big boys eat by themselves, and the small boys by themselves; the girls club together for their food. In ordinary daily life, the men eat their food first by themselves, and give what is left over to the women and children. But at a party, the children have the best of everything. The food may consist of the following: beef, mutton, goat, and old hens; these are always boiled, unless small portions are cooked over the fire on little wooden skewers, or are placed on the embers. In addition to meat there is usually sour milk, pumpkins, fried locusts, Indian corn, and mice. But the favorite food is beef. A number of small birds, caught in traps, are sure to be found roasting over the fire. Such birds are cooked with their feathers on, and without receiving any cleaning.

Kafir youngsters are very fond of making small toy clay plates and dishes, which they dry in the sun and afterwards bake in the fire.

These are arranged on the floor for the small guests, for tables and chairs are unknown. Wooden spoons are supplied for these parties. In Basutoland the children imitate their elders and make, not small plates of earthenware, for Basutos do not use such things, but small grass mats and baskets to eat food from. Small toy pots are also made to cook portions of food in.

One privileged girl is allowed to preside at the pot of the girls which is the Kafir equivalent to pouring tea at a tea party, and a big boy presides at the boys' pot. Most of the food is eaten out of the fingers because forks are unknown. Big boys, however, frequently have pocketknives nowadays, and feel very proud in producing them at parties.

When it is about an hour or so past midnight the great event of the party—so far as the boys are concerned—takes place. For this the boys have been watching all the evening. The headman tells the big boys—what they knew hours ago—that he has a sheep cooking for them in a large pot. The boys all fly off to the vessel, pull out the cooked sheep and tear it to pieces with their hands. Then they all rush off to some hill close by, where wood for fires has been collected before the party commenced; campfires are made, and the boys have a royal feast. At such times, everything is confusion in the kraal.

Sound Familiar?

The boys produce from their pockets the most marvelous things. Most boys carry under their arms a small bag which is suspended from the

A Kafir girl in her brass wire party finery kneels respectfully to salute the village headman (left). At right is a village like that described in this article.

South African Gov't Info. Off.

British Information Services

neck. This bag does duty for a pocket. Mothers always complain about what the pockets of boys can hold, but the Kafir boys must be champions in this field. Here is a list of things found in the pockets of a few Kafir boys: string made from grass, mice, old pieces of food, bangles, dead birds, pins, needles for sewing frayed skins, wooden spoons, edible roots, Indian hemp and a small horn to smoke it with, tobacco pipes made from roots of trees, caterpillars, and, finally lizards. A weird confusion of such articles is turned out beneath the silent stars, and all that is edible is cooked over the fire and eaten along with the sheep.

When the mutton has vanished—all except the skin and the bare bones which have been gnawed clean, broken, and robbed of the marrow—the boys wax fat and scrappy. Everyone seems to develop a fighting spirit. Sides are soon formed, possibly one set of kraals fighting another set as in real life. The boys all pretend to be soldiers; there may be as many as twenty or thirty boys on each side. To prevent confusion in the dark, the boys of one side deck themselves with white paint. If there should be no men looking on, a war dance is indulged in, the war song being sung slowly and solemnly in low voices, for in all things the boys imitate their elders. The excitement grows as the song increases in volume and rhythm. Before long the chant becomes boisterous and noisy; then the fighting commences in real earnest. Sticks are freely used, and many are the bruises received, and many are the scalps cut open. There is such a strong sense of honor amongst the boys that they would scorn to "sneak" about their injuries. Wounds are patched up with a free coating of mud, and if any awkward questions should be asked next morning, the boys account for the suspicious-looking marks of mud by saying that they fell down hill in the dark, or got cut while playing games.

Before returning to the huts at the first streak of dawn, the boys sit around the fire telling stories, all bragging of their abilities. At length a move is made to the huts, and an uproarious crowd of naked boys is seen sweeping down the hill with blankets waving from many an arm. A race is being held, and blankets are carried on the arm so as not to impede the movement.

All the time the boys have been enjoying their midnight orgy on the hill, the girls have been occupied with quieter amusements; some have been playing with clay dolls, and others have been gossiping about their sweethearts, or have coaxed an old grandmother into a good temper and have persuaded her to tell them some of the old nursery tales. During the night some of the smaller children have been sleeping peacefully in another hut, having been worn out with excitement.

We Had a Wonderful Time . . .

The return of the boys, who rush into the kraal like a hurricane, is the sign for the party to break up. Blankets are fetched out, and the tired children go to say goodbye to the headman, shake hands with the women, and then emerge from the hut on hands and knees. There are many last words between the departing guests, and slowly a number of straggling rows of children file off along the various pathways to their respective homes. The children walk home with wavering, unsteady gait, for most of them are tired, and all of them are grumbling and cross. When the children reach home the old people are cross at being roused too early from their slumber, and resent the barking of the dogs. Every one votes parties a nuisance; the girls wish they were boys to enjoy the midnight feast on the hill; the boys are aching in limb and bruised in body; the parents are suffering from being awakened. Yet with wonderful wisdom everybody will look forward to the next party with delight.

271

"The big boys eat by themselves, and the small boys by themselves." These young Basuto boys enjoy the party without bothering to dress up in paint or beadwork.

British Info. Serv.

How Do the Africans Say It?

Finding out about words and the way people use them can be fascinating fun. The people who live in the southern half of Africa speak the Bantu language and have very picturesque ways of describing things. Here is a list of descriptive Bantu expressions translated into English.
See how many you can understand without looking at the answers listed in the second column.
From **Fun and Festival from Africa** by Rose H. Wright, one of the **Fun and Festival** series. New York, Friendship Press, Copyright 1952. Used by permission.

Questions

1. In the world of nature, what would be the great ball of fire?
2. Who is Nyoka, the multicolored snake?
3. What is a slice of life?
4. What are the tom-toms on which the thunder beats?
5. What part of the anatomy is a bag of breath?
6. What is the hour when the sun bores through your head?
7. What do you mean when you say the clouds are crying?
8. When is "before the sun sleeps"?
9. When is water ready to roll in bad temper?
10. Who is The-One-Who-Put-Things-in-Order?
11. What is the face medicine the white woman is not strong without?
12. When does your stomach stick to your back?
13. When you tie your eyebrows, what do you do?
14. What are you doing when you wait small?
15. When is your liver in a temper?
16. When does your back feel heavy?
17. What is a book that makes trouble for the head?
18. What would be the town-of-the-men-of-the-tribe-of-God?
19. When is your heart let down?
20. When is your heart broken loose?
21. What do you mean when you say, "In my eye it is finished; in my heart it is not"?
22. What does it mean to have knives turning in your heart?
23. When are you laughed to sadness of heart?
24. When have you lost your heart?
25. When is your heart rolling from side to side?
26. When do you tie yourself in your heart?
27. When do you let your heart lie down good?
28. What do you mean when you say, "Did you plant the earth"?
29. What is a never-never land?
30. What is one rice season?

5. lungs
8. before sunset
10. God
14. waiting a minute
27. when you are happy
21. you appear to have forgiven when you haven't
13. frown
9. when it is ready to boil
26. when you promise something
1. sun
22. you are hating someone
28. that the person is so conceited he thinks he deserves more than other people; like "What do you think this is, your birthday?"
17. a study book
3. a day
16. you think someone is behind you, staring
23. when someone is making fun of you so that it really hurts
7. it's raining
19. when you are worried
4. clouds
29. a place where the speaker has never been
11. make-up
30. a year
6. noon
12. when you're hungry
20. when you have lost control of it and so become a treacherous person
25. when you can't make up your mind
2. rainbow
15. you're annoyed
24. you don't care what you do
18. the mission station

Pygmies of the Congo Jungle

In the Congo jungles that spread across Central Africa live some of the most fascinating people in the world—the pygmies. Here the story of how these small people battle the huge jungle with their skills and cleverness is told by Commander Attilio Gatti and his wife, Ellen, world-famous explorers of Africa. Condensed from **Here Is Africa** by Ellen and Attilio Gatti. Copyright 1943 by Charles Scribner's Sons. Used by permission of the publishers. Revised by editor, 1965.

The Ituri River in the eastern part of the Republic of the Congo marks the beginning of the ever green equatorial jungle, the infinite ocean of vegetation whose waves, rolling past the few islands of civilization scattered here and there, cross all central Africa to reach the shores of the Atlantic Ocean.

The deeper one tries to penetrate into this jungle the harder it seems to fight back. Climate, flora, and fauna increasingly become monstrous, exaggerated. Trees grow to unbelievable proportions. Trunks grow one across or over the other. Every slightest space between them is filled by a mad scramble of lianas (vines), creepers, mosses, thorns, caustic reeds, deadly mushrooms, poisonous knifelike leaves.

Biting ants are sometimes as long as a toe. Stinging beetles may be big as a fist. Venomous spiders grow to be as large as half of this page. Common are hogs five feet at the shoulder, crocodiles twenty-six feet in length, leopards nine to ten feet from nose to tail.

And what is the race of supermen who can withstand the strain and dangers of such a world? What extraordinary weapons do they possess to fight off and vanquish the stupendous monsters roaming and prowling through their somber kingdom?

Those "supermen" are the pure pygmies who variously call themselves Mambuti, Tikky-Tikky, Akka, Batwa, Bamoko, or Gulebako. Regardless of the difference in names, they are the same four-foot-six little mites of humanity at its most primitive stage. And, at the same time, they are sturdy, kind, brave, and carefree.

Except for the iron spearpoints which they obtain by barter with other, more advanced neighbors, their weapons are still those of the early ages. Their small bow has a creeper for cord. Their miniature arrow is a reed with a feather inserted as a stabilizer at one end, the other sharpened to a point by a cutting stone. The point is hardened in red embers, made lethal with a thick coat of vegetable poison. Their resourcefulness does the rest.

Poorly armed as they are, the leopard would

Some pigmies rest, while one straightens out a net used for hunting the jungle animals.

American Museum of Natural History

Pygmies laying magongo leaves over a layer of sticks to conceal the pit they have dug to trap an animal.

©Commander Gatti Expeditions

273

simply devour them, whenever it chose. Instead, they plant cleverly disguised nooses and traps all around the clearing where they are living. All night long they keep a great fire going in the middle of it. And the leopard, its shining eyes suffering from the flames, prowls around and around—until one of its paws gets caught. Then a dozen spears finish the great cat. And its skin, well cleaned with rocks chipped to a knife's shape, becomes the warm garment of a dwarf belle.

The elephant, the buffalo, the okapi, the hippopotamus, the giant hog, would smash and crush the pygmy hunter who dared to approach them. But to survive the pygmy needs plenty of meat. And each of these great animals can be easily killed, once it is imprisoned in the bottom of a deep hole. So the dwarf sees to it that many hundreds of such pits are always in readiness. Many of them have been dug by his ancestors. Many more are untiringly added the whole time. Light sticks are laid across the pit's mouth. Big *magongo* leaves are spread over this trellis. Then over them are strewn dead leaves and branches, even manure, small ant heaps, clods of moss—until not even the most suspicious eyes can detect a difference from the surrounding ground.

They Fly Through the Air . . .

If their hunting forces the dwarfs to cross a stream in which crocodiles abound, they don't even try their precious spears on the reptiles' tough hide. Instead, they get themselves some long lianas. They soften those natural ropes by twisting them over and over, tie them one to the other until the proper length is attained, climb up a convenient tree and fasten the liana to a solid branch. At the hanging end, they make a rough seat and one of the youngest hunters slips into it.

The rest of the tribe, by means of a vegetable cable thrust over the top branches of another tree, pull the hunter up—high, high up. Then they cut the rope and let him go. At dizzy speed the flying dwarf swings down toward the water, soars up toward the treetops on the opposite shore. Quick as a monkey, he grasps a branch. Helping himself with legs and

hands, he climbs out of his seat, ties it to the branch while he finds a heavy piece of wood. Once this is secured, he attaches it to the seat and lets the whole contraption swing back for another passenger.

If the whole tribe must cross the river, the hunters swing back and forth until several lianas are strung between the top of a tree on one shore and the top of a tree on the other. Slowly those main lianas are tied together with hundreds and hundreds of smaller ones. Rough stairs of sticks are fastened to the trunks of both trees. When it is finished, all that women, children, and old men have to do is to climb up, cross the swaying but perfectly safe bridge, and climb down the other side.

Thus in the same manner as their forefathers did tens of thousands of years ago, the pygmies face and cleverly overcome any of the endless difficulties, hardships, and dangers of their forbidding world.

In the Republic of the Congo alone their kingdom extends over a quarter of a million square miles. This kingdom is divided into hunting territories, each reserved to a clan.

The boundaries, majestic rivers and high mountains, are actually natural frontiers impassable to the dwarfs. But the pygmies believe that each of them was intentionally put there for no other purpose by Muungu himself, the greatest of their gods. "It is he," they say, "who is the maker and the owner of the world. It is he who sometimes comes on earth, when his steps shake the ground with earthquakes. But usually he lives in the skies. There, the sun is his fire by day, the moon his torch by night. The winds are his breath, the clouds the smoke of his pipe. The thunder is his voice, the hurricane his wrath."

Little People, Big Kingdoms

There are only five of these clans, which means that they have an average of fifty thousand square miles each. These enormous expanses are divided between the various tribes that compose each clan.

These tribe-families to which a man belongs from birth to death and into which womenfolk of other tribes of the same clan are merged

Pygmy engineers make jungle bridges to order by stringing woven vines between the trees on opposite sides of a river. The pygmy on the right is about to swing across the river with the first vine. At far right, the completed bridge.

Photos from HERE IS AFRICA by Ellen and Attilio Gatti, ©1943 by Chas. Scribner's Sons

from the moment of their marriage, are rabidly independent, thoroughly democratic little communities of forty or sixty individuals. One which we know intimately for having shared with it several years of jungle life, and which is typical of the thousand odd such tribes that compose the five clans, is that of sultani Makulu-Kulu.

The name of this four-foot-five chief literally means "Little Butterfly." In his close-knit community there is no place or reason for jealousy, envy, or hatred. Its 56 members can depend on no mercy from nature, on no outside assistance to help them overcome the fearful odds presented by every day. Each of them freely gives something to all. From all the others each individual freely gets what they best can give him.

Makulu-Kulu became his tribe's chief when his father grew too old, not because he was the oldest son, but because he was the ablest and the bravest of men.

As the tribe's sultan, he guides his hunters on the trail and directs them in the attack. He is the first in moments of great danger, the last in a perilous retreat. The welfare of the whole tribe is his burden, and he must see that fifty-five other stomachs are kept well filled. He decides what should be set aside for bartering with the Bantu people living at the edge of the jungle, leads the journeys to their villages and, once there, it is he who dramatically does all the bargaining.

He approves of marriages and decides the name of the newborn. He supervises the burying of the dead. Over each grave, a simple hole in the ground at half a day of march from where the tribe is at the time, he builds the altar of Muungu—some arched sticks covered with *magongo* leaves—in which he places offerings of meat and wild *tumbako* so that Muungu will come and take the dead's spirit into the great hunting territories of the above.

The tribe's little ones, eight plump babies still carried on their mothers' backs or sometimes on the top of their heavy loads, give joy and pride to their parents. The eleven other children of ages running up to fifteen help with numberless little tasks such as gathering dry wood and eatable roots, repairing hunting nets, and so on. And they are all abundantly fed, patiently taught.

The hunters, seven not yet married, six with a wife each, and two older ones with two wives, are Makulu-Kulu's younger brothers, his sons, cousins, or nephews. They, as well as he, make bows and arrows, machetes and spear handles, clay pots for cooking. They collect, dry, and prepare calabashes (gourds) for carrying water and for the water pipes which women and children share with the same zest. They gather wild tobacco, rare fruits, and mush-

275

rooms. They extract poison from the roots of the *kilabo* to smear the points of their arrows and spears. And they are responsible for most of the preparation of clothing from the bark of trees. This bark they cut in the proper size. The womenfolk repeatedly boil it. The men beat it with an ivory hammer until the material is thin and soft. Then the women dye it by boiling it with the dark yellow, brown, or purple wooden splinters which the hunters chip off certain jungle trees.

Most of the men's time, however, is devoted to tracking and trapping and hunting. And when they return from their hunting expedi-

tions, the meat they bring is for everybody, in equal parts. And so are the surplus meats to be smoked and the elephant ivory which later will be swapped with the Bantus for iron spear points, stems of bananas, baskets of manioca, beans, and sweet potatoes.

The womenfolk, thirteen wives and five girls of marrying age, take care of the children, fetch water, keep the huts in good repair. They crush seeds, cook meals, weave for the men rakish little straw hats, brilliantly crowned with tufts of feathers. And once in a while they find time also to prepare antelope hide shirts or child-carrying slings.

The Mysterious Ruins of Zimbabwe

A monumental ruin named Zimbabwe in Rhodesia has long been the source of controversy over both its age and the people who built it.

Early explorers who crossed the Limpopo River about a hundred years ago could not imagine that Zimbabwe had been built by the native Africans whom they were busy exploiting. And to explain the giant walls and towers that they found, they invented the myth that Zimbabwe was the "lost land of Ophir" from which, three thousand years ago, came the gold of King Solomon. The major fortress at Zimbabwe was described as

being a replica of Solomon's Temple, and near it was a copy of the palace of the Queen of Sheba. Other fantastic imaginings made the ruins the work of ancient Phoenicians.

There was, indeed, gold to be found in the vicinity of Zimbabwe. There were tools and artifacts of copper and iron. But more recent research, including work with radiocarbon dating, has placed the construction of the main wall at Zimbabwe not earlier than the 6th century A.D.; the ruins as a whole were probably occupied from about A.D. 500 to about A.D. 1750.

The problem of Zimbabwe, and almost two dozen other similar ruins also found in Rhodesia, have caused historians and archaeologists to change their opinions about the past of southern Africa. Once they had thought that the people had never known a culture high enough to have built such structures, or had possessed the civic organization which would have been necessary to carry out the design and construction of such works. But it now appears that Zimbabwe marks the site of an Iron Age civilization which flourished while Europe was in the Dark Ages.

But what happened to the people of Zimbabwe, and why their city was abandoned and allowed to fall into ruin, are questions not yet satisfactorily answered.

276

Ewing Galloway

The massive walls and towers of Zimbabwe are constructed from shaped stone, much of which has held together for a thousand years or more.

Photos by Commander Gatti Expeditions

The little-known Sonjo tribe of East Africa lives in a large village on a mountain which rises from the Serengeti Plains. Having been persecuted by the Masai, who continuously raided their cattle, the Sonjo surrounded their village with a strong fence. Through a recent epidemic of sleeping sickness, however, the Sonjo lost all their cattle and began raising herds of goats. The Masai, who will have nothing to do with goats, have left the Sonjo alone since then.

How Africans Live

From time to time the Masai herders bring some of their cattle to the trading centers to be sold at auction. In walled pits like this, the cattle are displayed to prospective buyers who may be European or Asiatic as well as African. The Masai seldom leave these auctions with any money because much of what they receive goes for payment of taxes. What is left is usually spent by the women of the families for wares from the merchants who set up shop around the auction site.

This picture was taken from the heights near Eshowe, the capital of Zululand in South Africa. Zululand is a country of rolling green hills, often swept by strong winds. Here the Zulus live much as they did several hundred years ago. Each family lives with their cattle in a separate kraal (group of huts), usually in a spot protected from the wind. The women take care of the huts and of the family, while the boys and girls tend the cattle. The men have few duties, and often work for a few months on sugar plantations in the vicinity.

Life in Dahomey: West Africa

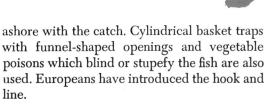

On the coastal lowlands under the big western hump of Africa is the land of the Dahomeans. More than any other of the Africans you read about in this section, these people are farmers and also fishermen. This selection from George Peter Murdock, Ph.D.: Our Primitive Contemporaries. Copyright 1934 by The Macmillan Company and used with The Macmillan Company's permission. Revised by editor, 1961.

The Guinea Coast of West Africa from Nigeria on the east to Senegal on the west, together with the nearby hinterland, is the home of the true Negro. In the heart of this region lies Dahomey, a once powerful Negro kingdom now incorporated in the much larger nation of the same name. The Dahomeans inhabit a strip of territory approximately 40 miles wide extending from the Atlantic Ocean on the south about 120 miles into the interior.

Hunting and Fishing

The Dahomeans have hunted the elephant for its ivory until it has become extinct in their territory. They also pursue the buffalo, which roams in small herds on the grassy plains, taking great care to appease the soul of a slaughtered animal in a special ceremony. Firearms are now more popular as weapons than the spear and the bow with poisoned arrows. Game is sometimes driven into ambush by means of grass fires. Antelopes, porcupines, and small edible rodents are captured in snares and pitfalls. A hunter lies in wait to spear the manatee, an aquatic mammal which visits the river banks at night to feed on the grass; a float attached by a long rope to the shaft of the barbed spear reveals the location of the animal in the morning, and it is secured from a boat. Once each year the king assembles his followers for an important community hunt.

The towns on the lagoons support themselves primarily by fishing. The inhabitants dry the fish in the sun or preserve them by smoking over a fire, and they carry on a flourishing trade in sea products with the inland people. The local fishermen employ spears and dip nets in shallow water. On the lagoons they set long seines from boats and haul them

Dahomeans are expert fishermen. How many methods of fishing can you find in this picture?

ashore with the catch. Cylindrical basket traps with funnel-shaped openings and vegetable poisons which blind or stupefy the fish are also used. Europeans have introduced the hook and line.

Herding

Although far indeed from being a herding people, the Dahomeans possess a fair number and variety of domesticated animals. The native dogs compete with the protected vultures as scavengers of the villages. A few cattle are raised but no use is made of their milk. Near the coast cattle do not thrive but sheep and goats are fairly numerous. The native sheep are small and have hair rather than wool. Pigs range freely in considerable numbers and are fed just enough to keep them in the neighborhood. Every yard has a clay shelter for poultry, which are plentiful and furnish the Dahomeans with their principal meat food.

Farmers First

Agriculture, however, forms the basis of the Dahomean economy. Every man, whatever his occupation, has his fields, although he leaves their cultivation, except the clearing of new land, mainly to the women of the family. Due to the foreign trade, the Dahomeans have adopted many foreign food plants, especially of American origin. The staple food crops are maize, yams, and manioc, but the oil palm is

279

Carlo Lamote

also of great economic importance. Other cultivated plants include millet, Guinea corn, sweet potatoes, beans, onions, okra, peppers, gourds, peanuts, bananas, oranges, limes, guavas, cashews, and papaws. Pineapples, tomatoes, cotton, and coconut palms grow freely with little or no cultivation. Before the rainy season begins, the farmers fire the stubble from the previous harvest and loosen the soil with an iron hoe lashed with thongs to a wooden handle. Climatic conditions enable them to reap two rich harvests each year. Since they use no fertilizers and do not rotate their crops, they must clear new land whenever their fields become exhausted.

Dining with the Dahomeans

The Dahomeans prepare the grains and vegetables upon which they mainly live according to a variety of recipes, of which the most universal is *akasan*—corn meal soaked in water until it begins to ferment, boiled to the consistency of porridge, allowed to harden, molded into balls the size of an orange, and wrapped in banana leaves. This local substitute for bread is rather sour but very nutritious. Another dish is the Creole *kalalu*, which consists of smoked fish cooked in palm oil and highly seasoned with peppers and other herbs. Fresh fish, fowls, and the flesh of wild and domesticated animals, including even monkeys, rodents, and lizards, are roasted, boiled, fried in palm oil, and made into savory stews and ragouts. When the fruit of the oil palm is crushed in troughs, mixed with water, and heated in vessels over a fire, there rises to the surface a reddish oil which, when refined, is an essential ingredient in most native dishes. The Dahomeans season their food with peppers and with an impure salt which they col-

280

lect at low tide on the muddy shores of the lagoons, where it forms like hoar frost because of rapid evaporation.

The cooking is done, except when it rains, in the open air in a corner of the court, where a pot is supported over the fire on three stones or balls of earth. Sometimes there is also a crude oven, consisting of an earthen vessel embedded on its side in sun-dried clay. The Dahomeans do not, however, prepare all their meals at home; they often buy their food, cooked and ready to eat, at the markets. They take a light breakfast, snatch a little food during the day, and eat a hearty meal just before retiring for the night—to induce sleep, since they believe that a person who "lies awake and counts the rafters" will shortly die. Wives serve their husbands and do not eat until their masters have finished. A host tastes the food before serving his guests—as a demonstration that it is not poisoned. Mats are placed on the floor, and the diners sit in a circle around the bowls or gourds containing the food. Each person takes a ball of *akasan* in his right hand, breaks off a piece, dips it into the sauce, seizes a piece of meat, fish, or ragout between the morsel and his thumb, and swallows the whole. When the food is eaten, drinks are served—water, palm wine, maize or millet beer, or imported liquors. After the meal each person scrupulously washes his hands, rinses his mouth, and brushes his teeth with the frayed end of a small stick.

Town Life

The Dahomeans rarely live in isolated homesteads. For the most part they dwell in villages consisting of houses scattered irregularly along narrow streets radiating from a central plaza or market place. The unit of residence is not the dwelling of an individual family but rather a compound or cluster of houses centering on a court and inclosed by a wattle (woven sticks) fence or a mud wall. Here, in separate buildings, reside the several wives of the owner with their children, the married sons and younger brothers of the owner with their families, and the household slaves. In addition, the compound contains storehouses, pens or stalls

British Info. Serv.

Every man is a farmer in Dahomey.

for animals, a fetish hut, and sometimes a cook-house or a bathhouse. The rectangular walls of the dwelling are made sometimes of reddish mud smeared over wattle, more often of sun-dried mud alone, laid in four tiers or courses. A gabled roof of lashed poles and neatly trimmed thatch covers the house and protects the walls from crumbling during the rains. A single rectangular doorway admits light and air to the inside, which is often divided into several rooms. In front, the roof usually projects considerably beyond the wall and is supported by a row of wooden pillars, forming a pleasant veranda. Here, on a clay bench which runs along the wall on either side of the doorway, the master entertains his guests and the family spends its leisure time.

The Household Furnishings

The most characteristic piece of Dahomean furniture is the stool. Those of important men are handsomely carved from a single block of wood, often in the form of an animal. Women own tiny stools, only a few inches high, which they carry wherever they go. Sometimes a house contains a low bamboo bedstead or two, but most of the people sleep on the floor on mats made from reeds. The household utensils include gourds, baskets, pots, a wooden mortar and pestle, and a stone mill. Gourds are made in almost any desired shape and size—from small drinking cups and bowls to huge tubs or barrels—by binding the growing fruit.

At the Market

Trade in Dahomey, except for the export of slaves and palm oil in exchange for European goods, takes place largely in markets, of which there is at least one in every village. In each market, police preserve order and a presiding official takes a toll from people who sell. Cross streets divide the larger markets into sections, each devoted to a special class of wares. The commodities sold include water, palm oil, amulets (religious articles), imported goods, raw and cooked provisions of all kinds, and the products of all the local handicrafts. They are displayed in low thatched booths raised on clay platforms a foot above the paths, which

A carved Dahomey stool.

are flooded during the rains. Purchases are made either through barter or by means of the cowrie shell money. Haggling is universal, and the women, who carry on almost all the trade, convert a market into a perfect bedlam with their loud arguments.

To prevent their dead from becoming harmful ghosts and the agents of sorcery, the Dahomeans make every effort to give them a proper funeral. Ancestor worship forms the core of Dahomean religion. In a clearing in front of every compound stands a fetish hut, a small square building with altars where the various ancestral spirits receive regular cult offerings.

Dahomey Art

The Dahomeans display considerable talent in the fine arts. Their wood carving, especially their staffs, stools, and statuettes are admired today by artists of other countries. The native musical instruments include horns, tongueless bells fixed to handles and struck with an iron rod, large drums hollowed from a log and covered with a goatskin, smaller gourd drums of hourglass shape yielding different notes as the thongs at the waist are pressed or relaxed, and gourd rattles containing shells or pebbles and covered with a netting to which snake verte-brae are attached. Vocal music is much superior to instrumental. The people are passionately fond of dancing, which is accompanied either by singing or by an orchestra. Adults amuse their young people with animal fables and entertain one another with more sophisticated tales and historical narrations. Their numerous and popular proverbs often suggest our own: "One tree does not make a forest"; "Clothes are men"; "No one chases two birds"; "Distant firewood is good firewood."

281

Brooklyn Mus.

Sculpture by Collamarini decorates the patio of the Presidential Palace at Abidjan, capital of Ivory Coast.

Nairobi, Kenya (right) began as a construction center for the railroad connecting Mombasa with Uganda.

African Cities South of the Sahara

This startlingly modern city (left), glittering with electricity, is Salisbury, capital of Southern Rhodesia. Below are two other African capitals. Léopoldville, Republic of the Congo (left), a bustling commercial city on the Congo River, was a trading post in Stanley's time. Accra, Ghana (right), with its airport, good schools, museums, libraries and an excellent university, is a center of modern African culture.

Right, aerial view of Cape Peninsula at the foot of Africa shows cosmopolitan Capetown, capital of Cape of Good Hope Province, Republic of South Africa.

Modern building in Ibadan, Nigeria, world's largest Negro city.

Street scene in Freetown, capital and port of Sierra Leone.

 **Other Books To Read**

The Land and People of South Africa, by Alan Paton. Published by J. B. Lippincott Co., Philadelphia. Revised edition, 1964.
This writer's literary works on the racial problems of his beloved South Africa are read the world over.

African Sketchbook, by Frederick Franck. Published by Holt, Rinehart and Winston, Inc., New York, 1961.
The author traveled through much of Africa, drawing pen-and-ink sketches and jotting down impressions of each country and its people.

African Encounter: A Doctor in Nigeria, by Robert Collis. Published by Charles Scribner's Sons, New York, 1961.
An Irish doctor reminisces about life in Nigeria, mingling information about politics with stories of the Nigerian way of life. Humor and a down-to-earth approach to African problems characterize this book.

Moroccan Roundabout, by Maureen Daly. Published by Dodd, Mead & Company, New York, 1961.
A popular author gives facts, but not dry facts, about Morocco's history, geography, and way of life.

African Kingdoms, by Basil Davidson. Published by Silver Burdett Co., Morristown, New Jersey, 1966.
Africa still is a largely unknown continent as regards its history south of the Sahara Desert. The story of kingdoms that flourished there before European colonization make a fascinating study.

283

This illustration (left) from a 17th-century book shows witches offering a child to the devil.

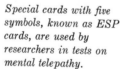

Special cards with five symbols, known as ESP cards, are used by researchers in tests on mental telepathy.

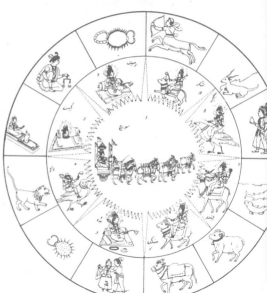

The twelve signs in the outer ring of this Hindu zodiac are the same as those of the European zodiac.

Superstition, Folklore, and Legend

It is customary for any culture to dismiss as superstitions any beliefs of people who lived before their own time or who do not share their own patterns of belief. But in many cases, when scientists have looked closely at some "superstitions," they have found much truth in them. Perhaps that truth was concealed beneath a myth, or it was something which has been passed down from one generation to another for so long that its original meaning was lost.

Many beliefs which are called superstitions today are remnants of the knowledge of nonscientific peoples. They could not always explain why they did certain things to make the crops grow, to make an epidemic cease or to bring good fortune in the hunt. Their thinking, however, was of a very practical kind; if a chant or prayer or ritual seemed once to have made a certain thing happen, the same action or ritual exactly repeated would make it happen again. And if it did not happen again, then the ritual had not been correctly performed.

The ancient wise women who were called witches used certain plants to heal the sick; modern doctors have found that these plants actually have important medicinal properties. The ancients were convinced that the planets had an influence on the earth; modern radio technicians have found that the sun, the planets and the earth are indeed linked in an electromagnetic network which affects solar storms and radio reception.

Some of the beliefs described in this section go far back into the earliest history of mankind on the earth. Some of them are interesting now only as curiosities; others are being studied today to see whether there is value in them for our own time. Some have been traced back to their beginnings, while others are still mysterious and unexplained. And no matter how strange some of them may sound, there are millions of people today who believe in each and every one of them.

—Arthur Louis Joquel, II

How Do Superstitions Begin?

Do you ever "knock on wood" or toss spilled salt over your left shoulder? Do you carry a rabbit's foot in your pocket or hunt carefully for four-leaf clovers whenever you have the chance? Most of us have pet superstitions that we learned from our family or our friends. Superstitious actions are a part of man's history from the very earliest times, as you will learn in this article. From **Superstitious? Here's Why!** Copyright, 1954, by Julie Forsyth Batchelor and Claudia de Lys. Reprinted by permission of Harcourt, Brace and Company, Inc.

How do superstitions begin? And what is the reason for them? To find the origin of most of the familiar beliefs, sayings, and customs of today we must travel back into the folklore of the past.

There is every reason to believe that the earliest superstitions grew out of pagan religions. Sun worship and moon worship were very important to primitive man. These heavenly bodies were viewed with great fear and respect, and it was believed both had the power to change human affairs. So thousands of beliefs sprang up about them.

These savage ancestors of ours were not stupid. In fact, most were more observant than people are today. With absolutely no knowledge about the laws of nature and man, they were constantly trying to figure out what made things happen. Everything was a mystery—lightning, shooting stars, eclipses, birth, and death, to mention a few of them. So there was always the question "Why?"; and, always, the fear of the unknown.

Early man's close observation led to a strong belief in unseen spirits. He saw that animals seemed to hear and sense things men couldn't. These must be ghosts or supernatural beings, he reasoned. Such things as the miracles of trees growing from tiny seeds and tadpoles becoming frogs also seemed to indicate help from invisible spirits.

Since life in those times was so difficult, primitive man assumed that there were many more bad spirits than good ones. The question was how to protect oneself, and how to appease these evil powers. So they invented all sorts of charms, amulets and talismans, as well as every kind of countermagic. When one failed they tried another. That's why today we have dozens of countercharms to break each spell or jinx early man imagined.

Like Brings Like

Many superstitions were based on "wishful thinking." The ancients expected a wish to come true if made while looking at or touching something connected with good fortune. This was sympathetic magic, or "like brings like."

A favorite countercharm was to do something in reverse, or to say something that was just the opposite of what you wanted. This was supposed to change bad luck to good luck. The instinct of trying to make bad luck over into good luck has been found among all the peoples of the world.

Thus superstitions grew, almost all of them based on lack of knowledge and fear. Each country added its beliefs and old wives' tales.

It must be granted that there often seems to be an element of luck at work, either good or bad. And we know that many people who have a strong faith can often make what they believe in come to pass. Therefore, despite facts and logic, the belief in good or bad luck influences many people today.

If carrying a rabbit's foot gives you confidence and faith in yourself, keep one in your pocket. But recognize it for what it is—a prop that only has the power your thinking gives it. Remember, too, that superstitions offer an immature individual an excuse for blaming some power beyond himself for his bad fortune. But instead of fighting these beliefs with scientific law let's view them with tolerance and amusement. For they are wonderful whimsy, and the stuff of which dreams are made.

Almost anything can stimulate a superstition as you can see from this strange assortment of a crow, a wishbone, and a ground hog, all of which are a part of superstitious lore.

Superstitions Old and New

There are literally thousands of superstitions. Every nation in the world has them and some superstitions are even international. In this article you will read about some of the most familiar and some of the strangest of these superstitions. You will find much more information about superstitions of all kinds in the excellent book from which this article was adapted. From **A Treasury of American Superstitions** by Claudia de Lys, published by Philosophical Library, Inc. Copyright, 1948, by Claudia de Lys and used by her permission.

Because there was so much in the world around him that man could not explain there are superstitions on nearly every subject under the sun (and including it!). Lots of these ancient superstitions are still followed today by people all over the world. Here are some of them.

One very old superstition about birds is that if a bird flies in the window of a house it is a bad omen and death will come to someone in the house within the year. This superstition may have originated from the fact that in ancient times birds were supposed to symbolize the spirit of departed souls.

The robin has been most often thought of as bringing good fortune. One old saying announces that if the first robin you see in the spring flies up you will have good luck; but if it flies down, you will have bad luck. Good luck will come if a robin builds a nest near your house. Make a wish when you see a robin and it will come true. It may be that robins are thought of as lucky because they seem to enjoy human company.

Like the robin, the crow has a reputation which is both good and bad. One rhyme says:

> Crow on the fence,
> Rain will go hence.
> Crow on the ground,
> Rain will come down.

Another old superstition has it that if you see a crow alone you should take your hat off or bow to the bird to forestall some calamity the crow might bring. If a crow flies to the left it is a sign of bad news, but flying on the right is a warning to be on guard that day. All these superstitions about the crow may stem from the fact that the bird is noisy, mischievous, and has a knack for thieving bright objects like beads and hiding them in odd places. This, its cawing, and other bad habits account for its strange place in the world of superstition.

Cats, Angry Bulls, Horsehairs, and the Ground Hog

Nearly everyone knows the old superstition that a cat has nine lives, but don't test the saying because there is another one that says that anyone who hurts or kills a cat can expect

286

It's the red cloth the bullfighter waves that enrages the bull. Fact or fancy?

Spanish Tourist Off.

at least nine years of ill fortune! The reasons for the cat's reputation for long life are simply its supple body and padded feet which make it easier for the cat to jump from high places and land safely.

Bulls have always been thought to become enraged when they see a red flag. The fact is that they are probably color blind and it is the movement of the cloth that the bull-fighter holds rather than its color which stimulates the bull to fight.

Many people, even today, think that if they put a horsehair in a water trough a snake will take its place. If you have ever tried this experiment we hope you did not wait too long because the only thing you would have noticed is the moisture of the water causing the horsehair to move a little, and perhaps curl—but never to turn into a snake.

On February 2 every year people hark back to an old Roman rite which we know today as ground-hog day—the day the ground hog comes out of his burrow to take a look at the weather. If the ground hog sees his shadow it is said there will be six weeks more of winter. If the day is cloudy the ground hog is expected to remain outside because it means spring is on its way. Naturally the weather bureau considers the ground hog a poor prophet. The ancient Roman rite which took place on the date we know as February 2, was in honor of the goddess Venus and celebrated the return

of Venus to its place as a morning star, and this symbolized the rebirth of nature and life in the springtime.

The Human Animal

My hair is gray, but not with years,
Nor grew it white
In a single night,
As men have grown with sudden fears.

Lord Byron, the English poet, in this portion of his poem, "The Prisoner of Chillon," was repeating an old superstition when he suggested that hair may turn white overnight from shock or fright. The facts are that hair may become gray from worry or physical disturbances— but the change is slow, never sudden.

Have you ever seen anyone take an eyelash that has fallen from his eye, carefully place it on his left hand, make a wish, and then blow it away in three tries or less? This superstition is based on an old idea that if an evildoer could get a hold of something from your body (a bit of skin, or nail, or hair) he could do you great harm. Making a wish on the eyelash was a way of counteracting the possible harm to be done by the evildoer. The ancients would have warned you that if you couldn't blow the eyelash off in three tries you must be certain to destroy the eyelash before the evildoer could get it.

When you make a wish do you keep your fingers crossed? This gesture grew out of the

287

UP

Do you know how the custom of throwing rice at newly-weds began? The answer is in this article.

288

fact that the cross was the symbolic sign of perfect unity—that is, when two straight lines cross and meet in the center of the two lines, the wish is held there and cannot slip away before it comes true!

Something Old, Something New

There are many superstitions about the wedding ceremony including the idea that the groom must never see his bride in her wedding gown before she comes to the altar during the ceremony. The most familiar of all these superstitions has to do with wearing something old, new, borrowed, and blue. The idea of wearing something old was based on "sympathetic magic"—if the bride wears something of an older woman who has had a happy marriage her happiness as a bride is insured. Something new may symbolize fresh happiness; something borrowed is most often a trinket of gold which recalls the ancient unity of the sun (the man) and the moon (the woman).

Rice throwing at weddings is a very ancient custom also. It is believed to be a survival of ancient religious rites of the Hindus and Chinese who thought of rice as a symbol of prosperity and fruitfulness. Another reason may be the very ancient superstitious belief that at the wedding evil spirits were supposed to be hovering about, and throwing rice at them would keep them busily eating and away from the groom of whom they were jealous.

Three Meals a Day

Here are some everyday eating superstitions: For seven people to eat together brings luck to all, but if thirteen eat together, one of the number will die before the year is out. If you take the last portion on a dish at the invitation of someone, you will have a handsome husband or wife, or if you are married—anything else you might want. There is still another superstition which says that if you take the last portion you will be an old maid. Eating before retiring is supposed to prevent sleep. Singing while eating is unlucky—"sing before breakfast and cry before supper."

Of the many food superstitions one of the most interesting concerns salt. When you spill salt you may quickly pick up a few grains and toss them over your left shoulder to avoid fighting with someone you love or to avoid bad luck in general. Saltiness is connected with tears and there are some people in New England who put particles of spilled salt on the stove—to dry up in advance the tears that are to be shed.

Salt's ancient and interesting history accounts for many of these superstitions and the phrases which we use each day: "I'll take that with a grain of salt," "He's not worth his salt," or "He's the salt of the earth." Salt was very rare and precious in ancient times. In Greece and Rome its value is indicated by the fact that soldiers, officials, and working people were paid with a portion of salt (in Latin called *salarium* and from which our word "salary" comes). In medieval times salt's preciousness is shown by the fact that an enormous saltceller divided the table of a nobleman; those who sat above the salt were titled nobility, those below the salt were less important.

A Few Health Superstitions

Long, long ago man believed that the basic essence of life was in the head in the form of air or breath which could be accidentally expelled for a short time or forever by a sneeze. To prevent calamities from taking place all kinds of superstitions were devised, among them our own expression "God bless you!", the German *Gesundheit,* the Italian *Felicita,* and the French *Que Dieu vous benisse,* etc.

Many people may still believe this verse:

Sneeze on Monday, sneeze for danger.
Sneeze on Tuesday, kiss a stranger.
Sneeze on Wednesday, receive a letter.
Sneeze on Thursday, something better.
Sneeze on Friday, sneeze for sorrow.
Sneeze on Saturday, see your lover tomorrow.
Sneeze on Sunday, your safety seek
Or the Devil will have you the rest of the week.

Long ago people were baffled by hiccoughs and believed that they were caused by the Evil Eye, the favorite explanation for all unpleasant things. Today there are still hundreds of weird cures for this discomfort—some of which strangely enough are scientifically approved. One old wives' tale has it that you should drink nine swallows of water without taking a breath, which often works; another device, that of blowing into a bag, held close to the mouth, and breathing in and out of it often succeeds because the oxygen in the bag is used up and an accumulation of carbon dioxide results which stimulates the normal breathing reflexes in the lung.

Are fat people gay and thin people sorrowful? Science disagrees with superstition here, as in many cases. Most fat people are not happy, primarily because they are overweight. They may look happy because you cannot see worry and wrinkles so clearly on their faces.

Coins, Wishbones, Pins, and Ladders

In olden times, superstitious people who could not arrive at a decision of their own, or who would not trust another individual, looked for the answer "yes" or "no" through various

Science has helped to disprove the old superstition that fat people are gay and thin people gloomy.

actions, among which the thumb played an important part. This is carried over into modern times in the familiar saying, "Heads you win, tails you lose," which combines the flick of the thumb with the tossing of a coin, to settle a question or to find out to whom the desired article is to go.

Historically coin-flipping dates back to the time of Julius Caesar, when his head was engraved on one side of every coin. When an argument arose, a coin was flipped, and if the side of Caesar's head showed, whoever chose the head was right, and this decision was final. Such was the power of Caesar!

And here's a pin, an object about which you can choose your superstition, depending on your frame of mind:

See a pin and pick it up,
All the day you'll have good luck.

Or "Pick up a pin, pick up sorrow." And then there is the saying, "Pass up a pin, pass up a friend," or "See a pin, let it lie, all the day you'll have to cry." There are as many reasons for these sayings as there are superstitions, but it is believed that superstitious fears pertaining to pointed objects began at the time of the earliest men when real danger was always present. Pin superstitions probably evolved as such from the danger attached to the primitive use of pin thorns, fish bones, fowl or animal leg bones, or the like in their crude garment making, tent making, or other fastening purposes.

A very ancient superstition that never seems

289

to lose its popularity is for two persons to make a wish and then pull the ends of a wishbone. The one who breaks off the larger piece will have the wish come true. In ancient birdlore, the hen and the cock were in great favor. Since the cock announced the coming of day, and the hen announced the laying of an egg, these fowl were looked upon as capable of revealing to men the answers to their problems, as interpreted by diviners and soothsayers of the day. As early as 322 B.C., the Etruscans (ancient inhabitants of Italy) had a "hen oracle," the medium by which a special god was called upon to reveal hidden knowledge and solve important matters. This sacred fowl was killed and the collar bone put to dry in the sun and the person seeking the answer from the god made a wish on it, which gave the name "wishbone." Afterwards, two persons snapped the dried wishbone, and whoever held the larger piece got his wish, or a "lucky break."

We all know the superstition that it is unlucky to walk under a ladder unless we stop long enough to make a countercharm such as crossing one's fingers or making a wish. There are many elaborate theories about the origin of this superstition, but it still makes good sense not to walk under a ladder because it might collapse on you or a worker might drop a tool or some other object that might hit you.

Numbers, Lucky and Otherwise

Do you know that there are some people who tear up two dollar bills? Why you may ask, do people do anything so foolish? The reason is that in gambling talk the word *deuce*, for the number two, the lowest value in cards, is derived from devil and means bad luck. When people get a two dollar bill they may tear off one corner, making a triangle, symbolizing the lucky number three which is another example of countermagic. The unfortunate superstitious person who gets the bill after all four corners have been torn off has no choice (he thinks) but to tear the bill up and prevent misfortune.

Just as three is considered a lucky number, and four because of its association with the four-leaf clover is thought to be lucky, so unlucky is thirteen. This may be because early man first counted his possessions by using tallies—numbers as such not being known then. He must have wondered at the triangularity of three, and the squareness of four. As he progressed, larger values, such as twelve, became easier to divide in all sorts of ways; while others, such as thirteen were impossible. In due time twelve became a noble generous symbol to him and the indivisible thirteen an outcast! Our universal use of twelve or the dozen, is evidence of its importance in our own modern age.

Putting the Evil Eye on Superstition

As you can see from the few examples of superstition in this article, most misbeliefs go far back in history and only a very few have any basis in fact. The next time you are tempted to lie in bed on Friday the 13th to avoid a calamity, or blow an eyelash into the wind think about the meaning of these ancient acts very carefully. If you enjoy them just because they are fun, go ahead and blow eyelashes all you like but remember it's up to you what kind of a day Friday the 13th turns out to be.

Weather Wisdom

Weather, like all the other parts of man's life, has given rise to many superstitious beliefs. In this article you'll learn just how much truth there is in some of the old observations about the weather. From **Eric Sloane's Weather Book**, published by Duell, Sloan & Pearce, Inc. Copyright 1949, 1950, 1951, 1952 by Eric Sloane.

In the course of modern living man has lost much of his weather "wisdom." What with air conditioning and improved travel facilities, we seem to go where we want, and to do what we wish, regardless of the weather. Except for an occasional rained-out ball game or called-off sailing trip or postponed air flight, we presume that weather has very little influence upon us.

Our forefathers and the men of ancient times had no weather maps, but they were, in the actual sense of the word, far more air-minded than we are.

Many people are surprised when it is pointed out that in Chapter 16 of Matthew there is a favorite of sailormen, a familiar weather quotation spoken by Christ: "When it is evening, ye say, It will be fair weather; for the sky is red. And in the morning, It will be foul weather today; for the sky is red and lowering." Few appear to be acquainted with that bit of weather lore in the Bible; but most of us know some version or other of the sailor's rhyme:

> Red sky in the morning
> Is a sailor's sure warning;
> Red sky at night
> Is the sailor's delight.

Folklore is generally frowned upon by scientific men, but many of its sayings and predictions have found scientific backing. The red sunset mentioned by Christ, for example, was a view of the sun through dust-laden air that would reach Him the next day. In most places, weather patterns tend to flow from west to east. If "tomorrow's air" lies westward as a mass of wet stuff, the sun shining through it appears a gray or yellowish disk, while, if this westward air is dry, the sun appears at its reddest.

Signs of Rain

Here is an old rhyme that is so crowded with weather lore evolved from accurate observation that the reader can almost feel the rain gathering and getting ready to come down:

> The hollow winds begin to blow:
> The clouds look black, the glass is low,
> The soot falls down, the spaniels sleep,
> And spiders from their cobwebs peep.
> Last night the sun went pale to bed,
> The moon in halos hid her head:
> The walls are damp, the ditches smell,
> Closed is the pink-eyed pimpernel.
> Hark how the chairs and tables crack!
> Old Betty's nerves are on the rack;
> Loud quacks the duck, the peacocks cry,
> The distant hills are seeming nigh.
> Low o'er the grass the swallow wings,
> The cricket, too, how sharp he sings!
> Through the clear stream the fishes rise,
> And nimbly catch incautious flies.
> The glow-worms, numerous and light
> Illumined the dewy dell last night;
> And see yon rooks, how odd their flight!
> They imitate the gliding kite,
> And seem precipitate to fall,
> As if they felt the piercing ball.
> 'Twill surely rain; I see with sorrow,
> Our jaunt must be put off tomorrow.

All these signs and portents can be sensed and observed before a rainfall, and although the poet did not know the scientific explanation of them, he recognized them as reputable

291

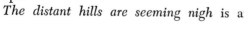

weather signs. Let us take the old rhyme apart meteorologically, line by line, and find the reasons behind its uncanny accuracy.

The hollow winds begin to blow refers to the hollowness of sound before a rain. This happens when the cloud ceiling lowers as during bad weather, the sounds then echoing back against the meteorological sounding board of the heavens.

The clouds look black, the glass is low is elementary; dark clouds are dark because they hold more precipitation and because they reflect the darkness of a dull-colored earth, rather than refracting the light of the sun, as the ceiling of a weather front moves in. The "glass," means the barometer.

The soot falls down indicates a lowering of air pressure: delicate soot is often kept in place within the chimney simply by the high pressure of good weather air; when the atmospheric pressure lowers (and the soot becomes heavy with humidity) chunks frequently fall into the fireplace below.

Last night the sun went pale to bed has already been commented upon in the explanation of Christ's words.

The moon in halos hid her head means that a mass of rain-bringing warm air has flowed in overhead, causing ice-crystal cloudform. When the sun or moon shines through ice-crystal clouds, a halo results.

The walls are damp, the ditches smell indicates humid air and a lessening of the atmospheric pressure that has held in much of the odor of swamps and wet places during the high pressure of good weather; when that pressure lowers, captive odors are released and things "smell more."

292

Hark how the chairs and tables crack hardly needs explanation, for we all know how wood "breathes," swelling and contracting with humidity and dryness.

But *Old Betty's nerves are on the rack* indicates that a drop in air pressure may affect the nerves by causing greater dehydration of the tissues; old wounds begin to ache, corns and bunions are felt, the minute the barometer drops.

The distant hills are seeming nigh is an often-noticed weather sign of sailors. Marine air is always rich with salt haze from evaporation during good weather, but becomes clear with the mixing action of unstable atmosphere. When the instability of pre-storm air invades the coast, the clearing away of salt haze results in great visibility.

Low o'er the grass the swallow wings is a weather sign that to my knowledge has never been researched. Yet we know that bats and swallows have extremely sensitive ears which they use as a sort of radar mechanism during flight, to avoid hitting obstacles and to locate insects in the air. When pre-storm pressure lowers abruptly, the pressure difference between the inside and outside of their heads becomes irritating, possibly painful. Therefore, bats and swallows will be seen seeking the relief of the highest pressure air, which of course is always found closest to the earth.

The cricket, too, how sharp he sings indicates that the old-timer observed the effect that weather has upon insects, especially crickets, which are astoundingly accurate atmospheric instruments. It has been recently learned that the cricket's reaction to temperature is often more immediate and accurate than that of the average thermometer, which has considerable lag and variation. The higher the temperature, the faster the crickets chirp.

Birds imitating *the gliding kite* would just indicate an unstable condition in the atmosphere. Strong noonday thermals (a current of rising warm air) soon build into towering afternoon storm clouds, so that an unstable morning atmosphere might well indicate an afternoon shower. Also when the air pressure lowers or the air becomes thin, birds must fly harder and faster in it in order to stay aloft; so much so, in fact, that before a hurricane or a stormy cyclonic atmosphere you will frequently find birds roosting or resting rather than staying aloft to face the strenuous flying conditions of the thining air.

All these observations are of the kind that make being weather-wise a pleasure. When you know what they mean, they cease to be folklore weather prophecies and become science.

The Stars Above Us

Whether astrology is a true science, as is claimed by its advocates, or a false one, as its critics aver, it has fascinated people for ages. Dante was a believer in it; the German author Goethe began his autobiography with the details of his horoscope. John Flamsteed, the first English Astronomer Royal and founder of Greenwich Observatory, was a believer; and when Edmund Halley made a slighting remark about the value of astrology after Sir Isaac Newton had defended it, Newton replied: "I have studied the subject, Mr. Halley; you have not." René Descartes, the mathematician, had to admit the accuracy of an astrological prediction. Thomas Jefferson made scholarly notes in the astrological books in his library. President Theodore Roosevelt and the financier J. P. Morgan are among those in the present century who found it of interest. This article, which surveys briefly the popular aspects of astrology, is reprinted by permission of the publisher, Abelard-Schuman, Inc., from **The Lore of Birthdays**, by Ralph and Adelin Linton. Copyright, 1952, by Abelard-Schuman, Inc.

A horoscope is a chart of the heavens at any particular time, and may be used to find the positions of the planets as seen from the earth. Astrologers divide the heavens into twelve "houses," and use symbols for the planets and the signs of the zodiac.

The idea of destiny linked with the regular movements of the stars may have originated in Babylonia. When the Greeks under Alexander conquered Mesopotamia (late in the fourth century B.C.), they found a learned religion based upon astronomical observation and a system of divination (system of foretelling the future) by which the stars revealed the secrets of the future and the destinies of man. Astrology, which was a mystical religion in the East, spread over Greece and later the Roman Empire, chiefly as a form of divination. Both Greeks and Romans had their horoscopes (a diagram of the heavens at specific time used in astrology to tell fortunes) read by experts and consulted astrologers before making important decisions. The heavenly bodies which are said to influence the horoscope still bear their Roman names: Jupiter, Saturn, Venus, Mars, Neptune, Uranus, Mercury, and Pluto, plus the sun and moon.

The desire to probe into the mysteries of the future is deeply rooted in human nature.

Anyone who claims to have the power to read these infinite secrets has always found a following. The sixteenth century was the period of the highest flowering of astrology, since it was a time of uncertainty and superstition which drove men in a feverish quest for some sort of assurance.

The Stars in Literature

All the great writers and philosophers of the Elizabethan period (so called because it corresponded to the reign of Queen Elizabeth I of England, 1558–1603) wrote constantly and confidently about the power of the stars over destinies of men. Bacon, Raleigh, Donne were all fascinated by astrology and refer to its findings. Shakespeare's writings are studded with astrological references, although his attitude is a wavering one. In *King Lear*, we find Kent, one of the king's retainers, saying:

> It is the stars,
> The stars above us, govern our conditions.

But in the same play we find Edmund ranting:

This is the excellent foppery of the world, that when we are sick in fortune—often the surfeit of our own behaviour—we make guilty of our disasters the sun, the moon, and the stars; as if we were villains by necessity, fools by heavenly compulsion: knaves, thieves and treachers by spherical predominence; drunkards, liars and adulterers by an enforced obedience of planetary influence.

Romeo and Juliet are known as the "star-crossed lovers," meaning that planetary influences opposed their love. Prospero, in *The Tempest*, says:

I find my zenith does depend upon
A most auspicious star, whose influences
If now I court not but omit, my
Fortunes will ever droop.

But Cassius says to Brutus, in *Julius Caesar:* "The fault, dear Brutus, is not in our stars, But in ourselves that we are underlings."

Your Future in the Stars?

The brief horoscopes (from *hora,* hour and *skopos,* watcher) which follow make no pretense of being serious or accurate. They are general character depictions which astrologers give to all persons born under each sign of the zodiac. They are presented here as a brief glimpse of one part of astrology, which some people consider an amusing myth and which others take very seriously.

Because the zodiac year begins on March 21st with Aries, the Ram, we start our horoscopes on that date rather than on January 1st.

Aries, March 21 to April 20

Those born with the sun in this position in the heavens are endowed with strength, vitality, and qualities of leadership. Symbolized by the Ram, an animal famous for his ability to force his way ahead against any obstacles, and ruled by Mars, a fiery and courageous god, this is a potent and aggressive sign. The native is independent and venturesome; he goes into any enterprise with enthusiasm and gusto. However, he is impatient of authority of routine and easily bored. His energy and initiative will bring success if he can persevere in what he undertakes.

Taurus, April 21 to May 21

This sign is symbolized by the Bull, the emblem of earthiness, and dominated by Venus, Goddess of Love. The Taurian has the easy-going nature of the bull. He is tolerant of others but, in turn, brooks no interference. When frustrated or aroused, he can be very headstrong and vehement. The influence of Venus makes for a warm, friendly attitude and love of beauty and luxury.

Gemini, May 22 to June 21

Ruled by Mercury and symbolized by the Twins, the fabled sons of the Greek god Zeus and Queen Leda, this sign gives those born under it a versatile, charming nature, and a fine intellect. However, Mercury, although an intellectual god, is also carefree and airy. The Gemini person therefore is interested in intellectual things but inclined to dabbling brilliantly in one thing after another and seldom following through in a practical constructive manner. A Gemini man should take up a profession in which quickness of mind, diplomacy, and intuition are necessary.

Cancer, June 22 to July 23

This sign is ruled by the Moon, the familiar satellite of our Earth. The Crab, a water creature, is the symbol and Cancerians love water and are happiest when they can live near a lake, a river or the sea. They are fond of travel, particularly ocean voyages. People born under this sign are sociable and fond of amusement, though they are often shy and sensitive, fearful of expressing their feelings too freely for fear of ridicule. They are dependent on friendship and need to be liked and admired.

Leo, July 24 to August 23

Here the lordly Lion is the sign and the great golden Sun the dominant body. This is the sign of those who were born to rule. The Leonine spirit is a dominating one, high-minded, tireless. It is difficult for Leo people to adapt themselves in an inferior position or to take orders, but with their intelligence and energy it is seldom necessary for them to do so.

They need a profession which makes use of the Leonine sense of responsibility and superior ability. They are dramatic and demonstrative. However, they are generous and never stoop to any petty or mean action.

Virgo, August 24 to September 23

The Virgin is the symbol here and Mercury the dominant planet, but his influence is very different here than in Gemini. There Mercury was airy and volatile. In Virgo, Mercury is an earth sign. He is the intellectual god, but here contributes sound intelligence and industry rather than restless brilliance. The native of Virgo is logical, systematic, and practical. He is usually successful in any enterprise he undertakes but wins his success by industry and devotion to the task. He disciplines himself and is apt to be intolerant of weakness or sentimentality in others. He is warm-hearted and kind and generous with those whom he feels deserve his help; however, his heart never rules his head. He keeps his emotions under control and considers the consequence of any romantic attachment before he acts. However, once he has made up his mind, he is dependable and loyal in business or love.

Libra, September 24 to October 23

Libra is the sign of beauty, symbolized by the scales which contribute balance and love of order. This sign is ruled by Venus, the Goddess of Beauty and the Arts. Children of Libra love beauty and justice. They see both sides of any arguments, which makes for fairness but sometimes also for indecision and hesitation. The Libra person is never driving and positive, not a go-getter with a single-track mind. He is swayed by his love of symmetry and justice to take an impartial position in all he does and thinks.

Scorpio, October 24 to November 22

The sign of the Scorpion is a fixed watery sign, executive and emotional and ruled by Mars. The native is passionate, energetic, proud, and obstinate. He goes into everything with gusto and energy, whether it is in the business world or the romantic sphere. He is an extremist in all he does; with him it's all or nothing. He is capable of deep devotion to people or to causes and will go to any lengths to achieve his ends. He is capable of great sacrifice and deep devotion where he loves but is also a furious hater.

Sagittarius, November 23 to December 22

This sign is ruled by Jupiter, noblest of the planets, and symbolized by the Archer, who shoots his arrow direct to the mark. The Jovian influence makes the native idealistic, high-minded and endows him with a "jovial" charm and gaiety. The Archer makes him honest to the point of bluntness. These people are high strung and for this reason can become restless and irritable although fundamentally their attitude is one of optimism and sincerity. The Sagittarian is generous and loyal in his personal relationship.

Capricorn, December 23 to January 20

Capricorn is ruled by Saturn, the great disciplinarian, and symbolized by the stubborn, sure-footed Goat. The Saturn influence makes the Capricornian reserved and thoughtful. They are the sort of people who direct and organize their lives and hew to the line with tireless energy and patience. They may be plodders, but with the surefootedness and determination of the goat, they reach their goals. They are likely to be more successful in later life than in youth, as it takes them a little time to get under way; no brilliant spurts or youthful precocity which burns out for the Capricorn.

Aquarius, January 21 to February 19

This is a sign of fame, for more great people who have left their imprint on history were born under this sign than any other. Uranus is exalted here and the symbol is a man pouring water. The men and women born under this sign give of themselves to the world. They are socially aware and eager to help humanity. Though they seldom accumulate wealth, their names and deeds are long remembered. As water brings forth the fertility of the earth, the Aquarian has the ability to stir men to action

The remaining six signs of the zodiac are (from the top), Libra (the Scales), Scorpio (the Scorpion), Sagittarius (the Archer), Capricorn (the Goat), Aquarius (the Water Bearer), and Pisces (the Fish). In the sky, these signs form the band through which the planets move.

and to change and improve the conditions in the world around them. Uranus' influence is toward change and originality. They are naturally intuitive and excellent judges of human nature. Therefore, they are able to influence others and to move and inspire them. The Aquarians have a long-range viewpoint and a sense of historical perspective. Abraham Lincoln was an Aquarian and Franklin Delano Roosevelt as well.

Pisces, February 20 to March 20

This is a mysterious and watery sign, ruled by Neptune, God of the Sea, and symbolized by two fishes, one swimming upstream and one downstream. Pisceans are lovers of beauty, inclined to be dreamy and impractical. They are very generous and frequently taken advantage of, as they dislike to hurt anyone. Unlike the generous Aquarian, the Piscean gives both wisely and unwisely. These people avoid competition and are sensitive, absent minded, and lacking in self-confidence. Because they lack the competitive spirit and are easily discouraged, they do better at quiet occupations where they can make use of their intuitive and artistic abilities and are not thrown into struggle against others. The Piscean has fine intelligence and great capabilities if he is not called upon to surmount obstacles.

Prediction and Prophecy

The desire to pull aside the veil which covers tomorrow has produced many types and manners of prediction and prophecy.

Many of these systems are based on the simple answering of a question, yes or no. The tossing of a coin is of this kind. But to the ancients, there was more than chance in the toss of a coin, or in any other method of indicating a choice. They believed that supernatural powers would take a hand, indicating what the answer should be.

Some systems of divination, as these attempts to view the future were termed, were much more complex. In geomancy, for example, a number of round objects were tossed to form a pattern, which was then interpreted according to fixed rules. The Chinese book called the *Yi King* indicates the reading to be made from a group of six sticks, solid in color on one side and divided into two on the other; they were tossed in the air, and when they fell were arranged in the form of one of sixty-four mystical characters.

In ancient Greek times, a person who had an important question would go to consult the oracle. There were a number of oracles, but the most famous one was at Delphi. One of the priestesses would seat herself in a chair which rose on a tripod over a crack in the earth. After inhaling the fumes which rose from the fissure, she would prophesy, usually in terms which had to be interpreted by the priests or by the inquirer. Sometimes the prophecy would be subject to several different interpretations. But it could always be shown that the oracle was never wrong.

Of the prophets of more recent times, perhaps none is more famous than Michel de Notredame, popularly known as Nostradamus, who lived from 1503 to 1566. A doctor who did much to try to help people stricken by the plagues that swept Europe, he made many predictions which were fulfilled while he was still alive.

One of these was that Henry II of France would "die in a golden cage." During a joust, the king's golden helmet was pierced by a splinter from his opponent's lance, and the king died—"in a golden cage."

Nostradamus wrote hundreds of prophetic verses, published in a book called the *Centuries*. Some people think that the prophecies are so obscure that they may be interpreted any way a person wishes; others believe that, somehow, Nostradamus was able to see events in the future, and concealed his visions in a kind of symbolic language which would not be understood until the event took place.

296

Lines, Bumps, and Moles:

The Belief in Character Reading

The belief that a person's character is revealed by certain marks on his body is an old one. It has produced several systems of analysis which, while not as yet verified by science, have many followers.

The analysis of character by the shape of the features of the face is called *physiognomy*. It was originated in the 16th century by several men, including Bartolomméo Cocle, who wrote a book on the subject. It was illustrated with hundreds of examples, showing how chins, lips, noses, eyes, and hair all were to be interpreted as keys to the personality of the individual. Giambattista della Portia (1538–1615) illustrated the title page of his book on the subject with comparative pictures of men and animals, attributing the traits of the animal to the man who looked like it. A Frenchman, Johann Lavater (1741–1801) also wrote many books on the subject.

Chiromancy, or palmistry as it is now called, had its origin at about the same time. The lines of the hand were supposed to provide a complete interpretation of the character. One line was given to the heart, another to the head; the length of a person's life was to be told by the life-line. Each of the joints of the fingers was assigned to one of the three faculties—intellect, intelligence, and instinct. The seven planets were assigned various places on the hand, and their influence interpreted in connection with the rules of astrology.

Still another variation of character reading developed during this period of enthusiasm for character study was one which assigned importance to the position of any moles which appeared on the body, and interpreted them according to elaborate charts. Some of the practitioners of physiognomy also used met-

oposcopy, which read the lines in the forehead as an index of character.

Much more recent is the practice of *phrenology*. Through this, the "bumps" on a person's head—actually the slight protrusions and depressions on the skull—were each assigned a quality. A bump meant strength in that characteristic, a dent meant weakness. Phrenological busts made of ceramic china may be found in many antique stores today as remnants of this belief of the last century.

While these systems described above were devoted mainly to character reading, some of the men who practiced them claimed to be able to tell a person's future destiny through them also. Thus Bartolomméo Cocle is said once to have told a nobleman of Bologna that the man would commit murder. Later Cocle angered Bentivoglio, the ruler of Bologna, by reading in his hand that he would be exiled and die in battle. Bentivoglio ordered Cocle assassinated; the man who did the deed was the nobleman of whom Cocle had made the prediction that he would be a murderer.

Related to the above systems is the reading of character in handwriting, or *graphology*. Some graphological rules are extremely simple, and are based on a logical interpretation of human traits. When a person is unhappy or depressed, for example, the lines of his writing are apt to slant downward; when happy or enthused, they will slant upward.

A person who fails to cross his *t*'s is considered absentminded; a Greek-style *e* is regarded as a sign of intelligence. Cramped writing or open writing, forward slanting or backward slanting are only a few of the points upon which graphologists base their analyses.

Of all the systems of character study mentioned here, graphology is the only one which has been given scientific study. For example, psychologists have found that the handwriting of mentally disturbed persons exhibits signs of such disturbance. Some business firms employ a professional graphologist and require all applications for positions to be written by hand; in this way they attempt to determine beforehand the type of person who will best fit into that company's employee system.

Reincarnation and Karma

This brief outline of the theory of reincarnation is taken from *Reincarnation: A Study of Forgotten Truth*, by E. D. Walker. Published by N. E. Wood, 1901.

Reincarnation is a doctrine rooted in the assurance of the soul's indestructibility. Reincarnation teaches that the soul enters this life, not as a fresh creation but after a long course of previous existences, on this earth and elsewhere, in which it acquired its present peculiarities, and that it is on the way to future transformations which the soul is now shaping.

Reincarnation claims that infancy brings to earth, not a blank scroll for the beginning of an earthly record nor a mere cohesion of atomic forces into a brief personality soon to dissolve again into the elements, but a soul that is inscribed with ancestral memories. Some are like the present scene; most of them are unlike it and stretch back into the remotest past.

These inscriptions are generally undecipherable, save as they are revealed in their molding influence upon the new career. The current phase of life will also be stored away in the secret vaults of memory for its unconscious effect upon the ensuing lives. All the qualities we now possess in body, mind and soul result from our use of ancient opportunities. We are indeed "the heirs of all the ages" and are alone responsible for our inheritances.

"Karma," the companion principle of reincarnation, is the Eastern word for a law of causation applied to personal experience. Briefly, the doctrine of karma is that we have made ourselves what we are by former actions and are building our future eternity by present actions.

Although largely rejected throughout Europe and America, reincarnation is accepted by the majority of mankind at the present time. And it has prevailed among a large part of humanity from the dawn of history.

It was taught as a precious secret by Pythagoras, Empedocles, Plato, Virgil and Ovid, who scattered its seeds through Greece and Italy. It is at the base of the religions of India. It was a cardinal element in the religion of the Persian Magi. Caesar found it among the Gauls.

The Cycle of Metempsychosis (a form of reincarnation) was an essential principle of the Druid faith. Among the Arab philosophers it was a favorite idea. In the old civilizations of Peru and Mexico it prevailed.

Reincarnation presumes that all will be favored with perfect poetic justice. Physical blessings, mental talents and moral successes are the laborious result of long merit. Sorrows, defects and failures proceed from negligence.

Reincarnation promotes the solidarity of mankind by destroying the barriers that conceit and circumstance have raised between individuals, groups, nations and races. It unites all the family of man into a universal brotherhood.

Other Books To Read

The New Golden Bough: A New Abridgement of the Classic Work by Sir James George Frazer, edited by Theodor H. Gaster. Published by Criterion Books, New York, 1959.
The Golden Bough: A Study in Magic and Religion, by Sir James George Frazer. One-volume abridged edition. Published by The Macmillan Company, New York, 1952
Either of these condensed versions of the monumental work on folklore will provide a fund of information on man's primitive beliefs and customs.

Diary of a Witch, by Sybil Leek. Published by Prentice-Hall, Inc., Englewood Cliffs, N.J., 1968.
A woman who claims to be a practicing witch tells about her beliefs, some interesting people she has met, and how "white" witches use their powers.

The History of Magic, by Kurt Seligmann. Published by Pantheon Books, New York, 1948.
A fascinating history of almost every topic which touches on the beliefs of magic, witchcraft, and prophecy. Includes a number of biographies.

Reincarnation: An East-West Anthology, edited by Joseph Head and S. L. Cranston. Published by The Theosophy Company, Los Angeles, 1961.
A collection of writings dealing with this belief.

Extra-sensory Perception, by J. B. Rhine. Published by Bruce Humphries, Boston, 1962.
The theories and experiments concerning the powers of the mind are discussed by a pioneer experimenter in this field.

The Mind Reaches Out:

ESP and Psi

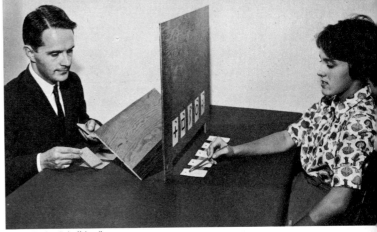

Thad W. Sparks—Duke University

The possibility that the human mind might have powers beyond those ordinarily recognized was suggested in the 17th century. The experiments of the pioneer researcher in hypnosis, Franz Mesmer, seemed to show that a subject in a hypnotic trance could exhibit qualities of telepathy, clairvoyance, and precognition.

Later the physiologist Charles Richet, Nobel Prize Winner in medicine (1913), was to show that such abilities could exist and be exercised by a person without resorting to a hypnotic condition.

The abilities of the subliminal mind—a term devised by W. H. Myers and meaning "beneath the threshold"—are now largely grouped under the terms extrasensory perception (ESP), or psi (for the Greek letter adopted to represent this field of research). "Parapsychology" is another term used to cover the entire field of research.

Clairvoyance is the asserted ability of a person to perceive something which could not be evident to any of the ordinary senses. It might, for example, be the ability to see the face of a playing card turned face down on a table—a frequent test for clairvoyance.

Telepathy is contact between the minds of two or more people and the ability to exchange thoughts. Many experiments have been conducted in which one person concentrates on a picture, object, or thought while another person many miles away makes notes on what he receives. Some very interesting results have been obtained from such tests.

Precognition, or "fore-knowing," is the ability to perceive things that have not yet occurred. A famous instance of this was recorded by J. W. Dunne, who saw an eruption of a volcano and the destruction of a village by it, and wrote down details of it long before the news reached him. Such precognition may be manifested in dreams.

Psychokinetics, or PK as it is referred to for short, is the ability of the mind to influence the motion or position of physical objects. A test for PK includes the rolling of dice down an inclined board, while the subject attempts to influence which way they will fall.

Laboratory tests on most of these psi powers have been carried on since the 1880's. However, the best-known research in this field has been conducted since the 1930's at Duke University by a laboratory under the direction of Dr. J. B. Rhine.

It was the Rhine laboratory that developed what are called ESP Cards—a deck of 25 cards about the size of playing cards, but having only five symbols; a star, cross, square, circle, and wavy lines.

In the beginning, testers were separated by a screen which kept the cards and movements of one person from being seen by other people involved in the test. Later, after numerous criticisms had been directed at such procedures as leading to the possibility of fraud, more complex safeguards were devised. Statistical analysis is used to a great extent by workers in this field, to try to determine whether favorable results which may be obtained are actually significant or are only chance.

Parapsychology is not as yet widely accepted by orthodox scientists, primarily because its results are uncontrollable and cannot be duplicated at will. Some feel that eventually psi abilities will be explained by present-day scientific theories; others believe that an entirely new formulation of physical laws may be necessary if parapsychology is found to be genuine.

299

In 1489, when witchcraft was strongly believed in, this illustration appeared in a book about witches and wizards. It shows three witches transformed into animals and riding to the Witches' Sabbath on a broom.

Witchcraft and Witch Hunting

In many parts of the world today, ignorant people have a fear of witches—that is, of anything or anyone that is different. This selection is from **Among My Books**, by James Russell Lowell, published by Houghton Mifflin and Company, 1895.

The notion of witch-gatherings which obsessed the Middle Ages and lasted until very recently was first suggested, there can be little doubt, by secret meetings of persisting or relapsed pagans or of heretics. Both, perhaps, contributed their share. Sometimes a mountain, such as the Blocksberg in Germany, sometimes a conspicuous oak or linden, and, later, a lonely heath, a cavern, gravel-pit or quarry, the gallows, or the churchyard were the places appointed for their diabolic orgies.

The three principal witch gatherings of the year were held on the days of great pagan festivals. One author supposes the witches' sabbath to be derived from the rites of Bacchus Sabazius, and accounts in this way for the Devil's taking the shape of a he-goat. But another writer assumes that the Devil is the same as the Greek Pan. In the popular mythology both of Celts and Teutons there were certain hairy wood-demons, called by the former *Dus* and by the latter *Scrat*. Our common names for the Devil of *Deuse* and *Old Scratch* are plainly derived from these.

It seems certain that the traditions of Vul-

can and Thor have converged at last in Satan. Like Vulcan, he was hurled from heaven, and, like him, he still limps across the stage in Mephistopheles, though without knowing why. In Germany, he has a horse's and not a cloven hoof, because the horse was a frequent pagan sacrifice and therefore associated with devil-worship under the new dispensation.

Most of the practices of witchcraft—such as the power to raise storms, to destroy cattle, to assume the shape of beasts by the use of certain ointments, to induce deadly sicknesses in men by waxen images or love by means of charms and philtres—were inheritances from ancient paganism.

Put the Blame on a Witch!

The Devil was an easy way of accounting for things that were beyond men's understanding. He was the simple and satisfactory answer to all the riddles of nature. And what the Devil had not time to bestow his personal attention on, the witch was always ready to do for him. Was a doctor at a loss about a case? How could he save his credit more cheaply than by pronouncing it witchcraft and turning it over to the parson to be exorcised? Did a man's cow die suddenly or his horse fall lame? Witchcraft! Unhappily, there were always ugly old women; and if you crossed them in any way, or did them a wrong, they were given to scolding and banning. If, within a year or two after, anything should happen to you or yours, why, of course, old Mother Bombie or Goody Blake must be at the bottom of it.

For it was perfectly well known that there were witches, and that they could cast a spell by the mere glance of their eyes, could cause you to pine away by melting a waxen image, could cause you a pain wherever they liked by sticking pins into a similar image. Worst of all, they could send a demon into your body. Meanwhile, you were an object of condolence to the whole neighborhood. What wonder if a lazy apprentice or servant-maid should prefer being possessed to working?

Suspicion of witchcraft was justified by general report, by the ill-looks of the suspected person, by her being silent when accused, by her mother's having been a witch, by flight, by the evidence of two witnesses, by the accusation of a man on his deathbed, by a habit of being away from home at night, by fifty other things equally grave. Anybody might be an accuser—a personal enemy, a child, parent, brother, or sister.

Once accused the culprit was not to be allowed to touch the ground on the way to prison, was not to be left alone there lest she have interviews with the Devil and get from him the means of resisting torture, was to be stripped and shaved in order to prevent her concealing some charm or to facilitate the finding of witch-marks. On half-proof or assumption, the judge could proceed to torture.

The Witches Confess

There was a terrible sameness about the confessions of the witches; a few samples will be representative of all.

Elizabeth Styles confessed "that the Devil about ten years since appeared to her in the shape of a handsome Man, and after of a black Dog. That he promised her Money, and that she should live gallantly, and have the pleasure of the World for twelve years, if she would with her Blood sign his Paper, which was to give her soul to him . . ."

The devil puts his mark on a witch in this picture from a 17th century book on witchcraft and demonology.

Juliana Cox confessed that "she had been often tempted by the Devil to be a Witch, but never consented. That one Evening she walkt about a Mile from her own House and there came riding towards her three Persons upon three Broomstaves, born up about a yard and a half from the ground. Two of them she formerly knew, which was a Witch and a Wizzard that were hanged for Witchcraft several years before."

The Witch-Burning Insanity

Toward no crime have men shown themselves so cold-bloodedly cruel as in punishing witchcraft, and the first systematic persecutions began in the south of France in the thirteenth century.

During this time all learning fell under suspicion, till at length the very grammar itself (the last volume in the world, one would say, to conjure with) gave to English the word *gramary* (enchantment) and in French became a book of magic, the *Grimoire*.

In the fifteenth century, witches were burned by thousands, and it may well be doubted if all paganism together was ever guilty of so many human sacrifices in the same space of time. In the sixteenth century, these holocausts were appealed to as conclusive evidence of the reality of the crime, terror was again aroused, and cruelty was the natural consequence. Men felt that they were surrounded by a long-lasting conspiracy whose extent they could not trace, though they might lay hold on one of its associates.

There is no more painful reading than the accounts of the tortures and trials of the witches. These awaken, by turns, pity, indignation, disgust: and dread—dread at the thought of what the human mind may be brought to believe not only probable but proven. Scepticism began at length to make itself felt, but it spread slowly. Toward the end of the seventeenth century, the safe thing to do was still to believe, or at any rate to profess belief. In France and Scotland it was not until the first quarter of the eighteenth century that a person might safely doubt the reality of witchcraft.

301

Men into Beasts:

The Were-Animal

Written especially for **Our Wonderful World**
by Sanford M. Cleveland.

The existence of the belief of therioanthropy —the ability of a human to change into animal form—is worldwide.

The particular area of this belief which has been studied most is that of the were-animal, and most especially the werewolf legend. It has found its way into literature in many countries, and forms a type of belief which is strong among all primitive peoples.

A typical story tells of an attack by a vicious animal against a man who managed to cut off the animal's leg or injure it in some way. Then, when the people of the village went to seek out the local magician, they would find him in human shape but injured just as the animal had been.

Wherever such stories are to be found, they almost always have one characteristic in common: the man-into-animal change takes the form of the fiercest, most fearsome and most feared animal in any given territory.

On the walls of the caves in southern France and northern Spain which were once occupied by Cro-Magnon Man, there are many drawings which seem to show men being transformed into animals through the putting on of masks. But there are some in which the change from man to animal seems to take place all in one flowing sweep, as if the artist had seen and believed in the actual act of shape-change and caught it at the halfway point. And it may be here, long before the origins of writing or history, that the belief in therioanthropy began—the change from human into animal form, and the return once more into the shape of man.

In the fifth century B.C. Herodotus, the "father of history," reported such a belief among the Scythians who lived north of the Danube River, but added, "though they affirm this, they do not persuade me." Pliny the Elder, writing in the first century A.D. in his *Natural History,* discusses the term "versipellis," or "changing the skin."

During the witch-trials of the 16th and 17th centuries in Europe, many reports were made that the witches and warlocks disguised themselves as animals and also that they could change themselves into animals at will.

In the Sudan and in Ethiopia, the were-hyena is strongly believed in. The weretiger and werefox are found in China, while in the Celebes there is a great fear of men and women who can change into crocodiles and other animals and roam about killing and maiming.

In Africa the wereleopard is well known, and this belief has given rise to the Human Leopard Societies, in which the members dress in leopard skins and fashion artificial metal claws with which to attack their victims; the wounds made by this device resemble the strokes of a real leopard.

The Plains Indians of North America believed that there were men who could turn themselves into wolves or buffalo. The Navajo Indians have a great fear of werewolves and werebears, and in the book *Spin a Silver Dollar* Alberta Hannum tells of the terror at a trading post caused by the belief that a certain Navajo man was a werewolf.

In the far north, the Eskimos of Alaska have many stories of men who change into wolves or bears. The Pomo Indians of northern California had a cult of shamans who were believed to change into bears.

Such beliefs are still held in many parts of the world. Reports in very recent years tell of werewolf scares in southern France and trials of members of the Human Leopard Society in Sierra Leone.

Two problems that researchers face are to explain, first, why a person can believe that he can change into an animal, and, second, why those who think they see the person in his transformation should believe that he is changed into that animal.

Anthropologists and psychologists have not been able to completely explain either the extent of such beliefs or why they have lasted so long and are still held.

302

The Spirit World

The belief that the dead can communicate with the living, or that those who have passed on may remain close to people or places on earth for a time, is a very ancient one. Several ancient Greek writers describe their experiences with ghosts, which were considered to be the still visible images of people who had once lived.

In the Middle Ages, particularly in England, the belief in ghosts was very strong. It occurs often, for example, in the plays of Shakespeare; there is the ghost of Hamlet's father, Banquo's ghost which appears to Macbeth, and the procession of ghosts of people murdered by King Richard III.

In the 16th and 17th centuries it was widely believed that through the use of the magical art called *necromancy* the spirit of a dead person could be called from the grave and forced to answer questions.

The noisy, stone-throwing ghost, or *poltergeist,* is frequently found in the literature about unusual occurrences.

The present-day movement which is called spiritualism actually had its beginnings in the phenomena which surrounded the family of John Fox of Arcadia, New York, beginning in 1848. The two young daughters of the family claimed to be able to communicate with the spirits of the dead through rappings on a table or similar noises.

While some investigators pronounced the phenomena to be a fraud, other people were convinced of its reality. Very soon large numbers of people were taking part in seances, or sessions where the deceased were contacted almost on a regular schedule. People who were particularly adept at making such contacts, which usually took place in a darkened room, were called *sensitives* or *mediums.*

Contacts with the dead gradually became more and more elaborate. Such things as spirit writing on slates, ghostly playing of musical instruments, production of photographs of the deceased persons, and the making of molds of the ectoplasm, or spirit substance, of which the hands of the spirit were supposed to be made, were all claimed as proof of the truth of spiritualism. The ouija board, supposed to be operated by spirits, was a popular fad.

However, two facts have made it difficult to solve the problem of the truth of spiritualism. One is that there are, and have been from its beginning, many false mediums. They pretend to make contact with the dead, and thus capitalize on the grief and suffering of people who sincerely wish for a consoling word from those who have passed on. There are even supply houses which sell equipment for unscrupulous would-be spiritualists to use to make their frauds more believable.

The other point is that every kind of spiritualistic phenomena, including spirit photography, can be duplicated by professional magicians, who therefore are inclined to claim that all mediumistic manifestations are hoaxes.

However, the believers point out that the fact that such things can be duplicated does not necessarily prove that the originals are not genuine. They insist that an honest investigation would show that cases do occur, both of spirit communication and of haunting by ghosts. The latter occurs particularly, they believe, where some violent crime has taken place, or because a person was so attached to a place or person in life that they refused to abandon the attachment even in death.

During the latter part of the 19th and first years of the 20th centuries, a number of presumably intelligent and critical men became firmly convinced of the reality of spirit communication. They included Sir Oliver Lodge, the astronomer Camille Flammarion, Sir William Crookes (inventor of the Crookes tube), the criminologist Caesar Lombroso, and Sir Arthur Conan Doyle. Psychical research societies were formed in England, France, and the United States. But despite all evidence which these men and organizations (and others since them) claim to have produced, the majority of scientists have always scoffed at spiritualism, or at the most have given it the verdict of "not proven."

The Divining Rod

The use of what is commonly called a divining rod to locate objects beneath the surface of the earth is extremely old. A scene painted on a rock wall in the Sahara desert perhaps 8,000 years ago appears to show a water diviner, or dowser, at work. Many reports from Greek and Roman antiquity seem to indicate that the people of the time were familiar with the subject, and by the sixteenth century its use was general.

In its most common form, the divining rod is a forked stick, usually of hazelwood. The operator holds the ends of the "Y" which the twig forms in his hands, with the point extended before him. When he walks above the substance or object which he is seeking, the twig suddenly dips downward (or in some cases, twists upward).

Scientists are skeptical of the use of a divining rod. They generally tend to label dowsers as frauds or impostors, claiming that they learned of the location of the object in some way, and simply put on a show to impress the people who have paid them to find water or whatever is being sought. But in some well-recorded cases, a diviner has walked across a field where only dry wells have resulted, indicated a particular spot, and a well sunk there produced water while the others remained dry.

While dowsing is the most common use of the forked twig, it has also been used to seek metals; in fact, an ancient medal worn by miners to protect them from hazards of work underground has the figure of a dowser on it.

If scientists are skeptical, many others, including government agencies, are not. The Government of India employed Major P. A. Pogson as official water diviner from 1925 to 1930, during which time he was recorded to have located 465 sites of water with a ratio of tries to successes of 97 per cent. Miss Evelyn Penrose was at one time official dowser to the Canadian province of British Columbia.

If the assumption is allowed that there is something to the idea of dowsing, even the diviners themselves do not agree as to how their ability works or how they received it. Some say quite frankly that the forked twig is only a device, and that it is a feeling in the body—such as a rise in the pulse—that tells them where to look.

One agency that has not scoffed at dowsers is the military. During World War II, a Royal Air Force unit stationed in the Sahara desert used a divining rod to locate water; a well was dug where the dowser indicated, and ample water for the encampment was obtained.

More recently, divining rods made of old metal coat hangers have been used in Vietnam to detect mines, underground tunnels of the enemy, and caches of arms hidden in the jungle. While it is pointed out that the official military training manuals do not list this rather unorthodox method of detection, engineer units of the First and Third Marine Divisions receive a demonstration of the coat hanger detector while at Camp Pendleton, California, and tests of the device have been made at other training schools.

In the military version, two L-shaped pieces of thin wire are held pointing in front of the operator. They will dip or spread apart to show the presence of underground material or tunnels. Not everyone who tries the gadget has success with it, but a large number of those who try do get results. The military writer for *The New York Times*, Hanson W. Baldwin, reported seeing such a demonstration, and then trying the rods out for himself. They indicated a tunnel which he did not know existed on the "Vietnam trail" at Camp Pendleton, a training area strewn with simulated booby traps and other hazards.

Physicists at Johns Hopkins University and with the Defense Department deny that the device can do what the engineers say that it does, but it is being used nonetheless. It has not, however, replaced the customary mine detectors and the procedure of probing with bayonets for buried objects.

Most dowsers, while unable to explain how their ability works, doubt that there is anything supernatural about it. Most of them suggest that more people have the ability than know about it.

304

Magic: Superstition or Advanced Technology?

The next time you read, in some old story or romance, that the hero drew his magic sword and smote his enemies, don't scoff at it.

He probably did.

It all depends on what is meant by magic. And some new light has been thrown on items such as this by the science writer, Arthur C. Clarke. Dr. Clarke has suggested that a "law" of his might be worth considering: "Any highly advanced technology is indistinguishable from magic." Highly advanced meaning, in this case, more highly advanced than that which the individual meeting it is used to.

Look at the wonders of electricity, for example, as they might seem to someone from a region of the earth so remote that Thomas Edison's inventions are there unknown. Light at a flip of a fingertip switch, cold from the refrigerator and heat from the electric oven, and all of this from no visible source whatever—obviously, magic!

Now, let us return to that little matter of the magic sword. The sword *was* magic, in that it was so powerful that no other sword could prevail against it.

Consider this imaginary scene: three or four soldiers of several thousand years ago are out on patrol when they encounter a strange warrior. They surround him and expect to make mincemeat of him in a short time; instead, one of the soldiers suddenly finds himself holding the handle and only the stump of the blade of his sword—the stranger's sword has chopped cleanly through it. When he gets back to the fort, he displays the cut-off weapon to his fellows, and they agree that it must have been magic. Incidentally, he was probably lucky that he escaped. Perhaps the others who met the magic sword weren't so fortunate.

What really happened was that the astounded soldier was armed with a bronze sword—and the stranger came from a society where the technology had developed iron. Bronze was a metal so widespread that history books still refer to the Bronze Age. But bronze swords were heavy; they got big nicks in them in any fight, and were hard to keep sharp in any case.

So when a smith discovered that the effort required to make a sword blade out of that hard-to-work metal iron was rewarded by the production of a blade that was light, took a keen edge and was hard to dent—and could slice through the older bronze weapons in the bargain—he probably had all the business he could handle. In his culture, of course, it was simply a matter of progress from one fairly good metal to a better one. But to the soldiers who met it for the first time in a fight, and its wielder was nearly invincible because of it, a "magic sword" was the only solution.

Eventually, of course, they too got iron, and things evened out some—until some industrious and enterprising metalworker discovered steel, which while not quite as superior to iron as iron is to bronze, still was superior enough to make the military profession sit up and take notice of the "magic swords" again. Someone's technology had gotten ahead once more—but to the person not familiar with it, it was magic, particularly if his culture was one with a good background of folk legends and stories of magic that lent themselves to being adapted or drawn on by the local storytellers.

Archaeologists are still working on the problems of just who King Arthur was and when he lived. But there seems a strong probability that Excalibur was an iron sword (possibly even a steel sword, made out of meteoric nickel-steel) which when compared to the bronze or even flint weapons prevalent in that early time would have seemed to be beyond any doubt enchanted. And many of the other magic swords of song and story may be traced to the same source. Achilles and Ulysses, of the ancient Greeks mentioned in Homer's *Odyssey*, had magic swords; so did Odin and Heimdall in Norse mythology. Perseus slew the Gorgon with a magic sword, and even King Charlemagne was given one by popular belief.

So the next time you encounter "magic" in a story, try substituting "advanced technology" for it, and see if it helps the explanation. It may not work all the time, but it will open some interesting lines of thought.

Classical Music and Its Composers

section **16**

There is no universal definition of classical music, but one dictionary defines it as music that appeals to "developed taste." Or you might say it is music of lasting value in contrast to music of passing interest. Some people call it "serious" music, instead.

If you're going to be technical, of course, "classical" can have only one of two meanings: music written in the period between 1770 and 1830 by such composers as Haydn and Mozart. Or, in a broader sense, music of the Classic type—music that is ordered, balanced, and objective—as opposed to the more dramatic music of the Romantic type.

Some classical music is easy to understand. Some requires effort and knowledge on the part of the listener. When the distinguished conductor, Leonard Bernstein, was in his teens, he found Johann Sebastian Bach's compositions dull except for a few pieces. In *The Joy of Music** he writes, "Why did these pieces touch me, when most of Bach's music didn't? It was because of their immediacy. They were instantly comprehensible to me as expressions of joy, or grief, or power, whereas the mainstream of Bach's work seemed to be nothing but endless pages of sixteenth notes, chugging along like a train. . . . But I was soon to learn that there are great beauties hidden in this music; only they are not so immediate as we expect them to be. They lie beneath the surface. But because they do, they don't rub off so easily; they last and last." Like any art, the more one learns about classical music, the more one enjoys it.

In this section you can learn about the forms or patterns in which classical music is written. You will also find stories about many famous composers and suggestions about compositions that make good listening.

*Copyright © 1954, 1955, 1956, 1957, 1958, 1959 by Leonard Bernstein

Harpsichord, harp, flute, guitar, recorder, and zither appear in this woodcut of an 18th-century orchestra.

A 20th-century symphony orchestra, like the New York Philharmonic, may have more than 100 players.

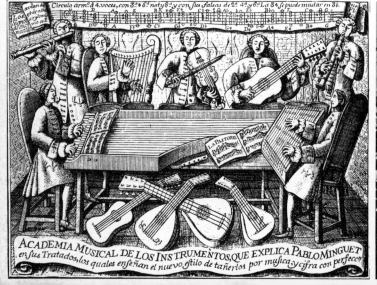

How We Listen

The distinguished American composer, Aaron Copland, shows you how to improve your ability to enjoy music. From **What to Listen for in Music**, rev. ed. by Aaron Copland. Copyright © 1939, 1957 by McGraw-Hill Book Company, Inc., and used with their permission.

The simplest way of listening to music is to listen for the sheer pleasure of the musical sound itself. This is the sensuous plane. It is the plane on which we hear music without thinking, without considering it in any way. One turns on the radio while doing something else and absent-mindedly bathes in the sound. Many people abuse that plane in listening. They go to concerts in order to lose themselves. They dream because of and apropos of the music, yet never quite listen to it.

The second plane on which music exists is what I call the expressive one. It is difficult to say precisely what it is that a piece of music means, to say it definitely, to say it finally so that everyone is satisfied with your explanation. But that should not lead one to the other extreme of denying to music the right to be "expressive."

My own belief is that all music has an expressive power, some more and some less, but that all music has a certain meaning behind the notes, and that that meaning behind the notes constitutes, after all, what the piece is saying, what the piece is about.

How close should one come to pinning a definite meaning to any particular work? No closer than a general concept, I should say. Music expresses, at different moments, serenity or exuberance, regret or triumph, fury or delight. It expresses each of these moods, and many others, in a numberless variety of subtle shadings and differences. It may even express a state of meaning for which there is no adequate word in any language.

The third plane on which music exists is the sheerly musical plane—the notes themselves and their manipulation. Most listeners are not sufficiently conscious of this third and important plane.

When the average person listens to the "notes themselves" with any degree of concentration, he is most likely to be aware of the melody and rhythm. But harmony and tone color are generally taken for granted, if they are thought of consciously at all. As for music's having a definite form of some kind, that idea seems never to have occurred to him.

It is very important for all of us to become more alive to music on its sheerly musical plane. The listener must be prepared to increase his awareness of the musical material and what happens to it. He must hear the melodies, the rhythms, the harmonies, the tone colors in a more conscious fashion. But above all he must, in order to follow the line of the composer's thought, know something of the principles of musical form. Listening to all of these elements is listening on the sheerly musical plane. I have split up the three planes on which we listen for the sake of clarity. Actually, we correlate them—listening in all three ways at the same time. It takes no mental effort, for we do it instinctively.

What the reader should strive for is a more *active* kind of listening. Whether you listen to classical or popular music, you can deepen your understanding of it only by being a more conscious and aware listener—not someone who is just listening, but someone who is listening *for* something.

Aaron Copland (1900–   ) is one
the most prominent figures in American
music. Discarding an overly romantic
style for more abstract musical
concepts, he has written ballets such as
Billy the Kid (*1938*) and
Appalachian Spring (*1944*), *both*
based on folk-music styles. He has
also composed symphonies and
other works.

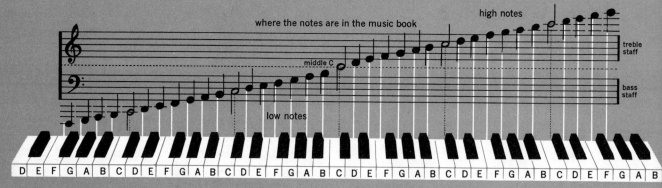

where the notes are in the music book

high notes

middle C

treble staff

bass staff

low notes

D E F G A B C D E F G A B C D E F G A B C D E F G A B C D E F G A B C D E F G A B C D E F G A B

where the notes are on the piano keyboard

Only a part of the piano keyboard is shown here. The ordinary piano has 88 keys. The trademark of a piano is always centered just above middle C.

The Alphabet of Music

Because of the system of writing down musical notes, it is possible for a German, an Italian, a Frenchman, a Russian, a Spaniard, and an American to sit down and play the same piece of music together, though none of them might be able to speak the language of the others. Here is a short description of the international language of music. From **Music: A Short History** by W. J. Turner. Copyright 1949 by A. & C. Black Ltd., London.

The great invention in musical notation came about some time around the eleventh century. It is called the staff. Because of the staff, a succession of tones could be written down so that their exact pitch was shown simply and clearly. This invention was perfected by an Italian monk of the eleventh century named Guido d'Arezzo. The principle of the staff is very simple. It consists merely of drawing a number of parallel lines and placing the dots and strokes upon these lines or between them, and by that means indicating whether the music is to go up or down in pitch.

A New Written Language

The invention of the staff was one of the great steps forward in the history of music, for it enabled musicians to put down their musical ideas clearly for others to understand. It was now no longer necessary to commit all music to memory and to pass it on by ear from one person to another. It could be committed to writing, and so the musical thought of every individual could be passed on immediately

from one country to another, and, of course, from one generation to another. It soon became apparent that a staff of five lines was all that was required for marking the pitch of musical tones. Every musical tone has a definite number of vibrations a second, and as we go up the scale of tones step by step we always come to a tone that has twice as many vibrations as the tone we started from. This is the eighth tone. Therefore we need only to have a method of writing down the pitch of eight tones and a way of indicating that at the eighth tone the same series of tones begins again, but an octave higher, to have a complete method of pitch notation. Any series of notes within one octave, sounding complete, is called a scale, which means a ladder of musical tones or steps. At the eighth note, or octave, the scale always begins again (see above).

1 and 2 and . . .

Once pitch could be written down exactly, it was easy to give a time value to the tones by giving the dots on the lines and spaces

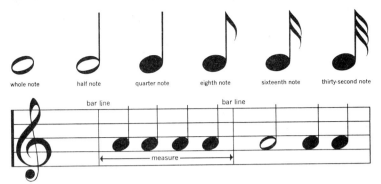

whole note   half note   quarter note   eighth note   sixteenth note   thirty-second note

bar line   bar line

← measure →

Each of the notes at left, above, is half the length of the preceding one. In this way a composer can write music in which each note will last exactly as long as he wants it to. In the musical staff (left, below), the two measures take up exactly the same amount of time, although they have a different number of notes.

different shapes according to the length of time it was intended each particular tone should last. For example, supposing we start with an open dot (the whole note) as our unit. If we want a tone to last only half as long we put a tail to it, and this note is known as a half note. Then by filling in the open dot and adding strokes to its tail we can get from one unit to ⅟₃₂ of that unit of time duration.

By this method musicians were able to write down not only the exact pitch of each tone but the exact time each tone was to last in relation to the unit decided upon.

Between the Notes

Other devices were now needed in order to make metric or measured music. This was done by the invention of pauses (or rests) and bars. A rest is the musical name for a pause and a number of signs were invented for rests or pauses. It was necessary that every note should have its equivalent rest; that is, there had to be a way of showing that there was to be silence for exactly the same length of time as each time note. Therefore, there are full rests, half rests, quarter rests, and so on, with a sepa-

rate sign for each. These rests are something like the punctuation marks in writing. The invention of bars resembles the invention of verse, that is, the writing of prose in lines of equal length. In musical notation a bar line is a vertical line across the five-lined staff which divides it into equal time parts called measures or bars. We can see how by using the bar line any number of tones in succession can be divided up into equal time groups, each time group being separated from its neighboring equal time group by a bar line.

With all the devices described, musicians could write down an indefinite number of tones in sequence, defining the exact pitch and the exact duration of each tone, and the relation in pitch and time of all the tones to one another, so that the whole could be grasped by the mind at sight. That is to say, the musicians now had a complete musical language or notation by means of which they could write down their ideas on paper. The whole of this development of musical notation took place in the Middle Ages, and our present system of notation was in general use by the fifteenth century.

While an octave has eight notes (octa = eight), a musical scale actually has twelve half tones in it. In a scale of eight notes, whole and half tones are arranged so as to make a "key," which may be major or minor. To indicate half tones, it may be necessary to use symbols for "sharp" (♯) and "flat" (♭)—a half tone higher or lower; a "natural" (♮) cancels the previous sign.

309

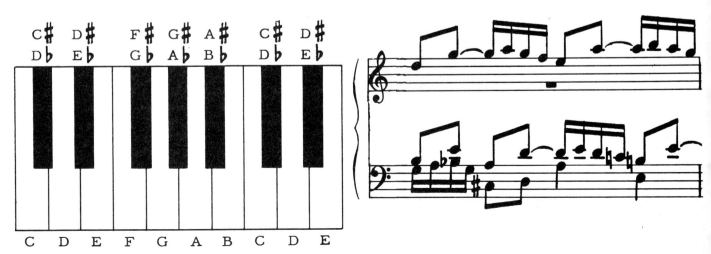

C♯ D♯   F♯ G♯ A♯   C♯ D♯
D♭ E♭   G♭ A♭ B♭   D♭ E♭

C D E F G A B C D E

Music Masters of Five Centuries

Giovanni Pierluigi da Palestrina   1525(?)–1594

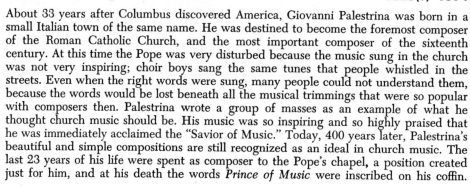

About 33 years after Columbus discovered America, Giovanni Palestrina was born in a small Italian town of the same name. He was destined to become the foremost composer of the Roman Catholic Church, and the most important composer of the sixteenth century. At this time the Pope was very disturbed because the music sung in the church was not very inspiring; choir boys sang the same tunes that people whistled in the streets. Even when the right words were sung, many people could not understand them, because the words would be lost beneath all the musical trimmings that were so popular with composers then. Palestrina wrote a group of masses as an example of what he thought church music should be. His music was so inspiring and so highly praised that he was immediately acclaimed the "Savior of Music." Today, 400 years later, Palestrina's beautiful and simple compositions are still recognized as an ideal in church music. The last 23 years of his life were spent as composer to the Pope's chapel, a position created just for him, and at his death the words *Prince of Music* were inscribed on his coffin.

Antonio Vivaldi   1675–1741

New York Public Library

Antonio Vivaldi, the great Italian composer and violinist, was born and educated in Venice. He studied music and theology, and in 1703 was ordained as a priest. In the following year he became a violin teacher and player at the Ospedale della Pietà, an orphanage in Venice, where from 1716–1740 he held the post of concert master. His contract with the school required him to write at least two concertos each month for the orchestra. Though much of his sacred music was unpublished he wrote many operas, sonatas, and cantatas and made occasional European tours. It must be remembered that Johann Sebastian Bach copied and imitated Vivaldi's work in his own concertos. (It was the custom for composers to borrow themes from each other, as most had patrons and were not concerned with copyright laws.) As a violinist the red-haired Vivaldi, sometimes called the Red Priest, was a great influence for the violinists and cellists of his time.

George Frederick Handel   1685–1759

If Handel's father, who was both a doctor and a barber in the town of Halle, Germany, had gotten his way, George Frederick Handel would have become a lawyer rather than one of the greatest composers of the eighteenth century. When Handel was only seven years old, he persuaded his aunt to smuggle a clavichord into the attic of his home. Secretly he practiced on the quiet little keyboard instrument. By the time Handel was twelve, his teacher said that he could teach him nothing more. In 1710, Handel went to England, where he was to spend the rest of his life and write his greatest orchestral and choral music, including the *Royal Fireworks*, the *Water Music*, and the glorious oratorio *The Messiah*, during the "Hallelujah Chorus" of which people still stand just as did King George II when he first heard this inspiring work.

Joseph Haydn   1732–1809

Because of his kindness, his goodness and humor, Joseph Haydn was affectionately known to his many friends as "Papa" Haydn. His childhood was filled with harsh discipline and poverty, but his musical studies, which he began at the age of six, kept him happy and good-natured. When he was 29, Haydn became musical director of the court of the music-loving Prince Esterházy of Vienna. A prolific composer, he produced over 100 symphonies, and dozens of concertos, oratorios, and pieces for smaller ensembles. When Haydn died in 1809, the Emperor Napoleon, who had just invaded Vienna, ordered his officers to accompany Haydn's body to its final resting place.

Wolfgang Amadeus Mozart   **1756–1791**

One of the most gifted of composers and performers, Wolfgang Amadeus Mozart was born in Salzburg on January 27, 1756. As a child he was extremely precocious; with the guidance of his father, Leopold, he was playing instruments at the age of three and began composing when only five. In the early years of his life, young Mozart visited and played for aristocracy all over Europe. His later years were occupied almost entirely with composing. His ability to improvise was remarkable, as was the quality and volume of his composition. He composed 22 operas (most of them quite short), 27 piano concertos, and 48 symphonies, as well as hundreds of other compositions. He was working on a Requiem when his untimely death occurred as the result of suspected poisoning. Fame he had, but money none; and he was buried in an unmarked pauper's grave.

New York Public Library

Felix Mendelssohn   **1809–1847**

Unlike many great composers, Felix Mendelssohn was extremely happy and successful throughout his life. In fact, even his first name, Felix, means "happy man" in Latin. He was born into a wealthy and cultured German family, and his childhood was filled with music and art and gaiety. But Felix worked hard at the things he loved; every morning at five he awakened to a day of studying piano, violin, drawing, and languages. By the time he was twelve years old, Felix had written many beautiful compositions in various musical forms. Also, at the age of twelve the young composer had the great fortune to be befriended by one of the greatest of all European writers, Johann von Goethe, who was then 72 years old. During his relatively short life he produced many brilliant compositions, including five symphonies, two piano concertos, a violin concerto which is one of the most popular among virtuosi, and the well-known incidental music to Shakespeare's *Midsummer Night's Dream*. Mendelssohn also brought to the attention of audiences the music of Johann Sebastian Bach, which had been neglected for many years.

From HARPER'S Mag.

Claude Debussy   **1862–1918**

In many ways, the French composer Debussy was the father of modern music. Even as a young student at the Paris Conservatory, Debussy many times angered his teachers and fellow students by writing music that seemed totally different from anything they had ever heard. "I can only make my *own* music," Debussy once said; he absolutely refused to imitate the music of past composers. But many critics and audiences did not understand his daring new style. One critic said, after the first performance of his opera, *Pelléas et Mélisande*, that it was "amusing in its absurdity"! The harmonies of Debussy's music do not seem strange now. Such works as *Clair de Lune* ("Moonlight"), and *Prélude à l'après-midi d'un faune* ("The Afternoon of a Faun") have probably never been surpassed in their descriptive delicacy. Debussy died in France in 1918 during World War I, but his influence can be heard in the work of many composers who have followed him.

Courtesy MUSIC NEWS

Igor Stravinsky   **1882–**

Igor Stravinsky is truly a man of the world. Born and educated in Russia, he moved to France in 1919 and soon became a citizen of that country. In 1939, he left France for the United States and became an American citizen. His music is as different from one group of compositions to the next as are the three countries that have been his home. He has written the music for nine ballets including *The Rite of Spring*, which had one of the most spectacular first performances in musical history. Part of the audience thought that the music was a work of genius, and they applauded and cheered, while others considered it a "musical outrage" and began to boo and whistle; the music was drowned out by the noise of the opponents; there were fist fights and even a challenge to a duel over it. But Stravinsky, who has said "I live neither in the past nor in the future; I can only know what the truth is for me today," is now considered rather conservative as a composer. His music for the ballets *The Firebird* and *Petrouchka*, and the *Dumbarton Oaks Concerto*, are standards of the concert hall.

311

Boosey & Hawkes, Inc.

Other Forms of Symphonic Music

The symphony is the biggest kind of work written for symphony orchestras to play, but if you attend a symphony concert you will probably hear a few other forms, also written for the symphony orchestra. This is a description of the forms played most often. From *Music—Its Appreciation* by C. Whitaker-Wilson. Copyright 1951 by W. & G. Foyle Ltd., London.

The Concerto

A good working definition of a concerto is a *sonata composition* (three movements) for a solo instrument accompanied by an orchestra.

The form for them seems to have been settled by Mozart; at least fifty of his concertos exist for various instruments, and they resemble each other in the main points of form. Beethoven wrote a number and, as usual, made a few changes; for one thing, he gave more prominence to the orchestra. With Mozart the orchestra really does accompany—and no more; with Beethoven it assumes symphonic importance and has much to say on its own account.

In a concerto the orchestra stops at one point, and the soloist goes on alone. This solo part is called the *cadenza*. The cadenza itself may have been written by the composer, or it might be written by the player. Usually it is the composer who writes it.

The original idea was to give the soloist—if he was good enough—a chance to improvise upon the themes of the concerto itself. That, however, is now only in theory; in practice it amounts to the solo player showing off the greatness of his technique—and indeed, the greatness of his instrument.

Sergei Prokofiev (1891–1953) tried to make his career as a musician in the United States after the Russian Revolution, but his music was considered too radical. Returning to Russia in 1933, he became a prolific and widely admired composer. His most popular works include the Classical Symphony, *the ballet* Romeo and Juliet, *and the* Lieutenant Kijé *suite.*

312

Sovfoto

Concertos To Hear

Beethoven: *Concerto in D major for Violin, Opus 61*
Tchaikovsky: *Concerto No. 1 in B-flat minor for Piano, Opus 23*
Grieg: *Concerto in A minor for Piano, Opus 16*
Haydn: *Concerto in E-flat major for Trumpet*
Taktakishvili: *Concerto for Piano and Orchestra (1951)*
Korngold: *Violin Concerto in D, Op. 35*
Gliere: *Harp Concerto in E Flat Major*
Dvorak: *Cello Concerto in B Minor, Op. 104*
Vivaldi: *Concerto for Sopronino Recorder*

The Symphonic Tone Poem

Franz Liszt, the Hungarian composer-pianist, began this form about 1850. His idea was to say in language of music what a poet says in language of words, but he had no intention of forsaking form. Form, to him, was a means to an end, but he preferred to create his own form (by developing his themes in an orderly fashion) to adopting a set pattern, such as the symphony, for his music.

It was not long before other composers snatched at so attractive an idea. Tchaikovsky used it in *Hamlet, Romeo and Juliet,* and *Francesca da Rimini.* Cesar Franck used it in several works; Sibelius in *Finlandia*—but Liszt's real successor in this respect was Richard Strauss: *Don Juan,* and *Don Quixote,* are tone poems. Another vivid example is *Till Eulenspiegel's Merry Pranks* which tells the story of a practical joker who annoyed people.

You may listen to any of these without the least notion of what the story behind it is, but you can never get away from the fact that powerful themes are being used and developed, and that the mind of the composer has been influenced by something in the way of a legend or story. For this reason symphonic tone poems make a pleasant change from the stricter forms of symphony.

 ## Tone Poems To Hear

Prokofiev: *Peter and the Wolf, Opus 67*
Saint-Säens: *Carnival of the Animals*
Debussy: *La Mer (The Sea)*

Magnavox Co.

The idea behind oratorio is not the same as that behind opera which has always been thought of as an entertainment. Originally oratorio was written to present to the uneducated something about religion which they could readily understand. St. Philip Neri, the Florentine saint of the sixteenth century, introduced the first of these sacred dramas into his church. In these days we associate oratorio with the names of Bach, Handel, Haydn, Mendelssohn, Spohr, Gounod, and Elgar. They are often played during the great Christian religious seasons, such as Christmas and Easter.

 Oratorios To Hear

Mendelssohn: _Elijah, Opus 70_
Bach: _Mass in B minor_
Elgar: _The Apostles_
Haydn: _The Creation_

In the space of a short life (1797–1828), the Austrian composer Franz Schubert wrote more than 1,200 musical compositions, although he was considered a failure by many during his lifetime. His nine symphonies (the eighth is the famous Unfinished Symphony), _his string quartets and his song cycles are his greatest works._

Chamber Music

This is music written for a small group of instruments, anything from one or two to a dozen. It is called chamber music because it was written to be played for a small audience, in a room or chamber, much smaller than the usual concert hall. The sonata form or dance forms are often used, and the music is usually played by the quieter instruments, the strings, and wood winds. Almost every wealthy eighteenth-century person who gave a party would hire a chamber music group to entertain his guests.

The Overture

Most overtures are written in "first movement" form of the symphony or sonata. Originally overtures were written for, and played in front of, operas, so that latecomers could get to their seats before the opera began. When you hear them played as concert pieces it is hardly possible to associate their themes with themes in the operas for which they were written—unless, that is, you happen to be familiar with the operas. The fact that they have been introduced into concert programs has brought about what are called concert-overtures, overtures written as independent compositions without any opera in mind.

 Overtures To Hear

Weber: _Oberon: Overture_
Gluck: _Alceste: Overture_
Smetana: _The Bartered Bride: Overture_
Mendelssohn: _The Hebrides ("Fingal's Cave"), Opus 26_
Wagner: _Overture to The Flying Dutchman_

 Chamber Music To Hear

Mozart: _Eine kleine Nachtmusik (A Little Night Music)_
Beethoven: _Trio No. 7 in B-flat major, Opus 97 ("Archduke")_
Schubert: _Quintet in A major, Opus 114 ("Trout")_
Brahms: _Quartet in G minor, Opus 25_

313

Other Sections To See

"Music from the Sea," Volume 2; "Exceptional People and Their Problems," (biographies of musicians), Volume 7; "Art and Music of the Frontier," Volume 8; "Musical Instruments," Volume 13; "Invitation to the Dance," "Careers in Entertainment," and "Popular Music and Its History," Volume 14.

Oratorio

An oratorio is a drama or sacred story set to music, in which there are solo voices, a chorus, and a full orchestra, but whose performance is given without costume or action. The last-mentioned restriction separates it from opera.

The Remarkable Bach Family

The most remarkable family in musical history was the Bach family of Germany. For over two centuries, members of this family were gifted musicians and composers in the towns of Eisenach, Arnstadt and Erfurt. The first member of the family to adopt music as a livelihood seems to have been Hans Bach, the great-grandfather of Johann Sebastian. After Hans, members of the early family were town and court organists, violinists and music masters.

Of all the Bachs, Johann Sebastian (1685–1750) attracted the most fame. He was born in Eisenach, Germany, on March 21, 1685. His parents both died when he was a boy, and he was sent to live at the home of his elder brother, Johann Christoph, at Ohrdurf. His father had already taught him the violin; his brother taught him the keyboard instruments.

When he was fifteen years old, Bach was forced to earn his living. He served as a chorister at St. Michael's Church at Luneburg and continued his schooling there also. At Luneburg, he was associated with the composer Georg Böhm and, in time, he developed into a competent organist.

In 1703, he joined the Weimar household of Duke Johann Ernst as an organist and string player. A series of posts followed. He served for Prince Leopold of Anhalt-Cöthen and was also appointed cantor of St. Thomas' Church at Leipzig.

In 1749, Bach became totally blind after an unsuccessful operation to restore his sight. He suddenly regained his sight in July 1750, but he was stricken with apoplexy and died in Leipzig.

While at his church posts, Bach wrote five sets of music for every Sunday and feast day of the year. Best known among his compositions are the six Brandenburg Concertos for chamber orchestra; *The Well-Tempered Clavier,* containing 48 preludes and fugues; and the St. Matthew and St. John *Passions.*

It is interesting to note that during his lifetime, Johann Sebastian Bach was not well known. His reputation did not extend beyond Germany, except as an organist, and only nine or ten of his compositions were actually published during his lifetime. He always worked in small towns and so developed musically along his own lines rather than contemporary ones. It was not until 1829, when Mendelssohn arranged for a performance of the *St. Matthew Passion,* that Bach's mastery of polyphonic art and invention was recognized and brought to the attention of the public.

Three of Johann Sebastian's sons were important members of the musical Bach family. The eldest son, Wilhelm Friedemann (1710–84), had inherited a great deal of his father's genius. He was an accomplished organist and also an extremely talented composer. However, his character was no match for his talent and he led the life of a "dissolute vagabond."

Johann Sebastian's third son, Carl Philipp Emanuel (1714–88), was the best known of the sons. He was a brilliant performer on the clavier and did much to establish the style and forms of the classical school. The composition of piano sonatas was his greatest achievement, and he brought order to the sonata by fixing its three-movement form.

Johann Christian (1735–82), the youngest of the sons, became noteworthy as an operatic composer and wrote a total of 12 operas. He composed widely in other genres also and had a considerable influence upon Mozart, Haydn, and Beethoven.

With the deaths of Johann Sebastian's sons, the family declined musically. The final member, Dr. Otto Bach, died in 1893 and took with him the last seeds of the Bach musical genius.

Much of the music of Johann Sebastian Bach was written for church use; he said that the aim of music should be for "the Glory of God."

Some Great Composers and Their Styles

WHO	WHEN	WHY HE IS FAMOUS	
Corelli	1653–1713	(Italian) Created the concerto grosso form in music	
Purcell	c.1659–1695	(English) Composer of the first true opera	
Scarlatti	1660–1725	(Italian) Considered founder of modern opera	BAROQUE
Vivaldi	c.1675–1741	(Italian) Wrote many concertos, sonatas, and operas	
Bach	1685–1750	(German) Master of church music	
Handel	1685–1759	(German) Classical oratorio composer	
Gluck	1714–1787	(German) Rebuilder of opera	
Haydn	1732–1809	(Austrian) "Papa" Haydn, first great master of symphony	CLASSICISM
Mozart	1756–1791	(Austrian) Master of both operatic and symphonic music	
Beethoven	1770–1827	(German) Developed and expanded musical forms	
Weber	1786–1826	Founder of German national opera	
Rossini	1792–1868	(Italian) Master of operatic comedy	
Schubert	1797–1828	(German) Master of the German song	
Berlioz	1803–1869	(French) Champion of "story" music	EARLY ROMANTICISM
Mendelssohn	1809–1847	German composer of musical atmospheres	
Chopin	1810–1849	(Polish) Noted composer of piano music	
Schumann	1810–1856	(German) Expressed human emotions in music	
Liszt	1811–1886	Hungary's foremost composer	
Wagner	1813–1883	Famous German opera composer	
Verdi	1813–1901	Greatest Italian opera composer	
Franck	1822–1890	Belgium's great composer	
Bruckner	1824–1896	(Austrian) A symphonist of the "big" orchestra	
J. Strauss	1825–1899	(Austrian) Immortal waltz king	
Brahms	1833–1897	German master of romantic nineteenth-century music	
Moussorgsky	1835–1881	Composer whose music described everyday life in Russia	
Saint-Saëns	1835–1921	French pianist and composer of "picture" music	LATE ROMANTICISM
Bizet	1838–1875	Glorifier of Spanish rhythm	
Tchaikovsky	1840–1893	Russia's great symphonist	
Dvorak	1841–1904	Interpreter of Bohemian music	
Grieg	1843–1907	Norway's most representative composer	
Rimski-Korsakov	1844–1908	(Russian) Composed symphonic poems, operas, songs	
Puccini	1858–1924	Verdi's greatest successor in Italian opera	
Mahler	1860–1911	Distinguished Bohemian conductor and composer	
Debussy	1862-1918	(French) Described personal impressions in music	IMPRESSIONISM
Ravel	1875-1937	(French) Impressionist with classical leanings	
Elgar	1857-1934	England's foremost composer	
MacDowell	1861-1908	Noted American composer	
R. Strauss	1864-1949	(German) Developed the symphonic tone poem	NEO-ROMANTICISM
Sibelius	1865-1957	Finland's great symphonist	
Rachmaninoff	1873-1943	Russian composer-pianist	
Shostakovich	1906-	Modern Russia's representative composer	
Stravinsky	1882-	(Russian) Innovator of the Neo-Classic movement	NEO-CLASSICISM
Hindemith	1895-	(German) Developed new contrapuntal style after Bach	
Schönberg	1874-1951	(Austrian-American) Devised 12-tone scale technique	
Bloch	1880-1959	(Swiss) Composer inspired by Bible stories and Hebrew music	
Béla Bartók	1881-1945	(Hungarian) Created highly original compositions based on folk music	MODERNISM
Webern	1883-1945	Austrian composer of atonal music	
Berg	1885-1935	(Austrian) Pupil of Schönberg. Wrote *Wozzeck*.	
Prokofiev	1891-1953	Russian composer of operas, ballets, orchestral music	

Adapted from FROM BACH TO GERSHWIN, Two and One-Half Centuries of Music;
A Musical Calendar prepared by Otto K. Eitel, President, Bismarck Hotel, Chicago.
Revised by editor.

What Is a Symphony?

If you were taking a vacation trip to a strange city, you would probably find out something about the place before you started. If you are getting acquainted with a kind of music that is strange to you, the same is true. From **A Guide to Great Orchestral Music** by Sigmund Spaeth. Reprinted by permission of Random House, Inc. Copyright 1943 by Random House, Inc.

A symphony is a large musical work, usually lasting at least a half hour or more. (The word *symphony* comes from two Greek words meaning "sounding together.") It regularly has four *movements* or sections, and these movements do not necessarily have any connection of key or melody.

The opening movement of a symphony is traditionally in the so-called *sonata* form, appearing also in actual sonatas, as well as in overtures, concertos, string quartets, etc. Sonata form is not at all hard to follow, so long as you know the tunes or themes of a symphony. It is similar to the structure of a play or a novel.

There are at least *two important themes*, corresponding to the hero and the heroine. They are generally in related keys but of contrasting character. These outstanding tunes are introduced early in the sonata form, and this part of the movement is called the *exposition*, as when the chief characters of a play are introduced. Each tune may have some slight development immediately, and there is often a connecting melody or *bridge* to hold them together.

The exposition is followed by the *development* or free fantasia, corresponding to the plot of the play or novel. Here the technique of the composer is allowed complete freedom, and this is the part of a symphony that is hardest for the beginning listener to follow. The tunes are broken up, turned upside down, put into different keys, played by various instruments, rhythmically distorted, treated in every possible way to create contrast, conflict, suspense, as in an actual plot.

Finally the leading melodies return in their original form, although often in new keys, and this section is called the *recapitulation,* or reminder, suggesting the happy or at least logical ending of the play or novel. There may be an additional section, often quite short, called the *coda,* literally a "tailpiece." Sometimes there is also an *introduction,* particularly in the older symphonies, and it was formerly customary to repeat the entire exposition before starting the development. Obviously sonata form is quite definite and logical, a fine example of the basic principle of statement, contrast, and reminder, which runs through all the related arts of music, literature, drama, and dance.

Sonata form, characteristic of the first move-

316

Wolfgang Amadeus Mozart, one of the first masters of symphonic form, was performing public concerts at the age of six. He and his sister, Maria Anna, are shown here playing the clavier, a predecessor of the piano, for Maria Teresa, then Empress of Austria.

ment of a symphony, may be conveniently outlined as follows:

Introduction: (sometimes used)
Exposition: (A) First Theme
(Bridge sometimes used here)
(B) Second Theme
(Repetition of exposition, older symphonies only)
Development: (using materials of A and B and possibly of introduction)
Recapitulation: Return of A and B, generally in new keys
Coda: (sometimes used)

With this outline in mind, and some familiarity with the melodies themselves, you can analyze the first movement of any symphony without difficulty, and follow its sonata form with mental as well as physical and emotional pleasure. A symphony is actually a sonata on a larger scale, written for a big orchestra. Hearing a piano or violin sonata is a good preliminary to its enjoyment.

The first movement of a symphony is generally the most important, but the other three may be equally beautiful and even more appealing on a first hearing. The second movement is likely to be in a slow tempo, in contrast to the livelier pace of the first. Sometimes it is a single theme with variations or musical decorations. This is a favorite form in the classic school of music, and has its counterpart in the decorations given to a popular tune by players of today, who often improvise their variations. The slow movement of a symphony may also be in the song form, with a first section, a contrasting second section, and a return to the first strain, once more employing the fundamental principle of statement, contrast, and reminder.

The third movement of a symphony is generally lively. In the old days it was traditionally a *minuet*, or *menuetto*, the latter representing a somewhat faster tempo than the regular dance. The minuet was always in triple time, rather slower than the modern waltz, and it had a definite form, again built on the A-B-A principle (statement, contrast, reminder). The first section contained the main theme, usually

Edward Alexander MacDowell (1861–1908), an American composer, was elected to the Hall of Fame in 1964. His work, in a highly romantic style, included two piano concertos, Woodland Sketches *and* Indian Suite.

in two parts, each of which was repeated. The middle section was called the *trio*, because it was originally played by only three instruments. This also consisted of two parts, with repetitions. Finally, the first section, or main theme, was played again, this time without repetition.

Beethoven upset the tradition of the *minuet*, as he did so many others, by substituting a still faster movement which he called *scherzo*, literally meaning "happy" or "jocular."

The *finale* of a symphony is more often fast than slow, perhaps balancing the mood and the pace of the first movement. A finale may have sonata form, possibly some form of variations, perhaps a dance form like the *rondo*. (This was originally a round dance, and it became popular with the classic composers as a form for instrumental music.) A rondo generally has several themes, of which the first is continually brought back after other tunes have been inserted for contrast. If each tune were lettered, the rondo form could be summed up as A, B, A, C, A, D, etc. A concluding coda is quite common. Occasionally an independent rondo has been written.

 ## Music To Hear

Bach: *Sonata No. 2 in D major for Clavier and Viol da Gamba* (piano and cello)
Brahms: *Symphony No. 1 in C minor, Opus 68*
Tchaikovsky: *Symphony No. 4 in F minor, Opus 36*
Schubert: *Symphony No. 8 in B minor ("Unfinished Symphony")*

Culver Pictures

317

The History and Value of Music

Music has always been a vital part of man's life. Here are a few highlights on the western tradition of music, as presented by Sir Arthur Sullivan, one of the most noted of British composers, who while famous for his collaboration in the Gilbert and Sullivan light operas also wrote much religious, symphonic and operatic music. From a lecture, "About Music," given in 1888, and printed in **Sir Arthur Sullivan: Life Story, Letters and Reminiscences** by Arthur Lawrence, published by Herbert S. Stone & Co., Chicago and New York, 1900.

In the account of the origin of mankind as given in the Biblical book of Genesis, we find society divided into three great divisions: (1) agriculturalists, "those that dwell in tents and have cattle," (2) manufacturers, "artificers in brass and iron," (3) musicians, "such as handle the harp and pipe," in other words, strings and wind instruments.

Music is put on a level with such essential pursuits as agriculture and manufacturing. And

A page from a 16th century book of religious music, showing old note form and 4-line staff.

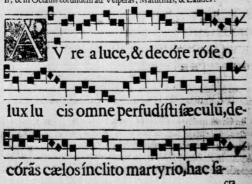

318

this equal share in the economy of the world music has maintained; but belonging as it does to the inmost part of man's nature, its presence is often overlooked. We are as unconcious of it as we are of the air we breathe, the speech we utter, the natural motion of our muscles, or the beating of our hearts.

In line with the descent of musical tradition in the west, in A.D. 550 there was a great gathering and competition of harpists at Conway, in Britain. In 866 King Alfred instituted a professorship of music at Oxford, and there must have been concert music in those Anglo-Saxon times, for in the British Museum is an old picture of a concert employing a six-stringed harp, a four-stringed fiddle, a trumpet, and a horn.

In the tenth century the monk Wulston gave a long description of a grand organ in Winchester Cathedral, and St. Dunstan, famous for his skill in metal work, at the same date fabricated an organ in Malmesbury Abbey, the pipes of which were of brass.

Long before the Conquest, in A.D. 1066, three-part harmony was practiced, and is spoken of by the chroniclers as the "custom of the country." In 1230 a piece of music was composed by the monk John of Fornsete of Reading in six-part harmony. Chaucer, in his "Princesses' Tale," mentions approvingly that young children were taught to sing as much as they were taught to read.

The constitution of military bands in England was also of a very early date. Henry VI, when he went to war with France, took with him a band consisting of ten clarion players and other instrumentalists, who played at headquarters morning and evening. This is the first military band of which we have a record. Queen Elizabeth improved upon it so far as to have a band which played during her dinner, of twelve trumpets, two kettledrums, pipes, cornets, and side drums, and it is written that "this musicke did make the hall ring for half an hour."

The universities of Cambridge and Oxford acknowledged the importance of music by making it a faculty, and granting doctors' degrees, analogous to those granted in Divinity, Law, and Medicine, at a very early date.

There are clear indications that up to the time of the Reformation music was in continual progress. But, unfortunately, the Wars of the Roses and the ruthless destruction which accompanied the suppression of the monasteries (the only homes of art of all kinds in those days) have obliterated almost all but the clearest indications. Following this period, however, there was a revival which paralleled the growth of music on the Continent.

I do not intend to explain why music should be cultivated, or to apologize for its existence, or to speak humbly of its merits; but I claim for it boldly and proudly its place among the great things and the great influences in the world; and I can only express pity for those who are ignorant and stupid enough to deny its importance in the world and in history.

Charles Darwin, in his *Descent of Man,* wrote: "Neither the enjoyment nor the capacity of producing musical notes are faculties of the least direct use to man in reference to his ordinary habits of life." Physiologically he is probably correct, but as soon as merely rudimentary actions are left, as soon as existence becomes life, his statement is completely false. Indeed, he does admit elsewhere that music is bound up in daily life, and is a necessity of existence.

Let us now consider several points about music—its usefulness, its necessity for the mind, and its influence in the world.

As to the practical matter of its use, what would commerce be without the music trades; without the workers who are necessary for the production of every kind of instrument; without those who engrave, typeset, and print music; without even the production of the millions of reams of paper used in music-printing and copying?

When we come to the question of the influence of music, we arrive at its greatest function —the area of its greatest power. Who shall measure the boundless influence of music on human feeling? Who shall dispute the mighty power it exercises over human passions, or deny the dynamic force which it has exerted in history?

In the ancient world it is constantly found associated with eventful episodes. The earliest records of the Bible contain more than one such case; for example, the greatest of the great wells which supplied the Israelites during their wandering in the wilderness is expressly stated to have been dug to the sound of a solemn national music.

In Greece we find that the first definite political revolution in Athens—the murder of Hipparchus the tyrant, and the establishment of free government, as early as 514 B.C.—was consecrated and probably accompanied by a song which is still preserved, the song of Harmodius and Aristogeiton. This song was for generations a rallying cry of the Greek advocates of liberty.

The Reformation in Germany was powerfully advanced by Martin Luther's famous hymn, *Ein feste Burg ist unser Gott* (A Mighty Fortress is Our God) and by his other chorales, which are known to have precipitated the conversion of whole towns to the reformed faith. I need also only mention the military songs such as the German *Wacht am Rhein* and the French *Marseillaise,* both of which fanned national fervor; and of course, for the Briton, there is the tune of mighty force which binds us all together, "God Save the Queen!"

But music needs one thing always—intelligent listeners. People must be educated to appreciate, and appreciation must come before production. But give us intelligent and educated listeners, and there will come forward composers and performers of corresponding worth.

Records To Hear

319

For the person who has some skill with an instrument, the *Music Minus One* records may provide hours of enjoyment. These are recordings of concertos, string quartets, and other similar classical compositions, performed by professional musicians but with either the solo part or one of the group parts omitted. The music for the missing part comes with the record, and the individual can play along with the recorded music as if he were a soloist or member of a group. Almost one hundred *Music Minus One* recordings are available.

How Composers Build Their Music

In order to compose music, one must have a knowledge and understanding of the elements of music—that is, what "building blocks" he has to work with. This article describes the most important of these elements and how they are used. By Judith Cuddihy.

Most of us have sung the scale—*do, re, mi, fa, sol, la, ti, do.* These are the 8 tones of an octave. However, if you play this scale on the piano you will see that there are 12 keys between *do* and the next higher *do*. In our system of music the octave is divided into 12 equal parts, or degrees, and each of these degrees is called a half step.

When a composer writes a piece of music, he usually chooses a pattern of 8 tones (or notes) from the 12 tones of the octave, and from this choice he establishes the main key of the musical piece. From these notes, the composer builds a melodic idea called a *motive* or *figure.* The motive may consist of only a few notes or it may contain several notes. A famous example of a melody, or motive, with only a few notes, is the famous theme on which the first movement of Beethoven's *Fifth Symphony* is composed.

There are several characteristics of the scale that the composer uses to construct his melody. First of all, he knows that certain notes in the scale are more stable than others; this is especially true of *do.* If he ignores *do* in his melody, the music appears aimless and seems to drift. However, if he returns to *do,* the music seems to have arrived somewhere. Thus *do* gives the music a focal point, or center of interest. The composer in constructing his melody must provide a proper balance between tones that lead to others and tones that are points of rest. Notes of longer duration than others are used to emphasize these resting points.

Another consideration the composer must bear in mind while constructing his melodic line is the steps by which the melody moves.

If the steps are narrow ones (conjunct), the melody usually seems emotional and expressive. But if the steps are wide (disjunct), the music seems static and reserved.

The composer also may take into consideration the principle of *musical gravity* in composing his melody. The natural movement of a musical line is downward, while ascending movement of the melody gives a characteristic of tension and energy to the music.

If the same melody were used over and over again in a musical composition, the piece soon would become boring to the listener. Thus the composer must bring variety to his composition by manipulating his motive. There are several methods he may use to do this. The motive can be played backwards, it can be turned upside down, or it can be tilted sideways. The notes of the figure may be changed drastically and the rhythm be maintained unchanged so that the new version is still related to the original motive. In each of these common methods of producing variety, some features of the original motive are maintained. Of course there are many more methods of producing variety with a main motive, and a good composer does this with originality and inventiveness.

When melody occurs by itself, without any additional elements or texture, it is called *monophonic* music. One good example of monophonic music is Gregorian chant. These monophonic melodies may be used to produce more complex types of music—*homophonic* and *polyphonic* music. In homophonic music, the melody is supported by harmonies, or chords, and in polyphonic music the melody is combined with one or more other melodies.

In homophonic music, the melody is the leading voice of the music and it is supported or accompanied by chords. A common example is the church hymn.

A chord is a series of notes sounded simultaneously. The study of these note combinations as blocks of sound is the science of *harmony.* In studying harmony, the composer learns how to handle the chords with the melody so that each chord enriches the meaning of the melody tone to which it is attached.

Each chord has its own quality, and this quality can be affected by chords that occur before or after it, by the melody tones with which it is played, and by variations in rhythm from that of the melody. The composer uses these principles to vary his effect in homophonic music.

We have already discussed ways of bringing variety to a motive, or melodic idea. However, these methods produce only short pieces of music. In order to produce a longer piece of music in the homophonic method, the melody must be developed. The melodic idea may simply be extended by adding new phrases made of material that has already been stated. The composer then may add to the original section (A) a new section that is in the same or in a similar key (B); the original section then may be repeated after the new section (A). This A B A form of music is known as *song form.*

A more complicated method of extending homophonic music is by the *theme and variation* method. The composer begins with a melody in song form: he simply repeats this melody, and each time he repeats it he makes a change in it. The change can be made in the melody or in the harmony, or in both. For instance, the composer may leave the melody and its harmony intact, but change the rhythm of the harmonic accompaniment. The theme and variations may be a separate composition, as the *Diabelli Variations* by Beethoven or the *Goldberg Variations* by Bach, or they may be a movement of a sonata as in the slow movement of Beethoven's *Appassionata Sonata.* A contemporary example of the use of theme and variation is jazz, where one or more musicians improvise many variations as they play.

Polyphonic music is the combination of several smaller voices (or parts), with the melodic interest transferring from one voice to another or even existing in several voices at the same time. Thus the composer begins with a melodic motive and uses it to produce a complicated musical texture quite different from homophonic music. Other terms for polyphonic music are *counterpoint* and *contrapuntal* music.

Because of its complexity, polyphonic music is more difficult to listen to than the types we have already discussed. However, this form is used extensively by all of the great composers.

There is one common type of polyphonic music that is easy to understand; this is the *round.* A common example is *Three Blind Mice.* The melody in a round always consists of sections of equal lengths that are designed to make good harmony with each other. In a three-voiced round, the pattern would be as follows:

Voices	Sections
1	A B C A B C
2	A B C A B
3	A B C A

Each voice repeats the melody several times.

An example of more difficult polyphonic music is the *fugue.* This is a form of music used to great effect by both Bach and Beethoven.

The fugue is based on a short melody which is stated at the beginning of the composition by one voice. It is then stated in succession by each of the other voices in the fugue. When a voice is not stating the subject, it plays freely invented counterpoint. The fugue may have only two voices or it may have as many as eight or more voices; these voices may enter the fugue in any order.

The first section of the fugue in which the theme appears at least once in each voice is called the *exposition.* Exposition sections are separated by *episode* sections that do not have a statement of the theme. Thus the overall structure of the fugue is an alternation between exposition and episode sections. In the first exposition section the statements of the theme are close together, but in later expositions, theme statements are more widely spaced.

Although some music is composed with greater emphasis on rhythm and tone color than on melodic motives, most music uses the techniques described here. These techniques are often combined and elaborated upon in a piece of music, but they usually can be identified through careful listening.

321

Resplendent in bright uniforms, the Band of the Grenadier Guards passes Buckingham Palace in London. Like bands everywhere, their precision of marching, gleaming brass instruments, and stirring music lend color and drama to public events.

Bands and Band Music

A band uses all the instruments of a symphony orchestra except strings. The many military and civic functions of bands often take place out of doors making it necessary to increase volume level so that the music may be heard. For this reason woodwinds are often used instead of strings.

The various kinds of bands have separate functions. For instance, a brass band uses no woodwinds at all and usually carries a large section of brass horns and percussion instruments. The military band is mainly brass and usually marches in parades. The concert band uses many woodwinds and percussion instruments and is often heard on summer weekends in parks in large cities, small towns and on college campuses.

One of the problems of band music is that there is so little of it. Most of the music is adapted from pieces originally written for orchestras. Most of these are not particularly noteworthy. Two band masters who composed especially for wind bands were John Philip Sousa and Edwin Franko Goldman. They also wrote books and articles about band conducting. Some orchestral composers who wrote interesting scores for wind bands were Arnold Schönberg, Ralph Vaughan Williams, Hector Berlioz, Darius Milhaud, Albert Roussel and Ottorino Respighi.

Many European towns of the sixteenth and seventeenth centuries hired their own bands of musicians to play at fairs and festivals, as well as to sound the hours from the church towers and provide trombone and cornet chorales at special hours. These first town bands were quite small, gradually increasing in number in the eighteenth century when they became regimented to perform both civic and military duties.

The Shakespearian theaters had a little tower high above the stage, where a small band of musicians played for the performances and sometimes during the entrance of an important member of the audience.

The very large wind bands began to appear during the French Revolution and during the reign of Napoleon I, when there were always many occasions for outdoor celebrations and demonstrations. Other countries adopted the idea of the large civic band and there emerged a rivalry between national bands, each having its own unique instrumentations.

College bands which perform during the half time break at football games usually must be able to march as well as to create the customary elaborate group formations on the field, thus providing additional entertainment for the spectators. Very often the same musicians also play in the schools' concert band or orchestra.

Your Musical Dictionary

Adagio: Slow time, hence a slow movement in a symphony.

Allegro: Literally "happy, cheerful," hence lively, in rapid time. Frequently applied to the first movement of a symphony, particularly after a slow introduction. *Allegretto:* not as fast as *Allegro*.

Alto: The deeper female voice, singing the second part in a mixed quartet also known as contralto. Often applied to the second part in any harmony, and to instruments playing such a part (especially horns).

Andante: Italian for "going, moving, walking"; hence a moderately slow pace in music, faster than *Adagio*, but slower than *Allegretto*. Frequently applied to the slow movement of a symphony.

Band: A company of musicians. Now applied specifically to a brass band, as differentiated from an orchestra, or to a jazz or dance band. Also used of one section of a symphony orchestra, such as the wood-wind or brass.

Baritone: The male voice between bass and tenor. Also an instrument in that range.

Brass: The adjective applied in general to all wind instruments made of metal (except the silver flute, which is included among the wood winds, as it was originally made of wood). The brass choir or section of a symphony orchestra includes trumpets, trombones, and bass tuba, as well as French horns, although these are generally seated with the wood winds. A brass band uses mostly metal instruments, including cornets, alto horns, etc.

Cadenza: Italian for an elaborate solo interlude, technically brilliant, to show off a soloist. *Cadenzas* are frequent in vocal music of the coloratura style.

Cantata: A type of vocal music, often sacred, using soloists and chorus, with instrumental accompaniment. (Originally any vocal piece.)

Cappella: Italian for chapel, hence choir, chorus, sometimes an orchestra or both combined.

Choral: Pertaining to a chorus or choir; applied to instrumental music that has the effect of choral voices. As a noun, also spelled *Chorale*, a sacred melody or hymn-tune of the German Protestant type, such as Bach arranged.

Chord: A harmony of tones, usually three or more, sounding together.

Chorus: A group of singers, or choir. Also the refrain in vocal music.

Chromatic: Literally, "colorful." The chromatic scale includes all the half tones (on the piano, black and white keys) in an octave, and has twelve different tones.

From *Great Symphonies: How To Recognize and Remember Them* by Sigmund Spaeth; distributed by Comet Press Books. Copyright 1952 by Sigmund Spaeth; used by permission of the author.

Clef: Literally, "key." A character or sign set at the start of a piece of music to indicate the pitch of all the following notes. Each line and space on the staff represents a different note, according to the clef at the start. The commonest clefs are the treble and bass, appearing regularly in piano music.

Coda: Italian for tail; hence the closing section of a movement.

Coloratura: In Italian, "colorful," referring to the brilliant technical feats of a singer with a flexible voice. Also applied to instrumental music containing such ornaments.

Contralto: See **Alto.**

Counterpoint: ("Counter" means "against") music written "point against point," or note against note, polyphonically, one melody harmonizing with another. **Countermelody:** a melody harmonizing with another.

Crescendo: Italian for "increasing in volume."

Diatonic: Literally "by tones," referring to the standard major or minor scale of eight notes. (See **Chromatic.**)

Duet: A composition or passage for two voices or instruments.

Expression mark: A sign, word or phrase, giving directions for the interpretation of a piece of music.

Finale: The closing movement in a symphony, sonata, concerto, etc. The final part.

Flat: A musical character which lowers the pitch of a note by half a tone. Used as a verb and adjective, referring to playing or singing below pitch (out of tune).

Grosso: Italian for great, grand, full. **Concerto grosso:** great concerto.

Harmony: The organizing factor in music which produces pleasing effects from the simultaneous sounding of two or more tones. A chord. The accompaniment to a melody.

Homophonic: Having a single melody, accompanied by chords, etc. Opposite of polyphonic.

Improvisation: Music composed and played on the spot.

Interlude: A connecting passage, not necessarily related to the preceding or following music.

Intermezzo: An elaborate form of interlude.

Key: The melodic and harmonic basis of a scale or composition. Keynote. The key of a piece is indicated by the signature (showing the number of sharps or flats).

Largo: Literally large, broad; hence, slow in time, stately.

Major and Minor: Literally "greater" and "lesser." Actually the difference between major and minor keys or chords is one of mood, the former often suggesting cheerfulness, the latter melancholy.

Motif: Motive. A short phrase or motto, containing basic melodic material, yet not a complete tune.

Movement: One of the divisions of a symphony, sonata, etc.

Octave: The eighth step in the diatonic scale. The interval between the first and the eighth tone. A series of eight tones in the diatonic scale.

Opus: Latin for "work." Often abbreviated to *Op.* The term applies to the works of a composer (sometimes to a group of works of the same type), each opus being given a number, according to the time of composition or publication. Low opus numbers usually indicate early works.

Overture: The instrumental introduction to an opera or a play.

Part: The music written for any one instrument in the orchestra. Also a division or section in any movement or composition.

Passage: Any logical succession of notes in a piece of music. A repeated figure or pattern.

Percussion: Instruments of percussion are those which are struck instead of blown or bowed or plucked, such as drums, cymbals, tambourine, castanets, bells, triangle, xylophone, piano.

Period: A complete musical theme, thought, or subject, from eight to twelve or sixteen measures in length, ending in a "cadence" or close.

Phrase: A short melodic pattern or figure, complete in itself, but possibly only part of a theme.

Polyphonic: Having several independent melodies or voices which harmonize with each other; contrapuntal; many-voiced.

Prelude: A musical introduction.

Program music: Music that tells a story, or paints a picture, rather than a mere pattern of tones.

Quartet: A group of four instruments or voices, or the music for it.

Quintet: A group of five instruments or voices (French, *Quintour*) or the music for it.

Refrain: A short chorus, repeated after each stanza of a song.

Rhythm: The organizing factor in music which regulates and measures the time beats or accents. Often used as meaning time in general, but actually a broader aspect of the measure of music, having to do with groups of tones, phrases.

Rondo: Originally a round dance; now an instrumental form of music in which the main theme alternates with others, ending in a *Coda*.

Scale: A regular progression of tones in major or minor key (diatonic). If all the half tones are included, the scale is called chromatic.

Scherzo: Literally, a "joke" or "jest." (Italian.) Applied by Beethoven and later composers to the fast movement of a symphony, formerly called *Menuetto*. Also used of independent compositions in that mood.

Score: The complete notation of a piece of music. (The conductor's score contains all the parts.)

Serenade: Literally, "evening song," hence a composition in that style.

Sextet: A group of six voices or instruments, or a composition for such a group.

Sharp: The sign that raises the pitch of a note by half a tone. Also used of any note so marked.

Solo: Italian for "alone." Hence a part or passage played by one instrument, or sung by one voice, or an entire composition of this type.

Sonata: Originally an instrumental piece, as contrasted with a *Cantata*, to be sung. Later, a solo (mostly for piano or violin) in three movements.

Song: A poem set to music. **Song form:** the form generally taken by a simple song, with two contrasting sections, A and B, ending in a repetition of A. (The A section is often repeated also before B.)

Soprano: The highest voice in a mixed quartet or chorus. Also applied to instruments playing such parts.

Suite: A set of dances or other forms of composition loosely strung together.

Symphony orchestra: An orchestra capable of playing a symphony (requiring generally at least sixty to eighty-five players).

Tempo: Italian for "time." Used for the rate of speed, not time in general.

Tenor: The high male voice, hence the corresponding part in a quartet or chorus.

Theme: A tune, a melody, a subject for development or elaboration in music.

Time: The measure of music, indicated by the grouping of beats. Duple time runs in multiples of two, triple time in multiples of three.

Tone: A musical sound, caused by regular vibrations of the air.

Tonic: The keynote of a scale or composition.

Trio: A composition for three instruments, or a group of three players or singers. Also part of a march.

Virtuoso: A highly skilled instrumental soloist.

Wood wind: The wooden wind instruments of an orchestra (including the flute).

Some Romantic, Impressionist and Modernist Composers

Robert Schumann
1810–1856

Outstandingly original among Romantic composers, Schumann, a German, intended to be a concert pianist. A lamed hand changed this, but led to his composing, in which his interests remained with the piano. His genius is best shown in his Piano Concerto and in his symphonies.

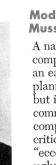

Modest Petrovitch Mussorgsky   1839–1881

A nationalistic Russian composer, Mussorgsky showed an early aptitude for music. He planned a career in the army, but in 1858 resigned his commission and turned completely to music. Early criticism called his works "eccentric and barbarously ugly." His best known work is *Boris Godunov.*

Peter Ilich Tchaikovsky
1840–1893

Born in Votkinsk, Russia, Tchaikovsky studied under Rubenstein at the St. Petersburg Conservatory and rapidly developed into a composer. His music has been described as "frankly sentimental." He composed in all genres; best known of his works are *Swan Lake,* his six symphonies, and the Piano Concerto No. 1, B Flat Minor.

Antonin Dvořák
1841–1904

The spirit of folk music, especially that of his birthplace, Bohemia, was the element that gave life to Dvořák's music. He studied in Prague, at first taking Schubert and Beethoven for models; later his music became more nationalistic. His famous *From the New World* Symphony was written in the United States.

Jean Sibelius
1865–1957

Sibelius stands as one of the greatest symphonists of the 20th century, and his music is a nationalistic monument to his native Finland. He began to compose at an early age while studying the violin. The history and legends of his country inspired his greatest works, including the stirring tone poem *Finlandia.*

Arnold Schönberg
1874–1951

Schönberg, born in Vienna, developed a new kind of music based on successions of fourths and a twelve-tone technique. His early work was tonal and somewhat romantic. His later work moved toward expressionism and atonality. His most often played work is the passionate *Verklärte Nacht* (Transfigured Night).

Maurice Ravel
1875–1937

Unjustly accused of plagiarizing Debussy, Ravel was, in truth, a composer of genius and originality. Born in Ciboure, France, he studied at the Conservatoire in Paris, making his public debut as a composer in 1898. His stirring *Bolero* and the ballet *Daphnis and Chloe* are extremely popular.

Dmitri Shostakovich
1906–

Honored by the State and at the same time decried as a composer of "jittery, noisy and neurotic music," Shostakovich is one of the most brilliant Soviet composers. He began composing early, after studying at St. Petersburg Conservatory, and has written an opera and many orchestral works.

Noah's Ark, drawn by artist Hans Fischer, on a schoolroom wall near Zurich, Switzerland.

Animal Art and Artists

Why are people so fascinated by animals?

We love them, yet fear them; we make them pets, yet enjoy hunting them. We read about them, watch them in movies, study them, and pay taxes to support zoos. Often we feel that we find human qualities in them.

Perhaps we feel this way because many animals have been our servants, guardians, and friends for thousands of years, while others have been traditional enemies or pests. We might not be here at all if early man had not learned to protect himself from animals and to use animals for food, clothing, tools, and weapons. And surely civilization would have grown much more slowly if animals had not been tamed to help with the heavy work of farming, building, and transportation.

So important have animals been that people have worshiped them as gods (the hawk-headed Osiris of Egypt), and men have been named for them—Chief Sitting Bull and King Richard I (Richard, the Lion-Hearted), for example. We still use them as national emblems, such as the American eagle and the British lion.

326

Today, because of the help of science and machines, we depend a little less directly on animals for our existence in some parts of the world, but who forgets old friends? Because of their beauty and grace, their interesting habits, they will always be fun to watch, to be with, and to study.

In these pages you will find an artists' zoo of animals formed from stone, paint, metal, clay, and cloth. They come from many ages, from all around the world. Animals have inspired some of our finest art, as you will see in this section. They will delight you as they did the people who created them.

—Margaret Tomec Zamiska

Will Burtin, SCOPE, The Upjohn Co.

Animal Art Around the World

The Japanese fish-print is made by a fascinating method which few people outside of Japan have mastered. To create as accurate and beautiful a print as the one above, the steps illustrated at the right are followed. 1, The freshly caught fish is carefully cleaned and pinned to a board while moderately wet. 2, A sheet of thin, strong rice paper is gently molded over the fish. 3, With a small wad of cotton wrapped in cloth, ink is lightly dabbed onto the paper. 4, The paper is carefully peeled off.

Early man spent much of his time hunting and fishing, and many paintings and sculptures which were made thousands of years ago are of animals. The ancient rock painting (below) is in the Rocky Mountain region near Vernal, Utah. The animals shown in the painting are still found in the Rocky Mountains; can you tell what they are?

1

2

3

4

Cities Serv. Co., by N. J. Parrino

This beautiful Chinese painting of a horse and willow tree is painted on silk. The artist was more interested in the twisted line that the rope forms than the straight, natural way in which a real rope hangs, but it is just this that makes this painting so pleasing to the eye.

Albrecht Dürer drew this picture of a little owl in 1508, when students of animal life were becoming very interested in such correct and exact drawings of specimens. Dürer may have seen some of Leonardo da Vinci's careful animal and plant drawings during a visit he made to Italy in 1495.

328

This ferocious cock was drawn in colored chalk by Pablo Picasso, the Spanish artist, in 1939. Picasso's style is simple, clear, and strong.

De naturis serpentum.

An English artist painted this giant serpent and struggling elephant for an animal book about A. D. 1200. The text of the book, partly true and partly rumors, was not as important to the book's owners as the pictures. As anyone who has seen an elephant can tell, the pictures were more beautiful than correct.

This picture of two elephants comes from a book made at a king's command. About A. D. 1290, the great Ghazan Khan, ruler of Persia, commanded that a book about animals be made. The pictures are fairly accurate in their detail, and often quite decorative as well.

About 150 years ago, an Indian artist made this fine picture of a prince riding an elephant. The lively colors help make it a most attractive animal picture.

329

Franz Marc, a German painter of the twentieth century, painted these deer in a simplified style. In 1937, German government officials took it from a museum and sold it because they didn't like it. Would you have kept it?

These sketches of birds by a Japanese artist show the soft coloring and carefully drawn lines typical of Oriental art. At the bottom of the picture is a sketch in which the artist tried to suggest the movement of a walking bird.

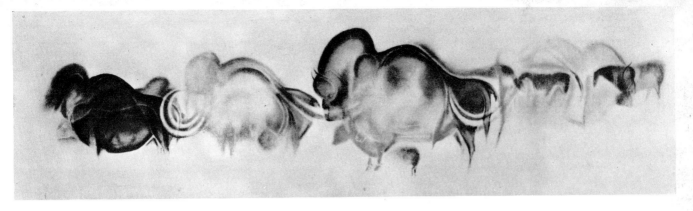

A frieze (decorative band) of mammoths, bison, horses, and reindeer from the cavern of
Font-de-Gaume, Dordogne, France. If you look closely you can see that the bigger animals have
been drawn right over some of the smaller ones by a later artist. Some people guess that the
hunters of the Ice Age believed these pictures would bring them good luck in hunting.

Animal Art Was the First Art

When the last of the great glaciers covered much of Europe, probably between 30,000 B.C. and
10,000 B.C., man was creating some of his first and finest art. The subjects he painted on the walls
of his cave home were the most important things in his life—animals. The cave paintings on
this page were found in southern France and northern Spain.

A five-year-old girl first discovered the beautiful
paintings like this in the Cave of Altamira,
northern Spain. The boar seems to have extra legs
because he is drawn directly over another one.
Many similar cave paintings in this area have
been found by boys and girls.

Another painting from Font-de-Gaume (left), this one a
beautifully clear picture of a woolly rhinoceros.
He is a little over two feet long and is outlined on a
light background. The colors of these cave paintings
range from pale yellow through reds, brown, and black
and were made from charcoal and minerals.

Photos on this page, Amer. Mus. Nat. Hist.

Animal Art of
Ancient Civilizations

The people of ancient civilizations have left many records of their interest in animals. On these pages you will find examples of animal art from Egypt, Assyria, Babylon, the island of Crete, Greece, and Rome—civilizations that once existed near the Mediterranean.

The ancient Egyptians believed that when life on this earth was over, all the good things of life would go with them into a new world. For this reason they filled their tombs with food, clothing, jewelry, and figures of the animals that they raised for food, hunted for sport, or kept as pets. Figures like this well-modeled bronze cat (above, left) are often found in tombs, many with saucers for milk beside them. Above, these jumping mice, called jerboas, were put into a tomb near the Nile Delta about 3,000 years ago. Perhaps they were meant to be food for a tomb cat. They are made of faience (a fine earthenware glazed with bright colors and designs).

332

The hippopotamus was once a favorite hunter's quarry along the banks of the Nile River. Perhaps that is why this friendly-looking hippo was included in a tomb household about 3,000 years ago. He is also made of faience, bright blue and green, and decorated with Nile lotus blossoms.

Photos on this page, Met. Mus. of Art

One of the most exciting hunting scenes ever created is this carving of the
Assyrian king, Ashurbanipal, hunting lions from his chariot.
Neighbors of the Egyptians, the Assyrians lived in what is now the
country of Iraq for about 2,000 years before the birth of Christ.

The Greeks were skilled potters, and one of them decorated this jug with
an imaginative parade of rams and tigers. The jug was made about
500 B.C.

Sheep were an important part of the wealth of the Babylonians,
neighbors and rivals of the Assyrians. This figure of a ram was used as
a weight in some Babylonian market long ago. It is carved from
basalt, a dark rock that forms when a flow of lava cools. The artist
merely suggested the figure, without using much detail.

Circuses on the island of Crete,
near Greece, were lively affairs.
The acrobats worked with bulls
instead of the horses used today.
This mural from the great
palace in the city of Knossos
shows a girl who has just
somersaulted between the horns
of a racing bull and is about to
be caught by a partner. This
painting was made about
1500 B.C.

Art Inst. of Chicago

The wolf is a favorite legendary figure in Roman history, since a wolf is supposed to have cared for two little orphaned boys, Romulus and Remus, who grew up to found the city of Rome. This extremely realistic wolf's head with a ring in its mouth was used to tie a Roman ship to the dock.

Met. Mus. of Art

The sculptors of Greece are admired for their artistry in carving human figures, but animals also played a great part in their decorations. This little bronze horse (right) who seems to be stepping out smartly, perhaps to military music, was probably once part of a procession. He was made about 470 B.C.

A dramatic moment from the life of the Roman emperor, Hadrian (A.D. 117–138). The stone medallion shows Hadrian about to bring down a wild boar. Though the men seem very calm, the artist has captured the fierceness of the boar and the excitement of the horses.

Boys and girls have probably always enjoyed playing with animal toys. These bronze oxen (below) yoked to a cart, were the plaything of a Roman child perhaps as long ago as 100 B.C.

Met. Mus. of Art

Thomas Bewick (1753–1828), an English wood engraver, made this illustration as well as many others for Aesop's fables. He was one of the finest wood engravers of all time and almost always chose animals as his subjects. (You can see more of Bewick's work in "Art and the Printed Word," in Volume 7.)

Thomas Hugo, BEWICK'S WOODCUTS, L. Reeve & Co., London

The Fox and the Crow

According to some legends, the man who first told this story was Aesop, a slave at the palace of the wealthy Greek king, Croesus, about two thousand years ago. He made up wonderfully funny tales about animals, which were really meant to show up the follies of people. From **Aesop's Fables** in a new translation for modern readers. Copyright 1941 by Peter Pauper Press.

A Fox once saw a Crow fly from a kitchen window with a piece of cheese in its beak, and settle in a tree to eat the delicacy. So the Fox walked up to the foot of the tree. "Crow," he cried, "How beautiful you are looking today! how glossy your feathers are, how bright your eyes! I am sure your voice, too, is more lovely than that of other birds!" At this the vain Crow began to caw her very best, but the moment she opened her mouth the piece of cheese fell to the ground, and was snatched by the Fox. "That will do," said he, as he ran away. "That was all I wanted, and in exchange I will give you a piece of advice: Don't trust flatterers."

 Other Books To Read

335

The Caves of the Great Hunters, by Hans Baumann. Published by Pantheon Books, Inc., New York, revised edition, 1962.
Exciting and true, the story of four boys who discovered one of the great picture-gallery caves of the Ice Age.

Born Free: A Lioness of Two Worlds, by Joy Adamson. Published by Pantheon Books, Inc., New York, 1960.
Elsa's two worlds were captivity and freedom. She was raised as the pet of an English couple who later retrained her, changing her from a family pet to a fierce lioness. Elsa's biography is illustrated with superb photographs of the heroine as a cub and as a young lioness.

Smoky, the Cow Horse, by Will James. Published by Charles Scribner's Sons, New York, 1929.
A story that has been a favorite since it was published. It is famous for its excellent animal illustrations done by the author.

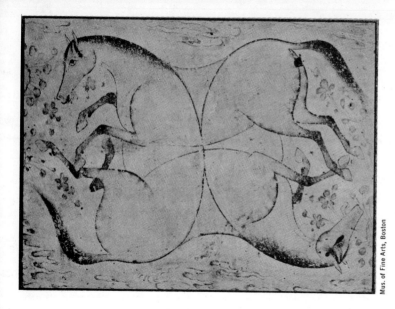

How many horses do you see? Turn the book around and you will see more. An early 17th-century Persian painter had fun making a picture puzzle while he was creating a beautiful horse drawing. You could make a puzzle drawing like this yourself.

Animal Art from the East

In the Eastern world there is an especially beautiful and pleasing tradition of using animals as art subjects. Examples from Persia, India, China, and Japan are shown here.

This embroidered square, made in India some time in the 18th century, shows how and what the men of India hunted. It is cotton gauze sewed with silk threads and tinsel. How many animals can you identify?

A zebra, with all his vibrating stripes, captured in paint by a famous Indian artist of the 17th century, Ustadi Mansur.

The Chinese sculptor who made this bronze seemed to think if one elephant was good, two would be better! The elephants are made very decorative with the raised designs swirled on their hides. It was probably made hundreds of years before the birth of Christ.

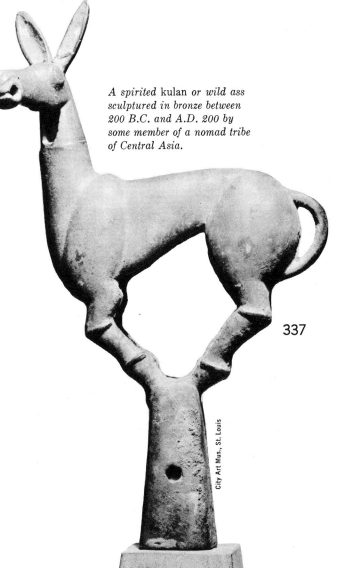

A spirited kulan *or wild ass sculptured in bronze between 200 B.C. and A.D. 200 by some member of a nomad tribe of Central Asia.*

337

Another embroidered square, this one from 18th-century China, centers a pleased tiger in a mass of color-ful trees, plants, and flowers.

Monkeys, birds, and a gnarled tree were used to make this beautiful design. Can you see the baby monkey on its mother's back at the far right? This Japanese painting was made in the 15th century.

These exquisitely "drawn" carp are not drawn at all, but woven of silk velvet. The textile was made in Japan in the last century.

338

The Japanese have been noted for centuries for their delicate skill in drawing and painting animal life. This ink drawing (12th century) is from a 41-foot panel which shows animals behaving like people. The frog on the right has told a good joke, and the rabbit is rolling on the ground with laughter.

*Made to be used in a medieval
church service, this copper dove
glitters like a real bird because
of enamel decorations in green,
yellow, turquoise, dark blue,
red, and black. The wings lift
up to show a space where the
communion wafer was kept. It
was made in France in the 1300's.*

Animal Art and Artists of Europe

The great artists of Europe have been as fascinated with animals as the unknown craftsmen
of ancient times. Italy, France, Spain, Holland, Germany, and England are represented on this and the
following two pages.

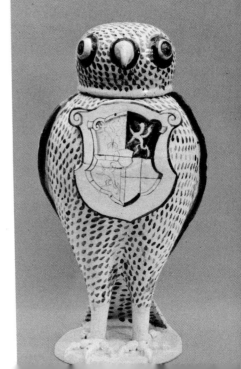

*A frivolous cow with bangs and flowers, made of tin-enameled
earthenware. She was modeled in the 1700's in Delft, Holland,
an important pottery center.*

*A pottery owl, used as a drinking vessel in 16th-century
Germany. Perhaps he looks so proud because he bears the
coat of arms of a royal German family, the Hohenzollerns.*

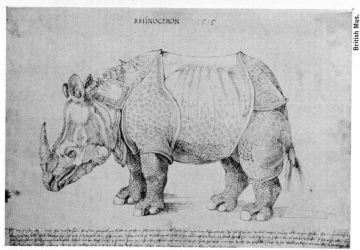

In the 1400's Europeans suddenly became interested
in natural science. Many famous artists helped this
new interest by making drawings of animals, birds,
and flowers from life or from eye witness accounts.
Albrecht Dürer, a German artist of the 1500's, did his
best to draw a rhinoceros from what he had heard
about them, but the result is rather a fantastic version.
Leonardo da Vinci, an Italian artist-scientist-
engineer of the same period, was much more successful
with his drawing of a goat.

340

One of the first successful equestrian (a man on horseback) bronzes to be made is this monument to a great
Italian soldier of the 15th century. The sculptor was
Andrea del Verrocchio, an Italian. Bronzes of such great
size and weight were extremely difficult to cast, but once
the problem had been solved such statues became a very
popular form of art.

Sir Edwin Landseer, (1802–1873) the English artist
who painted Shoeing the Bay Mare, is a favorite painter
of animals. He drew animals so well, even as a child,
that two of his drawings were shown at the Royal
Academy in London when he was only thirteen.
Landseer did many popular paintings like this scene
in the blacksmith shop.

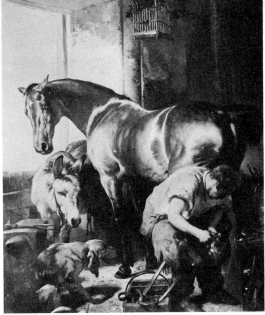

Courtesy Review Pictures, Review and Herald Publishing Association

Met. Mus. of Art

The Spanish feel that bullfighting is an art in itself, and
many of their best artists have been inspired by scenes
at the bull ring. Francisco Goya (1746–1828) caught
the life-and-death suspense of the bullfight in this
lithograph.

Detroit Inst. of Arts

341

Georges Braque (born
1882), modern French
artist, made fish the center
of attraction in his still
life, Red Mullet.
Compare them with the
Japanese carp on
page 338.

The Tropics and Their Animals

In the tropics, animals are probably as important to people today as they were hundreds of years ago. Perhaps that is why the people of the tropics are still creating some of the most interesting animal art in the world.

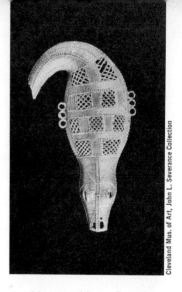

A golden crocodile, modern, from West Africa's Gold Coast, displays the same skill and taste for decoration as the workmanship of the Benin rooster.

Pork is a favorite food in the Pacific islands, so this pig (below) makes an appropriate bowl for food. He comes from one of the Solomon Islands. The wood has been dyed black and decorated with pieces of polished nautilus shell. Two cowrie shells make the eyes.

Met. Mus. of Art

The old kingdom of Benin (Nigeria, Western Africa) was producing bronze castings like this beautifully decorated rooster (above) when Europeans first visited there in 1472.

342

Photos on this page, not otherwise credited, by Friedrich Hewicker, KUNST DER SÜDSEE, Hauswedell & Co. Hamburg

From New Ireland (another Pacific island), a hawk, delicately carved of pale wood and painted black, white, and red. It holds a snake, and two small birds are on its wings. The artist has made the wings look like decorative panels. Figures like this are displayed at funerals.

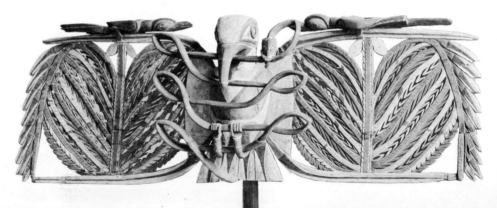

In the Americas

When man first arrived in the Americas is still something of a mystery. But wherever he has been he has left portraits of his animal companions. Here are a few examples of New World animal art.

Fat little ceramic dogs like this one have been made for hundreds of years by the Tarascan Indians around Colima, in southwestern Mexico. Originally they were put into tombs so that people would have them for companions on the way to the other world.

Museo Nacional de Antropologia, Mexico

Peabody Mus., Harvard Univ.

343

The graceful pottery fish (above) with its diamond-patterned scales is from the Andes Mountains of Peru. The shaggy-coated llama (right) was made of silver by an Inca Indian artist high in the Andes about 500 years ago.

Amer. Mus. Nat. Hist.

A stone pipe in the form of a hawk, made in Ohio by the Eastern Woodland Indians, possibly two thousand years ago.

Ohio State Mus.

This jaunty wooden rooster was a merry-go-round figure in the late 1800's, until American carousel makers found that boys and girls preferred to ride horses. Compare him with the African rooster on page 342.

The Lazy Lion, from Helen Wing's book of the same name, illustrated by Jan B. Balet. An example of the fine animal art to be found today in books for young people.

Nat'l Gallery of Art, Index of Amer. Design

Container Corp. of Amer.

Copr. 1932 James Thu
Orig. in THE NEW YOR

A thoughtful hound (right, above) drawn by James Thurber, American humorist. A Chinese dog (right, below) sculptured from jade centuries ago. Do you notice a resemblance?

Met. Mus. of Art

John James Audubon (1785–1851) was one of the world's truly fine animal artists. He also had a scientific interest in birds, insects, and animals and wanted to paint them accurately as well as beautifully. To do that he wandered down the Mississippi, drawing and painting wildlife in its natural surroundings and in characteristic poses. Today we have hundreds of his drawings, many of them precious records of species which have become extinct. Arctic Hare is an example of Audubon's rare skill in depicting animal life.

Modern photography has provided a new medium for animal art. Here are camera pictures of penguins and giraffes by Ylla, noted photographer of animals.

345

346

FIELD AND STREAM Mag., by W. M. Kretschmer

Fishing and Hunting

Fishing and hunting rate first and second, respectively, in popularity over all other sports in the United States. Four times more money is spent on fishing than on all other outdoor sports combined, except hunting. In one year during the early 1950's, nearly seventy million dollars were spent on hunting and fishing licenses alone! This fact surprises most people. So many other sports—baseball, basketball, and football, for instance—create more public excitement and take up more space in the sports sections of newspapers and magazines.

What are some of the probable reasons for the popularity of fishing and hunting? Most people like to be out of doors, and they like to hunt and fish because they can enjoy the beauty of streams, trees, hills, and clouds whether they have any game to take home or not. These are sports that can be done alone if a person craves solitude or with others if he wants companionship. And practically anyone can hunt and fish: boys and girls, young and old, city and country people, rich and poor. While it is true that many people can and do spend large sums of money on fishing tackle, rods, reels, guns, and ammunition, a lot of expensive equipment isn't necessary. In some countries in the past, fishing and hunting were sports of the wealthy classes only, because the landowners controlled most of the hunting and fishing grounds. Anyone caught taking game from these estates was severely punished for "poaching," as it was called. We are more fortunate today. It is true that there are game preserves where people are not allowed to fish or hunt, and there are laws against taking certain kinds of game during the spawning and breeding seasons. However, by making game birds, animals, and fish more plentiful, such laws actually improve the fishing and hunting in our country.

The Lure
of Lake and Stream

Do you know the difference between fly and bait
casting? Between a dry and a wet fly? Do you know which
insects are best for live bait? Ellsworth Jaeger is
famous as a writer and lecturer on camping, fishing,
and outdoor life in general. Here he shares with
you his wide knowledge of fresh-water fishing. This
selection from Ellsworth Jaeger: **Woodsmoke**. Copyright
1953 by The Macmillan Company and used with
The Macmillan Company's permission.

Fishing is an art, a skill, a relaxation, a sport.
A true fisherman is as delighted with the big
fellow that got away as with the trophies he
has in his den. In fact, the former makes a
better story—and what true fisherman doesn't
like a story? But the true fisherman is always
a sportsman. He always gives his quarry a
chance for its life. Fishing is one of the few
delights that are of lifetime duration. It will
give you adventure and thrills that are just
as keen at eighty as they are at eight.

However, the catching of fish alone is not

FIELD AND STREAM Mag.

Away to the brook,
All your tackle out-look,
Here's a day that is worth a year's wishing.
See that all things be right,
For 'twould be a spite
To want tools when a man goes a fishing.

Charles Cotton, *Cotton's Poems*, 1689

the chief aim or delight of angling. The true
fisherman realizes that the real pleasure in
this king of sports comes from fair play, sportsmanship, and the matching of skill and wits
with his finny antagonist, the fish.

There are four outstanding types of angling
—fly casting, bait casting, trolling, and bait
fishing.

What Is Fly Casting?

Fly casting is the most sportsman-like and perhaps the most difficult of all the fishing skills.
There are two types of fly casting, known as
wet- and dry-fly fishing.

Most fresh-water game fish are voracious
feeders of living insects, and will readily rise
for artificial fly lures. Trout, bass, and salmon
are at the top of the list when it comes to
flies. However, shad, rock bass, pickerel, and
others will readily respond to artificial flies.

Each type of fly fishing has its own tackle.
For instance, in wet-fly fishing, a nine and
one-half foot rod weighing about five and
one-half ounces is the favored type. It should
be pliant (bend easily), yet be strong enough
to carry a good length of line. Dry-fly rods
are less pliant than wet-fly types because
longer casts are necessary (that is, a greater
length of line is let out). Many fishermen
prefer expensive split bamboo rods, but beginners can find light fly rods at a price that
will fit most pocketbooks.

Fly-casting reels are usually of light metal
with a spool carrying sixty to one hundred
feet of line. Be sure that your reel fits the
rod, for reel attachments vary in design. Fish
line of the best enameled silk is preferred by
most fishermen. Leaders are lengths of light
but strong gut, about six feet long, used to
attach the flies to the line. The wet-fly leaders
have two or three loops for flies while the
dry-fly leader has no loops because dry-fly
fishermen never use more than one fly at a time.

Which Fly To Use?

There are hundreds of different types of artificial flies, of both wet and dry variety.

A dry fly floats upon the surface of the
water like a newly hatched or tired insect;

Dry flies are made of oiled materials to make them float on the water. The wings usually stand up at right angles to the body.

Royal Coachman   Stone Fly

Wet flies sink because they are made of absorbent materials. The wings usually sweep back in a horizontal line with the body.

A fly rod may be made of cane, fiber-glas, steel, or beryllium copper. The reel is attached to the bottom surface of the butt.

casting rod

Bait-casting rods may be made of cane, bamboo, laminated wood (layers of several woods glued together), steel, beryllium copper, fiberglas, or aluminum alloys.

From Johnston's Sport Shop, by John J. Rea

fly rod

a wet fly sinks beneath the surface of the water when it is pulled along. The flies are often good imitations of the insects in the water at the time you are fishing. Select the flies most like these insects, and you will be more likely to attract any fish that may be feeding in the vicinity. A fisherman needs to be a good observer and he has to have some knowledge of insect bait.

A few of the wet flies used to catch brook trout are the Parmachene Belle, Royal Coachman, Silver Doctor, Brown Hackle, Grizzly King, Professor, and Queen of the Waters. For rainbow trout, add Wickham's Fancy, Golden Spinner, and King of the Waters. Brown trout like, in addition to many of the above, such wet flies as Cahill, Great Dun, Cow Dung, and Hare's Ear, while bass may prefer Scarlet Ibis, Colonel Fuller, or Montreal. Salmon wet flies include Alexandria, Jock Scott, and Silver Doctor.

Dry flies, many of which have the same names as those mentioned in the wet-fly list, are also appetizing to brook, rainbow, and brown trout. Bass and salmon flies are gaily colored and tinseled, while trout lures usually are made to resemble insects as closely as possible.

The dry-fly fisherman usually goes to the foot of a pool and casts his fly *up the stream.* The dry fly which rests lightly on the surface, floats down; if a fish strikes (takes the bait) there is a rush and a whirl of water, and the fly disappears. The fisherman, as quick as a flash, will give a twist of his wrist to set the hook in the fish's jaws, otherwise the fish may get rid of the fly. When hooked, the trout will put up a real battle, and only skillful maneuvering will weary it enough for the net to be slipped under it.

Wet-fly fishing is done by casting the wet

FIELD AND STREAM Mag., Int'l News photo

The older fisherman teaches the younger some fine points in the art of fly fishing.

| Professor | Parmachene Belle | Silver Doctor | Western Bee | Red Ant | Scarlet Ibis |

fly *downstream* across the swift-running water. While the wet fly is designed for use under water, it is not allowed to sink more than an inch or so. It is most successful in swift water.

How To Fish with Plugs

Bait or plug casting requires a shorter fishing rod than fly casting. The rod should be about as tall as you are and should be quite stiff. The reel will be attached so that you hold the butt of the rod below it while your thumb regulates the spool. The reel has a free spool that allows the line to run out freely. The handle is used only to rewind the line.

The lines for this type of rod are of very flexible, braided nylon. The plugs are made to look like minnows, frogs, mice, and even birds. Spinners, spoons, and wigglers are also included. Plugs are usually made of wood painted various colors to attract the fish, and some are weighted to make them sink. Others may have fins to make them wobble about as they are pulled through the water. This type of bait will attract such game fish as bass, pickerel and pike, yellow perch, muskellunge, brown trout, and large brook trout.

A variation of bait casting, known as spinning, is becoming quite popular. This requires a special spinning reel in which the spool does not turn. As the cast is made, the line billows out, with very little resistance from the spool. An attachment on the reel rewinds the line.

How To Troll

Such fresh-water game fish as lake trout, landlocked salmon, bass, pike, pickerel, and perch are caught by trolling. A spoon troll—that is,

a metal spoonlike blade with a hook or hooks fastened to the end—is used. At times feathers or hair hide the hooks. The line is dropped into the water, then the boat is quietly paddled about, creating as little disturbance in the water as possible. Quite a lot of line is played out, so that the troll moves at a distance from the boat. The darting, flashing spoon attracts the game fish.

Just as in hunting and stalking land animals, make as little movement as possible, and then move slowly. The less attention you bring upon yourself the better.

Because no casting is required, an ordinary rod, line, and reel will do. However, the twisting spoon makes a braided fish line necessary.

How To Fish with Bait

Bait fishing is perhaps the oldest method of fishing. This is angling for fish with a hook and live bait such as worms, insects, frogs, and minnows.

Live bait may consist of insects, worms, mollusks, amphibians, crustaceans, and fish. Unlike flies, however, live bait must not only be collected but be kept alive and well to be of any use as bait. Crickets are wonderful trout and bass bait. May beetle grubs, fat and white, are often found in the decaying mold of rotten logs. They make good bait for trout, bass, perch, catfish, and sunfish. Almost any white grub will do as bait, however. They should be kept in a container in the moist, rotten mold in which they were found. Other examples are: goldenrod gall grubs, found in the enlarged or swollen parts of goldenrod stems; bluebottle fly grubs, commonly found in decaying garbage; meal worms, which can

349

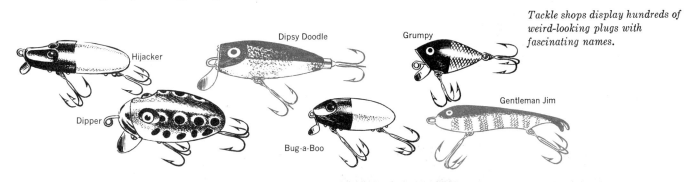

Tackle shops display hundreds of weird-looking plugs with fascinating names.

Hijacker

Dipsy Doodle

Grumpy

Gentleman Jim

Dipper

Bug-a-Boo

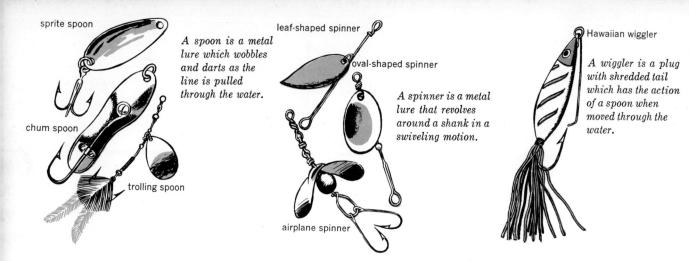

sprite spoon

chum spoon

trolling spoon

A spoon is a metal lure which wobbles and darts as the line is pulled through the water.

leaf-shaped spinner

oval-shaped spinner

A spinner is a metal lure that revolves around a shank in a swiveling motion.

airplane spinner

Hawaiian wiggler

A wiggler is a plug with shredded tail which has the action of a spoon when moved through the water.

be raised in musty corn meal. Grasshoppers, katydids, butterflies, and moths also make good bait.

The earthworm, or night crawler, is well known as a good bait for catching many fish including trout, bass, perch, eels, suckers, and bullheads. Collect earthworms at night on the front lawn, in the back yard after a rain, or after sprinkling the garden. Use a flashlight and grasp the worm close to the end near its burrow, for it disappears like a flash when disturbed. Worms can be stored for a time in a tin containing damp powdered peat moss or moist earth. Earthworms can be kept several days in this way.

Minnows are another well known kind of bait. To many people, any small fish is a minnow, but minnows are really distinct species of fish. A simple way to catch a supply for bait is to place a dip net under water and then drop bread crumbs upon the surface over it. When the minnows begin to feed, bring the net up under them. In using a live minnow for bait, push the hook up through the lower lip and out through the upper lip. This will not kill the minnow and will allow it to swim about freely, making it more tempting to bigger fish.

Bacon or salt-pork rind is sometimes used for bait. Other "dead" baits are pieces of potato or cheese, fins of fish, balls of dough, and bits of shiny fish skin.

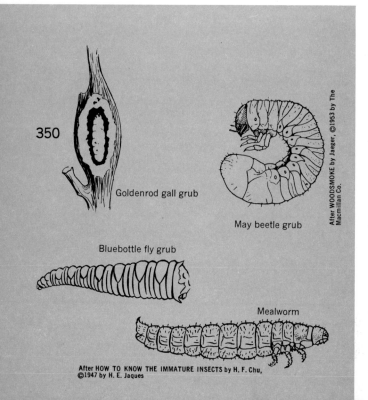

350

Goldenrod gall grub

May beetle grub

After WOODSMOKE by Jaeger, ©1953 by The Macmillan Co.

Bluebottle fly grub

Mealworm

After HOW TO KNOW THE IMMATURE INSECTS by H. F. Chu, ©1947 by H. E. Jaques

Other Books To Read

A Beginner's Book of Sporting Guns and Hunting, by Milton J. Shapiro. Published by Julian Messner, Inc., New York, 1961.

Everything the novice wants to know about firearms: how to buy a sporting gun, how to care for it, and, most important, how to use it safely. The book includes a short history of firearms.

The Young Sportsman's Guide to Game Animals, by Ray Ovington. Published by Thomas Nelson & Sons, New York, 1962.

Hunters, photographers, and nature students will be interested in this book about wild animals of the American woods and fields. There are tips on how to stalk animals, how to photograph them, and even how to stuff them as game trophies.

A Complete Guide to Fishing, by Vlad Evanoff. Published by Thomas Y. Crowell Company, New York, 1961.

Written especially for young anglers. Information about fish, fishing equipment, and techniques.

How To Clean and Cook a Fish

Freshly caught fish, fried to a crisp brown, make a delicious climax to the fisherman's day. Here are easy directions for cleaning and cooking your catch. This selection from Ellsworth Jaeger: Woodsmoke, Copyright 1953 by The Macmillan Company and used with The Macmillan Company's permission. Illustrations, not otherwise credited, adapted from Woodsmoke.

Fish should be killed and cleaned as soon as possible to preserve their flavor. They should be skinned or scaled, scraping from the tail toward the head, keeping the scales wet. (Brook trout merely need to have the usual slime scraped off. Bullheads or catfish, and smooth-skinned fish found in most ponds or creeks, have skins of a muddy flavor that must be removed before cooking. The step-by-step drawings on the right show how this is done.) To clean a fish, split it lengthwise along the belly. Remove the entrails and thoroughly rinse all blood from the inside, especially around the backbone. When it is thoroughly cleaned, wash it and dry.

Now you're ready to fry the fish. In a heavy skillet, melt enough shortening or margarine to make a half inch of fat in the bottom of the skillet. Dip the pieces of fish in corn meal, coating each piece thoroughly. Place in the hot fat. When one side has turned a golden brown, turn the fish. Finish cooking over low heat until the fish is tender when pierced with a fork. Sprinkle with salt and pepper, and serve.

It is fun to catch and eat fish, but cleaning and cooking them can be fun, too.

FIELD AND STREAM Mag.

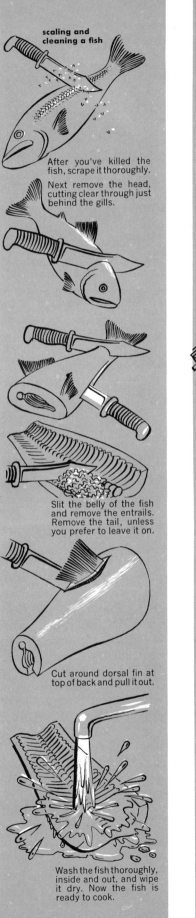

scaling and cleaning a fish

After you've killed the fish, scrape it thoroughly.

Next remove the head, cutting clear through just behind the gills.

Slit the belly of the fish and remove the entrails. Remove the tail, unless you prefer to leave it on.

Cut around dorsal fin at top of back and pull it out.

Wash the fish thoroughly, inside and out, and wipe it dry. Now the fish is ready to cook.

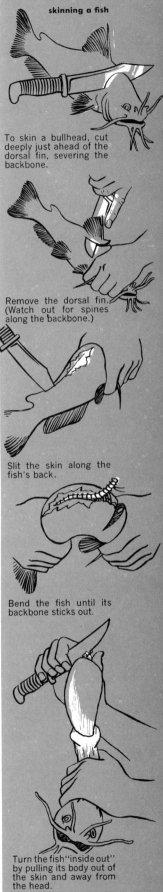

skinning a fish

To skin a bullhead, cut deeply just ahead of the dorsal fin, severing the backbone.

Remove the dorsal fin. (Watch out for spines along the backbone.)

Slit the skin along the fish's back.

Bend the fish until its backbone sticks out.

Turn the fish "inside out" by pulling its body out of the skin and away from the head.

Ancient Egyptians fishing.

The Art of Casting

This short article on casting is just a sample of the many helpful tips you'll find if you read Mr. Schneider's excellent little fishing book. From **The First Book of Fishing** by Steven Schneider. Copyright 1952 by Franklin Watts, Inc.

Some fish can be caught if you just drop your hook and bait into the water. But before you can fish well you must learn how to cast. Casting is whipping the line with hook and bait out over the water and making it come down just where you want it to in the water. This takes practice. In the beginning it's best to practice casting at the edge of a pond where there are no bushes or trees to catch your hook. (Stand away from your friends, too, so they won't get hooked.) The most important thing to learn is timing.

Get your rod all set up with about ten feet of line dangling from the tip. The pictures will show you what to do. After you've made a cast, don't be surprised if nothing happens. You can't expect to catch a fish on the first cast. Try it again. This time make the bait sink by giving the line a quick little pull as soon as the bait hits the water. If, after a few more tries, nothing happens, move on to another spot.

At last you feel a little tug and then a shivering pull. The fish has snapped at the bait. But he may not be hooked yet. Now it's up to you to get the barb of the hook into his jaw. Right here is where you may make a mistake. Don't try to pull the fish out of the water on the first heave.

Before you start to bring the fish in, you must sink the hook into his mouth with a quick little tug. Fishermen call this "setting the hook." With some fish you must wait a second or two before you set the hook. You will find out more about this after you have fished for a while.

Playing the Fish

If you've hooked a little fish, grasp the line with your free hand and pull it in. If you've hooked a big fish, you may have to let him pull and unwind some more of the line from the reel before he gets tired. To make it harder for him, you can let the line out slowly, making it drag between your finger and the rod. Keep the rod high, not pointing straight out. Then with your other hand, try to draw a little of the line in. If he pulls hard, let it out again. This is the most exciting part of fishing, called "playing the fish." It means tiring him out so that you can pull him in without breaking the line. The idea is to make the fish work as hard as possible and to keep the line tight at all times so that he cannot shake the hook from his jaw.

Try not to let the fish get too much line off the reel. Once he is tired, pull him in just as you pull a little fish, only more carefully.

How do you get the fish off the hook without catching yourself on it? First take hold of the line a little above the fish's mouth. With the other hand hold the fish behind the gills. Since some fish have sharp spines to watch out for, start at the nose and slide your hand down over the fish. Grip it firmly. If you have to let go, keep sliding your hand back toward the tail. This keeps the spines flat so that they can't stick you. Don't be upset if the first few fish get away. Even after you have learned how to play the fish well, a few will always get off the hook somehow.

How To Cast

Hold the rod in your right hand with your thumb stretched out *on top* and the reel underneath. With your left hand, grip the line loosely.

Snap the rod quickly upward, letting your wrist do most of the work. Don't swing your whole arm; keep your elbow low and quite close to your body. And don't swing the rod way back. When the rod is up and pointing slightly backward, stop. Now wait a second before you snap your wrist forward to cast; at the same time release the line from your left hand. This is the point where you have to learn timing. If your timing is just right, the line will zip out straight behind, then straight forward for a perfect cast.

Hook and bait hit the water. The rod should not be pointing toward the ground, but slightly upward. Your casts may not be perfect at first, but after you have practiced for a while they will get smoother. Keep practicing. Cast at a newspaper on the lawn. In time you will be able to hit just where you aim.

Fishing in Salt Water

Do you know why fishing is also called "angling"? The word comes from the angular shape of the hook or barb that is used for catching the fish. This article is full of tips on what kind of bait, tackle, and tactics are best for salt-water fishing; anglers (fishermen) who live inland will probably find it every bit as exciting as those who live near the sea. Text reprinted and illustrations, not otherwise credited, adapted from **Let's Fish** by Harry Zarchy, by permission of Alfred A. Knopf, Inc. Copyright 1952 by Alfred A. Knopf, Inc.

A few of the thousands of varieties of salt-water fish.

Wherever the coastline extends, you will find thousands of people enjoying salt-water fishing. Almost every coastal town has its fishing docks and piers, and there you will always find fishermen dropping their lines, swapping tall stories, and having a good time.

The ocean teems with life. There are many more fish here than could possibly exist in fresh water. The vast seas harbor thousands of species of fish, and there are uncounted millions of each species. They range all over, some preferring shallow water, while others live in the deep seas. Some are found only in the tropics, and others in the cold waters of the north.

There are fish of every size, as well. The ocean offers a wide variety of fish to the angler. He can fish from a dock for lafayettes, drift in a boat in sheltered bays for weakfish, or troll deep water for mighty tuna and other tackle busters.

Ocean fish have different habits from those which live in fresh water. Some, like the sal-mon, are anadromous—that is, they spend their adult lives in salt water but swim upstream in fresh water every year to spawn. Others remain in one locality, rarely if ever moving very far. Still others make yearly spawning migrations, remaining in salt water but covering vast distances. Many of these fish simply disappear for a time, returning to their accustomed haunts at the same time each year. Where some species go is still a mystery.

What Kind of Tackle Is Used for Ocean Fishing?

Salt-water tackle differs from that used in fresh water in two important respects. Since the fish you may catch are larger, the tackle is usually sturdier. You'll use a heavier rod and a stronger line. Reels and fittings must be able to withstand the corrosive effects of sea water.

You needn't have expensive tackle. You can have the time of your life with a simple hand line, fishing from a dock or a bridge Many

354

There's more than one way of catching fish in the sea. To bring in the big ones, you need heavy tackle and a boat, but you can have a lot of fun fishing from the shore with only a hook and line.

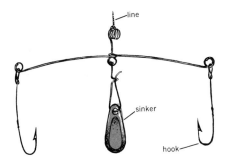

A tandem spreader for rigging hooks to the line, used also for bottom surf fishing from a drifting boat.

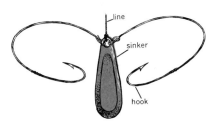

In this method of rigging a line for bottom fishing, the hooks are attached directly to the sinker.

a boy and girl has hauled in a good-sized striped bass while fishing for pan fish. You never know what may take your bait, and that's one of the thrills that every fisherman looks forward to.

If you live within a short distance of the ocean, why not try your luck? And remember every expert was once a beginner.

Fishing from the Shore

Most coastlines do not extend in straight lines, but twist and turn, forming countless coves, bays, and natural harbors. In these sheltered areas many species of fish are to be found. Some of these fish spend their entire lives in these relatively calm, shallow waters, others come inshore to spawn, and still others move in seeking food.

Depending upon which particular fish you are after, you will be bottom fishing, top fishing, drifting, or trolling. Each of these methods has its own technique.

Bottom fishing means doing exactly what you might think—fishing with your bait on the bottom. However, it's not quite so simple, for you must first locate a place where there are likely to be fish. Let's consider just what makes a good fishing ground. Fish must eat in order to live, and common sense tells us that they will be found in those places where the bottom offers them a good supply of food. They may feed upon worms, shrimp, crabs, clams, other shellfish, or bait fish. These, in turn, feed upon smaller organisms known as plankton—tiny forms of animal and plant life that are found in the water.

Some bottom areas are richer in marine life than others, and it is in these places that we find fish. Certain species like the flounder prefer mud or sand bottoms. Blackfish are found around piers, rocks, jetties, and wrecks, where they feed upon crabs. These fishing grounds are well known to the captains of fishing boats, who often treat their location as well-guarded secrets.

How To Keep the Bait on the Bottom

Let us suppose that you are going to fish from a bridge, dock, or jetty, with the simplest possible tackle—a hand line. All you need is from 50 to 100 feet of stout fishing line, thick enough to be gripped comfortably. You can buy hand lines, wound on small frames.

In order to get your bait down to the bottom, and what's more important, to *keep* it there, you will have to use a sinker. The exact weight will vary with each fishing situation. Here's how you can tell how heavy your sinker should be for hand-line fishing. Attach a sinker to the line, throw it out a short distance, then pull back so that there is some tension on the line. The sinker should be just heavy enough to hold bottom. If you are fishing in a strong current or tide, you will need a heavy sinker. If the water is not moving so rapidly, you can get by with a lighter one. Use the lightest sinker that you can, otherwise you won't feel small fish when they bite.

There are many ways of rigging hooks to a line for bottom fishing, and each fisherman has his favorite method. Two hooks are generally used. The drawing at the top right of this page shows how you can attach your hooks directly to the sinker. Another way to do this is by using a tandem spreader, as in the drawing above, left.

Now, bait your hooks and toss the whole assembly into the water. Be sure to hold the other end of the line or tie it securely to the dock; otherwise, you might find yourself out

355

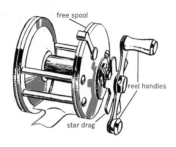

A salt-water reel equipped with a star drag and a free spool.

A homemade chum pot. When filled with chopped bait and trailed behind the boat, the chum pot is an inviting cafeteria, drawing the unsuspecting fish to your boat.

of business before you begin. Pull back enough to tense the line and wait for a bite. This may be signalled by one or a series of quick, sharp tugs. All you have to do is pull in your line, hand over hand, and you've got a fish.

At this point it is a good idea to say something about fishing manners. Wherever fishermen congregate on docks and piers, you will usually find some individuals "bolo" casting. The idea is to whirl the weighted end of the line around your head, get up enough momentum, then let it fly out over the water. It's true that you can cast a considerable distance by bolo casting, but it's also true that you are endangering everyone around you. Should your heavy sinker strike another person, it can cause a serious injury. As a matter of fact, you don't have to throw your line out any great distance when you are fishing from a dock. Fish usually come in quite close, and you may actually be casting out too far. A true sportsman always considers others; he will never knowingly hurt or embarrass anyone.

Fishing from a Boat

Now let's suppose you are fishing from a boat. The boat, of course, is anchored. Rig up your rod, reel, and hooks. Attach the sinker that will keep your bait on the bottom. Here again, use the lightest sinker that will do the job. Fasten a trial sinker to your line and let it go down into the water. It should hit bottom with a slight bump. Raise it about a foot, then let it drop again. Do this a few times; if the sinker has been moved by the current, it's too light.

Set the drag on your reel before you begin to fish. The drawing above shows a typical salt-water reel that has a star drag and a free spool. The purpose of the drag is to enable a hooked fish to pull out line even though you

may be reeling in. This keeps the fish under a steady tension which tires it so that it may be landed. The drag on your reel may be adjusted by turning the star wheel in either direction.

Try this experiment: Turn the star all the way to the right, tightening the drag, then have someone pull on your line. The line will not budge; it will snap if enough force is applied or if it is jerked hard enough. Should you hook a large fish with your drag tightened all the way, that's exactly what might happen. Now, with the same pull exerted on the line, slowly loosen the drag by turning it to the left. This will permit line to be pulled out. The spool will turn, even though the reel handles do not. Your drag should be adjusted so that line can be pulled out without breaking.

The drawing also shows the lever, which, when snapped forward, throws the reel into *free spool*. This means that the spool can revolve *freely*, while the reel handles are motionless. Put the reel into free spool when casting, or when you are dropping the line to the bottom for bottom fishing. Moving the lever back to its original position engages the handles, making it possible to reel in.

What Bait Is Used for Bottom Fishing?

Natural baits are usually best for bottom fishing. Depending upon your particular locality, you may use mussels, crabs, clams, squid, shrimp, sandworms, bloodworms, or whole or cut fish. Make a few inquiries; find out what the preferred baits are wherever you are going to fish.

Chumming is a practice that attracts fish to your boat. One way to chum is by using a wooden box, with a bottom made of half-inch wire mesh. This is known as a chum pot. It is filled with finely ground chopped fish, such as mossbunker, and is then lowered over the side into the water. Bits of fish are constantly escaping through the mesh, providing choice tidbits for fish in the vicinity, and sharpening their appetites. Another way to chum is by dropping a few grass shrimp into the water from time to time.

You can use almost any edible substance for chumming. Some fishermen add a tin of oily sardines to the chum pot. Try using ordinary dry oatmeal, simply dribbling it into the water. Boiled rice is good for chum, too. If you are using clams as bait, break up the shells and drop those into the water, together with the soft parts of the clam that won't stay on the hook. Don't chum if you are bottom fishing in a strong current, for it won't do you any good. The moving water will carry the chum far beyond the vicinity of your hook.

Drifting with the Tide

You may also fish the bottom while your boat is drifting with the tide. Use a tandem rig to attach the hooks to the line; and a sinker that is just heavy enough to hold bottom. As the current moves the boat, your bait is dragged along the bottom. Some fish establish stations for themselves, waiting for food to be carried along by the moving water. Others move in and out with the tides, feeding upon smaller fish that seek the protection of shallow water.

You can drift for weakfish. Bait up with a sandworm, and use a sinker that will keep your bait just a couple of feet below the water's surface. Sometimes just a split shot will do the trick. Fluke may also be caught when drifting, but here you must use a sinker that will drag along the bottom. For bait, use a live killie, a filet (boneless piece of meat) cut from a fluke's belly, spearing, or even a preserved minnow. If you rig your bait behind a spinner, you'll increase your chances of catching fish.

Some fishermen go after both weakfish and fluke at the same time by rigging their lines with a high and a low hook. Drifting gives you an opportunity to cover lots of ground and makes it possible to get your bait to the fish.

Trolling for Fish in Salt Water

Trolling in sheltered, inland waters differs from drifting because your boat is propelled by oars or an engine, and you can go wherever you please. More important is the idea that you can control the speed with which you are moving. This is very important, since not all lures can generally be trolled at faster speeds than underwater lures. The best way to judge the proper trolling speed is to watch the lure as it moves through the water. It should look as lifelike as possible.

The fisherman's first problem is to locate the fish. Sometimes this isn't so easy, for the surface of the water appears to be the same wherever you look. At a time like this you can only select the spots you are going to fish, then troll over the area systematically.

At other times, finding fish is a simple matter. Look for gulls, and where you see them wheeling and dipping down into the water, there you are reasonably certain of finding fish. The gulls are probably feeding on bait fish driven to the surface by larger fish.

How To Make a Skillful Approach

As you approach the school of feeding fish, you will often see them churning up the surface of the water. Many beginners make a mistake at this time, running their boats right over the school. This is a good way *not* to catch fish. Use a reasonable amount of caution. Run your boat alongside and past the feeding fish. Then, when you are well ahead of the school, make a sharp turn. This will bring your trolled lure directly through the fish. Another good method is to bring your boat to within a short distance of the fish, then cast into the school.

How much line do you let out when trolling? That depends upon what fish you are after and the kind of water in which you are fishing.

A bent eel squid, an example of the lifelike tin baits often used in surf fishing.

357

For example, school tuna are attracted by the white wake that is left by your boat, and will strike a lure about ten yards behind. For most trolling, your lure should be about one hundred feet behind the boat. Use a six-foot stainless steel wire leader, fastened to a swivel.

As a matter of simple courtesy, the other members of the fishing party reel in their lines whenever someone gets a strike from a large fish. This prevents the lines from becoming tangled as the fish is brought in and gives the lucky fisherman a chance to play his catch without interference.

Top Fishing from a Boat

Top fishing is done from an anchored boat. Select a place where the tide is strong, then set up a chum line. This is done by dribbling little bits of chum over the side from time to time. The chum drifts with the tide and attracts fish. Sometimes the fish will follow the chum right up to the boat. Grass shrimp make excellent chum for this kind of fishing; you'll need a few quarts for a day's sport.

Bait your line with shrimp and let it drift out with the chum. Put your reel into free spool and control the outgoing line with your thumb. Should you get a strike, flip your reel into gear, and reel in. If you have let out about one hundred feet of line with no results, reel in very slowly, examine your bait to see whether it's still there, then let it out again.

Sometimes your bait will ride too high in the water. A split shot attached to your leader will usually sink it deep enough.

Catching Fish by the Jigging Method

Jigging is a method of fishing in which your lure is moved rapidly up and down in the water. The usual equipment for jigging consists of a light bamboo pole about twelve feet long. To this is attached a piece of heavy weight leader, the same length as the pole. The lure you use depends upon what you are fishing for. Herring and whiting will go for small block tin squids or jigs, small spiral spinners, or natural bait such as spearing.

Cane poles are also used when fishing for snappers (young bluefish weighing less than a pound). You will use a float and bait up with spearing or any other small fish bait. Cast your line and be prepared for action. If snappers are feeding nearby, they'll strike savagely.

One of the nice things about jigging is the fact that you don't have to go out in a boat. You can fish from any handy dock or bridge, for many fish come quite close to shore.

The Joys of Surf Fishing

There are thousands of fishermen who feel that surf fishing is the most thrilling sport of all. Many of these people travel great distances in order to fish the surf. They cheerfully do without sleep, endure both broiling sun and freezing winds, and love every minute of it. The surf fisherman has an endless fund of patience and secretly hopes that the next cast will produce the biggest fish he has ever seen.

Surf fishing doesn't get you as many fish as fishing from a boat, but there's no denying that it's great fun. The person who fishes the surf is a free soul. He feels that he is not confined to a boat, but can move wherever he likes, whenever he feels the urge. If he doesn't catch anything in one place, he simply walks on to a better location.

How does the surf fisherman know where to fish? The beginner is likely to approach the water at any point, for all parts of the surf look alike to him, but the expert sees many things of interest. He looks for places where fish may find food.

The first sign of fish is the presence of

358

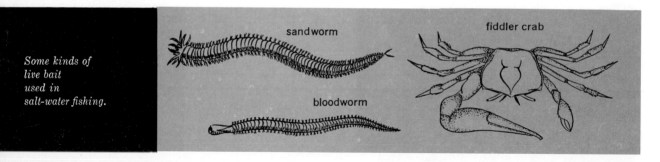

Some kinds of live bait used in salt-water fishing.

sandworm

fiddler crab

bloodworm

feeding gulls. If there are no gulls, the fisherman then looks for white water offshore. This usually indicates a sand bar, over which the waves are breaking. Small fish seek shelter from rough water inside these bars, and that is where you are likely to find big fish. They'll find a deep hole, then lie there waiting for food to come to them. Look for a break in the bar. The incoming water rushes through this opening, carrying food with it. Crabs and bait fish are temporarily helpless in this turmoil of water and are then gobbled up by larger fish.

Sometimes white water is formed by offshore rocks. The same conditions exist here. Big fish lie concealed in the turbulent water, then pounce upon anything that is swept by.

Tidal currents also produce fish. The best spots to fish are *rips,* or places where opposing currents meet. Here the bottom is always disturbed, food is constantly carried along by the water, and big fish lie there snatching the tidbits that are brought to them.

Now, let's suppose there are no offshore bars, no rocks, and no white water to be seen. In that case, you must trust to luck, and cover as much of the surf as you can. Work your way along the shore, casting at intervals of about fifty feet. You may strike a hole where a big fish is hiding.

Surf fishermen use special tackle which is designed for long, powerful casting.

Baits used for surf casting vary with the locality. Here are some common ones: bloodworms, sandworms, shrimp, crabs, squid, clams, eels, spearing, mullet, whiting, herring, menhaden or mossbunker, sand eels. Some surf fishermen do not use live bait. They cast and retrieve *squids,* which are heavy lures usually made of block tin. Sometimes the squids are plated to make them brighter; often they'll have bits of pork rind or feathers attached to the hook. They are shaped to resemble natural baits, such as mossbunker, butterfish, and sand eels.

Deep-Sea Fishing

Now we leave the sheltered bays and inlets and move out to the open sea. Vast schools of fish are constantly on the move, seeking food, or themselves being sought by larger fish. For example, mackerel eat smaller bait fish, and tuna eat mackerel.

Locating fish is again the angler's first consideration. Sometimes schools of fish are feeding on the surface and can be spotted by the commotion they make. Our old friends, the gulls, may be pointing out feeding fish. At other times the fish we seek may be down in the depths, leaving no clue to their presence. In any case, the deep-sea fisherman must go out after his fish instead of waiting for them to come to him.

Deep-sea fishing may be roughly divided into bottom fishing and trolling, done in the same way as for fishing near the shore. The main difference is in the heavier tackle used, for now we are after bigger fish.

Many different baits may be used, including bloodworms, sandworms, clams, crabs, cut-up squid, mullet, mossbunker, spearing, killies, and shrimp. Fish are most likely to go for those baits upon which they feed naturally, but they aren't always bound by strict rules.

Some of the fish that are taken by bottom fishing in northeastern Atlantic waters are pollack, croakers, porgies, kingfish, blackfish, fluke, sea bass, codfish, whiting, ling, and hake.

Some fish that can be caught by trolling, particularly off the north and central Atlantic coasts, are school tuna, weakfish, dolphin, amberjack, albacore, bluefish, striped bass, mackerel.

359

grass shrimp

killie

spearing

You and Your Gun

Here is a story—with wise advice and warnings—for any person who has ever wanted to own a gun. The author's experiences in learning about guns and how to handle them could be the experiences of any young would-be hunter. From **A Boy and His Gun**, by Edward C. Janes, copyright 1951 by Edward C. Janes. Used by permission of A. S. Barnes & Company, New York, publishers.

The town in which I grew up happened to be in New England, but it was, I think, typical of all small towns when the century was young, whether they were located in the midwestern prairies, the western mountains, or the southern cottonlands.

From the time I was old enough to hold a gun, I yearned to have one all my own. Slingshots and toy guns served at first, and many were the imaginary deer, foxes, and birds I killed in our backyard.

For years my pleas for a gun fell upon unsympathetic ears. My dad was county medical examiner at the time, and he had seen too many examples of thoughtless gun handling. Dad had gunned, too, and he knew that, properly handled, a gun is safe. But he also knew that a gun in reckless hands can be a treacherous, deadly instrument, and he wisely waited until he thought I was old enough to use a gun with good judgment.

Then came the day of days when he decided that the time was ripe for an eager boy to become a responsible person with a gun of his own. Then he gave me the gun, and with it, golden autumn days, tangy with the scent of woodsmoke, trees flaming scarlet and crimson, the shivering roar of grouse whirring up from the forest floor, the wide V's of wildfowl against a rosy dawn, and the companionship of good dogs and good men.

Hunting as a Sport

The pioneers were famous for their guns. This urge to own a gun is just as strong today as it was in years gone by. In my opinion, there is no more healthful sport than hunting and no sport more closely linked to the traditions of America's heritage. It is a safe sport when done in a commonsense manner. But changing times have brought changed conditions, and the boy who gets his first gun today will find a situation far different from that of years ago. For one thing, there are a lot more hunters today—about fifteen million of them—which is a much larger number than the entire population of the United States in 1830. For another thing, these fifteen million hunters have less room to hunt in than their fathers and grandfathers had. Cities have a way of spreading out, gobbling up the countryside for house lots and factory sites. Growing towns need more drinking water, so reservoirs are created in the surrounding hills. State and national wildlife refuges close more and more land to hunting and, finally, a lot of farmers have taken to posting their land these days.

To balance these conditions, today's hunter has some advantages on his side. One of them is the vast improvement in modern fire-arms and ammunition. Not so many years ago, loose shooting guns, misfires, and blowbacks were all too common and were accepted as necessary evils. Today there is nothing unusual in putting thousands of rounds of ammunition through the action of a gun without a single misfire of a shell or improper performance of the gun.

Conservation and the Hunter

For another thing, the men in charge of our conservation departments are doing a good job today in stocking and managing game birds and animals, and in creating better surroundings for them to live in. They are doing this by opening up public hunting areas, by planting food crops for game, by controlling destructive creatures such as cats, skunks, weasels, owls, hawks and crows, and by stocking game covers with birds from other countries.

Today strict laws limit the amount of game which a person may kill in a day or a season, but there is more to this business of conservation than just obeying the laws. It is something inside the hunter which makes him enjoy the sport rather than the actual killing. Years ago on the frontier men hunted for meat, and sport was secondary. Today it is the sport which is important, and the success of a day spent hunting cannot be measured by the weight of the game bag.

Shooting Is Only a Part of Hunting

Some of my pleasantest days afield have been those when I have returned empty-handed. It doesn't matter whether there is a duck or grouse or rabbit on the table. What does matter is the enjoyment of his day which the hunter brings home at night—the sweep of purple hills, the woodland sights and sounds and smells, the companionship he has shared, the stop at noon for lunch beneath a spreading pasture elm, the cup of spring water in the alders, the spine-tingling flight of a grouse—the true pleasures of hunting are made up of such things. Perhaps best of all are the memories of the shots you might have taken and didn't.

And this brings up the matter of killing cleanly. One of the most saddening experiences in hunting, and one which can spoil your whole day, is to watch a bird or animal which you have shot drag itself out of your reach to die a painful and lingering death.

What can we do to avoid this cruel suffering? Three things: first, we can learn to aim at vital spots when shooting game with a rifle—at the heart, lungs, or head. Second, by experimenting on the target, trap, or skeet range we can learn what our guns will do—how far they will shoot, the extent of their killing range (which is a far different thing), and for what game they are suited. Then, having discovered these facts, we will never fire at game beyond clean-killing range or at game too large for our guns. Every year, for example, numerous deer are shot with .22 rifles. Some of these are killed, but more often they escape with wounds which may later result

in death from infection or loss of blood. The .22 bullet is just not large enough nor propelled at sufficient speed for deer hunting, at least in the tiny rimfire cartridge size.

Safety First for Hunters

Needless to say, consideration of the safety factor in handling guns is very important. Your gun is completely impartial. It would just as soon shoot you or your companion as it would a tin can or a rabbit, and you only have to make one mistake. As a boy I learned never under any circumstances to point a gun, loaded or unloaded, at anything I didn't want to shoot at. The old Western plainsmen had a saying that is the basis of all gun handling: A GUN IS ALWAYS LOADED! If you remember that, you won't be apt to find yourself making the old and feeble alibi: "I didn't know it was loaded."

I learned always to empty my gun before bringing it into the house, although I shall have to confess that it took a BB pellet embedded in the living room ceiling, and consequently having to give up my gun for two weeks, to make that lesson stick. In the field I learned to carry my gun pointed downward or out to the side across my elbow so that if it discharged accidentally, it wouldn't shoot me or a companion. I learned that when no one is behind you, it is permissible to carry the gun over your shoulder but at such times the trigger guard should be on top so that the barrel points upward rather than down. And I learned to look closely at what I was shooting at, and to make certain what lay in the field of fire beyond the target, before I pulled the trigger.

These are the most important fundamentals of gun handling and the principles, which, when ignored, cause most of the firearms accidents. Too many hunters go into the woods and fields each season without any training in the use of guns, and, as a result, the papers are full of stories of accidents. It is these stories which make people who know little about hunting consider it a dangerous sport, but nine out of ten of these accidents could have been avoided.

361

Girl Sharpshooters

Pioneer heroes had to be sharpshooters. A man's gun was his friend in need. So it is not surprising that legends have sprouted like mushrooms after a rainy night. But don't think pioneer women left all the shooting to the men. The girls on this page did all right, too. From **Women Are Here To Stay** by Agnes Rogers. Copyright 1949 by Harper & Brothers.

Calamity Jane (1852–1903)

Recent students of the American frontier have been pretty hard on Martha Jane (Canary) Burke, popularly known as Calamity Jane, but there was a time when her reputation for bravery, for skill with firearms, and for horsemanship shone brightly. It is now believed that she excelled chiefly in the art of storytelling, and that her account of her activities as one of Custer's scouts was purely her own invention. She is shown on the right in the masculine clothes which she often wore.

362

Annie Oakley (1860–1926)

When little Phoebe Annie Oakley Mozee was nine years old, she could shoot the head off a running quail; this ability came in very handy in a household that couldn't afford butcher shops. In 1875, when she was fifteen, she went to Cincinnati to take part in a shooting match, and there met the dashing Frank Butler whom she married a little more than a year later. Annie Oakley toured with her husband for years in Buffalo Bill's Wild West Show and delighted audiences in America and Europe. She could split a playing card edgewise, knock the ash from Butler's cigarette, and one of her prettiest tricks was shooting the heart out of the ace of hearts with 25 shots at 25 yards—in 27 seconds. The shot-up cards that Annie left behind her probably account for the slang term "Annie Oakley," as applied to complimentary tickets, which must be punched by the gate-tender.

Anglers are said to be the only happy people. Even though people have poked fun at fishermen in cartoons, "fish" stories, and liars' tales, there are still more than twenty million fishing licenses issued each year in the United States. And in most states you need no license to fish if you're under sixteen, or if you are going to fish in salt water. Here are some of the most frequently caught fresh and salt water fish. The accompanying figures show sizes of large individual fish, which in all cases are well above the average.

Fresh Water

Yellow perch
(4¼ lbs.—16 in.)

Bluegill
(4¾ lbs.—15 in.)

Sebago salmon
(22½ lbs.—3 ft.)

Walleyed pike
(22⅓ lbs.—3 ft.)

Black crappie
(4 lbs.—18 in.)

Muskellunge
(110 lbs.—7 ft., 3 in.)

Brook trout
(14½ lbs.—31½ in.)

Large mouth bass
(22⅓ lbs.—32½ in.)

Brown trout
(39½ lbs.—3 ft.)

Rainbow trout
(37 lbs.—3 ft., 4½ in.)

Small mouth bass
(11 lbs., 15 oz.—27 in.)

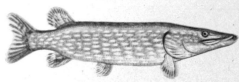

Chain pickerel
(9 lbs.—2½ ft.)

Salt Water

Amberjack
(120½ lbs.—5 ft., 2 in.)

Weakfish
(17½ lbs.—3 ft., 10 in.)

Striped bass
(73 lbs.—5 ft.)

Chinook salmon
(83 lbs.—4 ft., 10 in.)

Tarpon
(283 lbs.—7 ft., 3 in.)

Summer flounder
(20 lbs., 7 oz.—3 ft., 1 in.)

Atlantic salmon
(79 lbs.—about 5 ft.)

Tuna
(1,000 lbs.—15 ft.)

Dolphin
(76 lbs.—5 ft., 3 in.)

Pacific sailfish
(221 lbs.—10 ft., 9 in.)

Black sea bass
(7½ lbs.—over 2 ft.)

Common
pompano
(8 lbs.—18 in.)

Bluefish
(24¼ lbs.—3 ft., 5 in.)

Atlantic cod
(211¼ lbs.—6 ft.)

Red snapper
(35 lbs.—3 ft.)

Great barracuda
(103½ lbs.—5½ ft.)

Bonito
(39 lbs., 15 oz.—3 ft., 3 in.)

Albacore
(69 lbs.—3½ ft.)

365

Blue Marlin
(756 lbs.—14 ft.)

Blacktip shark
(300 lbs.—9 ft., 2 in.)

*Every fall, thousands of duck hunters put on their red caps and coats
and head for the fields or marshes. Here, in boats or from blinds, they tend
their strings of decoys and await the arrival overhead of the long V's of
waterfowl which will, they hope, come within shooting range.*

Hunting

*Fox hunting originated in England, and is considered the property of the
upper class there. Here, red-coated patricians ride out on a hunt in the eastern
United States. The purpose of the hunt is generally said to be the thrill of the
chase rather than the killing of the fox.*

Hunting With Bows and Arrows

Civilized man is still a hunter. Some men stalk their game with guns, others use cameras; but in the United States the bow, one of the oldest weapons, is rapidly gaining in popularity. Wherever hunting with a gun is permitted, bow hunting is a legal sport during specified seasons. Some states even allow a bow hunting season before the regular gun season starts.

Originally the bow and arrow were hunting weapons, as may be seen by both paintings and carvings on the walls of prehistoric caves. Later they were adapted for warfare; the bows used by medieval armies were large and powerful enough to down a knight dressed in full armor, from several hundred yards. The crossbow was even more powerful, and its quarrels, or arrows, had the piercing power of some modern high-velocity bullets; its kick, or recoil, was as powerful as that of a big-bore gun of today.

The hunting bow was smaller than the war bow, and could be easily carried through the woods without getting caught on low limbs or underbrush. The fiercest beast could be stopped by the bow hunter, who could move quietly and get close enough for an accurate aim. For this reason, today as in centuries past, the technique of hunting with a bow consists as much in stalking ability as in marksmanship.

The most common game for the bow and arrow hunter are squirrels and rabbits. Of large game, deer is the most widely hunted. Others are elk, moose, bear, and wild pigs. Carp and garfish are caught by the skillful bow fishermen who shoot from small boats or while wading in shallow water. Such bow fishing requires special patience and skill, in that it is necessary to allow for displacement of the object by refraction of the water and to aim accordingly.

There are two sides to arguments about the merits of bow hunting, especially for large game. Its advocates insist that since the hunter must get close to his target, the skill of stalking must be highly developed; thus the animal has a better chance to escape than if shot at by a high-powered rifle, whose bullets carry for long distances. Critics, on the other hand, insist that bow hunters are often able only to wound their game, which then makes an escape perhaps to bleed to death in a covert where the hunter cannot follow it. Arrows, they claim (and some bow hunters agree) have no "stopping power"; they usually only cause the animal to bleed to death.

With this in mind, some novice bow hunters select a bow with the heaviest "pull" that they can get, feeling that this gives their arrows more drive; however, it is penetrating power that counts, and a bow with a light pull can deliver an arrow almost as efficiently as a more powerful one. The American Indians once used bows with relatively light pull, yet they were able to kill game as big as the buffalo. A bow with strong pull may be able to shoot an arrow further—a virtue to the medieval bowman, perhaps—but this is not the aim of present-day bow hunters.

Bow hunting arrows have broad, razor-sharp points which do as much internal damage as possible to the game they hit, thus causing them to drop within range of the hunter.

While bow hunting in this country has been confined to the sport aspect, the armed forces have been experimenting with bow and arrows for some groups engaged in jungle warfare. As a weapon it is noiseless, thus confusing enemy search for the user; it has high penetrating power, as noted above; and arrows can be equipped with such special items as explosive charges and magnesium flares.

Bow hunters of all historical periods have sought out dangerous beasts to hunt, and the ancient Babylonians were no exception. This mural shows a royal lion hunt, with beaters on the ground clashing their shields to frighten the lions and drive them toward the king's chariot. One lion crouches wounded on the ground while another, charging at the chariot, is met by an arrow from a full-drawn bow.

British Museum

367

Back to camp.

Wisc. Conserv. Dept.

Winter Camping

You who are keen about camping—have you ever tried it in winter? In winter the woods are quieter than you thought possible, and the sun in the south makes long, blue shadows. Get snowshoes, or skis if you prefer, woolen underwear, good boots, and a mackinaw. This article is by Ross McKenney and will help you plan your trip. Mr. McKenney is a member of the Dartmouth Outing Club, a club for winter sport lovers that has helped to make Dartmouth College (Hanover, New Hampshire) famous around the world. From **The Dartmouth Book of Winter Sports**, edited by Harold Putnam. Copyright, 1939, by A. S. Barnes & Co., New York.

It's mostly skiing now up here in the North Country and everybody thinks the woods are only good to cut ski trails in so people can come whizzing down faster than the subways in New York City. But I have lived long enough to know that there is a lot more beauty and fellowship in the outdoors than merely skidding down a mountain as fast as you can. There's something I like better when the forests are banked with snow and the thermometer reads the way it did back in Paul Bunyan's time. (One morning Paul put the coffee outdoors to cool and it froze so quickly the ice was hot.) That something is winter camping.

Winter is a good time to wander through the forests with your pack on your back and a good pair of snowshoes on your feet, climbing hills, crossing streams, trailing the winter animals to see what they are doing, and how they live in the snow. You, too, can learn how to live in the snow and be warm and comfortable.

When you are going on a hiking trip, whether on skis or snowshoes, always go as light as possible. Avoid packing boxes or hard, square parcels. They have a way of working around in the pack so a sharp corner is forever digging into your back and making things uncomfortable. Small bags of canvas or waterproof material can be used for packing foodstuffs.

When you are getting food ready to pack, a box with small partitions is useful. Line these compartments with waxed paper. Then put in staple articles such as baked beans. Then place the box outside to freeze. Later the paper can be folded over the frozen beans, and the package can be tied with a string. The beans are then ready for the knapsack without the bother of an extra package. When the menu calls for beans, I thaw them out, remove the paper, heat them up, and have baked beans.

A quart of flour will feed one person for from six to eight meals, and it can be prepared before starting out. Other essentials for a short trip are: a cup of sugar, two or three tablespoons of salt, one pound of bacon, a cup of ground coffee, some good tea, a small can of evaporated milk or a small quantity of powdered milk.

A small steak tastes mighty good broiled over the coals the first night out, and a couple of medium-sized potatoes fried in bacon fat over the fire is a great dish. For cooking utensils you'll need: a small fry pan, some kind of a pail or can, a fork, and a spoon. And don't forget that good old tin cup.

If you have on good woolen underwear and a heavy mackinaw, you won't need so many blankets. I never carry one on the trap line, but one would be a help to a person who felt a bit scary about the cold. A light warm sleeping bag is always good, but it adds weight on a hiking trip. By no means leave without a good sharp axe, about two and a half pounds weight, and with a good sheath. It may sound a little light, but you can do a lot of work with an axe of that weight if it's sharp and you know how to use it.

As a precaution against some of the minor

Winter shelter

notched ends over
crossbar to prevent
slipping when loaded

trench wall of snow

lay boughs butts up
to-shed melting snow

Side view of shelter

or even major accidents that may occur in the woods, it's wise to take along some kind of first-aid kit: iodine, small box of Band-aids, a two- or three-inch bandage, a small jar of iodex salve or a tube of white vaseline (for those hot fat burns), and a roll of two-inch adhesive tape. Adhesive is good for anything from mending a cracked axe handle to drawing a cut together or mending a leg of your trousers where you got hung up on that dead stump when you made a fast turn.

Making Your Shelter

If you can find a natural windbreak, such as windfalls or a ledge of rock that stands up a few feet, it's a good idea to make camp in its shelter. Of course, in such a sheltered place, you may have to endure a little more smoke from your own campfire. A camp facing into the wind is better for the smoke problem, but not for warmth. Remember to start making camp in plenty of time before dark. Two hours is little enough to allow, if you are not well versed in woodlore. After darkness falls it's rather tough to get the things you want and the chance of accidents from ax cuts is greatly increased.

If you find that darkness is going to catch you before camp is made, get the material and drag it to your camp site where the fire light will aid you in erecting a lean-to. And be sure you have a supply of wood sufficient to last through the night, preferably hard wood, as soft woods snap when burning and throw sparks which may burn your blanket or clothing.

About an hour before dark I usually stop and make camp by digging a trench in the snow with my snowshoe, ten feet long, four feet wide, and down to the ground. This trench faces a big tree, which shelters the trench and reflects the heat from the fire.

Approximately four feet from the base of the tree, I drive a forked stake into the ground at each side of the snow trench. I then cut a crosspiece between these stakes level with the top of the snow, banking additional snow around the completed lean-to if the snow on the ground is not three or four feet deep. Then I notch ends of other poles to be hooked over the crosspiece, as in the picture above.

Big balsam or spruce boughs should be cut to cover this skeleton of poles. The inner walls of the completed shelter should be lined with boughs to keep the fire's heat from melting the snow. For maximum warmth the front crosspiece of the shelter should not be lower than three feet from the ground, or the heat from the fire will escape over the edge.

Some of the snow that banks the entire shelter melts, but the water is shed by the boughs which are put on in layers with their butts up. Boughs for the floor of the shelter complete this snug sleeping arrangement.

Build your fire close to the base of the protecting tree and about four feet in front of the shelter. Two large logs may be placed on either side of the tree, with the ends open, facing the shelter. Smaller logs may be placed across the base logs, and the fire lit beneath them. As fast as the cross logs burn, they can be placed on the fire.

369

Hundreds of mallard and pintail ducks find a home in this wildlife refuge in California. Through the work of the U.S. Fish and Wildlife Service and state and national conservation groups, our game birds and other wildlife are being protected and preserved.

What Conservation Means

Part of the fun of fishing and hunting comes from the thrill of capturing a hard-to-get fish or game animal. But if fish and game get too scarce or disappear altogether the sports of hunting and fishing will naturally die out, too. Robert Cushman Murphy, a renowned naturalist and member of the American Museum of Natural History staff, explains why it is important to protect all our natural resources—trees, water, and soil, as well as wildlife—if we want to keep our country beautiful and productive. From "Conservation for Everybody" by Robert Cushman Murphy. **Audubon Nature Bulletin**, Series No. 12, Bulletin No. 7. Published by National Audubon Society.

370

The word conservation has a thrifty meaning. To conserve is to save and protect, to leave what we ourselves enjoy in such good condition that others may also share the enjoyment. Conservation is the opposite of extravagance and wastefulness. It is an expression of good manners to nature and to our fellow men, including those of generations not yet born.

Only a little more than three hundred years ago the whole North American continent was in a state which had been very little altered by man. It was a temperate-zone Garden of Eden. In the forested parts trees not only covered the ground but they also grew to their greatest size and then continued to live until storms or lightning overthrew them, or until they died of old age. Other areas of the continent, where the average rainfall was somewhat less, were carpeted with long prairie grasses which served, like the forest and its undergrowth, to bind the soil. This prevented it from being washed away by rainfall and streams and so from being lost in the sea. The running waters were kept under control by this cover of vegetation and by the spongy humus in the ground, so that droughts and floods affected them much less than they do today. The water was clear, instead of muddy, and it furnished a suitable home for huge numbers of trout and other fresh-water organisms of many kinds.

The Natural Riches of North America

The extraordinary richness of the North American plant life in field, woodland, and river valley was unequalled in any other temperate part of the world. And the abundance of animal life quite matched that of the vegetation. The letters and diaries of all the earlier discoverers and travelers are filled with wonder at the richness of food resources in the ocean, the hordes of wild fowl, fur-bearers, deer, and many other kinds of beautiful and useful animals that flourished everywhere.

Our ancestors had no idea of how rapidly an expanding human population would outrun the supplies of raw materials; most of them, even until very recently, had the vague idea that the treasures were "limitless" and "inexhaustible." Most of the citizens of earlier generations knew little or nothing about the complicated and delicate system that runs all through nature, and which means that, as in a living body, an unhealthy condition of one part will sooner or later be harmful to all the others.

Fifty years ago nature study was not part of the school work; scientific forestry was a new idea; lumber was still cheap because it could be brought in any quantity from distant woodlands; erosion and river floods were not national problems; modern guns, smokeless powder, and automobiles had not yet raised the odds against native game; nobody had yet studied long-term climatic cycles in relation to proper land use; even the word "conservation" had nothing of the meaning that it has for us today.

What We Need To Know About Conservation

For the sake of ourselves and those who will come after us, we must now set about repairing the mistakes of our ancestors. Conservation should, therefore, be made a part of everyone's daily, workaday life. To know about the water table in the ground is just as important to us as a knowledge of the three R's. We need to know why all watersheds need the protection of plant life and why the running currents of brooks and rivers must be made to yield their full benefit to the soil before they finally escape to the sea. We need to be taught the duty of planting trees as well as of cutting them. We need to know the importance of big, mature trees, because living space for

most of man's fellow creatures on this planet is figured not only in square measure of surface but also in cubic volume above the earth. As John Muir wrote, "There is no dearth like the hole in the sky when a great tree is gone."

When Nature Is Upset, Man Pays the Price

We need to know the relations between climate, soil, and correct use of the land, because the laws that bind these together cannot be broken without bringing penalties. We cannot haphazardly kill off even insects on a large scale without danger of doing more harm than good, both to nature and ourselves. Most of the land-drainage projects have caused more damage than good.

The more we can keep, the more we shall all have. Many wild flowers are best enjoyed where they grow instead of in vases. Game is a crop, of which we can harvest only the surplus.

It should be our goal to restore as much of the original beauty of North America as we can. This task ought not to be looked upon as a hardship, because the conservation of our natural resources in the end makes a better life for us all. (Also see "Vanishing Animal Life" on page 176 and "A Nation Takes Stock of Its Resources" in Volume 12.)

Before you can hunt or fish in any of the 50 states or the provinces of Canada, you must buy a license or permit. Most state licenses cost residents only a dollar or two; out-of-state permits are slightly higher. The money is used to support the work of the conservation departments. For full details on where to buy your permit, write your state conservation department at your state capital, or inquire at a city or county courthouse. These offices can also tell you about the game laws in your area.

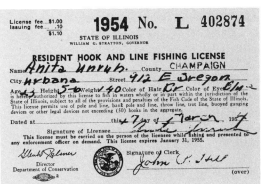

Reprod. courtesy Ill. Dept. of Conserv.

A red kite perches on its handler's glove in a demonstration of falconry at the Bronx Zoo.

Falconry

The art of hunting, using predatory birds, had all but died out by the twentieth century, when suddenly it saw a renaissance, inspired partly by the interest of both Prince Philip and Prince Charles of England. This article by Chloe Collis describes both the history and present standing of this exciting sport.

Falconry, or hawking, is both an art and a sport. A falconer is one who breeds, trains or hunts with birds of prey such as hawks, owls and eagles, called raptors. The most popular hunting bird, because it is the easiest to train, is the peregrine falcon (Falco peregrinus), a species of hawk found in almost every part of the world.

As a sport falconry has existed for hundreds of years throughout the world. It was practiced even before men learned to write. In the Middle Ages it was considered the sport of noblemen. The Crusaders brought the birds back with them from the Middle East and the Orient, as did other adventurers and merchants.

Although none of the hunting birds will retrieve game, they can be trained to kill a selected quarry. When deciding upon the type of hawk to train, the falconer must consider the type of game he wishes to hunt, the kind of country where it is to be found, and the fact that all birds do not kill in the same way.

For hunting rabbits, hares or pheasants, the goshawk with its long wings is the easiest to handle. It is best equipped for flight in open country where the game is most likely to be found. Goshawks usually chase their victims for a time, then finally they dive down to sink their powerful talons into the vital organs of the rabbit or fowl, and cling to the body until it is brought to the ground where men or dogs may capture or retrieve it.

The short-winged accipiters can maneuver easily in light forest areas and can be used for hunting smaller game such as quail, partridge, blackbirds or starlings. This falcon will kill its prey quickly in the air at the end of a very powerful dive and without clinging to the victim.

The falconer can either trap a wild hawk, or steal a young hawk (called an eyas) from the nest. The latter is easiest since the bird, though nearly mature, has not yet learned to fly. Only the larger female is properly called a falcon; the smaller male is called a tercel. An adult hawk is a haggard, while a young bird caught in flight is called a passager. It is advisable to try to train a young bird, an eyas, before trying to capture a wild adult.

Whether the hawk is trapped or captured, the training must be done with skill and patience. As soon as the bird is caught its head is covered with a soft leather hood called a rufter, a tiny bell is provided, and leg jesses are attached so that the hawk can be easily controlled. The falconer then begins to carry the bird perched on his fist, which is covered by a heavy leather glove which protects his arm (up to the elbow) from the sharp talons.

When the falcon has adjusted to the new environment and will eat unhooded while perched on the falconer's arm, it is then trained to hunt, and later to kill for itself.

Because of the fact that many of the favorite hunting grounds have been closed and restrictions placed on the killing of protected game animals and fowl, the sport of hawking has greatly diminished from what it was just a few

A common buzzard is here seen "flying to hand" during the Bronx Zoo's falconry demonstration.

New York Zoological Park

centuries ago. Also, the availability of the shotgun has turned hunters' interests elsewhere.

Some people are interested only in admiring the interesting birds and the artful technique of the falconer, and so are happy to collect the literature of falconry and take pride in owning the special hawk bells, of which those from India are most prized. The British Falconer's Club, founded in 1927, has members all over the world. However only a few individuals actually keep or fly hawks and fewer still are licensed to hunt.

Falconry in Europe was once supported by members of hawking clubs such as the Falconer's Society of England, which was founded in about 1770 and lasted until the death of its manager, Lord Berners, in 1838. Interest was then transferred to the Netherlands where in 1839 the Loo Hawking Club of England was founded; this was succeeded by the present British Falconer's Club.

The "bird of nobility" has been a symbol of the leisure afforded by the wealthy and carries a tradition of romance and sportsmanship unequaled in any other form of hunting.

The Fatal Hawking Match

Falconry, like many other diversions of the European Renaissance, developed its own special vocabulary for the actions and accessories of its birds. This scene is an excerpt from the play **A Woman Killed with Kindness** by Thomas Heywood, first performed in 1607. The two noblemen are rivals, and the flight of the hawks (which takes place invisibly off-stage) and their performance precipitate a brawl in which several men are wounded or killed. The hawking terms are numbered and defined in the notes at the end of the selection.

(Sound of horns. Enter Sir Charles Mountford, Cranwell, and Sir Charles' falconer and huntsmen; and Sir Francis Acton, Wendoll, and Sir Francis' falconer and huntsman.)

SIR CHARLES: So; well cast off! Aloft, aloft!
Well flown!
Oh, now she takes her at the souse,[1] and strikes her
Down to the earth, like a swift thunder-clap.

WENDOLL *(ruefully):* She hath struck ten angels out of my way.

SIR FRANCIS: A hundred pound from me.

SIR CHARLES: What, falconer!

SIR C.'S FALCONER: At hand, sir!

SIR CHARLES: Now she hath seized the fowl and begins to plume[2] her;
Rebeck[3] her not; rather stand still and check her!
So, seize her gets,[4] her jesses,[5] and her bells!
Away!

SIR FRANCIS: My hawk kill'd, too.

SIR CHARLES: Ay, but 'twas at the querre,[6]
Not at the mount like mine.

SIR FRANCIS: Judgment, my masters.

CRANWELL: Yours mist her at the ferre.[7]

WENDOLL: Ay, but our merlin first had plum'd the fowl,
And twice renewed[8] her from the river too. . . .

SIR CHARLES: 'Tis lost.

SIR FRANCIS: I grant it not. Mine likewise seiz'd a fowl
Within her talons, and you saw her claws
Full of the feathers; both her petty singles[9]
And her long singles grip'd her more than other;
The terrials[10] of your falcon's legs were stain'd with blood,
Not of the fowl only; she did discomfit
Some of her feathers; but she brake away.
Come, come; your hawk is but a rifler.[11]

SIR CHARLES: How!

SIR FRANCIS: Ay, and your dogs are curs!

SIR CHARLES: You stir my blood. You keep not one good hound in all your kennels.
Nor one good hawk upon your perch.
You will come short in all things.

SIR FRANCIS: Not in this!
Now I'll strike home! *(Strikes Sir Charles.)*
All they that love Sir Francis, follow me!

SIR CHARLES: All that affect Sir Charles, draw on my part!
(They divide themselves, draw swords and fight.)

373

Notes
[1]On the descent. [2]Strip the feathers from. [3]To call the falcon back. [4]Same as "jesses." [5]Leg-straps. [6]Similar to "souse." [7]Highest point. [8]Returned to the attack. [9]Talons. [10]Bottoms of the feet. [11]Bungler, incompetent.

American Museum of Natural History

Photo, Lisl Steiner

The Metropolitan Museum
of Art, Rogers Fund, 1947

An Inca artisan of Peru made this silver llama and rider (left); the medal of the Mexican-Ethiopian Institute of Cultural Relations shows the Lion of Ethiopia and the Eagle-and-Serpent of Mexico (center); the bronze bull is from the Achaemenian culture, Arabia, 6th century B.C.

Man and His Animals

Thousands of years ago some man with a lot of courage and patience became the first person to capture a wild animal, tame it, and use it for his own purposes. No one knows exactly where or when this happened, but it was probably somewhere in Asia, sometime during the New Stone Age which lasted in Asia from about 12000 to 5000 B.C. Before this time, and in many cultures for a long period thereafter, men often regarded certain animals as sacred, or as their *totem* —meaning that they were related to the animal and that it was their protector and adviser. In most cultures a man could not hunt or eat his totemic animal, but this did not apply to the totemic animals of others.

The taming of animals was a new step up the ladder of civilization. It gave man a more certain source of food (meat and milk). It gave him wool and hair which he learned to weave into cloth, and it gave him hides for making such things as tents, wine containers, water bottles, "books," and musical instruments. And the taming of animals gave man a source of power other than his own muscles. Now he had beasts to carry him and his burdens, to pull his loads and vehicles.

These animals that serve man in so many ways are known today as domestic animals or livestock. Compared with the total number of animals that exist in the world, the domestic animals make up a small group, but because of their usefulness they are more valuable to us than all the other animals combined. From the livestock that make up this group come many important products, as well as much of the meat for man's food supply. And besides this, animals have many other relationships to man; some of them symbolic and others so ancient and traditional that we take them for granted.

374

Animal Husbandry:

The Art and Science of Raising Livestock

If you have ever had a dog, cat, or some other kind of pet, then you know how much fun it is to own an animal. Also, you know that you have to take care of a pet, feed it and give it a place to sleep; if you take a vacation you either have to take your pet along or get someone else to take care of it until you come back.

When animals are tamed they are herded together or penned up and forced to live in a different way. They can't roam around and find their own food and shelter any longer. So, in return for the companionship, food, and work that we get from animals, we are responsible for taking care of them.

The work of breeding, feeding, and caring for livestock is called animal husbandry, and a person who does such work is called a husbandman. These names come from the word "husband" which is mainly used today to refer to the male member of a married couple. But hundreds of years ago when the word first came into use, a husband was a person who owned his house and land, and later, a person who tilled the soil or cared for livestock.

Animals were first tamed during the New Stone Age some ten or twelve thousand years before the time of Christ. In those days the husbandman simply herded his animals from place to place to find good grass and water for them. The nomads, as these wandering herdsmen were called, lived in natural shelters such as caves, or in tents which could be easily moved when it was time to drive the herd to greener pastures.

The story of Abraham in the Bible is a good example of this kind of animal husbandry. Abraham was a wealthy man who owned large numbers of cattle, sheep, goats, and camels. He hired servants to act as shepherds and take care of his flocks and herds. The shepherd's job was to see that none of the animals strayed too far from the main herd, to rescue those that might fall into ditches or holes, and to protect them against the preying of wild beasts.

Later, after the Mediterranean areas of Asia and Africa (where animal husbandry possibly began) became more settled and towns and villages were established, the livestock owners usually lived in towns near good grazing areas and they and their sons, or their servants, took turns going out to the pastures to take care of the animals. David, the shepherd boy who became a king, was a herdsman for his father, Jesse, who lived in Bethlehem. A thousand years after David's time, shepherds were still watching their flocks on the hillsides near Bethlehem the night Christ was born, and this is one of the few parts of the world where the

Animal husbandry is a combination of art and science. There is an old saying that "the eye of the master fattens his cattle." It means that a good husbandman observes his animals, knows when they are not doing well, and looks for ways to make them thrive.

Bob Taylor

375

An Arab shepherd boy of North Africa. In parts of Asia and Africa, sheep raising is still done in the manner of biblical times.

herding of animals in the ancient way of the nomads is still carried on today.

Animal Husbandry in America

In western America, however, there is a type of livestock farming that resembles that of the nomads. In the mountainous and semiarid (dry) grassland regions of the West and Southwest there are large ranches where cattle and sheep are raised. It takes up to 100 acres or even more to make enough grazing for one cow or six sheep. A single western rancher sometimes has as many as eight or ten thousand acres of this type of grassland which give him and his family only a modest income.

To keep track of his livestock on such a large pasture, the rancher makes regular inspection trips on horseback, or in a truck if there are roads on the ranch. In mountainous sections the cattle and sheep are driven into the mountains during the summer to eat the grass that grows on the slopes. In such cases, particularly if it is a sheep ranch, a herdsman usually stays with the stock at all times. He lives in a tent or trailer in the mountains and may go for months without seeing another

human being. In the autumn or early winter the animals are rounded up and driven down to the valleys to graze there until snow comes. When snow covers the grass, the animals must be fed hay or other feed such as soybean oil meal or linseed meal.

Where Men and Animals Must Be Hardy

In some parts of the West, especially in Utah, Colorado, and northern California, the country is extremely rough and barren. The only growing things among the rocks that cover the mountain slopes are short, thin grass, a few wild flowers, and some scraggly bushes. It takes hardy animals and hardy men to live in such country. But thousands of sheep are raised there and shipped to our markets each year. Most of the men who herd these sheep are Basques from the Pyrenees Mountains that border France and Spain. Few people would enjoy the lonely, uncomfortable, sometimes dangerous life in such desolate country, but the Basques thrive on it. Their people have been shepherds for hundreds of years in Europe. A special law makes it possible for numbers of Basques to come to the United States each year to serve as shepherds in the West. Ranchers are always glad to hire them because the Basques are devoted to the care of the sheep and have even been known to give their lives looking after the animals during severe blizzards, forest fires, and other times of danger.

The kind of animal husbandry practiced in the West is called livestock ranching. In other parts of the country livestock farming is usually combined with the raising of crops such as wheat and corn. The pasture land and all or part of the crops raised on such farms are fed to livestock either as hay, grain, or ensilage, also called silage (made by chopping green feeds such as corn, oats, or grass, putting them into a silo, and allowing them to ferment). Farms of this type are common throughout the Middle West, and parts of the South and Southwest.

Many Animals and Fewer Crops

There is still another type of livestock farming

in which large numbers of animals but few crops are raised. The dairy and poultry farms, found near big cities and in the thickly populated sections along the Atlantic and Pacific coasts, are examples of this type of livestock farming. The farms are small in area in proportion to the large number of animals found on them. There is very little, if any, pasture land and usually no crop land; all of the animal feeds are bought from feed dealers or other farmers. Millions of eggs and tons of milk and poultry meat are produced on such farms each year. The dairy cattle stay inside the barns for months at a time, and chickens are raised in "apartment houses," often never setting foot on outside ground from the time they are hatched until they are sold to the poultry processing plant.

Livestock and Good Living Go Together

Throughout the world, wherever livestock is raised you are likely to find a large number of people who have many comforts and conveniences of modern living. One exception, however, is India; although there are large numbers of cattle in India, religious laws forbid the use of cattle or their products.

"Animal agriculture," as livestock raising is also called, has reached a high stage of development in the United States, and animal husbandry has changed through the years from a simple art to a complex science. Millions of dollars are spent every year in our agricultural colleges and state and federal experiment stations to learn ways of improving and feeding livestock so that we may get more and better products from our animals.

The research covers three big areas—breeding, feeding, and management. The livestock breeders develop new breeds and improve those we already have in order to give us better animals to suit the purposes for which they are wanted—dairy cows that give more milk, beef cattle that yield more roasts and

Why there are fewer horses today. In the 1890's as many as 33 head of horses and mules were harnessed to one harvester; today one man and one tractor do the job.

J. I. Case Co.

Caterpillar Tractor Co.

The first cattle in North America looked like these Texas longhorns. Much of these animals' weight was in big bones and horns instead of beef.

There's more meat and less nonfood material such as bone on a modern beef animal—the result of experiments in cattle breeding.

steaks, chickens that lay more eggs. Research workers in livestock feeding and nutrition make studies to find out what animals should eat in order to yield more and better products. They plan balanced diets to meet these needs, and they experiment with new types of feeds to see if they may be profitably used by livestock. The specialists in livestock management study ways of controlling animal diseases, how to house animals on the farm, and how to take care of them in the best way with less work for the farmer.

Animal products make up nearly half of the total farm income in the United States today. The total number of livestock on our farms has increased steadily during the last 50 years, although there have been changes within the various classes of livestock. Cattle have increased from about 60 million head to 95 million, and hogs have increased from about 51 million to 55 million head. Sheep numbers have decreased from 48 million head to 28 million in the last 50 years, largely due to less use of lamb and mutton in favor of beef, pork, and poultry products.

The number of horses and mules has undergone a tremendous change, particularly since 1915 when there were almost 26½ million horses and mules on United States farms. The number has now dropped to slightly over 5½ million head.

378

Why We Have Fewer Horses Today

Horses and mules were once extremely important for transportation and for pulling farm machinery, but the invention of the automobile and the tractor put thousands of these animals out of work. Some horses are still raised for pleasure (riding and racing), for use as cowponies on ranches, and for draft (pulling farm machinery or vehicles) on small farms or farms in areas where the country is too hilly and rough for the use of machinery. The army retired horse cavalry only a few years ago.

Livestock is most important to us today as a source of meat, milk, eggs, and fats, which add to our diet's food value. Animals not only change corn and oats and other grains into meat, but they also eat other feeds that human beings don't eat—hay, grass, citrus pulp, cull apples and potatoes, dried meat scraps, and waste products of the brewing industry.

Boys and girls who live on farms where livestock is raised are fortunate in having many animals to care for and enjoy. Thousands of members of the Future Farmers of America and 4-H clubs have discovered that animal husbandry is one of the most satisfying kinds of farming. Each year more of them choose livestock raising in preference to all of the other worth-while projects sponsored by these clubs.

Cattle for Meat and Milk

Written by the editor.

The average person in the United States eats about 80 pounds of beef and uses more than 170 quarts of milk a year. This means that over 13 billion pounds of beef and 28 billion quarts of milk are being produced yearly to supply the needs of a population of about 180 million people.

How many cattle do you suppose it takes to produce this amount of food? At the start of 1960 there were nearly 100 million head of beef and dairy animals on United States farms. But the high production of meat and milk in the United States today is not made possible by large numbers of animals alone. It is also the result of scientific breeding, feeding, and management.

When people speak of the "breeding" of cattle they refer to the development of types that are built to do the job they are meant to perform: that is, beef animals that can produce the greatest amount of high quality meat in the shortest time on the least amount of feed, and dairy animals that can produce the most milk in proportion to the amount of feed they eat.

Improved practices in feeding and management of cattle go hand in hand to complete the job started by the breeder. Experiments are constantly under way in agricultural colleges and government experiment stations all over the United States to test new feeds and pastures and find new ways of combining them in rations that will get the most out of the animals in the form of meat and milk. Management comes into play when the cattleman or dairyman decides which breed of cattle he will raise, which crops he will grow for their feed, when and how he will sell his milk or meat, which machinery and equipment to buy, and how many animals he will raise.

How Beef Cattle Are Raised

Except in the more northern states and Canada where the winters are long and very cold, beef cattle spend a large part of their lives on the open range. Most of the calves are born in the

USDA, by Hunton

Dairy cattle carry less flesh and have finer bones than beef cattle; they change feed into milk instead of meat. This young herdsman can be proud of the good breeding of his heifer calf and two-year-old Jersey bull.

Products of dairy cattle

spring when the weather is mild. A beef calf weighs about 80 pounds at birth, and within a few hours it will be running on wobbly legs by its mother's side in the pasture. A good beef calf has a square, thick body, short neck, and short, straight legs. Female calves are called heifers and the males are called bulls. Steers are male calves that have been castrated—that is, their sex glands have been removed at an early age. This causes the animal to fatten more rapidly and makes its meat more tender; consequently most male calves are castrated.

A beef calf will eat grass when it is a few weeks old but it suckles its mother until it is six to eight months old. In the autumn the spring calves are weaned, or separated from their mothers and no longer allowed to nurse. The weanling calf weighs about 400 pounds and is nearly half grown. It is usually fed from eight months to a year longer and sold on the market as a fat (or finished) steer or heifer.

Many cattlemen prefer not to fatten the calves themselves because their land is not suited for growing grain, which is needed for the fattening process. In such cases, the feeder calves, as they are called, may be sold to local farmers or they may be shipped to a stockyards and sold to cattle feeders in the Corn Belt or other grain-producing parts of the

379

Products of
beef cattle

A Hereford cow showing motherly interest in her offspring. Contrast the heavier bones, shorter legs, and blockier frame of this calf with the build of the dairy calf on the preceding page.

Bob Taylor

country. The cattle raiser may decide, however, to keep the weaned calves on his pastures for another year and then sell them as grass-fed yearlings.

How Long Does It Take To Fatten a Calf?

Calves sold at weanling age are fed for about a year before they are fat enough for market; grass-fed yearlings are put "on feed," as the fattening process is called, for only six months or so before they are ready for market. In either case, the cattle are usually placed in pens or feedlots, which are large enough to give the animals room to exercise, but not large enough to allow them to run off their weight as fast as they put it on. The feed is placed in long, shallow feed boxes, and water tanks are provided where the cattle may drink. Water is very important; a feeder calf will drink an average of eight to ten gallons a day. In cold climates, special heaters are used to keep the water tanks from freezing over.

Feeds most commonly used to fatten beef cattle are corn, some type of protein-rich feed such as soybean oil meal or cottonseed meal, minerals, and hay or corn silage. Corn silage is feed made of coarsely chopped green corn stalks with the partly-formed ears left on; it is stored in an airtight structure called a silo.

All of the feed except the hay or silage is combined in a mixture before feeding. Most cattlemen mix their own feeds in large amounts at a time, although some farmers have their feeds mixed at a feed and grain store.

A feeder steer or heifer will eat from fifteen to twenty pounds of feed per day and will gain about two pounds per day in weight. The rate of weight gain depends on the animal's size, and the kind and amount of feed eaten. When they weigh about 1,000 pounds they are ready for market. Cattle can lose weight rapidly, however, during shipment to market or in the stockyards awaiting purchase.

On the Dairy Farm

The raising of beef cattle varies from one part of the country to another, but dairying is done in about the same way wherever you go. A dairy heifer does not give milk until she "freshens" or has her first calf. Usually this happens when the heifer is between two and three years old; after her first freshening she is called a cow. The newborn calf suckles its mother during the first few days after its birth; then it is put in a separate pen with other young dairy calves, and its mother is put with the other cows in the milking herd. The cow and calf are permanently separated from then on. They usually bawl for a few hours, but within a day or two they completely forget one another.

Most dairymen milk their cows twice a day, although some have three milking periods. The cows are driven into the milking barn and put in separate stalls or stanchions, where they are fed while the milking is done. The feed is a very nutritious mixture containing such things as ground corn, oats, wheat bran, soybean meal, alfalfa meal, and minerals such as salt and bone meal.

A good dairy cow is a living machine, working in the service of man. She is an expert at changing raw materials into milk—milk for babies and growing boys and girls, and for use in hundreds of foods for everyone. In comparison with a beef cow, a good dairy cow looks thin. Her hip bones stick up and her ribs show so plainly beneath her hide that they may easily be counted. A dairy cow is not supposed to be fat, if she puts on weight, or tends to be "beefy" as dairymen say, it shows that she is changing part of her feed into flesh instead of milk, and usually such cows are culled from the herd.

Milking Is Usually Done by Machine

Nowadays most dairy farmers use machines for milking because they are faster and more sanitary. The cows are milked in special areas often called "milking parlors." A good dairy cow enters the building with her udder swollen and gorged with milk and, when the milking is over, leaves the building with a limp and flabby udder. The cow enters the building and goes into a raised stall where the milking machines are located. Suctions cups are fitted over each teat and the electrically operated machine pulls them with a gentle, rhythmic motion. The cups are connected to a pipeline system which carries the milk to a bulk cooling tank. For each cow the total milking time is about five minutes.

The milk is kept cold in the tank at the farm until a special refrigerated tank truck picks it up each day for delivery to the plant where it will be processed. Bacteria thrive on milk, so every precaution must be taken to keep the milk clean and prevent spoiling until it can be pasteurized (heated to destroy bacteria) at the processing plant. After bottling (in rural areas) or being sealed into waxed or plasticized containers (for city distribution) the milk is ready for the consumer.

Cleanliness Helps Keep Milk Safe

The milking barn is washed clean after each milking and regularly sprayed to kill flies. The cows' udders are washed with a solution

Bob Taylor

Range cattle are often fed additional high-protein rations, especially in the winter when grazing is limited. These cattle are eating their "concentrate," as such feeds are called, from feed boxes called bunks.

containing an antiseptic (germ-killing substance) before milking, and all utensils and containers are washed in antiseptic solution and sterilized. People who work in dairies must keep themselves and their clothing as clean as possible and they must pass regular health examinations. Dairy barns are regularly inspected by health officials.

Some of the milk is used to feed the baby calves. Sometimes the calves plunge their heads into the pail of milk up to their eyes and come out coughing and spluttering before they learn to drink properly. Sometimes they are fed from a nipple pail which has a large rubber nipple the size of a cow's teat near the bottom of the pail.

Dairy calves are fed milk until they are about four months old. In addition they are given a mixed feed to help them grow. The young bull calves are usually sold for veal, but heifers are kept until they are old enough to breed and have calves, when they too will become part of the milking herd.

381

In the 1960's there were nearly 100 million head of cattle on United States farms. Over 80 million were beef cattle. Two-thirds of the cattle are produced west of the Mississippi; two-thirds of the products from cattle are consumed east of the Mississippi.

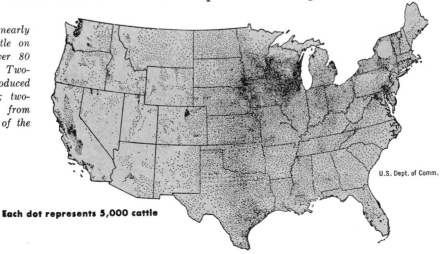

U.S. Dept. of Comm.

Each dot represents 5,000 cattle

The Story of Sheep and Goats

Did you know there is a sheep whose tail alone may weigh as much as 40 pounds, or where persian lamb fur coats come from, or what kind of milk is used for Roquefort cheese? There are answers to these questions in this article from **The Animal Kingdom**, Volume II, edited by Frederick Drimmer. Copyright, 1954, by The Greystone Press.

It is not always an easy matter to tell the goats from the sheep, in the wild. Both are mountain folk, dwelling in the high places of the earth. Both are chewers of the cud, have hairy coats and hollow horns. But although we may occasionally confuse a number of these creatures, there are ways in which sheep and goats differ.

The wild goat is generally a more sure-footed and adventurous animal than the wild sheep. It can live off the coarsest of food. Although it may browse and graze on grassy slopes, it will, after eating, retreat to a high crag for safety and slumber. Most male goats have a distinct beard and a strong goaty odor.

Both sheep and goats were domesticated before 3000 B.C., and probably much earlier than cattle. Wild goats are restricted to Europe, Central Asia, and North Africa. We find the wild sheep in the Northern Hemisphere, including North Africa. The Rocky Mountain bighorn sheep, the most spectacular animal of the American group, is not entirely a creature of the New World; close relatives occur in Siberia.

Goats produce milk, butter, cheese, and flesh for food. Like the wool of the sheep, goat hair is used for clothing. It is from Angora goats that we get the famous mohair. The cashmere goat is famed the world over for its fine fleece; a short-legged, graceful creature that is able to live on little food, the cashmere goat originally was a native of the Vale of Kashmir and the mountain ranges of the Himalayas.

The Agile Ibex and Other Wild Goats

The ibex, a native of Asia, North Africa, and Europe, is a common wild goat of the Old World. It dwells in the vicinity of precipitous

cliffs and mountain crags at high elevations close to the snow line at all seasons of the year. Even in winter it does not seek the shelter of timber; instead, it haunts steep hillsides where the snow is not deep.

The ibex has acute senses of sight, hearing, and smell. Usually one animal seems to act as a lone sentry, keeping watch for possible danger; it utters a shrill warning whistle to alert its fellows at the slightest suspicion of anything unusual. Extremely agile and sure-footed, the ibex can leap down a forty-foot precipice to a rocky ledge below with perfect control and calmness. Wild dogs and snow leopards are common enemies of this animal in the Himalayas.

Among the many kinds of these hardy animals, the Siberian ibex, *Capra sibirica,* is the largest and most handsome. The European ibex or steinbok is now extinct in the wild.

The ibex has enormous horns, sometimes spreading to 58 inches or more. Heavy ridges or bosses mark the top surface.

382

The hair of the cashmere goat is prized for its warmth and softness. It is used for making fine sweaters and fabrics.

J. C. Allen & Son

J. C. Allen & Son

A pair of Saanen kids (left). This breed, creamy white in color, originally came from the Saanen Valley in Switzerland. Many Saanens are polled, or hornless.

The native home of the Nubian goat (above right) is Nubia, in northeastern Africa. Long ears and short-haired coat of black, red, or tan mark this breed. Goat meat, called chevon, is an important food in some countries.

The brown and white Toggenburg, another Swiss breed, is the most numerous goat in America. The hair-covered tufts of skin, seen just above the collar on this doe's neck, are called wattles.

Bob Taylor

The domestic goat is a descendant of the pasang, Chetan ibex or wild goat, which roams in herds over barren, rocky hills. The pasang has the peculiar habit of selecting the narrowest of pinnacles on which to balance itself. This goat dwells in a territory that ranges from southeastern Europe to southwestern Asia and includes the neighboring islands.

Some of the wild goats are as much like sheep as they are goats, so they may be thought of as links between the two species. One of these, the Eastern tur, *Capra caucasica,* is a robust and handsome wild goat with comparatively smooth, short horns which curve outward and backward close to the neck. The Western tur, native to the western half of the main Caucasian Range, while still a wild goat, has heavy bosses (knobs) on the front of the horns like a true ibex, but the horns are shorter, heavier, and not so evenly arched. The turs like to live on lofty precipices above the snow line.

The Himalayan tahr, *Hemitragus jemlaicus,* is a beardless goat with short, evenly curved horns, that lives at high elevations in the Himalayas. Here it runs in herds of five to about 25, among the crags and rocky precipices near the timber line; old males may even enter thick timber. The tahrs are wary, sharp sighted and, like all goats, nimble on a steep terrain.

The markhor, *Capra falconeri,* has long, shaggy hair, and in old males the beard extends from the chin down the underside of the throat. This wild goat follows along the margin between deep forest and higher snow-capped peaks. It ranges from Kashmir in India to Afghanistan in western Asia. The Himalayan markhor is the biggest of the wild goats—it may stand over 40 inches high and weigh more than 200 pounds.

Some Breeds of Domestic Sheep

There is a vast difference between wild sheep and the 40-odd breeds of domestic sheep. The domestic sheep have long tails and woolly fleeces, whereas the wild varieties have short tails and stiff, hairy coats. It was man's selec-

383

tive breeding that made the sheep the valuable wool-bearer it is today. Most authorities are agreed that the domestic sheep was derived from the red sheep, *Ovis orientalis*. The red sheep is yellow or fox-red in summer and brownish in winter, with a gray saddle patch. The horns usually curve sharply backward and end behind the head. There are several species of red sheep that live in the arid rocky mountain ridges of Asia Minor, Persia (Iran), and Cyprus.

Sheep are the chief wealth of the rural tribes of Asia. In Turkestan the nomad (wandering) Kirghiz people live almost entirely on mutton, the meat of the sheep. They have developed a variety of sheep known as the dumba, which has an excess of fat on the buttocks. This breed possesses a long, fat tail that may weigh up to 40 pounds. The Kirghiz not only eat mutton but use the wool for clothing and beat it into heavy felt for covering their yurts, or tents.

The merino sheep of Spain is famous for its wool, which is often so thick that it covers the animal's eyes. The Spaniards introduced the merino into America at an early date, and it has also found a good home in Australia. This hardy, sociable animal is said to produce more and finer wool than any other sheep. Its mutton, however, is not highly esteemed.

It is from the caracul or karacul that we get persian lamb or broadtail, widely used for fur coats and fur trimmings. The best pelts are taken from caracul lambs when they are between a week and ten days old, for then the curl is at its best. Black pelts are the most desirable. These sturdy animals are at home in semiarid regions—particularly in Bokhara, in the Soviet Union.

A good deal of Australia's prosperity today is based on the raising of sheep. Western Asia and the western part of the United States are also responsible for much of the world's wool Britain, too, is a famed breeder of sheep for wool and mutton. The Cheviot sheep of Scotland, Southdown sheep, and Shropshire sheep are three noted British breeds. In Australia the sheep shearer is a vital person in the country's economy; his skill is admired and is the subject of folk songs.

In ancient times sheep were carefully tended. The thought of obtaining water and grass for his flock was uppermost in the shepherd's mind. The shepherd knew all his sheep by name and did not need to drive them. In those days, sheep were kept more for their milk than for their flesh. (Today our main product from the milk of these animals is Roquefort cheese, originally made in France.)

America's Wild Sheep

The Rocky Mountain bighorn sheep, *Ovis canadensis,* is considered to be America's finest game animal. The bighorn has extremely sharp eyesight and long-range vision. Its sense of smell is unusually acute and its ears can catch the faintest sound.

Goats are excellent climbers, but they by no means match the bounding swiftness of bighorn sheep. The feet of the bighorn have soft elastic pads that absorb the shocks of a bouncing gait and also provide a good grip on hard,

384

A herd of Rocky Mountain bighorn sheep, grazing in Pike National Forest, Colorado. Except for its white rump, which shows up brightly when the animal retreats, the bighorn is extremely difficult to see at a distance.

U.S. Forest Serv.

A merino ram has graceful, out-curving horns.

A caracul ram. The curly pelts used for fur coats come from the lambs.

rough, or slippery surfaces. There are few cliffs that bighorns cannot climb—not carefully and step by step like a mountain goat, but at a seemingly heedless and breakneck gallop. Observers have watched these sheep careening down steep cliffs, leaping 20 feet at a time and breaking their speed by bouncing without pause from one narrow ledge of rock to another. Near the bottom of the cliff they sail off into the air with a final majestic bound, to alight on all four feet on the floor of the valley.

Occasionally a bighorn does crash to its death in one of these magnificent charges, but it is usually the ram and not the ewe that dies this way. Barring fatal accidents and the possibility of being killed by wolves or bears, the bighorn can look forward to a long happy life on the sunlit mountain tops. The average mountain sheep has passed its prime at ten or twelve years of age and is old at sixteen; under very favorable conditions, it may live to the grand old age of twenty years, but this is unusual.

Full-grown bighorns may average 40 inches in shoulder height. Weight may range from 175 to 350 pounds. The horns of mature rams often form more than one full turn, the record length being a trifle short of 50 inches. Ewes have smaller horns seldom exceeding fifteen inches in length.

The bighorn's summer coat is dark (or grayish) brown; its winter covering is lighter and grayer. Its hair, like that of other wild sheep, is not woolly as in domestic sheep; instead, it is long, coarse, and full, like a deer's.

The Largest Living Sheep

The ammon or argali, *Ovis ammon*, the largest of all living wild sheep, lives on the highlands of central Asia. Here it is at home on grassy hillsides and meadows above the timber line. An agile mountain-climber, the argali can travel faster than any of the goats over dangerous crags and rugged mountain peaks.

The argali may attain a shoulder height of four feet and a weight of 350 pounds. The horns of the rams are large and massive, curling outward from the side of the head and frequently making more than one complete turn.

The fat-tailed sheep of Syria, like that of Turkestan, is valued as a source of meat, milk, and wool. This is the sheep of biblical times.

Other Sections To See

"How Animals Survive," Volume 1; "Birds of the Sea and Shore and Other Water Birds" and "Human and Animal Tools," Volume 2; "The Story of Horses and Their Masters" and "Fur Animals and Furs," Volume 3; "Whales," Volume 4; "Land Birds of North America," Volume 5; "The World of Reptiles" and "An Introduction to Dogs," Volume 6; "Insects" and "Cage Birds," Volume 7; "Big Game Animals" and "The Cat Family," Volume 8; "A Survey of the Animal Kingdom," "Rodents: Animals That Gnaw," and "Vanishing Animal Life," Volume 9; "Unusual Beasts of Burden," Volume 10; "Cattle, Sheep and Hogs," Volume 12; "The World of Fishes," "Water Animals Without Backbones," and "A Parade of Poultry," Volume 13; "Some Odd and Unusual Animals," Volume 14; "Amphibians: Animals With Two Lives," Volume 15; "Pests of the Animal Kingdom" and "Animal Behavior," Volume 16; "Presenting the Primates," Volume 17.

The Management and Feeding of Sheep

Sheep will eat plants that other animals ignore, and they can survive in rough and desolate country, but they depend on their herdsman to protect them from wild animals, to round them up in a storm, to lead them to a source of drinking water, to rescue them from ditches. In return, sheep provide food and clothing for man and a special kind of devotion for the shepherd that is summed up in the phrase from the Bible, "And the sheep follow him, for they know his voice." Only in certain areas of the Old World and in some parts of North America are sheep still herded as they were in biblical times, but they are still an important class of livestock. This article tells you how sheep are raised and fed today. From **Food and Life,** Yearbook of Agriculture, 1939. United States Department of Agriculture. (Revised according to the most recent data available.)

Most of the sheep produced in the United States are raised in the range country of the West and Southwest. In these areas they make use of land that is unsuited to most other types of farming and livestock production. Sheep are raised in every state in the union, but the leading states in sheep production are Texas, Wyoming, California, Montana, Utah, New Mexico, Colorado, Idaho, and Ohio.

Feeding and management practices vary with the area in which the sheep are found. Sheep generally have their lambs in the spring except for those breeds that produce an additional fall lamb crop. The bred ewes (females that are to have lambs) are separated from the rest of the flock some time before the lambing season begins so that the shepherd may give them extra attention.

Ewes sometimes don't claim their lambs after they are born and will not let them nurse. Also, when twin lambs are born, a ewe may claim one and not the other. In such cases the shepherd places the ewe and her lamb or lambs in a small, separate pen where the ewe can't escape when the lamb wants to nurse, and she usually claims her offspring after a short time. Twins, and even triplets, are not uncommon among sheep. Sometimes a ewe does not give enough milk to raise two or

USDA, by Osborne

Lambs appear to be frail and helpless, but they nurse with a great deal of energy.

three lambs, so the herdsman tries to get another ewe, who may have lost her own lamb, to take one of the "extras." Orphan lambs (those whose mothers die) are sometimes fed with a nursing bottle like those used for human babies, but the herdsman avoids bottle feeding because it means much extra work.

Docking, Shearing, Drenching, and Dipping

When the lambs are about ten days old, their tails are "docked" or cut off. The herdsman does the job with a quick cut of his pocket knife, and the lamb scarcely feels the operation. In ancient times sheep were allowed to keep their tails, and this is still the case in some countries today, but docking is generally practiced for reasons of cleanliness and ease of shearing.

Shearing of sheep—that is, removing their fleece or wool—takes place in the spring. Until fairly recent years this was a tedious hand process, but now practically all shearing of large flocks is done with electrically operated clippers. In areas where there are numerous flocks, shearers travel from farm to farm with their equipment, and the farmer pays them so much per head to have his sheep shorn. Sheep shearing is an art and a good workman can remove an entire fleece in one piece, with a minimum of discomfort to the sheep, in only a few minutes.

Sheep are bothered with parasites that live in their digestive tract. Worm-infested sheep do not grow or gain weight, so they must be dosed at least twice a year with a chemical compound that kills the worms and causes them to pass out of the sheep's body. Most farmers use a powdered type of worm remedy that can be mixed with sheep feed; others "drench" or dose each sheep with a liquid remedy which must be poured down the animal's throat.

Other insects, ticks and flies for example, cause damage to the sheep's hide. These pests are destroyed by walking the sheep through a vat containing a poisonous liquid; this process is known as "dipping."

What Do Sheep Eat?

Sheep are naturally adapted to grazing on pastures and ranges where there is a variety of forage plants (grasses and weeds). They do best on forage that is short and fine rather than high and coarse. They will eat a lot of brush, but they prefer choice grass and legumes and lush, juicy weeds. It is usually unnecessary to feed grain to breeding sheep or even to lambs when they can have an abundance of grazing forage. In some localities flocks can be kept in good condition and lambs can be raised to the marketing stage without the feeding of any grain.

Deep snows, extreme droughts, and overstocked pastures and ranges (where there is too much livestock for the amount of grass available) make it necessary, however, to feed sheep additional hay and grain. Sheep especially like alfalfa or clover hay and oats, corn, or barley. They are also fond of salt and eat a lot more of it than do cattle. Breeding sheep may eat nearly one-half ounce of salt per head daily, and fattening lambs from one-fifth to one-fourth ounce. The salt is usually mixed with bone meal and limestone to provide calcium, phosphorus, and other minerals the

sheep might need. The mineral mixture is placed in a separate feed box where the animals may eat as much as they want of it.

Sheep need plenty of fresh water. On dry feed, ewes drink from one to one-and-one-half gallons a day; fattening lambs drink one to two quarts a day. When succulent (juicy) feeds are provided, sheep drink less than when they are on strictly dry feeds, and when the weather is hot they drink more than when it is cool or cold. During late fall, winter, and early spring, range sheep get most of their water intake from snow.

How Fat Lambs Are Produced

Lamb producers in regions where there are lush pastures and ranges usually try to produce milk-fat lambs—that is, lambs that are fat enough to be slaughtered at weaning time. Many lambs, however, are raised on pastures and ranges that are not adequate for finishing (fattening) lambs at the weaning age of four to six months, and even on the best forage (pasture or hay) some mutton-type lambs and a large proportion of the lambs of the fine-wool type cannot be finished by weaning time. (For a discussion of the different wool types in sheep, see "Fibers Clothe the World," in Volume 3.) For these reasons a rather large proportion of the lamb crop of the United States must be fed on pasture or feed lots after weaning, until the lambs are fat enough for market.

Corn is the grain most often used in the United States as the chief fattening feed for lambs, but barley and oats are sometimes used. Alfalfa or clover hay is fed as roughage. When silage, especially corn silage, is available at reasonable cost, it may be used in the lamb-fattening ration together with a protein-rich meal such as cottonseed or linseed.

387

These yearling ewes of the Southdown breed are examples of the ideal mutton-type sheep. The sheep has a cleft underlip, which makes it possible for the sheep to crop grass closer to the ground than other types of grazing animals.

USDA

The range herdsman's life is a lonely one; except for the hundreds of sheep in his care he may see no living thing for days at a time.

Silage made from plants other than corn may be used—for example, silage made from peas and oats, pea vines, and corn and soybeans. Other feeds suitable for fattening lambs are turnips, rutabagas, wet beet pulp, beet tops, cabbage, and potatoes.

What Is a Hothouse Lamb?

Hothouse lambs are born in the fall or early winter and finished for slaughter as suckling lambs at the age of about two to four months at live weights of 40 to 60 pounds, or even less than 40 pounds if they are fat. The term "hothouse" is used because, like hothouse tomatoes or strawberries, such lambs are produced during an unusual season of the year, though not necessarily in quarters heated by a stove or furnace. If lambs are to be finished at such early ages and light weights, they must be able to develop and fatten rapidly, and their feeds and the feeds for their mothers must be of excellent quality. Hothouse lambs that measure up to the very special requirements for this product are often the offspring of Southdown rams and Dorset or Dorset-Merino ewes.

Hothouse lambs should be fed in a creep (a pen which the lambs can enter but the ewes can not) as soon as they will nibble at grain and roughage, which they will normally begin to do when they are about two weeks old. In order to get them to eat as much as possible, only the very choicest feed such as cracked corn and crushed oats should be offered and there should be nothing but fresh feed in the troughs and racks.

Feeding Sheep in Farm Flocks

In the eastern half of the United States and in the irrigated valleys and dry-land farming communities of the West, sheep are kept in small or moderate-sized flocks of about 20 to 100 head, or in some instances as many as 200 to 300. Most farm flocks glean much of their feed from stubble and stalk fields in the fall; after these feeds have been used, clover and grass pastures are grazed. In regions where winters are open (where there is no snow on the ground) a heavy stand (growth) of bluegrass will help to carry the flock through the winter in good condition. Green pastures of rye or wheat in late fall will provide succulent feed and furnish exercise for the flock. In the South, velvetbeans are found a great help in carrying the flock into January when pastures again become available.

In winter the feeding of the farm flock should be aimed at producing vigorous lambs and keeping the wool strong and in good condition. Clover or alfalfa hays, straws, and cornstalks usually form the main part of the winter rations. During the late spring, summer, and early fall, farm sheep in most regions can obtain most of their feed requirements from good pasture. When good pasture is not available it may be necessary to feed them the same as for the winter period. The quantity of feed should be increased for ewes nursing lambs. Rams may be fed the same kinds of feed as ewes but in slightly larger quantities. They need a good allowance of relatively high-quality feed just before and during the breeding season, when pasture is not available.

How Range Sheep Are Fed

In the western half of the United States a large majority of the sheep are produced in range bands varying in size from a few hundred to more than 2,000 head, but usually containing between 1,000 and 2,000. They live largely on the natural forage of the range, but deep snow, drought, and scanty forage on overgrazed or poor quality range make it necessary at times to feed hay and cottonseed cake or other high-protein feed. If there is not enough pasture for grazing in the early spring, the breeding ewes should receive some grain for about three weeks or a month before lambing. Breeding rams may be wintered on roughage and a small quantity of grain, as it is unnecessary to fatten them.

Danger! Poisonous Plants

Some of the most serious feeding problems encountered by range sheep producers result from poisonous plants that are eaten by sheep while grazing. Plants that cause sickness and death among sheep occur in all parts of the United States. However, because of the greater number of sheep on the range and the method of handling them, the main losses occur in the western range country. Where good grass is plentiful, sheep that are left to themselves seldom eat enough of any poisonous plant to suffer from its effects; but under the system of close herding that is practiced in many regions, where sheep eat practically all the vegetation as they move along, they are more liable to poisoning, and sometimes heavy losses occur.

The three groups of plants on the western ranges that cause the greatest destruction of sheep are the species of death camas found in the higher parts of the Great Plains and west to the Pacific; the locos, especially white loco, found on the Great Plains from Canada to Mexico; and the lupines, which are even more widely distributed than death camas. Lupine leaves rarely, if ever, injure sheep, but the pods and seeds, which are eaten during the summer and fall months, have caused heavy losses.

The laurels and leaves of wild cherries both in the East and in the West, the milk weeds and rayless goldenrod of New Mexico and Texas, the Colorado rubber plant of Colorado and New Mexico, and the coffee bean of Texas are some of the other plants that cause losses. The western sneezeweed is especially harmful in Utah and some parts of the Southwest.

No practical methods have been found for getting rid of most of these poisonous plants. However, a careful herder who is familiar with the plants and the places where they grow can cut down on plant poisoning by herding the sheep away from the danger.

The pioneer phase of the sheep industry has passed and cheap grazing is becoming more and more scarce. The need for economy in feeding methods is great, and careless and wasteful methods will lead to decreased numbers of sheep available for food and fiber. Sheep feeding and grazing must now be handled with the utmost care and research workers at the federal experiment stations and state agricultural colleges are constantly looking for improved methods of feeding and managing sheep.

389

Bob Taylor

Sheep eating silage. Additional feed is necessary when grazing is impossible in the winter and when sheep are to be finished for market.

Feeding her birds. Chickens make an ideal project for the beginner in animal husbandry.

USDA, by Boyer

How Poultry Is Raised

Many people who are professional stock or poultry raisers begin young; every year thousands of boys and girls, most (but not all) of whom are members of the 4-H Clubs or Future Farmers of America, get valuable experience in raising animals in ways such as this described for poultry. From **The 4-H Handbook** by H. A. Willman. Copyright 1952 by Cornell University Press. Revised by editor.

Some people, and even some farmers think that the chicken business is of small importance. Actually, in terms of the total farm income of the nation, poultry raising is one of the leading enterprises. In fact, on some farms and in some states, the value of poultry and eggs sold leads that of other farm commodities. Furthermore, more farms produce poultry and eggs than almost any other important farm crop.

There are many reasons for the immense production of poultry and eggs. A small flock fits the everyday needs of many families; it can provide the family with chicken dinners and often serves as the start of a larger commercial enterprise. Although the raising of chickens is of greatest importance, poultry raising may include ducks, turkeys, geese, swans, guineas, pigeons, and pheasants.

Keeping poultry does not require a large outlay of cash because much of the equipment needed, such as brooders, brooder coops, feeders, and fountains, can be made at home. Old buildings also may be remodeled and converted for poultry housing. If land is scarce, chickens can be produced successfully in buildings, but the use of green pasture throughout the summer helps to reduce costs.

Profit in poultry raising, like success with other farm animal enterprises, depends upon the person in charge, on the use of efficient stock, and on high, yet economical, production.

Beginners in poultry raising are usually advised to start their projects with day-old chicks, but they may begin either by pur-chasing some started pullets that are six to ten weeks old, or ready-to-lay birds, or breeding birds. It is well to keep in mind that the danger of bringing in disease is not so great with baby chicks as it is with older birds.

Whether the chicks are for meat or egg production, they must be from high-production ancestry. Like a calf, sow pig, or seed variety, well-bred chicks may cost more at the outset but will pay in the end through higher yields of meat or eggs. Good care and proper feeding and management are of the greatest importance because the effect of good breeding may be destroyed if the chicks are not given the care they need.

Which Breed Is Best?

The poultry raiser should decide his primary purpose in raising the birds and then select a breed and variety that is available and is suited to that purpose. Unusual breeds and varieties should be avoided, and in making a selection it is well to know that the strain or variety may be as important as the breed. For example, it is not unusual to find some strains of a general-purpose breed excelling, in productive capacity, an egg-production breed.

A breed is a group of fowls of very similar type and body shape. Some examples include Leghorns, Anconas, New Hampshires, Rhode Island Reds, Orpingtons, and Plymouth Rocks. Varieties are subdivisions of breeds and differ in such characteristics as color of plumage (feathers) and comb type. There are about

40 breeds and over 170 varieties and sub-varieties of chickens in the United States, and others in other parts of the world.

The size of the enterprise depends on the amount of time and space available, the size of brooder house and laying house, the available market, the number of people in the family and whether one expects to derive a major source of farm income from the sale of poultry and eggs.

Chicks should be bought from near-by flocks or from breeders and hatcherymen whose stock is known to be free from disease, especially pullorum. This is a disease of chicks which is transmitted to the chick by eggs from infected hens. Pullorum may cause heavy chick losses. It cannot be cured and therefore must be prevented by the use of hatching eggs from blood-tested stock found free of the disease infection.

Buy fewer good-quality chicks rather than more cheap ones if you have a limited amount of money to invest. When in doubt as to where to buy your chicks, consult your county extension agent or a successful local poultryman; and order your chicks early to make sure of getting the number you desire when you will be ready for them.

How Much Equipment Is Needed?

The equipment needed for raising chicks includes the following: (1) A warm brooder house, (2) water fountains (one gallon fountain for each 100 chicks), (3) feeders (one-inch space per chick at the start), (4) one thermometer, (5) a brooder stove (coal, oil, electric, or gas), (6) litter, and (7) feed.

When the baby chicks are removed from their shipping box, they should be placed under a brooder having a temperature of 95° F. as shown by a thermometer placed two inches off the floor at the edge of the hover (the hover is the umbrella-like canopy that fits over the brooder). There should be sufficient heat under the hover but the brooding room itself should be cool, but not chilly. The corners of the house should be closed off with circular material to prevent the piling up of chicks in the corners.

Reduce the temperature registered at the edge of the hover by 5° F. each week until the thermometer reads 80° F. Then, if the temperature and weather outside are not too severe, chicks will get along very well at 70°.

Feed the chicks when they are twenty-four hours old, using a ready-mixed starting mash available at any livestock feed store. Provide fresh clean water, and containers of grit, such as crushed oyster shell, which helps the chicks digest their feed and adds minerals to their diet.

Keep the ready-mixed starting mash constantly before the chicks for five or six weeks, then gradually shift to a growing mash when they are six weeks old. Also give them access to a scratch grain mixture in hoppers. (Scratch grain is a coarsely ground mixture of feeds.)

Cockerel chicks should be separated from the pullets before they are six weeks of age. (The cockerels will already be growing their combs.) Those that are to be sold for broilers may be continued on the all-mash starter and growing mashes. Those kept for roasters ought also to have free access to a mash and a grain mixture and may be raised either in pens or on pastures.

Well-grown pullets may show preparation for laying at five to six months. The signs are red combs, bright glossy feathers, some singing, and good weight. Of the males that were kept for roasters those that weigh four pounds or more and have plump breasts and very few pin feathers that are shorter than one-half inch should be fat enough to market.

How To Manage the Laying Flock

The pullets should be transferred to the laying house, which may be thought of as the hen's workshop and home. It is the place where she is expected to work. For her to do her best, she must be comfortable and be given a full opportunity to show her ability to lay eggs.

As with raising stock or crops, the husbandman must have a measure of his success. The henhouse must produce some return in dollars. In a sense, it is rented to the birds, the rent to be paid by the eggs produced.

Hens, like cows, may be referred to as ma-

water fountain

feed

litter

thermometer

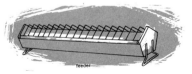

feeder

brooder

chines. They take raw materials (feeds) and manufacture a portion of them into eggs. Hens that are bred for high egg production will use a higher percentage of their feed for egg manufacturing. The average hen of average size may consume about 90 pounds of laying mash in a year. About 75 per cent of this feed is used for maintenance if the hen is in a laying condition. Therefore, about 25 per cent is left for egg production, and for growth if the hen is immature.

The following equipment would be adequate for about 100 pullets of a heavy breed such as New Hampshires or Plymouth Rocks: (1) A well-ventilated, lightly constructed house having a floor space of 350–400 square feet that is protected by a waterproof roof, (2) seventy feet of perch space, (3) twenty nests each containing about five inches of dry shavings or cut straw, (4) two four-gallon water fountains, (5) one four-foot grit and oyster-shell hopper, (6) ratproof bins for mash and grain, (7) thirty-six feet of mash feeder space, (8) a couple of pails and wire egg baskets, and (9) a catching hook and crate.

Proper ventilation and available drinking water are important.

During cold weather the drinking water should be kept from freezing because hens will drink more water and lay more eggs if all other conditions are favorable. Good ventila-

tion helps to keep the litter dry and guards chickens against respiratory diseases.

The poultryman should keep in mind that consumers do not like to buy dirty eggs. The bacteria from the manure and dirt penetrate the shell and lower the keeping quality of eggs. Washing will remove the dirt from the outside, but the washing process is usually costly in time and if not properly done may lower egg quality.

Some management practices that will aid in overcoming the problem of dirty eggs are: provide at least one nest for each five birds; keep nests clean and bedded with five inches of clean dry shavings, ground corn cobs, oat hulls, or cut straw; gather the eggs two or three times daily; keep the litter dry; and keep the birds penned up in the morning when it is wet outdoors, if practical.

Some other ways of improving market egg quality are: store the eggs in a well-ventilated cellar at temperatures below 65°; pack eggs in crates or boxes with small ends down; clean slightly dirty eggs with sandpaper and very dirty eggs by washing them with cool running water; and market the eggs in less than a week.

Some poultrymen recommend the use of lights in the henhouse. Certain rays of light penetrate a gland (the pituitary) near the base of the hen's skull, thereby stimulating the production of a substance called a hormone. This hormone on entering the blood stream increases the activity of the hen's ovaries (egg-producing organs), resulting in the increased development of egg yolks.

The value of lights probably has a greater effect on the lower producers than on birds which have a high egg-producing ability. Actually the use of lights may not increase yearly production very much in any flock. However, if used during the late summer, fall, and early winter when the hours of daylight are shortest, lights stimulate production. At this season, eggs are usually the highest in price. Actually, lights more nearly determine *when* the eggs are to be laid than the total number which will be produced.

Libr. of Congress

A well-fed, well-housed laying flock pays off in higher egg production.

Ah, the Bonny Cow!

Animals respond to good care but, being animals, they don't usually show their appreciation toward the persons who give them the care, as this story proves. Albert Bigelow Paine (1861-1937) a close friend of Mark Twain, wrote many novels, biographies, and books for boys and girls. This anecdote is from his book about an abandoned farm. From **Dwellers in Arcady** by Albert Bigelow Paine. Copyright 1919 by Harper & Brothers. Copyright 1947 by Louise Paine Moore, Joy Paine Cushman and Frances Paine Wade.

It was partly on account of the milk that we wanted Mis' Cow, partly because we wanted a cow in the landscape—a moving picture of her in the green pasture across the road—finally (and I believe principally) because we have a mania for restoring things and Mis' Cow looked as if she needed to be restored.

She was owned by a man who was moving away—moving because he had not made a success of chicken farming and still less of Mis' Cow. He was not her first owner, nor her second, nor her third. I don't know what his number was on her list of owners, but I know if he had kept her much longer he would have been her last one. Once we bought the mere frame of a haircloth couch, and took great pleasure in having it polished and upholstered, and made into a thing of beauty and service. It was with this view that we acquired Mis' Cow, who at the moment was a mere frame with a patchy Holstein covering and a feebly hanging tail.

We managed to get Mis' Cow up the hill and into her stall, where we could provide her with upholstery material. The little pasture across the road was getting green and she presently had the full run of it. The restoring progress began, as it were, overnight. If ever an article of furniture paid a quick return in the matter of looks, she did. She could never be a very fat Mis' Cow—she was not of that build. But a few days of good food and plenty of it certainly worked wonders. She filled out several of the most alarming hollows around her hips and along her ridgepole, she seemingly took on height and length. She grew smooth, even glossy; her tail no longer hung on her like a bell-cord, but became a lithe weapon of defense that could swat a fly with fatal precision on any given spot of her black-and-white area. It was only a little while until we were really proud to have her in the landscape, and the picture she made grazing against the green or standing in the apple shade was really gratifying. A visiting friend of Scotch ancestry was moved to exclaim, "Ah, the bonny cow!"

Then there was the matter of milk—she certainly earned herself a new reputation in that respect. From a quart or two of thin, pale unusable fluid her daily dividend grew into gal-

393

lons of foaming richness that became pitchers of cream and pounds of butter. All day Mis' Cow munched the new grass, and night and morning yielded a brimming pail. She was a noble worker, I will say that.

But there was another side to Mis' Cow— a side which her ex-owner didn't mention. Mis' Cow was an acrobat. When she had been on bran mash and clover for a few weeks she showed a decided tendency to be gay—to caper and kick up her heels—to break away into the woods or down the road, if one was not watching. But this was not all—this was mere ordinary cow nature. I was not surprised at these things—they were only a sign that she was getting tolerably restored, according to specifications. But when one day I saw her going down the road, soon after I had turned her into the pasture and carefully put up the bars, I realized that she had special gifts. Stone walls did not a prison make—not for her. My wife, Elizabeth, and I rounded her up and got her back into the pasture, and from concealment I watched her. She fed peacefully enough, for some time, then, doubtless believing herself unobserved, she took a brief promenade along the wall until she came to what looked like a promising place, and simply walked over it, like a goat.

We herded her into the barn, and I engaged a man to put a string of wire above the wall. That was effective as long as it was in repair. But it was Mis' Cow's business to see that it did not remain in repair permanently. She would examine it during idle moments, pick out a weak spot in the entanglement, pull it flat with her horns, and step over. If she could have been persuaded to do those things to order I could have sold her to a circus. It was necessary to reinforce the wire and add another string.

Even that was not always a cure. I came home from the city one night, after a hard day. Just as we reached the top of the hill on the way home from the station, a dim gray shadow met and passed us in the velvet dusk. It was Mis' Cow, starting out to spend the night. She was moving with a long, swinging trot, and in another second I was out and after her.

She had several rods' start and could run downhill better than I could, especially in the dark. It seemed to me that every step I went plunging out into space. By the time we had started up the next hill I had made up my mind to sell her—to give her away—to drive her off the premises. Some people were standing in front of the next house and they laughed as we went by, we being about neck and neck at the time. Then we came to the house of Mis' Cow's former owner and she darted in. She had remembered it as her home and wanted to return to it. Imagine wanting to go back to such a home!

A neighbor came, and we got a rope on her and led her uphill. I suppose I felt better in the morning, and it was about this time that our hired man, William, arrived on the scene. William loved Mis' Cow and did not mind chasing her up and down the road and through the bushes, though sometimes during the summer, when he had had a hard day with her, and our windows were open, we could hear him still hi-hi-ing and whooping in his sleep, chasing Mis' Cow through the woods of dream.

Other Books To Read

Written with Fire: The Story of Cattle Brands, by Edna Hoffman Evans. Published by Holt, Rinehart and Winston, Inc., New York, 1962.
How cattle brands came about, why they are necessary and how branding is done. Readers will be interested to discover that a brand may be so designed that an expert can tell whether the branded steer is from a ranch by a river or one near a mountain.

The Wonderful Egg, by G. Warren Schloat. Published by Charles Scribner's Sons, New York, 1952. Two boys visit an egg farm to learn about eggs and the hens that lay them. This book, for readers of any age, has many interesting photographs and diagrams to help tell the story.

Longhorns for Fort Sill, by Robert E. Trevathan. Published by Criterion Books, Inc., New York, 1962. An exciting novel about a boy and his family on a cattle drive through Texas and Oklahoma during the last century. The dangers of Indians, rustlers, and cattle stampedes are vividly presented.

Livestock Killers

Livestock diseases are a big worry to the animal husbandman. Every year they cause losses amounting to half a billion dollars throughout the United States. Even when the best feeding and management practices are followed disease sometimes strikes, but there are things that a farmer can do to help cut down on his disease losses. This article lists some of the worst livestock killers, how they are spread, and how they may be prevented. From "Fourteen Cases of Trouble," Humble Farm Family, September 1954.

Cattle

Blackleg: An old and well known disease, and still a big killer of young cattle.

Symptoms: Affected calves usually die just a few hours after they show up with visible symptoms. In fact, they are not often seen until after death, when they are found stiff and bloated with legs held stiffly in the air. The disease comes on suddenly, causing high temperature, lameness or stiffness, hard breathing, and swellings under the skin which give off a crackling sound when touched.

How it spreads: Cattle get blackleg by picking up the germ while grazing on infected ground. The germ has the ability to go into a resting, or spore, stage and survive for a long time—sometimes years when the ground is contaminated by the discharges of an affected animal or by the remains of an infected carcass.

Prevention: Vaccinate all calves before they are four months old. If calves are suspected of having blackleg, remove them to a spot which can be disinfected. Burn a calf if it dies from blackleg. Sprinkle chlorinated lime on areas where sick or dead animals have been. Wash floors and other surfaced areas with two per cent lye solution.

Anthrax: Another of the dread diseases which usually results in sudden death.

Symptoms: If the affected animal is seen before death, it will have few signs of illness, except for an extremely high temperature. An animal dead of anthrax will bloat and decompose rapidly.

How it spreads: By biting flies. Also by the improper use of live vaccine, and by contaminated soil or feed.

Prevention: In areas known to be infected with anthrax, vaccinate animals annually with vaccine of proper strength to suit the locality. It is a poor practice to vaccinate in other than an anthrax area.

Brucellosis: This is a real troublemaker that affects not only cattle but hogs, sheep, goats, and horses.

Symptoms: Sometimes an inflammation of the leg joints, causing "water on the knee." Pregnant cows lose their calves in many cases. The only sure method of diagnosing this disease, however, is by the use of the blood test.

How it spreads: Among the means known

Bob Taylor

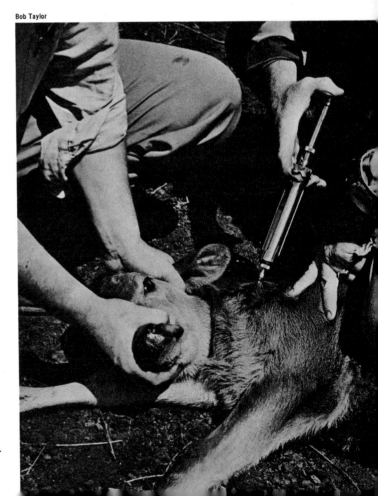

To prevent blackleg, killer of young cattle, calves should be vaccinated before they are four months old.

include eating feed or drinking water contaminated by discharges of infected animals; also through direct contact, as in breeding.

Prevention: If used properly, which means by a veterinarian, vaccine can give a fair degree of immunity if given to calves when four to ten months old. If diseased animals have died on the place, clean manure and rubbish out of barns, sheds and troughs, drain or fence off stagnant water holes and rake and burn accumulated litter in lots. Other important cattle diseases are shipping fever (hemorrhagic septicemia), tuberculosis, pneumonia, coccidiosis, and anaplasmosis.

Sheep

Enterotoxemia: A disease of young lambs, especially those on full feed in feedlots.

Symptoms: Usually lambs are found dead in the morning. If found before they die, lambs are usually on their sides, with heads drawn back and in convulsion. Death usually comes within two or three hours after lambs get sick.

How it spreads: Caused by a soil bacterium which may be in the feedlot or lowland soil. Causes trouble only in young, fat lambs that are getting lots of feed.

Prevention: In feedlot lambs, or in lambs to be turned on lowland pastures where the disease is known to be, vaccination should be carried out seven to ten days before feeding or grazing starts.

Poultry

Newcastle: One of the more serious of many disease problems in poultry.

Symptoms: In adult birds, difficulty in breathing. In chicks, difficult breathing for ten to fourteen days, perhaps followed by paralysis of wings or legs, head drawn over back or down between legs.

How it spreads: A virus infection, spread by contact with infected birds, contaminated sacks or utensils, attendants, shoes, and through the air.

Prevention: Keep the flock isolated from contact with outside birds. Buy all chicks as day-old birds, and vaccinate at purchase. Repeat vaccination when seven to twelve weeks old.

Leucosis: Biggest killer of poultry.

Symptoms: Blindness, lameness, fast weight loss, diarrhea, enlarged shanks, eye color fading to gray.

How it spreads: A virus or group of viruses spread through hatching eggs, by direct contact in young birds.

Prevention: Strict sanitation. Remove all affected birds immediately. Control all poultry parasites.

Swine

Cholera: Still a big hog killer, although it need not be since there is a dependable vaccine available.

Symptoms: These may vary from sudden unexpected death to an illness which lasts up to seven days. Affected swine show lameness, diarrhea, high fever, with eyes very sensitive to light.

How it spreads: By contact with cholera-infected hogs, or with hogs recently vaccinated with live virus. Many herd outbreaks result from improper use of live vaccine.

Prevention: All swine should be vaccinated, with vaccine suited to the particular requirements of the herd.

Necrotic Enteritis: A disease which is the direct result of poor sanitation.

Symptoms: Lengthy siege of diarrhea, with gradual loss of weight and stunted growth.

How it spreads: Unsanitary hog lots.

Prevention: Purchase of only healthy hogs from reliable sources. Proper feeding practices. Good sanitation.

"I wouldn't be caught dead there!"

Prime beef carcasses, the jewels of the meat-packing industry, hang in the chilling room to age before going under the butcher's knife.

Abernathy Live Stock Photo Co.

Bob Taylor

Meat for Your Table

Meat is the most important item in the diet of most United States families. Figures of the Department of Agriculture show that a family of four persons will use an average of six hundred pounds of meat a year for which they spend one-fourth or more of their total food money. To supply this demand for meat, it takes the work of thousands of people who make up the American meat industry. The industry divides into two major parts—the production of meat animals and the processing of the animals into cuts of meat ready for the kitchen. If you have read the section "Man and His Animals" which precedes this, you learned how livestock is fed and cared for, and how research in breeding and feeding has made it possible to produce animals that will yield more and better meat. This section tells the other half of the story—how livestock is shipped to market, sold to the meat packer, processed into ready-to-cook form, and shipped back to you, the consumer of meat. We usually think of an industry as an assembly, or putting together, of small parts to make a larger object such as a wrist watch, an electric toaster, or an automobile. The meat industry, however, is a dis-assembly operation in which live animals are reduced to meat cuts and other products. Meat packing is not a new industry in America, but it has only become a big industry within the last 75 years or so, since the invention of refrigeration and better transportation methods. The first American meat packer was Captain John Pynchon. In the 1640's in Springfield, Massachusetts, he made a business of packing pork, beef, venison, and bear meat in barrels and boxes with large amounts of salt to preserve the meat. That is how the expression "meat packing" came into use. From this small beginning sprang the gigantic American meat industry we know today.

—Lorena P. Neumann

397

Bob Taylor

Butchering day is a thing of the past on most farms today, but it once was an exciting yearly event. It meant hard work and lots of walking: out to the barnyard in the biting cold, into the steamy kitchen, up and down the cellar steps. At the end of the long day the farmer and his family sat down to a meal of fresh meat, a great treat in the days before refrigerators and freezers were in common use.

From Brine Barrel to Boxcar:

Meat Packing in America

Most people think that when there's meat on the table, the meal is made. Practically everybody likes meat and people are eating more of it every year. The United States' average annual consumption is about 160 pounds of beef, pork, lamb, and veal per person. Here is the interesting history behind the meats you can buy at your grocer's today. **Armour Food Source Map,** "From Brine Barrel to Boxcar—Meat Packing in America." Prepared by Armour and Company.

Until 1825 most of the meat eaten in the United States was produced near the place where it was eaten. Individual butchers slaughtered and dressed the animals, cured and smoked the hams and bacon, made the lard and the sausage.

Then new farm land opened in the West, and the settlers found that they could raise cattle and hogs there very easily. It took weeks, though, to drive the livestock to the eastern markets. The animals had to be fed on the way, and sometimes hogs escaped and ran wild in the woods of what is now the Middle West. There was no easy way to get them to market.

The First Packing Houses

To help solve the problem and supply a market for these hogs, packing houses were opened at many points in the territory. The entire hog carcass was cut into pieces and packed in barrels of brine, a mixture of salt and water. The salt preserved the meat, and the barrels could be shipped east by wagon or by boat. Later the railroads hauled the barreled and boxed meats to market.

All of the work had to be done in cold weather because the meat spoiled in warm weather before the action of the salt could

preserve it. When boat transportation was used, the packers had to wait for the spring floods on the rivers before shipping the meat to marketing centers.

The center of meat packing in the early days was Cincinnati, Ohio, which was nicknamed "Porkopolis." Shortly before the Civil War, Alton, Illinois, and St. Louis and Hannibal, Missouri, began to develop as markets, but when the war began, the center of the industry shifted to Chicago. There, new railroads were available to ship hogs quickly into the packing houses and to carry the cured pork east.

The packing of beef began at about this time. When the Civil War ended, beef packing centered around St. Louis and Kansas City. Cattle were driven up from Texas and other range areas, and the meat was shipped east as barreled (corned) beef.

That was the way the meat packing industry operated during the days before refrigeration.

Beginning of the Modern Meat Industry

The modern meat industry began with the invention of refrigerated rooms for chilling meat so that operations could be carried on in summer as well as in winter. At the same time, the pioneers realized that they needed refrigerated railroad cars so that fresh meat could be shipped to the East.

In 1872 Philip D. Armour opened the first large meat chilling room in the world at his Chicago plant. The meat was hung on hooks attached to the ceiling. The floor above was filled with blocks of natural ice cut from lakes and streams in winter and stored in huge ice houses. It seems like a crude process to us now, but year-around meat packing was a remarkable advance in its day.

Equally crude were the first refrigerator cars, patented by William Davis of Detroit in 1868. They were hardly more than an icebox on wheels and they didn't protect the meat very well. They could be used in cool weather, but not in midsummer.

The refrigerator car was later improved, and the next step in getting meat to the markets was to provide a place to keep refrigerated meat after it reached the eastern cities. To meet this problem, most meat-packing companies built refrigerated branch houses in the East.

Your Choice: Fresh, Canned, or Frozen Meat

With the use of refrigeration, shipment of fresh meats increased rapidly. Hams and bacon today are cured to bring out their flavor rather than to preserve them, as formerly.

Another branch of the meat industry, meat canning, began in the 1870's. The main prod-

Filling the ice compartment of a refrigerator car with dry ice. Most railroads use ordinary ice in their cars; and on long routes the train stops to take on a new supply.

uct at first was canned corned beef, and the reason for canning was to preserve the meat.

Modern canned meats are mostly "meal-in-a-can" dishes, and are popular because they are easy to use. Beef stew, corned beef hash, chopped ham and luncheon meat, chili, and various types of sausage are among the many varieties of canned meats found in the average store.

Freezing of meat has been practiced in the packing plants for many years. Beef and pork to be used in sausage, uncured hams and bacon, liver, and other variety meats were frozen in the fall and winter when supplies were plentiful and used in the summer when there were fewer numbers of livestock coming to market. Very little pork and almost no beef or lamb were frozen for later use as fresh meat.

Shortly before World War II, however, "quick-freezing" processes were developed which were a great step forward in improving

Air, chilled by ice in the ends of the refrigerator car, keeps meat fresh during shipment. The car holds about 25,000 pounds of meat. The meat is shipped from the packing plants to branch houses in large cities, or direct to smaller towns which have no branches.

399

our meat supply. Temperatures as low as 50 degrees below zero are used for freezing, and the frozen meats are marketed in packages in the stores.

Some meats are better suited to freezing than others. Poultry of all kinds, for example, is very satisfactory for freezing. Pork chops and cutlets, veal cutlets, cube steaks, and hamburger are among the most popular frozen meats in small packages. Larger steaks, roasts, and chops may be frozen successfully in the packing plant but seldom are because the process is usually not economical.

Lard, Shortening, Margarine, and Oil

Lard has always been a product of pork packing. Some of the fat meat is trimmed off in making pork cuts such as chops and roasts. This fat is then rendered (cooked) to separate the lard from the meat tissue.

Lard was sold in wooden barrels called tierces, and in tubs in the early days and store clerks "dipped" lard out of the barrel and wrapped it for individual customers' orders. Later, lard was sold in small tin pails and, finally, in the form most often seen today, waxed cardboard cartons.

Not only has the packaging of lard been improved, but the product, too, has been treated to make it snow-white and of better flavor. Until recent years, it was necessary to keep lard under refrigeration to prevent it from becoming mushy and rancid. We now have brands of lard which will remain sweet and

Power machinery plays an important part in the mass production of meat. Here, meats for sausage are mixed with seasonings in an automatic machine.

Armour & Co.

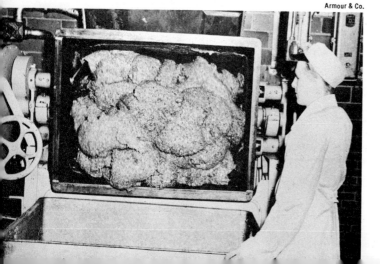

firm for many months at room temperatures.

In the 1880's, meat packers started making shortening and also oleomargarine which got its name from oleo oil, made from beef fat. The oleo oil was treated with milk to produce a milk-flavored spread for bread. The modern name of the product is margarine and it is now made almost entirely from vegetable oils such as cottonseed and soybean oils. The word "margarine" comes from margaric acid, one of the chemical compounds used in forming oleomargarine.

What Happens to the "Waste" Parts of Animals

A meat animal is not all meat. We get about 55 pounds of beef, 70 pounds of pork and lard, and 50 pounds of lamb for each 100 pounds of live weight of cattle, hogs, and sheep. Some of the remainder is lost as "shrinkage" when the animal is slaughtered, but the balance is used in nonfood products.

Up until 1882, a lot of animal material was wasted by the packing industry. It was buried in trenches or dumped into streams. Getting rid of it was a nuisance. Then the packers began finding uses for almost every part of the animal.

After the meat and other selected parts have been saved for various purposes, everything that is left is put in "tanks." Heat and pressure reduce the contents of the tanks to grease and "tankage." Grease is used for making soap, for making chemicals, and for several other purposes. Tankage, or "meat and bone scraps," is used for feeding livestock and poultry.

The work of finding new uses for meat and meat products still goes on and has increased in scope.

The big packing companies employ hundreds of scientists and assistants to develop better foods and improved nonfood products. These research workers believe that we have only scratched the surface in making useful things from meat animals in addition to food. They believe that science will develop still better meat foods, better ways of caring for our food, and more economy in the use of meat.

The Kansas City stockyards, one of the four largest in the country, sprawls over acres of flat land where the Missouri and Kansas (also called the Kaw) rivers come together.

To Market, to Market

Written by the editor.

You've often heard the nursery rhyme:
To market, to market to buy a fat pig.
Home again, home again, jiggety jig!
Ever since farmers began raising livestock they have had to find some way to sell the extra animals which they didn't need for their own use. Long ago, market days and fairs were held in most villages and towns, and the people of the countryside brought sheep, goats, pigs, and geese to sell at the market. The animals were usually tied or herded together at one corner of the village square. A buyer would come by, make the farmer an offer for a pig or goat, and after a satisfactory price was agreed upon he would drive his animal home.

For the most part, selling livestock is not such a simple process today. Two-thirds of the meat animals produced in the United States are raised west of the Mississippi, and two-thirds of the people—the users of the meat and products from these animals—live east of the Mississippi. The way in which livestock is moved from the West to the East, from the producer to the consumer, is an interesting chapter in the story of the United States meat industry.

Some farmers still sell their livestock at the local market in a nearby town or city. Today, however, the buyer usually doesn't keep the livestock for his own use. He in turn takes it, along with animals bought from other farmers, to a larger market, farther away—called a stockyards or terminal market—where the animals are sold again. Often a farmer hauls or ships his livestock direct to the terminal market, especially if he raises large numbers of animals.

A large share of the livestock sold in the United States now moves to market in huge semitrailer trucks. When sheep and hogs are hauled, a second floor, or double-deck, is added to the truck bed so that more animals may be shipped at one time. Practically all of the trucking takes place at night. This is done for two reasons: It is better for the animals, particularly in the summertime; and it gets the animals to the stockyards in time for the opening of the market in the morning.

Large numbers of livestock are also shipped to the stockyards by railroad in specially designed freight cars with open-air sides to allow ventilation. On long hauls the animals must be unloaded every 28 hours for feeding and watering.

At the Stockyards

The stockyards is a large, busy place. There are many runways, sheds and other buildings, and acres of pens stretching in all directions. All night long the animals arrive—cattle are

Abernathy Live Stock Photo Co.

Unloading hogs at the stockyards. The eight Corn Belt states which produce three-fifths of the United States' total corn crop, also produce almost 70 per cent of the country's market hogs.

USDA

Most of our sheep and lambs are raised on ranches in the West and Southwest. These sheep are being unloaded from a double-decked railroad car especially designed for hauling livestock.

unloaded in one part of the yards, sheep in another, and hogs in still another part. There is a lot of bawling, bleating, and squealing as the animals, frightened by the strange surroundings, are driven down ramps, out of the vehicles, along narrow alleys, and finally into pens. A stockyards official writes down the owner's name as the animals enter the yards. Workers are instructed to handle the animals with care. If they must use some kind of instrument to keep the livestock moving in the lanes, they use canvas slappers which will not bruise or otherwise injure the animals. Bruised spots must later be removed from the carcasses during the packing process, causing a waste of meat and money.

When he sells his animals through the stockyards, a farmer hires an agent to make the

A 40-foot-long cattle car will haul about 25 fat steers, 65 hogs, or 120 sheep. A double-decker will hold twice as many sheep or hogs.

Union Pacific RR.

actual sale for him. This is called "selling on consignment." The agent works for a company, known as a commission firm, which gets a certain amount of money for each animal sold, as a fee for being the farmer's agent.

The buyer, on the other hand, is usually a representative of one of the large packing companies.

Early each morning the buyers arrive at the yards to look over the day's "receipts," as the newly-arrived animals are called. A buyer usually specializes in one class of livestock, and whether he is a buyer of cattle, hogs, or sheep, he becomes an expert at estimating how much meat there is on a live animal, and whether the meat is likely to be high in quality. Each buyer has orders to buy a certain number of animals of various kinds for that day. For example, a typical day's order for a cattle buyer might be: 200 steers weighing 1,000 pounds each; 25 cows weighing 1,200 pounds; 50 veal calves, 10 bulls.

The Buyer at Work

In order to cover more ground in less time, the buyer usually rides a horse. He visits all of the cattle pens and each time he finds a pen of animals that might fill his order he makes an offer to the commission man who is in charge of the alley, or group of pens. Of course the buyer is trying to get the animals at the lowest possible price on behalf of the

Armour & Co.

Above, *a cattle buyer in action. By studying the appearance and movement of the animals, his trained eye can estimate within one per cent how much meat an animal's carcass will yield.*

Below, *the Chicago stockyard, one of the world's largest, at the height of the morning rush. After being sold, the animals are driven to the packing plants along the covered runways above the pens.*

Abernathy Live Stock Photo Co.

packing company he works for. On the other hand, the commission man is trying to get the highest possible price for the farmer whom he represents. So the two men usually bargain back and forth for a few minutes before each is satisfied with the price.

If the sale is agreed upon, each man makes a note in a memorandum book, but no other written record or contract is drawn up. It is a point of honor with both the buyer and the commission man that neither will go back on a sale once an agreement is reached. Millions of dollars worth of business have been transacted at the stockyards in this fashion and the men take pride in the fact that written contracts are never necessary.

If the buyer and the commission man cannot agree upon a price, the buyer moves on to look for another lot of animals. He may return later in the morning to make another offer in case the animals he originally bid on have not yet been sold and he has been unable to fill his orders elsewhere.

Animals that have been sold are weighed on

Abernathy Live Stock Photo Co.

A livestock auction. The auctioneer calls the bids over the microphone. When the buyers will go no higher on their offers, the auctioneer cries "all done," and one of his assistants writes down the buyer's name and the price he agreed to pay for the animals.

government-inspected scales and driven to the buyer's pens where they are held overnight. The next morning they are moved into the packing plant, and the buyer makes his rounds all over again, filling a new batch of orders.

Other Kinds of Livestock Marketing

This is the method that is most commonly used for buying and selling livestock—sheep and hogs, as well as cattle—at the stockyards. Sometimes, however, the buyer does not represent one of the large packing companies. He is what is called an "order buyer," that is, he has an office near the stockyards where he may receive orders from small packing companies, hotels, restaurants, and similar establishments that don't have full-time buyers in the yards.

Animals that are not sufficiently fat may be bought by farmers and taken back to farms for further feeding.

Two other important ways of marketing livestock are by auction and by direct sale. At a livestock auction, the animals are brought to a large sale barn and an auctioneer is the go-between for buyer and seller. In direct selling, the buyer for the packing company visits the farms of the livestock producers and makes offers on animals that are in his feed lots. This method is used, for the most part, in the great livestock feeding centers of the Corn Belt.

Leading Livestock Markets

The twenty leading public cattle markets in the United States are located in or near the heavy cattle-producing areas. Nearly half of all the cattle sent to market is sold at the seven leading markets: Chicago, Omaha, Kansas City, Sioux City, Denver, East St. Louis, and South St. Paul. From **Cattle and Calves.** Swift & Company, Agricultural Research Bulletin No. 15.

How the Sirloin Got Its Name

If you have eaten sirloin, you know how delicious it is and can understand why the king in this story would do what he did after tasting such steak for the first time. In this version of the legend James I (1566–1625) gave the sirloin its name. From "I Dub Thee Sir Loin," by Walter K. Putney, **Hearth & Home**, July-August 1953. Used by permission of Skelgas Division, Skelly Oil Company.

James I, King of England, was a very athletic man. He was fond of the outdoors and went on long walks. He fished and hunted and never was so happy as when off on some hike.

One day he and the Queen were making a long and rather tiresome trip through the country. When dinnertime came James the First was hungry. He came back to the lodge where the party was to dine and got ready to eat almost anything. Yet he was what one might call a very fussy eater. He wanted his food to be cooked just right.

A Puzzling Dish

He started to eat the dinner. The first course of soup was all right and King James praised it. Beverages were plentiful and likewise approved. Then came the main course, of meat. He had never eaten such meat before. It looked strange and he gazed at it for a moment before tasting it. The King took a large bite and chewed it for a moment. Then he stopped and asked, "Well, is this something new? I never had meat like this before."

Immediately everybody became confused. Consternation reigned. Something must be the matter with the meat. The Queen was worried. The servants were worried. The young ladies who were waiting on table actually trembled with fear. Again the King asked the same question, "Is this something new? What kind of meat is this?"

Meat Fit for a King

A servant rushed out to the kitchen to question the cook, or chef. He came back, trembling, and said that the meat was a special beef cooked for him and used by nobody else in all of England. The King took another bite and then asked, "What kind of beef is this? What part of the animal is it?"

Again, after a hurried rush to the kitchen the reply came, "It is loin, sire. Loin of beef."

Imagine the relief of all present when the King cut off another generous piece and said, happily, "The best meat I ever put into my mouth."

Then he stood up, drew his sword, laid it on the meat, and said, "I dub thee Sir Loin." From that time on, this particular cut of beef has been known as sirloin, but few who eat it realize that it was knighted by a king.

Livestock Language

Have you ever heard of green cattle? Do you know what heiferettes and warmed-up cattle are? Stockyards workers use a colorful language to describe the animals they work with. Here are some examples:

Heiferette—an older heifer that has failed to breed or a young cow that has raised one calf and still has the straight lines of a heifer.

Bologna bulls—older, thin bulls whose lean meat is ideal for grinding and mixing with water for making into bologna and sausage.

Green cattle—cattle which have been partly fattened on wheat pastures in the Southwest, or on grass and legume pastures in the Corn Belt.

Comeback—a lamb that has come to market once as a weanling, gone back to the country for fattening, and returned to market a second time as a fat lamb.

Warmed-up cattle—grass-fattened cattle which have been fed grain for only a very short time before slaughtering.

Canners and cutters—older, thin cows whose meat is cut from the bones for use in sausage and canned meats.

The Story of a Steak

A lot of things have to happen before the meat you eat reaches your table. This is the story of one particular calf and how it became a steak. Reprinted by permission of the American Meat Institute.

Drawings reprod. Courtesy Amer. Meat Inst.

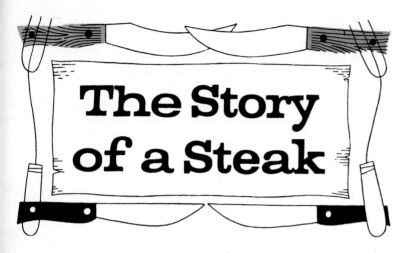

1. This calf was born on a Texas ranch. It suckled its mother for several months and ate grass, but probably received no other feed. It takes up to ten acres of range grazing land to support one cow and calf.

2. When it was about a year old the calf was sold to an Iowa farmer for finishing (fattening). In the feed lot, corn and high-protein feeds add extra pounds and extra flavor to beef.

3. After several months in the feed lot, our calf, now a full-grown steer, was sent by rail or truck to the stockyards. A marketing firm offered the steer for sale.

4. Buyers for several local and out-of-town meat-packing companies put in bids (made offers) and the highest bidder got the animal. This steer was one of a carload bought by an Ohio meat-packing company.

5. At the packing plant, the "beef crew" turned beef on the hoof into meat for the store. The beef carcass was inspected (examined for signs of disease), chilled, and cut into quarters for shipment.

6. In a refrigerated truck or boxcar, the quarters of beef were shipped to the packing plant's branch house in New York's wholesale meat district—1,500 miles from Texas, where the calf was born.

7. owner of a Brooklyn meat mar-
me to the branch house to
After comparing prices
the many carcasses,
a quarter of our steer.

8. In the store, the quarter of beef was cut into steaks, roasts, stew meat, and hamburger. The butcher arranged the beef cuts in his display case along with the pork, lamb and veal cuts.

9. A housewife came to the butcher shop and looked at all of the meats in the counter. After comparing values she decided on steak for her family's dinner that night.

Drawings reprod. courtesy Amer. Meat Inst.

It takes a lot of people besides the farmer to produce the steak (or other meat) that appears on your dining table today. Look at the people in this picture, for instance. Can you guess what part each of them plays in the production of meat? Check your guesses with the numbered answers in the column below. From the pamphlet ... **About Meat**, published by American Meat Institute.

How many people to produce a steak?

1. *The cowboy* who looks after the cattle.
2. *The banker* who lends money so the rancher may buy land, herd, and equipment.
3. *The chemist* who makes insect-killers and serums that help keep cattle healthy.
4. *The oil refiner* who provides the fuel for the power machinery which many ranchers use.
5. *The steelmaker* who makes items used by the rancher, from fencing and branding irons to filing cabinets.
6. *The brewer* ⎫
7. *The sugar refiner* ⎬ who furnish some of the by-products used to make
8. *The cotton ginner* ⎬ the livestock feeds which
9. *The flour miller* ⎭ cattle eat in addition to grass.
10. *The veterinarian* who looks after the health of the cattle.
11. *The blacksmith* who shoes the cowponies and repairs ranch machinery.
12. *The airplane pilot* who sprays ranges and fields, destroying pests.
13. *The lumberman* who provides the wood for corrals, barns, and pens.
14. *The windmill manufacturer* who makes the machinery that pumps water for the cattle.
15. *The feeder* who takes lean range cattle and puts about 25 per cent more beef on them by feeding them corn and other fattening feeds.
16. *The truck driver* ⎫ who haul cattle to mar-
17. *The railroader* ⎬ ket and meat to the consumer.
18. *The stockyards man* who provides "room and board" for the livestock that is waiting to be sold, and the *commission man* who is the sales agent for the cattle-feeder.
19. *The meat packer* who processes the beef.
20. *The retailer* who sells the meat.

407

A Pig Is More Than Pork:

The Story of Meat By-Products

Gustavus Swift, who established one of the larger meat-packing companies in the United States, once said that a person doesn't **make** money in the meat packing business, he **saves** it. This article about the by-products of the meat industry shows how the packers save many animal parts that once were wasted, and how they use them to make hundreds of important items. It shows that the saying "packers use every part of a pig except its squeal" is not too highly exaggerated these days. (The chart on page 410 discusses further the use of meat by-products.) From **Non-Food Products of Meat Packing.** Prepared by Armour and Company.

In the dawn of history when man hunted wild animals for meat and saved hides for clothing and bones for tools and weapons, by-products of the meat-packing industry were born. Very little progress was made, however, until the era of meat packing began in the second half of the nineteenth century. Since that time American meat packers have become more and more efficient in producing not only meat but a large variety of other valuable products from livestock. Formerly, the parts of meat animals unfit for food had simply been destroyed, dumped, or burned by the packers.

When research workers, largely chemists, were first employed by packing plants in the 1880's, their chief job was to find out better ways of getting rid of the waste products. The first step was to put all inedible parts (those unfit for food) except the hides and wool into a tank and "cook" it under high steam pressure. The fat came to the surface and could be drawn off for use principally in soap manufacture. The nonfat portion called "tankage" was dried and sold as fertilizer.

At first, the products of the "tanks" were sold for little more than the cost of removing them. Today, science has found so many uses for them that by-products now are a profitable branch of the packing industry. In addition to providing meat as a food, livestock processing gives us an ever-increasing variety of by-products to make our lives more pleasant.

Did you know that the shoes you wear, the soap you wash with, some of the clothes you buy, and the medicines you use are members of the meat-packing industry's family of non-food products? Here is a list of some of the more important products made from parts of animals that once were wasted:

Soaps

Tallow and grease are used to make scores of grades and varieties of soaps—toilet, laundry, and industrial—cleansers, washing powders, flakes, chips, granules, liquid soaps, and bars.

Glycerine

Glycerine, a syrupy red liquid that separates out from tallow, is a by-product of soap. There are more than 1,500 uses for glycerine in medicines and cosmetics, food products, auto polishes, parchment paper, sausage casings, and printers' rollers.

Pharmaceuticals

The lives and well-being of millions of people depend on such medicines as insulin, made from pancreas glands and used in treating diabetes; liver extract used for anemia; thyroid for a condition called cretinism. Many useful products are made from the pituitary gland, located at the base of the brain. One of them is ACTH, the hormone which controls the activity of the adrenal glands. (ACTH is an abbreviation of Adreno-Cortico-Tropin, the full name of the hormone.) It is used to treat such serious diseases as rheumatoid arthritis, rheumatic fever, gout, and asthma.

Leather

Leather is made from hides that are salted and cured, then tanned. There are all colors, textures, and weights of leather ranging from rough sole leather and belting to fancy sheep, kid, and pig-

408

skins. Some of the hair, which is removed from the hide with strong lime water, is used in making plaster, and in making felt, rugs, and carpet pads.

Wool

Most wool is shorn before the sheep are sold for slaughter. Pulled wool is that which is removed from sheep hides at the packing plant. It is generally used in soft-twist knitting yarns, bed blankets, carpets and rugs, woven paper, felts, and dress fabrics. Wool fat removed in cleaning the wool is refined into lanolin, a base for ointments.

Curled Hair

Some hair from cattle, especially the switches from the tails, goes into the manufacture of curled hair. After cleaning and sterilizing, the hairs are braided into long ropes and steamed, to "set" the curl. Each hair forms a tiny coiled spring which never loses its "bounce." Mattresses, furniture, and auto and railroad upholstery are made of curled hair.

Until a few years ago hog hair could not be used in high-grade upholstering material, but there is now a process through which hog hair can be curled and combined with latex (rubber). This product is used for upholstery filler and packaging material for delicate instruments.

Glue

Many varieties of glue are made from bones, hides, blood, sinews, and tannery scrap.

There is a difference between bone, blood, and hide glue. The raw materials for bone glue consist of cattle, sheep, and pig feet, skulls, jaw and rib bones, and shoulder blades. When glue is extracted from a vat of cattle feet, a by-product appears in the form of neat's-foot oil.

Large quantities of glue are used in the manufacture of paper, books, leather goods, oilcloth, musical instruments, trunks, billiard tables, corks, matches, carpets, cameras, pencils, toys, coffins, silks, whips, window shades, and sandpaper.

Ligatures and Casings

Ligatures are the "threads" which a surgeon uses to sew up tissues and wounds after surgery. Specially prepared strands of surgical gut are made from sheep intestines. It consists chiefly of collagen, a protein similar to that found in the connective tissues of the human body. Because it is absorbed readily by the body, the sheep gut—frequently called catgut—is in world-wide use as a material for ligatures and sutures.

The other main use for intestines is as sausage casings. Made from cattle, hog, and sheep intestines, natural casings are used to hold meat in sausage form, and to retain the natural juices and flavor of the meat. They serve the same purpose as nature's skin on fruits and vegetables. Because they are porous, natural casings let the smoke penetrate completely in curing the sausage.

Intestines are also used as cords in artificial limbs, in back of the reel that returns the carriage on typewriters, as drum snares, and as strings for tennis rackets, musical instruments, and looms.

Chemicals

A chemical called amine acetate, obtained from animal fats, has been found useful in the separation of minerals, a step in the manufacture of steel. Other chemicals made from packing-house products are used as detergents, synthetic soaps, solvents, wetting agents, polishes, paints, dyes, and germ killers.

Novelties

Bones find some use as combs, handles, pipe stems, chessmen, and such items.

Animal Feeds

Those parts of meat animals which cannot be used for some other purpose go into tanks where heat and pressure break down the tissues into grease and tankage. At one time tankage was used only for fertilizer, but it now is used for livestock and poultry feed.

Workers in the pharmaceutical division of a large packing plant prepare sterile bottles of ACTH, a drug made from the pituitary glands of meat animals. ACTH is used to treat such diseases as arthritis and rheumatic fever.

Armour & Co.

Meat By-Products and Their Uses

In the preceding article you learned about some of the by-products of animals. This chart shows the four main groups of by-products and the many ways in which they are used. From **Non-Food Products of Meat Packing.** Prepared by Armour and Company.

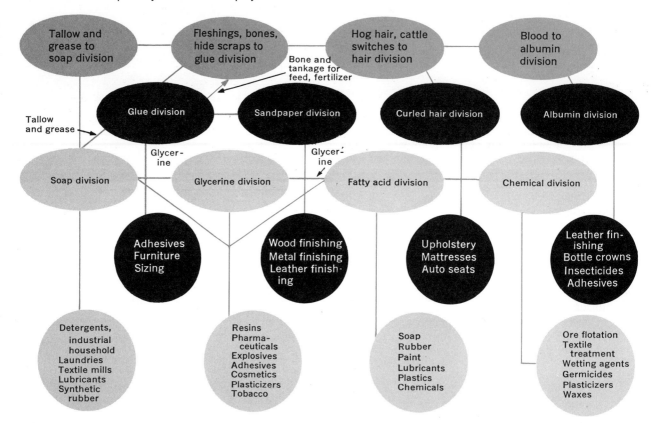

Tallow and grease to soap division

Fleshings, bones, hide scraps to glue division

Bone and tankage for feed, fertilizer

Hog hair, cattle switches to hair division

Blood to albumin division

Tallow and grease →

Glue division

Sandpaper division

Curled hair division

Albumin division

Glycerine

Glycerine

Soap division

Glycerine division

Fatty acid division

Chemical division

Adhesives
Furniture
Sizing

Wood finishing
Metal finishing
Leather finishing

Upholstery
Mattresses
Auto seats

Leather finishing
Bottle crowns
Insecticides
Adhesives

Detergents,
industrial
household
Laundries
Textile mills
Lubricants
Synthetic
rubber

Resins
Pharma-
ceuticals
Explosives
Adhesives
Cosmetics
Plasticizers
Tobacco

Soap
Rubber
Paint
Lubricants
Plastics
Chemicals

Ore flotation
Textile
treatment
Wetting agents
Germicides
Plasticizers
Waxes

How Much Steak in a Steer?

From **Cattle and Calves** Swift & Company, Agricultural Research Bulletin No. 15.

Only a little more than half of a steer is carcass beef, from which the meat cuts are made that you buy at your grocery store. Hides and other non-food by-products make up the remaining weight. (Sheep have about the same unusable material as cattle; in hogs, unusable material represents only about eighteen per cent of the live weight.)

A well-fed beef animal looks as if it would be practically all meat, but looks can be deceiving. There's far less "eating meat" than meets the eye on a 1,000-pound steer. To a meat packer a 1,000-pound steer looks like this.

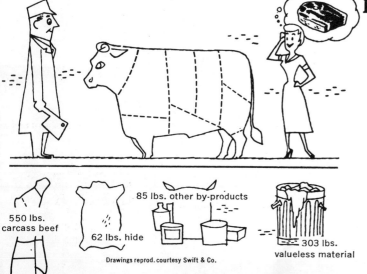

550 lbs. carcass beef

62 lbs. hide

85 lbs. other by-products

303 lbs. valueless material

Drawings reprod. courtesy Swift & Co.

Inside a Poultry Packing Plant

Whether it's baked turkey with dressing, stewed chicken with dumplings, duck with apple stuffing, roast goose, or fried chicken, most people think a meal is special when poultry is served. Here is the story of how poultry is processed and made ready for your table. From **Marketing Farm Poultry**, Farmers' Bulletin No. 2030. United States Department of Agriculture.

The word "poultry" refers to chickens, ducks, geese, and turkeys. (See the section on poultry in Volume 13 for more about breeds of chickens and other fowl.) Processing methods are practically the same for each type of poultry, with a few variations such as length of scalding time and method of packaging the finished product.

Birds are sent to market in crates or coops that have slats or rods in the tops and sides to allow plenty of ventilation. Huge open-sided trucks are used to haul poultry to market in areas where large numbers of chickens are produced.

Dressed poultry (that which has been killed and cleaned) is marketed in three forms—fresh, frozen, and canned. The method of dressing the birds is the same in all cases except that the dressed birds may be left whole or cut up in different ways depending upon the product desired.

At the poultry plant the birds are quickly killed by cutting their throats. Sometimes an electric knife is used, which numbs the bird, relaxes its muscles, and allows good bleeding. After the bird has bled thoroughly, it is ready to be picked.

Wax and Machines for Picking Chickens

There are several methods of picking or removing the feathers from the birds.

Wet picking means the picking of feathers after the birds have been dipped in, or sprayed with, hot water. The temperature of the water should be from 128° to 190° F. but the higher temperatures are used less often. Chickens and turkeys are often "wet picked" after being in water at a temperature of about 130°, for a period of approximately 30 to 35 seconds for young birds and from 40 to 50 seconds for adult birds. Ducks and geese are often dipped in water at temperatures of 148° to 150° F., for 2 to 2½ minutes.

In hand picking, after they have been scalded, the birds are hung on ropes and picked immediately. A fairly good picker can pick about twenty chickens or ten ducks in an hour.

Mechanical poultry pickers are used in most large poultry packing plants. They consist of

Processing Poultry in a Modern Packing Plant

drawing   washing   singeing   removing pinfeathers   picking by machine   scalding

inspecting   washing insides   cleaning giblets   washing outside   chilling   cutting up and packaging

Making the feathers fly. A chicken-picking machine removes all but the largest and the smallest feathers from a bird.

chicken

goose

duck

turkey

a revolving drum to which rubber fingers are attached. Such pickers have proved to be useful on both chickens and turkeys. With some mechanical variations, such pickers are also useful in the picking of ducks and geese.

With a mechanical picker, one man can pick ten chickens in about ten minutes. However, mechanical pickers need to be cleaned often to keep filth away from the carcasses.

Wax is sometimes used together with wet picking. Large feathers in the tail and wings and the greater proportion of the body feathers are first removed by hand after the birds have been dipped in the scald water. After drying, the birds are dipped into a tank holding wax at a temperature not over 130° F. Two dippings are required in order to build up a heavy coating of wax. After each dipping, the wax coat is allowed to dry until it is cool and hard. When the wax coating is stripped off, the remaining feathers come away with it.

The next step is to remove the pinfeathers. These are the horny new feathers that are just beginning to come through the skin. This is

A large frozen turkey is sawed into crosscut steaks three-fourths of an inch thick. New ways of selling turkey in small amounts make it possible for the average family to buy turkey more often.

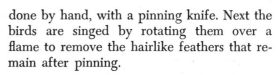

Photos, USDA

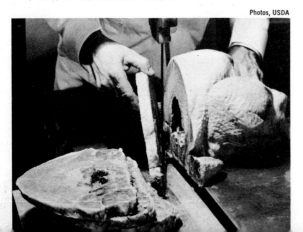

done by hand, with a pinning knife. Next the birds are singed by rotating them over a flame to remove the hairlike feathers that remain after pinning.

Getting the Birds Ready for the Store

If the birds are to be drawn, this takes place as the next step. Drawing consists of removing the internal organs—crop, gizzard, heart, intestines, and the like. The heart, gizzard, and liver are cleaned, wrapped in a piece of parchment paper, and placed with the bird when it is wrapped for sale. Some birds, particularly those sold in the eastern states, are not drawn and are sold with head and feet left on. In either case, the birds are next given a last thorough washing.

In the final washing, the carcass should be passed through a spray or sprays which provide a generous supply of fresh clean water. The birds are then chilled in crushed ice or ice water. Quick chilling of freshly killed poultry is important in keeping off-flavors from developing in the meat.

Many homemakers prefer to buy poultry ready for the pan, similar to the way they buy beef, pork, and lamb. Food chains and other retail stores that sell cut-up chickens, in the larger cities, report that the cutting up of broilers and fryers has increased the sales of these classes of poultry.

A completely cut-up bird consists of breast (may be cut into two or three pieces), two wings, two legs (thighs and drumsticks may be separated), back (whole or cut into two pieces), and neck, plus gizzard, heart, and liver.

Turkeys are sometimes sold by the half, or in fourths, in the form of disjointed pieces, crosscut steaks, and boneless steaks.

Inspection (examining the birds for signs of disease or other conditions that would make them unfit for food) takes place during dressing and cleaning or drawing. The final grading and inspection of the dressed birds should take place after the dressing operation, as the birds are being packaged for shipment or direct sale to the consumer.

Keeping Our Meat Safe To Eat

Written by the editor.

Scotland Yard, London's famous police force, has inspectors who go about in search of clues that may help solve murders and robbery cases. There are inspectors at stockyards all over the United States who are in search of clues, too, but instead of trying to solve crimes, they are looking for signs of disease in livestock sold at the yards. The job of the inspectors at the stockyards is to weed out the animals and meat products that are unfit for food.

These detectives who protect the health of the meat consumer are specially trained and licensed by the government. Most of them are veterinarians. Government inspectors are on hand in every packing plant in the United States that sells meat outside the state in which it is processed. It is estimated that at least three-fourths of all the meat processed in the United States has undergone federal inspection. Cities and states also have laws protecting the quality of meat sold within their boundaries.

What Does a Meat Inspector Look For?

The federal law covers meat and food products from cattle, sheep, hogs, and goats. The animals are inspected for the first time before they are slaughtered. (This is called ante-mortem inspection.) The inspector looks for outward signs of diseases such as shipping fever, pneumonia, and lump jaw. Animals that are obviously diseased are marked "Condemned" and must be destroyed. Doubtful cases are marked "Suspect" and will undergo further inspection, or they may be processed for uses other than human food, such as fertilizer.

Post-mortem inspection (that which takes place after an animal is slaughtered) occurs at various stages in the process of cleaning and

Swift & Co.

A United States government inspector examines the organs of a beef animal. If he finds signs of any disease or unhealthy condition the carcass is condemned and made into fertilizer instead of food.

dressing each carcass. In the case of a steer, for example: While the animal is being skinned by one of the workers, the inspector examines the head. He cuts open several of the lymph glands to look for signs of abscesses or tuberculosis; he cuts into the tongue and the outer cheek muscles looking for cysts or other abnormal conditions.

Another inspector stands by when the insides—the internal organs, or viscera, as they are called—are removed from the carcass. Under a strong light, the inspector examines the viscera with extreme care. The instant his trained eye notes some sign that might mean

The purple stamp of the federal meat inspector tells the buyer that precautions were taken to make sure the meat is safe for her family to eat.

413

USDA, by Forsythe

disease, he cuts into the suspicious-looking organ or tissue for further clues. Diseased or unsound carcasses and all their parts are tagged "U. S. Condemned" and are placed in special rooms until they can be removed to the fertilizer plants.

The Stamp of Approval

The final stage of inspection takes place after the carcass has been completely dressed and just before it goes to the chilling room. If the carcass gets by this last close examination, it is marked with a purple stamp containing a shortened form of the words "U. S. Inspected and Passed" enclosed within a circle. There is also a number on the stamp; this is the official number of the particular packing plant in which the carcass was processed. The purple dye used on the stamp is made of vegetable juices and is completely harmless, so it doesn't need to be washed off or cut away from the meat whenever it is prepared for cooking.

Products made from meat, such as lard, sausage, canned meats, and sandwich meats, must also be inspected and approved. Labels of cans and cartons containing such products are stamped "U. S. Inspected and Passed by Department of Agriculture."

There are also federal and local regulations that require packing plant operators to keep their premises in a clean and sanitary condition. This includes such items as water supply, light, ventilation, sanitary drainage system, scrub rooms where the workers may clean their hands and arms, clean outer clothing for workers, facilities for cleaning and disinfecting knives and other tools, and paved and drained passages where cars and vehicles are loaded with meat. The employees themselves must pass regular physical examinations.

What Are Government Graded Meats?

Another way in which the government protects the meat consumer is through its system of grading meats for quality. Although at the present time packers are not required to use the government grading system, many of them do; or they use a system of their own that

resembles the government system. The federal grades of beef are as follows:

Prime. Prime grade beef is produced from young, well-fed, beef-type cattle. Cuts have a thick outer layer of white fat, and the meat is well marbled—that is, there are streaks of fat mingled with the lean, red portions. This grade is preferred by hotel dining rooms and restaurants specializing in fine steaks.

Choice. This grade is preferred by most consumers. The meat is of high quality but has less fat than prime meat.

Good. Cuts of this grade are not as juicy as prime and choice cuts, but they contain a large percentage of lean meat in proportion to the amount of fat, which many consumers prefer.

Commercial. This is an economical grade of meat, produced largely from older animals. Unless carefully prepared, cuts of this grade are apt to be tough.

Utility. Cuts of this grade have very little fat, but when used as pot roasts or in ground meat dishes they are quite satisfactory with many people.

Veal and lamb are graded with a similar system. All meats that are federally graded will have the grade stamped along the outer, fatty edge of each meat cut.

Other Books To Read

The Indian and the Buffalo, by Robert Hofsinde (Gray-Wolf). Published by William Morrow and Company, Inc., New York, 1961.
An Indian tells how his people hunted the buffalo and how they used the meat, hides, and bones for food, clothing, shelter, and other needs.

Basic Leathercraft: A Worktext in Creative Design and Craftsmanship, by Robert A. McCoy. Published by Steck Company, Austin, Texas, 1961.
Data on preparing leather and making leather goods.

Free Grass to Fences: The Montana Cattle Range Story, by Robert H. Fletcher. Published by University Publishers, Inc., New York, 1961.
A readable combination history of the West's settlement and of the cattle industry's growth.

Fruitcake and Arsenic, by Josephine Hemphill. Published by Little, Brown and Company, Boston, 1962.
An interesting account of how the United States Food and Drug Administration protects consumers.

414

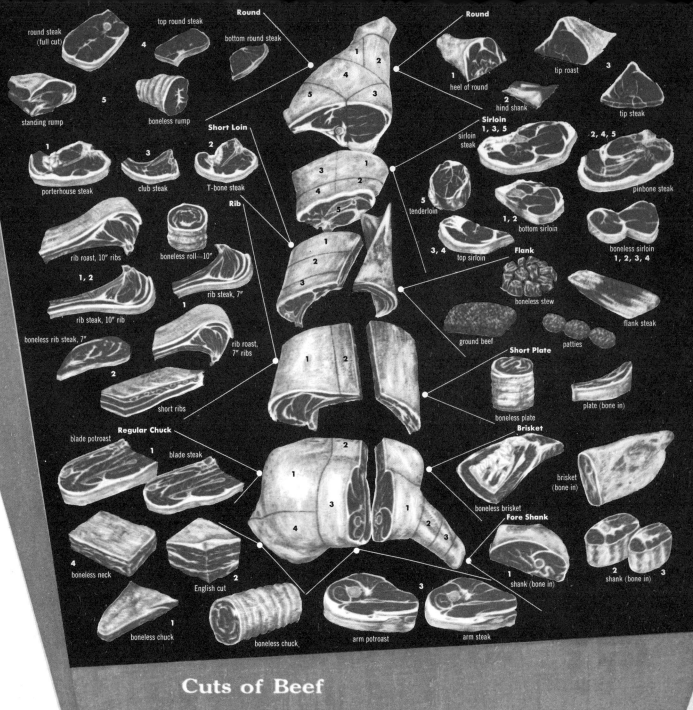

round steak (full cut) — 4 — top round steak — Round — bottom round steak — Round — tip roast — 3

5 — standing rump — boneless rump — heel of round — 1 — 2 — hind shank — tip steak

Short Loin — Sirloin 1, 3, 5 — sirloin steak — 2, 4, 5

1 — porterhouse steak — 3 — club steak — 2 — T-bone steak — pinbone steak

Rib — 5 — tenderloin — 1, 2 — bottom sirloin — boneless sirloin 1, 2, 3, 4

rib roast, 10" ribs — boneless roll—10" — 3, 4 — top sirloin — Flank

1, 2 — rib steak, 7" — boneless stew — flank steak

rib steak, 10" rib — 1 — ground beef — patties

boneless rib steak, 7" — rib roast, 7" ribs — Short Plate

2 — short ribs — boneless plate — plate (bone in)

Regular Chuck — blade potroast — 1 — blade steak — Brisket — brisket (bone in)

boneless brisket — Fore Shank

4 — boneless neck — 2 — English cut — shank (bone in) — 2 — shank (bone in) — 3

1 — boneless chuck — boneless chuck — arm potroast — arm steak — 3

Cuts of Beef

The above illustration shows how beef is cut for sale in butcher shops. Methods of cutting differ in various parts of the country; a Boston cut steer leaves three ribs on the hindquarter; the Chicago and New York methods leave one rib on the hindquarter, and Philadelphia cut steers have all ribs on the forequarter. A 1,000-pound steer cut Chicago style will yield 87 pounds of loin, 78 pounds of round steak, 163 pounds of roasts, 88 pounds of boiling or stew beef, 22 pounds of ground meat, and 50 pounds of boneless stew—a total of 488 pounds. There are also about 40 pounds of fat trimmings.

Processing Pork

The carcasses of freshly killed hogs emerge from being de-haired and washed, before final dressing. From the pen to the final meat product, cleanliness and sanitation are a must in modern meat processing plants. The meat packer's careful attention to health measures is supplemented by strict government inspection both before and after slaughtering.

A workman examines a product of the sausage department of a large meat-packing plant. To satisfy the tastes of sausage-lovers throughout America, the meat-packing companies manufacture many kinds of sausages containing minced pork, beef, and other meats. Although the most popular among these is undoubtedly the "hot dog," stores sell large quantities of other sausages like Genoa salami, Thuringer, pepperoni, and knackwurst.

The Meat Cook

Have you ever cooked a shishkabob or a pig-in-a-blanket, or roasted a wiener? If so, you've already had some experience as a meat cook. Cooking meat in a kitchen is just as easy as cooking it over a campfire if you know a few easy rules; in fact, it is even easier, because the average kitchen has regulated stoves and other equipment to help take the guesswork out of meat cookery. Whether you want to try them or just read them, the directions given below will tell you the difference between braising and broiling, roasting and stewing—and they'll give you the secrets of the fine art of meat cookery. Henrietta Fleck, **A Recipe Primer** (1949). Reprinted by special permission of D. C. Heath and Company, Boston, Mass.

Swift & Co.

A porterhouse steak, broiled to perfection, will win praises for any cook.

Successful meat cookery depends primarily on selecting the cut of meat best suited to the desired method of cooking. Suggested ways of cooking beef, lamb, pork, and veal cuts are given in the chart on page 419.

Meat may be cooked either by dry heat or by moist heat. Dry heat, such as roasting, broiling, or pan-broiling, is applied to tender cuts, such as steaks and chops. Moist heat, such as stewing and braising, is applied to less tender cuts, such as brisket and flank. The length of cooking time is another important item. Overcooked meat becomes dry and stringy. Temperature is important, too. High temperature induces needless shrinkage and produces a less palatable product.

How To Tell When Meat Is Done

To see if the meat is done as desired, cut a small gash in the meat near the bone and examine the color of the meat. For rare meat, stop cooking while there is still a distinct reddish look to the inside of the meat and the meat juices. For medium-rare, stop cooking when inside of meat still has a pinkish color. For well-done meat, continue cooking until the inside has lost all its pinkish color. All pork cuts should be cooked until well-done, that is, until whitish-gray inside.

How Meat Is Braised or Pot Roasted

Braising is a method of cooking meat by moist heat because the pan is covered for at least part of the cooking time. Steam collects on the lid and bastes, or drips down on, the meat.
1. Add a little fat to a hot frying pan or heavy kettle. If the fat begins to smoke, turn the heat down or set the pan off the burner.
2. Flour and season the meat. Salt, pepper, paprika, and other seasonings may be used.
3. Brown meat well on all sides in the hot fat.
4. Add a cup of liquid. Water, milk, tomato juice, and sour cream are some liquids used, depending on the recipe.
5. Place the meat on a rack to prevent it from overbrowning.
6. Cover with a close-fitting lid. Reduce temperature, and cook until tender. Time of cooking depends upon thickness of meat. Allow 30–60 minutes per pound.
7. Add additional liquid if necessary, but it is desirable to keep liquid at a minimum amount.
8. Meat may be cooked on top of the stove or in the oven.

417

How Meat Is Broiled

Broiling is a method of cooking meat by dry heat through direct exposure to the flame, or other source of heat such as the electric heating unit in an electric range.
1. Steaks should be at least 1-inch thick and chops ¾-inch thick.
2. Light the broiler and allow it to heat 10 minutes at 350° F.

3. Grease the rack of the broiler with a piece of fat.
4. Gash the fat edge of the meat every inch or so to prevent curling. (This is called scoring.)
5. Place meat on broiler rack.
6. Place rack so that meat will be three inches from broiler heat.
7. Follow directions on use of the broiler for your particular kind of stove. On some ranges the broiler door is left open, but in most models it is closed. In all cases the oven door is left open.
8. Length of time for broiling depends upon thickness, degree of doneness desired (rare, medium, or well-done), and weight of meat; an estimate for an inch-thick steak is 15–20 minutes to the pound. Time must be increased if meat is thicker.
9. When meat is half done, or when internal temperature reaches 113° F. for rare or 136° F. for medium to well-done, meat should be seasoned with salt and pepper and turned. Do not pierce meat with a fork because juices will be lost thereby. Insert fork in the fat portion.
10. Meat is done when temperature reaches 140° F. for rare and 150° F. for medium.
11. Bacon should be turned frequently. Drain on absorbent paper before serving.
12. Serve on a hot platter.
13. Melted butter or drippings may be poured over the meat.

How Meat Is Pan-Broiled

Pan-broiling is cookery by dry heat; the pan is kept uncovered and fat is poured off as soon as it accumulates.
1. Select a heavy frying pan large enough to hold the meat that is to be pan-broiled. A shallow pan (one with low sides) is best.
2. Heat the pan until a drop of water will sizzle on it.
3. Brush pan with fat.
4. Place meat in pan. Keep temperature low.
5. Turn meat occasionally to prevent burning. Do not pierce lean meat with fork because juices will be lost thereby. Place fork in fat portion.
6. Pour off fat as it accumulates in the pan. Do not add water at any time.
7. Bacon should be drained on absorbent paper when removed from the pan.
8. Serve on a hot platter.

How Meat Is Roasted

Roasting is cookery by dry heat, with the meat never coming in direct contact with the flame.
1. For beef, veal, and lamb, light the oven and set the regulator at 300° F.; for pork, set at 350° F.
2. Wipe the meat with a damp cloth.
3. Score the fat. (Cut through the fat edge several times with a knife.)
4. Season with salt and pepper.
5. Place the meat on a rack in the roaster. (In a standing rib roast, the ribs may serve as a rack.)
6. Insert a meat-cooking thermometer into the thickest part of meat. Place the meat into the oven. Roast without a cover. The meat is done when the thermometer registers the right temperature for a given degree of doneness—this varies with the kind of meat (beef, lamb, pork) being roasted.

If a thermometer is not available, roast from twenty to thirty minutes per pound for beef; roast twenty-five to forty minutes per pound for veal; roast twenty-five to forty-five minutes per pound for pork; and roast thirty to forty minutes per pound for lamb. Length of roasting time is determined by how well-done one desires the meat.

How Meat Is Stewed

Stewing is a moist-heat method of meat cookery, with the meat resting directly in water.
1. Cut the meat into small, uniform pieces about the size of two-inch cubes, unless it has already been cut in this way by the butcher.
2. If possible, cook the meat in a heavy kettle to prevent scorching.
3. For brown stew, dip the meat in flour and brown it well in hot fat. If unbrowned stew is desired, omit flouring and browning, and proceed with the next step.
4. Season with salt and pepper. Bay leaves, celery leaves, parsley, or spices may be used.
5. Add water just to cover.
6. Cover with a tightly fitting lid.
7. Simmer until meat is tender, but do not boil. Simmering time is from one and one-half to two hours.

Variations
1. If vegetables are to be added, put them in near the end of the cooking time, allowing enough time for vegetables to be done when the meat is done. Do not overcook. Potatoes, carrots, celery, onions, tomatoes, green peppers, string beans, and lima beans are vegetables often used.
2. Stew may be served with rice, boiled macaroni, or spaghetti; biscuits, toasted muffins, noodles, or dumplings.
3. A meat pie may be made of the stew by placing it in a casserole and topping it with baking powder biscuits or pastry cut in fancy shapes. Pastry and biscuits are baked on the stew, or they may be baked separately and placed on the stew just before serving to prevent sogginess.

How To Make a Hamburger

Hamburgers are a favorite meat dish with most boys and girls. Here is one way to make them:

1. To a pound of ground beef, add one beaten egg, ¼ teaspoon salt, and a sprinkling of black pepper.
2. Shape into balls about the size of a large egg. (This amount of meat will make five or six generous-sized hamburgers.)
3. Hamburgers may be broiled or pan-broiled. For broiling, press the balls of meat onto a cooky sheet, flattening them with a wide spatula. Place the cooky sheet beneath the broiler flame or unit, and cook a few minutes; turn and cook the other side.
4. To pan-broil the hamburgers, flatten the balls of meat on a preheated heavy skillet or pancake griddle. Have the flame turned low to prevent burning and spattering. Pour the fat off as it accumulates, and turn the hamburger after a few minutes to cook the other side.
5. Place the hamburgers on warmed buns and add your favorite seasonings: catsup, mustard, pickle relish, onion, sliced dill, or sour pickle.

Methods of Cooking Different Cuts of Meat

	Beef	Lamb	Pork	Veal
Braise or Pot-Roast These Cuts	Brisket Chuck Flank Heart Kidney Liver Neck Plate Round Rump Short ribs	Breast Heart Kidney Liver Neck slices Shank Shoulder	Chops Ham Heart Kidney Liver Shank Shoulder Spareribs Steak Tenderloin	Breast Chops Cutlet Heart Kidney Liver Shank
Broil These Cuts	Club steak Patties Porterhouse steak Tenderloin Top round (if top quality) T-bone steak	Loin chops Rib chops Shoulder chops Patties Steak	Bacon Ham Loin chops Rib chops Shoulder chops	Loin chops
Pan-Broil These Cuts	Beef patties Cubed steak Steaks, less than 1-inch thick Small steaks	Lamb chops Lamb patties	Ham Pork chops Sausage	
Roast These Cuts	Chuck ribs (if choice quality) Rolled ribs Rump Standing ribs Tenderloin Top round (if choice quality)	Crown roast Leg Loin Ribs Shoulder	Boston butt Crown roast Ham, fresh or smoked Loin Picnic shoulder	Leg Loin Shoulder
Stew These Cuts	Brisket Chuck Flank Heel of round Neck Organs Plate Shank Short ribs Tripe	Breast Flank Neck Organs Shoulder	Cottage butt Neck Organs Shank Spareribs	Breast Flank Neck Organs Shank Shoulder

After Fleck, A RECIPE PRIMER

419

Quiz for Meat Eaters

If you know the answers to most of these questions, you can hold your own in conversation with cowboys, meat economists, meat chefs, and market men. Reprinted by permission of the American Meat Institute.

Q. Which steer will make choice grade beef?

A. The grade of the meat can't be established definitely until *after* the steer is dressed. But to be a buyer for a meat packing plant you'd have to be able to judge not only what the grade will be, but the meat yield within one per cent.

Drawings reprod. courtesy Amer. Meat Inst.

Q. How much beef in a thousand-pound steer?

A. Dressing percentage varies from one animal to another but on the average, a steer that weighs in at 1,000 pounds "shrinks down" to 550 to 600 pounds of dressed beef. A steer that brings 25 cents per pound *on the hoof* (for example) actually costs the packer about 40 cents per pound for *the beef*.

420

Q. How many pork chops in a pig?

A. Only about five per cent of a pig is center-cut pork chops! That's about ten pounds, or 20 to 30 pork chops depending on size and thickness.

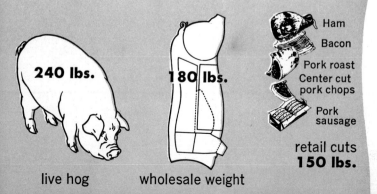

live hog   wholesale weight

240 lbs.   180 lbs.

Ham
Bacon
Pork roast
Center cut pork chops
Pork sausage

retail cuts
150 lbs.

Q. What is America's favorite meat?

A. Americans eat more beef than other meats. The average amounts of each meat consumed per person in 1960 were: beef, 80 pounds; pork, 70 pounds; veal, 8½ pounds; lamb and mutton, 4 pounds; chicken, 29½ pounds; turkey, 6 pounds.

Q. Where does sirloin steak come from?

A. On the side of beef pictured, the sirloin section is No. 4. Only about eight per cent of a side of beef is sirloin. There is over five times as much pot roast, stew meat, and hamburger as there is steak in a side of beef.

Round steak   Porterhouse   Sirloin
Chuck steak   Hamburger   Flank steak

Q. Which is the best steak for broiling?

A. If you named porterhouse, sirloin, and hamburger, you are right. Some people broil top quality round and chuck steak, but these cuts, and flank steak, are best if cooked by the braising method.

Q. Who invented the "hot dog"?

A. Antoine Feuchtwanger, a Bavarian sausage peddler, is usually given credit for inventing the hot dog in 1883, in St. Louis. Antoine let his customers borrow white gloves to wear while they ate the hot sausages which were his specialty. But the customers often walked away with the gloves, and with them went Antoine's profits. So he got the idea of putting the sausage in a bun, and that was the first hot dog. A New York cartoonist, Tad Dorgan, is believed to be the first to call them "hot dogs." He often used them in his cartoons and even gave them little speeches to say.

Careers in Agriculture

Agriculture is not only the oldest of all occupations, it's the job with the greatest future. Experts predict that by 1975 there will be nearly 225 million people in the United States. All of these people will have to be fed, clothed, and housed, and it will be up to agriculture to meet many of these needs.

Where will the increased agricultural production come from? There is a limit to the amount of land that is suitable for farming. In fact, as the population increases we will have even less land for agriculture than we have now. The cities and towns will expand, more land will be needed for houses and yards, for schoolgrounds, for factory sites where the things that the additional people need will be made and processed.

The increased agricultural production will have to come from the use of better farming methods, better seed, better breeds of livestock, better livestock feeding practices, better use of soil and water. So there will be jobs for farmers who are willing to meet the challenge of making the fullest use of our limited farm land. And back of every farmer there will be a need for hundreds of other workers—in laboratories, classrooms, processing plants, salesrooms, farm machinery factories, feed stores, greenhouses, fertilizer plants— workers to make the things the farmer needs and to process the things the farmer raises. These are just a few of the jobs waiting for you in agriculture.

"As a work of art, I know few things more pleasing to the eye, or more capable of affording scope and gratification to a taste for the beautiful, than a well-situated, well-cultivated farm."

—Edward Everett

Bob Taylor

Farming:

The Career for Those Who Love the Land

What is it about farming that makes many people prefer it to all other kinds of work? How can you tell if you are one of those who is likely to enjoy country living? How can you get started in farming? These are some of the questions answered in this absorbing article on farming as a career. From **Opportunities in Farming** by Paul W. Chapman. Copyright 1941, 1947 by Science Research Associates.

Farming, which is the oldest of all occupations, has lost none of its importance with the passing of time. All of us, regardless of where we live or what we do, depend upon farming for the food we eat, most of the fibers from which our clothes are made, and some of the materials used in the homes in which we live. If there were no farmers, each individual would have to spend the major portion of his time producing food for himself and his family.

Farming is thus the most essential of all occupations. In addition, it provides jobs for more than half of America's urban (city) workers. These jobs include buying, packing, processing, transporting, selling, and using farm commodities or products.

Farming is also a way of life, since the farmer must live on the land. But conveniences and improvements have made country life more attractive today. During recent years electricity has been made available to most rural sections. Telephone lines are being extended to rural homes everywhere. Highways are paved or hard surfaced. In fact, life in the country has been made so attractive that thousands of families have left the congested sections of cities to make their homes in suburban and rural communities. The number of part-time farms is increasing. These are small farms on which people live in order to enjoy the advantages of country life and, perhaps, to reduce living expenses, but which are not designed to provide all of the family's income. Usually the head of such families works in some non-farm job and goes daily to the office, factory, or store in which he works.

The fact that farming is a way of life has, no doubt, made it more popular as a vocation.

It is said that Thomas Jefferson loved his farm home at Monticello so much that he continued to spend money improving it even after his income and savings had been reduced through public service. Today, countless successful men who have accumulated a fortune turn to farming, not for the money they can make, but for the pleasure which farming and farm life make possible.

Here's Work That Satisfies

Why does farming appeal to so many men and women? Perhaps it is because farming is a business which satisfies the creative urge, the urge to make things, which is found in all persons with ambition and ability. Some people like to create books, pictures and music; others enjoy building houses, bridges, and roads. But there are no more satisfying materials with which to work than plants and animals.

Security is another factor which gives life on the land an appeal to many. But the majority of young men and women who choose farming as their vocation do so because they are the sons and daughters of farmers. In the past it has been fairly easy for them to get started in farming and difficult for them to enter other occupations because they knew little or nothing about other types of work. This is no longer true to the same extent that it has been in the past, and, as a result, a larger number of boys and girls have left the farm in recent years than ever before.

Personal interest should be one of the main factors in the selection of an occupation. To see if you are interested in farming think about these questions:

1. Do you like to work outdoors?

422

The farmer's touch turns soil and seed into a rich harvest of wheat which will make bread for a million tables.

Farmers have no such thing as a 40-hour work week. There are often times when the work won't wait and the tractors drone through the night. The farmer rests when the crop is in or the harvest is safely home.

2. Does living in the open country appeal to you?
3. Do you like plants and animals?
4. Are you interested in watching them grow from day to day?
5. Do you enjoy visiting farms and market places where farm products are sold?
6. Are you satisfied to spend much of your time alone?
7. Are you willing to work long hours during certain seasons of the year?
8. Do you like to plan your own work?
9. Do you have enough will power to control your own actions; to work when no one tells you to do so?
10. Can you manage your financial affairs successfully?
11. Are you strong enough to handle the tools that are used in farming?

If you can answer *yes* to all of these questions, you have some of the more important personal characteristics required for success in farming.

Not all persons who have the qualifications for success in farming will wish to choose this occupation as a career. Many will feel that they will be happier in some other type of work. Some may think that other types of employment offer greater chances for making money or other rewards in which they are interested. Such people will want to compare the advantages and disadvantages of farming with other work opportunities, although the advantages and disadvantages of any kind of work are, to a great extent, matters of personal opinion. What some people would call an ad-

vantage might be considered a drawback by others. Here are some of the advantages and disadvantages of farming as an occupation:

Advantages of Farming

1. A man works for himself.
2. It is healthful outdoor work.
3. A farmer is not in danger of losing his job.
4. There is a variety in the work to be done.
5. Personal and household expenses are small.
6. A farmer may be home with his family.
7. Farmers live well compared with city workers who earn the same amount of money.
8. Farming provides opportunities for improving crops and livestock and other creative achievements.

Disadvantages of Farming

1. Money is required to get established.
2. Income is uncertain.
3. There is no weekly or monthly pay check.
4. Farmers cannot as a rule set a price on their own products.
5. A farmer competes with untrained workers, making for low wage scales.
6. There may be overproduction and low prices.
7. Outdoor work must be done in bad weather.
8. Schools, churches, and entertainment facilities may not always be convenient in rural districts.
9. It is difficult to get away for vacations.
10. The achievements in farming are not recognized to the same extent as success in other lines of work.

Many of the former disadvantages of farming no longer exist. Improved machinery is

423

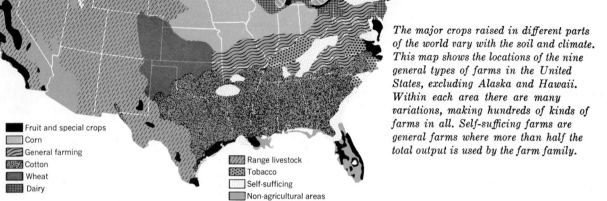

Major Types of Farming in the United States

Legend:
- Fruit and special crops
- Corn
- General farming
- Cotton
- Wheat
- Dairy
- Range livestock
- Tobacco
- Self-sufficing
- Non-agricultural areas

The major crops raised in different parts of the world vary with the soil and climate. This map shows the locations of the nine general types of farms in the United States, excluding Alaska and Hawaii. Within each area there are many variations, making hundreds of kinds of farms in all. Self-sufficing farms are general farms where more than half the total output is used by the farm family.

removing drudgery. Radios, highways, and cars now keep the farmer in touch with the rest of the world. There are better ways of marketing farm crops. Nationwide programs are trying to bring supply and demand closer together so there will be a more stable price for farm commodities. And, perhaps most important of all for young men who wish to enter the business, a loan program has been placed in operation by the federal government through which any young man with a farm background may borrow part of the money needed to buy and operate a farm, and be given as long as forty years to pay it back. This program has special provisions for war veterans. It is much easier for a young man to buy a farm for himself today than it was before this loan policy was established.

What Does the Future Hold for Farming?

The outlook for farming is, on the whole, quite promising. Our population has been increasing, and with it a greater demand for farm products has been created. This demand will doubtless remain at a permanently higher level; also, as our supply of natural resources is depleted, farm products are used more and more as raw materials for industry. Plastics are made from soybeans, fiberboard from sugar cane, upholstery from wool. In every section of the nation specialized crops are grown for industrial uses.

Through chemistry, scientists have learned that all organic (living) substances contain, in the main, the same elements. This means that through the processes of chemistry these substances can be changed from one form to another. This is why cloth can be made from coal; and rubber, from oil. Alcohol can be made from any starchy plant and converted into many useful products, including fuel to operate automobiles. All these scientific discoveries are helpful to both industry and agriculture. They will increase employment opportunities.

There Are Many Kinds of Farming

Farming is not just one occupation, but many, and today many kinds of farming are practiced in the United States. The United States Census Bureau classifies all farms into twelve groups. These are called *farm types.* The name of the type is taken from the crop which brings in 40 per cent or more of the total farm income. Thus, if 40 per cent or more of a farmer's income is derived from the sale of milk, his farm is known as a *dairy farm,* even though he produces products for sale other than those obtained through the management of dairy cattle. The twelve types of farms recognized by the Bureau of the Census are:

General—farms producing a great variety of products, no one of which accounts for as much as 40 per cent of the total gross income.

Cash-grain—farms depending on the sale of one or more of the following crops: wheat, corn, oats, barley, flax, rye, buckwheat, rice, and grain sorghum.

Cotton—farms deriving at least 40 per cent of their earnings from cotton (lint) and cottonseed.

Crop-specialty—farms selling sweet sorghum, sugar cane, sugar beets, maple sugar, soybeans, cowpeas, field peas and beans, tobacco, hay, peanuts, Irish potatoes, sweet potatoes, mushrooms, or other minor field crops.

Fruit—farms specializing in the production of apples, peaches, all tree fruits, nuts, grapes, strawberries, raspberries, cranberries, and other like crops.

Truck—farms growing and selling vegetables.

Dairy—farms producing and selling milk, cream, butter, dairy cows, and calves.

Animal specialty—farms specializing in the production and sale of cattle, sheep, hogs, goats, wool, mohair, and, possibly, slaughtered animals.

Stock-ranch—ranches, mostly in the West, devoted to the production of animals grown largely on grass.

Poultry—farms selling chickens, ducks, turkeys, geese, and eggs.

Self-sufficing—farms on which the value of the products used by the operator's family is 50 per cent or more of the total farm production.

Abnormal—includes five subtypes: farms of institution or country estates, farms operated on part time, boarding and lodging farms, farms emphasizing forest products, or farms operated by a dealer in livestock.

Locality Helps Decide Type of Farming

Climate, soil, rainfall, markets, and many other factors play a part in determining the type of farming in any section of the country. Apples, for example, cannot be grown profitably in all parts of the country. There are usually logical, practical reasons for the type of farming found in any community or section, based on the combined experience of all the people who have ever farmed in the locality.

While there are only twelve types of farming listed by the Bureau of Census, this list does not by any means present a complete picture of America's farming opportunities. Most of the types may be subdivided into different kinds of farming, each of which is a distinct occupation. For instance, there are about 150,000 fruit farmers in the United States. But this number includes men growing apples in Washington, peaches in Georgia, walnuts in California, and cranberries in New Jersey. Each is actually a separate occupation. In the same way, each type may be subdivided many times. There are, perhaps, around 100 kinds of farming in which one may engage. Each of these requires special training and know-how; each has different problems; and each has some special appeal which makes people want to try that kind of farming.

Different Kinds of Farm Work

Within each type of farming there are job possibilities for four classes of workers. These are: (1) *farm owners*, (2) *managers*, (3) *tenants*, and (4) *laborers*, often called "hired hands."

A "farmer" or "farm operator," according to the census, is a man who directs the operation of a farm. Hence, owners of farms, who do not themselves direct the operations, are not reported as farmers. Farmers are divided into three general classes, owners, managers, and tenants.

Farm owners include (1) farmers operating only their own land and (2) those operating their own land and some land rented from others.

Managers are farmers who are paid wages or salaries for managing farms for the owners.

Farm tenants are farmers who, as tenants, croppers, or renters, operate only hired land. Five classes of tenants are recognized as follows:

Share tenants—those who pay the owner of the land a certain share of the prod-

425

ucts, as one-half, one-third, or one-quarter, for the use of the farm but furnish their own farm equipment and animals.

Croppers—share tenants who do not furnish their work animals.

Share-cash tenants—those who pay a share of the products for part of the land rented by them and cash for another part.

Cash tenants—those who pay a cash rental, as $7 per acre for crop land, or $500 for the use of the entire farm.

Standing renters—those who pay a stated amount of farm products for the use of the farm, as three bales of cotton or 500 bushels of corn.

Hired hands are laborers employed for cash wages on either a temporary or a permanent basis.

Trends in Farming

To give some idea of the approximate number of workers in each group, when there were 4,782,416 farms reported for the United States, there were 2,744,708 owners, 20,894 managers, and 1,149,239 tenants. At the same time, about 1,925,000 hired hands were employed, largely on a seasonal or temporary basis.

For many years the number of "hands" required on farms has been decreasing. This is due mainly to the increased use of farm machinery.

Years ago, for example, thousands upon thousands of transient (traveling) workers and college students obtained summer employment in the wheat fields of the West. This work opportunity no longer exists, except for a limited few. At the opening of the century, many "hands" were needed to cut the grain, operate the threshing machine, and carry the wheat to the granary or elevator. Now a machine, called a combine, cuts and threshes the grain at one operation. Human labor has become a minor factor in the growing of grain.

Labor-saving machinery has also been designed for most other farm operations. Cotton was the last important crop in the nation to be produced entirely by hand, but now a mechanical cotton picker has been invented which will harvest as much cotton in a day as fifty people could pick by hand. In addition, other machines are used for cultivating and doing the other jobs once done by hand. In the South, the mule is being replaced to a large extent by the tractor. With mules, a farmer could take care of an average of only 25 acres, but using tractors and modern equipment he can easily manage 200 acres. This change has increased farm income per worker, but it has reduced the number of farm operators.

Most people think it is better to be a farm owner rather than a tenant. This is true insofar as ownership represents a capital reserve, or building up of earnings. It is not necessarily true, however, that a farm operator can earn more money as an owner than he can as a renter. Through wise management he may be able to get a larger income through investing his money in stock and equipment instead of land. Probably the majority of our better farmers rent land in addition to that which they own. This is a modern trend in farming which comes from the increased use of labor-saving machinery.

Farming occupations are so varied that any individual who desires to enter the business can find some opportunity suited to his means and experience.

USDA, by Hunton

One of the satisfactions of farming is growing your own food. Vegetables seem to taste better when you were the one who planted, weeded, watered, sprayed, cultivated, and harvested the crop.

Louis Bromfield describes . . .

The Joys of Farming

Although famous as a lecturer and writer of novels and nonfiction books, Louis Bromfield (1896-1956) was first and foremost a farmer at heart. In this short piece from one of his many well-known books, he showed his deep feeling for the earth and all that grows out of it. Malabar was the name of his farm near Lucas, Ohio. From **Out of the Earth** by Louis Bromfield. Published by The Curtis Publishing Company. Copyright 1948, 1949, 1950 by Louis Bromfield; used by permission of the author.

At Malabar when the shadows grow longer across the valley and each day the Big House falls earlier beneath the deep shadow of the low sandstone cliffs, we know that winter is closing in. On a still day when we hear the whistles of the big diesels on the Pennsylvania Railroad six miles away we know that we shall have fine clear weather, and when the sound comes from the opposite direction from the Baltimore and Ohio, we know that there will be clouds and rain. We know the time by the flight of the big planes going north and south, and some of the pilots know us so well that on summer nights they blink their lights in greeting as they pass through the clear, still sky overhead.

In the barns and the fields, Al and Simon know their cows—a hundred and twenty of them—by name, and they know their dispositions and what they like or do not like, from Jean, the bossy old Guernsey who must be started homeward first on her way from pasture before the others will go properly, to Inez, the Holstein, smart and temperamental, who once struck up a feud with Mummy, the feed-room cat, and was observed on two occasions shaking Mummy as a dog might shake her.

Fun and Adventure on the Farm

For the young people a farm is a kind of paradise. There is never any need to ask "Mama, what shall I do now?" On a farm no day is ever long enough for the young person to crowd into its meager twenty-four hours all there is to be done. There are fishing and swimming, explorations of the woods and the

Young people and young animals make good companions on the farm.

caves, trapping, messing about the big tractors, playing in the great haymows, a hundred exciting things to do which each day are new and each day adventurous.

But most of all there are the earth and the animals through which one comes very close to eternity and to the secrets of the universe. From Gus, the Mallard duck, who comes up from the pond every evening to eat with the dogs, from Stinker, the bull dog with his wise eyes and calm disposition, from all the dogs which run ahead leaping and barking and luring the small boys farther and farther into the fields, a child learns much. Most of all he discovers that warmth and love of nature which is perhaps the greatest of all resources, not only because its variety and beauty is endless but because slowly it creates a sense of balance and of values. It is not an accident that a large proportion of the great men and women of the nation and those who have built it have come from farms or villages.

Changes in Country Living

There is in all the world no finer figure than a sturdy farmer standing, his feet well planted in the earth, looking over his fields and his cattle. He has a security and an independence unknown to any other member of society, yet he is very much a part of society, perhaps its most important member. The sharp eyes with the wrinkles at the corners, the sunburned neck, the big strong hands, all tell a story of living not only overlooked but unknown to far too many of those who live wholly in an industrial civilization where time clocks and

427

Three Lions, by George Pickow

A farmer "paints" a landscape with fertile fields, trees, and neat houses and barns.

Bob Taylor

machines rule man instead of man ruling them.

Nothing is more beautiful than the big farm kitchen. It has changed with the times. The refrigerator, the electric stove, the quick-freeze, and the cold room have taken the place of the cellar, the root storage, and the great black old range with its tank of boiling water on the side. The woodpile is gone from outside the door and the horses no longer steam as they stand patiently while the farmer comes in for a cup of coffee and a cinnamon bun. We tell the time nowadays not by the whistle of the old steam locomotives but by the passage overhead of the big flying flag-ship. But the good smell is still there in the kitchen and the farmer's wife is the same at heart, although in these times she is not bent with rheumatism at forty years of age from carrying water and wood and bending over a washboard. At forty she is likely to be spry and young and busy with her clubs and neighborhood activities—as young-looking as her eighteen-year-old daughter who is a leader in the 4-H Club. And her husband does not rise at daylight and come in weary and bent long after dark. He keeps long hours some of the time, but during the day his work is half fun, because the drudgery has gone out of it. He is out of doors with the smell of fresh-turned earth rising to him from the furrow, the sight of a darting cock pheasant rising before his eyes in a kind of brilliant hymn to the morning. He, too, is young and sturdy at middle age and able to go places with his boys, to fish and hunt with them and attend their meetings.

A Farmer "Paints" a Landscape

A lot of things have changed on the farm of today, but the spirit and feeling of the farm and the open country remain the same. The freedom is unchanged and the sense of security and independence and the good food and the beauty that lies for the seeing eye on every side. And, above all, there is still that satisfaction, as great as that of Leonardo or Shakespeare or any other creative artist, in having made something great and beautiful out of nothing. The farmer may leave his stamp upon the whole of the landscape seen from his window, and it can be as great and beautiful a creation as Michelangelo's sculpture of David. The farmer who takes over a desolate farm, ruined by some unthinking previous owner, and turns it into a paradise of beauty and abundance is one of the greatest of artists.

Of course, I am talking about the good farmer, the real farmer, and not that group of men who remain on the land because circumstance dropped them there and who go on, hating their land, hating their work and their animals because they have never discovered that they do not belong there. The good farmer, working with nature rather than fighting or trying to outwit it, may have what he wants of those treasures which are the only real ones and the ones by which man lives—his family, and the deep, religious, humble sense of his own insignificance in God's creation.

The good farmer of today can have all the good things that his father knew and many that his father never knew, for in the modern world he lives with all the comforts of a luxurious city house plus countless beauties and rewards forever unknown to the city dweller.

428

Jobs in Agricultural Business

This article tells about the vital work of the people who deal in the processing and marketing of farm products and in selling supplies and goods needed by the farmer in his job. If you have a talent for the business end of things, you'll surely find a job here that interests you, whether it's selling seed or designing floral displays. From **Jobs in Rural Service**, second revised edition, by Paul W. Chapman. Copyright 1941, 1945, 1947 by Science Research Associates.

"I'd like to get a job as a representative of a farm machinery company in South America," said a member of a college graduating class to his counselor in the department of agricultural engineering. "Do you think I can get such a job?"

"Of course you can," replied the counselor, "but it may take several years."

"What do you mean?"

"Just this! If a company sends a man to South America as a representative, that man must know the line, he must know the policies of the company, and many other things. He might even have to speak Spanish or, in Brazil, Portuguese. But you can get such a position if that's your objective and you stick to it. The thing to do is to take any job you can get with the company you select—or the one that selects you. I'd let the personnel director know what I wanted to do, and, perhaps after several years of experience with this goal in mind, you will get the chance. Do you think it is worth the effort?"

He did—and took a job in one of the factories of a large farm machinery and implement company.

"I want to go into some kind of business. What can I do?"

This was the problem of a second member in the same engineering class. His training was much like that of the first, except that the second young man had specialized in rural electrification, while the first had majored in farm machinery.

"I know just the thing for you," replied the counselor. "Today I had a letter from a utility company that wants several young engineers to help get customers for rural electric lines."

"That would suit me fine," replied the lad, who knew that rural electric lines were expanding with the help of the government's Rural Electrification Administration. He knew, too, that the power companies wanted to point out to farmers how they could use more power with profit to themselves.

He got the job.

Beginners Start at the Bottom

A third young man, who had specialized in farm buildings, came to the counselor's office in a state of excitement. "I understand," he said, "that the Lowdwell Barn Company wants a sales manager in this part of the country. Do you think I could get the job?"

"I'm afraid not," replied the counselor with a smile. "I suppose they will want a man 35 or 40 years old, who has had experience in the farm building line, and who knows a lot of farm people all over this area. You see, the pay for such a position is excellent, and for such a salary they will expect to find someone with years of experience.

"You might get a job as a draftsman in the home office of the company, or you might work in the company's plant where they make barn equipment. But sales managers are men with years of experience—experience which includes some actual selling."

A fourth boy had prepared for work in the engineering aspects of soil conservation. He got a job building terraces for a farmers' cooperative association which owned a tractor and the necessary dirt-moving machinery. Some day, perhaps, this lad may become a sales manager for the company that makes the tractor which he is learning to operate and repair.

These are some of the opportunities in business open to young men with training in agricultural engineering. In this new division of the engineering profession there are four lines of specialization—*farm machinery, farm buildings, rural electrification,* and *soil and water conservation.* In each of these fields there are many jobs in industry and commerce open to college graduates.

farm machinery business

grain and feed

meat packing

farm credit

Farm Credit Services
Appraisers
Credit examiners
Credit executives
Insurance inspectors
Regional supervisors

Farm Co-operative Services
Accountants
Advertisers
Field agents
Inspectors
Managers
Salesmen
Scientific assistants

Farm Machinery Business
Designers
Foremen
Service specialists
Demonstrators
Salesmen
Service specialists

Fertilizer Business
Chemists
Demonstrators
Plant executives
Plant operatives
Salesmen
Scientific workers

Florist Business
Dealers
Flower growers
Gardeners
Greenhouse foremen
Salesmen

Fruit and Nursery Business
Foremen
Managers
Owners
Planting supervisors
Propagators (planters)

Grain and Feed Business
Buyers
Managers
Skilled operators
Advertising workers
Demonstrators
Salesmen
Scientific workers

Dairy Products Business
Accountants
Delivery men
Plant managers
Advertising workers
Bacteriologists
Butter makers
Dairy inspectors
Field buyers
Ice cream makers

Livestock Associations
Cow testers
Editors
Field men

Meat Packing
Buyers
Plant managers
Salesmen

Seed Business
Dealers
Field inspectors
Growers
Managers
Research workers
Salesmen

Produce Business
Canners
Country buyers
Dealers
Jobbers
Market masters
Truckers

After Chapman, JOBS IN RURAL SERVICE

Is a College Degree Always Needed?

430

Agricultural engineering is just one example of the business-career possibilities in lines related to farming for the college graduate. But there are jobs in business related to agriculture for which college training is not required. As a matter of fact, this field offers greater possibilities of employment for those without technical training than all other subdivisions or groups of agricultural jobs combined. Business jobs related to farming may appeal strongly to farm boys and girls who leave the land. They have the experience and viewpoints which will be most helpful in serving rural clients.

Business employs unskilled labor, skilled workers, technically trained personnel, members of the professional group, and executives. This means not only a wider range of employment opportunities compared with other types of agricultural occupations, but also greater differences in wages and salaries.

At the top, business can choose its employees from all of those in the field in which it is engaged. For example, the highest paid scientific men in America are working for business and industry. A successful business firm usually can go to any college or to any department of the federal government and hire the best men in the field. This statement, of course, does not apply to all individuals; there are those who enjoy the type of work in which they are engaged so much that higher pay will not take them away from it.

What are some of the businesses which offer employment opportunities to those interested in work related to farming? The businesses and jobs listed in the table (left) are examples of those which will appeal to persons with farm experience, agricultural training, or an interest in farming and rural life. This list suggests only a few of the opportunities for work in businesses related to farming. Within this group of jobs are all the industries serving the farmer and using the goods he produces, many commercial firms dealing with the marketing of farm products, and a number of rural-life service agencies.

Training for Jobs in Agricultural Business

Most persons get work through their friends. Boys and girls who want business jobs will, as a rule, find their best opportunities near home. In every town and city there are employment opportunities in businesses tied up with farming. By sticking to their search, the majority will be able to secure beginners' jobs, if only on a temporary basis. From a modest start, even without special training, it is possible for many persons to find successful and satisfying careers.

How Important Is College?

From **The Ford 1955 Farm-Ranch-Home Almanac**, edited by John Strohm. Copyright 1954 by Ford Motor Co., Simon and Schuster, Inc., and Artists and Writers Guild, Inc. Adapted by permission.

A seventeen year old farm boy was talking to his dad: "But I want to farm anyway—why should I finish high school?"

He probably would be surprised if he were told, "You'll get paid $40 a day for every day you go to high school."

Yet that's exactly what a recent survey has shown. Boys who graduate from high school can expect to earn $33,000 more during their lifetime than the grammar school graduates. And college graduates can expect to earn $72,000 more than the high school graduates, according to a study made at Pennsylvania State College.

It isn't so much whether a farm boy *should* go to college, however, as does he *want* to go to college. It's the decision he must make for himself.

But young people should remember this: Not just anybody can farm today. Farming probably takes more different kinds of knowledge than any other occupation on the face of the earth. And the parade of progress in agriculture is going forward at a mighty fast clip.

Where To Write . . .

For more information about careers in agriculture, write to:

The United States Office of Education, Washington, D.C., for information about training for jobs through the vocational agriculture program.

Your county agricultural agent, at the court house in your county seat, for booklets and information on agricultural careers in the Extension Service and 4-H Club work.

U.S. Government Printing Office, Washington 25, D.C., for these booklets:

Career Service Opportunities in the United States Department of Agriculture. Agriculture Handbook No. 45, 1960.

Getting Started in Farming. Farmers' Bulletin No. 1961, United States Department of Agriculture, 1954.

Employment Outlook for Agricultural Occupations. Bureau of Labor Statistics, Bulletin No. 1215-31, United States Department of Labor, 1960.

From Men to Machines

There are machines that milk cows, unload hay, dig post holes, grind and mix feeds, and plant, cultivate, and harvest most kinds of crops. It looks as if there will someday be a machine to do just about every job that needs to be done on a farm. Because machines work faster and for longer hours (they do not have to stop to rest as horses do), today one man can farm up to eight times as many acres as his grandfather could with horses.

The age of farm machinery also means that it takes more money to start farming than in the past. What is needed depends on where the farm is located, what kind of crops are grown, and the kind and amount of livestock raised. As an example: a grain and livestock farmer operating about 240 acres in the Midwest has from $17,000 to $30,000 invested in machinery.

▶ Other Sections To See

"Soil: More Valuable Than Gold," "Agriculture: Man's Most Important Industry," and "Workers and Jobs," Volume 3; "Selling and Service Occupations," Volume 10; "Exploring for Plants" and "Cattle, Sheep, and Hogs," Volume 12; "Inventing New Plants" and "New Directions in Agriculture," Volume 16.

A harvest crew at dinner. Gone are the days when "cooking for threshers" was a regular summer job for the wheat farmer's wife. Eighty-five per cent of the manpower once needed for the harvest has been replaced by huge combines, machines that cut thirty or more acres of grain per day.

Libr. of Congress

Ask Yourself

The best way to find out something about yourself is to ask yourself. If you ask yourself the questions on this page, you can find out something about what your job interests are in the field of agriculture. To play this "Ask Yourself" pretend that you can be one of the first people to inhabit a new planet. You are selected because of your interest and desire for a job in agriculture. Read each of the descriptions below and choose the five you like best. Don't worry about whether or not you can do these jobs; just for now, pretend that you could do any one of them if you wanted to. Write down on a separate sheet of paper all the letters in the parentheses following each job you chose. When you are all through, score yourself according to the instructions. The upside-down word at the end of each description is the name of the job to which the description refers. Do not look at this until you have completed the questionnaire.

Questions

1. You test the soil and suggest what will grow best. (A, C, F, G) (Agronomist)
2. Under your hands the soil produces food. (A, E, H) (Farmer)
3. You help folks plan what to grow and raise. (B, C, D, F, G) (Agricultural Economist)
4. You teach Johnny how to be a better farmer. (B, C, E, F, G) (Vocational Agricultural Teacher)
5. The equipment breaks down and you repair it. (A, F, H) (Farm Equipment Mechanic)
6. You decide whether or not Bill gets the farm loan he needs. (A, B, D, E) (Credit Examiner)
7. From your hothouses come new flowers everyone wants. (A, E, G, H) (Floriculturist)
8. Daily you visit farmers to get them to buy the seeds they need. (B, C, D, F, G) (Salesman)
9. Your hatchery is developing a new kind of chick. (B, D, F, H) (Poultry Husbandman)
10. Carefully you tend the vats that make the cheese. (A, F, H) (Cheese Maker)
11. After it is slaughtered you examine the animal carcass. (A, D, E, F) (Meat Inspector)
12. You keep track of the amount each co-op member contributes. (A, D, F) (Bookkeeper)
13. Each week you write a column on farm news. (A, C, F, G) (Writer)

14. You are called whenever farm animals get sick. (B, E, F, G, H) (Veterinarian)
15. The men wait for your orders in fighting the forest fire. (A, B, E, H) (Forest Ranger)

How To Score

Here is how you score your answers. Each one of the letters in the parenthesis represents an interest usually found in people holding that job. There are several letters after each job because every job has several interests associated with it.

Take your answer sheet and count how many times you put down each of the letters that followed the jobs you chose. Count how many A's, B's, etc. If your interests appear to be equal, reading more may help you discover which things you like best. Then look at the Job Interest Key. Usually, the more times a certain letter appears in your score, the greater your interest is in that kind of work.

432

Here is a list of the places in OUR WONDERFUL WORLD where you will find "Ask Yourself."

Mechanics	Vol. 4
Aviation	Vol. 5
Writing	Vol. 7
Medicine	Vol. 8
Agriculture	Vol. 9
Selling	Vol. 10
Law	Vol. 11
Teaching	Vol. 12
Office Work	Vol. 13
Entertainment	Vol. 14
Science	Vol. 15
Government	Vol. 16
Beauty and Fashions	Vol. 17

Job Interest Key

A Work with non-living things (machines, objects, devices, etc.)
B Work with living things (people, animals, etc.)
C Work using words (writer, speaker, salesman, etc.)
D Work using numbers (accountant, engineer, etc.)
E Work done outdoors (forest ranger, fisherman, etc.)
F Work done indoors (waitress, chemist, etc.)
G Work with ideas (scientist, teacher, etc.)
H Work with hands (machinist, carpenter, etc.)

The Solar System

"Which is more useful, the Sun or the Moon? The Moon is the more useful since it gives us light during the night, when it is dark, whereas the sun shines only in the daytime when it is light anyway."

This is the strange reasoning of the legendary philosopher Kuzma Prutkov, quoted in Professor George Gamow's book *The Birth and Death of the Sun.* The philosopher's statement is ridiculous, of course, because everybody would soon die and the moon would not be visible if it weren't for the sun. The moon shines only because the sun sheds its light upon it, and daytime is possible only because half of the earth is regularly turned toward the sun. The seasons, the weather, the growth of plants—all these things are what they are because of the heat and light sent out by the sun.

Our earth is only one member of the sun's family. There are eight other known planets, as the large bodies which circle the sun are called; and these have a combined total of at least 32 satellites or moons. There are also thousands of very small minor planets, called planetoids, that form a wide band between the planets Mars and Jupiter. In addition, there is an unknown, but very large, number of comets, meteors, and meteorites.

This sun-centered family is known as the solar system. (The word "solar" comes from the Latin *sol* meaning sun.) What keeps all the bodies in place? How much space does the solar system occupy? Will the sun ever "go out"? How old is the solar system? How was it formed? These are some of the questions that will be answered in the following section.

Four continents are visible in this view of the earth from ATS-3 (Applications Technology Satellite), photographed from its stationary orbit 22,300 miles above the Amazon River mouth. South America is in the center; clockwise from the upper left are: North America, Greenland, Europe, Africa, and Antarctica (at bottom).

What Is Our Solar System?

Ask almost anyone what the solar system is and he is apt to tell you: "It is the sun orbited by nine planets." That is right, of course, but it's a great deal more than that. Clifford Simak explains some of the new facts scientists are discovering about it in this article from his book, **The Solar System: Our New Front Yard.** Copyright 1962 by Clifford Simak. Adapted by permission of St. Martin's Press, New York.

The solar system is a wonderful mechanism. It operates by natural law, in an orderly manner, and it has been running for five to seven billion years. It should operate for uncounted billions more.

The solar system is composed of a star (the sun), nine known planets, 31 moons, upwards of 50,000 asteroids, vast numbers of meteors and other assorted debris, perhaps as many as 100 billion comets, and great clouds of radiation floating out in space.

What Are Planets Made Of?

Leaving out Pluto, about which little is known, there are two kinds of planets in the solar system. The terrestrial planets, Mercury, Venus, Earth, and Mars, are small planets fashioned of rock and metal. Jupiter, Saturn, Uranus, and Neptune are the giant gas planets —much bigger than the terrestrial planets, and probably with no rock or metal, as such, in them. They appear to be great balls of gas,

434

compressed until they resemble no earthly substance.

Some Other Solar System Members

The asteroids are small fragments of planetary material, most of which maintain an orbit between Mars and Jupiter. The largest, Ceres, is 450 miles in diameter. Some 1600 asteroids have had their orbits computed and another thousand have been listed. It is estimated that there may be 50,000 with diameters of more than a mile. The belt probably contains millions of asteroids basketball size or larger, and uncounted millions in sizes ranging down to gravel, sand, and tiny bits of rock. No matter what its size, every bit of material in the belt, even each grain of sand, is moving in an orbit of its own.

Just where one draws the line between a meteorite and an asteroid is almost impossible to determine. Many of the chunks of matter which fall upon the earth are actually members of the asteroid belt. In any case, a meteorite is a mass of solid matter which is either traveling in space or has finally landed on some surface. It can be almost any size, from less than the bulk of a grain of sand up to measurements of a mile or two in diameter. (A *meteor* is the light phenomenon which is produced by the passage of a meteorite through an atmosphere.) The total mass of the meteorites swept up by the earth every

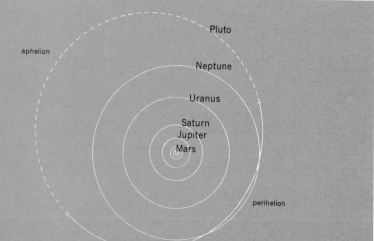

The orbits of the planets. The sun is only slightly off-center in relation to the paths most of the planets travel. Pluto and Mercury, the outermost and innermost planets, respectively, show greater variation, however. Perihelion (the point at which a planet is closest to the sun) and aphelion (the point of greatest distance) are shown on Pluto's orbit.

24 hours has been estimated at from 1000 to 10,000 tons.

Comets are generally members of the solar system, although occasionally there may be an intruder from outer space. They are largely composed of frozen gases, and range in size from about one to ten miles in diameter. There are a few, however, with diameters of 100 miles or more. Comets move in elongated orbits, coming in close to the sun, then going deep into space before they turn to travel inward toward the sun again.

The Solar Wind

Streaming out from the surface of the sun and reaching deep into the solar system is a solar wind made up of clouds of radiation and particles. Particles and radiations race out from the sun continuously; but at certain times, when the sun goes on a rampage of activity, they stream out in much thicker and more energetic clouds.

The average number of particles in space between the sun and the earth runs about 100 to 1000 per cubic centimeter, depending upon the activity of the sun and perhaps a number of other factors. A centimeter is about two-fifths of an inch.

While all indications for some time pointed to the existence of this wind, on-the-spot evidence of it was obtained in the spring of 1961 by a space probe which was sent aloft from Cape Canaveral.

The experiment was conducted by Dr. Bruno Rossi, professor of physics at Massachusetts Institute of Technology. He installed a rotating cup on the surface of the probe. When the sun-driven particles streamed through the cup opening, they were converted into electrical signals which were automatically transmitted back to earth.

Direction of the wind (showing that it did come from the sun) was determined by observing the intervals during which the cup recorded the electrical signals. The particles could enter the cup's opening only when it faced the sun. This produced a rhythmic signal which indicated that the particles were being caught only as the opening spun around to face the sun.

The wind travels at the speed of millions of miles an hour. Ordinarily, it takes between one and two days for it to travel from the sun to the earth. Suggestions have been made that the solar wind might be harnessed to drive spacecraft, with huge sails spread to catch the wind. There is a good deal of doubt, however, that the idea would work out. More will have to be known about the character of the wind.

Since the particles hurled out by the sun are for the most part highly ionized, magnetic fields move along with the gas. It is believed, however, that in most cases these magnetic fields remain connected with the sun, as if they had roots planted there.

Movement in the Solar System

The solar system does not simply spin like a wheel in space. It is on the move and going very fast. All the planets are spinning on their axes, some quickly, some comparatively slowly. Each is moving about the sun in something that is called an ellipse, which is, roughly, a slightly off-true circle.

435

From ASTRONOMIE by Rudaux and Vaucouleurs, ed. by Larousse

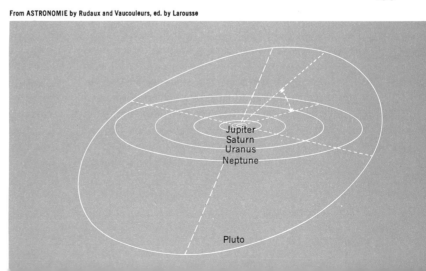

An "edgewise" view of the planets' orbits shows the angular tilt of Pluto's path. The other planets revolve more nearly on the same plane. (The scale of the drawing is so small that the orbits of the planets nearest the sun do not show.)

The earth spins on its axis at the rate of 1000 miles an hour—measured at the equator. In addition to this, the earth is moving around the sun at the rate of 66,600 miles an hour. The sun itself is moving through space, carrying the entire solar system with it, at 43,000 miles an hour. And the little cloud or neighborhood of stars to which the sun belongs is moving at a speed of 630,000 miles an hour, swinging in a great circle around the center of the galaxy of which this cloud of stars is a part.

Even moving at this speed, the sun and its neighbor stars need something like 200,000,000 years to swing clear around the great wheel of our galaxy.

If there is anything striking about our solar system it is the perfect order which it displays. Order is apparent even in the evenly spaced distances between the planets. This orderly distance is explained by something that is called Bode's law. You can read more about it on page 455.

Except for Pluto, all of the planets lie in the same plane, in line with the sun's equator.

And even Pluto's orbit is canted just a little. All the planets circle the sun in the same direction—in a counterclockwise motion if you look down at the system from a point above the sun's north pole.

With the exception of Uranus (and, possibly, of Venus), the planets rotate upon their axes in the same counterclockwise direction. The sun also rotates in the same direction. Uranus doesn't rotate in a clockwise direction. Rather it lies almost on its side, with one of its poles pointing at the sun, and rolls along the planetary plane. There is a possibility that Venus may rotate clockwise. All the moons which circle their planets, with a few exceptions, also orbit in the equatorial plane and in a counterclockwise direction.

Pluto, the farthest known planet, is an average of 3,666,000,000 miles from the sun, which makes the diameter of the solar system close to seven and a half billion miles. This does not take into account the comets, which are also members of the solar system. Some of them may reach out in their long orbits to many billions of miles beyond the sun.

Herschel's Model of the Solar System

Would you like to make a model of the solar system? Here is a plan suggested by a famous astronomer. All you will need is a globe, two mustard seeds, two peas, a peppercorn, two oranges, a cherry, a plum, and a few grains of sand. —Oh yes, you will also need time to walk two miles to put your outermost planet in place! From **Planets, Stars, and Atoms** by George Edwin Frost. Copyright 1939 by The Caxton Printers, Ltd., Caldwell, Idaho.

The following standard directions for making a model of our solar system to scale were originated by Sir John Herschel, a famous astronomer, many years ago: "On a wide level common, place a globe two feet in diameter to represent the sun. At a distance of 82 feet from it put a mustard seed to represent Mercury; a pea at 142 feet would stand for Venus, and another pea at 215 feet for the earth, whilst Mars would be indicated by a peppercorn at 327 feet. A fair-sized orange nearly a quarter of a mile from the central globe would stand for Jupiter, whilst the minor planets (the planetoids) would be represented by minute grains of sand, mostly from 500 to 600 feet from the center, though some would be as near as Mars, others as far as Jupiter. Saturn would be a small orange at two-fifths of a mile, Uranus a large cherry at three-quarters of a mile, and Neptune a plum at a mile and a quarter."

To this could now be added the planet Pluto, discovered in 1930, which is a little larger than Mercury, and might be represented by another mustard seed at a distance of about two miles from the central globe representing the sun. According to the same scale of distance, the nearest star would appear to be a minute point of light 7,500 miles from the sun.

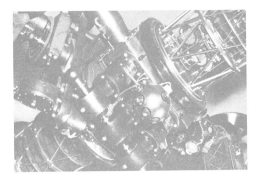

In addition to projecting images of the stars, an optical planetarium can show the ecliptic, meridian, and other imaginary lines (right). Below, a close-up of the many projectors which throw the star and planet images on the dome.

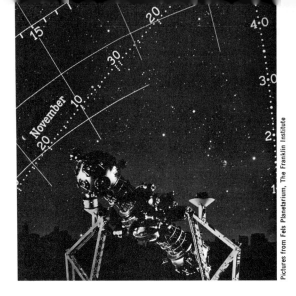

Pictures from Fels Planetarium, The Franklin Institute

Theater of the Heavens

In the last century and before, a planetarium was a mechanical device on which models of the planets moved around the sun. These models are still used in some classrooms. But the optical planetarium projector throws the image of every object in the night sky on a dome, and makes it move accurately and realistically. This article was written by Thomas D. Nicholson of the Hayden Planetarium, New York.

A planetarium is a place where people learn about the stars and about the science of astronomy. In every planetarium there is a special room called the sky theater where the sun, moon, planets, and stars appear in a man-made sky. Here audiences watch the sky while they listen to a story about astronomy. The sky theater is probably the most interesting part of a planetarium.

Every planetarium has its sky theater, but many also have telescopes for research and for public viewing. Some have exhibits on astronomy, libraries on astronomy and workshops for building telescopes and other instruments. In some there are classrooms where astronomy is taught to young people and adults. A planetarium is really an institution which specializes in teaching about astronomy. Special equipment and instruments are used to make astronomy more interesting and understandable.

The most exciting moment in a planetarium comes when visitors enter the sky theater.

Suddenly they find themselves looking at the stars, shining brightly and turning slowly just as they do in nature. Many people wonder where the stars come from when they see how real they appear in a planetarium sky. They are, of course, man-made stars. The planetarium sky is really the inside surface of a curved, white-painted ceiling. The stars come from a strange looking instrument at the center of the sky theater. This dumbbell-shaped instrument is a planetarium projector.

Projecting the Sky on the Ceiling

The idea of a projector that would make the sun, moon, stars and planets appear in a man-made sky came from a German scientist, Professor Walter Bauersfeld of the Carl Zeiss Company in Germany. The first planetarium projector, using Dr. Bauersfeld's design, was installed at the Deutches Museum in Munich, Germany, in 1925. Within a few years, a dozen more Zeiss projectors were supplied to new planetariums in Europe. Planetariums were introduced in the United States in the 1930's, first at Chicago, then at Philadelphia, Los Angeles, New York and Pittsburgh. All had Zeiss projectors.

Until World War II, the Zeiss projectors were the only ones available. After 1945, other planetarium projectors were developed. One kind is manufactured in the United States by Spitz Laboratories, Incorporated, of Yorklyn, Delaware. These new projectors are similar in some ways to the Zeiss projectors, but they

437

The Adler Planetarium in Chicago was built at the time of the 1933 World's Fair, and has presented planetarium shows to millions of visitors. In addition to its sky theater, there is a large collection of astronomical instruments both old and new. This planetarium and others often have displays of meteorites.

also have some unusual features of their own.

Inexpensive projectors for small sky theaters now make it possible for schools and museums in small cities to have planetariums of their own. Today there are several hundred small planetariums in the world, each with a seating capacity of a hundred people or so. Large institutions like the American Museum-Hayden Planetarium in New York, can seat over 800 people at a time.

A planetarium projector is really a great many projectors built into one large and complicated instrument. There are separate projectors for the sun, moon, and each planet. Each of these projectors has its own lamp and lens system. Each has a slide with an image of the object to be projected on the planetarium sky. Special motors and gears are used to turn these projectors so that the sun, moon, and planets appear and move in the right part of the sky.

Since the stars must appear all around the planetarium sky and all at the same time, they cannot all come from the same projector. The stars come from the two large balls at the ends of the planetarium projector. These two balls give the projector its strange dumbbell-like shape. There are many projectors in each ball. Each of these projectors contains a slide for making a picture of the stars appear in one part of the sky.

These pictures fill the entire planetarium sky with stars which are carefully matched to appear like the stars of nature. Motors on the planetarium projector turn the whole instrument slowly. In that way all the stars are made to move across the man-made sky as they appear to move outdoors. Stars which would appear below the horizon are cut off from the audience's view automatically by the projector. Curved, eyelid-shaped metal plates "wink" and shield the slides of the stars.

The Show in the Sky

The show in the sky theater of a large planetarium is much more than a view of the stars. An astronomer gives the lecture. While he talks, he controls the projector so that what he says can be illustrated by events in the sky. Music, sounds and colored lights are used to make the lecture more interesting and exciting. It might be about an eclipse of the sun or the moon, or about the birth and history of the stars. It might tell about the great observatories of the world, or about the exploration of the moon and the planets.

During the lecture, the dome-shaped ceiling in the planetarium becomes a man-made sky.

Often it is the sky of night sparkling with stars. A brilliant aurora may flicker across the dome. Sometimes it is the sky of day, with the sun drifting slowly through clouds. Suddenly the sky may be filled with a violent thunderstorm or a swirling snowstorm.

Different scenes are projected around the horizon of the sky theater. They may take the audience to a tropic island, to the frozen Arctic or to the lonely surface of the moon or Mars. Meanwhile special projectors may show the skies as they appear in great telescopes. The lecturer may also project and describe celestial bodies such as meteors, comets, asteroids.

Things to See and Do at the Planetarium

Visitors to a planetarium may see interesting astronomy exhibits while waiting for the sky show. The Fels Planetarium in Philadelphia, and the Griffith Planetarium in Los Angeles allow visitors to look through large telescopes. The Adler Planetarium in Chicago has an interesting collection of astronomical instruments. There is also an optical workship where visitors can see telescopes being made. Meteorites (meteors that have fallen to earth) are often displayed.

The Morehead Planetarium in Chapel Hill, North Carolina, and The American Museum-Hayden Planetarium in New York each have a second theater called a Copernican Room. There audiences can see a large model of the solar system in motion. At New York, there is also a real Viking rocket on display.

Many children and adults attend courses in astronomy at a planetarium. All of the large planetariums, and many smaller ones too, have special lectures during the week for school classes. Afternoon and Saturday classes

for children are offered at the large planetariums in Chicago, Pittsburgh, Philadelphia, New York, and Boston, and at many of the small planetariums attached to museums in other cities. Special summer sessions in astronomy for high school students are offered each year at some planetariums.

Today, there are large planetariums in nearly every major city in the world. More are being added each year. Many small cities have the new medium size projectors in sky theaters that seat 200 to 300 persons.

The most important thing about a planetarium, however, is not the size or kind of projector it uses. The planetarium is an educational institution. Its value depends upon the people who work there and how well they present astronomy to their visitors. There are many people on the staff of the large planetariums. Some are astronomers, and others are trained teachers of science. Artists and technicians design and build the exhibits and the special devices that make the heavens seem more real and understandable to visitors.

The astronomers and science teachers specialize in lecturing, teaching, studying astronomy or in planning the program for visitors. But all spend part of their time answering the questions of visitors or of people who write or call. They also help others to solve problems in astronomy and guide young people who are interested in a career in astronomy.

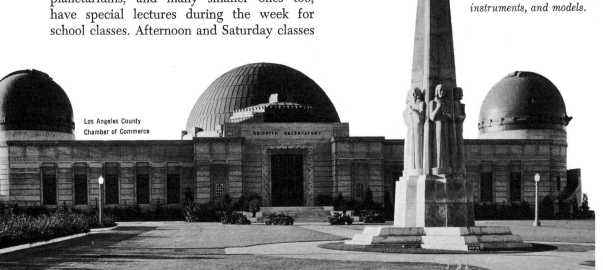

Griffith Observatory in Los Angeles has a sky theater, 12-inch telescope, solar telescope, and exhibits of astronomical photographs, instruments, and models.

439

The Structure of Space

When scientists speak of "space," they are not speaking of emptiness. They refer to something which, while it may seem to be nothing, must be considered as having a structure. It has dimensions which can be visualized and discussed—and which have led to some fascinating ideas about the universe around us.

Every object that we know has three dimensions—length, breadth, and depth (or height). But suppose we take an imaginary point, as mathematicians often have to do. This point is so tiny that it has no dimensions at all; therefore it can be said that it exists in *no* dimensions.

Move this point a given distance in an unchanging direction, and it will trace out a line, which has *one* dimension—that of *length*.

This line, moved in a direction at right angles to itself the same distance as its length, traces out a plane in the form of a square, which has *two* dimensions—those of *length* and *breadth*.

If the plane is then moved in a direction at a right angle to itself a distance equal to one of its sides, it will trace out the form of a cube. The cube has *three* dimensions—*length*, *breadth*, and *depth* or *height*.

But now, if you attempt to move the cube in a direction at right angles to the three directions which it contains, what happens? You do not create a figure having *four* dimensions —or do you?

Such a figure is called a *hypercube*, or *tesseract*. But we have no actual knowledge that such a figure exists, even though it would seem to follow from the creation of the figures that went before.

In mathematics, it is possible to raise any number to a power by multiplying it by itself. When a number is raised to the second power, it is squared, which corresponds to the square. When it is raised to the third power, it is cubed, corresponding to the cube. But while in mathematics it is possible to raise a number to the fourth power, there seems to be no corresponding physical figure which results which

can be seen, examined and analyzed.

A cube moved in space is the same cube as before—except that it is now in a different place. And in the moving it has gone through *time*, from the start of the move to the finish.

Is time the fourth dimension? Some people once thought so. But it seems more correct to say that time is only the way we, who are restricted to a world of three dimensions, can sense the fourth dimension.

If we could imagine a creature that lived in a world having only two dimensions, never knowing that "up" or "down" existed, how could it perceive something which entered its world from our own world—the world of the third dimension? It would see something suddenly entering its world in a mysterious manner that it could not explain, and then perhaps disappearing—when we would say that what happened was that the object went "up" or "down" and disappeared only because it was withdrawn from the two-dimensional area.

A two-dimensional creature would seem to us to have only partial perception of the

No matter how small a point is made, it still has three dimensions; we must imagine it as having no dimensions at all.

The line, generated by moving a point, also in reality has three dimensions; but mathematically we must regard it as having only one dimension.

Move the line in a direction perpendicular to itself, and it then makes the figure of a plane—a flat figure having two dimensions.

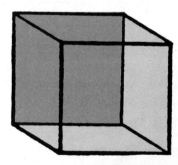

Moving the plane in a direction perpendicular to the plane makes a cube, a three-dimensional figure like all earthly things.

440

world, since there are three dimensions in it. But to carry the analogy further, do we in our three-dimensional world perceive things only in part, and is the phenomenon of time only our imperfect way of sensing the fourth dimension?

But to return to the idea of space as a structure which was mentioned earlier; if there is four-dimensional space, why could not five-, six-, and seven-dimensional space be a reality? Some scientists think that it is, since it is mathematically possible. And they have further suggested that there may be an indefinite number of dimensions in space, since each known dimension would appear to need a higher dimension to contain it.

We can draw zero-, one-, and two-dimensional figures on a sheet of paper. The point and line actually have three dimensions, but we can indicate what we mean by making them very small and very fine. But to illustrate a cube, we must make a model if we are to discover its exact shape. A drawing on paper will not be enough, although we can under-

stand and visualize the cube to some extent.

To draw four- and five-dimensional figures, however, is not to gain a real idea of their structure. A diagram or model of a tesseract either shows the eight three-dimensional cubes which comprise it as being edge-to-edge, or else only shows a part of each cube. It cannot possibly illustrate correctly the interpenetration of cubes which would take place in a tesseract. A five-dimensional figure, or *pentact*, would be more complex still.

How does this affect the earth, the other planets, the sun, and all of the other objects and bodies in space? As yet, scientists have found it only of theoretical interest. The planets rotate and revolve, the sun and stars move in their courses in the same way, so far as we are concerned, whether the universe has three or dozens of dimensions. But the existence of higher dimensions may in the not too distant future help to solve some of the riddles that still bother astronomers and physicists about the cosmos which surrounds us and of which we are a part.

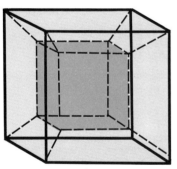

We cannot represent a four-dimensional figure in three dimensions; this is a suggestion only of how such a figure, a hypercube, *might appear.*

441

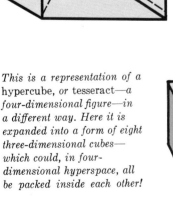

This is a representation of a hypercube, *or* tesseract—*a four-dimensional figure—in a different way. Here it is expanded into a form of eight three-dimensional cubes— which could, in four-dimensional hyperspace, all be packed inside each other!*

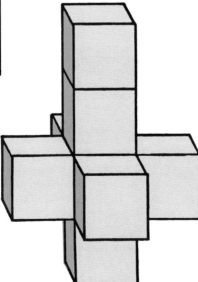

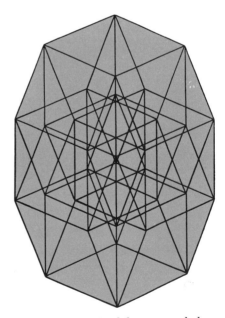

A five-dimensional figure can only be suggested by a drawing. The pentact *may, however, be only a simple figure in the multidimensional space around us.*

The Mystery of Cosmic Rays

Despite the intensive research which scientists have made, cosmic rays still remain much of a mystery. Flashing in from outer space, they bombard every square inch of the earth with a form of radiation which can be detected by instruments, but which apparently does little harm to life on our planet. Here is the story of the discovery of cosmic rays and what is definitely known about them. From "Where Do Cosmic Rays Come From?" by Bruno Rossi, **Scientific American**, September, 1953, Vol. 189, No. 34. Used by permission of the author and Scientific American.

The earth is under a ceaseless rain of particles from space. These cosmic rays, our only material contact with the vast universe outside our planetary system, have excited wonder and eager study ever since they were first discovered in 1912. They fall upon us with energies far beyond anything that can be produced on earth. They shatter the atoms of matter and make their nuclei explode into strange fragments. It is the investigation of cosmic rays that has been responsible for the discovery of so many new elementary particles in the past quarter-century: the positron, the various mesons, the lambda particles and others which are being discovered even as these lines are written. Besides this, cosmic rays are of great interest in biology, for they are believed to play a large role in the evolution of life on the earth.

Thus the cosmic rays have been very useful to science. But the big question remains: where do they come from, and how do they get their fantastic energy?

At six o'clock on the morning of August 7, 1912, a balloon took off from a field near the Austrian town of Aussig. It carried three men, one of them a young physicist named Victor Hess, and three sensitive instruments. Hess was out to learn something about the source of a certain mysterious radiation which physicists had been detecting for some time with laboratory instruments. His balloon rose to 16,000 feet, and he found the radiation much stronger there than at sea level. After analyzing his readings, he announced: "The results of my observations are best explained by the assumption that a radiation of very great penetrating power enters our atmosphere from above. . . ."

This was the first recognition of what the American physicist Robert Millikan later named cosmic radiation. The investigation that followed concerned itself first of all with finding out what the cosmic rays were.

Two Kinds of Cosmic Rays

Outside the earth's atmosphere, cosmic radiation consists mainly of protons (nuclei of hydrogen), varying widely in energy. Cosmic rays also contain nuclei of helium and of heavier elements. These rays outside the earth's atmosphere are called *primary* cosmic radiation. As the cosmic rays penetrate our atmosphere, many of them smash into atoms causing the latter to disintegrate completely. The products of this disintegration—neutrons, protons, gamma rays, so forth—are called *secondary* cosmic radiation.

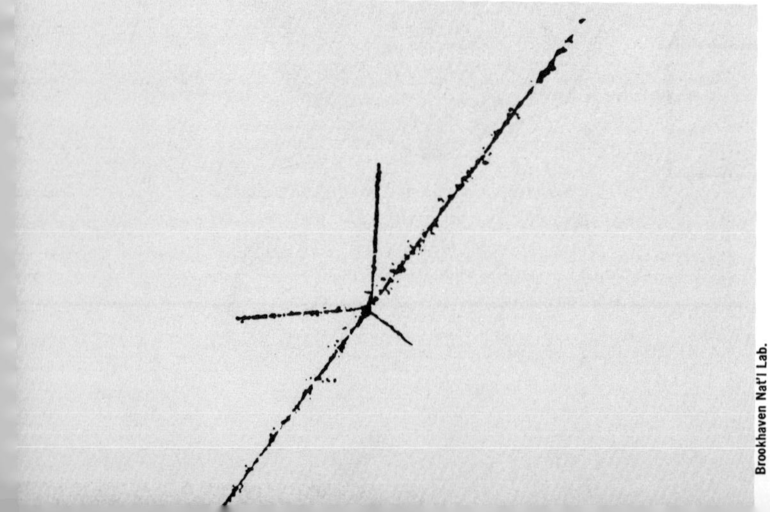

442

Brookhaven Nat'l Lab.

A cosmic ray whizzed through a photographic plate (shown here), leaving behind its trail. The long straight trail, from left to right, is the path of the cosmic ray. It collided with a nucleus, probably of a carbon atom. As a result of the collision, the carbon nucleus disintegrated into three alpha particles (an alpha particle consists of two protons and two neutrons and is the same as the helium nucleus). The alpha particles produce trails which the atomic physicists call a "three-pronged star."

It is interesting to note that the relative abundance of the different nuclei in cosmic rays corresponds closely to the relative abundance of those elements in the universe. Long before striking our atmosphere and beginning the series of collisions by which their energy is eventually lost, cosmic-ray particles are deflected by the earth's magnetic field. Some of them are thrown back into space; others reach the earth from a direction which may differ considerably from their original path.

Where Do Cosmic Rays Come From?

Suggestions as to where the cosmic rays may come from divide themselves into two general schools of thought. One school holds that the cosmic rays were created several billion years ago in a tremendous explosion that gave birth to the universe; since then they have been traveling through space with a speed of almost 186,000 miles per second. The trouble with this point of view is that it cannot be tested by any means whatever. It therefore seems more profitable to explore the second hypothesis, which can at least be tested by theory. This point of view assumes that cosmic rays are produced continuously somewhere in the system of stars which forms our galaxy.

The most attractive theory is that they come from the nearest star, our sun, for the farther away we place the source, the harder it is to account for the relatively heavy intensity of the cosmic-ray fall on the earth. The energy of this fall is very small compared to the energy of the light and heat we get from the sun, but it is almost the same as the light from the distant stars.

Some similarity between the intensity of cosmic radiation and activity in the sun has, in fact, been observed. Shortly after the appearance of a large flare on the sun, there is sometimes a sudden burst of extra cosmic radiation at the earth. Three such events are on record. On November 19, 1949, cosmic-ray meters at widely separated stations registered abnormally high intensities about one hour after a solar flare had reached its maximum. A detector of cosmic-ray neutrons at Manchester, England, went off the scale. At Climax, Colorado, a detector of cosmic-ray mesons registered a 180 per cent increase.

This does not necessarily mean that the sun is the sole source of cosmic rays. If they came only from the sun, their intensity should change very greatly with the position of the sun in the sky. Experiments have shown, however, that the change during the day's 24 hours is less than half of one per cent.

It is quite unlikely, then, that the sun contributes more than a small fraction of the total cosmic radiation observed at the earth, and we must continue to look for other possible sources of cosmic rays. If we keep in mind the required strength of the cosmic-ray sources, we must assume that the particles originate inside our galaxy, the Milky Way.

However, no hypothesis about the origin of cosmic rays is completely supported by theory or experiment today. Even worse, few of the many hypotheses that have been put forward can be definitely disproved. For this reason the question: "Where do cosmic rays come from?" is still a mystery in science. Nonetheless, scientists are working hard on this problem for its solution will give us a great deal of basic information about the universe.

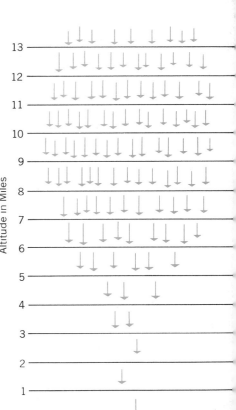

The intensity of cosmic rays for different heights above the surface of the earth is shown in this diagram. Each arrow stands for one cosmic ray passing through a square inch during a time of one minute. Ten arrows mean ten cosmic rays passing through a square inch each minute. Only cosmic rays going straight downward toward the earth are considered. The greatest intensity of cosmic radiation occurs about ten miles above the earth, then drops off to a steady value.

Planets and Radio

For many years scientists scoffed at any suggestion that the tiny planets might have any effect on the giant sun. But extended research by John H. Nelson, propagation analyst for RCA Communications, has shown that such effects do exist—and are vitally important to us on earth. This article, originally published in **The Story of Our Time: Encyclopedia Year Book, 1952,** has been revised by the author in 1964 to include results of his continuing research.

The earsplitting din of static has a way of spoiling your radio listening pleasure; it is also the nuisance for which shortwave radio engineers are ever on the lookout. With its discord it can drown out either long- or short-wave radio signals, making communication impossible. What is the cause of these costly and destructive disturbances?

Static is sometimes called "atmospherics" because its cause lies within the earth's atmosphere—in the ionosphere. The atmosphere is divided into three parts—the troposphere, which is nearest the earth's surface, the stratosphere, or middle layer, and the ionosphere, or outermost layer.

The ionosphere extends from about 50 to 250 miles above the earth's surface. Great numbers of atoms of gases within this layer are ionized—electrified—by the ultraviolet light of the sun. That is, from normally neutral atoms of gas an electron—an electrically

charged particle—is knocked away into space. There are three principal electrified layers within the ionosphere itself—the D layer, the E layer and the F layer, the highest of the three.

The higher surface of the ionosphere, the F layer, reflects long-distance shortwave radio signals back to the earth. The reflecting power of this layer is due to the presence of enormous numbers of unattached electrons. Without this reflection, long-distance communication by shortwave radio would be impossible. A radio wave travels in a straight line after leaving the transmitter: without the reflecting layer of the ionosphere it would travel on out into interplanetary space and be lost. However, when it reaches the ionosphere, it bounces back to earth and then up again to hit the ionosphere once more, and again back to earth. A news broadcast from Paris to New York has to be reflected from the ionosphere several

444

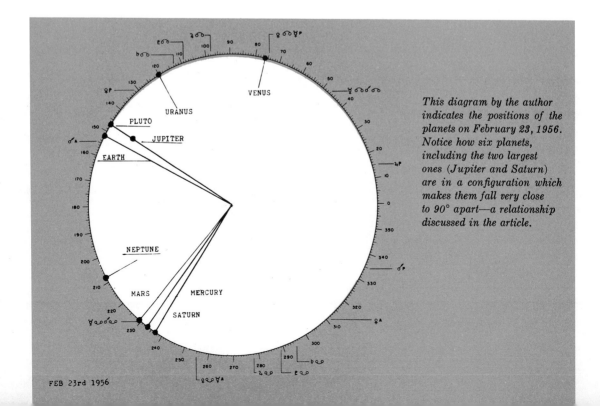

This diagram by the author indicates the positions of the planets on February 23, 1956. Notice how six planets, including the two largest ones (Jupiter and Saturn) are in a configuration which makes them fall very close to 90° apart—a relationship discussed in the article.

times before it reaches the American city.

Changes are constantly occurring in this higher reflecting layer of the ionosphere. Sometimes it becomes so disturbed that the signals reflected from it are badly distorted and cannot be understood by the listener at the distant end of the circuit. Such a disturbance is known as an ionosphere storm.

The Sun and the Ionosphere

Millions of dollars have been spent during the past twenty-five years by radio companies, research institutions and governments in trying to determine the cause of these storms and a means of overcoming them. It was soon found that there was some connection between these storms and the surface of the sun. Frequently a large, active sunspot can be observed at the time of an ionosphere storm. It was also found that the storms are most often confined to certain areas of the earth's surface and are noticed but slightly in other places. They are worse in the higher latitudes of the North Atlantic and the South Atlantic; the low latitudes in both hemispheres are least disturbed. It was a simple thing then to overcome, at least in part, the effects of the storms by routing radio signals over the unaffected parts of the earth. Then the radio companies realized

that it would be helpful if they could find out in advance when the storms were coming, so that preparations to meet them could be made.

In 1946, RCA Communications, Inc. in New York, assigned me as one of their engineer-astronomers, to do research on the sun for the purpose of developing a means of forecasting ionosphere storms. I was provided with an observatory housing a six-inch telescope at the Central Radio Office in New York. Here I studied sunspots and their relation to the behavior of radio signals.

After about two years of this type of research, I concluded that sunspots themselves were not the full answer to the problem. Their effects were too unreliable. Sometimes an ionosphere storm would coincide with a large sunspot. Sometimes no storm would occur under apparently identical conditions. In fact, more storms were associated with small, new, active sunspots than with large ones.

Ionosphere storms, coming in a random manner, suggested a random source. This led me to study the behavior of the planets as the possible cause of these storms; the relationships between the planets are extremely random and complex. I set to work to investigate the complicated patterns created by the ever changing positions of Mercury, Venus,

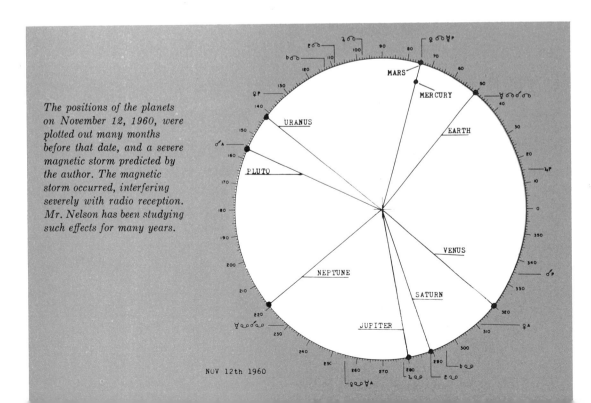

The positions of the planets on November 12, 1960, were plotted out many months before that date, and a severe magnetic storm predicted by the author. The magnetic storm occurred, interfering severely with radio reception. Mr. Nelson has been studying such effects for many years.

the earth, Mars, Jupiter and Saturn. My main purpose was to find out whether these changing patterns were connected with ionosphere storms.

Planetary Relationships

The planets move around the sun in almost circular paths, or orbits, and they move at different rates of speed. Each planet is separated from its nearest neighbor by many millions of miles. As we see these bodies from the earth, however, two or more of them may appear to be very close together in the sky. Or they may be halfway around the heavens from each other.

Measured in degrees, the entire distance around the sphere of the heavens is 360 degrees—the angular distance around any circle, no matter how big or how small. If the distance between two planets is just $\frac{1}{24}$ of the distance around the great circle of the sky, we say that the planets are 15 degrees apart, or that the angle between them is 15 degrees. We measure this angle by drawing an imaginary straight line from the center of the sun to each of the planets; the angle between two of these straight lines is the angular distance between the two planets. This angle is always changing as the planets move. It may be very small or it may be very large.

Early research conducted during the years 1948 to 1952, which compared planetary separation angles with the quality of high frequency (3 to 30 MC) radio signals indicated that signals of poorer quality often appeared on or near the dates when the planet Mercury, Venus, Earth or Mars was 0-90-180 or 270° from some other planet whose orbit was larger than its own.

Research of these arrangements showed that some of these angular separations did not coincide with poor signals, some coincided with moderately poor signals, and some with poor to very poor signals. Continued research produced the information that the poor signals came at a time when there were three or four planets associated in a 0, 90, 180, or 270° arrangement at the same time and all interconnected.

You will note that 90° is ¼ of 360°, 180° is ½ of 360°, and 270° is ¾ of 360°. Since 1952 research has also been conducted on smaller angles and it has been found that other angles which are exactly divisible into 360° are also important. These angles are known as "harmonics" and begin with 15° which is ⅙ of 90 and therefore any multiple of 15° becomes harmonic to 90, 180, 270°. In cases of poor or very poor signals there will often exist a series of planetary separations showing these smaller angles intermixed with 90, 180, 270° angles coming into operation at nearly the same time. Such arrangements are often associated with severe magnetic storms which appear at the same time.

Evidence of Planetary Influence

Since 1952 all of the sun's nine planets have been incorporated into systematic research and it has been definitely established that the planets even as far from the sun as Pluto play a part in the phenomena.

There is strong evidence also that the planets in these arrangements cause changes in the number of spots on the sun (sunspots). On February 10, 1956, the sunspot number was 30, rising to 260 by February 23, 1956. This is a very rare combination of planetary angles. Such a rapid increase in sunspot numbers is also rare.

The arrangement of the planets on November 12, 1960, was accompanied by one of the most severe radio blackouts and magnetic storms in several years. The magnetic storm was predicted by planetary arrangements 14 months in advance.

There is no physical law in nature known to the author that can explain how the planets cause changes in the solar atmosphere. It seems valid to rule out gravitation as a primary cause since the most distant planets— Uranus, Neptune, and Pluto—play an important part in this approach to forecasting. The planets Mercury (at perhelion), Venus and Jupiter do, however, have a pronounced gravitational pull on the sun.

It is the author's belief that the cause may possibly be related to electromagnetism.

How Was the
Solar System Formed?

By the editor.

Fools have said
That knowledge drives out wonder from the world;
They'll say it still, though all the dust's ablaze
With miracles at their feet.

—Alfred Noyes

This drawing illustrates Laplace's nebular theory of the origin of the solar system. At this stage the nebula has shed four gaseous rings which have begun to condense into planets as they rotate around the central mass.

How was the solar system formed? Astronomers, mathematicians, physicists, philosophers, geologists, chemists, scientists, and nonscientists have studied the problem for centuries, and all have come up with the same answer: Nobody knows what actually took place when the sun, moon, stars, and other bodies of the universe were formed.

There have been many theories, beliefs, and ideas on the subject. Some of the more likely ones have been handed down and discussed through the years. All or parts of some of the earlier theories have been proved wrong as new discoveries in astronomy were made, but new ideas were laid over the old, and scientists continue to wonder about the question in the light of the new facts that have been found. Now and then a man with courage and determination steps up to announce and defend his views on the solar system's origin.

Did It Come from a Gas Cloud?

One of the earliest theories was suggested by the German philosopher, Immanuel Kant, in the late eighteenth century. Kant proposed that the space now occupied by our solar system was once entirely filled with gases. The heavier gases attracted the lighter ones so that large masses began gradually to condense or take shape. As the condensing masses grew larger they were set in motion by opposite forces—one force attracted the masses, the other repelled them. The masses of whirling gas collided with one another and the larger bodies swallowed up the smaller ones until there were only a few masses left (the planets), all whirling in one direction around a still greater mass (the sun).

In 1796, Pierre Laplace, a French mathematician and astronomer, proposed a theory that closely resembled Kant's. Laplace believed that our solar system began as a great ball or globe of hot gas, called a nebula, that was slowly rotating in space. The nebula began to cool, and as it cooled it shrank and began to whirl faster. The great speed caused the ball to flatten, and finally a ring of the gas pulled away from the mid-region or equator of the nebula. Then other rings pulled away, each one smaller than the last, until there was a series of rings whirling around the remains of the original nebula. Each of the rings gradually formed into a globe of gas which finally condensed into the planets we know today.

Many scientists agreed to the main points of Laplace's theory and for nearly a century it probably had more followers than any other single theory on the solar system's origin. However, others have pointed out some of its weaknesses, the main one being that the angular momentum (the momentum of rotation) of the planets is far greater than the angular momentum of the sun, although the sun has much the greater mass. If the sun's mass had at one time spread throughout the solar system, its angular momentum would not have been great enough for the gas rings to form and condense into planets under such conditions as Laplace proposed.

447

Amer. Mus. Nat. Hist.

Astronomers once thought that this object in the constellation Canes Venatici was a nebula, or mass of gas, spinning in space and throwing off a smaller nebula which would cool to become a planet circling a sun. Then larger telescopes revealed it to be a galaxy, made up of millions of stars. Many people still confuse a nebula with a galaxy, and even astronomers who know better may refer to "spiral nebulae" when they mean galaxies.

Did It Start With a Solar Explosion?

In the early twentieth century two University of Chicago professors, T. C. Chamberlin, a geologist, and F. R. Moulton, an astronomer, developed an entirely new theory. They suggested that a great star once passed so close to the sun that it caused the sun to throw off great masses of material. The disturbance may have been somewhat like the solar prominences that can be seen through a telescope, except that those caused by the passing star were much more violent. Some of the material was probably drawn back into the sun, but much of it was attracted away by the passing star, and a great colony of tiny planets was formed. Chamberlin and Moulton called these tiny bodies "planetesimals." The larger planetesimals swallowed up the smaller ones and finally formed the planets of today.

448

Was a Passing Star Responsible?

The planetesimal theory was challenged by scientists who said such a solar eruption would be impossible. Two British scientists, Sir James Jeans and Harold Jeffreys, suggested that the passing star might have caused great tides in the sun—tides so strong that part of the sun was pulled away in streaming arms that whirled around the sun like a pinwheel as the disturbing star circled it. This material, Jeans and Jeffreys suggested, gradually condensed to form the planets.

Although it accounts for the fact that all the planets circle the sun in the same direction, the tidal theory has been criticized because it is more than likely that gases brought up from the depths of the sun would be so hot that they would explode and disappear into space instead of condensing into planets.

Perhaps the Planets Came from Cells?

In 1945, a German physicist, C. F. von Weizsacker, suggested what many people believe is the most likely theory of all. Von Weizsacker began by assuming that the sun was once surrounded by a flattened gaseous or nebular shell composed mainly of hydrogen and helium. The temperatures within the nebula were supposed to be equal to the temperatures of the planets and the liquid, solid, and gaseous elements were all revolving around the sun in separate orbits. Due to the different speeds of the various particles and their varying distances from the sun, and because of the attraction of the particles for one another, a system of cells was created within the nebula. In each cell the material moved clockwise, but the entire system was revolving counterclockwise. Pockets formed in the spaces between adjoining cells, and it was in these pockets that the planets took shape.

Although this theory, like the others, leaves several important steps unexplained, many scientists believe that Von Weizsacker's theory could account for the apparently regular progression of spacing between the planets as shown by Bode's Law.

[Continued on page 451]

How Did Our Solar System Begin?

Although no one really knows how our solar system began, there are many theories about it. Here and on the next page are an artist's conception of five of the best-known theories. Obviously, since no one knows which, if any, of these theories is correct, you should not believe any one of them is the true answer. On the other hand, the men who have developed these theories are among our greatest scientists, and each has put a tremendous amount of serious thought into his theory. Perhaps these highly simplified illustrations will make you want to find out more about the possible ways our solar system might have been formed. Fuller discussion of each of these theories appears in this section on the pages noted along with each theory.

The Kant-Laplace Theory

1

One of the earliest theories, this one claims that at first there was nothing but a ball of whirling gases. They contracted and whirled faster, bulging out at the "equator" so that rings of gas broke away. The rings later condensed into the sun and the planets. See page 447 for more about the Kant-Laplace theory.

The Chamberlin-Moulton Theory

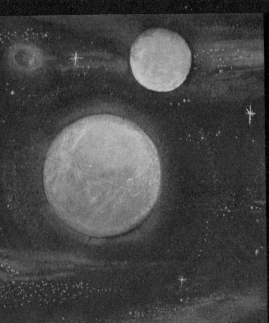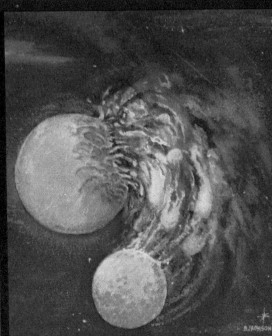

2

According to this theory, a great star once passed close to the sun and pulled great masses of the sun's material out into space, where it formed in clusters, and eventually solidified into the nine planets we now know. See page 448 for more about the Chamberlin-Moulton theory.

3

According to this theory, a star passed close to the sun, causing tidal bulges so strong that parts of the sun were pulled away in streaming arms that pinwheeled around it. This theory accounts for the fact that the planets formed from these parts circle the sun in the same direction. See page 448 for more about the Jeans-Jeffries theory.

The Jeans-Jeffries Theory
The Von Weizsäcker Theory

4

Many people believe this is the most likely theory of all. It suggests that the sun was once surrounded by a gaseous shell of about the same temperature as the planets now have. A system of cells was created within this gaseous shell. Gradually the "lumps" between the cells condensed, separated, and took shape as planets. See page 448 for more about Von Weizsäcker's theory.

The Hoyle Theory

5

This is one of the newer theories, and it suggests that once our sun was one of two stars. Something caused the sun's companion star to explode with tremendous force into pieces which shot far out into space. The planets were formed from some of these fragments. See page 451 for more about Hoyle's theory.

[Continued from page 448]

Suppose the Sun Had a Companion Star?

One of the newer theories on the solar system's origin suggests that the planets were formed from material that did not come from the sun, but from a companion star. The first man to suggest such a theory was Fred Hoyle, Cambridge, England. One of the reasons behind his theory is the great difference in chemical composition of the sun and the planets, a fact which was also pointed out by R. A. Lyttleton, also of Cambridge. Ninety-nine per cent of the sun's mass is made up of hydrogen and helium, but on the earth and the other planets, hydrogen and helium are found only in about the same amounts as more complex elements such as calcium, silicon, aluminum, and iron. This fact suggested that the source of the planets might have been a companion star that revolved around the sun. Something caused the star to explode and it blew apart with such tremendous force that pieces of it were shot far out into space. The theory maintains that the earth and other planets were formed from these star fragments. The sun's companion then moved to outer space.

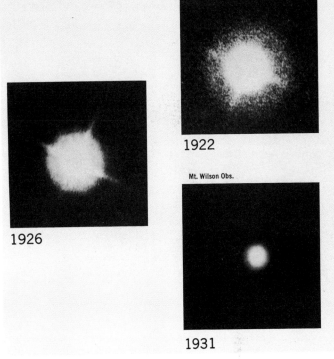

1926

1922

Mt. Wilson Obs.

1931

Some think our solar system was formed during the explosion of a star, or nova. These photographs show such an exploding star, Nova Aquila, which blazed forth on the night of June 8, 1918. It was the brightest nova in 300 years and was almost as brilliant as the beautiful white first magnitude star Vega, but it has since faded to less than eleventh magnitude. Later photographs of the nova show its expanding envelope of gases.

A pair of stars like the one suggested by Hoyle is called a binary system. Astronomers have discovered hundreds of such pairs with their telescopes. One example is the great white star Sirius near the constellation Orion which has a "twin" which astronomers have labelled Sirius B. (For more about the various kinds of stars, see "Stars and What We Know About Them" in Volume 8.)

A star explosion such as the one that might have caused the planets to form is called a nova. These, too, have been observed from time to time. Most astronomers think the Crab Nebula, in the constellation Taurus, is the remains of a supernova that exploded about 900 years ago, possibly the same one which, according to ancient Chinese records, was observed as a great explosion in that part of the sky in the year 1054.

There have been other theories about the solar system's origin, but these are some of the more widely discussed ideas.

The Crab nebula in the constellation Taurus (the Bull), best seen in southwestern skies in late winter or early spring. This photograph was made through the 200-inch telescope at Palomar.

Mt. Wilson & Palomar Obs's

451

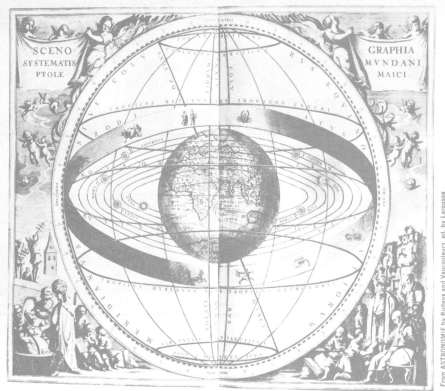

This old drawing of the sun and planets illustrates Ptolemy's theory that the heavenly bodies revolved around the earth.

The discoveries of Copernicus were remarkable because he had only the crudest of instruments to work with.

From ASTRONOMIE by Rudaux and Vaucouleurs, ed. by Larousse

Yerkes Obs.

The Man Who Made the Sun Stand Still

We know much more about the universe than was known fifty, twenty, or even ten years ago, largely due to discoveries made with the giant telescopes and other instruments. These new findings and our understanding of them would have been impossible if it hadn't been for the earlier discoveries made by hundreds of people through the centuries. Here is the story of Nicholas Copernicus, who might be called the father of modern astronomy because he proved that the sun, not the earth, is the center of our solar system. From **Heroes of Civilization** by Joseph Cottler and Haym Jaffe, by permission of Little, Brown and Company. Copyright 1931 by Joseph Cottler and Haym Jaffe.

In the second century A.D., a Greek named Ptolemy described all the astronomical knowledge of his time and earned the title of "Prince of Astronomers."

Ptolemy said the earth was the center of all things. He saw that during part of the year, the sun rose a little earlier every day and set a little later; then for the rest of the year, it rose a little later, and set a little earlier. He saw that the few stars which moved —the wanderers, which he called "planets"— moved in certain orderly ways. And he realized that the universe was a great system of laws. But what were these laws?

Ptolemy wrote a book in which he said, "We on earth are in the center of a vast globe. The firmament above us is solid and studded with stars. And like a wheel it turns round the earth. But this is very strange; the sun, moon, and each of the planets, all have their own peculiar paths around the earth."

Of course, he could not see these paths with his eyes. He calculated them. "If my picture of the heavens is true, then I can tell you where any planet will be at any moment in the future." And he made up tables of figures.

Astronomical measurements in Ptolemy's time, and for a long time after, could not be made as accurately as we can make them today. The result was that his tables worked fairly well; the planets were always near enough to the places he foretold. For many centuries there was no reason to disbelieve what Ptolemy had written.

Copernicus Comes
To Challenge Ptolemy

So thirteen centuries went by, and Ptolemy's word was unquestioned. But at length, in 1473, in Thorn, a small Prussian town belonging to Poland, a boy was born who was to challenge Ptolemy. He was Nicholas Copernicus, son of a successful Polish merchant. At the time Columbus was discovering the New World, Copernicus was studying at the University of Krakow. He then went to Italy, the center of learning at that time, where he stayed ten years, first as a student, then as a teacher.

His zeal for learning knew no bounds. He simply mastered everything: law, medicine, natural science, mathematics, civics. Upon his return to Poland, he was appointed a member of the Council of German States. He was once sent on a diplomatic mission to the King of Poland. He also wrote a book on economics, which was greatly admired by the learned.

His greatest interest, however, lay in astronomy. But in this study he was extremely handicapped. For there were no telescopes, nor any of the instruments we have today for observing the heavens. The few instruments he used, he had to make himself.

"Why do you have to worry about astronomy?" everybody said. "Ptolemy has said the last word on that subject." Nobody gave Copernicus any encouragement. But he needed none, for he had both genius and courage.

He looked long at Ptolemy's picture of the heavens. "Is it not queer," he thought, "that although all the planets move differently and are in different positions and of different sizes, yet they all seem to go around the earth once a day. It is unbelievable."

The more he pondered, the more unbelievable it seemed. One day a strange idea came to him. "If the earth spun around like a top once every day, then the planets would all seem to be turning around the earth once every day. That I can understand."

The Earth Moves?
How Ridiculous!

People laughed at the idea. "The earth moves! You must be joking, for that is contrary to common sense. If the earth moved, you could feel the motion." But Copernicus knew that if you were sailing on a smooth sea and you looked at the floor of your cabin, you could not detect any motion. Gaze out from the deck at the scenery, and you do see movement. But which is moving? You, or the scenery? Just so, if the earth were moving, the only way Ptolemy could observe it was by looking at the heavens, and then he thought it was the heavens that moved.

"Perhaps the earth does move!"

But the people of "common sense" had another objection.

"If a large body like the earth moved," they said, "it would travel with such speed that if you shot an arrow into the air, the earth would rush past under it before the arrow came down. Or if you took a high jump, the earth would whizz by, leaving you in the air. Since this does not happen, the earth does not move." The article on page 457 explains that the earth does rush past the flying arrow, but for such a short distance that we do not notice it. Only when we shoot very far, as with a long-range rocket, does it become noticeable. But neither Copernicus nor anyone else at that time knew of this.

But if you are sitting in your cabin, and you drop a penny, will it not fall at your feet? The penny will not be left in the air. It has the same motion as the cabin.

"Surely the earth moves," said Copernicus confidently. "It must, because it solves the problem of motion in the universe so simply."

But the followers of Ptolemy were not so easily convinced. "Absurd!" they insisted. "A moving earth would fly to pieces."

"Why should it?" retorted Copernicus. "Your moving heavens—have the stars dropped out of it?"

Copernicus Proves His Theory

Copernicus now used his mathematics. From youth to middle age he worked constantly to prove his theory. Then he wrote his conclusions in a book, which he did not publish until the very end of his life. He might not even then have done so, for he was modest

453

and very shy. His days were spent in ministering to the sick and poor, and he would have been content to end his days in that way. But some friends were ambitious for him and urged him to publish his thoughts on the universe. Copernicus always thought, "I am not ready yet. I can better my book. I shall wait . . ." And he might have kept on waiting to the end and never given us the book which proved one of the greatest events in the history of the world. It changed our whole thinking.

To begin with, Copernicus showed that his account of the facts of astronomy was simpler than Ptolemy's. The earth must move, because only then could the changing positions of all the stars, the seasons of the year, and the changes of night and day all occur simultaneously. The earth, Copernicus showed, is one of the planets. All the planets move around the sun which is the center. "Imagine a series of circles," said Copernicus, "one inside the other. The circles are the paths that the planets follow around the center point—the sun. As for our earth, it spins around like a top once a day, while at the same time it makes a journey around the sun that lasts a year. The spin gives us day and night. The motion around the sun gives us our seasons."

Wise men indeed saw how simple and beautiful was Copernicus's account compared with Ptolemy's. The learned men felt that, although the thought of living on an earth which moves was not a pleasant one, Copernicus was right.

How Small the Earth, How Vast the Universe!

The wonder of this solar system, as we now call it, was grasped slowly. What staggered everybody was the immensity of the universe, as Copernicus pictures it. Before his time the earth was regarded as the largest body in the heavens. We now know that the extent of our universe is difficult to imagine. We have counted thousands of millions of stars, the light from which takes thousands of years to reach our eyes. Copernicus himself did not realize how vast was the space he had opened up. Beyond the stars of our own galaxy lie other galaxies whose light, traveling at 186,000 miles a second, takes hundreds of millions of years to reach the earth. And we know that our sun, which is more than a million times as large as the earth, is only a small star.

Copernicus did not live to see the effect produced by his book on his fellow men. Scarcely had he given his consent to the publication of his book when he was stricken with paralysis. On May 24, 1543, just a few hours before he died, the printer placed the book in his hands. His life's end was the beginning of his immortality.

Years after, when Tycho Brahe, a great astronomer and believer in Copernicus, was given wooden instruments with which Copernicus had discovered a new heaven, he said: "The earth has not produced such a man for centuries. Copernicus has been able to stop the sun in its path across the sky, and has made the immovable earth move about the sun in a circle. About the earth he caused the moon to turn; he has changed for us the very face of the universe. This Copernicus has dared to do—with these small sticks. . . . He has done what was not permitted any other mortal to do since the beginning of the world. . . ."

454

A page from Copernicus' book, published in Nuremberg in 1543, shows his drawing of the solar system with the sun (sol) as the center.

Bode's Law: Divining Rod of the Solar System

A divining rod is a tree branch that is supposed to help some people discover water or metals underground. Here is the story of a mathematical "law" or relationship that helped predict where other members of our solar system might be located. The idea of the law was first suggested by John Daniel Titius, a professor at Wittenburg, Germany, but it was John Elert Bode (1747–1826), a German astronomer and director of the Berlin Observatory, who first published a paper on the subject. The law is called either the Titius-Bode law or simply Bode's law. The discoveries of the planet Uranus and of the planetoid Ceres (the "comet" referred to in the last paragraphs of this article) seemed to confirm the law, but it did not hold true for the later discoveries of Neptune and Pluto. The place which the law predicted would be occupied by Neptune is occupied by Pluto instead, and Neptune occurs about midway between Uranus and Pluto. However, many scientists believe that there may be a significance to Bode's law that is as yet unexplained. Here Bode himself discusses the law and how it works, in this translation from one of Bode's papers published in Berlin in 1802. By permission from **A Source Book in Astronomy** by Harlow Shapley, Ph.D., and Helen E. Howarth. Copyright 1929. McGraw-Hill Book Company, Inc.

In the second edition of my *Introduction to Knowledge of the Starry Heavens*, which I published while yet in Hamburg, in the year 1772, I speak on page 462 concerning the probable existence of other planets in the solar system than had up to that time been known. Should the boundary of the solar system indeed be limited to where we see Saturn? (Since 1781 we know of Uranus at a distance double that of Saturn.) . . . and for what reason the great space which is found between Mars and Jupiter, where so far no major planet is seen? Is it not highly probable that a planet actually revolves in the orbit which the finger of the Almighty has drawn for it?

And in a note at this place: This conclusion appears to follow especially from the very remarkable relation which the six, long-known major planets observe in their distances from the Sun. If we indicate the distance of Saturn from the Sun by 100 units, Mercury is four such units from the Sun. Venus is $4 + 3 = 7$; the Earth, $4 + 6 = 10$; Mars, $4 + 12 = 16$. Now, however, there comes a gap in this regular progression. From Mars outward there follows a space of $4 + 24 = 28$ units in which, up to now, no planet has been seen. Can we believe that the Creator of the world has left this space empty? Certainly not! From here we come to the distance of Jupiter through $4 + 48 = 52$, and finally to Saturn through $4 + 96 = 100$ units (and now to that of Uranus through $4 + 192 = 196$ units). . . . This progression proceeds only in small numbers and, therefore, gives only approximate results. In all my subsequent [later] astronomical writings I have, when occasion arose, spoken of this progression, presented it in sketches, and advanced many arguments for its correctness. The discovery of Uranus was the first happy verification [proof] of it.

Bode's Law in Larger Numbers

The progression agrees very well with observations even in small numbers. If, however, we put with Professor Wurm [another German astronomer of Bode's time] the actual mean distance of Mercury from the Sun at 387 (the distance of the Earth = 1,000) and take the distance between Mercury and Venus as 293, then the relative distances of the seven known planets are still more exactly represented. The distances from the Sun are in fact as follows:

			mean distance
Mercury	387 units		387
Venus	387+	293 = 680	723
Earth	387+	2×293 = 973	1,000
Mars	387+	4×293 = 1,559	1,524
probable planet between Mars and Jupiter	387+	8×293 = 2,731	
Jupiter	387+	16×293 = 5,075	5,203
Saturn	387+	32×293 = 9,763	9,541
Uranus	387+	64×293 = 19,139	19,082

On the 20th of March, 1801, I received from Dr. Joseph Piazzi, Royal Astronomer and Director of the Royal Observatory at Palermo,

Italy, a communication dated January 24th in which he writes as follows: "On the 1st of January I discovered a comet in Taurus [a constellation] in right ascension 51° 47′, northern declination 16° 8′. On the 11th it changed its heretofore (westward) retrograde [apparent backward] motion into (eastward) direct motion; and on the 23d was in right ascension 51° 46′, northern declination 17° 8′. I shall continue to observe it and hope to be able to observe throughout the whole of February. It is very small, and equivalent to a star of the eighth magnitude, without any noticeable nebulosity [gaseous character]. I beg of you to let me know whether it has already been observed by other astronomers; in this case I should save myself the trouble of computing its orbit."

The Missing Link Is Found

In the beginning of March, I had already found a notice of the discovery in foreign journals; there was, however, as little said on the place and motion as on the appearance of this remarkable comet.

When, however, I received from the observer himself the foregoing more exact notice of the object, it struck me immediately, upon reading through his letter, as remarkable, and I was convinced that this small star without noticeable nebulosity, at one time in eastern elongation, then appearing to stand still, thereafter again moving forward toward the east, was not a comet at all; Piazzi had, indeed, here discovered a very extraordinary object. It was most probably the eighth major planet of the solar system, which already thirty years before I had announced between Mars and Jupiter, but which until now had remained undiscovered—a planet whose distance from the Sun indicated a known progression of probably 2.80, and which in four years and eight months must run its course around the Sun.

How Long Will the Solar System Last?

If anything ever happened to change the sun and its relationship to our earth, it would naturally mean the end of our solar system as we now know it. Here a famous scientist gives you his ideas on how long our solar system is likely to last, and what may happen to cause its destruction. From **The Nature of the Universe**, by Fred Hoyle, published by Harper & Bros. Copyright, 1950, by Fred Hoyle.

How long will the Sun continue to radiate light and heat at just the rate required by living creatures on the Earth? Calculation shows that so long as the Sun is not seriously disturbed by processes occurring outside itself, the supply of hydrogen in the Sun will last for about 50,000,000,000 years. This does not quite answer our question, because after about 10,000,000,000 years the Sun will be getting too warm for our comfort. In other words, as more and more hydrogen gets con-verted into helium, the Sun will get hotter and hotter.

By the time the Sun has used about a third of its present store of hydrogen, the climate, even at the poles of the Earth, will be getting too hot for any forms of life that at present inhabit it. At a still later stage, the Sun will become so hot that the oceans will boil and life will become extinct, not because the Sun becomes too feeble, but because it becomes too hot.

As the Sun becomes hotter it will probably swell, at first slowly and then with increasing rapidity, until it swallows the inner planets one by one: first Mercury, then Venus, then the Earth. Mars is likely to be the last planet to suffer this fate, but it is just possible that an even further extension, as far as Jupiter, will occur. Such a happening would, of course, mean the end of our solar system.

The Curious Coriolis Effect

We know the earth spins on its axis, making one complete turn in 24 hours, but this fact seems to be of little importance beyond causing our night and day. But is that all? Did you know the rotation of the earth has quite a noticeable effect on airplane flight, artillery and rocket fire, and the weather? Here a professor of physics tells about one of the most fascinating facts about any planet which is rotating, and how a merry-go-round demonstrates it. From "The Coriolis Effect" by James E. McDonald. **Scientific American**, May, 1952. Used by permission of the author and **Scientific American**. Illustrations by Irving Geis.

It is a curious fact that all things which move over the surface of the earth tend to veer from their appointed paths—to the right in the northern hemisphere, to the left in the southern hemisphere. Probably few people realize that as they drive down a straight highway at 60 miles per hour this ever-present drift would carry them off the road to the right at the rate of some 15 feet per mile if it were not for the frictional resistance of the tires to any lateral (crosswise) motion.

This sidewise drifting tendency is called the Coriolis effect, after the nineteenth century French mathematician G. G. Coriolis, who made the first complete study of it. The effect is due simply to the rotation of the earth, and it appears in all motions as soon as we relate those motions to any fixed system with respect to the earth, for example, latitude and longitude.

Try This on a Merry-Go-Round

There is really only one satisfactory way to get a vivid impression of the nature of the Coriolis principle. That is to go to a carnival. Every carnival worth the name has a Coriolian coordinate system: namely a merry-go-round. With only a few balls as laboratory equipment, and two assistants, one on the merry-go-round with you and the other on the ground, you can carry out many interesting Coriolian experiments.

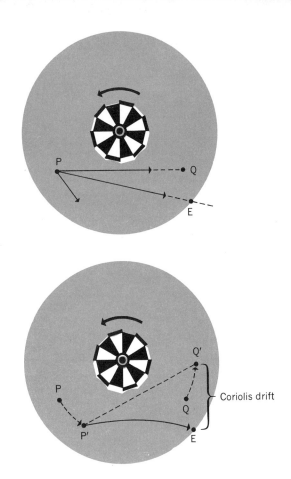

The merry-go-round experiment demonstrates Coriolis drift. In the top drawing, the merry-go-round is rotating counterclockwise and two men are standing on the merry-go-round at P and Q. The man at P tries to throw a ball to the man at Q, but the rotational motion causes the ball to head in the direction of PE. In the bottom drawing, by the time the ball has reached E, the man at P has rotated to P' and the man at Q to Q' and the ball misses its intended receiver by over six feet.

When the merry-go-round starts up, you begin a game of catch. Things will probably go very poorly for several throws (which is the reason why you should equip yourself with several balls). The ball will seem to veer from its thrown direction in the most amazing fashion. Let us say the merry-go-round turns counterclockwise, as does the earth when viewed from above the North Pole. If it makes one complete turn in 10 seconds, and you throw the ball at a speed of 20 feet per second toward an assistant standing 15 feet from you on the merry-go-round, the apparently curving ball will miss the assistant by a little over 6

457

feet to the right. When you throw a ball to your other assistant, in the outer world off the merry-go-round, it will again seem to drift rightward. This time, however, by great concentration you may be able to fix your attention on the nonrotating framework of the outer world sufficiently to sense that the ball is really moving as it ought to move, and you may even make proper allowance for the merry-go-round's rotation so that the ball reaches your assistant's hands.

Why Can't You Throw Straight?

The apparent strangeness of the ball's behavior in these experiments arises from the fact that you take the merry-go-round as your reference system, and in this system the laws of dynamics in their usual form simply do not hold. The drifting to the right which you seem to see is really due to the fact that your system is turning out from under the moving balls.

The earth is a spherical merry-go-round, and all of the Coriolis drifts we observe when we use terrestrial (earthly) coordinate systems are due to the fact that the earth, like the merry-go-round, is always spinning out from under us.

Now let us look at some interesting examples of the Coriolis effect. It is greatest near the North and South Poles (where the earth turns most rapidly under a moving object) and decreases to zero at the Equator. The extent of the effect also depends directly on the speed of the moving object.

Problems of an Airplane Pilot

An airplane experiences Coriolis drifts which would lead to astonishing errors in long flights if no allowance were made for them. A jet fighter that set out on a great-circle heading from Chicago to New York and flew at 600 miles per hour without changing its heading would miss New York by several hundred miles to the south (assuming no allowance for any wind). And if the same pilot tried to fly in a similar way from Seattle to New York, he would find himself down in South America by the time he crossed the meridian through New York!

Among all the ways in which the Coriolis effect plays a role, the most striking is the weather. If it were not for the Coriolis effect, winds on the earth would rush directly from higher-pressure areas to lower-pressure ones, and no strong "highs" or "lows" could develop. Hence there would be no opportunity for the build-up of the intense cyclones and the large anticyclones that control our weather, and our weather would be much less changeable than it is. This is precisely the situation in the Tropics, where the Coriolis effect is zero or very small. In that almost Coriolis-free belt any atmospheric pressure differences produced by heating of the air at the ground are quickly smoothed out, and the region has well earned the name of "the doldrums." Hurricanes and typhoons never form closer to the Equator than about five degrees of latitude.

Even the Water Is Pushed Around

People on the Pacific coast of North America are well acquainted with certain other consequences of the Coriolis effect, though not many realize this is the cause. Coriolis drift is mainly responsible for the well-known California fogs and the coldness of the water on California's beaches. Off the California coast, where the prevailing winds are from the northwest, the wind stress and Coriolis drift generally combine to make the coastal waters flow in a southwesterly direction. As water is carried away from the shore toward the southwest the water moving offshore is replaced by water rising from below. This brings up cold water from depths as great as several hundred feet. In summer the warm moist Pacific air streaming in from the northwest is cooled by the coastal water, and this is what forms the fogs for which California is sorry to be famous. A similar situation may be found off the coast of Peru and parts of the western coast of Africa.

All things that move over the surface of our spinning earth, whether birds, winds, rivers, ocean currents, explorers, cars, trains, bullets or rockets, are necessarily influenced by the Coriolis effect.

The shift in the position of the celestial north pole is shown in these astronomical photographs taken in 1925 (left) and 1935. The circular paths of the stars have moved in relation to the point about which they rotate in the heavens.

Yerkes Observatory

The Precession of the Equinoxes

How many motions does the earth have? There are two which are quite apparent to everyone—its rotation on its axis, which produces day and night, and its revolution around the sun, making the year and the seasons. But there are a number of others as well.

The earth is accompanying the sun on its movement through space; the sun is also taking part in the rotation of the galaxy; and the galaxy is, in turn, moving through space. These movements are all so large, and the immediate effects of them so small, that they concern the average person very little.

There is, however, a motion of the earth which is independent of all of these. It is the wobble on its axis which has been going on for a long time. A single individual would not notice it; yet it has caused enough change during the course of recorded history for its course to be accurately plotted.

This motion is called *precession,* and it can be exemplified by the motion of a spinning top or toy gyroscope. At the beginning, when the toy is spinning rapidly, it stands almost directly upright as it spins; but as the speed of spin gradually becomes slower, the axis of the toy begins to describe a circle around the vertical axis. This deviation becomes more prominent as the speed slows more and more, until at last the top or gyroscope falls over on its side.

This movement of the axis around the true center is called precession: it takes place with every spinning object, including the earth. The result as applied to the earth is that the north pole does not always point to the same place in the heavens, but changes over a period of about 26,000 years.

At about 4000 B.C., the two end stars in the constellation of the Great Dipper were closest to the celestial pole; a thousand years later, the pole had precessed so that the bright star Thuban was the pole star. At the beginning of the Christian era there was no prominent pole star, and it was not until about A.D. 1500 that the present star, termed Polaris because of its position on star maps of the time, came close enough to be usable as a guide to travelers wanting to know which direction was north.

By A.D. 8000 the star Alpha Cephei will be the pole star, and in A.D. 14000 Alpha Lyrae (Vega) will be in that position—very close to where it was in 12000 B.C., the last time the precession of the earth's pole pointed that way. But Vega itself will have moved its apparent position in the heavens, and will not be as good a pole star as before; the same will be true of the other stars when the cycle comes around again in its period of 25,800 years.

This wobble of the earth's axis is termed the *precession of the equinoxes,* because it makes the time of equal day and night move gradually in the calendar. It is of interest to many scholars, since because of it they can tell when certain temples or pyramids which were oriented to the skies were built.

459

Other Sections To See

"The Rocks Beneath Our Feet," Volume 1; "Our Neighboring Planets" and "The Exploration of Space," Volume 2; "Stars and What We Know About Them," Volume 8; "The Sun," Volume 10; "Earth's Long Past" and "Comets and Meteors," Volume 11; "Giant Telescopes and Their Discoveries," Volume 12.

Tides in the Atmosphere

The earth is like a great ball that is constantly being tugged back and forth by the forces of gravity from the moon and the sun. The oceans, being liquid and consequently more movable, show the effect of this pull in noticeable ways which we call tides. There are land and air tides, too, although we are not aware of them. This article compares the tidal forces of the sun and moon. From "Tides in the Atmosphere" by Sydney Chapman. Scientific American, May, 1954, Vol. 190, No. 5. Used by permission of the author and Scientific American.

Twice each day the oceans of the earth rhythmically rise and fall under the pull of the moon. Everyone knows of the sea tides. But very few people realize that the moon also creates tides in the atmosphere. Far over our heads daily moon tides heave and billow on the bosom of our ocean of air. This gentle "breathing" of the atmosphere is so much less apparent than the ocean tides and so masked by the much more powerful effects of the sun on atmosphere, that to detect it at all is a labor of infinite pains. Yet it has interested scientists since the time of Isaac Newton.

The moon's tidal pull acts on the solid as well as on the fluid parts of the earth. Although the solid matter cannot flow like the waters of the oceans, its elastic substance does bulge slightly toward and away from the moon. The twice-daily rise and fall of the earth under our feet is quite unnoticeable to our senses, but delicate instruments have detected it. The observations show that the earth as a whole is about as elastic as steel.

It was Newton, apparently, who first suggested that there must be tides in the atmosphere. He added that they would be so small as to be unnoticeable. Nevertheless, like the earth tides, they have been detected by careful measurements and analysis.

How Are Air Tides Measured?

The tidal rise and fall of the seas is visible and easily measured because the sea has a definite level with respect to the land. Tide gauges record the changing level of its surface. In mid-ocean the tides cannot be measured in this way. There, the only method of gauging the rise and fall of the surface is by changes in the weight or pressure of the water as measured by a pressure gauge on the sea bottom. The same type of device must be used to record the tides in the atmosphere, not only because there is no yardstick to measure the atmosphere's height, but because it thins away gradually and has no definite upper surface. The tide gauge for the atmosphere is a barometer, which measures the weight, and thereby the height, of the overlying air. High and low tide in the atmosphere correspond to higher or lower barometric pressure.

A century and a quarter ago, the great French mathematician and astronomer Pierre Laplace made the first systematic attempt to detect the moon tides in the atmosphere by means of barometric records. He had developed a theory of tides in an ideal ocean, and from an adaptation of this theory to the atmospheric ocean he calculated that the lunar (moon) tides should produce a daily rise and fall of one quarter of a millimeter of mercury in the tropics and less in other latitudes. Laplace analyzed a series of 4,752 daily barometric readings taken over an eight-year period at the Paris Observatory. He failed to find any important pattern and decided that at least 40,000 barometric readings would be needed. Other observers who followed up his work likewise failed, though one had 30,000 readings to analyze.

Which Pulls Harder, Moon or Sun?

There are two complications that make it difficult to detect the tiny pulling effect of the moon: irregular changes in air flow, and the tidal forces and daily thermal (heating) action of the sun. The sun exerts a tidal pull like that of the moon; but in spite of the sun's immensely greater mass, its tidal force on the sea is less than that of the moon. Tides are due to the difference between the pull at the center of the earth and the pull at other points. Thus while the sun's total attraction is greater, the difference at different points of the earth is smaller, because of its greater distance from us. The moon's tidal power in the sea is 2.4 times that of the sun.

However, in the atmosphere the sun tide drowns out the moon tide. One reason is that the atmosphere has a natural period of vibration which is nearly the sun's period of 12 hours. This helps to make the sun tide 15 to 20 times stronger than the moon tide in the atmosphere.

To use a musical comparison, the moon tide and the sun tide correspond to two pure notes of different pitch and intensity. The moon tide note has one vibration in 12 hours and 25 minutes; the sun tide note has a slightly higher pitch—one vibration in 12 hours. In a barometric recording of the music of the atmosphere in middle latitudes, the irregular surf of the winds is a deep, booming roar, the sun tide is a barely audible monotone, and the moon tide is a muted note which can be heard only by a specially attuned ear.

Measurement of the Moon's Air Tides

The height of the lunar air tide has now been determined at more than 60 places around the globe. It varies far less than the ocean tides, owing to the absence of "shores" in the atmosphere. The great Rocky Mountain chain seems to have a definite, though small, effect upon it. The most surprising feature of the moon tide is that the daily high tides come an hour or two later in January and February than in May and June.

In recent years we have found that the moon tide can be read on a natural tide gauge in the atmosphere. It is the ionosphere, the great layer of electrically conducting particles far above the earth. By bouncing radio signals from the ionosphere we can measure its height, and in this manner it has proved possible to follow the double wave of the moon tide around the earth. In the ionosphere the rise and fall of the moon wave is as much as a mile or more! (For more about ocean tides see "What Causes Tides?" in Volume 2.)

Directly below, variations in air tide caused by the moon's pull, as recorded on the barometer over a month's time at four different stations on the earth. In the lower diagram sea tides recorded at three stations during the same period of time. The dots on each curve indicate the recording at noon. The phases of the moon at corresponding times on the record are shown between the two sets of records. (Recordings of tides prepared by Dan Wilder of the University of Alaska under direction of Sydney Chapman.)

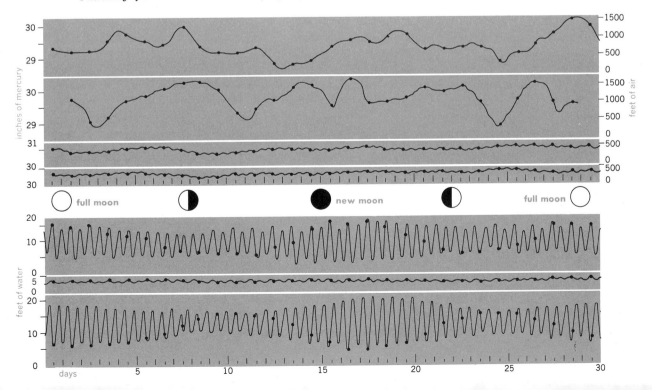

The Star Watchers

Ptolemy
about A.D. 100–170

Claudius Ptolemaeus, or Ptolemy, was born in Greece but lived in Alexandria, Egypt, which was the center of learning for all the civilized world. There he began to observe the stars and made a catalog showing the brightness and location of 1,028 of them. Not only did he map the skies; he mapped all of the earth that was known to men of his day. His famous work, *Almagest,* summed up ancient learning about the heavens. Some of the ancients had decided, correctly, that the earth traveled around the sun, but Ptolemy favored the theory of Hipparchus, who held that the earth was the center of the universe with the moon, sun, planets, and stars all revolving around it.

Tycho Brahe
1546–1601

Brahe, who was born at Knudstrup, in Skane, which was then part of Sweden, became a great practical astronomer without ever possessing a telescope. It is said that the irritable young aristocrat (part of his nose was cut off in a duel) became interested in astronomy because of an eclipse in 1560—not because of the eclipse but because it had been perfectly foretold. Sponsored first by Frederick II of Denmark and later by the German emperor, Rudolph II, Brahe lived at Prague where he built world-famous observatories and charted more accurately than any one before him the motions of the heavens. In his theories he greatly modified the Copernican theory. His view was a compromise: the earth was the center of the universe for him; around the earth revolved the sun, but the other planets revolved around the sun as it circled our globe.

Johannes Kepler
1571–1630

Kepler, the German astronomer who originally intended to become a minister, was taught the Copernican theory by Mastlin of the University of Tübingen. His first book brought him a friendly correspondence with Galileo and Brahe. Succeeding Brahe as imperial astronomer to Rudolph II, he completed Brahe's great charts of the skies and published (1609 and 1619) the three revolutionary ideas known as Kepler's laws. They may be summarized as follows: First, the planets move, not in circles, but in elliptical orbits, of which the sun is one focus. Second, the line joining the sun and the planet sweeps out equal areas of the planet's orbit in equal times; as a result a planet moves faster when it is in that part of its orbit that is closer to the sun. Third, the square of any planet's period (the time it takes to move around the sun) is proportional to the cube of the planet's mean distance from the sun. Despite his official position, Kepler died in poverty—actually while trying to collect his overdue salary.

Sir William Herschel
1738–1822
Sir John Frederick William Herschel
1792–1871

Musician and self-taught astronomer, William Herschel was born in Hanover, Germany. He became a builder of reflecting telescopes in his adopted country, England. (His largest telescope was 39 feet 4 inches long with an aperture of 4 feet.) With the help of his sister, Caroline, Herschel contributed much to astronomy. He discovered the planet Uranus and cataloged 800 binary stars, concluding that these twin stars revolve around each other according to the law of gravity. He also discovered that the sun and our solar system are actually moving through space. From his work on nebulae he even suspected the origin of new "worlds" from gaseous matter. His son, John, was also an astronomer and a chemist and pioneer in photography. (He invented the terms negative and positive, for instance.) Sir John's main work in astronomy was the correcting of his father's studies of nebulae and binary stars, and also the charting of the southern skies, begun in 1834, at the Cape of Good Hope.

Richard Anthony Proctor   1837–1888

Richard Proctor had been educated as a lawyer; however, by 1863 he had abandoned his study of law to devote his life to astronomy and mathematics. His monograph "Saturn and His Systems" appeared in 1865. In 1866 he became a science writer for the *Popular Science Review* and published his *Handbook of the Stars*. At the age of thirty-two, in 1869, he offered the then startling theory that distant spiral galaxies in space resembled our own Milky Way Galaxy in both size and shape, a theory that is accepted by modern astronomy. In that same year Proctor discovered that five of the seven stars making up the Big Dipper move across the sky in the same direction and with the same angular velocity—indicating that the dipper consists of a connected moving group of stars rather than a random moving group, as had been previously believed. In 1873 and 1879 he made lecture tours to America. In 1881 his weekly scientific journal *Knowledge* was founded. His book *Other Worlds Than Our Own* is an astronomical classic.

New York Public Library

Percival Lowell   1855–1916

A Boston-born member of the famous Lowell family, Percival Lowell spent the years from 1883 to 1893 in writing and traveling. His appreciation of the Orient is expressed in his book *The Soul of the Far East,* which appeared in 1888. His interest was turned to astronomy by the Martian observations of G. Schiaparelli and in 1894 he founded the Lowell observatory at Flagstaff, Arizona. His book *Mars and Its Canals,* enlarged upon his belief that Mars is a dying planet inhabited by intelligent beings who are trying to stay alive by using the water of polar snowcaps to irrigate huge bands of cultivated vegetation. He believed the canals of Mars to be these same bands. After making an exhaustive mathematical study of the movements of the planets Uranus and Neptune, Lowell began to suspect that there might be an unseen planet beyond Neptune. This led him to make a systematic search for the mysterious planet Pluto, which was discovered at his observatory in 1930, 14 years after his death.

New York Public Library

Harlow Shapley   1885–

Longtime director of the Harvard Observatory, Shapley was born in Nashville, Missouri, and was educated at the University of Missouri and Princeton. An ardent internationalist, he has brought a new understanding of the structure of the universe. Among other contributions, he has fixed the center of the Milky Way (in Sagittarius), has shown our galactic system to be a thousand times larger than was thought, and has suggested that the variations in some stars (known as Cepheid variables because their changes do not come from eclipses) are the result of pulsations.

Harvard Univ., by Walter R. Fleisher

Edwin Powell Hubble   1889–1953

E. P. Hubble was born in a small town in Missouri, educated in Chicago, a Rhodes scholar at Oxford, a major in World War I, and an amateur boxer. For a time he practiced law, but finally returned to his first love, astronomy, and began his pioneer study of the galaxies at California's Mount Wilson Observatory. He was the first to prove that the great galaxy in Andromeda was an island universe far from our own. Aided by the spectroscopic work of Milton L. Humason, Hubble found a measuring stick to chart the distances of remote galaxies. He found that the farther away a galaxy is, the more its light is reddened. This relationship led to the theory of the expanding universe.

Black Star by Sharland

Subramanyam Chandrasekhar   1910–

India-born astrophysicist and mathematician, Dr. S. Chandrasekhar, now an American citizen, has won many honors for his advanced study of stellar spectra, motions and atmospheres, and the strength of magnetic fields in interstellar space. He received his B.A. degree in Madras in 1930, his Ph.D. from Cambridge in 1933, and in 1942 he was given Cambridge's honorary doctor of science degree. Since 1937 he has been a member of the University of Chicago faculty. A nephew of Nobel prize winner C. V. Raman, Dr. Chandrasekhar is a Fellow of the Royal Society of London, councillor of the American Astronomical Society, former consultant in the Ballistic Research Laboratories at Aberdeen, Maryland and holder of the gold medal of the Astronomical Society of London, the Bruce Medal of the American Astronomical Society of the Pacific, the Adams Prize from Cambridge, and India's Padma Vibhushan.

Wide World Photos

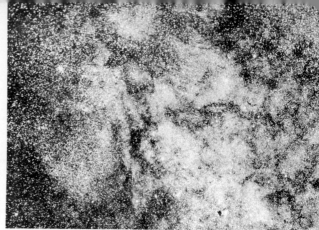

Non-luminous dust clouds obscure the edge of this spiral galaxy, which probably resembles our own galaxy if it were seen edge-on from space.

The center of the "Milky Way" galaxy, in which our solar system is located, is obscured by millions of stars as well as dark matter.

The Age of the Earth

The age of the earth's crust is now estimated at about 4,500,000,000 years. This is based on the laws of radioactive decay of naturally radioactive elements such as uranium, which becomes lead at a very slow and unchanging rate. Using only pure mineral in the form of crystals, scientists compare the ratio of uranium isotopes to lead isotopes to determine how long ago the transformation process began. This is possible since the rate of change is known and remains constant.

Astronomers, geophysicists and mathematicians have studied rock samples from the oldest undisturbed regions where it is believed that mountain building ceased very early in the formation of the earth's crust. Their researches indicate that the oldest samples have come from Africa, which means that this was probably the first continent to be formed.

Aside from analysis of meteorites which reach the earth from space, we as yet have no information about the amount of radioactive isotopes existing outside the earth. Early researchers thought that the helium content of meteorites might provide a clue to the age of the entire universe; however, this idea has proved false, or at least unreliable. It is probable that meteorites were formed by the breaking up of a small planet during the creation of the solar system; for this reason meteorites are probably about the same age as the earth and the rest of the objects in the Milky Way.

Does time have a beginning? There are two conflicting theories of origin. Does the universe expand eternally (this implies a beginning date for creation) or does it expand and contract in cycles, (meaning that time is infinite) returning to the original atomic state from which it came? It can only be said that scientists have established a minimum age for the earth; it may be older, and the solar system and the universe may be far older. Only future research can expand these fascinating details about the cosmos in which we live.

Other Books To Read

Astronomy and the Origin of the Earth, by Theodore G. Mehlin. Published by William C. Brown & Co., Dubuque, Iowa, 1968.
A summary of the findings of astronomical research dealing with the problems of how the earth came into being and how long ago this event occurred.

A Short History of the Universe, by Arthur S. Gregor. Published by The Macmillan Co., New York, 1962.
A clear explanation of what the universe is and how it may have come into existence.

The Structure of the Universe, edited by Webster P. True. Volume I of the Smithsonian Treasury of Knowledge. Published by Simon and Schuster, Inc., New York, in cooperation with The Smithsonian Institution, Washington, D.C.
A collection of interesting articles and papers on many aspects of planetary astronomy and other related subjects.

464

Photos, Yerkes Obs.

A Tapestry of Knowledge

THE INDIVIDUAL

	1	2	3	4	5	6	7	8
Your Body and How it Works				Machinery of the Body	Skin: The Body Covering	The Skeleton	Your Eyes	Muscles & Strength
Taking Care of Yourself				Food for the Body Engine		Familiar Diseases		Exercise and Physical Fitness
Living with Self and Others					Three Stages in Growing Up	Adolescence	Exceptional People and their Problems	How We Learn
Living and Learning with People		How To Study	Getting the Most Out of School	Mind Your P's and Q's	Your Club Life	Social Life		
Your Life Work	Careers in the Social Sciences	Workers of the Sea	Workers and Jobs	Workers with Machines	Careers in Aviation	Your Homemaking Career	Writing & Editing	Jobs in Medicine

THE PHYSICAL ENVIRONMENT

	1	2	3	4	5	6	7	8
Nature of Matter and Energy	Fire, Man's Friend and Foe	Wonders of Electricity	Chemical Elements		Heat and Cold	Everyday Devices for Everyday Living		Matter & Energy
The Earth We Live On	Rocks Beneath Our Feet	Seas that Lap Our Shores	Soil: More Valuable than Gold	Precious Metals & Gems	The Air Around Us		Climate	
Animals	How Animals Survive	Birds of Sea & Shore			Land Birds of N. Amer.	World of Reptiles	Insects	Big Game Animals
Animals and Man			Story of Horses & Their Masters / Fur Animals & Furs	Whales		Dogs	Cage Birds	Cat Family
World of Plants	Plants That Have Traveled	Grasses—World's Most Important Plants	Plants That Cannot Make Their Own Food / Wild Pl. Indians Used	We Live on Sunlight	House & Garden Plants			
Exploring the Universe		Neighboring Planets / Exploration of Space						Stars and What We Know About Them

MAN'S EFFORTS TO CONTROL HIS ENVIRONMENT

	1	2	3	4	5	6	7	8
Basic Inventions		Human & Animal Tools	Telling & Measuring Time	The Electron Tube / The Workshop & Its Tools	How Airplanes Work / Tools of Modern Science	Houses We Live In	Wheels & Gears	Pioneers of Atomic Energy
New Materials	Canada's Wealth		Fibers Clothe World / Story of Fabrics	Story of Metals	Aluminum & Magnesium			
Ample Food Supply				Let's Talk About Sugar	Fruits of the Tree	Food Preservation	Soybeans and Other Legumes	Diet in America
Conservation		Land from the Sea					Trees & Forests of the World	
Exploration	Explorers of New World / 3 Discoveries of Amer.	Conquest of Arctic / Conquest of Antarctic						
Transportation	Ships and Sailing / Railroads	Travel Beneath Sea	Westward Ho!	Roads: Life Line of Nations	Balloons & Their Kin / Modern Planes	Automobiles		
Better Health					Maintaining a Livable Environment	Accident Prevention	Bacteria & Disease	Pioneers of Medicine

MAN'S RELATION TO HIS FELLOW MAN

	1	2	3	4	5	6	7	8
How People Live and Work		Deep-Sea Diving	American Indians	The Negro in American Life			Flags of the World	Pioneer Life in America
How People are Governed			Indians of Today	How People Are Governed		The Law & You	Free Elections	Local Government
Economic Life						The Value of Money	World of Advertising	Paying for Government: Taxes & Tariffs
Technology and Mass Production				Manufacturing and Power			News & Newspapers	Oil: Fuel for Modern Machines
Communication	Written Word / Man: Speaking Animal / Codes & Ciphers	The Telegraph & the Telephone	Search for a World Language		Keeping Planes in the Air	Carrying the Mail	The Library & You	
Quest for World Peace						World Action for Man's Health		Warfare and Weapons
Communities of People	Southwestern States		The Midwest	New England States / British Isles	Countries of the Nile / Tropical So. Amer.	Middle Atl. States / Europe: Danube to Baltic	6 Nations W. Europe / New York City	Southern Mt. States / Canada

MAN'S RELATION TO HIS CULTURE

	1	2	3	4	5	6	7	8
Man's Ideal		Heroes & Heroism	Documents of American Democracy	Jewish Religion	Hindu & Moslem Religion	The Family		
The Past			The U.S. in the 20th Century	Landmarks of America	Man Learns To Fly / Pageant of History	Family Life in Amer.	Pirates, Outlaws, Imposters & Assassins	Folk Heroes: Real & Imaginary
Our Cultural Heritage			Americans All	Plays & Playwrights	World Literature: Asia	Fashions: Then & Now	World Literature: United States / World Lit.: Europe	
The Arts	Folk Customs / Humor in Words and Pictures	Sea and Art / Music from the Sea	Indian and His Art	Dolls and Puppets / Music in the Theater		Art & Design in Home	Art & Printed Word	Art & Music of Frontier / Modern Art
Enjoyment	Baseball—America's Sport	In & On the Water		Basketball			Puzzles from Past & Present	Football